Multimedia: Making It Work

Ninth Edition

Multimedia: Making It Work

Ninth Edition

Tay Vaughan

New York   Chicago   San Francisco
Athens   London   Madrid   Mexico City
Milan   New Delhi   Singapore   Sydney   Toronto

Sponsoring Editor
Meghan Manfre

Editorial Supervisor
Jody McKenzie

Project Editor
Howie Severson,
Fortuitous Publishing

Acquisitions Coordinator
Mary Demery

Technical Editor
Eileen Webb

Copy Editor
Bill McManus

Proofreader
Paul Tyler

Indexer
Jack Lewis

Production Supervisor
James Kussow

Composition
Cenveo Publishing Services

Illustration
Cenveo Publishing Services

Art Director, Cover
Jeff Weeks

Cataloging-in-Publication Data is on file with the Library of Congress

McGraw-Hill Education books are available at special quantity discounts to use as premiums and sales promotions, or for use in corporate training programs. To contact a representative, please visit the Contact Us pages at www.mhprofessional.com.

Multimedia: Making It Work, Ninth Edition

2 3 4 5 6 7 8 9 0 QVS QVS 19 18 17 16 15

ISBN   978-0-07-183288-5

MHID   0-07-183288-2

For Marcia Van Gemert

About the Author

Tay Vaughan is a widely known multimedia authority who has lectured and taught around the world. He has developed and produced projects for clients including Apple, Microsoft, Kodak, Lotus (IBM), Northern Telecom, Novell, Sun (Oracle), and Varian. He is president of Timestream, a multiformat design and publishing company.

About the Technical Editor

Dr. Eileen Webb is a Principal Lecturer and Subject Leader for Digital Media and Web Design in the School of Computing at Teesside University in the UK. She has worked at the university for 20 years, during which time she also completed a Ph.D. in Learning Technology. She has extensive experience of curriculum development and teaching in information technology, multimedia, and web design courses at both the undergraduate and postgraduate levels. She has presented at national and international conferences and is credited with a number of peer-reviewed conference and journal publications. Dr. Webb also holds a master's degree in Information Technology from Teesside University, a Postgraduate Certificate in Education from Huddersfield University, and a bachelor's degree in Biochemistry and Genetics from Newcastle University. She is a Member of the British Computer Society, a Certified IT Professional, and a Fellow of the Higher Education Society.

ABOUT THIS BOOK

Important Multimedia Skills

Multimedia offers many career paths that can lead to occupations in such fields as graphic design, web design, animation, audio and video production, and project management. To become competent in any multimedia field, however, you need to learn the fundamental multimedia concepts first.

Multimedia: Making It Work builds a foundation for success in the discipline of multimedia by introducing you to the multimedia building blocks of text, images, sound, animation, and video while going one step further to develop an understanding of the process of making multimedia.

Learning Objectives *set the goals of the chapter*

Quote *sidebars provide insight from experienced multimedia professionals*

Keywords, *identified in red, point out important vocabulary and definitions you need to know*

Notes, Tips *and* **Warnings** *create a road map for success*

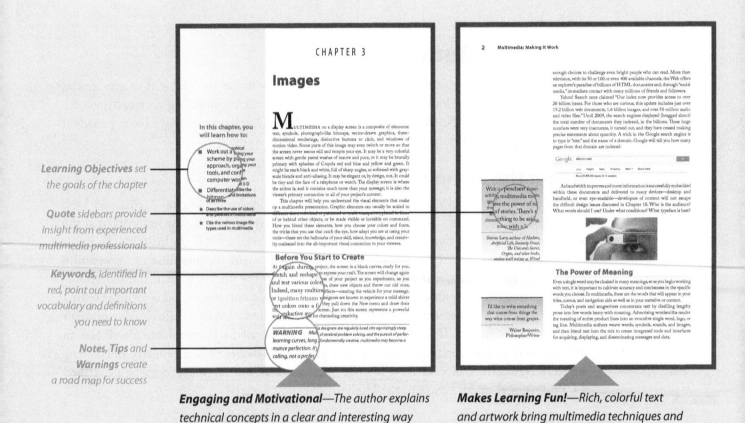

Engaging and Motivational—*The author explains technical concepts in a clear and interesting way using real-world examples.*

Makes Learning Fun!—*Rich, colorful text and artwork bring multimedia techniques and technologies to life.*

Proven *Learning Method Keeps You on Track*

Multimedia: Making It Work is structured to give you a comprehensive understanding of multimedia tools, technologies, and techniques. The book's active learning methodology guides you beyond mere recall and through thought-provoking sidebars, essay topics, and lab projects. It is designed to foster your creativity and the development of critical-thinking and communication skills.

Effective Learning Tools

This feature-rich book is designed to make learning easy and enjoyable as you develop the skills and abilities that will aid you in your multimedia education and career. Woven directly into the text are the author's own personal insights gained from more than 20 years in the multimedia industry. This expertise, combined with a personal and humorous style, makes learning interesting, motivational, and fun.

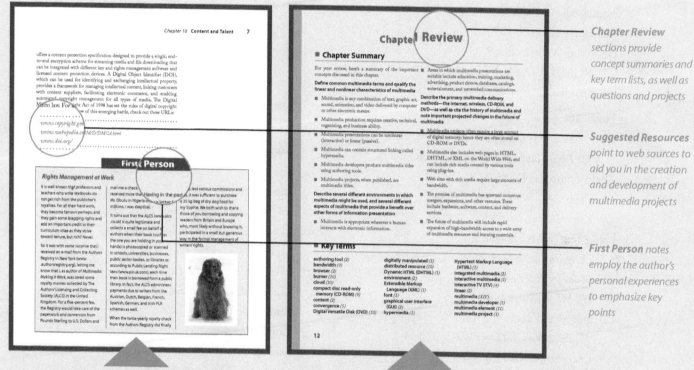

Chapter Review sections provide concept summaries and key term lists, as well as questions and projects

Suggested Resources point to web sources to aid you in the creation and development of multimedia projects

First Person notes employ the author's personal experiences to emphasize key points

Provides Professional Insight— Quotes from experts in the field and notes from the author put key concepts into the context of real-world situations.

Robust Learning Tools— Summaries, key terms lists, quizzes, essay questions, and lab projects help you practice skills and measure progress.

Each chapter includes:

- **Learning objectives** that set measurable goals for chapter-by-chapter progress
- Color **artwork** that makes difficult concepts easy to visualize and understand
- Shared personal expertise from experts in the field in the form of **First Person** notes, sidebar **quotes**, **Vaughan's Laws**, and **Vaughan's Rules**

- **Notes**, **Tips**, and **Warnings** that highlight important concepts and guide you through difficult areas
- Highlighted **Key Terms**, **Key Terms lists**, and **Chapter Summaries** that provide you with an easy way to review important concepts and vocabulary
- Challenging **End-of-Chapter Quizzes** that include vocabulary-building exercises, multiple-choice questions, essay questions, and lab projects

Contents

Acknowledgments

This ninth edition of *Multimedia: Making It Work* includes the cumulated input and advice of many colleagues and friends over almost a quarter century. Each time I revise and update this book, I am pleased to see that the acknowledgments section grows. Indeed, it is difficult to delete people from this (huge) list because, like the stones of a medieval castle still occupied, new and revised material relies upon the older foundation. I will continue accumulating the names of the good people who have helped me build this edifice and list them here, at least until my publisher cries "Enough!" and provides substantial reason to press the DELETE key.

At McGraw-Hill, Meghan Manfre and Mary Demery were instrumental in producing this ninth edition and keeping me on track. Jody McKenzie and Howie Severson provided superb design and production solutions, while Melinda Lytle oversaw graphic quality and Bill McManus and Paul Tyler copyedited and proofread, respectively. Erik Martin worked up interesting student projects and exercises. As technical editor for this edition, Professor Eileen Webb from the UK helped to bring current the detailed descriptions of the many elements of multimedia that are discussed in the book and helped me with the necessary pruning of accumulated old stuff. Not many people use floppy disks or VCRs today.

In past editions, Brad Borch, Tim Green, Jennifer Housh, Julie Smith, Jimmie Young from Tolman Creek Design, Joe Silverthorn, Chris Johnson, Jennie Yates, John and Kathryn Ross, Madhu Prasher, Frank Zurbano, Judith Brown, Athena Honore, Roger Stewart, Alissa Larson, Cindy Wathen, Eileen Corcoran, Megg Bonar, Robin Small, Lyssa Wald, Scott Rogers, Stephane Thomas, Bob Myren, Heidi Poulin, Mark Karmendy, Joanne Cuthbertson, Bill Pollock, Jeff Pepper, Kathy Hashimoto, Marla Shelasky, Linda Medoff, Valerie Robbins, Cindy Brown, Larry Levitsky, Frances Stack, Jill Pisoni, Carol Henry, and Linda Beatty went out of their way to keep me on track. Chip Harris, Donna Booher, Takis Metaxas, Dan Hilgert, Helayne Waldman, Hank Duderstadt, Dina Medina, Joyce Edwards, Theo Posselt, Ann Stewart, Graham Arlen, Kathy Gardner, Steve Goeckler, Steve Peha, Christine Perey, Pam Sansbury, Terry Schussler, Alden Trull, Eric Butler, and Michael Allen have contributed to making the work more complete since its first edition.

Since the fifth edition, peer reviewers Sandi Watkins, Dana Bass, David Williams, Joseph Parente, Elaine Winston, Wes Baker, Celina Byers, Nancy Doubleday, Tom Duff, Chris Hand, Scott Herd, Kenneth Hoffman, Sherry Hutson, Judith Junger, Ari Kissiloff, Peter Korovessis, Sallie Kravetz, Jeff Kushner, Theresa McHugh, Ken Messersmith, Marianne Nilsson, Lyn Pemberton, Samuel Shiffman, and Dennis Woytek have added significant structure to the book's foundation.

I would also like to acknowledge many friends in the computer and publishing industries who continue to make this book possible. They send me quotes and multimedia anecdotes to enliven the book; many arranged for me to review and test software and hardware; many have been there when I needed them. Some from editions past have changed companies or left the industry; my friend Dana Atchley, the well-known digital storyteller, has died. Whole companies in the list below have died, too, since the first edition of this book, but their discorporation is mourned differently from the heartfelt loss of the real people and real creators who launched the information age. I would like to thank them all for the time and courtesy they have afforded me on this long-legged project:

Grace Abbett, Adobe Systems
Jennifer Ackman, Edelman Worldwide
Eric Alderman, HyperMedia Group
Heather Alexander, Waggener Edstrom
Laura Ames, Elgin/Syferd PR
Kurt Andersen, Andersen Design
Ines Anderson, Claris
Travis Anton, BoxTop Software
David Antoniuk, Live Oak Multimedia
Yasemin Argun, Corel Systems

Cornelia Atchley, Comprehensive Technologies
Dana Atchley, Network Productions
Pamela Atkinson, Pioneer Software
Paul Babb, Maxon Computer
Ann Bagley, Asymetrix
Patricia Baird, *Hypermedia Journal*
Gary Baker, Technology Solutions
Richard Bangs, Mountain Travel-Sobek
Sean Barger, Equilibrium

Jon Barrett, Dycam
Kathryn Barrett, O'Reilly & Associates
Heinz Bartesch, The Search Firm
Bob Bauld, Bob Bauld Productions
Thomas Beinar, Add-On America/Rohm
Bob Bell, SFSU Multimedia Studies Program
George Bell, Ocron
Mike Bellefeuille, Corel Systems
Andrew Bergstein, Altec Lansing
Kathy Berlan, Borland International

Camarero Bernard, mFactory
Brian Berson, Diamondsoft
Bren Besser, Unlimited Access
Time Bigoness, Equilibrium
Ken Birge, Weber Shandwick
Nancy Blachman, Variable Symbols
Dana Blankenhorn, Have Modem Will Travel
Brian Blum, The Software Toolworks
Sharon Bodenschatz, International Typeface
Michele Boeding, ICOM Simulations
Donna Booher, Timestream
Gail Bower, TMS
Kellie Bowman, Adobe Systems
Susan Boyer, Blue Sky Software
Deborah Brown, Technology Solutions
Eric Brown, *NewMedia Magazine*
Russell Brown, Adobe Systems
Tiffany Brown, Network Associates
Stephanie Bryan, SuperMac
Ann Marie Buddrus, Digital Media Design
David Bunnell, *NewMedia Magazine*
Jeff Burger, Creative Technologies
Steven Burger, Ricoh
Bridget Burke, Gryphon Software
Dominique Busso, OpenMind
Ben Calica, Tools for the Mind
Doug Campbell, Spinnaker Software
Teri Campbell, MetaCreations
Doug Camplejohn, Apple Computer
Norman Cardella, Best-Seller
Tim Carrigan, *Multimedia Magazine*
Sara Chesiuk, Corel
Mike Childs, Global Mapper Software
Herman Chin, Computer Associates
    International
Curtis Christiansen, Deneba Software
Jane Chuey, Macromedia
Angie Ciarloni, Hayes
Kevin Clark, Strata
Cathy Clarke, DXM Productions
Regina Coffman, Smith Micro
Frank Colin, Equilibrium
David Collier, decode communications
Kelly Anne Connors, Alien Skin
David Conti, AimTech
Freda Cook, Aldus
Renee Cooper, Miramar Systems
Wendy Cornish, Vividus
Patrick Crisp, Caere
Michelle Cunningham, Symantec
Lee Curtis, CE Software
Eric Dahlinger, Newer Technology
Kirsten Davidson, Autodesk
Pete Daly, Porter Novelli /Nuance
John deLorimier, Kallisto Productions
John Derryberry, A&R Partners/Adobe Systems
Jeff Dewey, Luminaria
Jon Diaz, E Ink

Jennifer Doettling, Delta Point
Sarah Duckett, Sonic Solutions
Hank Duderstadt, Timestream
Mike Duffy, The Software Toolworks
Eileen Ebner, McLean Public Relations
Dawn Echols, Oracle
Dorothy Eckel, Specular International
Joyce Edwards, Timestream
Kevin Edwards, c|net
Mark Edwards, Independent Multimedia
    Developer
Dan Elenbaas, Amaze!
Ellen Elias, O'Reilly & Associates
Shelly Ellison, Tektronix
Heidi Elmer, Sonic Foundry
Kathy Englar, RayDream
Jonathan Epstein, MPC World
Jeff Essex, Audio Synchrosy
Sharron Evans, Graphic Directions
Kiko Fagan, Attorney at Law
Joe Fantuzzi, Macromedia
Lee Feldman, Voxware
Laura Finkelman, S & S Communications
Holly Fisher, MetaTools
Sean Flaherty, Nemetschek/VectorWorks
Terry Fleming, Timeworks
Patrick Ford, Microsoft
Marty Fortier, Prosonus
Robin Galipeau, Mutual/Hadwen Imaging
Kathy Gardner, Gardner Associates
Peter Gariepy, Zedcor
Bill Gates, Microsoft
Petra Gerwin, Mathematica
John Geyer, Terran Interactive
Jonathan Gibson, Form and Function
Brittany Gidican, Edelman
Karen Giles, Borland
Amanda Goodenough, AmandaStories
Danny Goodman, Concentrics Technology
Howard Gordon, Xing Technology
Jessica Gould, Corel
Jonathan Graham, Iomega
Catherine Greene, LightSource
Fred Greguras, Fenwick & West
Maralyn Guarino, Blue Sky Software
Cari Gushiken, Copithorne & Bellows
Kim Haas, McLean Public Relations
Marc Hall, Deneba Software
Johan Hamberg, Timestream
Lynda Hardman, CWI—Netherlands
Tom Hargadon, Conference Communications
Chip Harris, InHouse Productions
Scott Harris, Chief Architect
Sue Hart, FileMaker
Trip Hawkins, 3DO/Electronic Arts
Randy Haykin, Apple Computer
Jodi Hazzan, SoftQuad
Ray Heizer, Heizer Software

Dave Heller, Salient Software
Josh Hendrix, CoSA
Maria Hermanussen, Gold Disk
Allan Hessenflow, HandMade Software
Lars Hidde, The HyperMedia Group
Erica Hill, Nuance
Dave Hobbs, LickThis
Petra Hodges, Mathematica
Kerry Hodgins, Corel
John Holder, John V. Holder Software
Elena Holland, Traveling Software
Mike Holm, Apple Computer
Robert Hone, Red Hill Studios
Kevin Howat, MacMillan Digital
Joy Hsu, Sonnet Technologies
Tom Hughes, PhotoDisc
Claudia Husemann, Cunningham
    Communications
Les Inanchy, Sony CD-ROM Division
Tom Inglesby, Manufacturing Systems
Carl Jaffe, Yale University School of Medicine
Farrah Jinha, Vertigo 3D
Cynthia Johnson, BoxTop Software
Scott Johnson, NTERGAID
JoAnn Johnston, Regis McKenna
Neele Johnston, Autodesk
Jedidah Karanja, Genealogy.com
Dave Kaufer, Waggener Edstrom
David Kazanjian, AFTRA Actor
Jenna Keller, Alexander Communications
Helen Kendrick, Software Publishing
Benita Kenn, Creative Labs
Duncan Kennedy, Tribeworks
Trudy Kerr, Alexander Communications
Gary Kevorkian, ULead Systems
Deirdre Kidd, Nemetschek
David Kleinberg, NetObjects
Jeff Kleindinst, Turtle Beach Systems
Kevin Klingler, Sonic Desktop Software
Sharon Klocek, Visual In-Seitz
Christina Knighton, Play Incorporated
Lewis Kraus, InfoUse
Katrina Krebs, Micrografx
Kevin Krejci, Pop Rocket
Bob Kremers, Waggoner Edstrom
Larry Kubo, Ocron
Jennifer Kuhl, Peppercom
Howard Kwak, Multimedia SourceBook
Irving Kwong, Waggener Edstrom
Craig LaGrow, *Morph's Outpost*
Lisa Lance, Vectorworks
Kimberly Larkin, Alexander Communications
Kevin LaRue, Allegiant Technologies
Mark Law, Extensis
Nicole Lazzaro, ONYX Productions
Dick Lehr, Boston University
Alan Levine, Maricopa Community Colleges
Bob LeVitus, LeVitus Productions

Steven Levy, *MacWorld*
Kitten Linderman, LaserSoft Imaging
Leigh-Ann Lindsey, Mathematica
Rob Lippincott, Lotus
Mark Lissick, C-Star Technology
Jason Lockhart, G3 Systems
Elliot Luber, Technology Solutions
David Ludwig, Interactive Learning Designs
Kirk Lyford, Vivid Details
Jennifer Lyng, Aladdin Systems
John MacLeod, FastForward
Philip Malkin, Passport Designs
Kevin Mallon, FileMaker
Basil Maloney, Winalysis
Kathy Mandle, Adobe Systems
Audrey Mann, Technology Solutions
Lisa Mann, O'Reilly & Associates
Brent Marcus, Bender/Helper Impact
Nicole Martin, Netopia/Farallon Division
Jim Matthews, Fetch Software
Robert May, Ikonic
Georgia McCabe, Applied Graphics Technologies
Rod McCall, Runtime Revolution
Russ McCann, Ares Software
Kevin McCarthy, Medius IV
Charles McConathy, MicroNet Technology
Carol McGarry, Schwartz Communications
Peter McGill, Pilot and Photographer
Laurie McLean, McLean Public Relations
Amy McManus, Delta Point
Bert Medley, *The NBC Today Show*
Art Metz, Metz
Steve Michel, Author
Aline Mikaelian, Screenplay Systems
Nancy Miller, Canto Software
Doug Millison, *Morph's Outpost*
Karen Milne, Insignia Solutions
Brian Molyneaux, Heizer Software
Molly Morelock, Macromedia
Jeff Morgan, Radmedia
Rob Morris, VGraph
Glenn Morrisey, Asymetrix
Terry Morse, Terry Morse Software
Brendan Mullin, Peppercom
Rachel Muñoz, Caere
Philip Murray, Knowledge Management Associates
Heather Nagey, LiveCode/RunRev
Chuck Nakell, Inspiration Software
Kee Nethery, Kagi Engineering
Chris Newell, Musitek
Mark Newman, Photographer
Wendy Woods Newman, *Newsbytes*
Terry Nizko, AimTech
Glenn Ochsenreiter, MPC Marketing Council
Maureen O'Conell, Apple Computer
Jim O'Gara, Altsys

Eric Olson, Virtus
Karen Oppenheim, Cunningham Communications
Kim Osborne, Symantec
Nicole DeMeo Overson, GoLive Systems
Andy Parng, PixoArts
David Pawlan, Timestream
Naomi Pearce, Bare Bones Software
Susan Pearson, Waggener Edstrom
Lorena Peer, Chroma Graphics
Steve Peha, Music Technology Associates
Sylvester Pesek, Optical Media International
Christiane Petite, Symantec
Paul Phelan, INESC (Portugal)
Michael Pilmer, Alien Skin Software
Scott Pink, Bronson
Audrey Pobre, Quarterdeck
Dave Pola, Equilibrium
JB Popplewell, Alien Skin Software
Melissa Rabin, Miramar
Shirley Rafieetary, Medius IV
Tom Randolph, FM Towns/Fujitsu
Steven Rappaport, Interactive Records
Ronelle Reed, Switzer Communications
David Reid, Author
Diane Reynolds, Graphsoft
Laurie Robinson, Gold Disk
Chuck Rogers, MacSpeech
Connie Roloff, Software Products International
John Rootenberg, Paceworks
Amedeo Rosa, Alien Skin Software
Upasana Nattoji Roy, SWITCH!
Steve Rubenstein, *San Francisco Chronicle*
Jill Ryan, McLean Public Relations
Marie Salerno, AFTRA/SAG
John Sammis, DataDescription
Jay Sandom, Einstein & Sandom
Pam Sansbury, Disc Manufacturing
Richard Santalesa, R&D Technologies
Anne Sauer, Fast Electronic U.S.
Joe Scarano, DS Design
Sonya Schaefer, Adobe Systems
Rochelle Schiffman, Electronics for Imaging
Rachel Schindler, Macromedia
Melissa Scott, Window Painters
Sandy Scott, Soft-Kat
Brigid Sealy, INESC (Portugal)
Karl Seppala, Gold Disk
Peter Severin, WireframeSketcher
Chip Shabazian, Ocron
Ashley Sharp, Virtus
Philip Shaw, CodeStyle
Elizabeth Siedow, Macromedia
Adam Silver, Videologic
Stephanie Simpson, Adaptec
Marlene Sinicki, Designer
Chris Smith, VideoLabs

Brian Snook, Visual In-Seitz
Kent Sokoloff, Timestream
Simone Souza, Roxio
David Spitzer, Hewlett-Packard
Chris Sprigman, King & Spalding
Domenic Stansberry, Author
Ann Stewart, Interactive Dimensions
Polina Sukonik, Xaos Tools
Lisa Sunaki, Autodesk
Lee Swearingen, DXM Productions
Joe Taglia, Insignia Solutions
Meredith Taitz, Bare Bones Software
Marty Taucher, Microsoft
Bill Tchakirides, U-Design Type Foundry
Toni Teator, NetObjects
Amy Tenderich, Norton-Lambert
Lori Ternacole, SoftQuad
Dave Terran, WordPerfect
Leo Thomas, Eastman Kodak
Terry Thompson, Timestream
Bill Thursby, Thursby Software Systems
Alexandrea Todd, McLean Public Relations
Kim Tompkins, Micrografx
Tom Toperczer, Imspace Systems
Cara Ucci, Autodesk
Ross Uchimura, GC3
Jane Van Saun, Scansoft
David Vasquez, SFSU Multimedia Studies Program
Sally von Bargen, 21st Century Media
Dan Wagner, Miramar Systems
Helayne Waldman, SFSU Multimedia Studies Program
James J. Waldron, Visage
Arnold Waldstein, Creative Labs
Keri Walker, Apple Computer
Brad Walter, Leister Productions
Jon Ward, Tribeworks
Stefan Wennik, Bitstream
Chris Wheeler, TechSmith
Jim White, Alien Skin Software
Tom White, Roland
John Wilczak, HSC Software
Darby Williams, Microsoft
Laura Williams, Waggener Edstrom
Mark Williams, Microsoft
Shelly Williams, Prosonus
Hal Wine, Programmer
Sara Winge, O'Reilly & Associates
Warren Witt, Thursby Software Systems
Marcus Woehrmann, Handmade Software
Sandy Wong, Fenwick & West
Greg Wood, Corel
Chris Yalonis, Passport Designs
Alexandra Yessios, auto*des*sys
Karl-Heinz Zahorsky, LaserSoft Imaging
Barbara Zediker, Pioneer
Frank Zellis, KyZen

Image Credits

Illustration 2-2 on page 2 courtesy of Google, Inc.

Figure 2-7 used with permission from E Ink Corporation.

Figure 2-10 courtesy of Nickshanks with permission granted under the terms of the GNU Free Documentation License, Version 1.3, http://commons.wikimedia.org/wiki/Commons:GNU_Free_Documentation_License.

Illustration 2-17 on page 39 courtesy of Iron Bishop with permission granted under the terms of the Creative Commons Attribution 3.0 Unported License, http://creativecommons.org/licenses/by/3.0/legalcode.

Illustration 3-4 on page 92 courtesy of Marvin Raaijmakers with permission granted under the terms of the Creative Commons Attribution-ShareAlike 2.5 License, http://creativecommons.org/licenses/by-sa/2.5/legalcode.

Illustration 4-2d on page 109 courtesy of Axolotl Nr. 733 with permission granted under the terms of the Creative Commons Attribution 3.0 Unported License, http://creativecommons.org/licenses/by/3.0/legalcode.

Illustration 4-2e on page 109 courtesy of Quentar, Michal Starosta, Tomáš Solár with permission granted under the terms of the Creative Commons Attribution 3.0 Unported License, http://creativecommons.org/licenses/by/3.0/legalcode.

Figure 7-2 courtesy of XXV with permission granted under the terms of the Creative Commons Attribution-ShareAlike 3.0 Unported license, http://creativecommons.org/licenses/by-sa/3.0/legalcode.

Illustration 7-7 on page 216 courtesy of GRPH3B18 with permission granted under the terms of the Creative Commons Attribution 3.0 Unported License, http://creativecommons.org/licenses/by/3.0/legalcode.

Figure 12-3 courtesy of Aimee Daniells with permission granted under the terms of the Creative Commons Attribution-ShareAlike 2.0 License.

Illustration 7-8 on page 219 courtesy of Peter McGill.

Figure 8-5 courtesy of Upasana Nattoji Roy.

Illustration 10-3 on page 318 courtesy of Creative Commons, http://creativecommons.org.

Figure 10-6 courtesy of SAG-AFTRA.

Figure 12-1a courtesy of Bilby with permission granted under the terms of the Creative Commons Attribution 3.0 Unported License, http://creativecommons.org/licenses/by/3.0/legalcode.

Figure 12-1b courtesy of Square, Inc.

Illustration 12-1 on page 393 courtesy of Derzsi Elekes Andor with permission granted under the terms of the Creative Commons Attribution 3.0 Unported License, http://creativecommons.org/licenses/by/3.0/legalcode.

Illustration 12-2 on page 397 courtesy of Dannie-walker with permission granted under the terms of the Creative Commons Attribution 3.0 Unported License, http://creativecommons.org/licenses/by/3.0/legalcode.

Figure 12-4 courtesy of Mr3641 with permission granted under the terms of the Creative Commons Attribution 3.0 Unported License, http://creativecommons.org/licenses/by/3.0/legalcode.

Figure 12-5 courtesy of Tsaitgaist with permission granted under the terms of the Creative Commons Attribution 3.0 Unported License, http://creativecommons.org/licenses/by/3.0/legalcode.

Illustration 12-5 on page 399 courtesy of Samsung Belgium with permission granted under the terms of the Creative Commons Attribution-ShareAlike 2.0 Generic License, http://creativecommons.org/licenses/by/2.0/.

Illustration 12-7 on page 401 courtesy of ed g2s with permission granted under the terms of the Creative Commons Attribution 3.0 Unported License, http://creativecommons.org/licenses/by/3.0/legalcode.

Illustration 12-8 on page 405 courtesy of Google with permission granted under the terms of the Creative Commons Attribution 3.0 Unported License, http://creativecommons.org/licenses/by/3.0/legalcode.

Illustrations 12–13 on page 410 and 12–15 on page 415 courtesy of RunRev, Ltd.

Introduction

Since the first edition of this book in 1992, it has been necessary to update its content every few years. In writing this ninth edition, it is more than ever clear that changes in multimedia tools, technologies, and delivery platforms are occurring at an increasingly rapid pace. Indeed, the rate of change itself seems exponential as new ideas and new applications of multimedia are born, gain traction, and then bear yet newer ideas in often unpredictable and immediate follow-ons. Overnight, words like "tweet" and "selfie" enter the lexicon and explode through the Internet into common usage. With cloud computing and ever-more powerful browsers, cross-platform difficulties among Windows, Mac, and Linux systems are diminished, while the ubiquity of tablets, mobile devices, and smartphones presents new miniaturization and serious human interface issues. With modern mechanical designs, new tools are invented: "spudgers" are as necessary now as screwdrivers in the world of computer and electronic gear repair.

Happily for the longevity of this book, the fundamental concepts and techniques required to work with the elements of multimedia remain unchanged, and there are serious learning curves to climb before you can make your multimedia-capable computer stand up and dance!

This is a book about the basic parts of multimedia as much as about how to sew these parts together with current technology and tools. It is a book that shows you how to use text, images, sound, and video to deliver your messages and content in meaningful ways. It is about design-

This "Black Stick" opens Apple iPhones and iPods, Mac Laptops and Desktops. Also used to open MP3/MP4 Players, Mobile Phones, Laptops, PCs, and any other Electronic Device. Will not scratch surfaces. Temperature resistant. Flat (screwdriver) end for spudging wire leads. Notch end for hooking and pulling wires or components. Pointed end used to form leads, probe, point, and hold objects for soldering. 6" long.

Spudger: Three Tools In One!

ing, organizing, and producing multimedia projects of all kinds and avoiding technical and legal pitfalls along the way. Above all, it is a practical guide to making multimedia, complete with keywords, quizzes, exercises, tips, pointers, and answers.

The first part deals with the basic elements of multimedia and the skills required to work with them. Hardware and software tools are described in detail. You will learn about the importance of text and how to make characters look pretty, about making graphic art on your computer and how to choose colors, and about how to digitize sound and video segments. You will learn about human interaction and how to design a user-friendly computer interface. Then you will be introduced to the step-by-step creative and organizing process that results in a finished multimedia project. Today, the fastest moving wavefront in multimedia may be seen on the Internet, so I have updated and enlarged the chapters about designing, creating, and delivering multimedia for the Web and for Internet-connected multimedia devices. Indeed, with this ninth edition, I have included a new chapter about mobile devices, tablets, and smartphones.

I have written this book for people who make or want to make multimedia, for people who gladly take up new challenges and are unafraid of intensely creative work. The words and ideas of this book are the harvest of many years in the computer industry and of hands-on experience deep in the factory where multimedia is being made. The book is intended to be, above all, useful.

I have made a great effort to include in this book references to as much multimedia software and hardware as I could, trying not to miss any players. But because the industry is fast paced and rapidly evolving, and because, while writing this book, I have rediscovered the finite limits of my own time, I am sure some have fallen into the bit bucket anyway. Immutable physical laws have prevented me from including the fine details of 40 or 50 hardware and software manuals and technical resources into the pages allowed for this book. The distillation presented here should, however, point you toward further information and study. I have also made a great effort to double-check my words and statements for accuracy; if errors have slipped past, they are mine alone.

Two decades ago, people's experience on the information highway was a smooth ride paved with behavioral etiquette and with many kindnesses evolved from properly socialized dot-EDU users. Commerce was prohibited. Discourse and idea exchange through e-mail and newsgroups was encouraged. Language shortcuts such as IMHO (In My Humble Opinion) and smiley faces were de jure. RTFM was reserved for only the most surly.

Who could have predicted the impact of commerce, when the dot-com top-level domain was opened for business? Well, Adam Smith's free hand of capitalism is at work, straining First Amendment rights to free speech and inciting road rage on the information highway. Now you can buy a million e-mail addresses, and if only half a percent of recipients respond to your body part enhancement, vitamin, or mortgage rate spam, you can make a fortune. Not only are computer platforms and multimedia implements changing, so is our notion of etiquette. With the tools described in this book, you will be able to shape the very nature of information and how it is accessed and presented, and you will invent the future. Remember to be polite: some people suggest that if you go flying back through time and you see somebody else flying forward into the future, it's probably best to avoid eye contact.

Many years ago, after completing a book about HyperCard, I swore never to write another. Writing a book is much like childbirth, I believe. In the beginning, it gestates slowly, usually over a few months. Then it ramps up inexorably and quickly toward deadline, until all attention is focused upon the delivery itself, and the pain and workload are great. Editors cry, "Push." Afterwards, you remember it was rough, but memories of the pain itself become diffused, and one is only too easily persuaded to do it again. I am glad to share my multimedia experiences with you, and hope that in reading this book you will become better at what you do.

Tay Vaughan
Scientists' Cliffs
Port Republic, Maryland
May 2014

INSTRUCTOR AND STUDENT ONLINE LEARNING CENTER

For instructor and student resources, check out the Online Learning Center, www.mhprofessional.com/VaughanMultimediaOLC9e.com.

Additional Resources for Students

The Student Center on the Online Learning Center features more information about the book's author, table of contents, and key features, as well as an electronic sample chapter.

Additional Resources for Instructors

Instructor support materials are provided on the Online Learning Center's Instructor Download page. The Instructor Download page features the following:

- **Password protection** to ensure instructor-only use
- **Answer Keys** for the end-of-chapter textbook quizzes
- **Instructor's Manual** that contains learning objectives, classroom preparation notes, instructor tips, and a lecture outline for each chapter
- Engaging **PowerPoint slides** on the lecture topics with color artwork from the book
- **Test Bank** of questions organized by chapter in Microsoft Word and EZ Test formats
    - Access to EZ Test Online, which allows you to generate a wide array of tests, with automatic grading
    - Hundreds of questions and a wide variety of question types and difficulty levels, enabling you to customize each test to maximize student progress
- **LMS cartridges** may also be available upon request; contact your sales representative

To access the Instructor Download page, click the Instructor Requests link on the left side of the main Online Learning Center page to log in. If you do not have a username and password, click the Contact My Sales Rep link to request your username and password from your local sales representative.

Contributors to the Instructor Resources

Writer
Laura Osterweis
Associate Professor
Communication Arts Department
Framingham State University

Technical Editor
Iain Thomson
Journalist
The Register

CHAPTER 1

What Is Multimedia?

MULTIMEDIA is an eerie wail as two cat's eyes appear on a dark screen. It's the red rose that dissolves into a little girl's face when you press "Valentine's Day" on your iPhone. It's a small window of video laid onto a map of India, showing an old man recalling his dusty journey to meet a rajah there. It's an e-catalog of hybrid cars with a guide to help you buy one. It's a real-time video conference or e-meeting with colleagues in Paris, London, and Hong Kong, using whiteboards and microphones on your office computer. At home, it's an interactive geometry lesson for a fifth-grader. At the arcade, it's goggle-faced kids flying fighter planes in sweaty, virtual reality. On a DVD, it's the interactive video sequences (or screen hot spots) that explain how the *Harry Potter* movies were made.

Multimedia is any combination of text, art, sound, animation, and video delivered to you by computer or other electronic or digitally manipulated means. It is richly presented sensation. When you weave together the sensual elements of multimedia—dazzling pictures and animations, engaging sounds, compelling video clips, and raw textual information—you can electrify the thought and action centers of people's minds. When you give them interactive control of the process, they can be enchanted.

This book is about creating each of the elements of multimedia and about how you can weave them together for maximum effect. This book is for computer beginners as well as computer experts. It is for serious multimedia producers—and for their clients as well. It is for desktop publishers and video producers who may need a leg up as they watch traditional methods for delivery of information and ideas evolve into new, technology-driven formats. This book is also for hobbyists who want to make albums and family histories on the World Wide Web; for mainstream businesses who want to illustrate word-processed documents and spreadsheets with audio, video, and graphic animations; for public speakers who want to use animation and sound on large monitors and auditorium projection systems to present ideas and information to an audience; for information managers who want to organize and distribute digital images, sound, video, and text; and for educators and trainers who want to design and present information for learning.

If you are new to multimedia and are facing a major investment in hardware, software, and the time you will need to learn each new tool, take a gradual approach to these challenges. Begin by studying each element of multimedia and learning one or more tools for creating and editing that element. Get to know how to use text and fonts, how to make and edit colorful graphic images and animate them into movies, and how to record and edit digital sound. Browse the computer trade periodicals that contain the most up-to-date information. Your skills will be most valuable if you develop a broad foundation of knowledge about each of the basic elements of multimedia.

Producing a multimedia project or a web site requires more than creative skill and high technology. You need organizing and business talent as well. For example, issues of ownership and copyright will be attached to some elements that you wish to use, such as text from books, scanned images from magazines, or audio and video clips. The use of these resources often requires permission, and even payment of a fee to the owner. Indeed, the management and production infrastructure of a multimedia project may be as intense and complicated as the technology and creative skills you bring to bear in rendering it. Keys to successful development of a multimedia project are management of digital tools and skill sets, teamwork, general project management, documenting and archiving the process, and delivering the completed product on time and within budget.

> The implementation of multimedia capabilities in computers is just the latest episode in a long series: cave painting, hand-crafted manuscripts, the printing press, radio, and television.... These advances reflect the innate desire of man to create outlets for creative expression, to use technology and imagination to gain empowerment and freedom for ideas.
>
> Glenn Ochsenreiter, Director, Multimedia PC Marketing Council

Definitions

Multimedia is, as described previously, a woven combination of digitally manipulated text, photographs, graphic art, sound, animation, and video elements. When you allow an end user—also known as the viewer of a multimedia project—to control what and when the elements are delivered, it is called interactive multimedia. When you provide a structure of linked elements through which the user can navigate, interactive multimedia becomes hypermedia.

Although the definition of multimedia is a simple one, making it work can be complicated. Not only do you need to understand how to make each multimedia element stand up and dance, but you also need to know how to use multimedia computer tools and technologies to weave them together. The people who weave multimedia into meaningful tapestries are called multimedia developers.

The software vehicle, the messages, and the content presented on a computer, television screen, mobile device, or smartphone together constitute a multimedia project. If the project is to be shipped or sold to consumers or end users, typically delivered as a download on the Internet but also on a CD-ROM or DVD in a box or sleeve, with or without instructions, it is a multimedia title. Your project may also be a page or site on the World Wide Web, where you can weave the elements of multimedia into documents with Hypertext Markup Language (HTML), Dynamic HTML (DHTML), a collection of software technologies including HTML, JavaScript and CSS), or Extensible Markup Language (XML) and play rich media files created in such programs as Adobe's Flash or Apple's

QuickTime by installing plug-ins into a browser application such as Microsoft Internet Explorer, Apple Safari, Google Chrome, or Mozilla Firefox. Browsers are software programs or tools for viewing content on the Web. See Chapter 11 for more about plug-ins, multimedia, and the Web.

A multimedia project need not be interactive to be called multimedia: users can sit back and watch it just as they do a movie or the television. In such cases a project is linear, or starting at the beginning and running through to the end. When users are given navigational control and can wander through the content at will, multimedia becomes nonlinear and user interactive, and is a powerful personal gateway to information.

Determining how a user will interact with and navigate through the content of a project requires great attention to the message, the scripting or storyboarding, the artwork, and the programming. You can break an entire project with a badly designed interface. You can also lose the message in a project with inadequate or inaccurate content.

Multimedia elements are typically sewn together into a project using authoring tools. These software tools are designed to manage individual multimedia elements and provide user interaction. Integrated multimedia is the "weaving" part of the multimedia definition, where source documents such as montages, graphics, video cuts, and sounds merge into a final presentation. In addition to providing a method for users to interact with the project, most authoring tools also offer facilities for creating and editing text and images and controls for playing back separate audio and video files that have been created with editing tools designed for these media. The sum of what gets played back and how it is presented to the viewer on a monitor is the graphical user interface (GUI, pronounced "gooey"). The GUI is more than just the actual graphics on the screen—it also often provides the rules or structure for the user's input. The combination of hardware and software that governs the limits of what can happen here is the multimedia platform or environment.

Where to Use Multimedia

Multimedia is appropriate whenever a human user is connected to electronic information of any kind, at the "human interface." Multimedia enhances minimalist, text-only computer interfaces and yields measurable benefit by gaining and holding attention and interest; in short, multimedia improves information retention. When it's properly constructed, multimedia can also be profoundly entertaining as well as useful.

Multimedia in Business

Business applications for multimedia include presentations, training, marketing, advertising, product demos, simulations, databases, catalogs, instant messaging, and networked communications. Voice mail and video

---

> Multimedia is a very effective presentation and sales tool. If you're being driven somewhere in the back seat of a car, you may not remember how you got to your destination. If you had been driving the car yourself, chances are you could get there again. Studies indicate that if you're stimulated with audio, you will have about a 20 percent retention rate. With audio-visual, retention is up to 30 percent and in interactive multimedia presentations, where you are really involved, the retention rate is as high as 60 percent.
>
> Jay Sandom,
> Einstein & Sandom

> For viewers presented with graphics and words, not just words alone, there was a 23 percent increase in retention (ability to remember information) and an 89 percent increase in transfer (ability to creatively apply information).
>
> From *Multimedia Learning* by Richard E. Mayer, Cambridge University Press, 2001

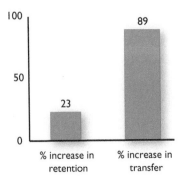

conferencing are provided on many local and wide area networks (LANs and WANs) using distributed networks and Internet protocols.

After a morning of mind-numbing presentations delivered from the podium of a national sales conference, a multimedia presentation can make an audience come alive. Most presentation software packages let you make pretty text and add audio and video clips to the usual slide show of graphics and text material.

Multimedia is enjoying widespread use in training programs. Flight attendants learn to manage international terrorism and security through simulation. Drug enforcement agencies are trained using interactive videos and photographs to recognize likely hiding places on airplanes and ships. Medical doctors and veterinarians can practice surgery methods via simulation prior to actual surgery. Mechanics learn to repair engines. Salespeople learn about product lines and leave behind software to train their customers. Fighter pilots practice full-terrain sorties before spooling up for the real thing. Increasingly easy-to-use authoring programs and media production tools even let workers on assembly lines create their own training programs for use by their peers.

Multimedia around the office has also become more commonplace. Image capture hardware is used for building employee ID and badging databases, for scanning medical insurance cards, for video annotation, and for real-time teleconferencing. Presentation documents attached to e-mail and video conferencing are widely available. Laptop computers and high-resolution projectors are commonplace for multimedia presentations on the road. Mobile devices and smartphones utilizing 4G, WiFi, and Bluetooth communications technology make communication and the pursuit of business more efficient.

As companies and businesses catch on to the power of multimedia, the cost of installing multimedia capability decreases, meaning that more applications can be developed both in-house and by third parties, allowing businesses to run more smoothly and effectively. These advances are changing the very way business is transacted by affirming that the use of multimedia offers a significant contribution to the bottom line while also advertising the public image of the business as an investor in technology.

> History has proven that advances in the way we communicate can give rise to entirely new communication cultures. Much like the transition from radio to TV, the evolution from text messaging to multimedia messaging (MMS) marks a whole new era of mobile communications, combining images with sound and text.
>
> Jorma Ollila, Chairman and CEO of Nokia

Multimedia in Schools

Schools are perhaps the destination most in need of multimedia. It is in schools that the power of multimedia can be maximized for the greatest long-term benefit to all.

Many schools in the United States today are chronically underfunded and, consequently, occasionally slow to adopt new technologies. The U.S. government has challenged the telecommunications industry to connect every classroom, library, clinic, and hospital in America to the information superhighway. Funded by telephone surcharges collected per the Universal

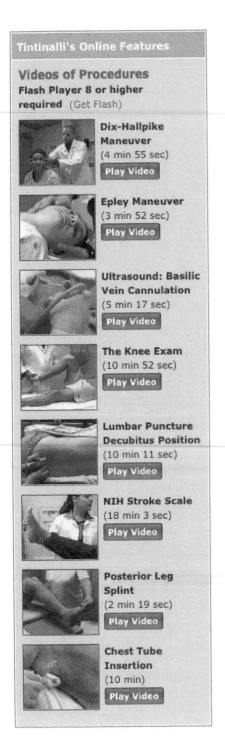

Tintinalli's Online Features

Videos of Procedures
Flash Player 8 or higher required (Get Flash)

Dix-Hallpike Maneuver
(4 min 55 sec)
[Play Video]

Epley Maneuver
(3 min 52 sec)
[Play Video]

Ultrasound: Basilic Vein Cannulation
(5 min 17 sec)
[Play Video]

The Knee Exam
(10 min 52 sec)
[Play Video]

Lumbar Puncture Decubitus Position
(10 min 11 sec)
[Play Video]

NIH Stroke Scale
(18 min 3 sec)
[Play Video]

Posterior Leg Splint
(2 min 19 sec)
[Play Video]

Chest Tube Insertion
(10 min)
[Play Video]

Figure 1-1 Multimedia e-learning is a powerful, convenient, and cost-effective tool for both instructors and students. From *Tintinalli's Emergency Medicine: A Comprehensive Study Guide*, available online at http://accessemergencymedicine.com.

Service Program for Schools and Libraries (E-Rate), most schools and libraries in the United States are now connected. Steps have also been taken to provide governmental support for state-of-the-art technology in low-income rural and urban school districts.

Multimedia will provoke radical changes in the teaching process during the coming decades, particularly as smart students discover they can go beyond the limits of traditional teaching methods. There is, indeed, a move away from the transmission or passive-learner model of learning to the experiential learning or active-learner model. In some instances, teachers may become more like guides and mentors, or facilitators of learning, leading students along a learning path, rather than the more traditional role of being the primary providers of information and understanding. The students, not teachers, become the core of the teaching and learning process. E-learning is a sensitive and highly politicized subject among educators, so educational software is often positioned as "enriching" the learning process, not as a potential substitute for traditional teacher-based methods.

Figure 1-1 shows a selection of instructional videos used for training emergency medicine specialists. Such online e-learning provides a cost-effective vehicle to learn clinical techniques outside of the hospital setting. From real-time echocardiographic images to explanations of the chemistry of synaptic transmission, multimedia is used as an effective teaching medium in medicine and other disciplines.

An interesting use of multimedia in schools involves the students themselves. Students can put together interactive magazines and newsletters, make original art using image manipulation software tools, and interview students, townspeople, coaches, and teachers. They can even make video clips with cameras and mobile phones for local use or uploading to YouTube. They can also design and run web sites. As schools become more a part of the Internet, multimedia arrives by glass fiber and over a network.

Interactive TV (ITV) is widely used among campuses to join students from different locations into one class with one teacher. Remote trucks containing computers, generators, and a satellite dish can be dispatched to areas where people want to learn but have no computers or schools near them. In the online version of school, students can enroll at schools all over the world and interact with particular teachers and other students—classes can be accessed at the convenience of the student's lifestyle while the teacher may be relaxing on a beach and communicating via a wireless system. Washington On Line (www.waol.org), for example, offers classes to students who do not wish to spend gas money, fight traffic, and compete for parking space; they even provide training to professors so they can learn how best to present their classes online.

Multimedia at Home

From gardening, cooking, home design, remodeling, and repair to genealogy software (see Figure 1-2), multimedia has entered the home. Eventually, most multimedia projects will reach the home via displays with built-in interactive user inputs—either on old-fashioned color TVs or on new high-definition (HDTV) sets. The multimedia viewed on these sets will likely arrive on a pay-for-use basis along the data highway.

Today, home consumers of multimedia may own a computer with an attached CD-ROM, DVD, or Blu-ray disc drive and Internet access, an Internet-capable mobile device such as an e-reader, tablet, or smartphone, or a set-top player that hooks up to the television, such as a Nintendo Wii, Microsoft Xbox, or Sony PlayStation machine. There is increasing **convergence** or melding of computer-based multimedia with entertainment and games-based media traditionally described as "shoot-em-up." Nintendo alone has sold many millions of game players worldwide (see www.nintendo.co.jp/ir/en/sales/hard_soft/index.html). Users with TiVo technology (www.tivo.com) can store 450 hours of high-definition television viewing and gaming on a stand-alone hard disk.

Figure 1-2   Genealogy software such as Reunion from Leister Productions lets families add text, images, sounds, and video clips as they build their family trees.

An interactive episode of *Wild Kingdom* might start out with normal narration. "We're here in the Serengeti to learn about the animals." I see a lion on the screen and think, "I want to learn about the lion." So I point at the lion, and it zooms up on the screen. The narration is now just about the lion. I say, "Well that's really interesting, but I wonder how the lion hunts." I point at a hunt icon. Now the lion is hunting, and the narrator tells me about how it hunts. I dream about being the lion. I select another icon and now see the world from the lion's point of view, making the same kinds of decisions the lion has to make—with some hints as I go along. I'm told how I'm doing and how well I'm surviving. Kids could get very motivated from experiencing what it's like to be a lion and from wanting to be a competent lion. Pretty soon they'd be digging deeper into the information resource, finding out about animals in different parts of the world, studying geography from maps displayed on the screen, learning which animals are endangered species....

Trip Hawkins, Founder, Electronic Arts

First Person

From time to time during my childhood I would hear bits and pieces of family lore about my great-grandfather, Victor C. Vaughan, who had been, at least it seemed from snatches of occasional conversation, a Famous Person many years ago. Not until adulthood, though, did I come across his autobiography and have a chance to meet him as a real person. Today he comes to mind when we discuss "radical changes in the teaching process." He was educated the old-fashioned way on a small farm in Missouri; I'll let him tell you what it was like:

… I received the better part of my education at home. My wise mother did not pretend to dictate my instruction. She simply placed the books she desired me to read within my reach and supplied no others. I sat many a night into the wee small hours and absorbed, by the light of a sycamore ball floating in a cup of grease, the wonderful stories of Walter Scott. I knew every one of his characters in detail and sought their prototypes among those about me. I clothed the farm and the neighboring hills and dales with romance. Rob Roy's cave was a certainty. I discovered it in a high bluff on the creek. I read the works of Dickens and Thackeray with like avidity and recited the *Prisoner of Chillon* and the *Corsair*. These and books of like character filled my library shelves. There were also volumes of ancient history and I remember with what eagerness and enthusiasm I read the *Decline and Fall of the Roman Empire.* "Poor training," a present-day educator would say, for one whose adult life was to be devoted to science. This may be true, but I am reciting facts. I cannot deny that my scientific work might have been more productive had my early training been different. However, I am not making a plea for a handicap, and I remain grateful to my mother for the books I read in childhood. They continue to be associated with her hallowed memory. I never open one of these now ancient volumes without seeing her face, as with lighted candle she came to my room and gently urged me to go to bed.

Victor C. Vaughan continued to learn and apply eagerness and enthusiasm to every subject. Among his accomplishments, he became Dean of the Medical School at the University of Michigan and President of the American Medical Association. He was Surgeon General during the great Spanish Flu pandemic of 1918 and, it is said, he remained bitter to his last days that science, his great love, was unable to unravel the causes of that disaster.

It may be that today's multimedia and interactive distance learning using video and audio delivered across broadband connections may not be sufficient to compete with the light of a sycamore ball floating in a cup of grease. It may be that the fundamental driver toward the success of any person's education remains, simply and plainly, eagerness and enthusiasm.

Live Internet pay-for-play gaming with multiple players has also become popular, bringing multimedia to homes on the broadband Internet, often in combination with CD-ROMs or DVDs inserted into the user's machine. MSN Games (http://zone.msn.com/) and Sony Online Entertainment (https://www.soe.com) boast more than a million registered users each—Microsoft claims to be the most successful, with tens of thousands of people logged on and playing every evening.

Multimedia in Public Places

In hotels, airport terminals, train stations, shopping malls, museums, libraries, and grocery stores, multimedia is already available at stand-alone terminals or kiosks, providing information and help for customers. Multimedia is piped to wireless devices such as smartphones and tablets. Such installations reduce demand on traditional information booths and personnel, add value, and are available around the clock, even in the middle of the night, when live help is off duty. The way we live is changing as multimedia penetrates our day-to-day experience and our culture.

Figure 1-3 shows two screens from Scoop, a mobile shopping app for Android that provides shopping tools and information about local malls, stores, and brands. At museums, kiosks are used to guide patrons through the exhibits and, when installed at each exhibit, provide great added depth, allowing visitors to browse through richly detailed information specific to that display.

The power of multimedia has been part of the human experience for many thousands of years, and the mystical chanting of monks, cantors, and shamans accompanied by potent visual cues, raised icons, and persuasive

My wife, the keeper of remotes, has rigged an entertainment system in our house that includes a remote controlled, ceiling mounted 96" × 96" drop-down screen, a 27" 16 : 9 format LCD screen, and an 1100 lumin Dell LCD projector connected to Wavecable, our Internet provider. We can watch our own CDs or Internet or Wavecable's TV/HDTV on our big screen while we track a sports show on the smaller screen off another Wavecable box. We have three cable boxes in our house.

Joe Silverthorn, Interactive Media Professor, Olympic College

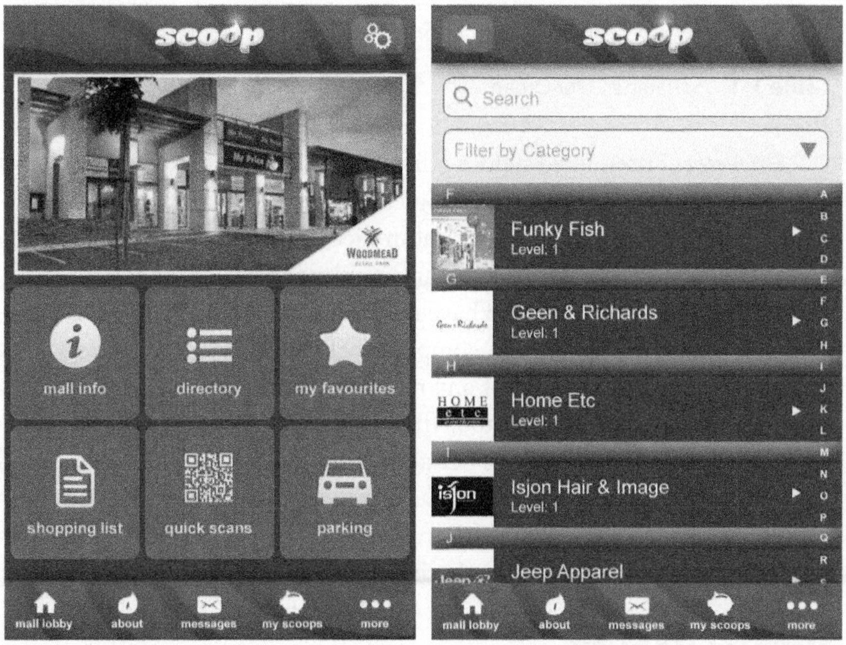

Figure 1-3 Shopping apps can make everyday life at the mall simpler.

text has long been known to produce effective responses in public places. Scriabin, the 19th-century Russian composer, used an orchestra, a piano, a chorus, and a special color organ to synthesize music and color in his Fifth Symphony, *Prometheus*. Probably suffering from synesthesia (a strange condition where a sensory stimulus, such as a color, evokes a false response, such as a smell), Scriabin talked of tactile symphonies with burning incense scored into the work. He also claimed that colors could be heard; Table 1-1 lists the colors of his color organ.

Frequency (Hz)	Note	Scriabin's Color
256	C	Red
277	C#	Violet
298	D	Yellow
319	D#	Glint of steel
341	E	Pearly white shimmer of moonlight
362	F	Deep red
383	F#	Bright blue
405	G	Rosy orange
426	G#	Purple
447	A	Green
469	A#	Glint of steel
490	B	Pearly blue

Table 1-1   Scriabin's Color Organ

Prometheus premiered before a live audience in Moscow in 1911, but the color organ had proved technologically too complicated and was eliminated from the program. Then Scriabin died suddenly of blood poisoning from a boil on his lip, so his ultimate multimedia vision, the Mysterium, remained unwritten. He would have reveled in today's world of MIDI synthesizers (see Chapter 4), rich computer colors, and video digitizers, and, though smell is not yet part of any multimedia standard, he would surely have researched that concept, too. The platforms for multimedia presentation have much improved since Scriabin's time. Today, multimedia is found in churches and places of worship as live video with attached song lyrics shown on large screens using elaborate sound systems with special effects lighting and recording facilities. Scriabin would have loved this.

Virtual Reality

At the convergence of technology and creative invention in multimedia is virtual reality, or VR. Goggles, helmets, special gloves, and bizarre human interfaces attempt to place you "inside" a lifelike experience. Take a step forward, and the view gets closer; turn your head, and the view rotates. Reach out and grab an object; your hand moves in front of you. Maybe the object explodes in a 90-decibel crescendo as you wrap your fingers around it. Or it slips out from your grip, falls to the floor, and hurriedly escapes through a mouse hole at the bottom of the wall.

VR requires terrific computing horsepower to be realistic. In VR, your cyberspace is made up of many thousands of geometric objects plotted in three-dimensional space: the more objects and the more points that describe the objects, the higher the resolution and the more realistic your view. As you move about, each motion or action requires the computer to recalculate the position, angle, size, and shape of *all* the objects that make up your view, and many thousands of computations must occur as fast as 30 times per second to seem smooth.

On the World Wide Web, standards for transmitting virtual reality worlds or scenes in VRML (Virtual Reality Modeling Language) documents (with the filename extension .wrl) or VRML's successor, X3D, have been developed. Intel and software makers such as Adobe have announced support for new 3-D technologies.

Using high-speed dedicated computers, multimillion-dollar flight simulators built by Thales, Link, and others have led the way in commercial application of VR. Pilots of F-16s, Boeing 787s, and Rockwell space shuttles have made many simulated dry runs before doing the real thing. At the Maine Maritime Academy and other merchant marine officer training schools, computer-controlled simulators teach the intricate loading and unloading of oil tankers and container ships.

Virtual reality is an extension of multimedia—and it uses the basic multimedia elements of imagery, sound, and animation. Because it requires instrumented feedback from a wired-up person, VR is perhaps interactive multimedia at its fullest extension.

> People who work in VR do not see themselves as part of "multimedia." VR deals with goggles and gloves and is still a research field where no authoring products are available, and you need a hell of a computer to develop the real-time 3-D graphics. Although there is a middle ground covered by such things as QuickTime VR and VRML that gives multimedia developers a "window" into VR, people often confuse multimedia and VR and want to create futuristic environments using multimedia-authoring tools not designed for that purpose.
>
> Panagiotis Takis Metaxis,
> Assistant Professor of
> Computer Science,
> Wellesley College

Delivering Multimedia

Multimedia requires large amounts of digital memory when stored in an end user's library, or large amounts of bandwidth when distributed over wires, glass fiber, or airwaves on a network. The greater the bandwidth, the bigger the pipeline, so more content can be delivered to end users quickly.

CD-ROM, DVD, Flash Drives

Compact disc read-only memory (CD-ROM, see Chapter 13) discs can be mass-produced for pennies and can contain up to 80 minutes of full-screen video, images, or sound. The disc can also contain unique mixes of images, sounds, text, video, and animations controlled by an authoring system to provide unlimited user interaction.

Discs can be stamped out of polycarbonate plastic as fast as cookies on a baker's production line and just as cheaply. Virtually all personal computers sold today include at least a CD-ROM/DVD reader/burner, and the software that drives these computers is commonly delivered on a disc. Multilayered **Digital Versatile Disc** (DVD) technology increases the capacity and multimedia capability of CDs to 4.7GB on a single-sided, single-layered disc to as much as 17.08GB of storage on a double-sided double-layered disc. Pioneer has recently improved Blu-ray storage to 500GB using 20 layers. Disc **burners** are used for reading discs and for making them, too, in audio, video, and data formats. DVD and Blu-ray authoring and integration software allows the creation of interactive front-end menus for both films and games.

In the longer term, however, CD-ROM, DVD, and Blu-ray discs are but interim memory technologies that will be replaced by new devices such as flash drives and thumb drives that do not require moving parts. As high-speed connections become more and more pervasive and users become better connected, copper wire, glass fiber, and radio/cellular technologies may prevail as the most common delivery means for interactive multimedia files, served from the **cloud** across the broadband Internet or from dedicated computer farms and storage facilities.

The Broadband Internet

These days telecommunications networks are global, so when information providers and content owners determine the worth of their products and how to charge money for them, information elements link up online as **distributed resources** in a data cloud, where you pay to acquire and use multimedia-based information and services.

Curiously, the actual glass fiber cables that make up much of the physical backbone of the Internet and the cloud are, in many cases, owned by railroads and pipeline companies who simply buried the cable on existing rights of way, where no special permits and environmental studies are necessary. One railroad company in the United States invested more than a million dollars in a special cable-laying trenching car; in the United Kingdom, fiber-optic cable runs in the towpaths of the decaying 19th-century canal and barge system. Bandwidth on these fiber-optic lines is leased to others, so competing retailers such as AT&T, Verizon, and Sprint may even share the same cable.

Full-text content from books and magazines is downloadable; feature movies are played at home; real-time news feeds from anywhere on earth are available; lectures from participating universities are monitored for education credits; street maps of cities are viewable (with recommendations for restaurants, in any language); and online travelogues include testimonials and video tracks. Just think—each of these interfaces or gate-ways to information is a multimedia project waiting to be developed!

. . . .

www.google.com/earth

www.google.com/maps/views

www.moviefone.com

www.netflix.com

www.travelocity.com

www.nytimes.com

www.5pm.co.uk

www.zagat.com

Maps, show times, restaurants, vacation trips, and current news items are quickly available on the Web.

. . . .

Interactive multimedia is delivered to many homes throughout the world. Interest from a confluence of entertainment mega-corps, information publishers and providers, cable and telephone companies, and hardware and software manufacturers is driving this inevitable evolution, and profound changes in global communications strategy are on the drawing boards. What will be piped through this new system for entertainment, reference, and lifelong learning experiences are the very **multimedia elements** discussed in the chapters of this book, including text, graphics, animation, sound, and video.

The actual content provided, let us hope, will be excellent fare, generated by thinking and caring creative people using ideas that will propel all of us into a better world. Entertainment companies that own content easily converted to multimedia projects are teaming up with cable TV companies. Film studios are creating new divisions to produce interactive multimedia, and wealthy talents have formed new companies to join in on the action. Google is scanning millions of books and periodicals. Even without a clear business model with known profits, large media corporations are uniting to create huge conglomerates to control the content and delivery of tomorrow's information.

Some companies own the routes for carrying data, while other companies own the hardware and software interfaces at the end of the line, at offices and homes. Some knit it all together and provide supply-on-demand and billing services. Regardless of who owns the roadways and the hardware boxes, multimedia producers create the new literature and the rich content sent along them. This is a fresh and exciting industry that is coming of age, but one that is still faced with many growing pains.

Chapter 1 Review

■ Chapter Summary

For your review, here's a summary of the important concepts discussed in this chapter.

Define common multimedia terms and qualify the linear and nonlinear characteristics of multimedia

- Multimedia is any combination of text, graphic art, sound, animation, and video delivered by computer or other electronic means.

- Multimedia production requires creative, technical, organizing, and business ability.

- Multimedia presentations can be nonlinear (interactive) or linear (passive).

- Multimedia can contain structured linking called hypermedia.

- Multimedia developers produce multimedia titles using authoring tools.

- Multimedia projects, when published, are multimedia titles.

Describe several different environments in which multimedia might be used, and several different aspects of multimedia that provide a benefit over other forms of information presentation

- Multimedia is appropriate wherever a human interacts with electronic information.

- Areas in which multimedia presentations are suitable include education, training, marketing, advertising, product demos, databases, catalogs, entertainment, and networked communications.

Describe the primary multimedia delivery methods—the Internet, wireless, CD-ROM, and DVD—as well as cite the history of multimedia and note important projected changes in the future of multimedia

- Multimedia projects often require a large amount of digital memory; hence they are often stored on CD-ROM or DVDs.

- Multimedia also includes web pages in HTML, DHTML, or XML on the World Wide Web, and can include rich media created by various tools using plug-ins.

- Web sites with rich media require large amounts of bandwidth.

- The promise of multimedia has spawned numerous mergers, expansions, and other ventures. These include hardware, software, content, and delivery services.

- The future of multimedia will include rapid expansion of high-bandwidth access to a wide array of multimedia resources and learning materials.

■ Key Terms

authoring tool *(2)*
bandwidth *(9)*
browser *(2)*
burner *(10)*
cloud *(10)*
compact disc read-only memory (CD-ROM) *(9)*
content *(2)*
convergence *(5)*
Digital Versatile Disk (DVD) *(10)*

digitally manipulated *(1)*
distributed resource *(10)*
Dynamic HTML (DHTML) *(1)*
environment *(2)*
Extensible Markup Language (XML) *(1)*
font *(1)*
graphical user interface (GUI) *(2)*
hypermedia *(1)*

Hypertext Markup Language (HTML) *(1)*
integrated multimedia *(2)*
interactive multimedia *(1)*
interactive TV (ITV) *(4)*
linear *(2)*
multimedia *(1)*
multimedia developer *(1)*
multimedia element *(11)*
multimedia project *(1)*

multimedia title *(1)*   platform *(2)*   storyboarding *(2)*
nonlinear *(2)*   scripting *(2)*   web site *(1)*

■ Key Term Quiz

1. _____ is any combination of text, graphic art, sound, animation, and video delivered to you by computer or other electronic means.

2. _____ allows an end user to control what elements are delivered and when.

3. _____ is a structure of linked elements through which the user can navigate.

4. A(n) _____ multimedia project allows users to sit back and watch it just as they do a movie or the television.

5. A(n) _____ is software designed to manage individual multimedia elements and provide user interaction.

6. The sum of what gets played back and how it is presented to the viewer on a monitor is the _____.

7. The combination of hardware and software that governs the limits of what can happen is the multimedia _____ or _____.

8. The information that makes up a multimedia presentation is referred to as _____.

9. CD and DVD _____ are used for reading and making discs.

10. HTML, DHTML, and XML web pages or sites are generally viewed using a(n) _____.

■ Multiple-Choice Quiz

1. LAN stands for:
   a. logical access node
   b. link/asset navigator
   c. local area network
   d. list authoring number
   e. low-angle noise

2. A browser is used to view:
   a. program code
   b. storyboards
   c. fonts
   d. web-based pages and documents
   e. videodiscs

3. The "ROM" in "CD-ROM" stands for:
   a. random-order memory
   b. real-object memory
   c. read-only memory
   d. raster-output memory
   e. red-orange memory

4. The software vehicle, the messages, and the content presented on a computer or television screen together make up:
   a. a multimedia project
   b. a CD-ROM
   c. a web site
   d. a multimedia title
   e. an authoring tool

5. A project that is shipped or sold to consumers or end users, typically in a box or sleeve or on the Internet, with or without instructions, is:
   a. a CD-ROM
   b. an authoring tool
   c. a multimedia project
   d. a multimedia title

6. The 19th-century Russian composer who used an orchestra, a piano, a chorus, and a special color organ to synthesize music and color in his Fifth Symphony, *Prometheus*, was:
   a. Rachmaninoff
   b. Tchaikovsky
   c. Scriabin
   d. Rimsky-Korsakov
   e. Shostakovich

7. Which one of the following *is not/are not* typically part of a multimedia specification?
   a. text
   b. odors
   c. sound
   d. video
   e. pictures

8. VR stands for:
   a. virtual reality
   b. visual response
   c. video raster
   d. variable rate
   e. valid registry

9. According to one source, in interactive multimedia presentations where you are really involved, the retention rate is as high as:
   a. 20 percent
   b. 40 percent
   c. 80 percent
   d. 60 percent
   e. 100 percent

10. Which of the following is displayable on a web page after installation of a browser plug-in?
    a. Windows 8
    b. Adobe Flash
    c. Mozilla
    d. Internet Explorer
    e. Firefox

11. Which is not dedicated game-playing hardware:
    a. Wii
    b. Xbox
    c. Blackberry
    d. PlayStation
    e. None of the above

12. The glass fiber cables that make up much of the physical backbone of the data highway are, in many cases, owned by:
    a. local governments
    b. Howard Johnson
    c. television networks
    d. railroads and pipeline companies
    e. book publishers

13. DVD stands for:
    a. Digital Versatile Disc
    b. Digital Video Disc
    c. Duplicated Virtual Disc
    d. Density-Variable Disc
    e. Double-View Disc

14. Genealogy software is used to
    a. Study benthic sediments
    b. Organize class reunions
    c. Display family trees
    d. Compute shortest routes for ambulances
    e. Open e-mail

15. Which of the following is *not* a technology likely to prevail as a delivery means for interactive multimedia files?
    a. copper wire
    b. glass fiber
    c. radio/cellular
    d. floppy disk
    e. DVD

■ Essay Quiz

1. Briefly discuss the history and future of multimedia. How might multimedia be used to improve the lives of its users? How might it influence users in negative ways? What might be its shortcomings?

2. You are a marketing director for a small telecommunications company. You are considering using multimedia to market your company's product. Put together an outline detailing the benefits and drawbacks of using a DVD presentation, a multimedia web site, or a television advertisement.

3. Multimedia is shifting from being localized (contained on a DVD) to being distributed (available on the World Wide Web or from the cloud). What are some of the implications of this? Who will have access to the presentation? How will you keep it secure? How will you distribute it?

Lab Projects

■ Project 1.1

You have been given the task of creating an interactive web presentation for marketing a new video game. Visit four different game web sites using a suitable search tool. For each web site you visit, write in the table below the name of the site and its URL, and:

1. Describe each site in terms of its multimedia incorporation.

2. Discuss whether its multimedia content is appropriate and where and how additional media content might improve the site.

3. Describe what multimedia presentation formats it uses. Video? Virtual reality? 3-D animations?

Site 1	
URL (address)	
Describe the GUI. What navigational elements does it have? What colors does it use? Is it cluttered?	
Is the content relevant and appropriate? What additions/ deletions of content might improve the site?	
Describe any multimedia presentations of specific products. What formats do they use?	
Site 2	
URL (address)	
Describe the GUI. What navigational elements does it have? What colors does it use? Is it cluttered?	
Is the content relevant and appropriate? What additions/ deletions of content might improve the site?	
Describe any multimedia presentations of specific products. What formats do they use?	

Site 3	
URL (address)	
Describe the GUI. What navigational elements does it have? What colors does it use? Is it cluttered?	
Is the content relevant and appropriate? What additions/deletions of content might improve the site?	
Describe any multimedia presentations of specific products. What formats do they use?	
Site 4	
URL (address)	
Describe the GUI. What navigational elements does it have? What colors does it use? Is it cluttered?	
Is the content relevant and appropriate? What additions/deletions of content might improve the site?	
Describe any multimedia presentations of specific products. What formats do they use?	

■ Project 1.2

Review an educational online game (you should be able to find one with a quick Google search). Then fill out the following table:

Title of CD	
Describe the GUI. What navigational elements does it have? What color scheme(s) does it use? Is it cluttered?	
Describe the educational content. Is it well organized?	
Would you be able to easily learn the subject matter using this package?	
Describe the product in terms of its multimedia incorporation.	
Discuss whether its multimedia content is appropriate and where and how additional media content might improve the site.	

■ Project 1.3

Contact a local multimedia development company. Ask them what kinds of products they develop and whether they would describe two projects they have recently completed. Be sure that they provide you with enough information to answer each of the following questions.

Multimedia Project 1

1. Name of project.

2. Kind of product created.

3. What authoring tool or tools were used to create the project?

4. Who made up the development team for the project?

5. How did the production of the project develop?

6. How long did the project take to complete?

7. What problems were encountered?

Multimedia Project 2

1. Name of project.

2. Kind of product created.

3. What authoring tool or tools were used to create the project?

4. Who made up the development team for the project?

5. How did the production of the project develop?

6. How long did the project take to complete?

7. What problems were encountered?

■ Project 1.4

Use a mobile device to capture a photo and then exchange that photo with a classmate. Using the tools available to you, significantly alter the image. Try to change the original look, feel, and message of the image you received as much as possible to convey a very different idea or emotion from the original. Then re-exchange images with your classmate and discuss your method, reasoning, and results.

Text

USING text and symbols for communication is a very recent human development that began about 6,000 years ago in the Mediterranean Fertile Crescent—Mesopotamia, Egypt, Sumeria, and Babylonia—when the first meaningful marks were scraped onto mud tablets and left to harden in the sun. Only members of the ruling classes and the priesthood were allowed to read and write the pictographic signs and cuneiforms. The earliest messages delivered in written words typically contained information vital to the management of people, politics, and taxes. Because this new medium did not require rote memorization by frail human gray matter, written messages became popular among the elite. Unlike their memory-based counterparts, these new "written" messages were less likely to perish due to acts of God, and certainly weren't going to die from dysentery or suffer from amnesia. Even if a message were intercepted by foes or competitors, it would still be indecipherable—except by those few who had acquired reading skills (see Figure 2-1).

In fact, because those who could read probably attended the same private school or shared the same tutors, in those days reading, writing, and power politics were naturally intertwined. In some former eras it was a capital offense to read unless you belonged to the proper social class or possessed a patent granted to you by your rulers. In modern times it may still be a capital offense to access, decrypt, or read documents declared by a government to be secret in a national interest.

Today, text and the ability to read it are doorways to power and knowledge. Reading and writing are expected and necessary skills within

Figure 2-1 "Gifts from the High and Mighty of Adab to the High Priestess, on the occasion of her election to the temple." Dated 26th century BC (4,700 years ago).

most modern cultures. Now, depending upon your proficiency with words, you may be awarded a doctorate instead of the death penalty. And, as has been the case throughout history, text still delivers information that can have potent meaning.

Since the explosion of the Internet, the World Wide Web, and text messaging services for handheld devices, text has become more important than ever. Indeed, the native language of the Web is **HTML** (Hypertext Markup Language), originally designed to display simple text documents on computer screens, with occasional graphic images thrown in as illustrations (see Chapter 11 for more history of the Internet). Academic papers, magazine articles, complex instruction manuals, and even the contents of entire books are now available for reading with a web browser. Add a built-in function that links, with a click of the mouse or a touch on the screen, selected words and phrases to other related and perhaps more-detailed material (the "hypertext" part of HTML, discussed later in this chapter), and you can surf the Net in a medium much richer than the paper pages of a book.

The social impact of this text-based medium on the way people access and use information has been profound. In contrast to today's television medium, which consists of sound and images with a few text headlines "dumbed down" to the level of a perceived lowest common denominator of passive audience, the Web offers an active experience laden with

While the specifics of how our intelligence agencies carry out this cryptanalytic mission have been kept secret, the fact that NSA's mission includes deciphering enciphered communications is not a secret, and is not news. Indeed, NSA's public website states that its mission includes leading "the U.S. Government in cryptology …in order to gain a decision advantage for the Nation and our allies."

Office of the Director of National Intelligence (ODNI) Statement on the Unauthorized Disclosure of NSA Cryptological Capabilities, September 6, 2013 (http://icontherecord.tumblr.com/)

First Person

In the 15th century, when the Church was a strong power throughout Europe, Johann Gensfleisch zum Gutenberg, a trained goldsmith from Mainz, Germany, invented movable type for printing presses. He used this new invention for the money-making task of producing religious literature, indulgence slips, and the Holy Bible. In the case of the Bible, he sold his copies to people who could read Latin and pay the equivalent of three years of a clerk's wage to own a personal copy of this Great Work. Other printers, including the Estienne family in France and Aldus Manutius in Italy, soon entered the publishing marketplace to compete,

and together they changed the fabric of society. The mass production of identical copies of text enabled an information-based paradigm shift that changed the human universe in a substantial way. Lots of scribes and illuminators were put out of business.

By way of pointing out that some elements of the human equation may be constant throughout history, I would remark that like many adventurers surfing the waves of today's continuing dot.com revolution, Gutenberg took on a financial investor, Johann Fust. Gutenberg, who was a visionary craftsman perhaps better suited to lab and shop work, defaulted

on a payment to Fust in 1455, was sued, and lost his press and all its profits. Toward the end of his life, it is said that he was granted a place as courtier to the archbishop of Mainz. This position offered perhaps better remuneration for a destitute inventor than a diminishing social security plan that rewards today's surfer who wipes out while hanging ten at the leading edge of the business world.

(From a speech by Tay Vaughan to the jointly held World Conference on Educational Multimedia and Hypermedia and World Conference on Educational Telecommunications, Freiburg, Germany, June 1998)

enough choices to challenge even bright people who can read. More than television, with its 50 or 100 or even 400 available channels, the Web offers an explorer's paradise of billions of HTML documents and, through "social media," immediate contact with many millions of friends and followers.

Yahoo! Search once claimed, "Our index now provides access to over 20 billion items. For those who are curious, this update includes just over 19.2 billion web documents, 1.6 billion images, and over 50 million audio and video files." Until 2009, the search engines displayed (bragged about) the total number of documents they indexed, in the billions. These huge numbers were very inaccurate, it turned out, and they have ceased making precise statements about quantity. A trick in the Google search engine is to type in "site:" and the name of a domain. Google will tell you how many pages from that domain are indexed:

Google   site:cnn.com   🔍

Web   Images   Maps   Shopping   More ▾   Search tools

About 20,500,000 results (0.14 seconds)

As bandwidth improves and more information is successfully embedded within these documents and delivered to many devices—desktop and handheld, or even eye-readable—developers of content will not escape the difficult design issues discussed in Chapter 9. Who is the audience? What words should I use? Under what conditions? What typeface is best?

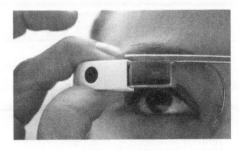

> With its penchant for inter-activity, multimedia too often ignores the power of narra-tive, of stories. There's really something to be said for documents with a beginning, middle, and end.
>
> ....
>
> Steven Levy, author of *Hackers, Artificial Life, Insanely Great, The Unicorn's Secret, Crypto,* and other books; senior staff writer at *Wired*

> I'd like to write something that comes from things the way wine comes from grapes.
>
> ....
>
> Walter Benjamin, Philosopher/Writer

The Power of Meaning

Even a single word may be cloaked in many meanings, so as you begin working with text, it is important to cultivate accuracy and conciseness in the specific words you choose. In multimedia, these are the words that will appear in your titles, menus, and navigation aids as well as in your narrative or content.

Today's poets and songwriters concentrate text by distilling lengthy prose into few words heavy with meaning. Advertising wordsmiths render the meaning of entire product lines into an evocative single word, logo, or tagline. Multimedia authors weave words, symbols, sounds, and images, and then blend text into the mix to create integrated tools and interfaces for acquiring, displaying, and disseminating messages and data.

The words "Barbie," "green," and "lite" may each easily trigger a rush of different meanings. A piercing cry in the night, the sight of fire engines leaving your street as you steer your car into your neighborhood, the scent of drying kelp along the seashore, the feel of rough pine bark against your chest as you climb, fingernails on a chalkboard—all these raw sensory messages are important only because of what they mean to you. Indeed, you alone know the words that will stop you dead in your tracks with anger, or, better, soothe you seductively over a quiet dinner for two. These words have meaning.

All of these examples demonstrate the following multimedia principle: it's important to design labels for title screens, menus, and buttons or tabs using words that have the most precise and powerful meanings to express what you need to say. Understand the subtle shadings. GO BACK! is more powerful than Previous; TERRIFIC! may work better than That Answer Was Correct. Experiment with the words you plan to use by letting others try them. If you have the budget, set up a focus group to have potential users experience your words. Watch them work. See if users flinch, balk, or click the Help button in confusion. See if they can even find the Help button.

Words and symbols in any form, spoken or written, are the most common system of communication. They deliver the most widely understood meaning to the greatest number of people—accurately and in detail. Because of this, they are vital elements of multimedia menus, navigation systems, keyword lists, and content. You will reward yourself and your users if you take the time to use excellent words. Let your poet loose!

TIP *Browse through a thesaurus. You will be surprised at the number of synonyms and related words that are closely associated to the word you start with, and you will certainly find the one word that most perfectly fits your need. The majority of today's popular word processors ship with a bundled electronic thesaurus; many are also available for free on the Internet.*

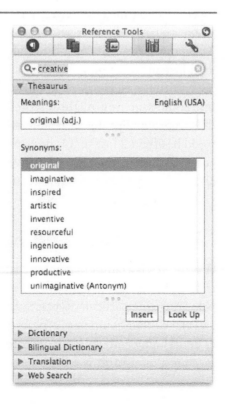

When we have a technical meeting with engineers coming from Germany, France, Spain, Sweden, Japan, and other countries, people say "Hello!" when they walk into the room; English is clearly the international common language of business and commerce and science. Sometimes the etiquette of polite speech is even more fascinating: when you have a room with a group of Germans talking to each other in German and suddenly a foreign visitor comes in, from one sentence to the other, they seamlessly switch to English.

Dipl.-Ing. Roland Cuny, Karlsruhe, Germany

The Power and Irregularity of English

If you are reading this book in English, you might consider yourself lucky. A study by the British Council estimated that one billion people spoke English by the beginning of the second millennium as a first, second, or "foreign" language. English is the official or joint official language of more than 75 countries, and Algeria, when it dumped French in favor of English as the second language in schools, irritated a great many Parisian intellectuals. More than two-thirds of the world's scientists read English, and three-quarters of the world's mail is written in English. It is estimated that 80 percent of the world's information that is stored on computers is written in English. As Dutch-born Professor Boeree of Shippensburg University has said, "Unfortunately for learners of English, it still has several irregular verbs (e.g., to be and to have) and a large number of strong verbs (e.g., sing-sang-sung), plus a few irregular plurals (e.g., child-children, man-men...). Nevertheless, people around the world find English relatively easy, with one huge exception: English has the worst spelling of any language using the Latin alphabet!"

The most recent changes in English spelling have been driven by technology limits as SMS (Short Message Service) text messages commonly used by social networking sites such as Twitter and Facebook to communicate and "tweet" allow only about 160 characters per message (140 bytes). As today's most pervasive method of human-to-human data communication (more than three billion texters worldwide sending trillions of short text messages from phone to phone each year), users speaking many languages quickly developed word shortcuts to pack the most meaning into the fewest characters. NetLingo (www.netlingo.com, where you will discover recent additions "twerk," "frape," "mopper," and "sockpuppet") maintains a list of almost two thousand English acronyms and instant messaging "chat-speak" or "text-speak" words such as XOXO (hugs & kisses), U (you), and NME (enemy). When assembled into a message, you might discover "were I a tear in ur eye i wood roll down onto ur lips. but if u were a tear in my eye i wood never cry as i wood be afraid 2 lose u!" Or perhaps your poetry receives the ID10T error code. With the arrival of MMS (Multimedia Messaging Service), which allows for 350,000-byte transmissions, perhaps these shortcut spellings will fade away. But perhaps not.

About Fonts and Faces

A typeface is a family of graphic characters that usually includes many type sizes and styles. A font is a collection of characters of a single size and style belonging to a particular typeface family. Typical font styles are boldface and italic. Your computer software may add other style attributes, such as underlining and outlining of characters. Type sizes are usually expressed in points; one point is 0.0138 inch, or about 1/72 of an inch. The font's size is the distance from the top of the capital letters to the bottom of the descenders in letters such as *g* and *y*. Helvetica, Times, and Courier are typefaces; Times 12-point italic is a font. In the computer world, the term font is commonly used when typeface or face would be more correct.

A font's size does not exactly describe the height or width of its characters. This is because the **x-height** (the height of the lowercase letter *x*) of two fonts may vary, while the height of the capital letters of those fonts may be the same (see Figure 2-2). Computer fonts automatically add space below the descender (and sometimes above) to provide appropriate line spacing, or **leading** (pronounced "ledding," named for the thin strips of lead inserted between the lines by traditional typesetters).

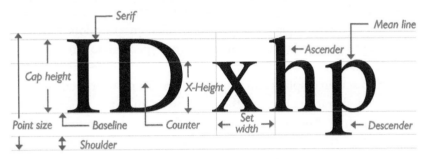

Figure 2-2   The measurement of type

Leading can be adjusted in most programs on both the Macintosh and the PC. Typically you will find this fine-tuning adjustment in the Text menu of image-editing programs or the Paragraph menu of word processing programs, though this is not an official standard. No matter where your application has placed the controls for leading, you will need to experiment with them to achieve the best result for your font. With a font editing program like Fontographer from Fontlab, Ltd. at www.fontlab. com (you'll see an example of it later in the chapter), adjustments can also be made along the horizontal axis of text. In this program the character metrics of each character and the kerning of character pairs can be altered. **Character metrics** are the general measurements applied to individual characters; **kerning** is the spacing between character pairs. When working with PostScript, TrueType, and Master fonts—but not bitmapped fonts— (see "Computers and Text" later in this chapter), the metrics of a font can be altered to create interesting effects. For example, you can adjust the body width of each character from regular to **condensed** to **expanded**, as displayed in this example using the Sabon font:

Regular
Condensed
Expanded

Or you can adjust the spacing between characters (**tracking**) and the kerning between pairs of characters:

Tighter Track

Looser Track

Av Av

Kerned   Unkerned

When it converts the letter *A* from a mathematical representation to a recognizable symbol displayed on the screen or in printed output (a process called **rasterizing**), the computer must know how to represent the letter using tiny square **pixels** (picture elements), or dots. It does this according to the hardware available and your specification, from a choice of available typefaces and fonts. Search the Web for "free fonts." High-resolution screen displays and printers can make more attractive-looking and varied characters because there are more fine little squares or **dots per inch (dpi)**. And today's broad selection of software fonts makes it easier to find the right typeface and font for your needs. The same letter can look very different when you use different fonts and faces:

A A A A A A A A A

Cases

In centuries when type was set by hand, the type for a single font was always stored in two trays, or *cases*; the upper tray held capital letters, and the lower tray held the small letters. Today, a capital letter is called **uppercase**, and a small letter is called **lowercase**.

TIP   *Studies have shown that words and sentences with mixed upper- and lowercase letters are easier to read than words or sentences in all caps (uppercase). While uppercase can make your message appear important or urgent, use this sparingly; in online messaging it's known as "SHOUTING" or "YELLING" and can be annoying, if not offensive.*

In some situations, such as for passwords, a computer is **case sensitive**, meaning that the text's upper- and lowercase letters must match exactly to be recognized. But nowadays, in most situations requiring keyboard input, all computers recognize both the upper- and lowercase forms of a character to be the same. In that manner, the computer is said to be **case insensitive**.

WARNING   *The directory names and filenames used in Uniform Resource Locator (URL) addresses on the Internet are case sensitive! Thus, http://www. timestream .com/info/people/biotay/biotay1.html points to a different directory and file than http://www.timestream.com/info/people/bioTay/biotay1.html. On the other hand, the record type (HTTP) and the domain name (www.timestream. com), and e-mail addresses (tay@timestream.com) as well, are usually case insensitive. Read more about addresses on the Internet in Chapter 11.*

Company and product names such as WordPerfect, ByWater, FedEx, FileMaker, and LoJack have become popular. Placing an uppercase letter in the middle of a word, called an **intercap** or a **CamelCase**, is a trend that emerged from the computer programming community, where coders discovered they could better recognize the words they used for variables and commands when the words were lowercase but interCapped.

Serif vs. Sans Serif

Typefaces can be described in many ways, just as a home advertised by a realtor, a wine described by a food critic, or a political candidate's platform can all be described in many ways. Type has been characterized as feminine, masculine, delicate, formal, capricious, witty, comic, happy, technical, newsy—you name it. But one approach for categorizing typefaces is universally understood, and it has less to do with the reader's response to the type than it does with the type's mechanical and historical properties. This approach uses the terms **serif** and **sans serif**.

Serif versus sans serif is the simplest way to categorize a typeface; the type either has a serif or it doesn't (*sans* is French for "without"). The serif is the little decoration at the end of a letter stroke. Times, New Century Schoolbook, Bookman, and Palatino are examples of serif fonts. Helvetica, Verdana, Arial, Optima, and Avant Garde are sans serif. Notice the difference between serif (on the left) and sans serif.

On the printed page, serif fonts are traditionally used for body text because the serifs are said to help guide the reader's eye along the line of text. Sans serif fonts, on the other hand, are used for headlines and bold statements. But the computer world of standard, 72-dpi screen resolution is not the same as the print world, and it can be argued that sans serif fonts are far more legible and attractive when used in the small sizes of a text field on a screen. Indeed, careful selection of a sans serif font designed to be legible in the small sizes (such as Tahoma or Verdana) makes more sense when you are presenting a substantial amount of text on the screen. The Times font at 9-point size may look too busy and actually be difficult and tiring to read. And a large, bold serif font for a title or headline can deliver a message of elegance and character in your graphic layout. Use what is right for your delivery system, which may not necessarily be the same as what is right when you're printing the material to paper. This is because when you're printing out what you create on a display screen, WYSIWYG (What You See Is What You Get) is more of a goal than an absolute fact.

Using Text in Multimedia

Imagine designing a project that used no text at all. Its content could not be at all complex, and you would need to use many pictures and symbols to train your audience how to navigate through the project. Certainly voice and sound could guide the audience, but users would quickly tire of this because greater effort is required to pay attention to spoken words than to browse text with the eye.

A single item of menu text accompanied by a single action (a mouse click, keystroke, or finger pressed to the screen) requires little training and is clean and immediate. Use text for titles and headlines (what it's all about), for menus (where to go), for navigation (how to get there), and for content (what you see when you get there).

TIP   *In designing your navigation system, bring the user to a particular destination with as few actions and as short a wait as possible. If the user never needs the Help button to get there or never has to click the Back button when at a dead end, you're doing everything right!*

Designing with Text

Computer screens provide a limited workspace for developing complex ideas. At some time or another, you will need to deliver high-impact or concise text messages on the screen in as condensed a form as possible. From a design perspective, your choice of font size and the number of headlines you place on a particular screen must be related both to the complexity of your message and to its venue.

If your messages are part of an interactive project or web site where you know the user is seeking information, you can pack a great deal of text information onto the screen before it becomes overwhelmingly busy. Seekers want dense material, and while they travel along your navigational pathways, they will scroll through relevant text and study the details. Here is where you must strike a balance, however. Too little text on a screen requires annoying page turns and unnecessary mouse clicks and waits; too much text can make the screen seem overcrowded and unpleasant.

On the other hand, if you are creating presentation slides for public-speaking support, the text will be keyed to a live presentation where the text accents the main message. In this case, use bulleted points in large fonts and few words with lots of white space. Let the audience focus on the speaker at the podium, rather than spend its time reading fine points and subpoints projected on a screen.

TIP   *A lengthy text document read by a web browser may scroll for hundreds of lines without annoying the user because it's expected. As a rule of thumb, however, try to make your web pages no longer than one-and-a-half to two screenfuls of text. In a 1024x768-pixel window, for example, you have about 600 pixels in height to work with before scrolling is necessary. Limit the width of your lines by using columns—reading a line of text across an entire 21-inch display screen is cumbersome, if not uncomfortable. For printing text documents, provide a separate link to a complete document in either plain text (.txt), rich text format (.rtf), word processor format (.doc, .odt, or .wpd), or Adobe PDF format (.pdf) instead of relying on a browser's print facilities. It is often more convenient to print and read a document than to scroll through many pages of text on a screen.*

Choosing Text Fonts

Picking the fonts to use in your multimedia presentation may be somewhat difficult from a design standpoint. Here again, you must be a poet, an advertising psychologist, and also a graphic designer. Try to intuit the potential reaction of the user to what is on the screen. Here are a few design suggestions that may help:

- For small type, use the most legible font available. Decorative fonts that cannot be read are useless, as shown at right.

- Use as few different faces as possible in the same work, but vary the weight and size of your typeface using italic and bold styles where they look good. Using too many fonts on the same page is called ransom-note typography. Visit www.letterplayground.com/generator.php to make your own ransom notes.
- In text blocks, adjust the leading for the most pleasing line spacing. Lines too tightly packed are difficult to read.
- Vary the size of a font in proportion to the importance of the message you are delivering.
- In large-size headlines, adjust the spacing between letters (kerning) so that the spacing feels right. Big gaps between large letters can turn your title into a toothless waif. You may need to kern by hand, using a bitmapped version of your text.
- To make your type stand out or be more legible, explore the effects of different colors and of placing the text on various backgrounds. Try reverse type for a stark, white-on-black message.
- Use anti-aliased text where you want a gentle and blended look for titles and headlines. This can give a more professional appearance. **Anti-aliasing** blends the colors along the edges of the letters (called **dithering**) to create a soft transition between the letter and its background.
- ⊤ry drop caps (like the *T* to the left) and initial caps to accent your words. Most word processors and text editors will let you create drop caps and SMALL CAPS in your text. Adobe and others make initial

Roboto Thin
Roboto Thin Italic
Roboto Light
Roboto Light Italic
Roboto
Roboto Italic
Roboto Medium
Roboto Medium Italic
Roboto Bold
Roboto Bold Italic
Roboto Black
Roboto Black Italic
Roboto Light Condensed
Roboto Light Condensed Italic
Roboto Condensed
Roboto Condensed Italic
Roboto Bold Condensed
Roboto Bold Condensed Italic

Helvetica Neue Light
Helvetica Neue Light Italic
Helvetica Neue Roman
Helvetica Neue Italic
Helvetica Neue Bold
Helvetica Neue Bold Italic
Helvetica Neue Condensed
Helvetica Neue Condensed Oblique
Helvetica Neue Condensed Bold

Figure 2-3 System font examples of the Roboto typeface designed by Christian Robertson for Google's Android devices and Helvetica Neue used by Apple's iOS

If you are older than eleven years, never *ever* use the Comic Sans face or the "fantasy" CSS attribute on a web page.

Brad Borch, Designer

caps (such as the one shown to the left from Adobe, called Gothic). The letters are actually carefully drawn artwork and are available in special libraries as Encapsulated PostScript files (EPS).

■ Coding an initial cap for a web page is simple. Use CSS attributes:

```
p:first-letter { font-size: 200%; }
p:first-line { line-height: 100%; }
```

■ If you are using centered type in a text block, keep the number of lines and their width to a minimum.

■ For attention-grabbing results with single words or short phrases, try graphically altering and distorting your text and delivering the result as an image. Wrap your word onto a sphere, bend it into a wave, or splash it with rainbow colors.

■ Experiment with drop shadows. Place a copy of the word on top of the original, and offset the original up and over a few pixels. Then color the original gray (or any other color). The word may become more legible and provide much greater impact. With web sites, shadowed text and graphics on a plain white background add depth to a page. Surround headlines with plenty of white space. **White space** is a designer's term for roomy blank areas, while programmers call the invisible character made by a space (ASCII 32) or a tab (ASCII 9) white space. While CSS should always be used for presentational purposes, some web designers use a nonbreaking space entity ( ) to force spaces into lines of text in HTML documents.

■ Pick the fonts that seem right to you for getting your message across, then double-check your choice against others' opinions. Learn to accept criticism.

■ Use meaningful words or phrases for links and menu items.

■ Text links (**anchors**) on web pages can accent your message: they normally stand out by color and underlining. Use link colors consistently throughout a site, and avoid iridescent green on red or purple on puce.

■ Bold or emphasize text to highlight ideas or concepts, but do not make text look like a link or a button when it is not.

■ On a web page, put vital text elements and menus in the top 320 pixels. Studies of surfer habits have discovered that only 10 to 15 percent of surfers *ever* scroll *any* page.

■ If you are designing for a mobile operating system such as iOS or Android, be sure to follow that platform's design guidelines. In those environments text can be manipulated to be large or small and scrolled to be readable. For legibility on smaller mobile devices, consider using the device's system font: many hours have gone into the design of these (see Figure 2-3).

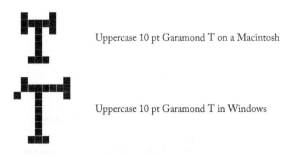

Uppercase 10 pt Garamond T on a Macintosh

Uppercase 10 pt Garamond T in Windows

Figure 2-4   Examples of Garamond typeface displayed on a Macintosh (top) and in Windows

---

TIP   *Characters identified in a particular font (say, Garamond 10-point) do not always look the same on a Macintosh as they do on Windows displays. Typically, what is called 12-point on a Macintosh will be a 10- or 9-point size in Windows. And the actual shape of the characters may be different (see Figure 2-4). Take care to visually test the flow of your text on all platforms.*

Installed Fonts   Before you can use a font, it must be recognized by the computer's operating system (see Figure 2-5). That is to say, if you ask the computer to write onto the screen a large 24-point uppercase T in a Palatino font face, the computer must be able to locate the precise

> My parents offered my brother and sister $50 to teach me the alphabet, but that didn't work. So I flunked second grade. I had the same nun again, and she was mean. She paddled me for two years, but I still didn't learn the alphabet or how to read. By the time I was 15 or 16, I could get by in class with reading. But I could never spell. I was a woodshop major in high school, and my typical report card was two Cs, three Ds, and an F. I just got used to it. Though reading is still difficult for me, I do like readers. I like the written language because I like photocopying. I believe in double-spacing, since it helps my business!
>
> Paul Orfalea, founder of Kinko's [now FedEx Office], discussing his reading disability

Aharoni	Aharoni
Aldhabi	Aldhabi
Andalus	خط الأندلس
Angsana New	อังสนา นิว
AngsanaUPC	อ้างสนา ยูพีซี
Arabic Typesetting	خط الطباعة العربي
Arial	Arial
Arial Black	**Arial Black**
Batang	바탕
Browalia New	โบรวาเลีย นิว
BrowaliaUPC	โบรวาเลีย ยูพีซี
Calibri	Calibri
Cambria	Cambria
Cambria Math	Cambria Math
Candara	Candara
Comic Sans MS	Comic Sans
Consolas	Consolas
Constantia	Constantia
Corbel	Corbel
Cordia New	คอร์เดีย นิว
CordiaUPC	คอร์เดีย ยูพีซี
Courier New	Courier New

Al Bayan البيان (Regular, **Bold** خط ضخمة)
American Typewriter (Condensed Light, Condensed, **Condensed Bold**, Light, Regular, **Bold**)
Andale Mono (Regular)
Apple Casual (Regular)
Apple Chancery (Regular)
Apple Garamond (Light, *Light Italic*, Book, *Book Italic*, **Bold**, ***Bold Italic***)
Apple Gothic 애플고딕 (Regular 보통)
Apple LiGothic 蘋果儷中黑 (Medium 太字)
Apple LiSung (Light)
Apple Myungjo 애플명조 (Regular 보통)
Apple Symbols (Regular ⊟▧♭)
Arial (Condensed Light, Narrow, *Narrow Italic*, Narrow Bold, *Narrow Bold Italic*, Regular, *Italic*, **Bold**, Rounded Bold, ***Bold Italic***, **Black**)
Arial Hebrew (Regular רגיל, **Bold מודגש**)
Baghdad بغداد (Regular)
Baskerville (Regular, *Italic*, **Semi-bold**, ***Semi-bold Italic***, **Bold**, ***Bold Italic***)
Beijing 北京 (Regular)
BiauKai 標楷 (Regular 體)
Big Caslon (Medium)
Brush Script (Italic)
Chalkboard (Regular)
Charcoal (Regular)
Charcoal CY (Regular Обычное)
Chicago (Regular)
Comic Sans (Regular, **Bold**)
Cooper (Black)
COPPERPLATE (LIGHT, REGULAR, **BOLD**)
Corsiva Hebrew (Regular רגיל, **Bold מודגש**)
Courier (Regular, *Oblique*, **Bold**, ***Bold Oblique***)
Courier New (Regular, *Italic*, **Bold**, ***Bold Italic***)

Figure 2-5   Fonts that come with Windows (left) and Macintosh computers (*Continued*)

Font	Sample
DaunPenh	DaunPenh
David	David
DFKai-SB	微軟標楷體
DilleniaUPC	ดิลลีเนีย ยูพีซี
DokChampa	ดอกจำปา
Dotum	Dotum
Estrangelo Edessa	Estrangelo Edessa
EucrosiaUPC	ยูโครเชีย ยูพีซี
Euphemia	Euphemia
Gautami	గౌతమి
Georgia	Georgia
Gulim	굴림
Impact	**Impact**
IrisUPC	ไอริส ยูพีซี
Iskoola Pota	ඉස්කෝල පොත
JasmineUPC	จัสมิน ยูพีซี
KodchiangUPC	กอดเชียง ยูพีซี
Leelawadee	ลีลาวดี
LilyUPC	ลิลลี่ ยูพีซี
Lucida Console	Lucida Console
Lucida Sans Unicode	
Malgun Gothic	맑은 고딕
Mangal	मंगल
Meiryo	メイリオ
Microsoft JhengHei	微軟正黑體
Microsoft YaHei	微软雅黑体
MingLiU, PMingLiU	微軟新細明體
MS Mincho, MS PMincho	MS 明朝 / MS P明朝
NSimSun	新宋体
Palatino Linotype	Palatino
Segoe UI	Segoe UI
SimHei	黑体
SimKai	楷体
Simplified Arabic	الخط العربي
SimSun	宋体
Sylfaen	
Tahoma	Tahoma
Times New Roman	Times New Roman
Trebuchet MS	Trebuchet MS
Tunga	తుంగ
Verdana	Verdana
Vijaya	300x30px
Vrinda	বৃন্দা
Webdings	▶ 🏠 ♨ ♥ ① ● 🔲 ?
Wingdings	✿ ❋ ■ ☼ ♌ ✠ ■ ♊ ✦

Devanagari देवनागरी (Regular, **Bold देवनागरी**)
Didot (Regular, *Italic*, **Bold**)
Fang Song 仿宋 (Regular)
Futura (Condensed Medium, **Condensed Extra Bold**, Medium, *Medium Italic*)
Gadget (Regular)
Geeza Pro جيزا Pro (Regular, **Bold** حروف ضخمة)
Geezah جيزه (Regular)
Geneva (Regular)
Geneva CY (Regular Обычное)
Georgia (Regular, *Italic*, **Bold**, ***Bold Italic***)
Gill Sans (Light, *Light Italic*, Regular, *Italic*, **Bold**, ***Bold Italic***)
Gujarati ગુજરાતી (Regular, **Bold ગુજરાતી**)
Gung Seouche 궁서 (Regular 보통)
Hangangche (Regular 보통)
HeadlineA 헤드라인A (Regular 보통)
Hei 黑 (Regular 體)
Helvetica (Regular, *Oblique*, **Bold**, ***Bold Oblique***)
Helvetica CY (Regular Обычное, *Oblique Наклонное*, **Bold Полужирное**, ***Bold Oblique Полужирное и Наклонное***)
Helvetica Neue (Condensed Bold, **Condensed Black**, Ultra-light, *Ultra-light Italic*, Light, *Light Italic*, Regular, *Italic*, **Bold**, ***Bold Italic***)
HERCULANUM (REGULAR)
Hiragino Kaku Gothic Pro ヒラギノ角ゴ Pro (W3, W6 太字)
Hiragino Kaku Gothic Std ヒラギノ角ゴ Std (W8 太字)
Hiragino Maru Gothic Pro ヒラギノ丸ゴ Pro (W4 體)
Hiragino Mincho Pro ヒラギノ明朝 Pro (W3, W6 太字)
Hoefler Text (Regular, *Italic*, **Black**, ***Black Italic***, Ornaments ☙❦❧)
Impact (Regular)
Jung Gothic 고딕 (Medium 미디엄)
Kai 楷 (Regular 體)
LiHei Pro 儷黑 Pro (Medium 太字)
LiSong Pro 儷宋 Pro (Light)
Lucida Grande (Regular, **Bold**)
Marker Felt (Thin, Wide)
Monaco (Regular)
Monaco CY Монако (Regular Обычное)
New Peninim (Regular ניו, *Inclined נטוי*, **Bold מודגש**, ***Bold Inclined מודגש נטוי***)
New York (Regular)
Optima (Regular, *Italic*, **Bold**, ***Bold Italic***, **Extra Black**)
Osaka 大阪市 (Regular 體, Monospace 等幅)
Palatino (Regular, *Italic*, **Bold**, ***Bold Italic***)
Papyrus (Regular)
PCMyungjo PC명조 (Regular 보통)
Pilgi 필기 (Regular 보통)
Plantagenet Cherokee ᏣᎳᎩ (Regular)
Raanana רעננה (Regular רגיל, **Bold מודגש**)
Sand (Regular)
Seoul 서울 (Regular 보통)
Shin Myungjo Neue 새 명조 (Regular 보통)
Skia (Variable)
Song 宋 (Regular)
STFangSong 华文仿宋 (Regular 體)
STHeiti 华文黑体 (Light 細, Regular 體)
STKaiti 华文楷体 (Regular 體)
STSong 华文宋体 (Regular 體)
Symbol (Regular Ψϑϖ)
TaeGraphic 태그래픽 (Regular 보통)
Tahoma (Regular, **Bold**)
Techno (Regular)
Textile (Regular)
Times (Regular, *Italic*, **Bold**, ***Bold Italic***)
Times CY (Regular Обычное, *Italic Курсив*, **Bold Полужирное**, ***Bold Italic Полужирное и Курсив***)
Times New Roman (Regular, *Italic*, **Bold**, ***Bold Italic***)
Trebuchet (Regular, *Italic*, **Bold**, ***Bold Italic***)
Verdana (Regular, *Italic*, **Bold**, ***Bold Italic***)
Zapf Chancery (Medium Italic)
Zapf Dingbats (Regular ✈❀✄)
Zapfino (Regular)

Figure 2-5 Fonts that come with Windows (left) and Macintosh computers

description for a Palatino uppercase T before it can tell the screen to energize exactly the proper tiny dots that will "draw" the T. Additional fonts are included with application packages such as Microsoft Office or Adobe InDesign, and they are added to your available fonts when the application is installed on your computer.

Use of **Cascading Style Sheets (CSS)**, preferred over the deprecated HTML <font> tag, allows you to be quite precise about font faces, sizes, and other attributes when writing HTML code for the Web (see Table 2-1).

Although in HTML and using CSS for building Web pages you can specify a base font size, color, and other attributes for displaying text, you still have no guarantee that the font is installed in the user's system. Fortunately, if your specified font is missing, a browser will attempt to substitute a similar font. But the look is not guaranteed to be exactly the same as the one you have designed. In the font-family property you can build a **font stack**, which can include the exact names of both Windows and Macintosh fonts. Using this comma-separated list, a browser will look on the computer for the first font specified in the list; if it is not available, the browser will check for the next, then the next, and so on until it finds a match. At the end of your list, it is best to place a **generic font** catch-all ("serif" or "sans serif") to cover an instance in which all specified fonts are unavailable.

Property	Value	Description
color	color	Sets the color of text
direction	ltr rtl	Sets the text direction; use with the unicode-bidi property
letter-spacing	normal length	Increases or decreases space between characters
line-height	normal number length %	Sets the distance between lines
text-align	left right center justify	Aligns the text in an element
text-decoration	none underline overline line-through blink	Adds decoration to text
text-indent	length %	Indents the first line of text in an element
text-shadow	none color length	Shadows the text
text-transform	none capitalize uppercase lowercase	Controls the letters in an element
unicode-bidi	normal embed bidi-override inherit	Used for languages that run from left to right or right to left; works with the direction property
vertical-align	baseline sub super top text-top middle bottom text-bottom length %	Sets the vertical alignment of an element
white-space	normal pre nowrap	Sets how white space inside an element is handled
word-spacing	normal length	Increases or decreases space between words

Table 2-1 Available Text Properties Using Cascading Style Sheets (CSS)

Some font stacks for paragraph text might look like:

```
font-family: Baskerville, "Times New Roman", Times, serif;
font-family: Garamond, "Hoefler Text", "Times New Roman", Times, serif;
font-family: "Gill Sans", Calibri, "Trebuchet MS", sans-serif;
font-family: "Helvetica Neue", Arial, Helvetica, sans-serif;
```

And for titles, font choices might look like:

```
font-family: Georgia, Times, "Times New Roman", serif;
font-family: Baskerville, Times, "Times New Roman", serif;
font-family: "Gill Sans", "Trebuchet MS", Calibri, sans-serif;
font-family: Verdana, Tahoma, Geneva, sans-serif;
```

Note that if a font name includes a space, it must be enclosed in quotes.

If the right look is important to you, provide a way to download the font to the end user's computer. Or, for the Web, either use the CSS3 @font-face rule to provide a link to the font(s) on your own server or, for a small annual fee, purchase a font-linking service and choose from hundreds of fonts on that service's server. If the look is crucial, use a bitmap image of the text drawn in the selected font.

To address copyright and cross-platform font issues, Microsoft hired type designer Matthew Carter of Carter & Cone Type, Inc. (http://new .myfonts.com/foundry/Carter_and_Cone_Type_Inc./) to design a serif font and a sans serif font that display well on a computer screen. The two fonts Carter designed are Georgia (the serif font) and Verdana (the sans serif font), both of which Microsoft makes available for free. Since they are freely available and designed specifically for screen display, many designers recommend them as a "first choice" when specifying font faces for web pages. For mobile devices, Roboto and Helvetica Neue are a good font choice (see Figure 2-3 earlier in this section).

In addition to serif and non-serif fonts, the generic fonts available in CSS also include monospace, cursive, and fantasy:

font-family: Verdana, Arial, Helvetica, sans-serif;

font-family: Times, "Times New Roman", Georgia, serif;

font-family: Impact, Arnoldboecklin, Oldtown, fantasy;

font-family: "Zapf Chancery", "Comic Sans", "Comic Sans MS", cursive;

font-family: "Lucida Console", Courier, monospace;

Animating Text   There are plenty of ways to retain a viewer's attention when displaying text. For example, you can animate bulleted text and have it "fly" onto the screen. You can "grow" a headline a character at a time. For speakers, simply highlighting the important text works well as a pointing device. When there are several points to be made, you can stack keywords and flash them past the viewer in a timed, automated sequence (as in the roadside Burma Shave ads—signs placed every half mile or so along the highway, each offering the motorist just a few more words toward a complete slogan). You might fly in some keywords, dissolve others, rotate or spin others, and so forth, until you have a dynamic bulleted list of words that is interesting to watch. But be careful—don't overdo the special effects, or they will become boring. For simple presentations, PowerPoint (see the Custom Animation palette at right) has bells and whistles to reveal a line of text one word or one letter at a time, or to animate an entire line.

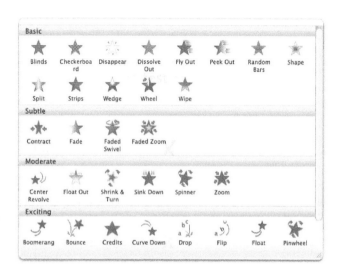

Symbols and Icons

Symbols are concentrated text in the form of stand-alone graphic constructs. Symbols convey meaningful messages. The trash can symbol, for instance, tells you where to throw away old files; the hourglass cursor tells you to wait while the computer is processing. Though you may think of symbols as belonging strictly to the realm of graphic art, in multimedia you should treat them as text—or visual words—because they carry meaning. Symbols such as the familiar trash can and hourglass are more properly called **icons**: these are symbolic representations of objects and processes common to the graphical user interfaces (**GUI**—pronounced "gooey") of many computer operating systems.

Certainly text is more efficient than imagery and pictures for delivering a precise message to users. On the other hand, pictures, icons, moving images, and sounds are more easily recalled and remembered by viewers. With multimedia, you have the power to blend both text and icons (as well as colors, sounds, images, and motion video) to enhance the overall impact and value of your message.

Word meanings are shared by millions of people, but the special symbols you design for a multimedia project are not; these symbols must be learned before they can be useful message carriers. Some symbols are more widely used and understood than others, but readers of even these common symbols must grow accustomed to their meanings. Learning a system of symbols can be as difficult as lessons in any foreign language.

WARNING   *Do not be seduced into creating your own language of symbols and icons.*

Here are some symbols you may already know:

And here are some astronomers' symbols from the days of Kepler and Galileo that you may not have learned. Still in heavy use by astrologers, they represent the 12 constellations of the zodiac:

But why are there 13 icons in the preceding illustration? Or did you notice? Find the sign for the planet Venus among the constellations. Not easy if you are unfamiliar with the meaning of these symbols.

When early computers began to display bitmapped pictures as well as lines of text, there was a flurry of creative attempts by graphic artists to create interesting navigational symbols to alleviate the need for text. The screens were pure graphic art and power—all lines and angles and stunning shadows. But many users were frustrated because they could not get to the data right away and had to first wade through help and guidance material to learn the symbols. In this context it is clearly safer, from a product design point of view, to combine symbols with text cues. This ensures the graphic impact of the symbols but allows prompting the user on their meaning. The Macintosh trash can icon, incidentally, also has a text label, "Trash," just in case people don't get the idea from the symbol. Indeed, long arguments occur among designers dealing with clarity of meaning and ambiguity: the Macintosh trash can was used to obliterate files but also to eject discs and mounted volumes, which are not actually "trashed" when ejected. Apple now replaces the trash can icon with the Eject symbol when dragging CDs and other volumes to it.

Nonetheless, a few symbols have emerged in the interactive multimedia world as an accepted lexicon of navigation cues that do not need text. These symbols are by no means universal, but Figure 2-6 shows some that have roots in the consumer electronics world and in social networking. Even for these "common symbols," text labels are often added to the graphic icons to avoid uncertainty. Microsoft Word and Adobe Acrobat, for example, use an icon representing a 3.5-inch diskette to indicate "Save to Disk." While this storage medium has been relegated to museums, the iconic meaning persists. Some Japanese-invented ideograms or pictographs, called **emoji** (*e* for "picture" and *moji* for "letter"), have been incorporated into Unicode (described later in this chapter)

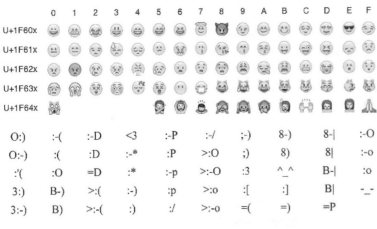

Figure 2-6 Some symbols, like Rewind, Pause, Play, Stop, and Fast Forward, are easily recognized but may still be more precise with text titles.

and are used in phones and e-mail services as well as being available in both the Macintosh and Windows operating systems.

"Smiley" symbols, or **emoticons**, used in Internet conversation to express mood, once were made up entirely of text and punctuation characters. These have been replaced by both custom-made graphic symbols and official type characters as part of the international Unicode library (Block 1F600..1F64F). Indeed, as you can see in Figure 2-6, sometimes it's difficult to know what a smiley really *means*! ☺

Menus for Navigation

An interactive multimedia project or web site typically consists of a body of information, or content, through which a user navigates by pressing a key, clicking a mouse, or pressing a touch screen. The simplest menus consist of text lists of topics. Users choose a topic, click it, and go there. As multimedia and graphical user interfaces become pervasive in the computer community, certain intuitive actions are being widely learned.

For example, if there are three words on a computer screen, the typical response from the user, without prompting, is to click one of these words to evoke activity. Sometimes menu items are surrounded by boxes or made to look like push buttons. Or, to conserve space, text such as Throw Tomatoes, Play Video, and Press to Quit is often shortened to Tomatoes, Video, and Quit. Regardless, the user deduces the function.

Text is helpful to users to provide perpetual cues about their location within the body of content. When users must click up and down through many layers of menus to reach their goal, they may not get lost, but they may feel transported to the winding and narrow streets of a medieval city where only the locals know the way. This is especially true if the user moves slowly from screen to screen en route to that goal. If Throw Tomatoes leads to Red or Green, then to Paris or Prague, then to Prime Minister or President, then to Forehead or Chest, then to Arrested or Got Away, and so on, the user can end up tangled in the branches of a navigation tree without cues or a map. However, if an interactive textual or symbolic list of the branches taken (all the way from the beginning) is continuously displayed, the user can at any time skip intervening steps in a nonlinear manner or easily return to one of the previous locations in the list.

    Tomatoes
        Red
           Paris
              Prime Minister
                  Chest
                      Arrested

The more locations included in the menu list, the more options available for navigation. On the Web, designers typically place on every page at least a Main Menu of links that offers the user a handhold and mechanism for returning to the beginning. Often they will also place a list, such as

Store > Home & Garden > Patio & Grilling > Gas Grills & Accessories > Gas Grills > Burners

along the tops of storefronts to let shoppers know where they are currently located within the store. Inventive interface developers first referred to this array of menu items as "**breadcrumbs**," for they represent a map of the virtual forest and often the "trail" users have taken, like the edible markers so intelligently placed by Hänsel und Gretel along the way to the witch's house in the Brothers Grimm's famous fairy tale.

Navigation methodologies and navigation maps are discussed in greater detail in Chapter 11.

Hänsel wirft Brotkrümel auf den Weg.

TIP   *Avoid using more than a few levels of GO BACKs or RETURNs if you do not provide a map. Too much tunneling in and out with repetitive mouse clicks will frustrate users and discourage exploration. Display a perpetual menu of interactive text or symbolic cues so users can always extricate themselves from any place in the tunnel. In a web browser, this can be handled by a Back or Prev.*

Buttons for Interaction

In most modern cultures a doorbell is recognized by its context (next to the door itself, possibly lit); but if you grew up in a high-rise apartment, you may have seen 50 or more buttons at the entrance. Unless you knew that yours was the third from the top on the left, you could find your button only by reading the printed or scrawled name beside it. And certainly your Aunt Barbara needed this text cue to avoid having to push the Help button, which in this case rang in the building superintendent's apartment.

In multimedia, **buttons** are the objects, such as blocks of text, a pretty blue triangle, or a photograph, that make things happen when they are clicked or tapped. They were invented for the sole purpose of being pushed or prodded with cursor, mouse, key, or finger—and to manifest properties such as highlighting or other visual or sound effects to indicate that you are over or have hit the target. Buttons and the art of button design and human interaction are discussed in detail in Chapter 9. For now, remember that the rules for proper selection of text and fonts in your projects apply to buttons as well as headlines, bulleted items, and blocks of text.

The automatic button-making tools supplied with multimedia and HTML page authoring systems are useful, but in creating the text for you, they offer little opportunity to fine-tune the look of the text. Character- and word-wrap, highlighting, and inverting are automatically applied to your buttons, as needed, by the authoring system. These default buttons and styles may seem overused or trite, but by using common button styles, shapes, borders, and highlights, you increase the probability that users will know what to do with them—especially when they are also labeled. Many applications that use icon buttons also provide **tooltips**, sometimes called "hover boxes" or "screen tips," that display information about the icon when the mouse pointer or cursor hovers for a short time above the icon. Tooltips are not found on mobile devices because they have no pointer.

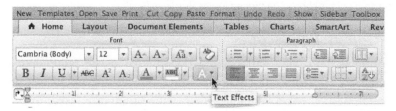

Pick a font for buttons that is, above all, legible; then adjust the text size of the labels to provide adequate space between the button's rim and the text. You can choose from many styles of buttons and several standard methodologies for highlighting. You will want to experiment to get the right combinations of font, spacing, and colors for just the right look.

In most authoring platforms, it is easy to make your own buttons from bitmaps or drawn objects. In a message-passing authoring system, where you can script activity when the mouse button is up or down over an object, you can quickly replace one bitmap with another highlighted or colored version of the bitmap to show that the button has been "pushed" or that the mouse is hovering over it. Making your own buttons from bitmaps or drawn objects gives you greater design power and creative freedom and also ensures against the missing font problem. On the other hand, this custom work may require a good deal more time. You can also implement these graphic image **rollovers** on web pages, using JavaScript or CSS to replace the image when there is a MouseOver or hover event; when a MouseUp event occurs on the image, the user can be directed to another page (see "Clickable Buttons" in Chapter 11). Typically the destination address (URL) is displayed in the status bar of the browser when the mouse is over a linked image or text element. So users know first if the mouse is over an active button and second, where that button will take them if they click.

Whether default or custom, treat the design and labeling of your buttons as an industrial art project: buttons are the part of your project the user touches.

Fields for Reading

Unless the very purpose of your multimedia project or web site is to display large blocks of text, try to present to the user only a few paragraphs of text per page. Use a font that is easy to read rather than a prettier font that is illegible. Try to display whole paragraphs on the screen, and avoid breaks where users must go back and forth between pages to read an entire paragraph.

> When I was four years old, a button was the little plastic knob mounted in brass next to the front door. When I pushed it, a muffled ringing sound worked its way through the house from the kitchen. Sometimes I would push the button a lot and somebody would always come to the door. As an adult, I'm still pushing buttons to make things happen.
>
> Ann Stewart, Multimedia Developer, Smyrna, Tennessee

WARNING   *Research has shown that when people read text on a computer screen, they blink only 3 to 5 times per minute, but they blink 20 to 25 times per minute when reading text on paper. This reduced eye movement may cause dryness, fatigue, and possibly damage to the eyes. Research also suggests that desktop displays should be placed lower than eye level.*

Portrait vs. Landscape

Traditional hard-copy and printed documents in the taller-than-wide orientation are simply not readable on a typical display with a wider-than-tall **aspect ratio**. The taller-than-wide orientation used for printed documents is called **portrait**; this is the 8.5-by-11-inch (21.6 cm by 27.9 cm) letter size unique to the United States, Canada, Mexico, and a few other countries or the internationally designated standard A4 size, 21 cm by 29.7 cm (8.3 by 11.7 inches). The wider-than-tall orientation normal to computer displays is called **landscape**. Shrinking an 11-inch-tall portrait page of text into your available display screen height usually yields illegible chicken tracks. There are four possible solutions if you are working with a block of text that is taller than what will fit:

- Put the text into a scrolling field. This is the solution used by web browsers.
- Put the text into a single field or graphic image in a project window, and let the user move the whole window up or down upon command. This is most appropriate when you need to present text with page breaks and formatting identical to the printed document. This is used by Adobe's popular Acrobat Reader for displaying PDF files.
- Break the text into fields that fit on screen-sized pages, and design control buttons to flip through these pages.
- Design your multimedia project for a special display that is taller than it is wide (portrait) or a normal display rotated onto its side. At one time "page view" displays were expensive and used for commercial print-based typesetting and layout. Today, you can turn the display on its side and the video controller can rotate the text 90 degrees for you:

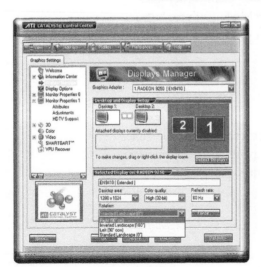

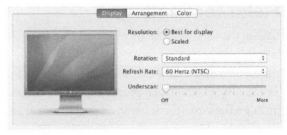

eBooks, E-Readers, and Tablet Computers

eBooks are books digitized and formatted to be read using an **e-reader**. E-readers display text, graphics, and multimedia—most using E Ink screens between five and ten inches diagonal, some with touch screens, some with Wi-Fi and 3G connectivity, and all with varying and sometimes nonstandard input formats (see Table 2-2). Among devices handy for reading eBooks are the Amazon Kindle, Apple iPad, Barnes & Noble Nook, Bookeen Cybook, Google Nexus, DistriRead Icarus, Ectaco Jetbook, Rakuten Kobo, Microsoft Surface, and the Sony Reader.

Format	Filename Extension
ArghosReader	.aeh
Broadband eBook	.lrf, .lrx
DjVu	.djvu
EPUB	.epub
eReader	.pdb
FictionBook	.fb2
HTML	.html
Kindle	.azw
Microsoft Reader	.lit
Mobipocket	.prc, .mobi
Multimedia EBook	.exe
Plain text	.txt
Portable Document Format	.pdf
PostScript	.ps
Tome Raider	.tr2, .tr3
WOLF	.wol

Table 2-2 E-Readers Can Read Many File Formats, Some Proprietary

Electronic ink is a proprietary material of E Ink® Corporation that is processed into a film for integration into electronic displays. Revolutionary in concept, electronic ink is a straightforward fusion of chemistry, physics and electronics to create this new material. The principal components of electronic ink are millions of tiny microcapsules, about the diameter of a human hair. Each microcapsule contains positively charged white particles and negatively charged black particles suspended in a clear fluid. When a negative electric field is applied, the white particles move to the top of the microcapsule where they become visible to the user and pull the negatively charged black particles to the bottom of the capsule, hidden behind the white. This makes the surface appear white at that spot or pixel. The opposite happens if a positive electric field is applied causing the black particles to come to the surface and the white are pulled to the bottom, causing a black pixel. Gray can be achieved by removing the electric field when the particles have only travelled part of the way and hence are partially mixed.

To form an E Ink electronic display, the ink is printed onto a sheet of plastic film that is laminated to a layer of circuitry called a Thin Film Transistor (TFT) array. The TFT array forms a grid pattern of pixels that can then be controlled by a display driver.

During the manufacturing process, the microcapsules are suspended in a liquid "carrier medium" allowing them to be printed or laminated using existing screen printing processes onto virtually any surface, including glass, plastic, fabric, and even paper. Electronic ink can turn almost any surface into a display, bringing information out of the confines of traditional devices and into the world around us.

From E Ink Corporation
(www.eink.com)

The E Ink screen is a technology for "electronic paper," designed to imitate the appearance of ordinary ink on paper (see sidebar and Figure 2-7). E Ink displays can be used in direct sunlight and boast a long battery life. But E Ink is not required to read eBooks, which can be viewed on most computers and many mobile devices using format converting/reading software such as Adobe Digital Editions.

Figure 2-7   Electronic paper and e-reader devices have changed the way we do things.

HTML Documents

The standard document format used for displaying text pages on the Web is called Hypertext Markup Language (HTML). In an HTML document you can specify typefaces, sizes, colors, and other properties by "marking up" the text in the document with **tags**. The process of marking up documents or "styling" them is simple: Where you want text to be bold, surround it with the tags <b> and </b> or <strong> and </strong>; the text between the tags will then be displayed by your browser application in bold type. Where you have a header, surround it with <h1> and </h1>. For an ordered list of things (1, 2, 3, … or a, b, c, …, etc.), surround your list with <ol> and </ol>. There are many tags you can use to lay out a page. Although HTML Version 5 (HTML5) is not case sensitive, it is convention to use lowercase tags. Cascading Style Sheets (CSS) work in conjunction with HTML and provide fine tuning and control of text and layout. How HTML and CSS work together is discussed in greater detail in Chapters 12 and 13, and there are many good learning guides and references available on the Web.

· ·

www.w3.org/TR/html5/

www.w3.org/MarkUp/Guide/

www.w3schools.com/html/default.asp

www.w3schools.com/css/default.asp

www.w3.org/Style/CSS/

Check out these web sites for more information about HTML and CSS.

· ·

The remarkable growth of the Web is straining the "old" designs for displaying text on computers. Indeed, while marked-up text files (HTML documents) remain at the foundation of Web activity, when you visit a well-designed web site, you often discover graphic images, animations, and interactive work-arounds contrived to *avoid* displaying text. The neat paragraphs, indented lists, and formats for text documents for which HTML was originally intended are evolving into multimedia documents, not text documents, and the original HTML method and standard is consequently suffering great stress.

HTML5 is a redesign that stretches the Web into a multimedia delivery vehicle, making HTML no longer just a text display tool with assorted attachments and plugged-in objects. The new <canvas> element allows a box to be defined on a web page in which 2-D graphics can be drawn under program control. Video and audio (timed media) playback is supported. Still, HTML doesn't provide you with much flexibility to make pretty text elements, which are often done as graphical bitmaps placed within the HTML document's layout with image (<IMG>) tags or incorporated into Flash animation files. Indeed, using plain HTML, you do not know what font a reader will use to view your document—the default display font is a preference that can be set in the viewer's browser, which knows it's installed on that viewer's machine. So some viewers may read your words in serif Times Roman, others in sans serif Helvetica or Arial.

Computers and Text

Very early in the development of the Macintosh computer's display hardware, Apple chose to use a resolution of 72 pixels per inch. This almost exactly matches the standard measurement of the printing industry (72 points per inch) and allows desktop publishers and designers to see on a display screen what their printed output will look like (WYSIWYG). In addition, Apple made each pixel square-shaped, providing even measurements in all directions. Until the Macintosh was invented, and the VGA video standard set for the PC (at 96 pixels per inch), pixels were typically taller than they were wide. The aspect ratio for a pixel on older EGA displays, for example, is 1.33:1, taller than it is wide. Screen resolutions for both Macintosh and Windows display pixels at an aspect ratio of 1:1 (square). With square pixels, there has been a steady increase in display resolution and screen size, and aspect ratios are no longer fixed at 4:3 (see Chapter 7 for more detail).

The Font Wars Are Over

In 1985, the desktop publishing revolution was spearheaded by Apple and the Macintosh computer, in combination with word processing and page layout software products that enabled a high-resolution 300-dpi laser printer using special software to "draw" the shapes of characters as a cluster of square pixels computed from the geometry of the character. This special software was the **Adobe PostScript** page description and **outline font** language. It was licensed by Apple and included in the firmware of Apple's LaserWriter laser printer.

PostScript is really a method of describing an image in terms of mathematical constructs (Bézier curves, described in more detail in Chapter 3), so it is used not only to describe the individual characters of a font but also to describe entire illustrations and whole pages of text. Because each PostScript character is a mathematical formula, it can be easily scaled bigger or smaller so it looks right whether drawn at 24 points or 96 points, whether the printer is a 300-dpi LaserWriter or a high-resolution 1200-, 2400-, or even 3600-dpi image setter suitable for the finest print jobs. And the PostScript characters can be drawn much faster than in the old-fashioned way. Before PostScript, the printing software looked up the character's shape in a **bitmapped font** table (see Figure 2-8) containing an exact representation of the pixels of every character in every size. PostScript quickly became the de facto industry font and printing standard for desktop publishing and played a significant role in the early success of Apple's Macintosh computer.

There are two kinds of PostScript fonts: Type 3 and Type 1. Type 3 font technology is *older* than Type 1 and was developed for output to printers; it is rarely used by multimedia developers. There are currently over 6,000 different Type 1 typefaces available. Type 1 fonts also contain **hints**, which are special instructions for grid-fitting to help improve resolution. Hints can apply to a font in general or to specific characters at a particular resolution.

Other companies followed Adobe into the desktop publishing arena with their own proprietary and competitive systems for scalable

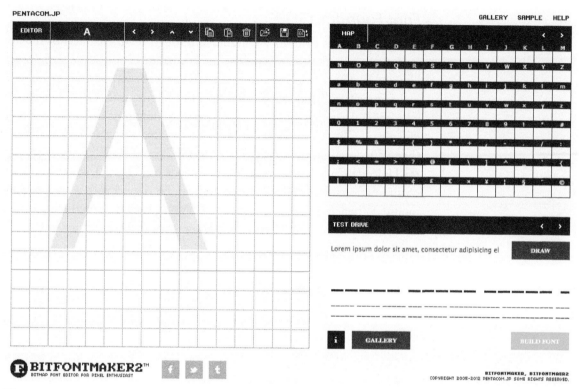

Figure 2-8   BitFontMaker2 (www.pentacom.jp/pentacom/bitfontmaker2/) is an online tool for building bitmapped fonts.

outline fonts. In 1989, Apple and Microsoft announced a joint effort to develop a "better and faster" quadratic curves outline font methodology, called **TrueType**. In addition to printing smooth characters on printers, TrueType would draw characters to a low-resolution (72 dpi or 96 dpi) display. Furthermore, Apple and Microsoft would no longer need to license the PostScript technology from Adobe for their operating systems. Because TrueType was based on Apple technology, it was licensed to Microsoft. Adobe and Microsoft then developed a new and improved font management system incorporating the best features of both PostScript and TrueType, and by 2007, **OpenType** became a free, publicly available international standard. The font wars were over.

WARNING   *TrueType, OpenType, and PostScript fonts do not display (or print) exactly the same, even though they may share the same name and size. The three technologies use different formulas. This means that word-wrapping in a text field may change. So if you build a field or a button that precisely fits text displayed with a PostScript font, be aware that if you then display it with the same font in TrueType or OpenType, the text may be truncated or wrapped, wrecking your layout.*

Font Foundries

Today collections of fonts are available through retail channels or directly from their manufacturers. Typefaces are created in a **foundry**, a term (much like *case*) that has carried over from times when lead was poured into molds to make letter faces. There are also special interest groups (SIGs) where people who enjoy designing and making interesting fonts post them for others to download. Check out the Fonts SIG at the free software Fedora Project (https://fedoraproject.org/wiki/Category:SIGs?rd=SIGs#Fonts). Also visit the Unicode Code Charts page (www.unicode.org/charts/), where hundreds of international fonts are cataloged and can be viewed with a click of your mouse. When you purchase some applications, such as CorelDraw, Adobe Illustrator, or Microsoft Word, many extra fonts are included for free.

· ·

www.3ipfonts.com/

www.myfonts.com/

www.bitstream.com/

www.esperfonto.com/

These gateways are commercial type foundries and font sites, and they lead a discussion of fonts and where to find them. With *Esperfonto*, Will Harris provides an interesting tool for making font decisions: Casual or Formal, Body or Display, Friendly or Serious, Cool or Warm, Modern or Traditional.

· ·

WARNING   *It is easy to spend hours and hours downloading neat and interesting fonts; they are like the midnight snack table on a Caribbean cruise liner—ice carvings and delectable goodies laid out as far as the eye can see.*

Character Sets and Alphabets

Knowing that there is a wide selection of characters available to you on your computer and understanding how you can create and use special and custom-made characters will broaden your creative range when you design and build multimedia projects.

The ASCII Character Set

It all began with a set of characters called **ASCII**, for the American Standard Code for Information Interchange. ASCII was initially invented and standardized for analog teletype communication before the digital age began; it was in place and available when computers needed a system to display or print characters. As seen in Figure 2-9, this simple system assigns a binary value to 128 characters (7 bits), including both lower- and uppercase letters, punctuation marks, Arabic numbers, and math symbols.

Also included in the 128 are 32 control characters used for device control messages such as carriage return, line feed, tab, and form feed.

Teletype machine

ASCII code numbers represent a letter or symbol within the English alphabet, so a computer or printer can work with the number that represents the letter, regardless of what the letter might actually look like on the screen or printout. To a computer working with the ASCII character set, the number 65, for example, always represents an uppercase letter *A*. Later, when the computer is asked to display the number 65 on a screen or print it, it converts the number into the letter shape using the specified font information.

dec/hex	char	dec/hex	char	dec/hex	char	dec/hex	char	dec/hex	char	dec/hex	char	dec/hex	char	dec/hex	char
0 / 0x00	NUL	16 / 0x10	DLE	32 / 0x20		48 / 0x30	0	64 / 0x40	@	80 / 0x50	P	96 / 0x60	`	112 / 0x70	p
1 / 0x01	SOH	17 / 0x11	DC1	33 / 0x21	!	49 / 0x31	1	65 / 0x41	A	81 / 0x51	Q	97 / 0x61	a	113 / 0x71	q
2 / 0x02	STX	18 / 0x12	DC2	34 / 0x22	"	50 / 0x32	2	66 / 0x42	B	82 / 0x52	R	98 / 0x62	b	114 / 0x72	r
3 / 0x03	ETX	19 / 0x13	DC3	35 / 0x23	#	51 / 0x33	3	67 / 0x43	C	83 / 0x53	S	99 / 0x63	c	115 / 0x73	s
4 / 0x04	EOT	20 / 0x14	DC4	36 / 0x24	$	52 / 0x34	4	68 / 0x44	D	84 / 0x54	T	100 / 0x64	d	116 / 0x74	t
5 / 0x05	ENQ	21 / 0x15	NAK	37 / 0x25	%	53 / 0x35	5	69 / 0x45	E	85 / 0x55	U	101 / 0x65	e	117 / 0x75	u
6 / 0x06	ACK	22 / 0x16	SYN	38 / 0x26	&	54 / 0x36	6	70 / 0x46	F	86 / 0x56	V	102 / 0x66	f	118 / 0x76	v
7 / 0x07	BEL	23 / 0x17	ETB	39 / 0x27	'	55 / 0x37	7	71 / 0x47	G	87 / 0x57	W	103 / 0x67	g	119 / 0x77	w
8 / 0x08	BS	24 / 0x18	CAN	40 / 0x28	(	56 / 0x38	8	72 / 0x48	H	88 / 0x58	X	104 / 0x68	h	120 / 0x78	x
9 / 0x09	TAB	25 / 0x19	EM	41 / 0x29	)	57 / 0x39	9	73 / 0x49	I	89 / 0x59	Y	105 / 0x69	i	121 / 0x79	y
10 / 0x0A	LF	26 / 0x1A	SUB	42 / 0x2A	*	58 / 0x3A	:	74 / 0x4A	J	90 / 0x5A	Z	106 / 0x6A	j	122 / 0x7A	z
11 / 0x0B	VT	27 / 0x1B	ESC	43 / 0x2B	+	59 / 0x3B	;	75 / 0x4B	K	91 / 0x5B	[	107 / 0x6B	k	123 / 0x7B	{
12 / 0x0C	FF	28 / 0x1C	FS	44 / 0x2C	,	60 / 0x3C	<	76 / 0x4C	L	92 / 0x5C	\	108 / 0x6C	l	124 / 0x7C	|
13 / 0x0D	CR	29 / 0x1D	GS	45 / 0x2D	-	61 / 0x3D	=	77 / 0x4D	M	93 / 0x5D	]	109 / 0x6D	m	125 / 0x7D	}
14 / 0x0E	SO	30 / 0x1E	RS	46 / 0x2E	.	62 / 0x3E	>	78 / 0x4E	N	94 / 0x5E	^	110 / 0x6E	n	126 / 0x7E	~
15 / 0x0F	SI	31 / 0x1F	US	47 / 0x2F	/	63 / 0x3F	?	79 / 0x4F	O	95 / 0x5F	_	111 / 0x6F	o	127 / 0x7F	

Figure 2-9 The 128-character ASCII character set showing each character's decimal and hexadecimal value

Unicode provides a consistent way of encoding multilingual plain text and brings order to a chaotic state of affairs that has made it difficult to exchange text files internationally. Computer users who deal with multilingual text—business people, linguists, researchers, scientists, and others—will find that the Unicode Standard greatly simplifies their work. Mathematicians and technicians, who regularly use mathematical symbols and other technical characters, will also find the Unicode Standard valuable.

The design of Unicode is based on the simplicity and consistency of ASCII, but goes far beyond ASCII's limited ability to encode only the Latin alphabet. The Unicode Standard provides the capacity to encode all of the characters used for the written languages of the world. To keep character coding simple and efficient, the Unicode Standard assigns each character a unique numeric value and name.

The Unicode Standard and ISO/IEC 10646 support three encoding forms (UTF-8, UTF-16, UTF-32) that use a common repertoire of characters. These encoding forms allow for encoding as many as a million characters. This is sufficient for all known character encoding requirements, including full coverage of all historic scripts of the world, as well as common notational systems.

. . . .

The Unicode® Standard: A Technical Introduction (www.unicode.org/unicode /standard/principles.html)

The ASCII Extended Character Set

A byte, which consists of 8 bits, is the most commonly used building block for computer processing. ASCII uses only 7 bits to code its 128 characters; the eighth bit of the byte is unused. This extra bit allows another 128 characters to be encoded before the byte is used up, and computer systems historically used these extra 128 values for an extended character set. The extended character set is most commonly filled with ANSI (American National Standards Institute) standard characters, including often-used symbols, such as ¢ or ∞, and international diacritics or alphabet characters, such as ä or ñ. This fuller set of 255 characters is also known as the ISO-Latin-1 character set; it was commonly used to program the text of HTML web pages but has been replaced by Unicode's UTF-8 as the most common character set on the Internet. It is backward compatible with the ASCII set.

Unicode

As the computer market became more international, one of the resulting problems was handling the various international language alphabets. It was at best difficult, and at times impossible, to translate the text portions of programs from one script to another. For example, the differences between the Latin script used by Western European writers and the kanji script used by Japanese writers made it particularly challenging to transfer innovative programs from one market to another.

Since 1989, a concerted effort on the part of linguists, engineers, and information professionals from many well-known computer companies has  been focused on a 16-bit architecture for multilingual text and character encoding. This architecture is now an international standard called Unicode. The original standard accommodated up to about 65,000 characters to include the characters from all known languages and alphabets in the world.

Where several languages share a set of symbols that have a historically related derivation, the shared symbols of each language are unified into collections of symbols (called scripts). A single script can work for tens or even hundreds of languages (for example, the Latin script used for English and most European languages). Sometimes, however, only one script will work for a language (such as the Korean Hangul). Figure 2-10 shows a map of writing systems used in the world today.

The Unicode standard includes more than 18,000 Han characters (ideographs for Japanese, Chinese, and Korean) as well as obsolete alphabets such as cuneiform, hieroglyphs, and ancient Han characters. In addition, character space is reserved for users and publishers to create their

Figure 2-10 Writing systems currently in use around the world. Unicode provides a consistent methodology for encoding the characters of any alphabet.

own scripts, designed especially for their own applications. For example, a carpenter might develop a script that includes a character meaning "half-inch Sheetrock," another character meaning "three-quarter-inch plywood," and so forth. HTML allows access to the Unicode characters by numeric reference. Thus 水 (in hexadecimal) represents the Chinese character for water:

Mapping Text Across Platforms

If you build your multimedia project on a Windows platform and play it back on a Macintosh platform (or vice versa), there may be subtle (and sometimes not-so-subtle) differences. Fonts are perhaps the greatest cross-platform concern, because they must be mapped to the other machine. If a specified font doesn't exist on the target machine, a substitute must be provided that does exist on the target. This is **font substitution**. In many cross-platform-savvy applications, you can explicitly define the **font mapping**.

TIP   *Never assume that the fonts you have installed on your computer will also be installed on another person's computer. Pay attention to the way you include fonts in a project so that you never face the nightmare of your carefully picked fonts being replaced by an ill-suited default font like Courier (see the next "First Person"). If your work is being distributed to sites that may not have the fonts you are using, or if you do not license these fonts for distribution with your work, be sure to bitmap the special font text you use for titles, headlines, buttons, and so forth. For text to be entered by users, it is safest to stay with the installed Windows or Macintosh fonts, because you know they are universally available on that platform. In Windows, use the TrueType fonts installed during the Setup procedure.*

First Person

We had a short break between sessions to install the software for a panel discussion about multimedia. It was a big auditorium in Boston. Four of us brought media with discussion material. Our moderator installed her presentation first, and we heard her wail, "Something's wrong with my fonts!" We all looked at her ugly 48-point Courier and felt sorry for her; we knew her mistake. The beautiful fonts she had installed on her home system were not installed in the system of the computer being used for the big-screen projector, and she had failed to bring the fonts along so she could install them. By then, it was too late anyway.

Figure 2-11   BBEDIT, a serious text editor for creating HTML documents and creating program code, provides a choice of Unicode character sets. Choose UTF-8 and BBEDIT creates a meta tag for your HTML document, <meta charset="utf-8" />, to declare it to be using the most widely used (and "safest") set among all web documents, UTF-8.

Always be sure your fonts travel with your application when you are delivering software to run on a hardware platform other than the one you used to create the application. To avoid many font display problems, particularly for menus and headlines, you may wish to snap a picture of your text with a screen capture utility and use this image, or bitmap, instead of text that you type into a text field. (Chapter 3 describes bitmaps and how to capture and edit images.) This will ensure that the screen always looks right, regardless of what hardware platform you use or what fonts are installed.

It is not just fonts that are problematic; characters, too, must be mapped across platforms. **Character mapping** allows bullets, accented characters, and other curious characters that are part of the extended character set on one platform to appear correctly when text is moved to the other platform. In documents created using a Western Latin set, for example, curly quotes may not properly display across platforms. Documents created using the more complete and better-organized UTF-8 set (see Figure 2-11) are readable on most all platforms.

First Person

While we were in the early phases of producing my CD-ROM, *Multimedia: Working It Out!* I sold the rights to distribute it into Korea and Mainland China. Nobody on the production team had ever seen a computer that typed short-form Mandarin, and we knew that even when the English was localized, we would be hard pressed to recognize any of the text, much less edit or alter it in its new form.

So we devised a structured system of labels and names for *Multimedia: Working It Out!* and converted all the text in the project (about 600 "pages" of about a paragraph each) into 1-bit bitmaps in an Adobe Director movie. Donna Booher edited and formatted the text in Microsoft Word, Dan Hilgert bitmapped and screen-captured each page with Capture and Photoshop, and Peter Wolf imported the image files into Director (by the hundreds) as cast members. Each cast member had a unique (but systematic) name associated with a Director movie, a heading, and various icons. It took a while.

The localizers across the Pacific, then, would simply translate a page or a series of pages using their own native-language word processor and capture their own bitmaps. Finally, we would substitute the new bitmaps for the old using the unique identification labels. No language skills required!

When we started, Terry Thompson devised a color-coded master filing system and database so that all the word-processed text and the screen-captured bitmaps would remain neatly side by side and concurrent. This is called *version control*. By the time this project shipped, Donna's computer was crashing four or five times a day and we had lost files, Dan had gone back to school, Peter and I were slapping miscellaneous text elements into the project without tracking where they came from, and we were changing labels and moving cast members around as we streamlined performance, debugged, and staggered toward a golden master and the FedEx drop-off. We had converted Terry's neatly organized system into chaos.

After the CD-ROMs were pressed, and there wasn't anything anybody could change anymore anyway, we did a tricky thing with Lingo programming, image processing, and optical character recognition (OCR) to convert the final project's bitmapped text back into word processor text.

First we collected all the bitmapped text into a single Director movie (we weren't interested in pretty pictures, QuickTime, sounds, or other types of cast members, just text). Then we placed each page of bitmapped text into a movie frame (Cast to Time), neatly labeled that frame at the top with the identifying code of the image using a Lingo handler, and saved all of the frames as bitmapped images (an automatic command in Director's Export menu). With DeBabelizer, we batch-converted these hundreds of images from 72 dpi (screen capture resolution) to 300 dpi (printer resolution) and saved each as a 1-bit TIFF image. The process was automatic.

We then batch-processed the image files using an OCR program to turn them into nicely formatted word processing documents. Bingo! They came out as archival word processing files. Then we sent the word files to Guido Mozzi in Italy so that his team of translators could begin localizing there.

Some efforts are cyclical, we have discovered. The trick is to learn something and improve the process each time the task comes around!

The written Japanese language consists of three different types of character sets, namely: kanji, katakana, and hiragana. Kanji was originally taken from the Chinese language and is essentially a pictographic representation of the spoken word. Each kanji has two different readings, "on-yomi" and "kun-yomi," respectively, the "Chinese rendering" and the "Japanese rendering." Both are used depending on the conjugation of the kanji with other kanji.

Due to certain incompatibilities between the Japanese spoken word and kanji, two sets of kana or phonetic syllabary (alphabet) were developed. Katakana is the "square" kana and is used today for writing only foreign words or onomatopoeic expressions. Hiragana is the "cursive" kana and can be used alone to represent a certain word or combined with kanji to form other words and sentences. Romaji, a more recent addition to the alphabets of Japan, allows for the phonetic spelling of the Japanese language using the Roman characters familiar to the Western world.

Ross Uchimura, Executive Vice-President, GC3 Ltd., a cross-cultural expert

Languages in the World of Computers

In modern Western languages, words are made up of symbols or letters strung together, representing as a whole the sounds of a spoken word. This is not so for Eastern languages such as Chinese, Japanese, and Korean (and the ancient languages of Sumeria, Egypt, and Mesopotamia). In these languages, an entire concept might be represented by a single word symbol that is unrelated to a specific phonetic sound.

The letters or symbols of a language are its alphabet. In English, the alphabet comprises more than 3,000 *kanas*, or whole words. The Russian alphabet, made up of Cyrillic characters based on the ancient Greek alphabet, has about the same number of letters as a Roman alphabet. All languages, from Navajo to Hebrew, have their own unique alphabets.

Most modern alphabets share one very important attribute: the graphic shapes and method for writing the Arabic numbers 0 1 2 3 4 5 6 7 8 9. This is a simple system for representing decimal numbers, which lends itself to easy reading, writing, manipulation, and calculation. Expressing and performing

$$16 + 32 = 48$$

is much easier in Arabic numbers than in Roman or Greek numerals:

$$XVI + XXXII = XLVIII$$

$$\iota\varsigma + \lambda\beta = \mu\eta$$

Use of Arabic notation has gradually spread across the world to supplant other systems, although Roman numerals are still used today in Western languages in certain forms and contexts.

Translating or designing multimedia (or any computer-based material) into a language other than the one in which it was originally written is called **localization**. This process deals with everything from the month/day/year order for expressing dates to providing special alphabetical characters on keyboards and printers. Even the many Western languages that share the Roman alphabet have their own peculiarities and often require special characters to represent special sounds. For example, German has its umlaut (¨); French its various accents (é, for example), the cedilla (ç), and other diacritics; and Spanish its tilde (ñ). These characters are typically available in the extended character set of a font.

Special Characters in HTML

In HTML, **character entities** based upon the ISO-Latin-1 set make up an alphabet that is required by the HTML standard to be recognized by all browser software. All of the usual characters of an English keyboard are included (the 7-bit ASCII set is built in), but to use characters from the extended set that includes tildes, umlauts, accents, and special symbols, you must use an escape sequence to represent them. A character entity is represented either by a number or by a word and is always prefixed by an ampersand (escape) and followed by a semicolon. For example, the name for the copyright symbol is "copy" and its number is 169. The symbol may be inserted into a document either as © or as ©—either way, the character © is generated by the browser. The list of character entities allowed in standard HTML is growing and will soon include mathematical symbols and even icons to represent things like trash cans, clocks, smileys, and disk drives. Word processors for languages other than English automatically insert the necessary character entities when a document is saved in HTML format.

Entities			
Decimal	Hex	Entity	Character
34	22	&quot;	"
38	26	&amp;	&
60	3C	&lt;	<
62	3E	&gt;	>
160	A0		
161	A1	&iexcl;	¡
162	A2	&cent;	¢
163	A3	&pound;	£
164	A4	&curren;	¤
165	A5	&yen;	¥
166	A6	&brvbar;	¦
167	A7	&sect;	§
168	A8	&uml;	¨
169	A9	&copy;	©
170	AA	&ordf;	ª
171	AB	&laquo;	«

First Person

When I was in Germany some years ago, I read a curious report in the *Frankfurter Allgemeine* about a fellow who was suing the local electric utility for not correcting the spelling of his name to its proper form in the German alphabet. His name had an umlaut in it (Wörm), but his bill always read Woerm. In German, the letter *ö* sounds different from the letter *o*, so I can't say I blamed him. At first he didn't pay his bill, claiming that he wasn't that person; then the courts told him to pay anyway. So he initiated a civil suit to protect his name.

It seems the utility was using a legacy IBM system with a high-speed chain printer to produce the monthly bills, and none of the umlaut characters were available on the ASCII-based chain. By long-standing convention, when you are limited to the English alphabet, the letter *e* immediately follows any umlautless vowel, to indicate that the umlaut should be there but isn't. Today, with high-speed laser printers and special fonts, the problem has probably gone away.

More recently, there are reports that the California Department of Motor Vehicles cannot handle blank spaces in the name fields of its massive database, so Rip Van Winkle's name was changed to Rip VanWinkle without his permission. Expect a lawsuit.

. . . .

www.w3.org/TR/REC-html40/sgml/entities.html

An encyclopedic discussion and reference for HTML character entity references

. . . .

Multilanguage Web Pages

When building a project in more than one language for the Web, consider translating the languages that use Roman fonts and displaying them as text in the browser in the normal way. Languages other than English may have many escaped characters, as you can see in Figure 2-12. If Chinese or Japanese or Arabic is desired, translate the Roman text onto a computer running an operating system using that native language. For the web page, the translator can then capture a screen image of the translated text, and you can embed that image into your web page. This process takes precise coordination among the designers, the content providers, and the translators, but it can be done smoothly with careful labeling of the bits and pieces.

```
<p>
What can this integrated network solution offer your business? Lower
costs, increased flexibility, and greater reliability by supporting all voice
and data requirements, including:</p>
<p>
O que esta solu&ccedil;&atilde;o de rede integrada pode oferecer a sua
empresa? Menores custos, elevada flexibilidade, e maior confiabilidade,
pelo suporte a todos os requisitos de voz e dados, incluindo:</p>
<p>
Qu&eacute; puede ofrecerle a su negocio esta soluci&oacute;n integrada de
redes? Menores costos, mayor flexibilidad y mayor fiabil-idad mediante la
compatibilidad con todos los requisitos para voz y datos, incluso:</p>
<p>
<img src="images/chinese/story 1-1.gif">
```

這種綜合性的網路產品能為您的公司企業帶來哪些好處呢？它能降低成本，提昇服務的靈活性，以及具有更大的可靠性，因為它能支持各種話音與數據傳輸的要求，包括：

```
</p>
<p>
<img src="images/japanese/story 1-1.gif">
```

この統合的ネットワークソリューションは、以下を含む音声・データ要件のすべてに対応し、費用節減、フレキシビリティや信頼性の向上を実現させます。

求，包括：

```
</p>
```

Figure 2-12 Portion of a five-language web site using normal HTML code for the Roman languages and screen-captured graphic images to display the Chinese and Japanese translations

Translation web services are available that attempt to make text in one language readable in another, even from Western languages to Eastern languages and vice versa. Google's online translator will even speak the words to you:

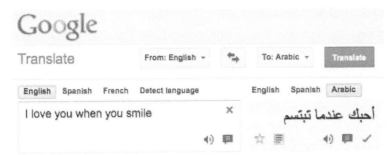

Font Editing and Design Tools

Special font editing tools can be used to make your own type, so you can communicate an idea or graphic feeling exactly. With these tools, professional typographers create distinct text and display faces. Graphic designers, publishers, and ad agencies can design instant variations of existing typefaces.

Typeface designs fall into the category of industrial design and have been determined by the courts in some cases to be protected by patent. For example, design patents have been issued for Bigelow & Holmes' Lucida, International Typeface Corporation's ITC Stone, and Adobe's Minion.

WARNING   *If your commercial project includes special fonts, be sure that your license agreement with the font supplier allows you to distribute them with your project.*

Occasionally in your projects you may require special characters. With the tools described in the paragraphs that follow, you can substitute characters of your own design for any unused characters in a character set. You can even include several custom versions of your client's company logo or other special symbols relevant to your content or subject right in your client's text font.

. . . .

www.fontfoundry.com

www.larabiefonts.com

There are hundreds of sites for downloading free and shareware fonts drawn by others. For starters, try these two.

. . . .

Fontographer

Fontlab, Ltd., located at www.fontlab.com, specializes in font editors for both Macintosh and Windows platforms. You can use this software to develop PostScript, TrueType, and OpenType fonts for Macintosh, Windows, and Sun workstations. Designers can also modify existing typefaces, incorporate PostScript artwork, automatically trace scanned images, and create designs from scratch. A sample of the Fontographer screen is shown in Figure 2-13.

Fontographer's features include a freehand drawing tool to create professional and precise inline and outline drawings of calligraphic and script characters, using either the mouse or alternative input methods (such as a pressure-sensitive pen system). Fontographer allows the creation of multiple font designs from two existing typefaces, and you can design lighter or heavier fonts by modifying the weight of an entire typeface.

Making Pretty Text

To make your text look pretty, you need a toolbox full of fonts and special graphics applications that can stretch, shade, shadow, color, and anti-alias your words into real artwork. Pretty text is typically found in bitmapped drawings where characters have been tweaked, manipulated, and blended into a graphic image. Simply choosing the font is the first step. Most designers find it easier

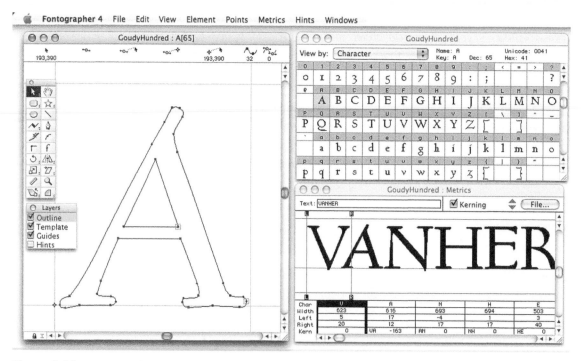

Figure 2-13   Fontographer from Fontlab, Ltd. is a powerful font editor for Macintosh and Windows.

to make pretty type starting with ready-made fonts, but some will create their own custom fonts using font editing and design tools.

With the proper tools and a creative mind, you can create endless variations on plain-old type, and you not only choose but also customize the styles that will fit with your design needs. Using **Dynamic HTML (DHTML)** with Cascading Style Sheets (CSS), you have great flexibility and type choices ranging from line height to margin width to font face.

Most image-editing and painting applications (see Figure 2-14 for a PowerPoint example) let you make text using the fonts available in your system. You can colorize the text, stretch, squeeze, and rotate it, and filter it through various plug-ins to generate wild graphic results.

> When they first invented typesetting, there were variants cut of each character so that text would look as if it had been handwritten by a monk! Desktop designers have been fighting so hard to get their setting to look like it's come from a Berthold system, that most of the new potential of desktop typography has been overlooked.
>
> David Collier, Author of *Collier's Rules for Desktop Design and Typography*

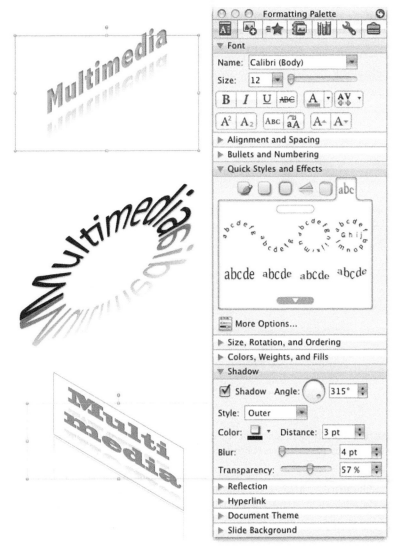

Figure 2-14 PowerPoint lets you manipulate text in many ways.

As a multimedia developer, you may only need to be concerned about how your fonts look on the screens, not how they are printed to paper—unless, of course, you are printing perfect proposals, bids, storyboards, reports, and above all, invoices ☺. TrueType, OpenType, and PostScript outline fonts allow text to be drawn at any size on your computer screen without jaggies:

The Jaggies

Jaggies are avoided by anti-aliasing the edges of the text characters, making them seem smoother to the eye. Note the improved look of the anti-aliased letters in the bottom row of letters in Figure 2-15. Pasting an image that was anti-aliased against a light background onto a darker-colored background using transparency (so that the new, dark background is seen, instead of the old, light one) can be problematic: the blending pixels along the edge will show as a halo and may have to be edited pixel by pixel.

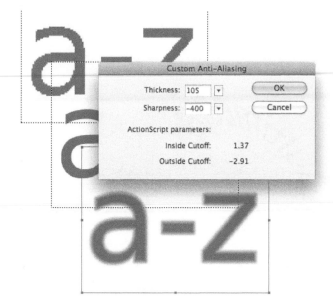

Figure 2-16 In some authoring programs, anti-aliasing can be fine-tuned.

Figure 2-15 Anti-aliasing text and graphics creates "smooth" boundaries between colors. The top row of letters is not anti-aliased; the bottom row is.

Macintosh and PCs handle anti-aliasing differently. Authoring programs such as Adobe Flash allow you to fine-tune anti-aliasing settings for text fields (see Figure 2-16), useful when you want a different look for text that will be static versus text that will be animated.

Hypermedia and Hypertext

Multimedia—the combination of text, graphic, and audio elements into a single collection or presentation—becomes interactive multimedia when you give the user some control over what information is viewed and when it is viewed. Interactive multimedia becomes **hypermedia** when its designer provides a structure of linked elements through which a user can navigate and interact.

When a hypermedia project includes large amounts of text or symbolic content, this content can be indexed and its elements then linked together to afford rapid electronic retrieval of the associated information. When words are keyed or indexed to other words, you have a **hypertext system**; the "text" part of this term represents the project's content and meaning, rather than the graphical presentation of the text. Hypertext is what the World Wide Web is all about.

When text is stored in a computer instead of on printed pages, the computer's powerful processing capabilities can be applied to make the text more accessible and meaningful. The text can then be called **hypertext**; because the words, sections, and thoughts are linked, the user can navigate through text in a nonlinear way, quickly and intuitively.

Using hypertext systems, you can electronically search through all the text of a computer-resident book, locate references to a certain word, and then immediately view the page where the word was found. Or you can create complicated Boolean searches (using terms such as AND, OR, NOT, and BOTH) to locate the occurrences of several related words, such as "Elwood," "Gloria," "mortgage," and "happiness," in a paragraph or on a page. Whole documents can be linked to other documents.

A word can be made into a hyperlink (made "hot"), as can a button, thus leading the user from one reference to another. Click on the word "Elwood," and you may find yourself reading a biography or resume; click on "mortgage," and a calculator pops up. Some authoring systems incorporate a hypertext facility that allows you to identify words in a text field using a bold or colored style, then link them to other words, pages, or activities, such as playing a sound or video clip related to that hot word. You cannot do this kind of nonlinear and associative navigation in a sequentially organized book. But on a CD-ROM or DVD or on the Web, where you might have more than 100,000 pages of text to investigate, search, and browse, hypertext is invaluable.

Because hypertext is the organized cross-linking of words not only to other words but also to associated images, video clips, sounds, and other exhibits, hypertext often becomes simply an additional feature within an overall multimedia design. The term "hyper" (from the Greek word "over" [υπερ]) has come to imply that user interaction is a critical part of the design, whether for text browsing or for the multimedia project as a whole.

[Vannevar] Bush identified the problem—and the need to provide new ways to access information—but was he right about how the mind works? I suspect a purely associative model of human memory and mental processes is too simplistic.

Philip Murray, *From Ventura to Hypertext*, Knowledge Management Associates, Danvers, MA

When interaction and cross-linking is then added to multimedia, and the navigation system is nonlinear, multimedia becomes hypermedia.

In 1945, Vannevar Bush wrote a seminal eight-page article, "As We May Think," for the *Atlantic Monthly* (www.theatlantic.com/magazine /archive/1945/07/as-we-may-think/303881/). This short treatise, in which he discusses the need for new methodologies for accessing information, has become the historic cornerstone of hypertext experimentation. Doug Englebart (inventor of the mouse) and Ted Nelson (who coined the term "hypertext" in 1965) have actively championed the research and innovations required of computer technology for implementing useful hypertext systems, and they have worked to combat the historic inertia of linear thought. Nelson would claim that the very structure of thought is neither sequential nor linear and that computer-based hypertext systems will fundamentally alter the way humans approach literature and the expression of ideas during the coming decades.

The argument against this theory of associative thought is that people are, indeed, more comfortable with linear thinking and are easily overwhelmed by too much freedom, becoming quickly lost in the chaos of nonlinear gigabytes. As a practical reminder, it is important always to provide location markers, either text-and-symbol menus or illustrative maps, for users who travel the threads of nonlinear systems.

The Power of Hypertext

In a fully indexed hypertext system, all words can be found immediately. Suppose you search a large database for "boats," and you come up with a whopping 1,623 references, or *hits*—among them, Noah's Ark (open boat in water), television situation comedies (*The Love Boat*), political criticisms of cabinet members who challenged the status quo (rocked the boat), cabinet members who were stupid (missed the boat), and Christmas dinner trimmings (Grandmother's gravy boat). So you narrow your search and look for "boats" and "water" when both words are mentioned on the same page; this time you get 286 hits. "Boats," "water," and "storms" gets you 37; "boats," "water," "storms," and "San Francisco," a single hit. With over a thousand hits, you are lost. With one hit, you have something! But you still may not find what you are looking for, as you can see in this fictional example:

The *storm* had come and gone quickly across the Colorado plains, but *water* was still puddled at the foot of the house-high bank of mud that had slid into town when the dam burst. In front of the general store, which had remained standing, four strong men carefully lifted a tiny *boat* onto the large dray wagon borrowed from the woodcutters. On a layer of blankets in the bilge of the *boat*, the undertaker had carefully laid out the remains of both the mayor and his paramour.

The mayor had not drowned in the flood, but died of a heart attack in the midst of the panic. Children covered the *boat* with freshly cut pine boughs while horses were quickly harnessed to the wagon, and a strange procession began to move slowly down *San Francisco* Street toward the new cemetery. ...

The power of such search-and-retrieval systems provided by a computer for large volumes of data is immense, but clearly this power must be channeled in meaningful ways. Links among words or clusters of information need to be designed so that they make sense. Judgments must be made about relationships and the way information content is organized and made available to users. The lenses through which vast amounts of data are viewed must necessarily be ground and shaped by those who design the access system.

The issue of who designs the lenses and how the designers maintain impartial focus is troubling to many scientists, archivists, and students of cognitive thinking. The scientists would remain "hermeneutically" neutral; they would balance freedom against authority and warn against the epistemological unknowns of this new intellectual technology. They are aware of the forces that allow advertising and marketing craftspeople to intuitively twist meanings and spin events to their own purposes, with actions that can affect the knowledge and views of many millions of people and thus history itself. But these forces remain poorly understood, are not easily controlled by authority, and will express themselves with immeasurably far-reaching, long-term impact on the shape of human culture.

The multimedia designer controls the filtering mechanisms and places the lenses within the multimedia project. A manufacturer, for instance, that presents its products using interactive multimedia can bring abundant information and selling power within reach of the user, including background information, collateral marketing material, pricing statistics, and technical data. The project design will be, of course, biased—to sell more of the manufacturer's products and generate more profit; but this bias is assumed and understood in these circumstances. When the assumptions and understandings of inherent bias in any information base break down, when fiction or incomplete data is presented as full fact, these are the times when the powerful forces of multimedia and hypermedia can have their greatest deleterious effect.

WARNING   *Bad multimedia projects will not alter the collective view of history; really bad projects might.*

Using Hypertext

Special programs for information management and hypertext have been designed to present electronic text, images, and other elements in a database fashion. Commercial systems have been used for large and complicated

The hype about hypertext may be justified. It can provide a computer-supported information environment which can add to our appreciation of the text, can go some way towards aping the mental agility of the human mind, can allow navigation along patterns of association, can provide a nonlinear information environment. But the problems of constructing nonlinear documents are not few and can prove to be very complex.

....

Patricia Baird, Editor of *Hypermedia*, a scientific journal published in the United Kingdom

Hypermedia on its own simply functions as a reference tool. But when it is integrated within a goal-based activity, it becomes a powerful learning resource.

....

Brigid Sealy and Paul Phelan, INESC, Porto, Portugal (conclusions from research funded by the European Commission's Human Capital and Mobility Program)

mixtures of text and images—for example, a detailed repair manual for an Airbus 330 aircraft, a parts catalog for Rolls Royce jet turbine engines, an instant reference to hazardous chemicals, and electronic reference libraries used in legal and library environments. Such searchable database engines are widely used on the Web, where software robots or "bots" visit millions of web pages and index entire web sites. Hypertext databases rely upon proprietary indexing systems that carefully scan the entire body of text and create very fast cross-referencing indexes that point to the location of specific words, documents, and images. Indeed, a hypertext index by itself can be as large as 50 percent to 100 percent the size of the original document. Indexes are essential for speedy performance. Google's search engine generates more than half a billion hits in less than a third of a second!

Commercial hypertext systems were developed historically to retrofit gigantic bodies of information. Licenses for use and distribution of these commercial systems are expensive, and the hypertext-based projects typically require the large mass-storage capability of dedicated gigabyte or terabyte hard disks. Simpler but effective hypertext indexing tools are available for both Macintosh and Windows, and they offer fairly elaborate features designed to work in concert with many multimedia authoring systems. Server-based hypertext and database engines designed for the Web are now widely available and competitively priced.

About 651,000,000 results (0.32 seconds)

TIP *Rather than designing an elaborate, fully cross-referenced hypertext system for your multimedia project, you can "hardwire" the links between the most salient words (highlight them in your text) so that a mouse click leads to a topic menu specific to the chosen word. Though this constrains the user's movement through the text, the user will not perceive it as such, and you can thus maintain strict control over your navigation pathways and design.*

Searching for Words

Although the designer of a hypermedia database makes assumptions, he or she also presents users with tools and a meaningful interface to exercise the assumptions. Employing this interface, users can tailor word searches to find very specific combinations. Following are typical methods for word searching in hypermedia systems:

- **Categories** Selecting or limiting the documents, pages, or fields of text within which to search for a word or words.
- **Word relationships** Searching for words according to their general proximity and order. For example, you might search for "party" and "beer" only when they occur on the same page or in the same paragraph.

- **Adjacency**   Searching for words occurring next to one another, usually in phrases and proper names. For instance, find "widow" only when "black" is the preceding adjacent word.
- **Alternates**   Applying an OR criterion to search for two or more words, such as "bacon" or "eggs."
- **Association**   Applying an AND criterion to search for two or more words, such as "skiff," "tender," "dinghy," and "rowboat."
- **Negation**   Applying a NOT criterion to search exclusively for references to a word that are not associated with the word. For example, find all occurrences of "paste" when "library" is not present in the same sentence.
- **Truncation**   Searching for a word with any of its possible suffixes. For example, to find all occurrences of "girl" and "girls," you may need to specify something like **girl#**. Multiple character suffixes can be managed with another specifier, so **geo*** might yield "geo," "geology," and "geometry," as well as "George."
- **Intermediate words**   Searching for words that occur between what might normally be adjacent words, such as a middle name or initial in a proper name.
- **Frequency**   Searching for words based on how often they appear: the more times a term is mentioned in a document, the more relevant the document is to this term.

Hypermedia Structures

Two buzzwords used often in hypertext systems are link and node. **Links** are connections between the conceptual elements, that is, the **nodes**, which may consist of text, graphics, sounds, or related information in the knowledge base. Links connect Caesar Augustus with Rome, for example, and grapes with wine, and love with hate. The art of hypermedia design lies in the visualization of these nodes and their links so that they make sense, not nonsense, and can form the backbone of a knowledge access system. The term anchor is used for the reference from one document to another document, image, sound, or file using HTML on the Web (see Chapter 11).

Links are the navigation pathways and menus; nodes are accessible topics, documents, messages, and content elements. A **link anchor** is where you come from; a **link end** is the destination node linked to the anchor. Some hypertext systems provide unidirectional navigation and offer no return pathway; others are bidirectional.

The simplest way to navigate hypermedia structures is via buttons that let you access linked information (text, graphics, and sounds) that is contained at the nodes. When you've finished examining the information, you return to your starting location. A typical navigation structure might look like the following:

Pages of text with hot words linked to InfoBites only

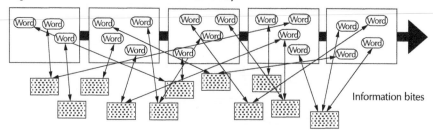

Information bites

Navigation becomes more complicated when you add associative links that connect elements not directly in the hierarchy or sequence. These are the paths where users can begin to get lost if you do not provide location markers. A link can lead to a node that provides further links, as shown here:

Pages of text with hot words linked to InfoBites linked to pages and to other InfoBites

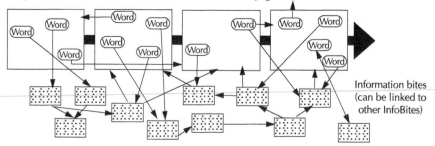

Information bites (can be linked to other InfoBites)

When you offer full-text search through an information base, there may be links between any number of items at your current node and any number of other nodes with items that meet your relationship criteria. When users are browsing freely through this system, and one page does not follow the next (as expected in the linear metaphor of books and literature), users can get lost in the associative maze of the designer's content:

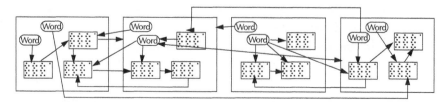

One publisher of hypermedia products claims that becoming lost in "hyperspace" may not be all that bad. The struggle to find your way back can be valuable in itself, and certainly a learning experience.

Hypertext Tools

Two functions are common to most hypermedia text management systems, and they are often provided as separate applications: building (or authoring) and reading. The builder creates the links, identifies nodes, and generates the all-important index of words. The index methodology and the search algorithms used to find and group words according to user search criteria are typically proprietary, and they represent an area where computers are carefully optimized for performance—finding search words among a list of many tens of thousands of words requires speed-demon programming.

Hypertext systems are currently used for electronic publishing and reference works, technical documentation, educational courseware, interactive kiosks, electronic catalogs, interactive fiction, and text and image databases. Today these tools are used extensively with information organized in a linear fashion; it still may be many years before the majority of multimedia project users become comfortable with fully nonlinear hypertext and hypermedia systems. When (and perhaps if) they do, the methodology of human thought and conceptual management—indeed, the way we think—will be forever changed.

Hypermedia can take advantage of powerful capabilities that are becoming clearer as the new multimedia medium matures, giving us a greater choice in exploration, if not in outright plot definition, for example. From my experiences with "Playa Sirenas," the real challenge facing storytellers in this new medium is allowing readers appropriate choices (some authorship of the story, really) while they navigate through the hypermedia experience, without destroying the successful and basic patterns that have been part of storytelling since people first gathered around campfires.

There is something organic about these time-proven storytelling patterns. As an author in the new medium, you must first design the DNA or template of your story, then allow (and promote) mutation along evolutionary lines that you, as the author, have created as part of the template...

Hermann Steffen, hypermedia novelist, San Jose, Costa Rica

Chapter 2 Review

Chapter Summary

For your review, here's a summary of the important concepts discussed in this chapter.

Recognize the importance of word choice

- With the relatively recent explosion of the Internet and the World Wide Web, text has become more important than ever. Words and symbols in any form, spoken or written, are the most common system of communication. It's important to design labels for title screens, menus, and buttons using words that have the most precise and powerful meanings to express what you need to say. Experiment with the words you plan to use by letting others try them.

Describe the difference between a typeface and a font and list at least three attributes of a font, for example, upper/lowercase, serif/sans serif, PostScript/TrueType/OpenType

- A typeface is a family of graphic characters that usually includes many type sizes and styles.

- Serif versus sans serif is the simplest way to categorize a typeface.

- A font is a collection of characters of a single size and style belonging to a particular typeface family.

- Three common font styles are bold, italic, and underline, but there are several others; some, such as superscript, emboss, or strikethrough, have specialized uses.

- Type sizes are usually expressed in points (about 72 per inch).

- Leading is the space between lines.

- Kerning is the space between individual characters.

- Alignment can be left, right, centered, or justified.

Discuss the importance of text and ways text can be leveraged in multimedia presentations

- Size, color, background color, style, and leading are factors that affect the legibility of text.

- On the printed page, serif fonts are traditionally used for body text because the serifs are said to help guide the reader's eye along the line of text. Sans serif fonts, on the other hand, are used for headlines and bold statements. But sans serif fonts are far more legible and attractive when used in the small sizes of a text field on a screen.

Discuss the presentation of text on Windows, Macintosh, eBook, tablet, and mobile platforms

- The fonts installed in Windows and Macintosh operating systems are not the same.

Find sources for free and shareware fonts

- Search for "free fonts" for access to thousands of free downloadable fonts.

Define hypermedia, hypertext, links, anchors, and nodes and be able to discuss both the potential and limitations of hypertext and hyperlinking systems

- Multimedia—the combination of text, graphic, and audio elements into a single collection or presentation—becomes interactive multimedia when you give the user some control over what information is viewed and when it is viewed. Interactive multimedia becomes hypermedia when its designer provides a structure of linked elements through which a user can navigate and interact.

- When a hypermedia project includes large amounts of text or symbolic content, this content can be indexed and its elements then linked together to afford rapid electronic retrieval of the associated information. When words are keyed or indexed to other words, you have a hypertext system; the "text" part of this term represents the project's content and meaning, rather than the graphical presentation of the text. Hypertext is what the World Wide Web is all about.

- When text lives in a computer instead of on printed pages, the computer's powerful processing capabilities can be applied to make the text more accessible and meaningful. The text can then be called hypertext; because the words, sections, and thoughts are linked, the user can navigate through text in a nonlinear way, quickly and intuitively. Because hypertext is the organized cross-linking of words not only to other words but also to associated images, video clips, sounds, and other exhibits, hypertext often becomes simply an additional feature within an overall multimedia design.

- Links are connections between the conceptual elements, that is, the nodes containing text, graphics, sounds, or related information in the knowledge base. The term anchor is formally used in HTML as the reference from one document to another document, image, sound, or file. Links are the navigation pathways and menus; nodes are accessible topics, documents, messages, and content elements. A link anchor is where you come from; a link end is the destination node linked to the anchor.

- The standard document format used for pages on the Web is called Hypertext Markup Language (HTML). In an HTML document you can specify typefaces, sizes, colors, and other properties by "marking up" the text in the document with tags. The remarkable growth of the Web is straining the "old" designs for displaying text on computers. Dynamic HTML (DHTML) uses Cascading Style Sheets (CSS) to define choices ranging from line height to margin width to font face. HTML character entities are represented either by a number or by a word and always prefixed by an ampersand (escape) and

followed by a semicolon. In modern web design, presentation (for example color, font, font size and style) should be declared using CSS.

Decimal	Hex	Entity	Character
188	BC	¼	¼
189	BD	½	½
190	BE	¾	¾
191	BF	¿	¿
192	C0	À	À
193	C1	Á	Á
194	C2	Â	Â
195	C3	Ã	Ã
196	C4	Ä	Ä
197	C5	Å	Å
198	C6	Æ	Æ
199	C7	Ç	Ç
200	C8	È	È
201	C9	É	É
202	CA	Ê	Ê
203	CB	Ë	Ë
204	CC	Ì	Ì
205	CD	Í	Í
206	CE	Î	Î
207	CF	Ï	Ï
208	D0	Ð	Ð
209	D1	Ñ	Ñ
210	D2	Ò	Ò
211	D3	Ó	Ó
212	D4	Ô	Ô
213	D5	Õ	Õ
214	D6	Ö	Ö
215	D7	×	×
216	D8	Ø	Ø
217	D9	Ù	Ù
218	DA	Ú	Ú
219	DB	Û	Û
220	DC	Ü	Ü
221	DD	Ý	Ý
222	DE	Þ	Þ
223	DF	ß	ß
224	E0	à	à
225	E1	á	á
226	E2	â	â
227	E3	ã	ã
228	E4	ä	ä
229	E5	å	å
230	E6	æ	æ
231	E7	ç	ç
232	E8	è	è
233	E9	é	é
234	EA	ê	ê
235	EB	ë	ë
236	EC	ì	ì
237	ED	í	í
238	EE	î	î
239	EF	ï	ï

- You can search and view potentially billions of documents and files (information), but you can also become "lost in hyperspace."

Key Terms

Adobe PostScript *(42)*
anchor *(28)*
anti-aliasing *(27)*
ASCII *(44)*
aspect ratio *(38)*
attribute *(22)*
bitmapped font *(42)*
breadcrumbs *(36)*
buttons *(36)*
CamelCase *(25)*
Cascading Style Sheets
  (CSS) *(31)*
case insensitive *(24)*
case sensitive *(24)*
character entity *(51)*
character mapping *(48)*
character metrics *(23)*
chat-speak *(22)*
condensed *(23)*
dithering *(27)*
dots per inch (dpi) *(24)*
Dynamic HTML (DHTML) *(55)*
eBook *(39)*
emoji *(34)*
emoticon *(35)*
e-reader *(39)*

expanded *(23)*
font *(22)*
font mapping *(47)*
font stack *(31)*
font substitution *(47)*
foundry *(44)*
generic font *(31)*
GUI *(33)*
hint *(42)*
HTML *(19)*
hypermedia *(57)*
hypertext *(57)*
hypertext system *(57)*
icon *(33)*
intercap *(25)*
jaggies *(56)*
kerning *(23)*
landscape *(38)*
leading *(23)*
links *(61)*
link anchor *(61)*
link end *(61)*
localization *(50)*
lowercase *(24)*
Multimedia Messaging
  Service (MMS) *(22)*

nodes *(61)*
OpenType *(43)*
outline font *(42)*
pixel *(24)*
point *(22)*
portrait *(38)*
rasterizing *(24)*
rollovers *(37)*
sans serif *(25)*
scripts *(46)*
serif *(25)*
software robot *(60)*
style *(22)*
tags *(40)*
text-speak *(22)*
tooltip *(37)*
tracking *(24)*
TrueType *(43)*
typeface *(22)*
Unicode *(46)*
uppercase *(24)*
white space *(28)*
WYSIWYG *(26)*
x-height *(23)*

Key Term Quiz

1. Type sizes are usually expressed in _____.

2. When a password must be entered in upper- or lowercase in order to match the original password, it is said to be _____.

3. Symbolic representations of objects and processes common to the graphical user interfaces of many computer operating systems are called _____.

4. Special HTML characters, always prefixed by an ampersand (escape) and followed by a semicolon, are called _____.

5. "What you see is what you get" is spoken as _____.

6. Translating or designing multimedia (or any computer-based material) into a language other than the one in which it was originally written is called _____.

7. The little decoration at the end of a letter stroke is a(n) _____.

8. Designers call roomy blank areas _____.

9. _____ blends the colors along the edges of the letters (called dithering) to create a soft transition between the letter and its background.

10. Conceptual elements consisting of text, graphics, sounds, or related information in the knowledge base are called _____.

Multiple-Choice Quiz

1. A family of graphic characters that usually includes many type sizes and styles is called a:
   - a. typeface
   - b. font
   - c. point
   - d. link
   - e. node

2. Which of the following is a term that applies to the spacing between characters of text?
   - a. leading
   - b. kerning
   - c. tracking
   - d. points
   - e. dithering

3. Intercapping, the practice of placing a capital in the middle of a word, is a trend that emerged from the computer programming community because:
   - a. it looks cool
   - b. they wanted to copy marketing practices in the electronics industry
   - c. they found they could see the words used for variables and commands better
   - d. one of the first computer programmers had a faulty SHIFT key on his keyboard
   - e. it increases security in case-sensitive passwords

4. Dynamic HTML uses _____ to define choices ranging from line height to margin width to font face.
   - a. Cascading Style Sheets
   - b. font mapping
   - c. font substitution
   - d. software robots
   - e. Encapsulated PostScript

5. If a DHTML document includes a font face that is not installed on the user's computer, a browser will:
   - a. automatically download the correct font
   - b. refuse to load the page
   - c. leave a blank space where that text is
   - d. crash
   - e. try to substitute the font with a similar looking font

6. In the URL http://www.timestream.com/info/people/biotay/biotay1.html, which part is case sensitive?
   - a. the record type: "http://"
   - b. the domain name: "timestream.com"
   - c. the subdomain "www"
   - d. the document path: "info/people/biotay/biotay1.html"
   - e. all are case sensitive

7. Multimedia becomes interactive multimedia when:
   - a. the user has some control over what information is viewed and when it is viewed
   - b. the information is displayed by a computer with a touchscreen or other input device
   - c. the information is available on the Web—either the Internet or a local area network
   - d. quizzes and tests with evaluations and scoring are included
   - e. the user can change such attributes as volume and type size

8. Interactive multimedia becomes hypermedia when:
   - a. the information is available on the Web—either the Internet or a local area network
   - b. quizzes and tests with evaluations and scoring are included
   - c. it includes a structure of linked elements through which a user can navigate and interact
   - d. the user can change such attributes as volume and type size
   - e. the content formatting complies with the American Standard Code for Information Interchange

9. Web pages are coded using:
   - a. Unicode
   - b. ASCII
   - c. File Transfer Protocol
   - d. Hypertext Markup Language
   - e. Encapsulated PostScript

10. Which of the following provides a system for dynamically displaying a font?
    a. Apache
    b. PostScript
    c. HTTPD
    d. serif
    e. WYSIWYG

11. A printed page might be presented in which of these orientations?
    a. newsscape
    b. portrait
    c. flat-file
    d. x-height
    e. node

12. Which of the following is a character encoding system?
    a. FontTab
    b. HTML
    c. CSS
    d. WYSIWYG
    e. Unicode

13. The reference from one document to another document, image, sound, or file on the Web is a(n):
    a. sweetspot
    b. anchor
    c. node
    d. tag
    e. button

14. Which of the following is a problem that might apply to hypermedia?
    a. Users' eye movements affect their ability to link.
    b. Users will be turned off by excessive animation.
    c. Hypermedia software might create inappropriate links.
    d. Current hyperlinking technology far exceeds what today's desktop computers can handle.
    e. Search results generally are too granular to be useful.

15. Which of the following is a typical method for word searching in a hypermedia system?
    a. best fit
    b. adjacency
    c. popularity
    d. tracking
    e. localization

■ Essay Quiz

1. Describe what characteristics a block of text might have.

2. Describe what characteristics a typeface might have.

3. Discuss the problems encountered using text across computer platforms and in different languages.

4. Discuss the differences among multimedia, interactive multimedia, hypertext, and hypermedia.

5. Your boss wants you to create a hypermedia system for web visitors to find technical support information about your company. What are some of the implications in creating this system? Should you hand-build the links or use an automatic indexing system? Why?

Lab Projects

■ Project 2.1

Visit three foreign television news or newspaper web sites from different cultures around the world (such as CNN, BBC, CNTV, Reuters, or Al Jazeera). Describe the text fonts and styles used by each for headlines, paragraph content, and menus.

Now visit a local news web site in your own country or local area. If there are differences, explain them. Choose the web site from all that you visited that best presents information through use of text. Describe why this is so.

■ Project 2.2

Using a laptop or desktop computer, visit three web sites. Then visit the same three web sites using a mobile smartphone device with a smaller screen. Compare the presentations of each web site on the mobile and non-mobile devices and describe differences in text style, fonts, and readability. Describe some ways that you might alter fonts and text on these web pages to improve legibility and ease of use when delivered to a mobile device.

■ Project 2.3

Install on your computer two presentation programs that allow you to manipulate text, such as PowerPoint from Microsoft, Keynote from Apple, Prezi, Kingsoft, LibreOffice, or Apache Open Office. If the program is not free, it can often be downloaded as a free trial for limited-time use.

Open each program and write a few sentences of text. Explore the program's customization options for text color, style, and font. Animate your text to "fly" or "grow" or change color as the screen opens or a button is clicked.

Visit the Presentation Library of the American Association of Variable Star Observers (AAVSO) at www.aavso.org/presentation-library-0. View *Cataclysmic Variables for Visual Observers* by Mike Simonsen, *¡Aprenda cómo divertirse haciendo observaciones de estrellas variables!* by Chuck Pullen (translated into Spanish by Jaime García, 2001), and *Pourquoi pas observer les étoiles variables?* by Pierre de Ponthiere (2007). Describe the different ways each handles the presentation of text.

■ Project 2.4

Using a word processor or text editor like Notepad or TextEdit, write two sentences that are 140 characters in length—without using any abbreviations or word shortcuts. Now write the same sentence with as much "chat-speak" as you can possibly apply. Consider how your message's meaning might be changed by using chat-speak, and the pros and cons of doing so.

Now go online and navigate to Twitter.com, or an equivalent platform in your country. Find a prominent celebrity or figure, and describe his or her use of chat-speak. List each use of a chat-speak word.

■ Project 2.5

Use a web browser to locate the free online bitmap font editor BitFontMaker2 (www.pentacom.jp/pentacom/bitfontmaker2/; refer to Figure 2-8 earlier in the chapter). Create several letters to make a new font. Click the Build Font button to download your new font to your computer as a TTF file. Install this font on your computer. Open a text editor and write a few lines using your new font.

Images

Multimedia on a display screen is a composite of elements: text, symbols, photograph-like bitmaps, vector-drawn graphics, three-dimensional renderings, distinctive buttons to click, and windows of motion video. Some parts of this image may even twitch or move so that the screen never seems still and tempts your eye. It may be a very colorful screen with gentle pastel washes of mauve and puce, or it may be brutally primary with splashes of Crayola red and blue and yellow and green. It might be stark black and white, full of sharp angles, or softened with gray-scale blends and anti-aliasing. It may be elegant or, by design, not. It could be tiny and the face of a telephone or watch. The display screen is where the action is, and it contains much more than your message; it is also the viewer's primary connection to all of your project's content.

This chapter will help you understand the visual elements that make up a multimedia presentation. Graphic elements can usually be scaled to different sizes, colorized or patterned or made transparent, placed in front of or behind other objects, or be made visible or invisible on command. How you blend these elements, how you choose your colors and fonts, the tricks that you use that catch the eye, how adept you are at using your tools—these are the hallmarks of your skill, talent, knowledge, and creativity coalesced into the all-important visual connection to your viewers.

Before You Start to Create

At the beginning of a project, the screen is a blank canvas, ready for you, the multimedia designer, to express your craft. The screen will change again and again during the course of your project as you experiment, as you stretch and reshape elements, draw new objects and throw out old ones, and test various colors and effects—creating the vehicle for your message. Indeed, many multimedia designers are known to experience a mild shiver or **ignition frisson** when they pull down the New menu and draw their first colors onto a fresh screen. Just so; this screen represents a powerful and seductive avenue for channeling creativity.

WARNING *Multimedia designers are regularly lured into agonizingly steep learning curves, long nights of cerebral problem solving, and the pursuit of performance perfection. If you are fundamentally creative, multimedia may become a calling, not a profession.*

Plan Your Approach

Whether you use templates and ready-made screens provided by your authoring system, incorporate clip art or objects crafted by others, or even simply clone the look and feel of another project, there will always be a starting point where your page is "clean." But even before reaching this starting point, be sure you have given your project a good deal of thought and planning. Work out your graphic approach, either in your head or during creative sessions with your client or colleagues. There are strong arguments against drawing on a fresh screen without such foresight and preparation. To get a handle on any multimedia project, you start with pencil, eraser, and paper. Outline your project and your graphic ideas first: make a flowchart; storyboard the project using stick figures; use three-by-five index cards and shuffle them until you get it right.

You may not "nail it" with the first design you submit to a client. Get a few examples from them or have them look at templates from a site such as www.templatemonster.com. When you have a clear idea what they want, submit a few variations—different visual designs, color palettes, and layouts.

The organizing and creative process begins with drawings in pen or pencil on paper. Too many times we are enthused about the color and the computer graphics tools, but they can overwhelm the creative design process.

Dennis Woytek, Assistant Professor, Duquesne University

Organize Your Tools

Most authoring systems (discussed in Chapter 9) provide the tools with which you can create the graphic objects of multimedia (text, interactive buttons, vector-drawn objects, and bitmaps) directly on your screen. If one of these tools is not included, the authoring system usually offers a mechanism for importing the object you need from another application. When you are working with animated objects or motion video, most authoring systems include a feature for activating these elements, such as a programming language or special functions for embedding them. Likely, too, your tools will offer a library of special effects—including zooms, wipes, and dissolves. Many multimedia designers do not limit their toolkits to the features of a single authoring platform, but employ a variety of applications and tools to accomplish many specialized tasks.

I like "do-overs," where you make quick and dirty buttons now, or live text now, but go back later and replace those placeholders with more refined images or pretty bitmapped text. This do-over approach lets you work two ends against the middle—you can get right into designing navigation and animation, but know that you will put in the "good" images later.

Sherry Hutson, Lecturer, University of Illinois at Springfield

Configure Your Computer Workspace

When developing multimedia, it is helpful to have more than one monitor to provide lots of screen **real estate** (viewing area). In this way, you can display the full-screen working area of your project or presentation and still have space to put your tools and other menus. This is particularly important in an authoring system such as Flash or Director, where the edits and changes you make in one window are immediately visible in the presentation window—provided the presentation window is not obscured by your editing tool! During development there is a lot of cutting and pasting among windows and among various applications, and with an extra monitor, you can open many windows at once and spread them out. Both

Macintosh and Windows operating systems support this extra hardware. If you are using a laptop computer to develop your project, it is helpful to have access to cloud storage. In any case, with your project files stored in the cloud, other team members can access your materials using different devices.

NOTE   *A few weeks of having to repeatedly bring windows to the front, and then hide them again to see the results of your editing, will probably convince you to invest in a second monitor.*

TIP   *Your operating system has keyboard shortcuts for moving among windows and applications, accessing your desktop, and for standard commands such as cut, copy, paste, and undo. Learning to use these commands—and using them consistently—will enable you to work efficiently.*

Making Still Images

Still images may be small or large, or even full screen. They may be colored, placed at random on the screen, evenly geometric, or oddly shaped. Still images may be a single tree on a wintry hillside; stacked boxes of text against a gray, tartan, or Italian marble background; an engineering drawing; a snapshot of your department manager's new BMW. Whatever their form, still images are generated by the computer in two ways: as **bitmaps** (or paint graphics) and as **vector-drawn** (or just plain "drawn") graphics. Bitmaps may also be called **raster images**. Likewise, bitmap editors are sometimes called "painting" programs. And vector editors are sometimes called "drawing" programs.

Bitmaps are used for photorealistic images and for complex drawings requiring fine detail. Vector-drawn objects are used for lines, boxes, circles, polygons, and other graphic shapes that can be mathematically expressed in angles, coordinates, and distances. A drawn object can be filled with color and patterns, and you can select it as a single object. The appearance of both types of images depends on the display resolution and capabilities of your computer's graphics hardware and monitor. Both types of images are stored in various file formats and can be translated from one application to another or from one computer platform to another. Typically, image files are compressed to save memory and disk space; many bitmap image file formats already use compression within the file itself—for example, **GIF**, **JPEG**, and **PNG**.

Still images may be the most important element of your multimedia project or web site. If you are designing multimedia by yourself, put yourself in the role of graphic artist and layout designer. Take the time necessary to discover all the tricks you can learn about your drawing software.

Competent, computer-literate skills in graphic art and design are vital to the success of your project. Remember—more than anything else, the user's judgment of your work will be heavily influenced by the work's visual impact.

Bitmaps

A **bit** is the simplest element in the digital world, an electronic digit that is either on or off, black or white, or true (1) or false (0). This is referred to as **binary**, since only two states (on or off) are available. A map is a two-dimensional matrix of these bits. A bitmap, then, is a simple matrix of the tiny dots that form an image and are displayed on a screen or printed.

First Person

A few years ago a large corporation asked my company and one other multimedia developer to bid on a long-term contract for computer-based training. Though busy with other active projects, we didn't want this possibly lucrative opportunity to slip by, so we spent a few days hastily putting together a demonstration of our technical skills for building nifty databases, designing tricky telecommunications systems, and integrating live video. We even "wire-framed" a bit of a working multimedia database with real data we got from the corporation.

We showed our demo to about a dozen management and training executives, in a fancy boardroom that had a built-in projector and sound system with mixers and light dimmers—a place where we could knock the socks off anybody. But within 30 seconds, the disaster bells started tinkling: most of our presentation was going way over their heads. Afterward, there were one or two vague questions and some thank-you's.

Our competitor's presentation, on the other hand, provided a slick series of finely rendered bitmapped screen images and elegant visuals. It was heavy on pretty menu screens and very light on how-it-is-done technology. We later learned that one of their graphic artists had worked for two solid weeks on the color bitmaps for that demo. In the follow-up phone call, we were told by our potential clients that the competition's "incredible artwork" had won out over our "excellent technology demonstration."

To cover our disappointment, we mumbled something to ourselves about not wanting to work with computer illiterates, anyway—people who could be taken to the cleaners by fresh paint. But we knew we'd missed a hefty piece of contract work because we hadn't invested serious graphic art talent in our demonstration. We decided that's why the real peas in the can are never the same bright green as the ones on the label. So we learned a marketing lesson.

A one-dimensional matrix (1-bit depth) is used to display monochrome images—a bitmap where each bit is most commonly set to black or white. Depending upon your software, any two colors that represent the on and off (1 or 0) states may be used. More information is required to describe shades of gray or the more than 16 million colors that each picture element might have in a color image, as illustrated in Figure 3-1. These picture elements (known as **pels** or, more commonly, **pixels**) can be

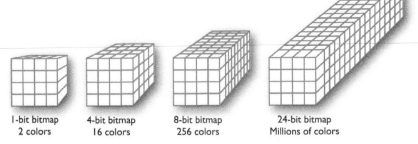

1-bit bitmap
2 colors

4-bit bitmap
16 colors

8-bit bitmap
256 colors

24-bit bitmap
Millions of colors

Figure 3-1 A bitmap is a data matrix that describes the characteristics of all the pixels making up an image. Here, each cube represents the data required to display a 4×4-pixel image (the face of the cube) at various color depths (with each cube extending behind the face indicating the number of bits—zeros or ones—used to represent the color for that pixel).

Is there a colour scheme that will appear coloured or at least solid black for the colour-impaired?
If you're gathering empirical evidence, I have something called red-green colour blindness (it is quite common in males). It doesn't mean that you don't know which traffic light is showing! What it means mainly is that the *tone* of red-type colours doesn't seem so different to the tone of greens—the obvious case is a poppy field. I can see the poppies as red OK if I look carefully or they are pointed out to me, but other people see them kind of exploding out of the green... For people like me, a vibrant yellow always works. I read somewhere that black on yellow is a reliable "strong" combination. Certainly it is used by one of the motoring organisations in the UK for special diversion notices and the like.
....

Graham Samuel, Educational Software Developer, The Living Fossil Co., London

either on or off, as in the 1-bit bitmap, or, by using more bits to describe them, can represent varying shades of color (4 bits for 16 colors; 8 bits for 256 colors; 15 bits for 32,768 colors; 16 bits for 65,536 colors; 24 bits for 16,777,216 colors). Thus, with 2 bits, for example, the available zeros and ones can be combined in only four possible ways and can, then, describe only four possible colors:

Bit Depth	Number of Colors Possible	Available Binary Combinations for Describing a Color
1-bit	2 (2^1)	0, 1
2-bit	4 (2^2)	00, 01, 10, 11
4-bit	16 (2^4)	0000, 0001, 0011, 0111, 1111, 0010, 0100, 1000, 0110, 1100, 1010, 0101, 1110, 1101, 1001, 1011

Together, the state of all the pixels on a computer screen makes up the image seen by the viewer, whether in combinations of black and white or colored pixels in a line of text, a photograph-like picture, or a simple background pattern. Figure 3-2 demonstrates various color depths.

Bitmap Sources

Where do bitmaps come from? How are they made? You can do the following:

- Capture a bitmap using a camera.
- Capture a bitmap from a photo or other artwork using a scanner to digitize the image.
- Make a bitmap from scratch with a paint or drawing program.
- Grab a bitmap from an active computer screen with a screen capture program, and then paste it into a paint program or your application.

Once made, a bitmap can be copied, altered, e-mailed, and otherwise used in many creative ways. If you do not want to make your own bitmaps, you can get them from suppliers of clip art, and from photograph suppliers who have already digitized the images for you. Libraries of clip art are available online and images are downloadable (usually for a fee). Many graphics applications are shipped with clip art and useful graphics. A clip art collection may contain a random assortment of images, or it may contain a series of graphics, photographs, sound, and video related to a single topic.

You can also download an image bitmap from a web site: in most browsers right-click over the image to see a menu of options. Choose "Download image to disk," "Copy Image," or "Save picture as...." Regardless of the source of the image, you should be aware of who owns the copyright to the image you wish to use and what is required to reproduce the image legally.

WARNING   *To avoid legal problems, always assume that an image on the Web is protected by copyright, even if there is no copyright notice shown. Just because you can easily download an image from a web site doesn't mean that you can reuse that image in your own work without permission or paying a license fee. See Chapter 10 for more about copyright protection.*

Legal rights protecting use of images from clip art libraries fall into three basic groupings. Public domain images were either never protected by a copyright or their copyright protection has ended. Generally these can be freely used without obtaining permission or paying a license fee, though there still may be an ownership issue for a particular work of art (such as a painting owned by an art gallery). Royalty-free images are purchased and then used without paying additional license fees. Rights-managed images require that you negotiate with the rights holder regarding terms for using the image and how much you will pay for that use.

Figure 3-3 shows a page of thumbnails describing a commercially available resource of royalty-free images called Photodisc, a part of Getty Images (www.gettyimages.com). The Photodisc collections

 1-bit, dithered. Each pixel is either on or off. The image is dithered by the computer to best represent the whole.

 8-bit, grayscale. Each pixel is represented by a value of up to 256 shades of gray.

 8-bit, not dithered. Each pixel is represented by a value drawn from a palette of up to 256 colors.

 8-bit, dithered. Each pixel is represented by a value drawn from a palette of up to 256 colors. Neighboring pixels have been dithered.

 24-bit. "True color." Each pixel is represented by a value ranging from 1 to 256 each for red, green, and blue yielding 16,777,216 possible colors.

Figure 3-2   This image has been divided into several common color depths. When file size (download time) is important, you can reduce and dither (discussed later in the chapter) bitmap files to the lowest color depth that will still provide an acceptable image. Note that 8-bit grayscale images are sometimes superior to 8-bit color images.

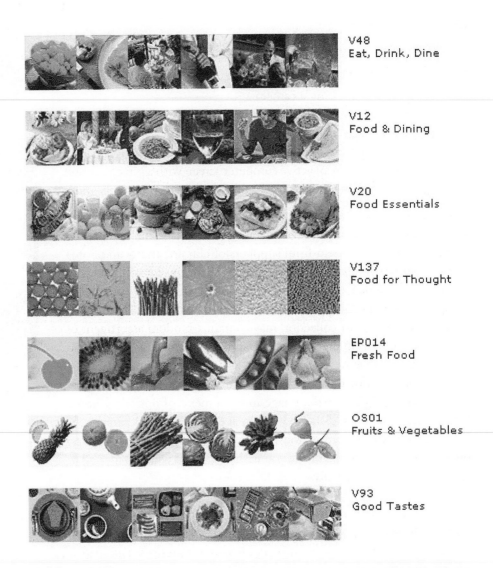

V48
Eat, Drink, Dine

V12
Food & Dining

V20
Food Essentials

V137
Food for Thought

EP014
Fresh Food

OS01
Fruits & Vegetables

V93
Good Tastes

Figure 3-3   A page of thumbnails showing the content of various royalty-free Photodisc collections from Getty Images

contain high-resolution bitmaps with a license for their "unlimited use." But you should note that "unlimited use" often contains caveats: in many cases there is an upper limit to the number of "units" of your own product that you may distribute without paying more, so you need to read the fine print. These additional fees are usually reasonable, however, and affect only commercial multimedia publishers.

Regardless of the source, once you have a bitmap, you can manipulate and adjust many of its properties (such as brightness, contrast, color depth, hue, and size). You can also cut and paste among many bitmaps using an image-editing program. If the clip art image is high resolution (aimed at 300- or 600-dpi printers, not 72-dpi display monitors), you may discover that you can grab just a tiny portion of the high-res image—say, a sheep in the far corner of a farmyard or a car in a parking lot—and it will look great when displayed at monitor resolution.

Bitmap Software

The abilities and features of painting and image-editing programs range from simple to complex. Many programs are available in versions that work the same on both Windows and Mac platforms, and the graphics files you make can be saved in many formats, readable across platforms and by mobile devices.

Macintosh computers do not ship with a painting tool, and Windows provides only a rudimentary Paint program (see Figure 3-4), so you will need to acquire this very important software separately. Many multimedia authoring tools offer built-in bitmap-editing features. Director, for example, includes a powerful image editor that provides advanced tools such as "onion-skinning" and image filtering using common plugins. Adobe Photoshop, however, remains the most widely used image-editing tool among designers worldwide; it is available without some bells and whistles in a less-expensive version, Photoshop Elements, which may have all the features you need for your projects.

Figure 3-4 The Paint program shipped with Windows is too primitive to be a useful tool for building multimedia projects.

Many designers also use a vector-based drawing program such as Adobe's Illustrator or InDesign or Corel's CorelDRAW to create curvy and complicated looks that they then convert to a bitmap. You can use your image-editing software to create original images, such as cartoons, symbols, buttons, bitmapped text, and abstract images that have a refined "graphic" look, but it is virtually impossible to create a realistic-looking photo from scratch using an image-editing program. The artistic painting tools offered by Corel's Painter (www.corel.com/painter) include hundreds of brushes, sprays, watercolors, inks, and textures to mimic the output of natural media in a bitmap (see Figure 3-5).

There are also many open source and free bitmap editors available—just type "graphics editors" in a search engine. Regardless of your program of choice, learning to use a high-powered paint program and image editor is a necessary investment in your multimedia future.

Capturing and Editing Images The image you see on your monitor is a digital bitmap stored in video memory, updated about every 1/60 of a second. As you assemble images for your multimedia project, you may often

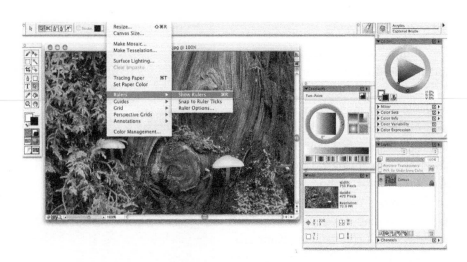

Figure 3-5   Painter is used for creating original artwork; for book, medical, and architectural illustration; to transform photographs into realistic-looking paintings; to build seamless patterns for fabrics; and for storyboarding scene concepts and costumes for movies and theater.

need to capture and store an image directly from your screen. The simplest way to capture what you see on the screen at any given moment is to press the proper keys on your computer keyboard. This causes a conversion from the screen buffer to a format that you can use.

■ Both the Macintosh and Windows environments have a **clipboard**—an area of memory where data such as text and images is temporarily stored when you cut or copy them within an application. In Windows, when you press PRINT SCREEN, a copy of your screen's image goes to the clipboard. From the clipboard, you can then paste the captured bitmap into an application.

■ On the Macintosh, the keystroke combination COMMAND-SHIFT-3 creates a PNG-format file showing your entire screen, names it Screen Shot, and places it on your desktop. COMMAND-SHIFT-4 allows you to drag a selection rectangle to make your Screen Shot file from just a part of the screen. You can then import this image into your multimedia authoring system or image-editing program. You can also press COMMAND-CONTROL-SHIFT-4 to drag a rectangle on your screen and copy what is inside the rectangle onto the clipboard ready for pasting (without making a file).

Figure 3-6   Image-editing programs let you add and delete elements in layers.

The way to get more creative power when manipulating bitmaps is to use an image-editing program, likely one of the programs named previously. These are the king-of-the-mountain programs that let you not only retouch the blemishes and details of photo images, but also do tricks like placing an image of your own face at the helm of a square-rigger or right at the sideline of last year's World Cup. Figure 3-6 shows just such a composite image, made from two photographs. It was created by graphic artist Frank Zurbano and shows his fiancée, Brandy Rowell, chasing after wedding gifts on the lawn where they will be married. Isolating and extracting parts of an image is an essential skill in multimedia production. Most bitmap editors have "lasso" type tools that select areas by drawing a path. This selection can be "feathered," or made to include partially transparent pixels outside the selected area.

In addition to letting you enhance and make composite images, image-editing tools allow you to alter and distort images. A color photograph of a red rose can be changed into a purple rose, or blue if you prefer. A small child standing next to her older brother can be "stretched" to tower over him. **Morphing** is another effect that can be used to manipulate still images or to create interesting and often bizarre animated transformations. Morphing (see Figure 3-7) allows you to smoothly blend two images so that one image seems to melt into the next, often producing some amusing results.

Image-editing programs may, indeed, represent the single most significant advance in computer image processing during the late 1980s, bringing truly amazing power to PC desktops. Such tools are indispensable for excellent multimedia production.

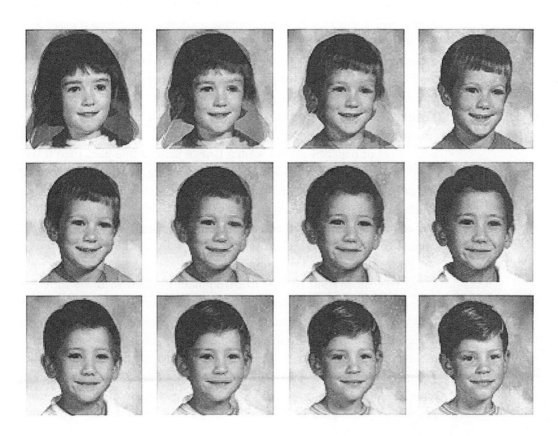

Figure 3-7 Morphing software was used to seamlessly transform the images of 16 kindergartners. When a sound track of music and voices was added to the four-minute piece, it made a compelling video about how similar children are to each other.

We have to keep saturation in mind *all* the time when doing our web pages...viewing the graphics on both Macs and PCs before actually using them. For instance, when doing our Halloween pages, we used a very cool pumpkin background that was beautifully saturated on the Mac side. On Windows, though, it was way too dark, and you couldn't read the overlying text. We had to lighten the GIF on the Mac side a few times before using it cross-platform.

....

Rich Santalesa, Editor,
NetGuide Magazine

NOTE   *When you import a color or grayscale bitmap from the Macintosh to Windows, the colors will seem darker and richer, even though they have precisely the same red, green, and blue (RGB) values. In some cases, this may improve the look of your image, but in other cases you will want to first lighten (increase the brightness and possibly lower the contrast) of the Macintosh bitmap before bringing it into Windows.*

Scanning Images   After poring through countless clip art collections, you still haven't found the unusual background you want for a screen about gardening. Sometimes when you search for something too hard, you don't realize that it's right in front of you. Everyday objects can be scanned and manipulated using image-editing tools, such as those described in the preceding section, to create unusual, attention-getting effects. For example, to enliven a screen with a gardening motif, scan a mixture of seeds, some fall foliage, or grass-stained garden gloves. Open the scan in an image-editing program and experiment with different filters, the contrast, and various special effects. Be creative, and don't be afraid to try strange combinations—sometimes mistakes yield the most intriguing results.

Another alternative to computer-generated graphics is to create artwork using traditional methods: watercolors, pastels, and even crayons. You can then scan the image, make necessary alterations, and tweak pixels on the computer. Too many designers have fallen into the trap of trying to draw detailed sketches using a mouse or drawing tablet, when a pencil or pen on paper would have produced better results quicker. In Chapter 9, Figure 10-6 shows part of a web page that uses a large image map of a seacoast village for navigation. The picture of the village was drawn on a large sheet of paper by artist Carolyn Brown using a fine pen. Then it was digitized in sections because the original drawing was too large for the scanner top. Four scans were stitched together into a single image using Photoshop layers, and the image was resized to fit the web page. Finally, it was colorized to look "old" and reduced in color depth to 4 bits so that it would load quickly on the Internet as a GIF.

Powerful filters and plug-ins are offered by most image-editing programs (see illustration to left) to manipulate bitmaps in many different ways. Experiment with your filters and plug-ins. Alien Skin's Exposure, for example, brings the creative tools of film photography to the world of digital editing with presets for many looks: discontinued films, dark room tricks, lo-fi camera quirks like Holga and Lomo, vintage looks like Technicolor movie film and old Kodachrome that are distressed with dust, scratches, and lens blur, warped vignettes, and funky colors from cross-processing (see Figure 3-8).

Figure 3-8 Exposure from Alien Skin, offering photography effects, is one of hundreds of commercial plug-ins and filters available for manipulating bitmapped images. Here a digital color image has been processed to look like it came from a photographer's darkroom.

Vector Drawing

Most multimedia authoring systems provide for use of vector-drawn objects such as lines, rectangles, ovals, polygons, complex drawings created from those objects, and text.

- Computer-aided design (CAD) programs have traditionally used vector-drawn object systems for creating the highly complex and geometric renderings needed by architects and engineers.
- Graphic artists designing for print media use vector-drawn objects because the same mathematics that put a rectangle on your screen can also place that rectangle (or the fancy curves of a good line-art illustration) on paper without jaggies. This requires the higher resolution of the printer, using a page description format such as Portable Document Format (PDF).
- Programs for 3-D animation also use vector-drawn graphics. For example, the various changes of position, rotation, and shading of light required to spin an extruded corporate logo must be calculated mathematically. (Animation is discussed in Chapter 5.) Some 3-D modeling programs incorporate libraries of premade 3-D models into the application, allowing you to drag and drop these common objects into a scene.

How Vector Drawing Works

A **vector** is a line that is described by the location of its two endpoints. Vector drawing uses **Cartesian coordinates** where a pair of numbers describes a point in two-dimensional space as the intersection of horizontal and vertical lines (the x and y axes). The numbers are always listed in the order x,y. In three-dimensional space, a third dimension—depth—is described by a z axis (x,y,z). This coordinate system is named for the French philosopher and mathematician, René Descartes. So a line might be simply

```
<line x1="0" y1="0" x2="200" y2="100">
```

where x1 and y1 define the starting point (in the upper-left corner of the viewing box) and x2 and y2 define the ending point.

A simple rectangle is computed from starting point and size: your software will draw a rectangle (rect) starting at the upper-left corner of your viewing area (0,0) and going 200 pixels horizontally to the right and 100 pixels downward to mark the opposite corner. Add color information like

```
<rect x="0" y="0" width="200" height="100" fill="#FFFFFF" stroke="#FF0000"/>
```

and your software will draw the rectangle with a red boundary line and fill it with the color white. You can, of course, add other parameters to describe a fill pattern or the width of the boundary line. Circles are defined by a location and a radius:

```
<circle cx="50" cy="50" r="10" fill="none" stroke="#000000" />
```

SVG

Type the following code into a text editor and save it as plain text with a .svg extension. This is an **SVG (Scalable Vector Graphics)** file. Open it in an HTML5-capable browser (File | Open File) and you will see:

```
<svg xmlns="http://www.w3.org/2000/svg"
    xmlns:xlink="http://www.w3.org/1999/xlink"
    width="200"
    height="200"
    viewBox="-100 -100 300 300"><rect x="0" y="0" fill="yellow" stroke="red" width="200" height="100"/>
<text transform="matrix(1 0 0 1 60 60)" font-family="'TimesNewRomanPS-BoldMT'" font-size="36">SVG</text>
</svg>
```

Because these SVG files can be saved in a small amount of memory and because they are scalable without distortion (try changing the width and height of the view box in the preceding code), SVG (Tiny) is supported by browsers on most mobile phones and tablets. The SVG specification also includes time-based changes or animations that can be embedded within the image code (see www.w3.org/TR/SVG11/animate.html#AnimationElements). Figure 3-9 shows Adobe Illustrator saving a file in SVG format. Vector drawing tools use **Bézier** curves or paths to mathematically represent a curve. In practical terms, editing software shows you points on the path, each point having a "handle." Changing the location of the handle changes the shape of the curve. Mastering Bézier curves is an important skill: these curves not only create graphic shapes but represent motion paths when creating animations.

In a Bézier curve, the distance between P0 and P1 determines "how long" the curve moves into direction P1 before turning towards P3.

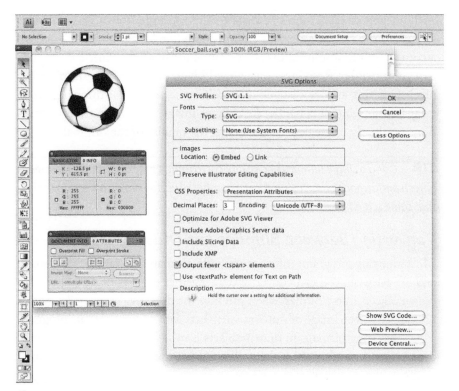

Figure 3-9 Drawing software such as Adobe Illustrator can save vector graphics in SVG format.

Vector-Drawn Objects vs. Bitmaps

Vector-drawn objects are described and drawn to the computer screen using a fraction of the memory space required to describe and store the same object in bitmap form. The file containing the vector-drawn colored rectangle described in the preceding section is less than 698 bytes of alphanumeric data (even less—468 bytes—when the description is tokenized or compressed as .svgz). On the other hand, the same rectangle saved as a .gif image with a 64-color palette takes 1,100 bytes.

Because of this file size advantage, web pages that use vector graphics as SVG files or in plug-ins such as Flash download faster and, when used for animation, draw faster than pages displaying bitmaps. It is only when you draw many hundreds of objects on your screen that you may experience a slowdown while you wait for the screen to be refreshed—the size, location, and other properties for each of the objects must be computed. Thus, a single image made up of 500 individual line and rectangle objects, for example, may take longer for the computer to process and place on the screen than an image consisting of just a few drawn circle objects.

A vector-drawn object is created "on the fly"; that is, the computer draws the image from the instructions it has been given, rather than displaying a precreated image. This means that vector objects are easily scalable without loss of resolution or image quality. A large drawn image can be shrunk to the size of a postage stamp, and while it may not look good on a computer monitor at 72 dpi, it may look great when printed at 300 dpi to a color printer. Resizing a bitmapped image requires either duplicating pixels (creating a blocky, jagged look called **pixelation**) or throwing pixels away (eliminating details). Because vector images are drawn from instructions on the fly, a rescaled image retains the quality of the original.

TIP *Using a single bitmap for a complicated image may give you faster screen-refresh performance than using a large number of vector-drawn objects to make that same screen.*

Converting Between Bitmaps and Drawn Images

Most drawing programs offer several file formats for saving your work, and, if you wish, you can convert a drawing that consists of several vector-drawn objects into a bitmap when you save the drawing. You can also grab a bitmapped screen image of your drawn objects with a screen capture program.

Converting bitmaps to drawn objects is more difficult. There are, however, programs and utilities that will compute the bounds of a bitmapped image or the shapes of colors within an image and then derive the polygon object that describes the image. This procedure is called **autotracing** and is available in vector drawing applications such as Illustrator or CorelDraw. Flash has a Trace Bitmap menu option that converts a bitmapped image into a vector image. Be cautious: the size of your Flash file may actually balloon because the bitmapped image is replaced by hundreds or even thousands of tiny vector-drawn objects, leading to slow processing and display.

WARNING *Some bitmap applications allow vector images to be pasted into them. Be careful to save your vector drawing separately because you will not be able to edit the curves once they are bitmapped.*

3-D Drawing and Rendering

Drawing in perspective or in 3-D on a two-dimensional surface takes special skill and talent. Creating objects in three dimensions on a computer screen can be difficult for designers comfortable with squares, circles, and other x (width) and y (height) geometries on a two-dimensional screen. Dedicated software is available to help you render three-dimensional scenes, complete with directional lighting and special effects, but be prepared for late nights and steep learning curves as you become familiar with nurbs, deformations, mesh generations, and skinning! From making 3-D text to creating detailed walkthroughs of 3-D space, each application will demand study and practice before you are efficient and comfortable with its feature set and power.

form•Z, the 3-D form synthesizer, is above all a 3-D modeling program, even though it also includes drafting, rendering and animation. Additional photorealistic rendering is offered by form•Z Render-Zone Plus. It combines solids and surface modeling. It also combines faceted (boundary) representations with parametric spline representations, NURBS, patches, and metaballs. This unique mixture of modeling personalities allows you to create any form, existing or imaginary, while working in a single package.

Marketing literature from AutoDesSys, Inc. *(www.formz.com)*

The production values of multimedia projects have increased dramatically, and as the production bar has risen, end users' expectations have also ratcheted upward. The multimedia production bar moves like a high jump or pole vault competition—as each new project improves on the last, competitors must jump to meet the new, higher standard. Flat and colorless 2-D screens are no longer sufficient for a successful commercial multimedia project. 3-D-rendered graphic art and animation has become commonplace since the late 1980s, providing more lifelike substance and feel to projects. Luckily, in an arena where only high-powered workstations could supply the raw computing horsepower for effective 3-D designing, inexpensive desktop PCs and excellent software have made 3-D modeling attainable by most multimedia developers.

Today many products—including Daz3D (www.daz3d.com) and form•Z (www.formz.com)—are touted as essential tools for illustration, animation, and multimedia production. NewTek's LightWave (www.lightwave3d.com) and Autodesk's Maya (www.autodesk.com/Maya) are industry-standard, high-end animation programs used for everything from multimedia programs and game designs to special effects in films and even feature-length movies. For experimenting with 3-D, Trimble Navigation's SketchUp (www.sketchup.com) provides a simple (and free) cross-platform tool. To delve deeply into 3-D, the open-source Blender (www.blender.org) is a powerful tool—but its complex interface presents a steep learning curve.

For 3-D, the depth (**z dimension**) of cubes and spheres must be calculated and displayed so that the perspective of the rendered object seems correct to the eye. As illustrated in Figure 3-10, most 3-D software packages provide adjustable views so that you can see your work from the top, bottom, or sides.

A great deal of information is needed to display a 3-D scene. **Scenes** consist of **objects** that in turn contain many small elements such as blocks, cylinders, spheres, or cones (described using mathematical constructs or formulas). The more elements contained in an object, the more complicated its structure will be and, usually, the finer its resolution and smoothness.

Objects and elements in 3-D space carry with them **properties** such as shape, color, texture, shading, and location. A scene contains many different objects. Imagine a scene with a table, chairs, and a background. Zoom into one of the objects—the chair, for example, in Figure 3-11. It has 11 objects made up of various blocks and rectangles. Objects are created by **modeling** them using a 3-D application.

To model an object that you want to place into your scene, you must start with a **shape**. You can create a shape from scratch, or you can import a previously made shape from a library of geometric shapes called **primitives**, typically blocks, cylinders, spheres, and cones. In most 3-D applications,

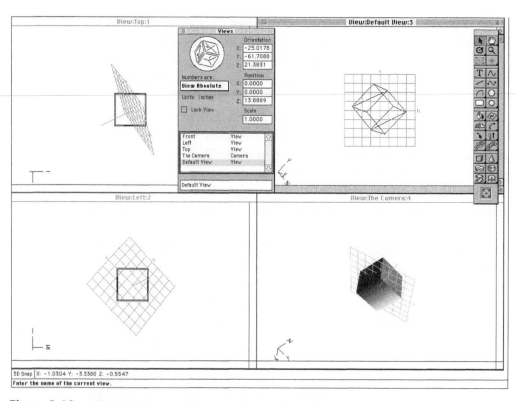

Figure 3-10 3-D applications provide x, y, and z axes and adjustable perspective views.

Figure 3-11 A chair modeled in 3-D is made up of various blocks and rectangles.

you can create any 2-D shape with a drawing tool or place the outline of a letter, then extrude or lathe it into the third dimension along the z axis (see Figure 3-12). When you **extrude** a plane surface, its shape extends some distance, either perpendicular to the shape's outline or along a defined path. When you **lathe** a shape, a profile of the shape is **rotated** around a defined axis (you can set the direction) to create the 3-D object. Other methods for creating 3-D objects differ among the various software packages.

Once you have created a 3-D object, you can apply **textures** and colors to it to make it seem more realistic, whether rough and coarse or shiny and smooth. You can also apply a color or pattern, or even a bitmapped picture, to texture your object. Thus you can build a table, apply an oak finish, and then stain it purple or blue or iridescent yellow. You can add coffee cup rings and spilled cheese dip with appropriate coloring and texturing.

To model a scene, you place all of your objects into 3-D space. Some complex scenes may contain hundreds (if not thousands) of elements. In modeling your scene, you can also set up one or more lights that will create diffuse or sharp shades and shadows on your objects and will also reflect, or **flare**, where the light is most intense. Then you can add a background and set a camera view, the location and angle from which you will view the final rendered scene.

Extruding   Lathing

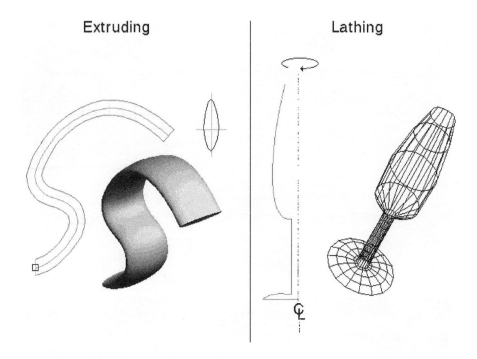

Figure 3-12 A free-form object created by extrusion and a wine flute created by lathing

Shading can usually be applied in several ways. As illustrated in Figure 3-13, flat shading (*b*) is the fastest for the computer to render and is most often used in preview mode. Gouraud shading (*a*), Phong shading (*d*), and ray tracing (*c*) take longer to render but provide photorealistic images.

When you have completed the modeling of your scene or an object in it, you then must render it for final output. **Rendering** is when the computer finally uses intricate algorithms to apply the effects you have specified on the objects you have created. Figure 3-14 shows a background, an object, and the rendered composite.

Rendering an image requires great computing muscle and often takes many hours for a single image, and you will feel the strength (or weakness) of your hardware. Indeed, some multimedia and animation companies dedicate certain computers solely for rendering. The final images for the classic animated movie *Toy Story* were rendered on a "farm" of 87 dual-processor and 30 quad-processor 100-MHz SPARCstation 20s. It took 46 days of continuous processing to render that film's 110,000 frames at a rate of about one frame every one to three hours.

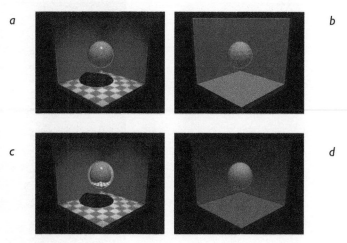

Figure 3-13 A scene rendered with four different methods of shading

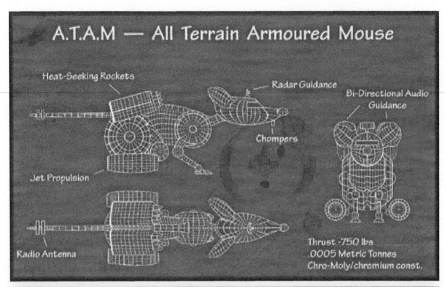

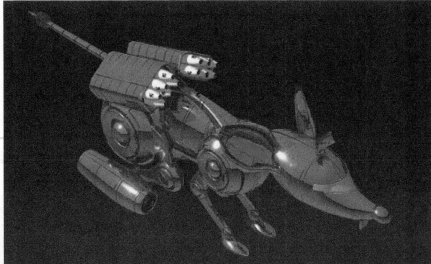

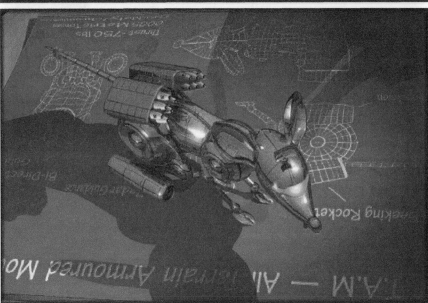

Figure 3-14 A background and object rendered into an image with shadows and lighting effects

> **NOTE** *Farms of many computers hooked together may also be called "clusters of workstations," or COWs. There is occasionally humorous contention regarding proper nomenclature: it seems that developers who live and work in cities tend to prefer the notion of computer farms; developers in rural communities already familiar with farms prefer to call these beasts COWs. The engineer who maintains such a* render farm *is, of course, a "render wrangler."*

COLLADA (from Collaborative Design Activity, http://collada.org) is an ISO standard XML file format for passing 3-D files among applications. COLLADA files are called DAE files (for "digital asset exchange") and use the extension .dae. Development of the standard is supported by an open source organization of game developers, CAD designers, and VFX (visual effects) and animation specialists.

Panoramas

For 360-degree rotations, software such as ArcSoft's Panorama Maker (www .arcsoft.com/panorama-maker/), Easypano's Panoweaver (www.easypano .com/panorama-software.html), or Smoky City Design's Panorama Factory (www.panoramafactory.com) works by importing a sequence of photos and letting you adjust them precisely into a single seamless bitmap, where the right edge attaches to the left edge and the color and lighting differences among the image are smoothed. The images are stitched together. You should allow some overlap when you take each photo for a 360-degree panorama, and you may need to adjust each photo's contrast, brightness, hue, and saturation while stitching, if that feature is not provided by your software. Most programs also allow you to adjust perspective to compensate for different focal lengths or camera heights. *QuickTime* VR files go a step further and let you view as "virtual reality" a single surrounding image as if you were "inside" the picture and able to look up or down, turn, or zoom in on features.

Color

Color is a vital component of multimedia. The next few sections explain where color comes from and how colors are displayed on a computer monitor. Management of color is both a subjective and a technical exercise. Picking the right colors and combinations of colors for your project can involve many tries until you feel the result is right. But the technical description of a color may be expressed in known physical values (humans, for example, perceive colors with wavelengths ranging from 400 to 600 nanometers on the electromagnetic spectrum), and several methods and models describe color space using mathematics and values (see Figure 3-15).

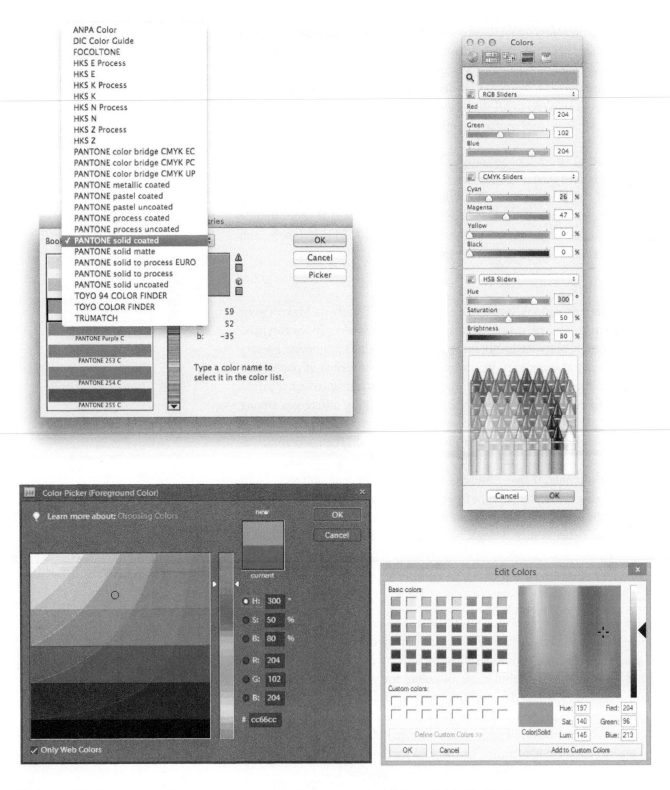

Figure 3-15   Color pickers allow you to select a color using one or more different models of color space.

Understanding Natural Light and Color

Light comes from an atom when an electron passes from a higher to a lower energy level; thus each atom produces uniquely specific colors. This explanation of light, known as the **quantum theory**, was developed by physicist Max Planck in the late 19th century. Niels Bohr, another physicist, later showed that an excited atom that has absorbed energy and whose electrons have moved into higher orbits will throw off that energy in the form of quanta, or photons, when it reverts to a stable state. This is where light comes from.

Color is the frequency of a light wave within the narrow band of the electromagnetic spectrum to which the human eye responds. The letters of the mnemonic **ROY G. BIV**, learned by many of us to remember the colors of the rainbow, are the ascending frequencies of the visible light spectrum: red, orange, yellow, green, blue, indigo, and violet. Light that is infrared, or below the frequency of red light and not perceivable by the human eye, can be created and viewed by electronic diodes and sensors, and it is used for television and other controllers or "remotes," for wireless communications among computers, and for night goggles used in the military. Infrared light is radiated heat. Ultraviolet light, on the other hand, is beyond the higher end of the visible spectrum and can be damaging to humans.

The color white is a noisy mixture of all the color frequencies in the visible spectrum. Sunlight and fluorescent tubes produce white light (though, technically, even they vary in color temperature—sunlight is affected by the angle at which the light is coming through the atmosphere, and fluorescent tubes provide spikes in the blue-green parts of the color spectrum); tungsten lamp filaments produce light with a yellowish cast; sodium vapor lamps, typically used for low-cost outdoor street lighting, produce an orange light characteristic of the sodium atom. These are the most common sources of light in the everyday (or every night) world. The light these sources produce typically reaches your eye as a reflection of that light into the lens of your eye.

The cornea of the eye acts as a lens to focus light rays onto the retina. The light rays stimulate many thousands of specialized nerves, called rods, which cover the surface of the retina. Receptors in the cones are sensitive to red, green, and blue light, and all the nerves together transmit the pattern of color information to the brain. The eye can differentiate among about 80,000 colors, or **hues**, consisting of combinations of red, green, and blue.

As color information is sent to the brain, other parts of the mind massage the data en route to its point of cognitive recognition. Human response to color is complicated by cultural and experiential filters that cause otherwise straightforward color frequencies to carry pleasant, unpleasant, soothing, depressing, and many other special meanings. In Western cultures, for example, red is the color of anger and danger; in Eastern cultures, red is the color of happiness. Red is the traditional color for Chinese restaurant motifs, to make them attractive and happy places; Western restaurants are often decorated in quieter pastels and earth tones. White, not black, is the color of funerals in Chinese culture.

Green, blue, yellow, orange, purple, pink, brown, black, gray, and white are the ten most common color-describing words used in all human languages and cultures. Komar and Melamid's interesting tongue-in-cheek study of the "most wanted" and "least wanted" paintings in the world (http://awp.diaart.org/km/painting.html) has determined that the world's favorite color is blue (http://awp.diaart.org/km/surveyresults.html).

See what an image looks like to someone with glaucoma, cataracts, macular degeneration, or a color deficit:

. . . .

www.vischeck.com/examples

http://webaim.org/simulations/lowvision

. . . .

Computerized Color

Because the eye's receptors are sensitive to red, green, and blue light, by adjusting combinations of these three colors, the eye and brain will interpolate the combinations of colors in between. This is the psychology, not the physics, of color: what you perceive as orange on a computer monitor is a combination of two frequencies of green and red light, not the actual spectral frequency you see when you look at that namesake fruit, an orange, in sunlight. Various color models are illustrated in Figure 3-15 shown earlier. Although the eye perceives colors based upon red, green, and blue, there are actually two basic methods of making color: additive and subtractive.

Additive Color

In the **additive color** method, a color is created by combining colored light sources in three primary colors: red, green, and blue (**RGB**). This is the

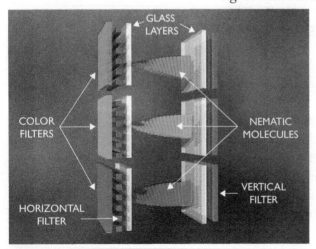

process used for cathode ray tube (CRT), liquid crystal (LCD), and plasma displays. On the back of the glass face of a CRT are thousands of phosphorescing chemical dots. These dots are each about 0.30 mm or less in diameter (the **dot pitch**), and are positioned very carefully and very close together, arranged in triads of red, green, and blue. These dots are bombarded by electrons that "paint" the screen at high speeds (about 60 times a second). The red, green, and blue dots light up when hit by the electron beam. Your eye sees the combination of red, green, and blue light and interpolates it to create all other colors. As illustrated by Marvin Raaijmakers and Angelo La Spina, like CRTs, LCD and plasma screens utilize minute red, green, and blue elements energized through tiny transparent conductors.

Subtractive Color

In the subtractive color method, color is created by combining colored media such as paints or ink that absorb (or subtract) some parts of the color spectrum of light and reflect the others back to the eye. Subtractive color is the process used to create color in printing. The printed page is made up of tiny halftone dots of three primary colors: cyan, magenta, and yellow (designated as CMY). Four-color printing includes black (which is technically not a color but, rather, the absence of color). Since the letter *B* is already used for blue, black is designated with a *K* (so four-color printing is designated as CMYK). The color remaining in the reflected part of the light that reaches your eye from the printed page is the color you perceive.

All these factors make computerized color pretty tricky to manage. The fact that a paint program uses RGB to create the colors on your monitor, while your printer uses CMYK to print out your image, explains the problem of matching what you see on the screen with your printout. High-end image-editing programs such as Photoshop deal with this problem by allowing you to calibrate your monitor with your printer.

The following chart shows the three primary additive colors and how, when one of the primary colors is subtracted from this RGB mix, the subtractive primary color is perceived. The numbers in parentheses indicate the amount of red, green, and blue (in that order) used to create each of the colors in 24-bit color, which is described in the next section. A 0 indicates a lack of that primary color, while 255 is the maximum amount of that color.

RGB Combination (R,G,B)	Perceived Color
Red only (255,0,0)	Red
Green only (0,255,0)	Green
Blue only (0,0,255)	Blue
Red and green (blue subtracted) (255,255,0)	Yellow
Red and blue (green subtracted) (255,0,255)	Magenta
Green and blue (red subtracted) (0,255,255)	Cyan
Red, green, and blue (255,255,255)	White
None (0,0,0)	Black

Computer Color Models

Models or methodologies used to specify colors in computer terms are RGB, HSB, HSL, CMYK, CIE, and others. Using the 24-bit RGB (red, green, blue) model, you specify a color by setting each amount of red, green, and blue to a value in a range of 256 choices, from 0 to 255. Eight bits of memory are required to define those 256 possible choices, and that has to be done for each of the three primary colors; a total of 24 bits of memory ($8 + 8 + 8 = 24$) are therefore needed to describe the exact color, which is one of "millions" ($256 \times 256 \times 256 = 16,777,216$). When web browsers were first developed, the software engineers chose to represent the color amounts for each color channel in a hexadecimal pair. Rather than using one number between 0 and 255, two **hexadecimal** numbers, written in a scale of 16 numbers and letters in the range "0123456789ABCDEF," represent the required 8 bits ($16 \times 16 = 256$) needed to specify the intensity of red, green, and blue. Thus, in HTML, you can specify pure green as #00FF00, where there is no red (first pair is #00), there is maximum green (second pair is #FF), and there is no blue (last pair is #00). The number sign (#) specifies the value as hexadecimal.

Red	Green	Blue	Color
255 (#FF)	255 (#FF)	255 (#FF)	White (#FFFFFF)
255 (#FF)	255 (#FF)	0 (#00)	Yellow (#FFFF00)
255 (#FF)	0 (#00)	255 (#FF)	Magenta (#FF00FF)
0 (#00)	255 (#FF)	255 (#FF)	Cyan (#00FFFF)
255 (#FF)	0 (#00)	0 (#00)	Red (#FF0000)
0 (#00)	255 (#FF)	0 (#00)	Green (#00FF00)
0 (#00)	0 (#00)	255 (#FF)	Blue (#0000FF)
0 (#00)	0 (#00)	0 (#00)	Black (#000000)

As illustrated in Figure 3-16, there are many valid color names you can use when writing HTML and CSS code. They are officially listed by The World Wide Web Consortium (www.w3.org/TR/css3-color/#svg-color) and can be used in place of #Hex values.

In the **HSB** (hue, saturation, brightness) and **HSL** (hue, saturation, lightness) models, you specify hue or color as an angle from 0 to 360 degrees on a color wheel, and saturation, brightness, and lightness as percentages. Saturation is the intensity of a color. At 100 percent saturation a color is pure; at 0 percent saturation, the color is white, black, or gray.

Lightness or brightness is the percentage of black or white that is mixed with a color. A lightness of 100 percent will yield a white color; 0 percent is black; the pure color has a 50 percent lightness.

Color name	Hex rgb	Decimal
aliceblue	#F0F8FF	240,248,255
antiquewhite	#FAEBD7	250,235,215
aqua	#00FFFF	0,255,255
aquamarine	#7FFFD4	127,255,212
azure	#F0FFFF	240,255,255
beige	#F5F5DC	245,245,220
bisque	#FFE4C4	255,228,196
black	#000000	0,0,0
blanchedalmond	#FFEBCD	255,235,205
blue	#0000FF	0,0,255
blueviolet	#8A2BE2	138,43,226
brown	#A52A2A	165,42,42
burlywood	#DEB887	222,184,135
cadetblue	#5F9EA0	95,158,160
chartreuse	#7FFF00	127,255,0
chocolate	#D2691E	210,105,30
coral	#FF7F50	255,127,80
cornflowerblue	#6495ED	100,149,237
cornsilk	#FFF8DC	255,248,220
crimson	#DC143C	220,20,60
cyan	#00FFFF	0,255,255
darkblue	#00008B	0,0,139
darkcyan	#008B8B	0,139,139
darkgoldenrod	#B8860B	184,134,11
darkgray	#A9A9A9	169,169,169
darkgreen	#006400	0,100,0
darkgrey	#A9A9A9	169,169,169
darkkhaki	#BDB76B	189,183,107
darkmagenta	#8B008B	139,0,139
darkolivegreen	#556B2F	85,107,47
darkorange	#FF8C00	255,140,0
darkorchid	#9932CC	153,50,204
darkred	#8B0000	139,0,0
darksalmon	#E9967A	233,150,122
darkseagreen	#8FBC8F	143,188,143
darkslateblue	#483D8B	72,61,139
darkslategray	#2F4F4F	47,79,79
darkslategrey	#2F4F4F	47,79,79
darkturquoise	#00CED1	0,206,209
darkviolet	#9400D3	148,0,211
deeppink	#FF1493	255,20,147
deepskyblue	#00BFFF	0,191,255
dimgray	#696969	105,105,105
dimgrey	#696969	105,105,105
dodgerblue	#1E90FF	30,144,255
firebrick	#B22222	178,34,34
floralwhite	#FFFAF0	255,250,240
forestgreen	#228B22	34,139,34
fuchsia	#FF00FF	255,0,255

Color name	Hex rgb	Decimal
gainsboro	#DCDCDC	220,220,220
ghostwhite	#F8F8FF	248,248,255
gold	#FFD700	255,215,0
goldenrod	#DAA520	218,165,32
gray	#808080	128,128,128
green	#008000	0,128,0
greenyellow	#ADFF2F	173,255,47
grey	#808080	128,128,128
honeydew	#F0FFF0	240,255,240
hotpink	#FF69B4	255,105,180
indianred	#CD5C5C	205,92,92
indigo	#4B0082	75,0,130
ivory	#FFFFF0	255,255,240
khaki	#F0E68C	240,230,140
lavender	#E6E6FA	230,230,250
lavenderblush	#FFF0F5	255,240,245
lawngreen	#7CFC00	124,252,0
lemonchiffon	#FFFACD	255,250,205
lightblue	#ADD8E6	173,216,230
lightcoral	#F08080	240,128,128
lightcyan	#E0FFFF	224,255,255
lightgoldenrodyellow	#FAFAD2	250,250,210
lightgray	#D3D3D3	211,211,211
lightgreen	#90EE90	144,238,144
lightgrey	#D3D3D3	211,211,211
lightpink	#FFB6C1	255,182,193
lightsalmon	#FFA07A	255,160,122
lightseagreen	#20B2AA	32,178,170
lightskyblue	#87CEFA	135,206,250
lightslategray	#778899	119,136,153
lightslategrey	#778899	119,136,153
lightsteelblue	#B0C4DE	176,196,222
lightyellow	#FFFFE0	255,255,224
lime	#00FF00	0,255,0
limegreen	#32CD32	50,205,50
linen	#FAF0E6	250,240,230
magenta	#FF00FF	255,0,255
maroon	#800000	128,0,0
mediumaquamarine	#66CDAA	102,205,170
mediumblue	#0000CD	0,0,205
mediumorchid	#BA55D3	186,85,211
mediumpurple	#9370DB	147,112,219
mediumseagreen	#3CB371	60,179,113
mediumslateblue	#7B68EE	123,104,238
mediumspringgreen	#00FA9A	0,250,154
mediumturquoise	#48D1CC	72,209,204
mediumvioletred	#C71585	199,21,133
midnightblue	#191970	25,25,112
mintcream	#F5FFFA	245,255,250

Color name	Hex rgb	Decimal
mistyrose	#FFE4E1	255,228,225
moccasin	#FFE4B5	255,228,181
navajowhite	#FFDEAD	255,222,173
navy	#000080	0,0,128
oldlace	#FDF5E6	253,245,230
olive	#808000	128,128,0
olivedrab	#6B8E23	107,142,35
orange	#FFA500	255,165,0
orangered	#FF4500	255,69,0
orchid	#DA70D6	218,112,214
palegoldenrod	#EEE8AA	238,232,170
palegreen	#98FB98	152,251,152
paleturquoise	#AFEEEE	175,238,238
palevioletred	#DB7093	219,112,147
papayawhip	#FFEFD5	255,239,213
peachpuff	#FFDAB9	255,218,185
peru	#CD853F	205,133,63
pink	#FFC0CB	255,192,203
plum	#DDA0DD	221,160,221
powderblue	#B0E0E6	176,224,230
purple	#800080	128,0,128
red	#FF0000	255,0,0
rosybrown	#BC8F8F	188,143,143
royalblue	#4169E1	65,105,225
saddlebrown	#8B4513	139,69,19
salmon	#FA8072	250,128,114
sandybrown	#F4A460	244,164,96
seagreen	#2E8B57	46,139,87
seashell	#FFF5EE	255,245,238
sienna	#A0522D	160,82,45
silver	#C0C0C0	192,192,192
skyblue	#87CEEB	135,206,235
slateblue	#6A5ACD	106,90,205
slategray	#708090	112,128,144
slategrey	#708090	112,128,144
snow	#FFFAFA	255,250,250
springgreen	#00FF7F	0,255,127
steelblue	#4682B4	70,130,180
tan	#D2B48C	210,180,140
teal	#008080	0,128,128
thistle	#D8BFD8	216,191,216
tomato	#FF6347	255,99,71
turquoise	#40E0D0	64,224,208
violet	#EE82EE	238,130,238
wheat	#F5DEB3	245,222,179
white	#FFFFFF	255,255,255
whitesmoke	#F5F5F5	245,245,245
yellow	#FFFF00	255,255,0
yellowgreen	#9ACD32	154,205,50

Figure 3-16   There are many valid color names you can use when writing HTML and CSS code. They can be used in place of #Hex values.

The CMYK color model is less applicable to multimedia production. It is used primarily in the printing trade where cyan, magenta, yellow, and black are used to print process color separations.

Color	Degrees
Red	0°
Yellow	60°
Green	120°
Cyan	180°
Blue	240°
Magenta	300°

Other color models include CIE, YIQ, YUV, and YCC. **CIE** (developed by the International Commission on Illumination in the 1930's) describes color values in terms of frequency, saturation, and illuminance (blue/yellow or red/green, which in turn corresponds to the color receptors in the cones of the eye). CIE more closely resembles how human beings perceive color, but certain devices such as scanners are unable to replicate the process.

YIQ and **YUV** were developed for broadcast TV (composite NTSC). They are based on luminance (brightness) and chrominance (color) expressed as the amplitude of a wave and the phase of the wave relative to some reference. Detail is carried by luminance (black and white), so reduction in color does not result in the loss of image definition detail. This analog process can be translated to a number value so that the computer can use a palette to assign a color to a pixel.

The Photo **YCC** model was developed by Kodak to provide a definition that enables consistent representation of digital color images from negatives, slides, and other high-quality input. YCC is used for PhotoCD images.

Color Palettes

Palettes are mathematical tables that define the color of a pixel displayed on the screen. The most common palettes are 1, 4, 8, 16, and 24 bits deep:

Color Depth	Colors Available
1-bit	Black and white (or any two colors)
4-bit	16 colors
8-bit	256 colors (good enough for color images)
16-bit	Thousands of colors (65,536; excellent for color images)
24-bit	More than 16 million colors (16,777,216; totally photorealistic)

To generate a palette which is best for representing a particular image, we support Heckbert's median cut algorithm. This algorithm first builds a three-dimensional table (a histogram cube) indicating how popular any given colour in the RGB cube is in the image being converted.

It then proceeds to subdivide this histogram cube (by dividing boxes in half) until it has created as many boxes as there are palette entries.

The decision as to where to divide a box is based on the distribution of colours within the box. This algorithm attempts to create boxes which have approximately equal popularity in the image. Palette entries are then assigned to represent each box. There are other methods of generating a palette from an image, but Heckbert's algorithm is generally regarded as the best trade-off between speed and quality.

....

Allan Hessenflow of HandMade Software, makers of Image Alchemy, describing how an 8-bit palette is made

When color monitors became available for computers, managing the computations for displaying colors severely taxed the hardware and memory available at the time. 256-color, 8-bit images using a color lookup table or palette were the best a computer could do. 256 default system colors were statistically selected by Apple and Microsoft engineers (working independently) to be the colors and shades that are most "popular" in photographic images; their two system palettes are, of course, different. Web authorities also decided on a palette of 216 "web-safe" colors that would allow browsers to display images properly on both Macintosh and Windows computers.

GIF files using 256-color palettes are saved in a lossless format. The PNG format also uses palettes (24 bits, or 32 bits if an "alpha" mask is included for transparency), and is lossless. It was developed for the Internet (it supports only the RGB color space) to expand GIF's limited 256 colors to PNG's millions of colors.

In 24-bit color systems, your computer works with three channels of 256 discrete shades of each color (red, green, and blue) represented as the three axes of a cube. This allows a total of 16,777,216 colors (256 × 256 × 256). Just as the 44.1-KHz sampled-sound standard for CD music on compact discs that is discussed in Chapter 4 covers the range of human hearing, the color range offered by 24-bit systems covers what the human eye can sense.

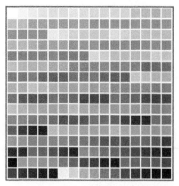

Macintosh System

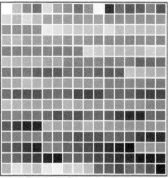

Windows System

Dithering

If you start out with a 24-bit scanned image that contains millions of colors and need to reduce it to an 8-bit, 256-color image, you get the best replication of the original image by **dithering** the colors in the image. Dithering is a process whereby the color value of each pixel is changed to the closest matching color value in the target palette, using a mathematical algorithm. Often the adjacent pixels are also examined, and patterns of different colors are created in the more limited palette to best represent the original colors. Since there are now only 256 colors available to represent the thousands or even millions of colors in the original image, pixels using the 256 remaining colors are intermixed and the eye perceives a color not in the palette, created by blending the colors mixed together. Thus any given pixel might not be mapped to its closest palette entry, but instead to the average over some area of the image; this average will be closer to the correct color than a substitute color would be. How well the dithered image renders a good approximation of the original depends upon the algorithm used and whether you allow the image-editing program to select the best set of 256 colors from the original image (called an adaptive palette) or force it to use a predetermined set of 256 colors (as, for example, with the browser-safe

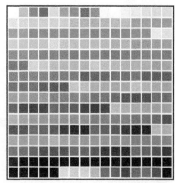

Web-Safe

Figure 3-17 This 24-bit, 72-dpi JPG image was dithered in Photoshop to an 8-bit color depth using the Windows system palette and, at first, no special algorithm. Then three different dithering algorithms (diffusion, pattern, and noise) were applied as seen in the 4X thumbnails at left. Note the blotchy nature of the converted image when no dithering is applied.

> Multimedia is just another way to transform ambiguity. There were so many ambiguous colors in this scan, I decided to make them unambiguous. How do you like the purple?
>
> Lars Hidde, explaining why he dithered a perfectly fine 256-color image into a 16-color default palette

web palette). Figure 3-17 compares the same scanned image dithered from millions of colors to the 256 colors in the Windows system palette using various dithering formulas.

Dithering concepts are important to understand when you are working with bitmaps derived from RGB information or based upon different palettes. The palette for the image of a rose, for example, may contain mostly shades of red with a number of greens thrown in for the stem and leaves. The image of your pretty Delft vase, into which you want to electronically place the rose, may be mostly blues and grays. Your software will use a dithering algorithm to find the 256 color shades that best represent both images, generating a new palette in the process.

Dithering software is usually built into image-editing programs and is also available in many multimedia authoring systems as part of the application's palette management suite of tools.

Image File Formats

Most applications on any operating system can manage JPEG, GIF, PNG, and TIFF image formats. An older format used on the Macintosh, PICT, is a complicated but versatile format developed by Apple where both bitmaps and vector-drawn objects can live side by side. The **device-independent bitmap (DIB)**, also known as a BMP, is a common Windows palette–based image file format similar to PNG. PCX files were originally developed for use in Z-Soft MS-DOS paint packages; these files can be opened and saved by almost all MS-DOS paint software and desktop publishing software. TIFF, or Tagged Interchange File Format, was designed to be a universal bitmapped image format and is also used extensively in desktop publishing packages. Often, applications use a proprietary file format to store their images. Adobe creates a PSD file for Photoshop and an AI file for Illustrator; Corel creates a CDR file. DXF was developed by Autodesk as an ASCII-based drawing interchange file for AutoCAD, but the format is used today by many computer-aided design applications. IGS (or IGES, for **Initial Graphics Exchange Standard**) was developed by an industry committee as a broader standard for transferring CAD drawings. These formats are also used in 3-D rendering and animation programs. KML (Keyhole Markup Language) and KMZ (a zipped package of KML files and images) are XML (Extensible Markup Language) text-based formats used by Google in its mapping software and on mobile devices to place lines, overlays, images, polygons, 3-D models (working with COLLADA 3-D files), text, placemark locations, and interactive buttons onto maps. Each item placed onto a map using KML always contains latitude, longitude, and altitude data.

JPEG, PNG, and GIF images are the most common bitmap formats used on the Web and may be considered cross-platform, as all browsers will display them. Adobe's popular PDF (Portable Document File) file manages both bitmaps and drawn art (as well as text and other multimedia content), and is commonly used to deliver a "finished product" that contains multiple assets.

First Person

The fire department had received a new laptop computer for its attack truck and wanted to install a list of the fire hydrants in town. Instead of a simple text list, we suggested creating a KML overlay for Google Earth, so en route to the scene, the firefighter riding shotgun could graphically see which hydrants or water sources were closest to the fire and advise the driver about the best route to the scene. An attack truck carries a very limited supply of water to spray on the fire right away, but as it approaches the fire it can reel out hundreds of feet of high-capacity 4-inch hose, which is stored on top of the water tank. That hose will connect it to the closest source so it can draw water up the hose when the onboard tank runs dry. Having accurate, information-rich maps on board would be a tactical advantage.

The local water department, whose job it was to supply water to the hydrants, provided a spreadsheet of information: a record for each hydrant with fields for ID, capacity, pressure, longitude, and latitude. We converted this to a tab-delimited text file (Figure 3-18).

Then we wrote a short routine using LiveCode to work through each item in the text file and generate the KML code to enable placemarks for Google Earth (Figure 3-19). We made a custom icon and made each icon clickable to bring up an info box containing relevant data about that hydrant.

The end result was a KMZ file that contained the overlay of all hydrants in the town (Figure 3-20).

```
                    📄 rockportHydrantDat.txt
RT-34   1615   78   -69.0700015708201    44.199723376828
RT-35   1312   75   -69.0717027104951    44.1952226872458
RT-36   1781   91   -69.0718793635868    44.1893412040448
RT-37   1127   10   -69.0708331043585    44.1881821466438
RT-38   1393   00   -69.0689296956672    44.1868475263758
RT-39   802    00   -69.0671397906289    44.1866157941379
RT-40   343    90   -69.0656920862429    44.183304626704
RT-41   437    10   -69.0701039187456    44.1835159770518
RT-42   1084   90   -69.0703475045864    44.1857171160825
RT-43   683    92   -69.061059156081     44.1078197401871
```

Figure 3-18   Tab-delimited text file with water department information

```
<Placemark>
    <name>RT-40</name>
    <Snippet maxLines="0"></Snippet>
    <description><![CDATA[<table width="250" border='0' padding='0'>
        <tr><td>Municipallity:</td><td>Rockport</td></tr>
        <tr><td>ID:</td><td>RT-40</td></tr>
        <tr><td>Type:</td><td>Muni</td></tr>
        <tr><td>Flow_at_20:</td><td>343</td></tr>
        <tr><td>StaticPressure:</td><td>90</td></tr>
        <tr><td>Lat:</td><td>44.183304626704</td></tr>
        <tr><td>Long:</td><td>-69.0656920862429</td></tr>
        <tr><td>Last Updated:</td><td>April 4, 2009</td></tr>
        <tr><td> </td><td> </td></tr>
        <tr><td>Source:</td><td>Aqua Maine</td></tr>
        </table>]]>
    </description>
    <styleUrl>#HydrantMuni</styleUrl>
    <Point>
        <coordinates>-69.0656920862429,44.183304626704,0</coordinates>
    </Point>
</Placemark>
```

Figure 3-19   KML code enabling placemarks for Google Earth

Figure 3-20   An overlay of all the hydrants in town

Figure 3-21 As you can see in the bottom image, a few generations of edits and saves at low compression have rendered this JPG image very messy.

Image File Compression

Particularly for bitmapped images, the file format you choose for editing an image and saving it is important. This is because file formats are either **lossless** or **lossy**, depending on the method used to compress the image's content. With a lossy file format, each time you save an image, a bit of the file's accuracy is lost. If you open it again, edit a while, and save it again, even more data will be lost; these cycles of opening, compressing, and saving are called "generations." Figure 3-21 shows an example of four generations of loss. JPEG files are lossy. Common formats that are lossless or nearly lossless are PSD, PSP, GIF, PNG, BMP, TIFF, and RAW. Always edit and save using a lossless format! File compression is also discussed in Chapter 11.

Chapter 3 Review

■ Chapter Summary

For your review, here's a summary of the important concepts discussed in this chapter.

Work out a graphical scheme by planning your approach, organizing your tools, and configuring your computer workspace

- What you see on a multimedia computer screen is the viewer's primary connection to all of your project's content.

- Work out your graphic approach before you begin, either in your head or during creative sessions with your client or colleagues.

- To get a handle on any multimedia project, start with pencil, eraser, and paper. Outline your project and your graphic ideas first: make a flowchart; storyboard the project using stick figures; use three-by-five index cards and shuffle them until you get it right.

- Most authoring systems provide simple tools for creating the graphic objects directly on your screen. Most can also import objects from other applications.

- Multimedia designers employ a variety of applications and tools to accomplish many specialized tasks.

Differentiate between bitmap, vector, and 3-D images and describe the capabilities and limitations of all three

- Bitmaps are an image type most appropriate for photorealistic images and complex drawings requiring fine detail.

- Limitations of bitmapped images include large files sizes and the inability to scale or resize the image easily while maintaining quality.

- A bitmap is a simple information matrix describing the individual dots of an image, called pixels.

- The image's bit-depth determines the number of colors that can be displayed by an individual pixel.

- You can grab a bitmap image from a screen, scan it with a scanner, download it from a web site, or capture it from a camera.

- You can then manipulate and adjust many of its properties, and cut and paste among many bitmaps using image-editing software.

- Vector images are most appropriate for lines, boxes, circles, polygons, and other graphic shapes that can be mathematically expressed in angles, coordinates, and distances.

- A vector object can be filled with color and patterns, and you can select it as a single object.

- Vector-drawn objects use a fraction of the memory space required to describe and store the same object in bitmap form.

- Most drawing programs can export a vector drawing as a bitmap.

- Converting bitmaps to vector-drawn objects is difficult; however, autotracing programs can compute the boundaries of shapes and colors in bitmapped images and then derive the polygon object that describes those bounds.

- For 3-D, the depth (z dimension) of cubes and spheres must be calculated and displayed so that the perspective of the rendered object seems correct to the eye.

- Objects and elements in 3-D space carry with them properties such as shape, color, texture, shading, and location.

- To model an object that you want to place into your scene, you must start with a shape.

- When you extrude a plane surface, it extends its shape some distance, either perpendicular to the shape's outline or along a defined path.

- When you lathe a shape, a profile of the shape is rotated around a defined axis (you can set the direction) to create the 3-D object.

- Rendering is when the computer finally uses intricate algorithms to apply the effects you have specified on the objects you have created.

Describe the use of colors and palettes in multimedia

■ Color is the frequency of a light wave within the narrow band of the electromagnetic spectrum to which the human eye responds.

■ Different cultures associate certain colors with different meanings.

■ For 8-bit GIF images, the computer uses a palette of 256 colors to determine which colors to display.

■ Dithering is a process whereby the color value of each pixel is changed to the closest matching color value in the target palette, using a mathematical algorithm.

■ If you are using a specialized application to make bitmaps or drawings, make sure your multimedia authoring package can import the image files you produce, and that your application can export such a file.

Cite the various image file types used in multimedia

■ GIF and PNG images use palettes of colors and provide lossless files.

■ Windows uses device-independent bitmaps (DIBs) as its common image file format, usually written as BMP files.

■ TIFF, or the Tagged Interchange File Format, was designed to be a universal bitmapped image format and is also used extensively in desktop publishing.

■ For handling drawn objects across many platforms, there are three common formats: DXF, IGS, and SVG. JPEG, GIF, and PNG images are the most common bitmap formats used on the Web and may be considered cross-platform, as all browsers will display them.

■ Key Terms

additive color *(92)*
autotracing *(84)*
Bézier *(82)*
binary *(73)*
bit *(73)*
bitmap *(72)*
BMP *(99)*
Cartesian coordinates *(81)*
CDR *(99)*
CIE *(96)*
clipboard *(78)*
CMYK *(93)*
COLLADA *(89)*
DAE *(89)*
device-independent bitmap (DIB) *(99)*
dithering *(97)*
dot pitch *(92)*
DXF *(99)*
extrude *(86)*
flare *(86)*
GIF *(72)*
hexadecimal *(94)*
HSB *(94)*

HSL *(94)*
hue *(91)*
ignition frisson *(70)*
IGS or IGES (Initial Graphics Exchange Standard) *(99)*
JPEG *(72)*
KML *(99)*
KMZ *(99)*
lathe *(86)*
lossless *(101)*
lossy *(101)*
modeling *(85)*
morphing *(79)*
object *(85)*
palette *(96)*
PCX *(99)*
pel *(73)*
PICT *(99)*
pixel *(73)*
pixelation *(84)*
PNG *(72)*
primitive *(85)*
property *(85)*
quantum theory *(91)*

raster image *(72)*
real estate *(71)*
render farm *(89)*
rendering *(87)*
RGB *(92)*
rotated *(86)*
ROY G. BIV *(91)*
scene *(85)*
shading *(87)*
shape *(85)*
stitch *(89)*
subtractive color *(93)*
SVG (Scalable Vector Graphics) *(82)*
texture *(86)*
TIFF *(99)*
vector *(81)*
vector-drawn *(72)*
YCC *(96)*
YIQ *(96)*
YUV *(96)*
XML *(99)*
z dimension *(85)*

Key Term Quiz

1. The working area of a computer display is sometimes called _____.

2. The type of image used for photorealistic images and for complex drawings requiring fine detail is the _____.

3. The type of image used for lines, boxes, circles, polygons, and other graphic shapes that can be mathematically expressed in angles, coordinates, and distances is the _____.

4. The picture elements that make up a bitmap are called _____.

5. _____ allows you to smoothly blend two images so that one image seems to melt into the next.

6. The process that computes the bounds of the shapes of colors within a bitmap image and then derives the polygon object that describes that image is called _____.

7. _____ is when the computer uses intricate algorithms to apply the effects you have specified on the objects you have created for a final 3-D image.

8. _____ is the blocky, jagged look resulting from too little information in a bitmapped image.

9. A collection of color values available for display is called a(n) _____.

10. _____ is a process whereby the color value of each pixel is changed to the closest matching color value in the target palette, using a mathematical algorithm.

Multiple-Choice Quiz

1. What is the best way to start creating your project's interface?
    a. Start with pencil, eraser, and paper.
    b. Outline your project and graphic ideas.
    c. Storyboard using stick figures.
    d. Use three-by-five index cards and shuffle them.
    e. All of the above

2. Which image file type is best for photographs?
    a. vector
    b. Encapsulated PostScript
    c. bitmap
    d. Shockwave
    e. laser

3. A 24-bit image is capable of representing how many different colors?
    a. 2
    b. 16
    c. 256
    d. 65,536
    e. 16,772,216

4. Vector-drawn objects are used for all of the following *except*:
    a. lines
    b. circles
    c. polygons
    d. photographs
    e. boxes

5. "Unlimited use" of stock photography may actually impose a limitation on:
    a. the number of units you can distribute without paying more
    b. the number of changes you can make to the image
    c. converting the image to another file format
    d. the filters you may use to alter the image
    e. the price you can charge for your product

6. Name the area of memory where data such as text and images is temporarily stored when you cut or copy within an application.
    a. scrapbook
    b. notepad
    c. junkyard
    d. filedump
    e. clipboard

7. Perhaps the single most significant advance in computer image processing during the late 1980s was the development of:
   a. digital cameras
   b. 3-D modeling programs
   c. image-editing programs
   d. scanners
   e. electronic crayons

8. When an image created on a Macintosh is viewed on a PC:
   a. it appears darker and richer because the values have changed
   b. it appears lighter and less saturated because the values have changed
   c. it appears darker and richer even though the values have not changed
   d. it appears lighter and less saturated even though the values have not changed
   e. it appears exactly the same

9. Graphic artists designing for print media use vector-drawn objects because:
   a. they can contain more subtle variations in shading than bitmap graphics
   b. printing inks respond better to them
   c. they can be converted across platforms more easily
   d. they can be scaled to print at any size
   e. they can be viewed directly in web browsers

10. The 3-D process of extending a plane surface some distance, either perpendicular to the shape's outline or along a defined path, is called:
    a. lathing
    b. rendering
    c. modeling
    d. extruding
    e. skinning

11. A GIF image may contain:
    a. 8 bits of color information per pixel
    b. 16 bits of color information per pixel
    c. 24 bits of color information per pixel
    d. 32 bits of color information per pixel
    e. 48 bits of color information per pixel

12. Which of these is the correct HTML hexadecimal representation of magenta (red + blue)?
    a. 00GGHH
    b. #FF00FF
    c. 255,0,255
    d. %R100-%G0-%B100
    e. <color = "magenta">

13. Which of the following is *not* a color specification format?
    a. RGB
    b. HSB
    c. GIF
    d. CMYK
    e. CIE

14. Which of the following is *not* a native Windows graphics file format?
    a. BMP
    b. DIB
    c. TIFF
    d. PCX
    e. PICT

15. TIFF stands for:
    a. Transitional Image File Format
    b. Total Inclusion File Format
    c. Tagged Interchange File Format
    d. Temporary Instruction File Format
    e. Table Index File Format

■ Essay Quiz

1. Discuss the difference between bitmap and vector graphics. Describe five different graphic elements you might use in a project; for example, a background, buttons, icons, or text. Would you use a vector tool or a bitmap tool for each element? Why?

2. You are assigned to create an interface that will look good across platforms. What is the difference between images shown on a Macintosh and on a Windows PC? How would you deal with this problem?

3. List several simple geometric shapes. If you have a 3-D modeling program available, using these shapes, extrude or lathe them to create various objects, such as a teapot, a tree, a car, a table, or a lamp. Think of some other objects. How would you use the simple geometric shapes (called "primitives") to create the 3-D object?

4. You are a designer given the task of creating a web site for a new division of your company. Start by defining the characteristics of the customers of the company and the kind of image the company wishes to present to its customers. Then specify a color palette to be used for the design of the site. Defend your color choices by discussing the associations people have with the colors and how they relate to your customers and the company's image.

Lab Projects

■ Project 3.1

Visit three web sites that include images, one site reaching out to a local audience, one to a general global audience, and one to a special niche (for example, gaming, auctions, or weight loss). Use a screen capture tool, such as the one built into your operating system, to capture an entire page from each. Then in an image-editing program, reduce the size of each web page image by 50 percent and line them up in a new image, side by side. Save this image as a PNG file. Analyze the different approaches each site has used with images. Prepare a report of your findings using a text editor and insert into your report your PNG image.

■ Project 3.2

Use a smartphone or a tablet to take a photo. Upload the photo to a computer and open it in an image editor. Make some changes. Save the image using the native format of your editor (such as PSD for Photoshop), and then as a JPG, then as a PNG, and finally as a GIF. Record the file size for each of the files. Choose the smallest-sized file and attach it to an e-mail addressed to yourself. Back on your mobile device, get your e-mail, download the image attachment into your image library memory (sometimes called the "Camera Roll"), and view it.

■ Project 3.3

Using a black pen or pencil, draw a picture on a piece of plain white paper. Using a scanner or camera, make a bitmapped image of your drawing and save it on a computer. Open the image in a vector-based editing program such as Adobe Illustrator. Using the autotrace function, autotrace part or all of the raster image into a vector-based one. If using Illustrator, make sure you hit the Expand button after you've autotraced; that turns your image into a set of vector-based paths. Reorient the new autotraced lines by selecting them individually (they should now be individual vector paths) and moving them. Make the vector-drawn lines either red or green. Export the modified image as a JPG when you are done.

■ Project 3.4

Install SketchUp (free from Trimble Navigation at www.sketchup.com), which can export to a Google Earth KMZ file and a COLLADA DAE file. Open the template called "Google Earth Modeling – Meters." Use the Rectangle tool (small rectangle icon with a line through it) to lay out a 50×50-meter square on the ground. Then use the Push/Pull tool (small rectangle icon with an arrow pointing away from it) to select the square; pull it upward to a length of 200 meters. To verify your model's measurements, use the Tape Measure tool (tape ruler icon), selecting the endpoints both vertically and horizontally.

Select File | Export | 3D Model. Name the file **tower.kml** and export it as a Google Earth file. Now export the file as **tower.dae** in the COLLADA format. Each file contains only text. Explain the difference in file size.

■ Project 3.5

Download and install Google Earth (from www.google.com/earth/download/ge/) if it is not already available on your computer. Run Google Earth, select File | Open, and choose the file tower.kml, saved during Lab Project 3.4.

In the dialog box, name the imported object **Tower** and adjust its placement on Earth—for example, enter a latitude value of **86S** and a longitude value of **155W**. Beneath the Latitude and Longitude fields, select the View tab, and enter the same values you did for the latitude and longitude. When you click OK, the object(s) in the file will appear in the left sidebar (in My Places) as Tower. Double-click this name and you will fly to its location on Earth. You have proudly built your tower in Antarctica! To become an alien invasion, you could import that file into Google Earth again and again, setting the tower's position to Athens, Sydney, Delhi, Denver, and London.

Sound

Sound is perhaps the most sensuous element of multimedia. It is meaningful "speech" in any language, from a whisper to a scream. It can provide the listening pleasure of music, the startling accent of special effects, or the ambience of a mood-setting background. Some feel-good music powerfully fills the heart, generating emotions of love or otherwise elevating listeners closer to heaven. How you use the power of sound can make the difference between an ordinary multimedia presentation and a professionally spectacular one. Misuse of sound, however, can wreck your project. Try testing all 56 of your ringtones on a crowded bus: your fellow passengers will soon wreck your day.

The Power of Sound

When something vibrates in the air by moving back and forth (such as the cone of a loudspeaker), it creates waves of pressure. These waves spread like the ripples from a pebble tossed into a still pool, and when they reach your eardrums, you experience the changes of pressure, or vibrations, as sound. In air, the ripples propagate at about 750 miles per hour, or Mach 1 at sea level. Sound waves vary in sound pressure level (amplitude) and in frequency or pitch. Many sound waves mixed together form an audio sea of symphonic music, speech, or just plain noise.

Acoustics is the branch of physics that studies sound. Sound pressure levels (loudness or volume) are measured in decibels (dB); a decibel measurement is actually the ratio between a chosen reference point on a logarithmic scale and the level that is actually experienced. When you quadruple the sound output power, there is only a 6 dB increase; when you make the sound 100 times more intense, the increase in dB is not hundredfold, but only 20 dB. A logarithmic scale (shown below) makes sense because humans perceive sound pressure levels over an extraordinarily broad dynamic range.

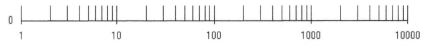

A logarithmic scale is also used for measuring the power of earthquakes (the Richter scale) and stellar magnitudes (a first magnitude star is 100 times as bright as a typical sixth magnitude star, which is at the limit of human visual perception—magnitude 31.5 is the faintest visible light object detectable by the Hubble Space Telescope). You can recognize logarithmic scales because they use divisions that are multipliers (1, 10, 100, 1000) instead of additions (1, 2, 3, 4).

The decibel scale, with some examples, is shown in Table 4-1; notice the relationship between power (measured in watts) and dB.

dB	Watts	Example
195	25–40 million	Saturn rocket
170	100,000	Jet engine with afterburner
160	10,000	Turbojet engine at 7,000-pounds thrust
150	1,000	ALSETEX splinterless stun grenade
140	100	Two JBL2226 speakers pulling 2,400 watts inside an automobile
130	10	75-piece orchestra, at fortissimo
120	1	Large chipping hammer
110	0.1	Riveting machine
100	0.01	Automobile on highway
90	0.001	Subway train; a shouting voice
80	0.0001	Inside a 1952 Corvette at 60 mph
70	0.00001	Voice conversation; freight train 100 feet away
60	0.000001	Large department store
50	0.0000001	Average residence or small business office
40	0.00000001	Residential areas of Chicago at night
30	0.000000001	Very soft whisper
20	0.0000000001	Sound studio

Table 4-1 Typical Sound Levels in Decibels (dB) and Watts

Sound is energy, just like the waves breaking on a sandy beach, and too much volume can permanently damage the delicate receiving mechanisms behind your eardrums, typically dulling your hearing in the 6 kHz range. In terms of volume, what you hear subjectively is not what you hear objectively. The perception of loudness is dependent upon the frequency or pitch of the sound: at low frequencies, more power is required to deliver the same perceived loudness as for a sound at the middle or higher frequency ranges. You may feel the sound more than hear it. For instance, when the ambient noise level is above 90 dB in the workplace, people are likely to make increased numbers of errors in susceptible tasks—especially when there is a high-frequency component to the noise. When the level is above

80 dB, it is quite impossible to use a telephone. Experiments by researchers in residential areas have shown that a sound generator at 45 dB produces no reaction from neighbors; at 45 to 55 dB, sporadic complaints; at 50 to 60 dB, widespread complaints; at 55 to 65 dB, threats of community action; and at more than 65 dB, vigorous community action, possibly more aggressive than when you tested your ringtones on the bus. This neighborhood research from the 1950s continues to provide helpful guidelines for practicing rock musicians and multimedia developers today.

Human hearing is less able to identify the location from which lower frequencies are generated. In surround sound systems, subwoofers can be placed wherever their energy is most efficiently radiated (often in a corner), but midrange speakers should be carefully placed.

There is a great deal more to acoustics than just volume and pitch. If you are interested, many texts will explain why middle C on a cello does not sound like middle C on a bassoon; or why a five-year-old can hear a 1,000 Hz tone played at 20 dB, while an older adult with presbycusis (loss of hearing sensitivity due to age) cannot. Your use of sound in multimedia projects will not likely require highly specialized knowledge of harmonics, intervals, sine waves, notation, octaves, or the physics of acoustics and vibration, but you do need to know how to record and edit sounds on your computer and incorporate them into your multimedia work

Digital Audio

Digital audio is created when you represent the characteristics of a sound wave using numbers—a process referred to as digitizing. You can digitize sound from a microphone, a synthesizer, existing recordings, live radio and television broadcasts, and popular CD and DVDs. In fact, you can digitize sounds from any natural or prerecorded source.

Digitized sound is sampled sound. Every *n*th fraction of a second, a **sample** of sound is taken and stored as digital information in bits and bytes. The quality of this digital recording depends upon how often the samples are taken (**sampling rate** or frequency, measured in kilohertz, or thousands of samples per second) and how many numbers are used to represent the value of each sample (**bit depth**, **sample size**, resolution, or dynamic range). The more often you take a sample and the more data you store about that sample, the finer the resolution and quality of the captured sound when it is played back. Since the quality of your audio is based on the quality of your recording and not the device on which your end user will play the audio, digital audio is said to be **device independent**.

The three sampling rates most often used in multimedia are 44.1 kHz (**CD-quality**), 22.05 kHz, and 11.025 kHz. Sample sizes are either 8 bits or 16 bits. The larger the sample size, the more accurately the data will describe the recorded sound. An 8-bit sample size provides 256 equal measurement units to describe the level and frequency of the sound in that slice of time. A 16-bit sample size, on the other hand, provides a staggering 65,536 equal units to describe the sound in that same slice of time. As you can see in Figure 4-1, slices of analog waveforms are sampled at various frequencies, and each discrete sample is then stored either as 8 bits or 16 bits (or more) of data.

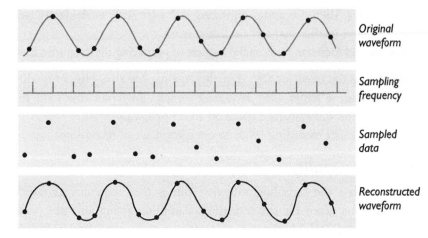

Original waveform

Sampling frequency

Sampled data

Reconstructed waveform

Figure 4-1 It is impossible to reconstruct the original waveform if the sampling frequency is too low.

The value of each sample is rounded off to the nearest integer (**quantization**), and if the amplitude is greater than the intervals available, **clipping** of the top and bottom of the wave occurs (see Figure 4-2). Quantization can produce an unwanted background hissing noise, and clipping may severely distort the sound.

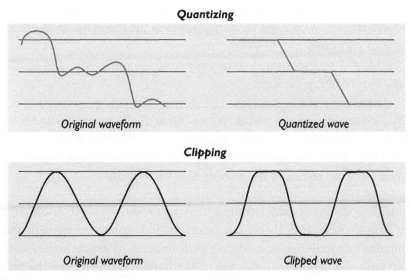

Quantizing

Original waveform   Quantized wave

Clipping

Original waveform   Clipped wave

Figure 4-2 Examples of quantizing and clipping

I have a 20-second sample of a song which I play to my class at 8K, 22K, 44K, and 48K, and I have the students listen and compare quality. They comment that 8K does not sound all that bad *until* they hear the 44K and 48K. They also see (hear) very little difference between 44K and 48K.

....

Dennis Woytek, Assistant Professor of Multimedia Technology, Duquesne University

Making Digital Audio Files

Making digital audio files is fairly straightforward on most computers. Plug a microphone into the microphone jack of your computer. If you want to digitize archived analog source materials—music or sound effects that you have saved on videotape, for example—simply plug the "Line-Out" or "Headphone" jack of the device into the "Line-In" or microphone jack on your computer. Then use audio digitizing software such as Audacity (see Figure 4-3 later in this chapter) to do the work.

You should focus on two crucial aspects of preparing digital audio files:

■ Balancing the need for sound quality against file size. Higher quality usually means larger files, requiring longer download times on the Internet and more storage space on a CD or DVD.

■ Setting proper recording levels to get a good, clean recording.

File Size vs. Quality

Remember that the sampling rate determines the frequency at which samples will be taken for the recording. Sampling at higher rates (such as 44.1 kHz or 22.05 kHz) more accurately captures the high-frequency content of your sound. Audio resolution (such as 8- or 16-bit) determines the accuracy with which a sound can be digitized. Using more bits for the sample size yields a recording that sounds more like its original.

WARNING   *The higher the sound quality, the larger your file will be.*

Stereo recordings are more lifelike and realistic because human beings have two ears. Mono recordings are fine but tend to sound a bit "flat" and uninteresting when compared with stereo recordings. Logically, to record stereo you need two microphones (left and right), and the sound file generated will require twice as much storage space as the mono file for the same length of play time.

Table 4-2 provides some commonly used sampling rates and resolutions, with resulting file sizes.

TIP   *The only reason to digitize audio at a higher specification than can be used by the target playback device is for archiving it. As playback technologies and bandwidth improve over time, you may wish (someday) for higher-quality original files when you upgrade a product. Save the originals!*

Consumer-grade audio compact discs provide stereo at a sampling rate of 44.1 kHz and 16-bit resolution. Sound studios using high-end equipment digitally record and edit performances at much higher sampling rates and depths than this target distribution platform, and the final mix is downsampled before mass replication.

Sampling Rate	Resolution	Stereo or Mono	Bytes Needed for 1 Minute	Comments
44.1 kHz	16-bit	Stereo	10.5MB	CD-quality recording; the recognized standard of audio quality.
44.1 kHz	16-bit	Mono	5.25MB	A good trade-off for high-quality recordings of mono sources such as voice-overs.
44.1 kHz	8-bit	Stereo	5.25MB	Achieves highest playback quality on low-end devices such as most of the sound cards in Windows PCs.
44.1 kHz	8-bit	Mono	2.6MB	An appropriate trade-off for recording a mono source.
22.05 kHz	16-bit	Stereo	5.25MB	Darker sounding than CD-quality recording because of the lower sampling rate, but still full and "present" because of high bit resolution and stereo. Preferred for CD-ROM projects.
22.05 kHz	16-bit	Mono	2.5MB	Not a bad choice for speech, but better to trade some fidelity for a lot of disk space by dropping down to 8-bit.
22.05 kHz	8-bit	Stereo	2.6MB	A popular choice for reasonable stereo recording where full bandwidth playback is not possible.
22.05 kHz	8-bit	Mono	1.3MB	A thinner sound than the previous choice, but very usable. About as good as listening to your TV set.
11 kHz	8-bit	Stereo	1.3MB	At this low a sampling rate, there are few advantages to using stereo.
11 kHz	8-bit	Mono	650KB	In practice, probably as low as you can go and still get usable results; very dark and muffled.
5.5 kHz	8-bit	Stereo	650KB	Stereo not effective.
5.5 kHz	8-bit	Mono	325KB	About as good as a bad telephone connection.

Table 4-2   One-Minute Digital Audio Recordings at Common Sampling Rates and Resolutions

Audiophiles (listeners seriously interested in perfect sound reproduction) have driven a small market for very high-end equipment that can play back SACD (Super Audio CD) or DVD-Audio formats written on special audio-only DVDs that require dedicated players and a system with as many as five full-frequency speakers and a subwoofer. This sound is typically sampled at a depth of 24 bits and a frequency of 96 kHz. It is said by some that, while the limit of human hearing may be about 21 kHz, the unheard higher frequency harmonics (easily heard by dogs to 60 kHz, bats to 120 kHz, and dolphins to 150 kHz) "flood" the brain with pleasure-causing endorphins and lead to a fuller sensory experience.

Here are the formulas for determining the size (in bytes) of a digital recording. For a monophonic recording:

sampling rate × duration of recording in seconds × (bit resolution / 8) × 1

For a stereo recording:

sampling rate × duration of recording in seconds × (bit resolution / 8) × 2

Remember, sampling rate is measured in kHz, or thousand samples per second, so to convert from kHz to a whole number, you must multiply by 1,000. Resolution is measured in bits per sample. Since there are 8 bits in a byte, you have to divide the bit resolution by 8. Thus the formula for a 10-second recording at 22.05 kHz, 8-bit resolution would be

$$22050 \times 10 \times 8 / 8 \times 1$$

which equals 220,500 bytes. A 10-second stereo recording at 44.1 kHz, 16-bit resolution (meeting the CD-quality Red Book Audio standards—an international recording standard discussed later in this chapter) would be

$$44100 \times 10 \times 16 / 8 \times 2$$

which equals 1,764,000 bytes. A 40-second mono recording at 11 kHz, 8-bit resolution would be

$$11000 \times 40 \times 8 / 8 \times 1$$

which equals 440,000 bytes.

Fortunately, for hard disk storage requirements at least, and for ring-tone files sent over a mobile phone, user expectations of audio quality are somewhat lower than for Grammy Award–winning recordings. (See Vaughan's Law of Multimedia Minimums later in this chapter.)

Setting Proper Recording Levels

A distorted recording sounds terrible. If the signal you feed into your computer is too "hot" to handle, the result will be an unpleasant crackling or background ripping noise. Conversely, recordings that are made at too low a level are often unusable because the amount of sound recorded does not sufficiently exceed the residual noise levels of the recording process itself. The trick is to set the right levels when you record.

Any good piece of digital audio recording and editing software will display digital meters to let you know how loud your sound is. Watch the meters closely during recording, and you'll never have a problem. Unlike analog meters that usually have a 0 setting somewhere in the middle and extend up into ranges like +5, +8, or even higher, digital meters peak out. To avoid distortion, do not cross over this limit. If this happens, lower your volume (either by lowering the input level of the recording device or the output level of your source) and try again. Try to keep peak levels between –3 and –10. Any time you go over the peak, whether you can hear it or not, you introduce distortion into the recording. In digital meter displays, if you see red, you are over the peak.

Editing Digital Recordings

Once a recording has been made, it will almost certainly need to be edited. Shown in Figure 4-3 with its special effects menu, Audacity is a free, open-source sound-editing application for Windows, Macintosh, and Linux (http://audacity.sourceforge.net). With such a tool you can create sound tracks and digital mixes. The basic sound-editing operations that most multimedia producers need are described in the paragraphs that follow.

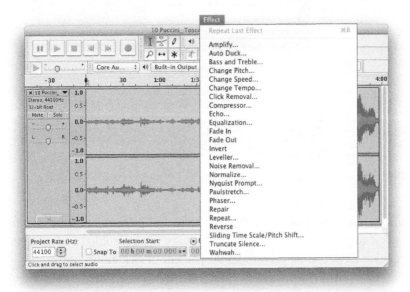

Figure 4-3   Audacity is an open-source, cross-platform editing tool for digitizing and editing sound (http://audacity.sourceforge.net/).

Trimming   Removing "dead air" or blank space from the front of a recording and any unnecessary extra time from the end is your first sound-editing task. **Trimming** even a few seconds here and there might make a big difference in your file size. Trimming is typically accomplished by dragging the mouse cursor over a graphic representation of your recording and choosing a menu command such as Cut, Clear, or Erase.

Splicing and Assembly   Using the same tools mentioned for trimming, you will probably want to remove the extraneous noises that inevitably creep into a recording. Even the most controlled studio voice-overs require touch-up. Also, you may need to assemble longer recordings by cutting and pasting together many shorter ones. In the old days, this was done by splicing and assembling actual pieces of magnetic tape.

Volume Adjustments   If you are trying to assemble ten different recordings into a single sound track, there is little chance that all the segments will have the same volume. To provide a consistent volume level, select all the data in the file, and raise or lower the overall volume by a certain

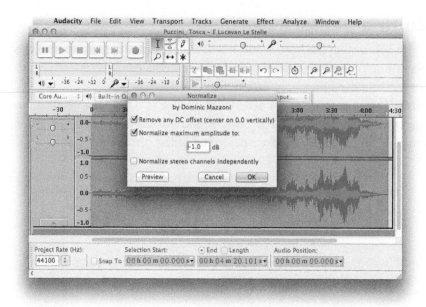

Figure 4-4 Normalizing evens out the sound level in an audio file.

amount. Don't increase the volume too much, or you may distort the file. It is best to use a sound editor to **normalize** the assembled audio file to a particular level, say 80 percent to 90 percent of maximum (without clipping), or about –16 dB. Without normalizing to this rule-of-thumb level, your final sound track might play too softly or too loudly. Even pros can leave out this important step. Sometimes an audio CD just doesn't seem to have the same loudness as the last one you played, or it is too loud and you can hear clipping. Figure 4-4 shows the normalizing process at work.

Format Conversion In some cases, your digital audio editing software might read a format different from that read by your presentation or authoring program. Most sound-editing software will save files in your choice of many formats, most of which can be read and imported by multimedia authoring systems. Data may be lost when converting formats. If, for example, you have a **Digital Rights Management (DRM)**–protected M4P file downloaded from the iTunes store and burn that file to an Audio CD track, the DRM data will be lost because the Audio CD format does not provide for managing DRM data. The now-unprotected tune on the CD can then be ripped into a playable **MP3** format. You will lose some audio quality as well as the DRM protection.

Resampling or Downsampling If you have recorded and edited your sounds at 16-bit sampling rates but are using lower rates and resolutions in your project, you must **resample** or **downsample** the file. Your software will examine the existing digital recording and work through it to reduce the number of samples. This process may save considerable disk space.

Fade-ins and Fade-outs   Most programs offer enveloping capability, useful for long sections that you wish to fade in or fade out gradually. This enveloping helps to smooth out the very beginning and the very end of a sound file.

Equalization   Some programs offer **digital equalization (EQ)** capabilities that allow you to modify a recording's frequency content so that it sounds brighter (more high frequencies) or darker (low, ominous rumbles).

Time Stretching   Advanced programs let you alter the length (in time) of a sound file without changing its pitch. This feature can be very useful, but watch out: most **time-stretching** algorithms will severely degrade the audio quality of the file if the length is altered more than a few percent in either direction.

Digital Signal Processing (DSP)   Some programs allow you to process the signal with reverberation, multitap delay, chorus, flange, and other special effects using **digital signal processing (DSP)** routines. Being able to process a sound source with effects can greatly add to a project. To create an environment by placing the sound inside a room, a hall, or even a cathedral can bring depth and dimension to a project. But a little can go a long way—do not overdo the sound effects!

TIP   Once a sound effect is processed and mixed onto a track, it cannot be further edited, so always save the original so that you can tweak it again if you are not happy with the result.

Reversing Sounds   Another simple manipulation is to reverse all or a portion of a digital audio recording. Sounds, particularly spoken dialog, can produce a surreal, otherworldly effect when played backward.

Multiple Tracks   Being able to edit and combine multiple tracks (for sound effects, voice-overs, music, etc.) and then merge the tracks and export them in a "final mix" to a single audio file is important.

MIDI Audio

MIDI (Musical Instrument Digital Interface) is a communications standard developed in the early 1980s for electronic musical instruments and computers. It allows music and sound synthesizers from different manufacturers to communicate with each other by sending messages along cables connected to the devices. MIDI provides a protocol for passing detailed descriptions of a musical score, such as the notes, the sequences of notes, and the instrument that will play these notes. But MIDI data is not digitized sound; it is a shorthand representation of music stored in numeric form. Digital audio is a recording, MIDI is a score—the first depends on the capabilities of your sound system, the other on the quality of your computerized musical instruments *and* the capabilities of your sound system.

A MIDI file is a list of time-stamped commands that are recordings of musical actions (the pressing down of a piano key or a sustain pedal, for example, or the movement of a control wheel or slider). When sent to a MIDI playback device, this results in sound. A small, concise MIDI message can cause a complex sound or sequence of sounds to play on an instrument or synthesizer; so MIDI files tend to be significantly smaller (per second of sound delivered to the user) than equivalent digitized waveform files.

Composing your own original score can be one of the most creative and rewarding aspects of building a multimedia project, and MIDI is the quickest, easiest, and most flexible tool for this task. Yet creating an original MIDI score is hard work. Knowing something about music, being able to play a keyboard, and having a lot of good ideas are just the prerequisites to building a good score; beyond that, it takes time and musical skill to work with MIDI.

Happily, you can always hire someone to do the job for you. In addition to the talented MIDI composers who charge substantial rates for their services, many young composers are also available who want to get into multimedia. With a little research, you can often find a MIDI musician to work for limited compensation. Remember, however, that you often get what you pay for.

The process of creating MIDI music is quite different from digitizing existing recorded audio. If you think of digitized audio as analogous to a bit-mapped graphic image (both use sampling of the original analog medium to create a digital copy), then MIDI is analogous to structured or vector graphics (both involve instructions provided to software to be able to re-create the original on the fly). For digitized audio you simply play the audio through a computer or device that can digitally record the sound. To make MIDI scores, however, you will need **notation software** (see Figure 4-5),

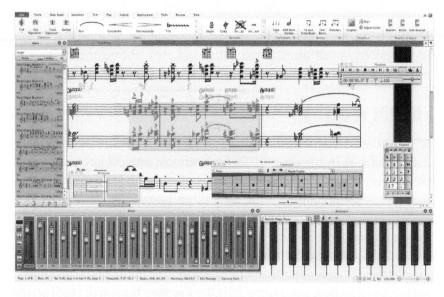

Figure 4-5 Notation and composition software such as Sibelius provides a way for composers and musicians to create and arrange scores using MIDI instruments.

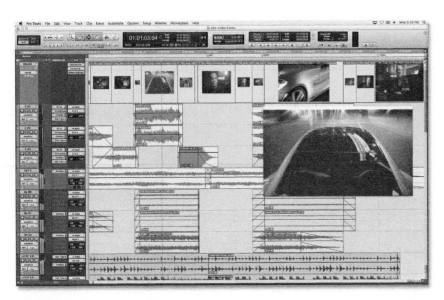

Figure 4-6 Sequencer software such as Pro Tools allows you to record, edit, and save music generated from a MIDI keyboard or instruments and blend it with digital audio.

sequencer software (see Figure 4-6), and a **sound synthesizer** (typically built into the software of multimedia players in most computers and many handheld devices). A **MIDI keyboard** is also useful for simplifying the creation of musical scores.

Rather than recording the sound of a note, MIDI software creates data about each note as it is played on a MIDI keyboard (or another MIDI device)—which note it is, how much pressure was used on the keyboard to play the note, how long it was sustained, and how long it takes for the note to decay or fade away, for example. This information, when played back through a MIDI device, allows the note to be reproduced exactly. Because the quality of the playback depends upon the end user's MIDI device rather than the recording, MIDI is **device dependent**. The sequencer software quantizes your score to adjust for timing inconsistencies (a great feature for those who can't keep the beat), and it may also print a neatly penned copy of your score to paper.

An advantage of structured data such as MIDI is the ease with which you can edit the data. Let's say you have a piece of music being played on a honky-tonk piano, but your client decides he wants the sound of a soprano saxophone instead. If you had the music in digitized audio, you would have to re-record and redigitize the music. When it is in MIDI data, however, there is a value that designates the instrument to be used for playing back the music. To change instruments, you just change that value. Instruments that you can synthesize are identified by a **General MIDI** numbering system that ranges from 0 to 127 (see Table 4-3). Until this system came along, there was always a risk that a MIDI file originally

ID	Sound	ID	Sound	ID	Sound
0	Acoustic grand piano	42	Cello	84	Lead 5 (Charang)
1	Bright acoustic piano	43	Contrabass	85	Lead 6 (Voice)
2	Electric grand piano	44	Tremolo strings	86	Lead 7 (Fifths)
3	Honky-tonk piano	45	Pizzicato strings	87	Lead 8 (Bass + lead)
4	Rhodes piano	46	Orchestral harp	88	Pad 1 (New Age)
5	Chorused piano	47	Timpani	89	Pad 2 (Warm)
6	Harpsichord	48	String ensemble 1	90	Pad 3 (Polysynth)
7	Clarinet	49	String ensemble 2	91	Pad 4 (Choir)
8	Celesta	50	SynthStrings 1	92	Pad 5 (Bowed)
9	Glockenspiel	51	SynthStrings 2	93	Pad 6 (Metallic)
10	Music box	52	Choir aahs	94	Pad 7 (Halo)
11	Vibraphone	53	Voice oohs	95	Pad 8 (Sweep)
12	Marimba	54	Synth voice	96	FX 1 (Rain)
13	Xylophone	55	Orchestra hit	97	FX 2 (Soundtrack)
14	Tubular bells	56	Trumpet	98	FX 3 (Crystal)
15	Dulcimer	57	Trombone	99	FX 4 (Atmosphere)
16	Hammond organ	58	Tuba	100	FX 5 (Brightness)
17	Percussive organ	59	Muted trumpet	101	FX 6 (Goblins)
18	Rock organ	60	French horn	102	FX 7 (Echoes)
19	Church organ	61	Brass section	103	FX 8 (Sci-Fi)
20	Reed organ	62	Synth brass 1	104	Sitar
21	Accordion	63	Synth brass 2	105	Banjo
22	Harmonica	64	Soprano saxophone	106	Shamisen
23	Tango accordion	65	Alto saxophone	107	Koto
24	Acoustic guitar (nylon)	66	Tenor saxophone	108	Kalimba
25	Acoustic guitar (steel)	67	Baritone saxophone	109	Bagpipe
26	Electric guitar (jazz)	68	Oboe	110	Fiddle
27	Electric guitar (clean)	69	English horn	111	Shanai
28	Electric guitar (muted)	70	Bassoon	112	Tinkle bell
29	Overdriven guitar	71	Clarinet	113	Agogo
30	Distortion guitar	72	Piccolo	114	Steel drums
31	Guitar harmonics	73	Flute	115	Wood block
32	Acoustic bass	74	Recorder	116	Taiko drum
33	Electric bass (finger)	75	Pan flute	117	Melodic tom
34	Electric bass (pick)	76	Bottle blow	118	Synth drum
35	Fretless bass	77	Shakuhachi	119	Reverse cymbal
36	Slap bass 1	78	Whistle	120	Guitar fret noise
37	Slap bass 2	79	Ocarina	121	Breath noise
38	Synth bass 1	80	Lead 1 (Square)	122	Seashore
39	Synth bass 2	81	Lead 2 (Sawtooth)	123	Bird tweet
40	Violin	82	Lead 3 (Calliope lead)	124	Telephone ring
41	Viola	83	Lead 4 (Chiff lead)	125	Helicopter
				126	Applause
				127	Gunshot

Table 4-3 General MIDI Instrument Sounds

ID	Sound	ID	Sound	ID	Sound
	Percussion Keys	50	High tom	66	Low timbale
35	Acoustic bass drum	51	Ride cymbal 1	67	High agogo
36	Bass drum 1	52	Chinese cymbal	68	Low agogo
37	Side stick	53	Ride bell	69	Cabasa
38	Acoustic snare	54	Tambourine	70	Maracas
39	Hand clap	55	Splash cymbal	71	Short whistle
40	Electric snare	56	Cowbell	72	Long whistle
41	Low-floor tom	57	Crash cymbal 2	73	Short guiro
42	Closed high-hat	58	Vibraslap	74	Long guiro
43	High-floor tom	59	Ride cymbal 2	75	Claves
44	Pedal high-hat	60	High bongo	76	High wood block
45	Low tom	61	Low bongo	77	Low wood block
46	Open high-hat	62	Mute high conga	78	Mute cuica
47	Low-mid tom	63	Open high conga	79	Open cuica
48	High-mid tom	64	Low conga	80	Mute triangle
49	Crash cymbal 1	65	High timbale	81	Open triangle

Table 4-3   General MIDI Instrument Sounds *(Continued)*

composed with, say, piano, electric guitar, and bass, might be played back with piccolo, tambourine, and glockenspiel if the ID numbers were not precisely mapped to match the original hardware setup. This was usually the case when you played a MIDI file on a MIDI configuration different from the one that recorded the file.

TIP   *Making MIDI files is as complex as recording good sampled files; so it often pays to find someone already set up with the equipment and skills to create your score, rather than investing in the hardware, software, and the learning curve. Once you have gathered your audio material, you will need to edit it to precisely fit your multimedia project. As you edit, you will continue to make creative decisions. Because it is so easy to edit MIDI data, you can make many fine adjustments to your music as you go along.*

Since MIDI is device dependent and the quality of consumer MIDI playback hardware varies greatly, MIDI's true place in multimedia work may be as a production tool rather than a delivery medium. MIDI is by far the best way to create original music, so use MIDI to get the flexibility and creative control you want. Then, once your music is completed and fits your project, lock it down for delivery by turning it into digital audio data.

In addition to describing the instrument and the note, MIDI data can also describe the **envelope** of the sound, which is made up of the **attack** (how quickly a sound's volume increases), the **sustain** (how long the sound continues), and the **decay** (how quickly the sound fades away).

TIP Test your MIDI files thoroughly by playing them back on a variety of hardware devices or with different MIDI players before you incorporate them into your multimedia project. Windows Media Player and QuickTime will play MIDI on your computer.

MIDI vs. Digital Audio

In contrast to MIDI data, digital audio data is the actual representation of a sound, stored in the form of thousands of individual numbers (*samples*). The digital data represents the instantaneous amplitude (or loudness) of a sound at discrete slices of time. MIDI data is to digital audio data what vector or drawn graphics are to bitmapped graphics. That is, MIDI data is device dependent; digital data is not. Just as the appearance of vector graphics differs depending on the printer device or display screen, the sounds produced by MIDI music files depend on the particular MIDI device used for playback. Similarly, a roll of perforated player-piano score played on a concert grand would sound different than if played on a honky-tonk piano. Digital data, on the other hand, produces sounds that are more or less identical regardless of the playback system. The MIDI standard lets instruments communicate in a well-understood language.

MIDI has several advantages over digital audio and two huge disadvantages. First, the advantages:

- MIDI files are much more compact than digital audio files, and the size of a MIDI file is completely independent of playback quality. In general, MIDI files will be 200 to 1,000 times smaller than CD-quality digital audio files. Because MIDI files are small, they don't take up as much memory, disk space, or bandwidth.
- Because they are small, MIDI files embedded in web pages load and play more quickly than their digital equivalents.
- In some cases, if the MIDI sound source you are using is of high quality, MIDI files may sound better than digital audio files.
- You can change the length of a MIDI file (by varying its tempo) without changing the pitch of the music or degrading the audio quality. MIDI data is completely editable—right down to the level of an individual note. You can manipulate the smallest detail of a MIDI composition (often with submillisecond accuracy) in ways that are impossible with digital audio.
- Because they represent the pitch and length of notes, MIDI files can generally be converted to musical notation, and vice versa. This is useful when you need a printed score; in reverse, you can scan a printed score and convert it to MIDI for tweaking and editing.

Now for MIDI's disadvantages:

- Because MIDI data does not represent sound but musical instruments, you can be certain that playback will be accurate only if the MIDI playback device is identical to the device used for production. Imagine the emotional humming chorus from *Madame Butterfly* sung by a chorus of chipmunks—same score, wrong instrument. Even with the General MIDI standard (see the General MIDI table of instrument sounds in Table 4-3), the sound of a MIDI instrument varies according to the electronics of the playback device and the sound generation method it uses.

- Also, MIDI cannot easily be used to play back spoken dialog, although expensive and technically tricky digital samplers are available.

In general, use MIDI in the following circumstances:

- Digital audio won't work because you don't have enough memory or bandwidth.
- You have a high-quality MIDI sound source.
- You have complete control over the machines on which your program will be delivered, so you know that your users will have high-quality MIDI playback hardware.
- You don't need spoken dialog.

The most important advantage of digital audio is its consistent playback quality, but this is where MIDI is the least reliable! With digital audio you can be more confident that the audio track for your multimedia project will sound as good in the end as it did in the beginning when you created it. For this reason, it's no surprise that digital audio is used far more frequently than MIDI data for multimedia sound delivery.

There are two additional and often more compelling reasons to work with digital audio:

- A wider selection of application software and system support for digital audio is available for both the Macintosh and Windows platforms.
- The preparation and programming required for creating digital audio do not demand knowledge of music theory, while working with MIDI data usually does require a modicum of familiarity with musical scores, keyboards, and notation, as well as audio production.

In general, use digital audio in the following circumstances:

- You don't have control over the playback hardware.
- You have the computing resources and bandwidth to handle digital files.
- You need spoken dialog.

Multimedia System Sounds

You can use sound right off the bat on your computer because beeps and warning sounds are available as soon as you install the operating system. Open the Sound preference pane to listen to your system sounds, change them, or make a new, custom sound (see Figure 4-7).

In Windows, system sounds are WAV files (**Waveform Audio File Format**). As you can see in Figure 4-7, you can assign these sounds to system events such as Windows startup, warnings from other applications, or clicks outside of an open dialog box (which causes the default beep in Windows). And you can create schemes of sounds according to your mood. You can also add your own sound files and install them so they play when system events occur: place the WAV sound files into your ~\Windows\Media directory and use the Sound Control Panel to select them.

In OS X on a Macintosh, you can only change your system alert sound. Put your custom sound file (in **AIFF**—Audio Interchange File Format) into your folder ~/System/Library/Sounds, then select it in the Sound preference pane. The Library folder on a Mac is by default invisible. To make it visible, launch the Terminal program (in Applications/Utilities/) and enter the following command:

```
chflags nohidden ~/Library/
```

and the Library folder will become immediately visible. To hide it again, enter

```
chflags hidden ~/Library
```

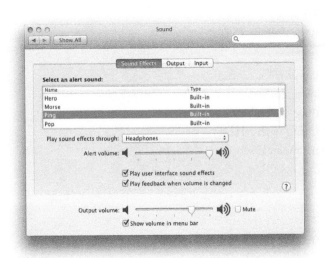 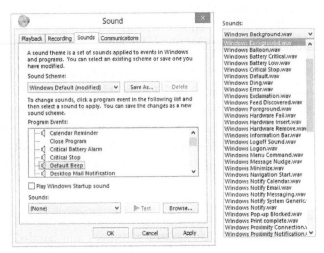

Figure 4-7 Sound preference panes for Macintosh and Windows

TIP   *If you are new to computers, your first multimedia sound experience might be simply finding one of these system sounds in the Sound preference pane and testing it.*

Audio File Formats

When you create multimedia, it is likely that you will deal with file formats and translators for text, sounds, images, animations, or digital video clips. A sound file's format is simply a recognized methodology for organizing and (usually) compressing the digitized sound's data bits and bytes into a data file. The structure of the file must be known, of course, before the data can be saved or later loaded into a computer or device to be edited and/or played as sound. The **filename extension** (letters and numbers after the last dot) identifies which method of storage is used.

There are many ways to store the bits and bytes that describe a sampled waveform sound. The method used for consumer-grade music CDs is called **Linear Pulse Code Modulation (LPCM)**, often shortened to PCM. An audio CD provides up to 80 minutes of playing time, which is enough for a slow-tempo rendition of Beethoven's Ninth Symphony. Incidentally, being able to contain a slow rendition of Beethoven's Ninth Symphony is reported to have been Philips's and Sony's actual size criterion during early research and development for determining the length of the sectors and ultimately the physical size of the compact disc format itself. The **CD-ROM/XA (extended architecture)** format for reading and writing CDs was developed later so you could put several recording sessions of music or data onto a single CD-R (recordable) disc. LPCM tracks from an audio CD are usually converted and stored on a computer in uncompressed AIFF or **wave format (WAV)** files when copied from the CD.

AIFF is historically used for Macintosh sound files. The WAV format was introduced by Microsoft when Windows was first released. Both formats contain uncompressed sound data. But there are huge numbers of sound file formats and "multimedia containers" that store sound data (more than 300 different filename extensions are used for various sound files), and often a converter is required to read or write sound files in the format you need. Hoo Technologies (www.hootech.com), for example, offers MP3 to SWF, SWF/FLV to MP3, AIFF to MP3, MIDI to MP3, WMA to MP3, WAV to MP3, and OGG to MP3 converters. Hoo's AIFF MP3 Converter will read the following formats: 3G2, 3GP, 3GP2, 3GPP, 4XM, AAC, AC3, ADX, AFC, AIF, AIFC, AIFF, ALAW, AMR, AMV, APE, ASF, AU, AVI, AWB, CAF, CDA, CDATA, DIF, DIVX, DTS, DV, DVD, DVR-MS, DXA, FLAC, FLC, FLI, FLIC, FLV, FLX, GSM, GXF, H261, H263, H263+, H264, IT, KAR, M1A, M1V, M2A,

M2TS, M2V, M4A, M4B, M4V, MID, MIDI, MJ2, MJPEG, MJPG, MKA, MKV, MLP, MLV, MMF, MO3, MOD, MOV, MP+, MP1, MP2, MP3, MP4, MPA, MPC, MPE, MPEG, MPG, MPGA, MPP, MPV, MTM, MTS, MTV, MVI, MXF, NSA, NSV, NUT, NUV, OGA, OGG, OGM, OGV, OGX, OMA, PSP, PSX, PVA, QCP, QT, RA, RAM, RM, RMI, RMVB, ROQ, RPL, S3M, SDP, SHN, SMK, SND, SOL, SPX, STR, SWF, TS, TTA, UMX, VFW, VID, VMD, VOB, VOC, VQF, W64, WAV, WAVE64, WM, WMA, WMD, WMV, WV, XA, XM, XVID, XWMV, and YUV. And it will output to AAC, AMR, AWB, M4A (MPEG-4 audio), M4B (MPEG-4 audiobook), MP3, MP4, OGG, WAV, and WMA formats. But rest easy—you will likely only work with a handful of sound file types.

The MP3 format was developed by the Moving Picture Experts Group (**MPEG**) and evolved during the 1990s into the most common method for storing consumer audio. It incorporates a "**lossy**" compression algorithm to save space. An audio CD, for example, may hold an hour or so of uncompressed LPCM sound. That same CD, using MP3 compression, can store almost seven hours of music, but with a slight loss of quality. WMA (Windows Media Audio) is a proprietary Microsoft format developed to improve MP3. OGG was developed as an open-source and royalty-free "container" for sound compressed using Vorbis algorithms similar to MP3—because the Vorbis sound data resides within an Ogg container, these audio files are normally called "Ogg Vorbis."

MP4 is a format based on Apple's **QuickTime movie (.mov)** "container" model and is similar to the MOV format, which stores various types of media, particularly time-based streams such as audio and video. The .mp4 extension is used when the file streams audio and video together. The .m4a extension is used when the file contains only audio data. M4P files contain only audio, but are encrypted for Digital Rights Management (DRM). M4R files are used for ringtones on Apple's iPhone. Other GSM (Global System for Mobile Communications) mobile phones use 3GP files for their ringtones, a format also based on the MPG container model.

The AAC (Advanced Audio Coding) format, which is part of the MP4 model, was adopted by Apple's iTunes Store, and many music files are commercially available in this format. ACC is the default format for iPod, iPhone, PlayStation, Wii, DSi, and many mobile phones including Motorola, Nokia, Philips, Samsung, Siemens, and Sony Ericsson. The SWF format is a container for vector-based graphics and animations, text, video, and sound delivered over the Internet. Typically created using Adobe's Flash, SWF files require a plug-in or player be installed in the user's browser. Adobe claims that the Flash Player is installed in more than 98 percent of web users' browsers and in more than 800 million handsets and mobile devices. Flash video files (FLV) contain both a video stream and an audio stream, and the FLV format has been adopted by YouTube, Google, Yahoo, Reuters.com, BBC.com, CNN.com, and other news providers for Internet delivery of content. When Apple introduced its iOS operating system for the iPhone, iPod touch, and iPad, Adobe's Flash was intentionally disabled in favor of using HTML5 solutions for playing video (see Chapter 6).

TIP   *The most common sound formats you might use are WAV, AIF, AAC, FLV, MP3, MP4, MOV, SWF, WMA, OGG, or for ringtones, M4R, AAC, MIDI, MMF, 3G2, 3GP, 3GP2, and 3GPP. Be sure your audio software can read and write the formats you need.*

A **codec** (compressor-decompressor) is software that compresses a stream of audio or video data for storage or transmission, then decompresses it for playback. There are many codecs that do this with special attention to the quality of music or voice after decompression. Some are "lossy" and trade quality for significantly reduced file size and transmission speed; some are "lossless," so original data is never altered. While editing your audio files, be sure to save your files using a lossless format or codec—with repetitive saves in a lossy format (see Figure 3-17 in previous chapter for an example of data loss in a JPG image), you will notice a quality degradation each time. A container format such as MP4, MOV, or OGG may encapsulate data streams that use one of many codecs allowable in that container.

Vaughan's Law of Multimedia Minimums

A classic physical anthropology law (Liebig's Law of the Minimum) proposes that the evolution of eyesight, locomotor speed, sense of smell, or any other species trait will cease when that trait becomes sufficiently adequate to meet the survival requirements of the competitive environment. If the trait is good enough, the organism expends no more effort improving it. Thus, if consumer-grade electronics and a handheld microphone are good enough for making your sound, and if you, your client, and your audience are all satisfied with the results, conserve your energy and money and avoid any more expenditure. And keep this Law of the Minimum in mind when you make all your trade-off decisions involving other areas of high technology and multimedia, too.

Vaughan's Law of Multimedia Minimums

There is an acceptable minimum level of adequacy that will satisfy the audience, even when that level may not be the best that technology, money, or time and effort can buy.

Adding Sound to Your Multimedia Project

The original 128K Macintosh, released in January 1984, was technically a multimedia-capable machine. It displayed bitmapped graphics (albeit in black and white) and, more significantly, boasted 8-bit digital audio capability right on the motherboard. In fact, the very first Macintosh actually introduced itself by voice when it was unveiled by Steve Jobs.

Here's a little history: In order to use the Apple moniker, the original founders of Apple Computer, Inc., worked out an arrangement with the Beatles (yes, *those* Beatles). One part of that agreement stipulated that Apple Computer, Inc., would never venture into the music business. To Steve Jobs and Steve Wozniak, working out of their garage in the late 1970s on a machine that could barely manage a convincing system beep, that clause probably seemed a harmless one. Little did they know that years later their computer and the Apple itself would become the most popular provider of music in the world through its iTunes facility. The company did finally pay representatives of the Beatles about $30 million to settle the issue once and for all.

Whether you're working on a Macintosh or in Windows, you will need to follow certain steps to bring an audio recording into your multimedia project. Here is a brief overview of the process:

1. Determine the file formats that are compatible with your multimedia authoring software and the delivery medium(s) you will be using (for file storage and bandwidth capacity).

2. Determine the sound playback capabilities (codecs and plug-ins) that the end user's system offers.

3. Decide what kind of sound is needed (such as background music, special sound effects, and spoken dialog). Decide where these audio events will occur in the flow of your project. Fit the sound cues into your storyboard (see Chapter 9), or make up a cue sheet.

4. Decide where and when you want to use either digital audio or MIDI data.

5. Acquire source material by creating it from scratch or purchasing it.

6. Edit the sounds to fit your project.

7. Test the sounds to be sure they are timed properly with the project's images. This may involve repeating steps 1 through 4 until everything is in sync.

When it's time to import your compiled and edited sounds into your project, you'll need to know how your particular multimedia software environment handles sound data. Each multimedia authoring program or web browser handles sound a bit differently, but the process is usually fairly straightforward: just tell your software which file you want to play and when to play it. This is usually handled by an importing or "linking" process during which you identify the files to play.

Scripting languages such as LiveCode (RunRev), Lingo (Director), and ActionScript (Flash) provide a greater level of control over audio playback, but you'll need to know about the programming language and environment. In multimedia authoring environments, it is usually a simple matter to play a sound when the user clicks a button, but this may not be enough. If the user changes screens while a long file is playing, for example, you may need to program the sound to stop before leaving the current screen. If the file to be played cannot be found, you may need to code an entire section for error handling and file location. Sample code is generally provided in both printed and online documentation for software that includes sound playback. For web pages, you will need to point to your sound file using HTML5 code.

Space Considerations

The substantial amount of digital information required for high-quality sound takes up a lot of storage space, especially when the quantity is doubled for two-channel stereo. It takes about 1.94MB to store 11 seconds of uncompressed stereo sound.

If monaural sound is adequate for your project, you can cut your storage space requirement in half or get double the playing time in the same memory space. With compression codecs, you might be able to store the sound in one-eighth the space, but you will lose some fidelity. Further, to conserve space you can downsample, or reduce the number of sample slices you take in a second. Many multimedia developers use 8-bit sample sizes at 22.05-kHz sampling rates because they consider the sound to be good enough (about the quality of AM radio), and they save immense amounts of digital real estate.

The following formula will help you estimate your storage needs. If you are using two channels for stereo, double the result.

$$(\text{sampling rate} \times \text{bits per sample}) / 8 = \text{bytes per second}$$

If you prefer to solve for kilobytes (KB), not bytes, then try:

$$\text{sample rate} \times \text{sample size} / 8 \times \text{\# seconds} \times 2 \text{ (if stereo)} = \text{file size in KB}$$

For example, 60 seconds of stereo in Red Book (CD) Audio:

$$44.1 \times 16 / 8 \times 60 \times 2 = 10{,}584\text{KB} @ 10.59\text{MB}$$

This is an approximate result using 1,000 instead of 1,024 bytes per KB, but yielding the quick handy answer "…about ten and a half megabytes."

You face important trade-offs when deciding how to manage digitized sound in your multimedia project. How much sound quality can you sacrifice in order to reduce storage? What compression techniques make sense?

Will compressed sound work in your authoring platform? What is good enough but not amateurish? Can you get away with 8 bits at 11.025 kHz for voice mail, product testimonials, and voice-overs and then switch to higher sampling rates for music?

Many people feel that MP3s files sampled at 128 Kbps provide decent audio quality for music, especially when played through small speakers. For better quality, sample your music at 192 Kbps. Because the human voice does not use a wide range of frequencies, you can sample speech or voice at 96 Kbps or even 64 Kbps.

TIP *The sound of the human voice comes from one point (the mouth), so there is not much to gain by recording (or playing) it in stereo.*

Audio Recording

If your project requires CD-quality digitized sound at 44.1 kHz and 16 bits, you should hire a sound studio. High-fidelity sound recording is a specialized craft, a skill learned in great part by trial and error, much like photography. If you do decide to do it yourself at CD-quality levels, be prepared to invest in an acoustically treated room, high-end amplifiers and recording equipment, and expensive microphones.

As already stated, there are many trade-offs involved in making multimedia. For example, if you are satisfied with 22.05 kHz in your project or are constrained to this rate by storage considerations, any consumer-grade digital or analog recorder of reasonable quality will do fine. This, of course, also applies to conversations recorded from the telephone, where a sampling rate of 11.025 kHz is adequate. Noise reduction circuits and metal tapes are helpful to remove hiss, but at a sampling rate of 22.05 kHz you are only going to be digitizing audio frequencies as high as about 11 kHz, anyway. Both the high and low ends of the audio hearing spectrum are therefore less important to you, and that is OK, because those areas are precisely the add-value focus of very elaborate and expensive consumer equipment.

Digital audio tape (DAT) systems provide a tape-based 44.1-kHz, 16-bit record and playback capability. You may, however, find that DAT is high-fidelity overkill for your needs, because the recordings are too accurate, precisely recording glitches, background noises, microphone pops, and coughs from the next room. A good editor can help reduce the impact of these noises, but at the cost of time and money.

Mobile phones can often record audio (and video), and applications and hardware attachments are available to manage external microphones and file transfer. USB and flash memory recorders range in quality, some suitable for voice only, some generating compressed MP3 files, and some

With the collaboration of composer Dave Soldier, Komar & Melamid's Most Wanted Paintings project (www.diacenter.org/km/index.html) was extended into the realm of music. A poll, written by Dave Soldier, was conducted on Dia's web site (www. diacenter.org). Approximately 500 visitors took the survey. Dave Soldier and Nina Mankin used the survey results to write music and lyrics for the Most Wanted and Most Unwanted songs.

A Note from the Composer

This survey confirms the hypothesis that popular music indeed provides an accurate estimate of the wishes of the vox populi. The most favored ensemble, determined from a rating by participants of their favorite instruments in combination, comprises a moderately sized group (three to ten instruments) consisting of guitar, piano, saxophone, bass, drums, violin, cello, synthesizer, with low male and female vocals singing in rock/r&b style. The favorite lyrics narrate a love story, and the favorite listening circumstance is at home. The only feature in lyric subjects that occurs in both most wanted and unwanted categories is "intellectual stimulation." Most participants desire music of moderate duration (approximately 5 minutes), moderate pitch range, moderate tempo, and moderate to loud volume, and display a profound dislike of the alternatives. If the survey provides an accurate analysis of these factors for the population, and assuming that the preference for each factor follows a Gaussian (bell-curve) distribution, the combination of these qualities, even to the point of sensory overload and stylistic discohesion, will result in a musical work that will be unavoidably and uncontrollably "liked" by 72 plus or minus 12 percent (standard deviation; Kolmogorov-Smirnov statistic) of listeners. The most unwanted music is over 25 minutes long, veers wildly between loud and quiet sections, between fast and slow tempos, and features timbres of extremely high and low pitch, with each dichotomy presented in abrupt transition. The most unwanted orchestra was determined to be large and features the accordion and bagpipe (which tie at 13 percent as the most unwanted instrument), banjo, flute, tuba, harp, organ, synthesizer (the only instrument that appears in both the most wanted and most unwanted ensembles). An operatic soprano raps and sings atonal music, advertising jingles, political slogans, and "elevator" music, and a children's choir sings jingles and holiday songs. The most unwanted subjects for lyrics are cowboys and holidays, and the most unwanted listening circumstances are involuntary exposure to commercials and elevator music. Therefore, it can be shown that if there is no covariance—someone who dislikes bagpipes is as likely to hate elevator music as someone who despises the organ, for example—fewer than 200 individuals of the world's total population would enjoy this piece.

Dave Soldier, composer and musician, who provides the Most Wanted Song and the Most Unwanted Song on a CD at www.diaart.org/publications/main/61

recording in CD-quality stereo. Recordings can be directly downloaded as digital files using a USB cable or flash memory card reader.

Keeping Track of Your Sounds

In an elaborate project with many sounds, it is important to maintain a good database, keeping a physical track of your original material—just in case you need to revert to it when your disk drive crashes or you accidentally delete the work file. A database is particularly important because you may need to give your sound files such unhelpful names as janesEyes OpenWide.aiff or Chapter11inSpanish03.wav; these names contain some clues about the files' actual content, but you may need a more descriptive cross-reference. You don't want to have to load and play many sound files just to find the one you need.

Acoustic Fingerprints

Databases containing information about CD recordings and their individual tracks are commonly used to identify and provide metadata for digital music. These databases use an **acoustic fingerprint** of your musical sample (a combination of tempo, spectrum, and other components that identify the sound) to match it against tens of thousands of known samples either systematically gathered or submitted by users. Some music recognition and database systems are patented and commercial, such as LASSO, Audible Magic, or the Fraunhofer Institute's AudioID. Sony's Gracenote database is said to contain about 100 million identified songs or tracks compiled since the mid-1990s from more than 1 billion submissions. This is perhaps the most widely used commercial database, with clients such as iTunes, Yahoo! Music Jukebox, AOL, Amazon MP3, Spotify, Winamp, Pandora, Google Music, Bose, Panasonic, Philips, Sony, and Samsung. MusicBrainz is an open-source, free database containing information about more than 12 million tracks. MusicBrainz Picard can be used to automatically identify your audio files; it understands most audio formats, including AAC, MP3, MP4, Ogg Vorbis, WAV, and WMA.

Audio CDs

The method for digitally encoding the high-quality stereo of the consumer CD music market is an international standard, called ISO 10149. This is also known as the Red Book Audio standard (derived simply from the color of the standard's book jacket). Developers of this standard claim that the digital audio sample size and sampling rate of Red Book Audio (16 bits at 44.1 kHz) allow accurate reproduction of all the sounds that humans can hear. Until recently, dedicated professional sound-studio equipment was used for this high-fidelity recording; today most off-the-shelf computers will record and play 16-bit sampled sound at 44.1 kHz and at 48 kHz. Converter and burning software such as Toast and Creator from Roxio (www.roxio.com) can translate the digital files of Red Book Audio found on consumer compact discs directly into a digital sound file format such as MP3 or WAV. Unlike DVDs, audio CDs do not contain information about artists, titles, or track lists of songs.

Sound for Your Mobile Phone

Ringtones are perhaps the most widely- and often-heard sounds in today's world. Unlike plain old telephones, where a pulsating 90-volt signal is sent down copper wires to energize a hammer that klangs a bell, there is no bell in a digital mobile telephone. When the mobile receives a notice that someone is calling, the unit's software takes over and, depending on the programmed options, plays the user's choice of ringtone—either generated by internal MIDI software or played from a stored sound file. Ringtones play on a very small speaker and often compete in a noisy environment. Perhaps an urban myth, it is reported that an inventive sales executive recorded herself coughing and sent that awful sound to her phone as a ringtone. When she received an incoming call during a meeting, she would quickly cover her mouth, continue the cough, and excuse herself from the room in order to take the call. Ringtones aren't the end of it. Into the daily lexicon have entered answertones, ringbacktones, truetones, realtones, singtones, videotones, and "ringles." Most are for sale from enterprising small and large businesses all over the world. MP3 files will play on most mobiles; check your phone's manual to be sure. See Chapter 12 for more about multimedia and mobile devices.

Sound for the Internet

There are several methods for playing digital or MIDI sound from a web page. The sound is actually not part of the web page but is a separate file with its own address on the Internet, which is "embedded" in the page. Web browsers associate files with applications and plug-ins: Figure 4-8 shows the Preferences panel from Firefox, which lets you specify what to do when the browser downloads a particular file type. The simplest way to embed a sound file in a web page is to call it from an inline HTML anchor:

```
<a href="mysound.wav">Click here to play MySound!</a>
```

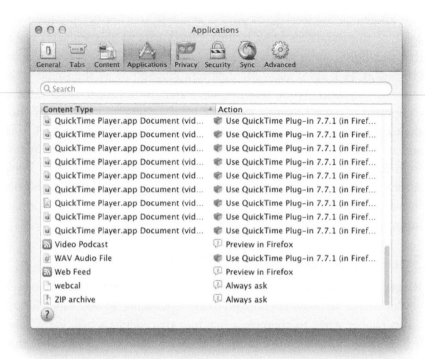

Figure 4-8   Web browsers must be told what to do when they download file types.

As an HTML anchor, the text "Click here to play MySound!" will usually be underlined, and when that link is clicked, the browser will find the file mysound.wav (in this case, in the same directory as the web page), will download it, and, depending on how the user has instructed the browser to manage WAV files, will open a player and play the sound.

Media players are designed to play files as soon as enough of the data is cached in your computer's **buffer** (a place where data is stored temporarily). The downloading continues to fill the buffer faster than you empty it by playing the sound file, allowing the sound file to stream into your computer in the background, keeping ahead of what has already been played so the playback doesn't pause or break up. **Streaming** files are dependent upon connection speed: you must wait longer (**streaming latency**) before the streamed sound begins to play when using a dial-up modem (low bandwidth) than when using a high-speed glass fiber connection (high bandwidth).

TIP   *See Chapter 11 for more about the HTML5 <audio> tag, which can be used to play sound on a web page without requiring a special player or helper application.*

Adobe's Flash allows you to integrate the sound tracks that you have made using a sound editor into a web-based multimedia presentation, including both event sounds like button clicks and streaming sounds like background music. Because it can read and save MP3 files, Flash offers web designers serious and powerful options for solving the quality conundrum of high-quality (big) files and slow downloads versus low-quality (small) files and speedy delivery—with nice results. Because it must break a sound into "frames" so it plays in sync with the timeline, Flash resamples the audio track if you ask it to "stream" in a movie clip; for the best quality, import an uncompressed audio clip into the Flash library and let Flash do the compression.

Testing and Evaluation

Putting together all the media components of your project can be tough, but testing and evaluating what you've done can be even tougher—especially if your project involves a complicated live presentation, or if you're shipping a commercial multimedia application. Unless you plan ahead, problems will not emerge until you begin testing.

TIP   *During editing and authoring, regularly test the sound-and-image synchronization of your project. If you are delivering your sound on the Web, test it with different browsers and different connection speeds.*

Don't forget to evaluate your sound storage medium. How much RAM does your project need to run effectively? Some authoring and delivery packages will stream sound directly off the hard disk or CD-ROM; others require the sound to be loaded into memory from the hard disk before they play. Sometimes you will need to break a sound or a music file into smaller parts. And MIDI files that sound terrific with expensive General MIDI during development will not have the same quality on a low-end FM-synthesis device at the end user's site or on a handheld.

In the world of professional film and video production, sound is incorporated during **post-production,** or a **post-session,** after all the film and video footage has been assembled. Just so with multimedia—and don't give it short shrift because of time or budget constraints. The sound track can make or break your project!

Copyright Issues

Ownership rights are significant issues for multimedia producers who would love to use a few bars of Beyonce's latest hit or a nostalgic background of Bach suites played by Pablo Casals. Producers may rightfully fret about copyrights and permissions. Most developers play it safe by always making their own custom music from scratch in a sound studio, or with synthesizers, or by using sounds that have a clear and paid-for ownership and permission trail. Others simply take a risk and break the law.

WARNING _You are breaking the law if you record and use copyrighted material without first securing the appropriate rights from the owner or publisher of the material._

As more and more multimedia is produced by more and more developers who are hungry for sound content, the copyright of sounds and images has become a major issue—not so much about who owns something, but how much of it they own. Because it is so easy to manipulate and edit a sound, just how much of someone's original work do you have to change before it then becomes your own? There are separate licensing issues for use of a musical composition (even if you create a MIDI performance of it yourself) and for use of a particular recording of a musical composition (as when you make a copy of a song downloaded from iTunes). Different licensing arrangements may be required, depending upon exactly how you use the music in different types of multimedia programs—from a presentation you create for a client's annual stockholders meeting, to a musical foundation beneath a commercial application. As this suggests, music licensing is a specialized and complicated area, so you should make sure you have cleared all the necessary rights before using any music in a product. The Harry Fox Agency (www.harryfox.com), for example, represents more than 27,000 music publishers and is the premier licensing resource for the mechanical use of music reproduced in all formats and media. Copyright issues and methods of securing permission for use (equally relevant for sounds, still images, and motion video) are discussed in more detail in Chapter 10.

A number of software vendors have entered the multimedia marketplace by selling digitized clip sounds with an unlimited-use, royalty-free license. Some of these products include musical clips, and some just include sound effects (e.g., doors closing, dogs barking, and water dripping). Other products have a mixture of both. But beware of sources claiming to be public domain that offer clips of Bella Swan and Edward in the Twilight Saga, or one-liners from Humphrey Bogart movies, because these sounds have likely been used without permission. Also, carefully read the licensing terms that come with any collection you purchase. Although the box may claim that the sounds are "unlimited-use, royalty free," the fine print inside most likely limits their use to your personal machine and does not include the right to use them in any commercial use or republication in a form that would allow others to obtain them (such as using them on a web site).

WARNING _Taking a camera or a tape or video recorder to some public events may be illegal without proper permission._

Police Fight Cellphone Recordings

Witnesses taking audio of officers arrested, charged with illegal surveillance

Simon Glik, a lawyer, was walking down Tremont Street in Boston when he saw three police officers struggling to extract a plastic bag from a teenager's mouth. Thinking their force seemed excessive for a drug arrest, Glik pulled out his cellphone and began recording.

Within minutes, Glik said, he was in handcuffs.

"One of the officers asked me whether my phone had audio recording capabilities," Glik, 33, said recently of the incident, which took place in October 2007. Glik acknowledged that it did, and then, he said, "my phone was seized, and I was arrested."

The charge? Illegal electronic surveillance.

Jon Surmacz, 34, experienced a similar situation. Thinking that Boston police officers were unnecessarily rough while breaking up a holiday party in Brighton he was attending in December 2008, he took out his cellphone and began recording.

Police confronted Surmacz, a web-master at Boston University. He was arrested and, like Glik, charged with illegal surveillance.

There are no hard statistics for video recording arrests. But the experiences of Surmacz and Glik highlight what civil libertarians call a troubling misuse of the state's wiretapping law to stifle the kind of street-level oversight that cellphone and video technology make possible.

In 1968, Massachusetts became a "two-party" consent state, one of 12 currently in the country. Two-party consent means that all parties to a conversation must agree to be recorded on a telephone or other audio device; otherwise, the recording of conversation is illegal. The law, intended to protect the privacy rights of individuals, appears to have been triggered by a series of high-profile cases involving private detectives who were recording people without their consent.

In arresting people such as Glik and Surmacz, police are saying that they have not consented to being recorded, that their privacy rights have therefore been violated, and that the citizen action was criminal.

It took five months for Surmacz, with the American Civil Liberties Union (ACLU), to get the charges of illegal wiretapping and disorderly conduct dismissed. Surmacz said he would do it again.

"Because I didn't do anything wrong," he said. "Had I recorded an officer saving someone's life, I almost guarantee you that they wouldn't have come up to me and say, 'Hey, you just recorded me saving that person's life. You're under arrest.'"

Excerpted from http://necir-bu.org/ with permission. The New England Center for Investigative Reporting at Boston University is an investigative reporting collaborative. This story was done under the guidance of BU professors Dick Lehr and Mitchell Zuckoff.

Chapter 4 Review

■ Chapter Summary

For your review, here's a summary of the important concepts discussed in this chapter.

Describe the components and measurements of sound

■ How you use the power of sound can make the difference between an ordinary multimedia presentation and a professionally spectacular one. Misuse of sound, however, can wreck your project.

■ When something vibrates in the air by moving back and forth, it creates waves of pressure. These waves spread, and when they reach your eardrums, you experience the vibrations as sound.

■ Acoustics is the branch of physics that studies sound.

■ Sound pressure levels (loudness or volume) are measured in decibels (dB).

Use digital audio to record, process, and edit sound

■ Digital audio data is the actual representation of a sound, stored in the form of thousands of individual samples that represent the amplitude (or loudness) of a sound at a discrete point in time.

■ How often the samples are taken is the sampling rate.

■ The three sampling frequencies most often used in multimedia are CD-quality 44.1 kHz (kilohertz), 22.05 kHz, and 11.025 kHz.

■ Digital audio is not device dependent, and sounds the same every time it is played. For this reason digital audio is used far more frequently than MIDI data for multimedia sound tracks.

■ You can digitize sounds from any source, live or prerecorded.

■ The amount of information stored about each sample is the sample size and is determined by the number of bits used to describe the amplitude of the sound wave when the sample is taken.

■ Sample sizes are either 8 bits or 16 bits.

■ The value of each sample is rounded off to the nearest integer (quantization).

■ The preparation and programming required for creating digital audio do not demand knowledge of music theory.

Use MIDI and understand its attributes, especially relative to digitized audio

■ MIDI data is not digitized sound; it is a shorthand representation of music stored in numeric form.

■ MIDI files tend to be significantly smaller than equivalent digitized waveform files.

■ MIDI data is device dependent; its playback depends on the capabilities of the end user's system.

■ Because they are small, MIDI files embedded in web pages load and play more quickly than their digital equivalents.

■ You can change the length of a MIDI file (by varying its tempo) without changing the pitch of the music or degrading the audio quality. MIDI data is completely editable.

■ MIDI cannot easily be used to play back spoken dialog.

■ Working with MIDI requires familiarity with musical scores, keyboards, and notation as well as audio production.

Compare and contrast the use of MIDI and digitized audio in a multimedia production

■ MIDI is analogous to structured or vector graphics, while digitized audio is analogous to bitmapped images.

■ MIDI is device dependent, meaning the quality of the playback is dependent upon the hardware installed on the user's machine, while digitized audio is device independent.

- Use MIDI only when you have control over the playback hardware and know your users will be using a high-quality MIDI device for playback.

- MIDI files are much smaller than digitized audio, so they may be used for delivery of music under the right circumstances.

- Use digitized audio for spoken dialog.

List the important steps and considerations in recording and editing digital audio

- The file size (in bytes) of a digital recording is sampling rate × duration of recording in seconds * (bit resolution / 8) × number of tracks (1 for mono, 2 for stereo).

- Consumer-grade audio compact discs are recorded in stereo at a sampling rate of 44.1 kHz and a 16-bit resolution. Other sampling rates include 22.05 and 11 kHz, at either 16 or 8 bits.

- When recording (digitizing) audio, it's important to keep the recording level near the maximum without going over it.

- Important steps in digital sound editing include removing blank space from the start and end of a recording and normalizing the sound to bring all clips to approximately the same level.

- The native sound file format for most Macintosh sound-editing software is the AIFF format, and most authoring systems will read these formats. In Windows, the native sound file format for most sound-editing software is a WAV file.

- Many audio editors provide tools such as resampling, fade-ins and -outs, equalization, time stretching, various digital signal processing effects, and reversing sounds.

Determine which audio file formats are best used in a multimedia project

- MIDI scores require sequencer software and a sound synthesizer.

- The General MIDI format standardizes a set of MIDI instruments, ensuring that the MIDI sequence is played correctly.

- Streaming files begin playing when part of the file has been buffered into the computer's memory and are dependent upon connection speed.

- Adobe's Flash provides powerful tools for integrating and streaming sounds, including the MP3 format.

- Apple's QuickTime is a file format that, among other capabilities, enables digital audio to be blended with video information.

Cite the considerations involved in managing audio files and integrating them into multimedia projects

- Because sounds are time based, you may need to consider what happens to sounds that are playing in your project when the user goes to a different location.

- Appropriate use of sound requires technical considerations of disk space or bandwidth as well as the abilities of the authoring system to use various file formats and compression algorithms.

- Do not use equipment and standards that exceed what your project requires.

- Keep track of your audio files, and be sure to back them up.

- Regularly test the sound-and-image synchronization of your project.

- Evaluate your sound's RAM requirements as well as your users' playback setup.

- Be sure you understand the implications of using copyrighted material. You are breaking the law if you record and use copyrighted material without first securing the appropriate rights from the owner or publisher.

- You can purchase and use digitized clip sounds with an unlimited-use, royalty-free license.

■ Key Terms

acoustic fingerprint *(132)*
acoustics *(108)*
AIFF *(124)*
attack *(121)*
audio resolution *(112)*
bit depth *(110)*
buffer *(134)*
CD-quality *(110)*
CD-ROM/XA (extended architecture) *(125)*
clipping *(111)*
codec *(127)*
decay *(121)*
decibels (dB) *(108)*
device dependent *(119)*
device independent *(110)*
digital audio *(110)*
digital audio tape (DAT) *(130)*

digital equalization (EQ) *(117)*
digital signal processing (DSP) *(117)*
downsample *(116)*
Digital Rights Management (DRM) *(116)*
envelope *(121)*
filename extension *(125)*
General MIDI *(119)*
Linear Pulse Code Modulation (LPCM) *(125)*
lossy *(126)*
MIDI *(117)*
MIDI keyboard *(119)*
MP3 *(116)*
MPEG *(126)*
normalize *(116)*
notation software *(118)*

post-production, post-session *(135)*
quantization *(111)*
QuickTime movie (.mov) *(126)*
Red Book Audio *(133)*
resample *(116)*
sample *(110)*
sample size *(110)*
sampling rate *(110)*
sequencer software *(119)*
sound synthesizer *(119)*
streaming *(134)*
streaming latency *(134)*
sustain *(121)*
time stretching *(117)*
trimming *(115)*
wave format (WAV) *(125)*

■ Key Term Quiz

1. The branch of physics that studies sound is _____.

2. Sound pressure levels (loudness or volume) are measured in _____.

3. To adjust the level of a number of tracks to bring them all up to about the same level is to _____ them.

4. When audio is measured in order to be digitally stored, the value of each measurement is rounded off to the nearest integer in a process called _____.

5. A reduction in the number of separate measurements in an audio file is called a(n) _____ or _____.

6. The standard file format for displaying digitized motion video on the Macintosh is _____.

7. The most common file format for editing sound on the Macintosh is _____.

8. The audio file format introduced by Microsoft and IBM with the introduction of Windows is the _____.

9. The process of playing a sound file while part of the file is still downloading is called _____.

10. Some software allows you to begin playing a downloading sound file as soon as enough of the sound is cached in your computer's _____.

■ Multiple-Choice Quiz

1. The file format that uses a shorthand representation of musical notes and durations stored in numeric form is:
   a. AIFF
   b. CD-ROM/XA
   c. DSP
   d. MIDI
   e. QuickTime

2. Which of these statements regarding the MIDI audio format is *not* true?
   a. The sound can easily be changed by changing instruments.
   b. Spoken audio can easily be included.
   c. Sound tracks can be created using sequencing software.
   d. Files are generally smaller than the same digital audio sound.
   e. Sounds can be stretched and timing changed with no distortion of the quality.

3. The primary benefit of the General MIDI over the previous MIDI specification is that:
   a. the file sizes are much smaller due to the compression scheme
   b. users can easily edit and adjust the data structures
   c. it can be easily converted into the CD-ROM/XA format
   d. MIDI files can be easily integrated into the computer's operating system as system sounds
   e. the instruments are the same regardless of the playback source

4. What happens when an audio signal exceeds the recording device's maximum recording level?
   a. The signal is compressed to an appropriate level.
   b. "Clipping" of the signal occurs, introducing distortion.
   c. The audio clip is extended to accommodate the extra data.
   d. The entire clip's volume is reduced correspondingly.
   e. The extra bits go into a buffer for later use.

5. As one story goes, the criterion used to set the length of the sectors and ultimately the physical size of the compact disc format was based on the length of:
   a. the Beatles' "White Album"
   b. Handel's *Messiah*
   c. Beethoven's Ninth Symphony
   d. Bach's *St. John's Passion*
   e. Iron Butterfly's live rendition of "In-A-Gadda-Da-Vida"

6. The process of recording a sound, stored in the form of thousands of individual measurements, each at a discrete point in time, is called:
   a. sampling
   b. synthesizing
   c. sizing
   d. quantizing
   e. streaming

7. The file size of a five-second recording sampled at 22 kHz, 16-bit stereo (two tracks) would be about:
   a. 110,000 bytes
   b. 220,000 bytes
   c. 440,000 bytes
   d. 550,000 bytes
   e. 880,000 bytes

8. Which of the following sound file characteristics does *not* directly affect the size of a digital audio file?
   a. sample rate
   b. sample size
   c. tracks (stereo vs. mono)
   d. volume
   e. compression

9. Each individual measurement of a sound that is stored as digital information is called a:
   a. buffer
   b. stream
   c. sample
   d. capture
   e. byte

10. Audio recorded at 44.1 kHz (kilohertz), 16-bit stereo is considered:
    a. phone-quality
    b. voice-quality
    c. FM-quality
    d. CD-quality
    e. AM-quality

11. Removing blank space or "dead air" at the beginning or end of a recording is sometimes called:
    a. quieting
    b. pre-rolling
    c. quantizing
    d. trimming
    e. flashing

12. DSP stands for:
    a. dynamic sound programming
    b. data structuring parameters
    c. direct splicing and partitioning
    d. delayed streaming playback
    e. digital signal processing

13. Sequencing software:
    a. places audio clips in order in a soundtrack
    b. records and edits MIDI data
    c. applies filters to digital audio clips in a predetermined order
    d. manages a project by creating a timeline of events
    e. helps synchronize images with a sound track

14. The slower a user's connection, the longer the user must wait for enough of the sound to download so that the entire file will have downloaded by the time the sound reaches the end. This effect is called:
    a. streaming latency
    b. post-processing
    c. compression
    d. digital signal processing
    e. multitap delay

15. The Red Book standard was so named because:
    a. the standard was pioneered in the former Soviet Union
    b. red is an acronym for "Registered Electronic Data"
    c. the standard's book jacket was red
    d. it was so expensive to produce CDs early on that most producers were "in the red"
    e. the dye in the first recordable CDs had a reddish tint

■ Essay Quiz

1. Imagine you are a journalist tasked with a large investigative story for which you will interview some 30 people. You plan to record each interview, many in informal settings where background noise might also be an issue. Discuss how you would approach this process with regard to recording, editing, and organizing your audio files into a database.

2. Discuss the implications of remixing someone else's audio work for your own use. Consider the current copyright law and system of acquiring rights in your essay. When is it OK to remix another's work? When is it not OK? Discuss why you do or do not agree with the current copyright system.

3. You have been assigned to design and produce the audio portions of a multimedia project. The program will be delivered on a CD-ROM, and video clips will take up most of the CD. You have only 50MB of storage space to store 20 one-minute clips of speech, 10 songs averaging three minutes long, and a background sound loop. What sampling rates and depths should you use for the speech, for the music, and for the background sound? Why? Roughly calculate the file size totals for these specifications, and be sure that you end up with less than the 50MB of storage space allotted. Discuss your reasoning.

4. Describe what MIDI is, what its benefits are, and how it is best used in a multimedia project.

5. List the steps you would go through to record, edit, and process a set of sound files for inclusion on a web site. How would you digitally process the files to ensure they are consistent, have minimum file size, and sound their best?

Lab Projects

▪ Project 4.1

Go online and locate three sound editors (either from a shareware site or demo versions of commercial software). Document their capabilities. What file formats can they import from and export to? How many tracks can they handle? What DSP effects do they provide?

▪ Project 4.2

Record three sounds using a simple recording device—most mobile phones should be capable of this. One sound should be speech, one should be music, and one should be recorded outdoors. Connect your recording device to a computer and download the three recording files. Depending on the recorder you used, you may need to convert the file type to MP3, WAV, or AIFF. To do this, use an online converter such as media.io (http://media.io). Save all three files in a location where you can find them again.

▪ Project 4.3

Download and install the free audio-editing program Audacity (http://audacity.sourceforge.net/). Spend a few minutes familiarizing yourself with the program. Open one of the music files you made for Project 4.2. From the Audacity menu bar, choose Effect | Change Tempo. Using the pop-up slider, change the tempo by +20 percent, and then −20 percent. Describe the difference. Now open a speech file. Choose Effect | Change Pitch. Change the pitch by +20 percent, and then −20 percent. Describe the result.

▪ Project 4.4

Open the outdoors file you recorded for Project 4.2. Listen to the recording and make note of the background ambient noises, such as birds or the wind. Highlight a small portion of the recording with such a noise. Now choose Effect | Noise Removal. In the Noise Removal dialog box, click the Get Noise Profile button. Select the full audio track, and then choose Effect | Noise Removal again. This time, click the OK button in the dialog box. After the process is complete, listen to the file all the way through, making note of differences from the original.

▪ Project 4.5

Locate three web sites that offer "royalty-free" or "buyout" music. Such sites almost always allow visitors to listen to low-quality samples. What formats are the samples provided in? Listen to some of the samples. Try to identify which are synthesized and which are actual instruments playing the music. What are the license arrangements for using the music? Document your findings, noting the various lengths and formats the music is provided in.

▪ Project 4.6

Visit the web site for the Harry Fox Agency (www.harryfox.com) and check the licensing terms for different uses of musical compositions and recordings of music. Briefly describe the terms for using music for which you have created a performance, for using a recording of a piece of music in a multimedia program, and for selling a product that contains music. Identify differences in rates for use of music in different types of media (for example, using as part of a one-time presentation to a limited audience, using in a multimedia product for commercial release, and using as part of a radio or TV broadcast).

Animation

BY definition, animation makes static presentations come alive. It is visual change over time and can add great power to your multimedia projects and web pages. Many multimedia development and authoring applications for both Macintosh and Windows provide animation tools.

The Power of Motion

You can animate your whole project, or you can animate here and there, accenting and adding spice. For a brief product demonstration with little user interaction, it might make sense to design the entire project as a video and keep the presentation always in motion. For speaker support, you can animate bulleted text or fly it onto the screen, or you can use charts with quantities that grow or dwindle; then, give the speaker control of these eye-catchers. In a parts-assembly training manual, you might show components exploding into an expanded view.

Visual effects such as wipes, fades, zooms, and dissolves are available in most multimedia authoring packages, and some of these effects can be used for primitive animation. For example, you can slide images onto the screen with a wipe, or you can make an object implode with an iris/close effect. Figure 5-1 shows an example of fire effects that you might choose to add to your animation when using Corel's MotionStudio 3D.

But animation is more than wipes, fades, and zooms. Animation is an object actually moving across or *into* or *out of* the screen; a spinning globe of our earth; a car driving along a line-art highway; a bug crawling out from under a stack of papers, with a screaming voice from the speaker telling you to "Shoot it, now!" Until video became more commonplace (see Chapter 6), animations were the primary source of dynamic action in multimedia presentations.

WARNING   *Overuse of animation and annoying visual effects can ruin a multimedia project.*

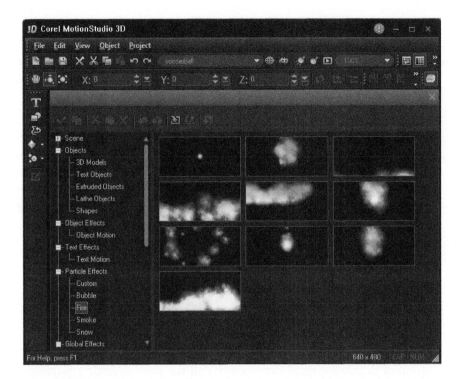

Figure 5-1 Many animation effects (such as fire, as shown here) can be added to your project using Corel's MotionStudio 3D.

Principles of Animation

Animation is possible because of a biological phenomenon known as persistence of vision and a psychological phenomenon called phi. In persistence of vision, an object seen by the human eye remains chemically mapped on the eye's retina for a brief time after viewing. Combined with the human mind's need (phi) to conceptually complete a perceived action, this makes it possible for a series of images that are changed very slightly and very rapidly, one after the other, to seemingly blend together into a visual illusion of movement. The illustration shows a few cels, or frames, of a rotating logo. When the images are progressively and rapidly changed, the arrow of the compass is perceived to be spinning.

Digital television video builds 24, 30, or 60 entire frames or pictures every second, depending upon settings; the speed with which each frame is replaced by the next one makes the images appear to blend smoothly into movement. Movies on film are typically shot at a shutter rate of 24 frames per second, but using projection tricks (the projector's shutter flashes light through each image twice), the flicker rate is increased to 48 times per second, and the human eye thus sees a motion picture. On some film projectors, each frame is shown three times before the pull-down claw moves to the next frame, for a total of 72 flickers per second, which helps to eliminate the flicker effect: the more interruptions per second, the more continuous the beam of light appears.

Quickly changing the viewed image is the principle of an animatic, a flip-book, or a zoetrope. To make an object travel across the screen while it changes its shape, just change the shape and also move, or **translate**, it a few pixels for each frame. Then, when you play the frames back at a faster speed, the changes blend together and you have motion and animation. It's the same magic as when the hand is quicker than the eye, and you don't see the pea moving in the blur of the sidewalk swindler's shells.

Animation by Computer

Using appropriate software and techniques, you can animate visual images in many ways. The simplest animations occur in two-dimensional (2-D) space; more complicated animations occur in an intermediate "2½-D" space (where shadowing, highlights, and forced perspective provide an illusion of depth, the third dimension); and the most realistic animations occur in three-dimensional (3-D) space.

In 2-D space, the visual changes that bring an image alive occur on the flat Cartesian x and y axes of the screen. A blinking word, a **color-cycling** logo (where the colors of an image are rapidly altered according to a formula), a cel animation (described more fully later in this chapter), or a button or tab that changes state on mouse rollover to let a user know it is active are all examples of **2-D animations**. These are simple and static, not changing their position on the screen. **Path animation** in 2-D space increases the complexity of an animation and provides motion, changing the location of an image along a predetermined path (position) during a specified amount of time (speed). Authoring and presentation software such as Flash or PowerPoint provide user-friendly tools to compute position changes and redraw an image in a new location, allowing you to generate a bouncing ball or slide a corporate mascot onto the screen. Combining changes in an image with changes in its position allows you to "walk" your corporate mascot onto the stage. Changing its size from small to large as it walks onstage will give you a 3-D perception of distance.

In **2½-D animation**, an illusion of depth (the z axis) is added to an image through shadowing and highlighting, but the image itself still rests on the flat x and y axes in two dimensions. Embossing, shadowing, beveling, and highlighting provide a sense of depth by raising an image or cutting it into a background. Zaxwerks' 3D Invigorator (www.zaxwerks .com), for example, provides 3-D effects for text and images and, while calling itself "3D," works within the 2-D space of image editors and drawing programs such as Illustrator, Fireworks, and After Effects from Adobe and PaintShop from Corel.

In **3-D animation**, software creates a virtual realm in three dimensions, and changes (motion) are calculated along all three axes (x, y, and z), allowing an image or object that itself is created with a front, back, sides, top, and bottom to move toward or away from the viewer, or, in this virtual space of light sources and points of view, allowing the viewer to wander around and get a look at all the object's parts from all angles. Such animations are typically rendered frame by frame by high-end 3-D animation programs such as NewTek's LightWave or Autodesk's Maya.

Today, computers have taken the handwork out of the animation and rendering process, and commercial films such as *Shrek*, *Coraline*, *Toy Story*, and *Avatar* have utilized the power of computers. (See Chapter 3 for an account of the historic "computer wall" of 117 Sun SPARCstations used to render the animated feature *Toy Story*.) As shown in the next illustration, most tools provide ready-made complex shapes and 3-D models to save time and effort.

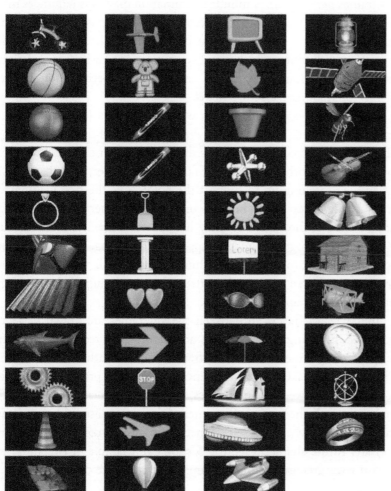

Animation Techniques

When you create an animation, organize its execution into a series of logical steps. First, gather up in your mind all the activities you wish to provide in the animation. If it is complicated, you should create a written script with a list of activities and required objects and then create a storyboard to visualize the animation. Choose the animation tool best suited for the job, and then build and tweak your sequences. This may include creating objects, planning their movements, texturing their surfaces, adding lights, experimenting with lighting effects, and positioning the camera or point of view. Allow plenty of time for this phase when you are experimenting and testing. Finally, post-process your animation, doing any special renderings and adding sound effects.

Cel Animation

The animation techniques made famous by Disney use a series of progressively different graphics or cels on each frame of movie film (which plays at 24 frames per second). A minute of animation may thus require as many as 1,440 separate frames, and each frame may be composed of many layers of cels. The term **cel** derives from the clear celluloid sheets that were used for drawing each frame, which have been replaced today by layers of digital imagery. Cels of famous animated cartoons have become sought-after, suitable-for-framing collector's items.

Cel animation artwork begins with **keyframes** (the first and last frame of an action). For example, when an animated figure of a woman walks across the screen, she balances the weight of her entire body on one foot and then the other in a series of falls and recoveries, with the opposite foot and leg catching up to support the body. Thus the first keyframe to portray a single step might be the woman pitching her body weight forward off the left foot and leg, while her center of gravity shifts forward; the feet are close together, and she appears to be falling. The last keyframe might be the right foot and leg catching the body's fall, with the center of gravity now centered between the outstretched stride and the left and right feet positioned far apart.

The series of frames in between the keyframes are drawn in a process called tweening. **Tweening** is an activity that requires calculating the number of frames between keyframes and the path the action takes, and then actually sketching with pencil the series of progressively different outlines. As tweening progresses, the action sequence is checked by flipping through the frames. The penciled frames are assembled and then actually filmed as a **pencil test** to check smoothness, continuity, and timing. Later in the chapter, Figure 5-5 shows an example of tweening; you can visit www.greensock.com/tweenmax/ for an online demo.

I grew up using cel techniques and a huge animation crane to photograph with. I can tell you the static electricity caused hell with dust on the cels. Do you know why most 2-D animated characters in the past, like Mickey Mouse, wore white gloves? It was an inside joke…We all wore white gloves to protect the cels! And the reason most animated characters had only three fingers and a thumb inside their gloves was because it saved us time and money to drop that extra finger.

Joe Silverthorn, Integrated Multimedia Professor, Olympic College

When the pencil frames are satisfactory, they are permanently inked, photocopied onto cels, and given to artists who use acrylic colors to paint the details for each cel. Women were often preferred for this painstaking inking and painting work as they were deemed patient, neat, and had great eyes for detail. In the hands of a master, cel paint applied to the back of acetate can be simply flat and perfectly even, or it can produce beautiful and subtle effects, with feathered edges or smudges.

The cels for each frame of our example of a walking woman—which may consist of a text title, a background, foreground, characters (with perhaps separate cels for a left arm, a right arm, legs, shoes, a body, and facial features)—are carefully registered and stacked. It is this composite that becomes the final photographed single frame in an animated movie. To replicate natural motion, traditional cel animators often utilized "motion capture" by photographing a woman walking, a horse trotting, or a cat jumping to help visualize timings and movements. Today, animators use reflective sensors applied to a person, animal, or other object whose motion is to be captured. Cameras and computers convert the precise locations of the sensors into x,y,z coordinates and the data is rendered into 3-D surfaces moving over time.

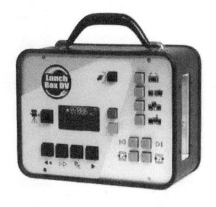

TIP *For experimenting with frame editing and timing, LunchBox DV from Animation Toolworks (www.animationtoolworks.com) requires only a video camera and a monitor to get started.*

Computer Animation

Computer animation programs typically employ the same logic and procedural concepts as cel animation and use the vocabulary of classic cel animation—terms such as layer, keyframe, and tweening. The primary difference among animation software programs is in how much must be drawn by the animator and how much is automatically generated by the software (see Figure 5-2). In path-based 2-D and 2½-D animation, an animator simply creates an object (or imports an object as clip art) and describes a path for the object to follow. The computer software then takes over, actually creating the animation on the fly as the program is being viewed. In cel-based 2-D animation, each frame of an animation is provided by the animator, and the frames are then stitched (usually with some tweening help available from the software) into a single file of images to be played in sequence. Creabit Development's GIF Animator (www.gif-animator .com) and Alchemy Mindworks' GIF Construction Set Professional (www .mindworkshop.com) simply string together your collection of frames.

For 3-D animation, most of your effort may be spent in creating the models of individual objects and designing the characteristics of their shapes and surfaces. It is the software that then computes the movement of the objects within the 3-D space and renders each frame, in the end stitching

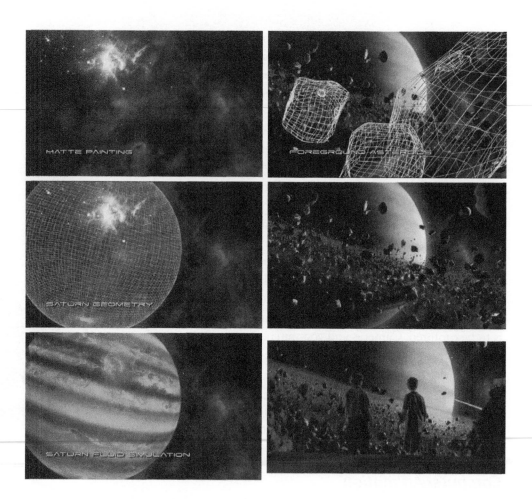

Figure 5-2 Several cels or digital image layers that have not yet been composited into a final frame from the movie *Zathura* (Columbia Pictures/Imageworks)

them together in a digital output file or container such as an AVI or Quick-Time movie. (See Chapter 6 for more information about video containers.)

On the computer, paint is most often filled or drawn with tools using features such as gradients and anti-aliasing. The word **inks**, in computer animation terminology, usually means special methods for computing color values, providing edge detection, and layering so that images can blend or otherwise mix their colors to produce special transparencies, inversions, and effects.

You can usually set your own frame rates on the computer. 2-D cel-based animated GIFs, for example, allow you to specify how long each frame is to be displayed and how many times the animation should loop before stopping. 3-D animations that are output as digital video files can be set to run at 15, 24, or 30 frames per second. However, the rate at which changes are computed and screens are actually refreshed will depend on the speed and power of your user's display platform and hardware, especially for animations such as path animations that are being generated by the computer on the fly. Although your animations will probably never push the limits of a monitor's scan rate (about 60 to 70 frames per second), animation does put raw computing horsepower to task. If you cannot compute all your changes and display them as a new frame on your monitor within, say, 1/15th of a second, then the animation may appear jerky and slow. Luckily, when the files include audio, the software maintains the continuity of the audio at all cost, preferring to drop visual frames or hold a single frame for several seconds while the audio plays.

TIP *The smaller the object in path-based 2-D animation, the faster it can move. Bouncing a 10-pixel-diameter tennis ball on your screen provides far snappier motion than bouncing a 150-pixel-diameter beach ball.*

3-D animations are typically delivered as "pre-rendered" digital video clips. Software such as Flash or PowerPoint, however, renders animations as they are being viewed, so the animation can be programmed to be interactive: touch or click on the jumping cat and it turns toward you, snarling; touch the walking woman and...

Kinematics   Kinematics is the study of the movement and motion of structures that have joints, such as a walking man. Animating a walking step is tricky: you need to calculate the position, rotation, velocity, and acceleration of all the joints and articulated parts involved—knees bend, hips flex, shoulders swing, and the head bobs. Smith Micro's Poser (http://poser.smithmicro .com), a 3-D modeling program, provides preassembled adjustable human models (male, female, infant, teenage, and superhero) in many poses, such as "walking" or "thinking." As you can see in Figure 5-3, you can pose figures in 3-D and then scale and manipulate individual body parts. Surface

Figure 5-3   Smith Micro's Poser understands human motion and inverse kinematics: move an arm, and the shoulders follow.

textures can then be applied to create muscle-bound hulks or smooth chrome androids. **Inverse kinematics**, available in high-end 3-D programs such as LightWave and Maya, is the process by which you link objects such as hands to arms and define their relationships and limits (for example, elbows cannot bend backward). Once those relationships and parameters have been set, you can then drag these parts around and let the computer calculate the result.

Morphing   Morphing is a popular (if not overused) effect in which one image transforms into another, as discussed in Chapter 3. Morphing applications and other modeling tools that offer this effect can transition not only between still images but often between moving images as well. Figure 5-4

Figure 5-4   Morphing software was used to seamlessly transform the 8-bit images of 16 kindergartners. When a sound track of music and voices was added to the four-minute piece, it made a compelling video about how similar children are to each other. Matching key points (red) in the start and end image guide each morphing transition.

illustrates part of a morph in which 16 kindergarten children are dissolved one into the other in a continuous, compelling motion video.

The morphed images were built at a rate of eight frames per second, with each transition taking a total of four seconds (32 separate images for each transition), and the number of key points was held to a minimum to shorten rendering time. Setting key points is crucial for a smooth transition between two images. The point you set in the start image will move to the corresponding point in the end image—this is important for things like eyes and noses, which you want to end up in about the same place (even if they look different) after the transition. The more key points, the smoother the morph. In Figure 5-4, the red dot on each child's temple is a matching key point.

Animation File Formats

Some file formats are designed specifically to contain animations, so they can be ported among applications and platforms with the proper translators. Those formats include Director (.dir and .dcr), AnimatorPro (.fli and .flc), 3D Studio Max (.max), GIF89a (.gif), and Flash (.fla and .swf). Because file size is a critical factor when downloading animations to play on web pages, file compression is an essential part of preparing animation files for the Web. A Director's native movie file (.dir), for example, must be preprocessed and compressed into a proprietary Shockwave animation file (.dcr) for the Web. Compression for Director movies is as much as 75 percent or more with this tool, turning 100K files into 25K files and significantly speeding up download/display times on the Internet. Flash, widely used for web-based animation, makes extensive use of vector graphics (see Chapter 3) to keep the post-compression file size at absolute minimums. As with Director, its native .fla files must be converted to Shockwave Flash files (.swf) in order to play on the Web. To view these animations within a web page, special plug-ins or players are required (see Chapter 6). COLLADA (Collaborative Design Activity) is an open source standard for passing 3-D animation files among applications. It uses the .dae file extension and is supported by many software tools.

In some cases, especially with 3-D animations, the individual rendered frames of an animation are put together into one of the standard digital video file containers, such as the Windows Audio Video Interleaved format (.avi), QuickTime (.qt, .mov), or Motion Picture Experts Group video (.mpeg or .mpg). These can be played using the media players shipped with computer operating systems.

Motion with SVG in HTML5

HTML5 can deliver in a browser animation built within an SVG (Scalable Vector Graphics) file, where graphic elements can be programmed to change over time (www.w3.org/TR/SVG11/animate.html). In the following simple code, a patch of red expands within a rectangle, filling it in three seconds. Type this code into a text processor and save it as plain text with a .svg extension. Open the file with File | Open from an HTML5-compliant web browser to see it work. Change some parameters (duration, colors, location) and reload or refresh it to see the effects of your changes.

```
<svg width="8cm" height="3cm" viewBox="0 0 800 300" xmlns="http://www.w3.org/2000/svg" version="1.1">
    <rect x="1" y="1" width="800" height="300" fill="none" stroke="rgb(255,0,255)" stroke-width="4" />
    <rect id="RectElement" x="300" y="100" width="300" height="100" fill="rgb(255,0,0)"  >
        <animate attributeName="x" attributeType="XML" begin="0s" dur="3s" fill="freeze" from="300" to="0" />
        <animate attributeName="y" attributeType="XML" begin="0s" dur="3s" fill="freeze" from="100" to="0" />
        <animate attributeName="width" attributeType="XML" begin="0s" dur="3s" fill="freeze" from="300" to="800" />
        <animate attributeName="height" attributeType="XML"
        begin="0s" dur="3s" fill="freeze" from="100" to="300" />
    </rect>
</svg>
```

Making Animations That Work

Animation catches the eye and makes things noticeable. But, like sound, animation quickly becomes trite if it is improperly applied. Unless your project has a backbone of movie-like, animated imagery, use animation carefully (and sparingly) like spice to achieve the greatest impact. Your screens may otherwise become busy and "noisy."

Multimedia authoring systems typically provide tools to simplify creating animations within that authoring system, and they often have a mechanism for playing the special animation files created by dedicated animation software. Although disabled in Apple's popular iOS, Adobe's Flash remains the most widely used tool for creating multimedia animations for Macintosh and Windows environments and for the Web. Flash directly supports several 2½-D features, including z-axis positioning, automatic sizing and perspective adjustment, and kinematics. External libraries can extend Flash's capabilities: open source Papervision3D (http://blog.papervision3d .org) provides extensive support for true 3-D modeling and animation. Figure 5-5 shows a very basic interactive demo for GreenSock's TweenLite (www.greensock. com/tweenmax), which provides sophisticated tweening capabilities in Flash.

Figure 5-5   Plug-ins for Flash can make tweening easier.

A Rolling Ball

First, create a new, blank image file that is 100×100 pixels, and fill it with a sphere.

Create a new layer in Photoshop, and place some white text on this layer at the center of the image.

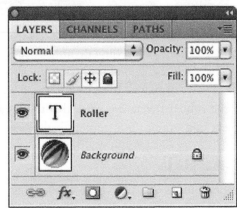

Make the text spherical using Photoshop's Spherize distortion filter, and save the result.

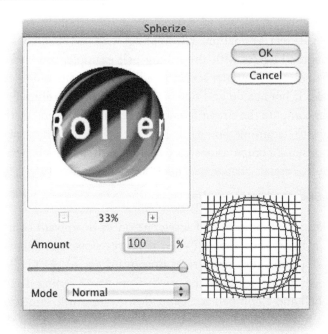

To animate the sphere by rolling it across the screen, you first need to make a number of rotated images of the sphere. Rotate the image in 45-degree increments to create a total of eight images, rotating a full circle of 360 degrees. When each is displayed sequentially at the same location, the sphere spins:

For a realistic rolling effect, the circumference (calculated at pi times 100, or about 314 pixels) is divided by 8 (yielding about 40 pixels). As each image is successively displayed, the ball is moved 40 pixels along a line. Being where the rubber meets the road, this math applies when you roll any round object in a straight line perpendicular to your line of sight.

A Bouncing Ball

With the simplest tools, you can make a bouncing ball to animate your web site using GIF89a, an image format that allows multiple images to be put into a single file and then displayed as an animation in a web browser or presentation program that recognizes the format. The individual frames that make up the **animated GIF** can be created in any paint or image-processing program, but it takes a specialized program to put the frames together into a GIF89a animation. (Animating with GIF89a files is discussed in Chapter 11.) As with the rolling ball example, you simply need to flash a ball on the computer screen rapidly and in a different place each time to make it bounce up and down. And as with the rolling ball, where you should compute the circumference of the ball and divide by the number of images to determine how far it rolls each time it flashes, there are some commonsense computations to consider with a bouncing ball, too. In the formula, *s* equals distance, *a* equals acceleration due to gravity, and *t* equals time:

$$s = \tfrac{1}{2} \, at^2$$

Gravity makes your bouncing ball accelerate on its downward course and decelerate on its upward course (when it moves slower and slower until it actually stops and then accelerates downward again). As Galileo discovered while dropping feathers and rocks from the Leaning Tower of Pisa, a beach ball and a golf ball accelerate downward at the same rate until they hit the ground. But the real world of Italy is full of air, so the feather falls gently while the rock pounds dirt. It is in this real world that you should compose your animations, tempering them always with commonsense physics to give them the ring of truth.

Unless your animation requires precision, ignore the hard numbers you learned in high school (like 32 feet per second per second), and simply figure that your ball will uniformly accelerate and decelerate up and down the pixels of your screen by the squares: 1, 4, 9, 16, 25, 36, 49, 64, 81, 100 are the squares of 1, 2, 3, 4, 5, 6, 7, 8, 9, and 10. This is illustrated in Figure 5-6. In the case of a perpetual-motion bouncing ball (even better than silly putty), it goes up the same way it comes down, forever, and this makes the job easy, because the up and down movements are symmetrical. You can use the same images for downward motion as you use for upward—as in frames 11 through 18 in Figure 5-6—by *reversing* them. You might also add a squash frame (not shown in Figure 5-6) when the ball hits the floor. The amount of squash would be determined by the type of ball—a steel ball or a balloon or a very soft rubber ball. The ball would squash when it hit and un-squash as it bounced up again. With a bit of programming, you might allow the user to choose the elasticity of the object, the amount of gravity, and the length of fall. Some animation software provides tools for this: it's called **easing**.

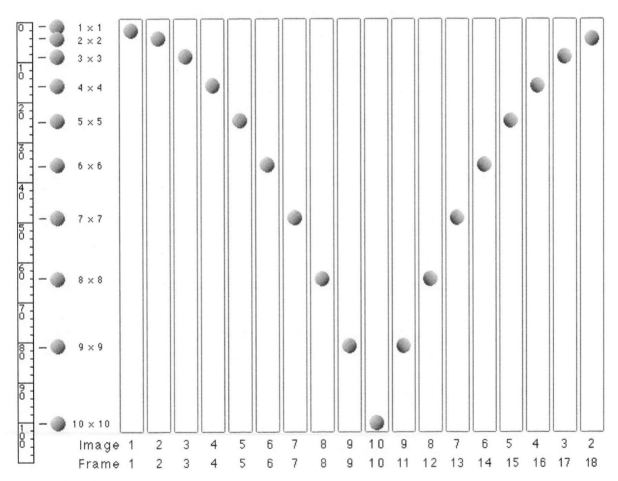

Figure 5-6 To make a bouncing ball seem natural, don't forget the acceleration effects of gravity. If you loop the 18 images shown here, the ball will bounce forever.

Open a graphics program and paint a ball about 15 pixels in diameter (if you have an odd-number diameter, there is a middle pixel that can be your center alignment point). If you wish to be fancy, make the ball with a 3-D graphics tool that will shade it as a sphere. Then duplicate the ball, placing each copy of it in a vertical line at the ten locations 1, 4, 9, 16, 25, 36, 49, 64, 81, and 100. The goal is to create a separate image file for each location of the ball, like the pages of a flip-book. With Photoshop, you can create a single file with ten layers to contain each ball at its proper location, and you can add an eleventh background layer, too. Then save each layer showing against the background as a separate file. (Use numbers in your filenames, like ball01, ball02, and so on, to keep them organized.)

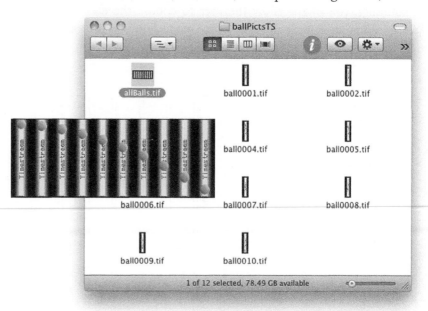

This is a construction process also easily managed with Director or Flash, in which you can place the same cast member or object (the ball) where you wish on the presentation stage.

You can also add a background and other art elements, and when you are done, you can export each frame as a graphics file using the export function. You will probably also wish to set the size of your stage to a small area just sufficient for your animation, say 32×120 pixels. The smaller the better if users will be downloading this animated GIF file into their web browsers.

To turn your collection of images into a GIF89a animation, you need an application like Stone Design's GIFfun (for Macintosh; see Figure 5-7) or Creabit's GIF Animator (for Windows) or online at www.gifmaker.me. These tools organize the sequence of images to be shown, set timing and transparency, and (most importantly) let you save the final GIF file in the proper format. See Chapter 11 for more details about animated GIF files and where to use them.

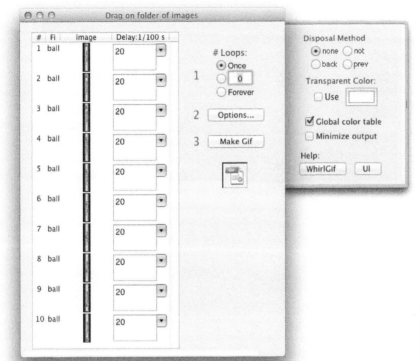

Figure 5-7   Many applications are available for Windows and Mac that will help build animated GIF files. Shown here is GIFfun for Mac, free from Stone Design (www.stone.com/GIFfun/), for organizing images and creating animations.

Creating an Animated Scene

A creative committee organized a brief storyboard of a gorilla chasing a man. From a stock library containing many images licensed for unlimited use, a photograph was chosen of Manhattan's Central Park where a bridge crossed a small river and high-rise apartments lined the horizon. The chase scene would occur across the bridge. To produce frames of the running man, a real actor was videotaped running in place against an Ultimatte chroma-keyed blue background in a studio; a few frames of this were grabbed, and the blue background was made transparent in each image. The gorilla was difficult to find, so a toy model dinosaur about 25 centimeters tall was used; again, a few frames were captured and the background made transparent to form a composite. That was all that was required for image resources.

As illustrated in Figure 5-8*a*, the background was carefully cut in half along the edge of the bridge, so that the bridge railing could be placed in front of the runners. The running man was organized in a series of six frames that could be repeated many times across the screen to provide the pumping motions of running. The same was done for the dinosaur, to give him a lumbering, bulky look as he chased the little man across the bridge (see Figure 5-8*b*). The result, in Figure 5-8*c*, was simple and quickly achieved.

Figure 5-8 (*a*) The upper portion of the photo was placed behind the runners (*b*) and the lower portion in front of them, to make them appear to run behind the bridge railing (*c*).

First Person

The animation storyboard called for a photorealistic monster chasing a running man through a city park amid screams of terror. The man was already in Director's cast, running in great strides across an arched footbridge in a woodsy scene with high-rises in the background; he even looked over his shoulder a few times in panic. We were scouting around for an effective Godzilla when a friend dropped by with a motorized, 12-inch Tyrannosaurus rex from Toys"R"Us. It was perfect—opening a toothy, gaping mouth every few steps as it lumbered along on C batteries.

I took the dinosaur and a video camera home to the delight and fascination of my three-year-old daughter, who helped rig a white sheet in front of the living room fireplace and a cardboard-box runway where Mr. TRex could strut his stuff before the camera. A couple of lamps gave him a sweaty sheen. We recorded about five minutes of video as my daughter happily retrieved Mr. TRex each time he nosed off the "cliff" at the end of the stage.

I grabbed a still image about every fourth frame of the recording and imported the resulting files into Director as cast members. They needed a little cleanup and scaling, but the fellow looked really convincing when he was finally scored to run across the bridge. Next day, I mixed a bunch of sounds—singing birds, running footsteps, screams, roars, sirens, and gunshots—and it was done.

Chapter 5 Review

◼ Chapter Summary

For your review, here's a summary of the important concepts discussed in this chapter.

Define animation and describe how it can be used in multimedia

- By definition, animation is the act of making something come alive.

- Depending on the size of the project, you can animate the whole thing or you can just animate parts of it.

- Visual effects such as wipes, fades, zooms, and dissolves, available in most authoring packages, are a simple form of animation.

- Animation is an object actually moving across, into, or out of the screen.

Discuss the principles of animation

- Animation is possible because of a biological phenomenon known as persistence of vision and a psychological phenomenon called phi.

- With animation, a series of images are changed very slightly and very rapidly, one after the other, seemingly blending together into a visual illusion of movement.

- Digital display video builds 24, 30, or 60 entire frames or pictures every second. Movies on film are typically shot at a shutter rate of 24 frames per second.

Discuss the animation techniques of cel and computer animation and choose the correct file types for animations

- Cel animation, an animation technique made famous by Disney, uses a series of progressively different graphics on each frame of movie film.

- Cel animation artwork begins with keyframes; these are the first and last frames of an action.

- Tweening is an activity that involves creating the frames to depict the action that happens between keyframes.

- Computer animation programs typically employ the same logic and procedural concepts as cel animation.

- You can usually set your own frame rates on the computer, but the rate at which changes are computed and screens are actually refreshed will depend on the speed and power of your display platform and hardware.

- Kinematics is the study of the movement and motion of structures that have joints.

- Inverse kinematics is the process in which you link objects such as hands to arms and define their relationships and limits, then drag these parts around and let the computer calculate the result.

- Morphing is an effect in which one image transforms into another.

- Some file formats are designed specifically to contain animations, and they can be ported among applications and platforms with the proper translators.

Create computer-generated animations from multiple still images

- Multimedia authoring systems typically provide tools to simplify creating animations within that authoring system.

- The most widely used tool for creating multimedia animations for Macintosh and Windows environments is Adobe's Flash.

- With the simplest tools, you can make a bouncing ball to animate your web site using GIF89a.

- Making animations appear natural requires a basic understanding of the principles of physics. You should compose your animations using these principles, tempering them always with common-sense physics to give them the ring of truth.

■ Key Terms

2-D animation *(146)*
2½-D animation *(146)*
3-D animation *(147)*
animated GIF *(156)*
animation *(144)*
cel *(148)*
cel animation *(148)*

color cycling *(146)*
easing *(157)*
inks *(150)*
inverse kinematics *(152)*
keyframes *(148)*
kinematics *(151)*
morphing *(152)*

path animation *(146)*
pencil test *(148)*
persistence of vision *(145)*
phi *(145)*
translate *(146)*
tweening *(148)*

■ Key Term Quiz

1. An object seen by the human eye remains chemically mapped on the retina for a brief time after viewing. This phenomenon is called _____.

2. The human mind needs to conceptually complete a perceived action. This phenomenon is called _____.

3. To make an object travel across the screen while it changes its shape, just change the shape and also move or _____ it a few pixels for each frame.

4. The animation technique made famous by Disney involves showing a different image for each frame. This technique is called _____.

5. The first and last frames of an action are called _____.

6. The series of frames in between the first and last frames in an action are drawn in a process called _____.

7. In computer animation terminology, _____ usually refers to special methods that allow images to blend or otherwise mix their colors to produce special transparencies, inversions, and effects.

8. The study of the movement and motion of structures that have joints is called _____.

9. The effect in which one image transforms into another is known as _____.

■ Multiple-Choice Quiz

1. Most authoring packages include visual effects such as:
   a. panning, zooming, and tilting
   b. wipes, fades, zooms, and dissolves
   c. morphing
   d. tweening
   e. inverse kinematics

2. The term cel derives from:
   a. the concept of each action in a sequence being a separate element or "cell"
   b. the fact that the inks used in early animations were based on extracts from celery plants
   c. an abbreviation of the phrase "composite element"
   d. the fact that the first animations were the work of communist dissidents who were organized into cells
   e. the clear celluloid sheets that were used for drawing each frame

3. Which of these is *not* a reason why animation is perceived as motion?
   a. An image remains in the eye chemically for a brief time after viewing.
   b. Our mind tries to "connect the dots" by completing perceived actions.
   c. The use of darker colors for moving objects is interpreted by the mind as motion.
   d. A sequence of images is read as continuous motion.
   e. All of the above are valid reasons.

4. Movies on film are typically shot at a shutter rate of:
   a. 15 frames per second
   b. 24 frames per second
   c. 29.97 frames per second
   d. 30 frames per second
   e. 48 frames per second

5. The clear sheets that were used for drawing each frame of animation have been replaced today by:
   a. acetate or plastic
   b. titanium
   c. fiberglass
   d. epoxy resin
   e. digital paper

6. Today's computer animation programs most closely resemble:
   a. film "rotoscoping" techniques
   b. the "phi" phenomenon described by Carl Jung
   c. neuro-kinetics techniques pioneered by NASA
   d. traditional cel animation
   e. none of the above

7. The technical limitation you are likely to encounter in creating animations is:
   a. the monitor's refresh rate
   b. the computer's processing capability
   c. the ability to accurately calculate physical actions
   d. the "persistence of vision" phenomenon
   e. the monitor's color gamut

8. In general, the animation may appear jerky and slow if each frame is displayed for more than about:
   a. 1/30 of a second
   b. 1/15 of a second
   c. 1/4 of a second
   d. 1/2 of a second
   e. 1 second

9. The process in which you link objects such as hands to arms and define their relationships and limits (for example, elbows cannot bend backward), then drag these parts around and let the computer calculate the result is called:
   a. rotoscoping
   b. de-morphing
   c. meta-articulation
   d. cyber-motion
   e. inverse kinematics

10. To create a smooth transition between two images when morphing, it's important to set numerous:
    a. layers
    b. keyframes
    c. key points
    d. anchor tags
    e. splines

11. The standard frame rate of computer animations is:
    a. 10 frames per second
    b. 15 frames per second
    c. 24 frames per second
    d. 30 frames per second
    e. There is no standard; it depends on the file's settings.

12. Today, the most widely used tool for creating vector-based animations is:
    a. Adobe's Flash
    b. Adobe's GoLive
    c. Corel's CorelDraw
    d. Microsoft's KineMatix
    e. Activa's InterStudio

13. A COLLADA file format has which extension?
    a. .dae
    b. .fli or .flc
    c. .avi
    d. .qt or .mov
    e. .mpeg or .mpg

14. The file format that is most widely supported for web animations is:
    a. PICT
    b. .DCR
    c. GIF89a
    d. JPEG
    e. AIFF

15. To keep the post-compression file size at absolute minimums, Flash makes extensive use of:
    a. inverse kinematics
    b. cel-type animation
    c. vector graphics
    d. inks
    e. NURBS

■ Essay Quiz

1. Discuss the physical and psychological principles as to why animation works, as well as how it is usually presented.

2. Briefly discuss the origins of cel animation and the concepts that go into creating these animations. Be sure to include keyframes, tweening, and inks.

3. You need to create a simple animation of an animated logo. The logo depicts a planet orbiting the sun. Describe the motion in a storyboard. List the points in the action that would make good keyframes, and explain why. How would you need to manipulate the planet to make its motion look natural?

4. You need to create a simple animation of a man bowling, with the ball rolling down the alley, and striking the pins. Describe the sequence of motions in a storyboard. Discuss the various techniques and principles you might employ to accurately represent the motion of the man moving, the ball rolling, and the pins falling.

5. Discuss where and how you might use animation in one of the following projects. Be creative. Where would animation be appropriate? Where would it be distracting? How could it best be used to visually illustrate a concept?
    a. A web site for sports car enthusiasts
    b. A presentation to shareholders of a financial report
    c. A training CD on using a printing press
    d. A DVD that depicts the history of a railroad

Lab Projects

■ Project 5.1

Sketch a short storyboard showing the brief animation of a stick figure. Identify which keyframes should be included as the figure moves. Keep the sequence short and simple but include at least five keyframes.

■ Project 5.2

Install the free animation program Aseprite (www.aseprite.org/) and start a new file. Familiarize yourself with the drawing tools, including Line, Blur, and Paint Bucket. Draw the first frame of an animated stick figure. From the menu bar, choose Frame | New and then draw the second frame of your animation. In this way, draw five to ten frames and export your work as a GIF file. Open this file in a browser to play it.

■ Project 5.3

Pick an animation software package available for either the Macintosh or Windows that offers at least one form of animation (for example, 2-D cel animation, animated GIF, or 3-D animation). List its name and discuss its capabilities. Is the software capable of layers? Keyframes? Tweening? Morphing? Will it allow you to create cross-platform files for playback? Does it require a plug-in for viewing in a web browser?

■ Project 5.4

If not still available on your computer from Lab Project 3.4, download and install the 3-D modeling application SketchUp (www.sketchup.com/). Create a cube shape using the Rectangle and Push/Pull tools. On the menu bar, choose Window | Scenes to open the Scenes Manager. Use the Orbit tool to rotate your view. Next, click the Add Scene (+) button to add a new scene. Right-click on the "Scene 1" tab on the top left and select Play Animation from the context menu; your camera view should automatically shift between the two views you created. Export your animation as video (File | Export | Animation | Video) and play it.

Video

SINCE the first silent film flickered to life, people have been fascinated with "motion" pictures. To this day, motion video is the element of multimedia that can draw gasps from a crowd at a trade show or firmly hold a student's interest in a computer-based learning project. Digital video is the most engaging of multimedia venues, and it is a powerful tool for bringing computer users closer to the real world. It is also an excellent method for delivering multimedia to an audience raised on television. With video elements in your project, you can effectively present your messages and reinforce your story, and viewers tend to retain more of what they see. But take care! Video that is not thought out or well produced can degrade your presentation.

Using Video

Carefully planned, well-executed video clips can make a dramatic difference in a multimedia project. A clip of Mahatma Gandhi proclaiming "An eye for an eye only ends up making the whole world blind" in video and sound is more compelling than a scrolling text field containing that same speech. Before deciding whether to add video to your project, however, it is essential to have an understanding of the medium, its limitations, and its costs. This chapter provides a foundation to help you understand how video works, the different formats and standards for recording and playing video, and the differences between computer and television video. It also covers the equipment needed to shoot and edit video, as well as tips for adding video to your project.

Video standards and formats are still being refined as transport, storage, compression, and display technologies take shape in laboratories and in the marketplace and while equipment and post-processing evolves from its analog beginnings to become fully digital, from capture to display. Working with multimedia video today can be like a camping trip in the desert: you may pitch your tent on comfortable high ground and find that overnight the shifting sands have buried both your approach and your investment.

In this chapter, you will learn how to:

- Consider the implications of using digital video in multimedia

- Discuss analog and digital video technologies and displays

- Work with digital video containers and codecs to select the best video recording formats for multimedia projects

- Find and acquire video clips

- Shoot and edit video for use in multimedia

Of all the multimedia elements, video places the highest performance demand on your computer or device—and its memory and storage. Consider that a high-quality color still image on a computer screen could require as much as 1 megabyte (MB) or more of storage memory. Multiply this by 30—the number of times per second that the picture is replaced to provide the appearance of motion—and you would need at least 30MB of storage to play your video for one second, more than 1.8 gigabytes (GB) of storage to play your video for a minute, and 108GB or more to play your video for an hour. Just moving all this picture data from computer memory to the screen at that rate would challenge the processing capability of a supercomputer. Some of the hottest and most arcane multimedia technologies and research efforts have dealt with compressing digital video image data into manageable streams of information. Compression (and decompression), using special software called a codec (see "Codecs" later in the chapter), allows a massive amount of imagery to be squeezed into a comparatively small data file, which can still deliver a good viewing experience on the intended viewing platform during playback.

If you control the delivery platform for your multimedia project, you can specify special hardware and software enhancements that will allow you to work with high-definition, full-motion video, and sophisticated audio for high-quality surround sound. Or you can design a project to meet a specific compression standard, such as MPEG2 for **Digital Versatile Disc (DVD)** playback or MPEG4 (MP4) for home video or Flash (FLV) for the Internet. You can install a superfast **RAID (Redundant Array of Independent Disks)** system that will support high-speed data transfer rates. You can include instructions in your authoring system that will spool video clips into RAM, ready for high-speed playback *before* they need to play. Having control of the playback platform is always good, but it is seldom available in the real world, so as you develop your video elements, you will need to make many choices and compromises based upon your assessment of the "lowest common denominator" playback platform where your project will be used.

How Video Works and Is Displayed

When light reflected from an object passes through a video camera lens, that light is converted into an electronic signal by a special sensor called a **charge-coupled device (CCD)** or a **complementary metal-oxide semiconductor (CMOS) image sensor**. High-end video (and photographic) equipment uses CCD technology. Smartphones and tablets use CMOS technology because the power drain is 100 times less and CMOS technology is cheaper to manufacture than CCD technology. But CMOS devices are more susceptible to noise and less sensitive to light. Top-quality broadcast cameras and even camcorders may have as many as three CCDs

> Since multimedia gives you the ability to present information in a variety of ways, let the content drive the selection of media for each chunk of information to be presented. Use traditional text and graphics where appropriate; add animation when "still life" won't get your message across; add audio when further explanation is required; resort to video only when all other methods pale by comparison.
>
> David A. Ludwig, Interactive Learning Designs

(one for each color of red, green, and blue) to enhance the resolution of the camera and the quality of the image.

It's important to understand the difference between analog and digital video. Analog video has a resolution measured in the number of horizontal scan lines (due to the nature of early cathode-tube cameras), but each of those lines represents continuous measurements of the color and brightness along the horizontal axis, in a linear signal that is analogous to an audio signal. Digital video signals, on the other hand, consist of a discrete color and brightness value for each pixel on the screen. The more pixels, the higher the resolution.

For some multimedia projects, you may need to digitize legacy analog video. The following discussion will help you understand the differences between analog and digital video and the old and new standards for horizontal lines, aspect ratios, and interlacing.

Analog Video

In an analog system, the output of the CCD is processed by the camera into three channels of color information and synchronization pulses (sync) and the signals are recorded onto magnetic tape. There are several video standards for managing analog CCD output, each dealing with the amount of separation between the components—the more separation of the color information, the higher the quality of the image (and the more expensive the equipment). If each channel of color information is transmitted as a separate signal on its own conductor, the signal output is called **component** (separate red, green, and blue channels), which is the preferred method for higher-quality and professional analog video work. Lower in quality is the signal that makes up **Separate Video (S-Video)**, using two channels that carry luminance and chrominance information. The least separation (and thus the lowest quality for a video signal) is **composite**, when all the signals are mixed together and carried on a single cable as a composite of the three color channels and the sync signal. The composite signal yields less-precise color definition, which cannot be manipulated or color-corrected as much as S-Video or component signals.

The analog video and audio signals are written to tape by a spinning recording head that changes the local magnetic properties of the tape's surface in a series of long diagonal stripes. Because the head is canted or tilted at a slight angle compared with the path of the tape, it follows a helical (spiral) path, which is called **helical scan** recording. As illustrated in Figure 6-1, each stripe represents information for one field of a video frame. A single video frame is made up of two fields that are interlaced (described in detail later in the chapter). Audio is recorded on a separate straight-line track at the top of the videotape, although with some recording systems (notably for 3/4-inch tape and for 1/2-inch tape with high-fidelity audio), sound is recorded helically between the video tracks. At the bottom of

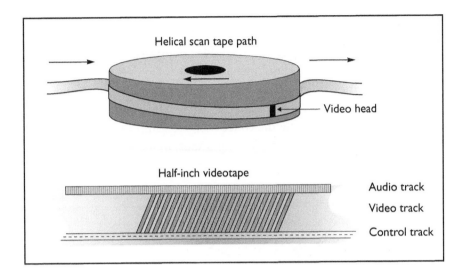

Helical scan tape path

Video head

Half-inch videotape

Audio track

Video track

Control track

Figure 6-1   Diagram of tape path across the video head for analog recording

the tape is a control track containing the pulses used to regulate speed. Tracking is a fine adjustment of the tape during playback so that the tracks are properly aligned as the tape moves across the playback head. These are the signals your grandmother's VCR reads when you rent *Singing in the Rain* (on video cassette) for the weekend.

Some consumer set-top devices like video cassette recorders (VCRs), cable and satellite receivers add the video and sound signals to a subcarrier and modulate them into a radio frequency (RF) in the FM broadcast band. This is the RF signal available at the Antenna Out connector of a cable box or a VCR and, depending on the geographical location, conforms to one of the three analog broadcast video standards commonly in use around the world: National Television Standards Committee (NTSC), Phase Alternate Line (PAL), and Sequential Color and Memory (SECAM). Usually the signal is modulated on either Channel 3 or Channel 4, and the resulting signal is demodulated by the TV receiver and displayed on the selected channel. An analog video cassette recorded in the United States (which uses the NTSC standard) will not play on a television set in any European country (which uses either PAL or SECAM), even though the recording method and style of the cassette is "VHS." Likewise, tapes recorded in European PAL or SECAM formats will not play back on an NTSC video cassette recorder. Each system is based on a different standard that defines the way information is encoded to produce the electronic signal that ultimately creates a television picture.

Television sets today usually provide a composite signal connector and an S-Video connector to connect to legacy analog devices, but typically they rely on a High-Definition Multimedia Interface (HDMI) connector for purely digital input. Displays for computers typically provide analog component (red, green, blue) input through a 15-pin VGA connector and also a purely digital component input through a Digital Visual Interface (DVI) connector and/or an HDMI connection.

Digital Video

In digital systems, the output of the CCD is digitized by the camera into a sequence of single frames, and the video and audio data are compressed before being written to a tape (see Figure 6-2) or digitally stored to disc or flash memory in one of several proprietary and competing formats. Digital video data formats, especially the codec used for compressing and decompressing video (and audio) data, are important; more about them later in this chapter.

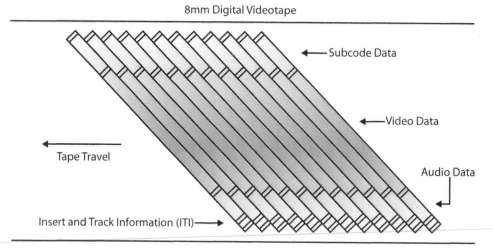

Figure 6-2   Diagram of tape path across the video head for digital recording

In 1995, Apple's FireWire technology was standardized as IEEE 1394, and Sony quickly adopted it for much of its digital camera line under the name i.Link. FireWire and i.Link (and USB 2) cable connections allow a completely digital, tape-free process, from the camera's CCD or CMOS sensor to the hard disk of a computer; and camcorders store the video and sound data on an onboard digital tape, writable mini-DVD, mini–hard disk, or flash memory.

HDTV

In the 1980s and 1990s broadcast television evolved from an analog standard to a digital standard. The new standards provided TV broadcasters with sufficient bandwidth to present four or five Standard Television (**STV**, providing the NTSC's resolution of 525 lines with a 3:4 aspect ratio, but in a digital signal) signals or one HDTV signal (providing 1,080 lines of resolution with a movie screen's 16:9 aspect ratio).

HDTV (High Definition Television) provides high resolution in a **16:9** aspect ratio (see Figure 6-3). This aspect ratio allows the viewing of Cinemascope and Panavision movies. There was contention between the broadcast and computer industries about whether to use interlacing or progressive-scan technologies (described in the next section). The broadcast

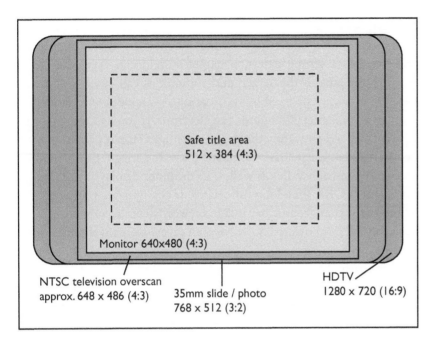

Safe title area
512 x 384 (4:3)

Monitor 640x480 (4:3)

NTSC television overscan
approx. 648 x 486 (4:3)

35mm slide / photo
768 x 512 (3:2)

HDTV
1280 x 720 (16:9)

Figure 6-3   Here you can see the difference between VGA and HDTV aspect ratios.

industry promulgated an ultra-high-resolution, 1920×1080 interlaced format (1080i) to become the cornerstone of the new generation of high-end entertainment centers, but the computer industry wanted a 1280×720 progressive-scan system (720p) for HDTV. While the 1080i (1920×1080) format provides more pixels than the 720p (1280×720 pixels) standard, the refresh rates are quite different. The higher-resolution interlaced format delivers only half the picture every 1/60 of a second, and because of the interlacing, on highly detailed images there is a great deal of screen flicker at 30 Hz. The computer people argued that the picture quality at 1280×720 pixels is superior and steady. Both formats have been included in the international HDTV standards, and, indeed, **1080p** (progressive scan, not interleaved 1080i) is the top of the line.

TIP   In a high-definition TV smaller than about 40 inches, there is little noticeable difference among the three main high-definition resolutions, 1080p, 1080i, and 720p. In larger screen sizes, however, there are noticeable differences: 1080p is the best.

Displays

Colored phosphors on a **cathode ray tube (CRT)** screen glow red, green, or blue when they are energized by an electron beam. Because the intensity of the beam varies as it moves across the screen, some colors glow brighter than others. Finely tuned magnets around the picture tube aim the electrons precisely onto the phosphor screen, while the intensity of the beam is varied according to the video signal. This is why you needed to keep speakers (which have strong magnets in them) away from a CRT screen. A strong external magnetic field can skew the electron beam to one area of the screen and sometimes can cause a permanent blotch that cannot be fixed by **degaussing**—an electronic process that readjusts the magnets that guide the electrons. If you had the misfortune to forget and wear a watch, the degausser might stop it permanently and then, if you are particularly unlucky, erase the magnetic strips on the credit cards in your wallet as well. If a computer displays a still image or words onto a CRT for a long time without changing, the phosphors will permanently change, and the image or words can become visible, even when the CRT is powered down. Screen savers were invented to prevent this from happening.

Flat screen displays are all-digital, using either **liquid crystal display (LCD)**, **light-emitting diode (LED)**, or **plasma** technologies, and have supplanted CRTs for computer use. Some professional video producers and studios, however, still prefer CRTs to flat screen displays, claiming colors are brighter and more accurately reproduced.

Full integration of digital video in cameras and on computers eliminates the analog television form of video, from both the multimedia production and the delivery platform. If your video camera generates a digital output signal, you can record your video direct-to-disc, where it is ready for editing. If a video clip is stored as data on a hard disk, CD-ROM, DVD, thumb-drive, or other mass-storage device, that clip can be played back on a computer's display without special hardware.

Interlacing and Progressive Scan

The process of building a single frame from two fields is called **interlacing**, a technique that helps to prevent flicker on CRT screens. Computer displays use a different **progressive-scan** technology, and draw the lines of an entire frame in a single pass, without interlacing them and without flicker. In television CRTs, the electron beam actually makes two passes on the screen as it draws a single video frame, first laying down all the odd-numbered lines, then all the even-numbered lines, as they are interlaced. On a computer display, lines are painted one-pixel thick and are not interlaced. Single-pixel lines displayed on a computer screen look fine; on a television, these thin lines flicker brightly because they only appear in every other field. To prevent this flicker on CRTs, make sure your lines are greater than two pixels thick and that you avoid typefaces that are very thin or have elaborate serifs. If you are capturing images from a video signal, you can filter them through a de-interlacing filter provided by image-editing applications such as Photoshop or Fireworks. With typefaces, interlacing flicker can often be avoided by anti-aliasing the type to slightly blur the edges of the characters. The term "interlacing" has a different meaning on the Web, where it describes the progressive display of lines of pixels as image data is downloaded, giving the impression that the image is coming from blurry into focus as increasingly more data arrives.

Most computers today provide video outputs to CRT, LCD, LED, or plasma displays at greater than 1024×768 resolution. Table 6-1 describes the various aspect ratios and width/heights in pixels used by computer displays since IBM's VGA standard was adopted in 1987. The VGA's once ubiquitous 640×480 screen resolution is again becoming common for handheld and mobile device displays.

Acronym	Name	Aspect Ratio	Width (pixels)	Height (pixels)
VGA	Video Graphics Array	4:3	640	480
SVGA	Super Video Graphics Array	4:3	800	600
XGA	eXtended Graphics Array	4:3	1024	768
XGA+	eXtended Graphics Array Plus	4:3	1152	864
WXGA	Widescreen eXtended Graphics Array	5:3	1280	768
WXGA	Widescreen eXtended Graphics Array	8:5 (16:10)	1280	800
SXGA	Super eXtended Graphics Array	4:3	1280	960
SXGA	Super eXtended Graphics Array	5:4	1280	1024
HD	High Definition (Basic)	16:9	1366	768
WSXGA	Widescreen Super eXtended Graphics Array	8:5 (16:10)	1440	900
HD+	High Definition (Plus)	16:9	1600	900
UXGA	Ultra eXtended Graphics Array	4:3	1600	1200
WSXGA+	Widescreen Super eXtended Graphics Array Plus	8:5 (16:10)	1680	1050
HD-1080	Full High Definition	16:9	1920	1080
WUXGA	Widescreen Ultra eXtended Graphics Array	8:5 (16:10)	1920	1200

Table 6-1 Screen Resolutions for Computer Displays

In the realm of **digital television (DTV)** displays, Table 6-2 shows the most common screen resolutions. Note that the highest resolution, 1080p, does not include a 60-per-second frame refresh rate. When the original digital standards were written in the early 1990s, that was simply too fast for the broadcast digital signal to keep up. Not shown is the 720×576 resolution used in PAL systems.

Scan Lines from Top to Bottom	Pixels from Left to Right	Aspect Ratio	Display Rate in Frames per Second
1080p (progressive)	1920	16:9	30, 24
1080i (interlaced)	1920	16:9	30
720p (progressive)	1280	16:9	60, 30, 24
480p (progressive)	704 or 640	16:9 or 4:3	60, 30, 24
480i (interlaced)	704 or 640	16:9 or 4:3	30

Table 6-2   Common Digital Television Resolutions

Overscan and the Safe Title Area

As illustrated earlier in Figure 6-3, it is common practice in the television industry to broadcast an image larger than will fit on a standard TV screen so that the "edge" of the image seen by a viewer is always bounded by the TV's physical frame, or bezel. This is called **overscan**. In contrast, computer displays show a smaller image on the display's picture tube (**underscan**), leaving a black border inside the bezel. Consequently, when a digitized video image is displayed on a CRT or television, there is a border around the image; and, when a computer screen is converted to video, the outer edges of the image will not fit on a TV screen. Only about 360 of the 480 lines of the computer screen will be visible. Video-editing software often will show you the safe areas while you are editing.

TIP   Avoid using the outer 15 percent of the screen when producing computer-generated graphics and titles for use in television video. The safe title area, where your image will not be affected by overscanning, even in the worst conditions, is illustrated in Figure 6-3.

Digital Video Containers

A digital video architecture is made up of an algorithm for compressing and encoding video and audio, a container in which to put the compressed data, and a player that can recognize and play back those files. Common containers for video are Ogg (.ogg, Theora for video, Vorbis for audio), Flash video (.flv), MPEG (.mp4), QuickTime (.mov), Windows Media Format (.wmv), WebM (.webm), and RealMedia (.rm). Containers may include audio and video data compressed by a choice of codecs, and media players may recognize and play back more than one video file container format.

Container formats may also include metadata—important information about the tracks contained in them—and even additional media besides audio and video. The QuickTime container, for example, allows inclusion of text tracks, chapter markers, transitions, and even interactive sprites. Totally Hip's LiveStage Professional (www.totallyhip.com/livestage.html) is an authoring tool that can produce interactive multimedia self-contained within a single QuickTime .mov container.

Codecs

To digitize and store a 10-second clip of full-motion video in your computer requires transfer of an enormous amount of data in a very short amount of time. Reproducing just one frame of digital video component video at 24 bits requires almost 1MB of computer data; 30 seconds of full-screen, uncompressed video will fill 1GB of hard disk. Full-size, full-motion uncompressed video requires that the computer deliver data at about 30MB per second. This overwhelming technological bottleneck is overcome using digital video compression schemes or **codecs** (*co*ders/*dec*oders). A codec is the algorithm used to compress a video for delivery and then decode it in real time for fast playback. Different codecs are optimized for different methods of delivery (for example, from a hard drive, from a DVD, or over the Web). Codecs such as **Theora** and H.264 compress digital video information at rates that range from 50:1 to 200:1. Some codecs store only the image data that changes from frame to frame instead of the data that makes up each and every individual frame. Other codecs use computation-intensive methods to predict what pixels will change from frame to frame and store the predictions to be deconstructed during playback. These are all lossy codecs where image quality is (somewhat) sacrificed to significantly reduce file size.

MPEG

The MPEG standards were developed by the **Moving Picture Experts Group** (**MPEG**, www.mpeg.org), a working group convened by the International Organization for Standardization (ISO) and the International Electro-technical Commission (IEC), which created standards for the digital representation of moving pictures as well as associated audio and other data. Using **MPEG-1** (specifications released in 1992), you could deliver 1.2 Mbps (megabits per second) of video and 250 Kbps (kilobits per second) of two-channel stereo audio using CD-ROM technology. **MPEG-2** (specifications released in 1994), a completely different system from MPEG-1, required higher data rates (3 to 15 Mbps) but also delivered higher image resolution, improved picture quality, interlaced video formats, multiresolution scalability, and multichannel audio features. MPEG-2 became the video compression standard required for digital television and for making DVDs.

The MPEG specifications since MPEG-2 include elements beyond just the encoding of video. As a container, **MPEG-4** (specifications released in 1998 and 1999) provides a content-based method for assimilating multimedia elements. It offers indexing, hyperlinking, querying, browsing, uploading, downloading, and deleting functions, as well as "hybrid natural and synthetic data coding," which will enable harmonious integration of natural and synthetic audiovisual objects. With MPEG-4, multiple views, multiple layers, and multiple sound tracks of a scene, as well as stereoscopic and 3-D views, are available, making virtual reality workable. MPEG-4 can adjust to varied download speeds, making it an attractive option for delivery of video on the Web. The MPEG-4 AVC standard (Advanced Video Coding, Part 10) requires the H.264 codec for Blu-ray discs.

Because the software behind MPEG-4 is patented by more than two dozen companies, developers who build video editors and players that read and write MPEG-4 files must purchase licenses and make royalty payments.

The Codec Wars

The high bit rate requirements of video and the (relatively) low bit rates available from CD-ROMs, and later from the Web, have led to a long and occasionally confusing progression in the development of codecs. Generally, the greater the compression, the more processing "horsepower" (and waiting time) is needed to compress and decompress the video. So only relatively new computers are capable of decompressing highly compressed video at a rate that can keep up with the video data stream. Using the best or "latest" codecs in your project is a good idea, but it must be balanced by ensuring that the video will play on the widest range of platforms.

Unencumbered by licensing and royalty fees, and supported by many but not all implementations of the HTML5 browsers' <video> tag (see Chapter 11), an Ogg container with the Theora video codec and the Vorbis audio codec is both platform independent and widely available, particularly within free and open-source video-editing software. At one point in the development of the HTML5 specification, Ogg (using Theora and Vorbis codecs) was the video container required to be available in all compliant browsers, thus providing a single video format web developers could count on. But some manufacturers complained that their own favored (but proprietary and patented) codecs worked better and no container should be specified at all. To the consternation of the open-source and web developer community, midway through the evolution of the draft HTML5 spec the language was changed from effectively requiring all compliant browsers to support at minimum Ogg Theora video and Ogg Vorbis audio, as well as the Ogg container format, to simply *suggesting* that browsers support the same codecs, thus leaving standardization of the <video> containers and codecs in limbo (see Table 6-3).

The Flash video container, which uses the older VP6 and a newer H.263 codec (depending upon version), is used by YouTube and at many

My client had just completed a production run of 5,000 CDs containing my project for them. I was pretty proud of it: it had a 3D fly-in opening, integrated testing, Flash elements, customizable printing, the ability to save paths through the program. I thought I had thoroughly tested the golden master. But late in development I had changed the audio codec in three of the video clips and, sure enough, the audio wouldn't play on the Macintosh on those three clips. The client tossed the production run. I was a victim of the killer codec.

Brad Borch, Activa Design

Browser	MP4	WebM	Ogg
Internet Explorer	Yes	No	No
Chrome	Yes	Yes	Yes
Firefox	No on Macintosh	Yes	Yes
	Yes on Windows and Android		
Safari	Yes	No	No
Opera	No	Yes	Yes

Table 6-3 Not All HTML5 Video Containers and Their Codecs Are Recognized As Playable by All Browsers

web sites but requires the Flash plug-in to be installed in the user's browser. For playing WMV containers, Macintosh computers require installing the Silverlight plug-in, a Microsoft development framework similar to Flash. The H.264 codec was developed by the Moving Picture Experts Group, is patented and proprietary, and is required on Blu-ray discs and used by YouTube, iTunes, and some broadcast services. Google's open-source VP8 codec works within the WebM container (www.webmproject.org), and was launched as an effort to replace Flash and H.264 on the Web. Google has re-encoded all its Flash holdings at YouTube to work with WebM and VP8 as well as with the H.264 codec.

Because of this codec and container war, for web developers wishing to place video elements onto their pages, programming with the HTML5 <video> tag (which was supposed to simplify and standardize inclusion of video at web sites) remains as complicated as ever (see Table 6-3). This is a constantly changing area of development, so check these browsers from time to time to see which codecs and containers are currently supported:

Chrome: www.chromium.org/

Safari: www.apple.com/safari/

Internet Explorer: http://ie.microsoft.com/testdrive/

Opera: www.opera.com/

Firefox: www.mozilla.com/

A discussion of the HTML5 <video> tag can be found in Chapter 11 along with snippets of code for launching your video using HTML5.

Video Format Converters

Be prepared to produce more than one version of your video (codecs in a container) to ensure that the video will play on all the devices and in all the browsers necessary for your project's distribution. DVD video uses

MPEG-2 compression. Blu-ray video uses MPEG-4 AVC compression. These are known standards and few choices are necessary: simply click "Save for DVD" or "Save for Blu-ray." But if you need to prepare a video file that will run on an iPod/iPad, a Droid, and an Atom-based tablet, as well as in all web browsers, you will need to convert your material into multiple formats. There are many free, shareware, and inexpensive file format converters available for multiple platforms. Figure 6-4 shows a menu of video format selections and profiles available in the free converter HandBrake for Mac and Windows (http://handbrake.fr).

Figure 6-4 Working with many video formats (containers and codecs) is made simpler with conversion software.

Obtaining Video Clips

After you've decided that your project should and will include video, consider whether you should shoot new "**footage**" (a legacy term from the film and analog world) or acquire preexisting content for your video clips. There are many sources for film and video clips: a friend's home movies may suffice, or you can go to a "stock" footage house or a television station or movie studio. But acquiring footage that you do not own outright can be a nightmare—it is expensive, and licensing rights and permissions may be difficult, if not impossible, to obtain. Each second of video could cost $50 to $100 or more to license. Even material from a "public domain clip" from the National Archives must be researched:

> Generally, materials produced by Federal agencies are in the public domain and may be reproduced without permission. However, not all materials appearing on this web site are in the public domain... Items found in our holdings may be copyrighted. Please note that it is your responsibility to identify the copyright owner and to obtain permission before making use of this material in any way.

NOTE   *Many companies sell royalty-free video stock specifically for multimedia productions—these are often lower resolution than broadcast quality and typically less than full-frame video.*

On some projects, you will have no choice but to pay the price for required footage. If it is absolutely essential that your project include a clip of Elvis Presley crooning "You Ain't Nothing But a Hound Dog," and an Elvis impersonator just won't do, you will have to negotiate for rights to use the real thing. If your budget can't cover the cost of licensing a particular video clip, you may want to consider using other alternatives. You could try locating a less expensive archival video source, using a series of still images rather than video, or shooting your own video. If you shoot your own video for a project, make sure you have talent releases from all persons who appear or speak and permission to use the audio effects and music you weave into it. Licensing, permissions, and legal issues are discussed more fully in Chapter 10.

For projects that are focused on training, particularly training people to use software applications, video screen capture of mouse and key activity is widely used along with a voice-over sound track. Video screen capture tools for both PC and Macintosh systems will generate video files that can then be edited and integrated with audio. One eLearning and courseware authoring program, Adobe's Captivate (www.adobe.com/products/captivate/), will not only capture your own screen activity but allow you to import video in a wide variety of formats (AVI, MOV, FLV, MPEG) and edit it into your final project.

TIP *Before nonlinear video-editing suites became commonplace in television studios, video was edited into a master using two tape decks (A and B). The A deck contained video of an event or the reporter doing an interview; the B deck contained ancillary and supporting material and scenery. "B-roll" is what editors call the collection of general footage that supports the main theme or narration. Locating and integrating B-roll, especially using royalty-free or public domain footage, can greatly enhance your project while keeping your costs down.*

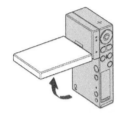

Scene Selection

☾ Twilight
   Shoots night scenes without losing the nighttime atmosphere.

☃ Twilight Portrait
   Shoots sharp images of people in a dark place without losing the nighttime atmosphere.

☺ Soft Snap
   Shoots images with a softer atmosphere for portraits of people, flowers, etc.

⛰ Landscape
   Shoots with the focus on a distant subject.

🏃 Hi-speed Shutter
   Shoots moving subjects outdoors or in other bright places.

🌴 Beach
   Shoots seaside or lakeside scenes with the blueness of the water captured more vividly.

☃ Snow
   Shoots snow scenes in white more clearly.

🎆 Fireworks
   Shoots fireworks in all their splendor.

♢ Candle
   Shoots candlelit scenes, without spoiling the atmosphere.

PART OF THE LEARNING CURVE

Shooting and Editing Video

Good videography requires good hardware and good shooting techniques. Piecing together your many shots, images, and sounds and delivering them as a finished product on DVD or the Internet requires editing software. Both your camera and your video editing software must be completely understood, too—be sure to thoroughly learn how each works! Read the manuals! Experiment! Time spent on the learning curves for your hardware and software is vital to your success!

Camcorders

Before you head out to the field with your camcorder in hand, it is important to understand at least the basics of video recording and editing, as well as the constraints of using video in a multimedia project.

Setting up a production environment for making digital video requires hardware that meets minimum specifications for processing speed, data transfer, and storage. There are many considerations to keep in mind when setting up your production environment, depending on the capabilities of your camcorder:

- Fast processor(s)
- Plenty of RAM
- Computer with FireWire (IEEE 1394 or i.Link) or USB connection and cables
- Fast and big hard disk(s)
- A second display to allow for more real estate for your editing software
- External speakers
- Nonlinear editing (NLE) software

Expensive professional video equipment and services may not yield proportionately greater benefits than if you used consumer-grade equipment and nonlinear editors. As with audio equipment, you need to make balancing decisions using Vaughan's Law of Multimedia Minimums (see Chapter 4). Most likely, your goal is to expend resources without diminishing returns—in other words, to produce multimedia that is adequate and does its job, but doesn't break your bank. If you can, experiment with various combinations of video recording and playback devices hooked to your computer, and test the results using your multimedia-authoring platform. You can do a great deal of satisfactory work with consumer-grade video cameras and recording equipment if you understand the limitations of the technology.

Never underestimate the value of a steady shooting platform. A classic symbol of amateur home movies is shaky camera work. Using a tripod or even placing the camera on a stable platform, such as a rolled-up sweater on the hood of a car, can improve a shot. With a little care, and careful adjustment of the lockdown screws, a sturdy conventional tripod can do wonders. If you must shoot handheld, try to use a camera with an electronic image stabilization feature for static shots, use a "steady-cam" balancing attachment, or use camera moves and a moving subject to mask your lack of steadiness. Even using a rolling office chair and sitting facing the back with the camera balanced on the chair-back makes a convenient, stable dolly. If you must shoot handheld, set the camera's lens to the widest angle: at a wide angle, camera motion becomes smaller relative to the field of view and is thus less apparent.

And invest in an external microphone, like a lavaliere. It will give you better audio than the on-camera microphone during interviews, and you can easily hide it in the scene during general use. Or use a "shotgun" mic on a boom, with an operator who can "ride levels" by monitoring the recorded volume.

Most important, learn the features and controls of your camera—there are many tiny icons and menu selections! Study the manual. Experiment and practice. Stay organized—keep your extra batteries, spare memory cards and tapes, your charger and cables, and even your manual (in case you haven't studied it hard enough) in a good camera bag. Learn how to connect the camera to your computer and how to access your video footage with nonlinear editing software. Learn how to use the editing software. If you are new to video, this is a steep learning curve with many small annoyances, but it is forgiving: if you mess up your video, there is often *something* from it that can be recovered and used.

Many digital camcorders will allow you to choose 4:3 or 16:9 aspect ratios for your recording, one or the other. Unfortunately, there is no easy way to convert between these aspect ratios, so you should decide up front which to use in your multimedia project. As shown in Figure 6-5, there are three ways to convert from a 4:3 aspect ratio for display on a 16:9 aspect ratio screen: you can *stretch* the 4:3 image to fill the 16:9 frame (this distortion can make people look fat), you can zoom the width of the image to fit the 16:9 frame (you lose part of the top and bottom of the image), or you can place the image into the center of the 16:9 frame (leaving empty **pillars** right and left).

As also shown in Figure 6-5, there are two ways to convert from 16:9 to 4:3. The *Letterbox* or hard matte method produces blank bars at top and bottom but leaves the original image untouched; *Pan and Scan*, on the

Converting 16:9 to 4:3

Original   Letterbox   Pan and Scan

Converting 4:3 to 16:9

Original   Pillars   Zoom   Stretch

Figure 6-5   Methods for converting 4:3 and 16:9 aspect ratios in video production

other hand, loses both sides of the original image. When using the Pan and Scan method for conversion, editors will carefully pan across wide scenes to capture the best area to show. Videographers and wide-screen movie-makers often consider a 4:3 "safe frame" area when setting up their wide shots, knowing that their work will be converted to 4:3 for the DVD after-market. Some DVDs use an **anamorphic widescreen** coding system to squeeze 16:9 widescreen image data into a DVD's standard 4:3 aspect ratio format; with a compatible player, these "Enhanced for Widescreen Televisions" discs will play the original video properly on a 16:9 screen.

TIP   *If your camera is HD-capable, it is a good idea to shoot your footage in HD. While it may be difficult to deploy HD video in your project due to bandwidth and memory constraints, you will have archived the footage at the highest resolution available to you. You can easily convert the high-definition source video to standard definition, but you cannot convert the other way without enhancer software that attempts to increase the resolution and make the video "good looking."*

Smartphones and Tablets

Smartphones and tablets were initially the home of cheap lenses, tiny sensors, and lower quality displays. That has changed. Onboard cameras for mobile devices typically provide 8 to 13 megapixels of resolution with good image and light quality. Many people now capture amateur video without the use of a specialized video camera or camcorder. Just shoot the video on your mobile and (seamlessly) upload it to social media or into the cloud. The many smartphone/cameras in Figure 6-6 were readily

Figure 6-6 Peaceful demonstrators raise smartphones to shine light on their government and let it know that it is being watched [from www.youtube.com/watch?v=Wmgqc4oiFZI].

available in a crowd of demonstrators. More detail about mobile devices for recording and playing video is available in Chapter 12.

TIP *If you have both memory and power, just let the video roll. It's easy to cut unwanted footage later, but hopeless if you have no footage at all.*

Storyboarding

Preplanning a video project is a factor that cannot be ignored without costing time loss, lots of unnecessary aggravation, and money that would be better spent elsewhere. Successful video production, of any sort, deserves the time it takes to make a plan to carry it out. It may take a little time at first, but you'll find it to be very helpful in the long run. Storyboards are like any sequential comic strip that appears daily in a newspaper, where every day there are three or four panels showing a progression of story or information. Take the time to structure your production by writing it down, and then engineer a sequential group of drawings showing camera and scene, shooting angles, lighting, action, special effects, and how objects move through from start to finish. A storyboard can get everyone on one page quickly.

Lighting

Perhaps the greatest difference between professional camcorders and consumer camcorders is their ability to perform at low light levels. With proper lighting, however, it may be difficult for uninitiated viewers to differentiate between shots taken with an expensive studio-grade video camera and an inexpensive camcorder. Using a simple floodlight kit, or even just being sure that daylight illuminates the room, can improve your image. Onboard battery lights for camcorders can be useful, but only in conditions where the light acts as a "fill light" to illuminate the details of a subject's face. As in photography, good lighting techniques separate amateurs from professionals in video shoots.

Illustrated in Figure 6-7 is a screen from The Lighting Lab. The standard lighting arrangement of a studio is displayed with fill, key, rim, and background lights. Changing any of these lights can make a dramatic difference in the shot. This project originally used a QuickTime container of several hundred single-frame images of the model as she is lighted by every permutation of lamp and intensity; clicking a light switch instantly

Figure 6-7 Good lighting is essential for quality video results.

shows the effect of that combination. If you are not convinced that lighting is critical to the success of a photo or video shoot, it will become immediately clear with this exercise! Try it at www.tayvaughan.com/multimedia /stuff/lightinglab.html.

Chroma Keys

Chroma keys allow you to choose a color or range of colors that becomes transparent, allowing the video image to be seen "through" the computer image. This is the technology used by a newscast's weatherperson, who is shot against a blue (or green) background that is made invisible when merged with the electronically generated image of the weather map. The weatherperson controls the computer part of the display with a small handheld controller.

A useful tool easily implemented in most digital video-editing applications is **blue screen**, **green screen**, **Ultimatte**, or **chroma key editing**. When Captain Picard of *Star Trek* fame walks on the surface of the moon, it is likely that he is actually walking on a studio set in front of a screen or wall painted blue. Actually placing Picard on the moon was, no doubt, beyond the budget of the shoot, but it could be faked using blue screen techniques. After shooting the video of Picard's walk against a blue background and shooting another video consisting of the desired background moonscape, the two videos were mixed together: wherever there was blue in the Picard shot, it was replaced by the background image, frame by frame.

Chroma key editing is a popular technique for making multimedia titles because expensive sets are not required. Incredible backgrounds can be generated using 3-D modeling and graphics software, and one or more actors, vehicles, or other objects can be neatly layered onto that background. Video-editing applications provide the tools for this.

When you are shooting blue screen, be sure that the lighting of the screen is absolutely even; fluctuations in intensity will make this **key color** appear choppy or broken. Shooting in daylight, and letting the sun illuminate the screen, will mitigate this problem. Also be careful about "color spill." If your actors stand too close to the screen, the colored light reflecting off the screen will spill onto them, and parts of their body will key out. While adjustments in most applications can compensate for this, the adjustments are limited. Beware of fine detail, such as hair or smoke, that wisps over the screen; this does not key well.

Figure 6-8 shows frames taken from a video of an actor shot against a blue screen on a commercial stage. The blue background was removed from each frame, and the actor himself was turned into a photorealistic animation that walked, jumped, pointed, and ran from a dinosaur.

When I worked in live video at KCAL in Los Angeles, one of our anchor women wore a blouse that was the same chroma-key blue that we could program into our Ultimatte. Actually, the anchor should have known better. We, being the naughty guys we were, keyed a closeup of two big eyes from one of the other anchors onto her blouse and fed it into the stage floor monitor and waited to see how long it would take before she noticed it. It was a couple of minutes, while everyone was trying to keep a straight face, before she saw what we had done. She threw her script at us, and we all broke up laughing.

Joe Silverthorn, Integrated Multimedia Professor, Olympic College

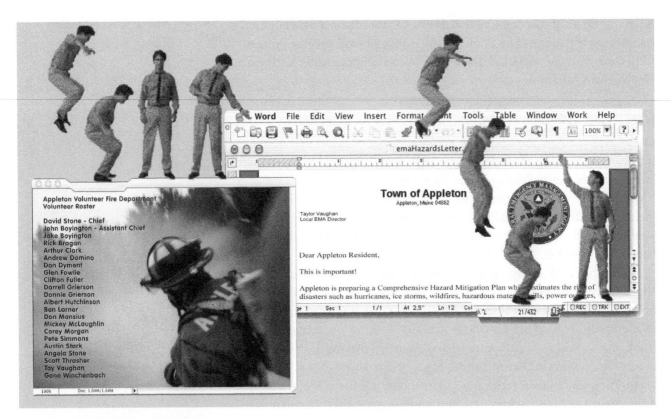

Figure 6-8 This walking, jumping, and pointing actor was videotaped against a blue screen.

Composition

The general rules for shooting quality video for broadcast use also apply to multimedia. When shooting video for playback in a small window, it is best to avoid wide panoramic shots, as the sweeping majesty will be lost. Use close-ups and medium shots, head-and-shoulders or even tighter. Depending upon the compression algorithm used (see the discussion on video codecs earlier in the chapter), consider also the amount of motion in the shot: the more a scene changes from frame to frame, the more "delta" information needs to be transferred from the computer's memory to the screen. Keep the camera still instead of panning and zooming; let the subject add the motion to your shot, walking, turning, talking.

Beware of excessive backlighting—shooting with a window or a bright sky in the background is a common error in amateur video production. Many cameras can be set to automatically compensate for backlighting. If you adjust for this, the background may be "blown out" (so bright the video signal peaks), but at least the foreground image you're focusing on will be visible. Of course, the best choice in this situation is to light the foreground.

Non-professional cameras are set to always adjust the iris (the opening in the lens) to keep the image's overall exposure at a constant level. When you go from a dark setting to a light setting, the camera will adjust, and you can often see this shift. Pro cameras allow the iris setting to be locked down to avoid this.

In different situations, white may not be white, depending on the color temperature (warmth or coolness) of the light source. **White balance** corrects for bluish, orange, or greenish color casts resulting from an uneven distribution of colors in the spectrum your eye tells you is white, but your less forgiving digital camera says is not quite white. Many cameras automatically set white balance with best guesses, but they also offer adjustable settings for daylight, shady, cloudy, tungsten, and fluorescent lighting conditions. Try to get the white balance correct when shooting; then you won't be spending time with your editing software to remove the greenish tinge from your client's white wedding dress.

Titles and Text

Titles and text are often used to introduce a video and its content. They may also finish off a project and provide credits accompanied by a sound track. Titles can be plain and simple, or they can be storyboarded and highly designed. For plain and simple, you can use templates (see Figure 6-9) in an image editor and then sequence those images into

Figure 6-9 Title templates are available for downloading. This template from "Westie" is at www.mediacollege. com/downloads/video/ titles/.

your video using your video-editing software. Or you can create your own imagery or animations and sequence them. More elaborate titles, typical for feature films and commercial videos, can become multimedia projects in themselves. Upasana Nattoji Roy's title design for director Indrajit Nattoji's film *Aagey Se Right*, for example, began with creative ideas (see Chapter 10), transitioned into a detailed storyboard and animations (see Chapter 7), and was finally rendered using Adobe After Effects (see Figure 6-10).

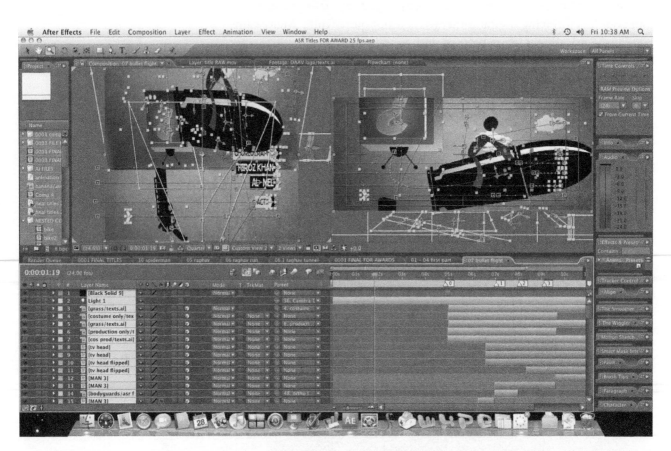

Figure 6-10   Elaborate titles are storyboarded, animated, and rendered to video using many multimedia tools. This title sequence was designed for a short film and stitched together using After Effects by Upasana Nattoji Roy. Check out www.artofthetitle.com/titles to view many other title sequences.

If you make your own, here are some suggestions for creating good titles:

- Fonts for titles should be plain, sans serif, and bold enough to be easily read.
- When you are laying text onto a dark background, use white or a light color for the text.
- Use a drop shadow to help separate the text from the background image.
- Do not kern your letters too tightly.
- If you use underlining or drawn graphics, always make your lines at least two pixels wide. If you use a one-pixel-wide line (or a width measured in an odd number of pixels), the line may flicker when transferred to video due to interlacing.
- Use parallel lines, boxes, and tight concentric circles sparingly. When you use them, draw them large and with thick lines.
- Avoid colors like bright reds and magenta that are too "hot"; they might twinkle and buzz.
- Neighboring colors should be markedly different in intensity. For example, use a light blue and a dark red, but not a medium blue and a medium red.
- Keep your graphics and titles within the safe area of the screen. Remember that CRT televisions overscan (see the earlier section "Overscan and the Safe Title Area").
- Bring titles on slowly, keep them on screen for a sufficient time, and then fade them out.
- Avoid making busy title screens; use more pages or a longer sequence instead.

Nonlinear Editing (NLE)

Top-of-the-line **nonlinear editing (NLE)** software includes Adobe's Premiere, Apple's Final Cut, and Avid's Media Composer, the "A Team" of professional video editors. These are feature-packed and expensive packages designed to work hand-in-hand with fast and powerful computers (6GB of RAM recommended) and dedicated file servers. Many hours of training and many days of experience are needed before users become proficient.

If your project involves simple cutting and editing of footage, with a few transitions and titles thrown in, then you may be satisfied with simpler software such as Microsoft's Windows Movie Maker (see Figure 6-11) or Apple's iMovie (see Figure 6-12) that come with the operating system.

Remember not to edit and re-edit and re-edit again. The video codecs used are lossy, so each time you finalize a file, it will be less true than the original material—this is called **generation loss**. Because NLE software works with **EDLs (edit decision lists)** based upon the raw source video, be sure you have sufficient disk space to store your original footage.

Figure 6-11 Windows Movie Maker comes free with Windows and can edit photos and videos, add special effects, and make DVDs and files for the Web.

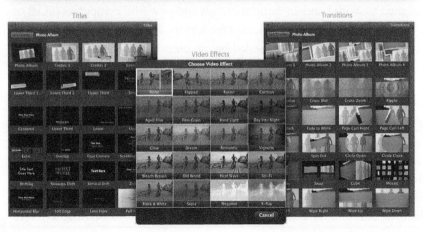

Figure 6-12 iMovie is a robust video editor that comes free with Macintosh computers and provides full libraries of title templates, video effects, and transitions.

Chapter 6 Review

■ Chapter Summary

For your review, here's a summary of the important concepts discussed in this chapter.

Consider the implications of using digital video in multimedia

- Video places the highest performance demand on any computer system.

- A massive amount of imagery must be squeezed into a comparatively small data file using compression (and decompression) software called a codec.

- You will need to make many choices and compromises based upon your assessment of the "lowest common denominator" playback platform where your project will be used.

Discuss analog and digital video technologies and displays

- A charge-coupled device (CCD) or a CMOS device converts the light that has been reflected from an object through the camera's lens.

- Four broadcast and video standards and recording formats are commonly in use around the world: NTSC, PAL, SECAM, and HDTV.

- HDTV provides high resolution in a 16:9 aspect ratio.

- Flat screen displays are all-digital, using either liquid crystal display (LCD), light-emitting diode (LED), or plasma technologies, and have supplanted CRTs for computer use.

- The process of building a single frame from two fields is called interlacing, a technique that helps to prevent flicker.

- Progressive-scan technology draws the lines of an entire video frame in a single pass, without interlacing them and without flicker.

- Don't place critical information such as text in the outer 15 percent of the screen. Keep it within the "safe title area."

Work with digital video containers and codecs to select the best video recording formats for multimedia projects

- Codecs are digital video and audio compression schemes that compress a video into a container for delivery and then decode it during playback.

- Video containers may include data compressed by a choice of codecs, and media players may recognize and play back more than one video file container format.

- The MPEG standards were developed by the Moving Picture Experts Group.

- The HTML5 <video> tag was supposed to simplify and standardize inclusion of video at web sites, but it remains embroiled in a codec and container war.

Find and acquire video clips

- There are many sources for digital video, but getting the rights can be difficult, time-consuming, and expensive.

- eLearning projects often employ screen capture programs to record mouse and keyboard activities to teach about a software application.

Shoot and edit video for use in multimedia

- Always shoot using a steady shooting platform.

- Storyboards are a useful exercise when planning a shoot.

- Good, even lighting is extremely important.

- Expensive stages are not required when using blue screen or Ultimatte techniques.

- Avoid wide panoramic shots and camera motion when shooting for a small computer window on CD-ROM or the Web.

- Fonts for titles should be plain, sans serif, and bold enough to be easily read.

- Most editing is now being done on computers using nonlinear editing (NLE) software such as Avid Media Composer, Adobe Premiere, and Apple Final Cut.

Key Terms

1080p *(171)*
16:9 *(170)*
anamorphic widescreen *(182)*
B-roll *(180)*
blue screen *(185)*
cathode ray tube (CRT) *(171)*
charge-coupled device (CCD) *(167)*
chroma key *(185)*
codec *(175)*
complementary metal-oxide semiconductor (CMOS) image sensor *(167)*
component *(168)*
composite *(168)*
degaussing *(172)*
DTV (Digital Television) *(173)*
Digital Versatile Disc (DVD) *(167)*
Digital Visual Interface (DVI) connector *(169)*
EDL (edit decision list) *(189)*
footage *(179)*
generation loss *(189)*
green screen *(185)*
HDTV (High-Definition Television) *(170)*
helical scan *(168)*
High-Definition Multimedia Interface (HDMI) *(169)*
interlacing *(172)*
key color *(185)*
light-emitting diode (LED) *(172)*

liquid crystal display (LCD) *(172)*
Moving Picture Experts Group (MPEG) *(175)*
National Television Standards Committee (NTSC) *(169)*
MPEG-1 *(175)*
MPEG-2 *(175)*
MPEG-4 *(175)*
NTSC (National Television Standards Committee) *(169)*
nonlinear editing (NLE) *(189)*
overscan *(174)*
Phase Alternate Line (PAL) *(169)*
pillars *(181)*
plasma *(172)*
progressive-scan *(172)*
RAID (Redundant Array of Independent Disks) *(167)*
safe title area *(174)*
Separate Video (S-Video) *(168)*
Sequential Color and Memory (SECAM) *(169)*
STV (Standard Television) *(170)*
Theora *(175)*
tracking *(169)*
Ultimatte *(185)*
underscan *(174)*
VGA connector *(169)*
video cassette recorder (VCR) *(169)*
white balance *(187)*

Key Term Quiz

1. A redundant hard-disk system that will support high-speed data transfer rates is called a(n) _____.

2. When you are shooting blue screen, blue is known as the _____ color.

3. Television screens use a process of building a single frame from two fields to help prevent flicker on CRTs in a technique called _____.

4. When creating graphics for conversion to video, do not place any critical information such as text in the outside 15 percent of the image. Instead, keep it within the _____ (three words).

5. High-Definition Television (HDTV) for Cinemascope is displayed in a(n) _____ aspect ratio.

6. The best HDTV image using the most pixels is called _____.

7. The digital video and audio compression schemes that compress a video for delivery and then decode it during playback are called _____.

8. When reformatting a 4:3 aspect ratio video to fit in the center of an HDTV screen, leaving the sides empty, the effect is called _____.

9. The video compression/decompression scheme used in an Ogg container is called _____.

10. MPEG is an acronym for _____.

■ Multiple-Choice Quiz

1. In a video camera, a sensor that picks up light may be called a CCD. CCD stands for:
   a. color-coding data
   b. custom color descriptor
   c. chroma-calculation daemon
   d. charge-coupled device
   e. carbon crystal digitizer

2. An HDTV display screen may be made from:
   a. long-chain polymers
   b. bakelite
   c. light-emitting diodes
   d. chrome retinas
   e. silver tubes

3. Removing a residual magnetic field that distorts the colors on a television screen is called:
   a. tracking
   b. dubbing
   c. streaming
   d. flattening
   e. degaussing

4. A video signal transmitted with all the signals mixed together and carried on a single cable is called:
   a. RGB video
   b. composite video
   c. component video
   d. multiformat video
   e. chroma-key video

5. Which of the following is *not* a television signal format?
   a. TIFF
   b. NTSC
   c. PAL
   d. SECAM
   e. HDTV

6. Computer displays draw the lines of an entire frame in a single pass; this technique is called:
   a. streaming
   b. progressive-scan
   c. packing
   d. flattening
   e. overscan

7. The video technique that allows you to choose a color or range of colors that becomes transparent, allowing the video image to be visible behind that color or range of colors in the overlying image, is known by all of the following *except*:
   a. blue screen
   b. Ultimatte
   c. chroma key
   d. interlacing
   e. green screen

8. Which of the following is a multimedia container format?
   a. JPEG
   b. DVD-RW
   c. ComponentY
   d. Hi-8
   e. Ogg

9. Red and green should be avoided as cue colors because:
   a. they represent negative ideas in some cultures
   b. they do not blend well with other colors
   c. color-blind individuals cannot see them correctly
   d. they are associated with "stop" and "go"
   e. they remind people of Christmas

10. Which of the following is *not* a good idea when creating titles (text) to be used in video?
    a. Fonts for titles should be plain, sans serif, and bold enough to be easily read.
    b. When you are laying text onto a dark background, use white or a light color for the text.
    c. Do not kern your letters too tightly.
    d. If you use underlining or drawn graphics, make sure your lines are only one pixel wide.
    e. Use a drop shadow to help separate the text from the background.

11. Which of the following is *not* a typical studio light?
    a. rim light
    b. fill light
    c. key light
    d. background light
    e. focal light

12. Which of the following is *not* a codec?
    a. H.264
    b. Theora
    c. NTSC
    d. VP6
    e. VP8

13. Generation loss occurs when:
    a. an analog tape is copied to another analog tape
    b. a digital file is copied to another hard disk
    c. a digital file is copied to another hard drive
    d. a video file is compressed and saved using a lossy codec
    e. your teenage son gets his tongue pierced

14. MPEG stands for:
    a. Multiformat Processed-Event Graphics
    b. Multi-Phase Element Grid
    c. Meta-Program Environment Graph
    d. Moving Picture Experts Group
    e. Micro-Phase Electronic Guidance

15. Which of the following HTML5 attributes is used in the display of multimedia video?
    a. <load>
    b. <animate>
    c. <forward>
    d. <play>
    e. None of the above

■ Essay Quiz

1. List the steps involved in capturing video, compressing the video, and preparing it for DVD. Briefly discuss the decisions you need to make with each step regarding compromises on image quality and other limiting factors.

2. Discuss how a computer display image differs from a television image. List the limitations in creating images on the computer destined for a television screen.

3. Discuss several considerations in shooting and editing video for multimedia. What techniques would you use to produce the best possible video, at a reasonable cost? Which of these techniques apply to *all* video, and which apply specifically to multimedia?

4. Briefly discuss how a digital video signal makes a moving picture on a television.

5. Define *codec* and list an example of a codec.

Lab Projects

■ Project 6.1

Go online and find three video cameras for sale. Compare their price and capabilities, such as memory storage, image stabilization, portability, autofocus quality, lens zoom, and range of customization. Make a list of the important features you would want in your video camera, and choose the camera that best matches your list. Document your findings.

■ Project 6.2

Create a short storyboard of a brief conversation or interaction between two people. Keep the interaction short, say, less than a minute. Your storyboard should include a number of different angles and shots. Note what kind of lighting, background noise, and other conditions should be present for the shot. Determine what amount of editing your shot would require and at which points in the storyboard sequence.

■ Project 6.3

Use a mobile device with video recording capability to record the short scene you planned in Project 6.2. If a video camera is not available, a smartphone that records video will suffice, but remember to hold the smartphone horizontally in landscape mode to record. Once finished, transfer the video to a computer. Using a simple video-editing program such as Windows Movie Maker, implement any simple edits necessary to prepare the video for distribution to friends. Explore effects such as fading in at the beginning, other dissolves, and adding text. Save your video in MP4 format and exit the program.

■ Project 6.4

Visit www.youtube.com. You will need to make an account to use the web site, or log in with a previous Google account. Once you have logged in, click (or tap) the Upload button at the top of the YouTube window. Select the video file you recorded for Project 6.3 and proceed to upload it (make sure the file is in one of YouTube's supported file types). Once the upload is complete, explore your options for displaying the video online, such as privacy settings, tags, and YouTube's own online video-editing tools. Once you have made your settings, save them and write down the web address where you can find your posted video.

## CHAPTER 7

Making Multimedia

In this chapter, you will learn how to:

- Describe the four primary stages in a multimedia project

- Discuss the intangible elements needed to make good multimedia

- Identify the typical members of a multimedia project team and describe the skills that they need for their work.

- Discuss the hardware most often used in making multimedia and choose an appropriate platform for a project

- Understand common software programs used to handle text, graphics, audio, video, and animation in multimedia projects and discuss their capabilities

- Determine which multimedia authoring system is most appropriate for any given project

IN this chapter, you will be introduced to the workshop where multimedia is made, with guidance and suggestions for getting started, and you will learn about planning a project. In later chapters, you will learn about producing, managing, and designing a project; getting material and content; testing your work; and, ultimately, shipping your project to end users or posting it to the Web.

The Stages of a Multimedia Project

Most multimedia and web projects must be undertaken in stages. Some stages should be completed before other stages begin, and some stages may be skipped or combined. Here are the four basic stages in a multimedia project:

1. **Planning and costing** A project always begins with an idea or a need that you then refine by outlining its messages and objectives. Identify how you will make each message and objective work within your authoring system. Before you begin developing, plan out the writing skills, graphic art, music, video, and other multimedia expertise that you will require. Develop a creative "**look and feel**" (what a user sees on a screen and how he or she interacts with it), as well as a structure and a navigational system that will allow the viewer to visit the messages and content. Estimate the time you'll need to do all the elements, and then prepare a budget. Work up a short **prototype** or **proof of concept**, a simple, working example to demonstrate whether or not your idea is feasible. The ease with which you can create materials with today's production and authoring tools tempts new developers to immediately move into production—jumping in before planning. This often results in false starts and wasted time and, in the long run, higher development cost. The more time you spend getting a handle on your project by defining its content and structure in the beginning, the faster you can later build it, and the less reworking and rearranging will be required midstream. Think it through before you start! Your creative ideas and trials will grow into screens and buttons (or the look and feel), and your proof of concept will help you test whether your ideas will work. You may discover that by breaking the rules, you can invent something terrific!

2. **Designing and producing**   Perform each of the planned tasks to create a finished product. During this stage, there may be many feedback cycles with a client until the client is happy.

3. **Testing**   Test your programs to make sure that they meet the objectives of your project, work properly on the intended delivery platforms, and meet the needs of your client or end user.

4. **Delivering**   Package and deliver the project to the end user. Be prepared to follow up over time with tweaks, repairs, and upgrades.

What You Need: The Intangibles

You need hardware, software, and good ideas to make multimedia. To make *good* multimedia, you need talent and skill. You also need to stay organized, because as the construction work gets under way, all the little bits and pieces of multimedia content—the six audio recordings of Alaskan Eskimos, the Christmas-two-years-ago snapshot of your niece, the 41 news articles still to scan with your optical character recognition (OCR) program—will get lost under growing piles of paper, CDs, videotapes, phone messages, permissions and releases, cookie crumbs, Xerox copies, and yesterday's mail. Even in serious offices, where people sweep all flat surfaces clear of paperwork and rubber bands at five o'clock, there will be a mess.

You will need time and money (for consumable resources such as DVD blanks and other memory or digital storage hardware, for telephoning and postage, and possibly for paying for special services and time, yours included), and you will need to budget these precious commodities (see Chapter 8).

You may also need the help of other people. Multimedia development of any scale greater than the most basic level is inherently a team effort: artwork is performed by graphic artists, video shoots by video producers, sound editing by audio producers, and programming by programmers. You will certainly wish to provide plenty of coffee and snacks, whether working alone or as a team. Late nights are often involved in the making of multimedia.

Creativity

Before beginning a multimedia project, you must first develop a sense of its scope and content. Let the project take shape in your head as you think through the various methods available to get your message across to your viewers.

The most precious asset you can bring to the multimedia workshop is your creativity. It's what separates run-of-the-mill or underwhelming multimedia from compelling, engaging, and award-winning products, whether we're talking about a short sales presentation viewed solely by colleagues within your firm or a fully immersive online game that may be played by thousands of users.

You have a lot of room for creative risk taking, because the rules for what works and what doesn't work are still being empirically discovered, and there are few known formulas for multimedia success. Indeed, companies that produce a terrific multimedia title are usually rewarded in the marketplace, but their success can be fleeting. This is because competitors often reverse-engineer the product, and then produce knockoffs using similar approaches and techniques, which appear on the market six months later. Good web site ideas and programming are easily cloned.

The evolution of multimedia is evident when you look at some of the first multimedia projects done on computers and compare them to today's apps. Taking inspiration from earlier experiments, developers modify and add their own creative touches for designing their own unique multimedia projects.

It is very difficult to learn creativity. Some people might say it's impossible—and that you have to be born with it. But, like traditional artists who work in paint, marble, or bronze, the better you know your medium, the better able you are to express your creativity. In the case of multimedia, this means you need to know your hardware and software first. Once you're proficient with the hardware and software tools, you might ask yourself, "What can I build that will look great, sound great, and knock the socks off the viewer?" This is a rhetorical question, and its answer is actually another question—which is simply, "How creative are you?"

WARNING   *If you are managing a multimedia project, remember that creative talent is priceless, so be certain to reward it well. If you don't, you may find that your talent takes a job elsewhere, even at lower pay!*

Organization

It's essential that you develop an organized outline and a plan that rationally details the skills, time, budget, tools, and resources you will need for a project. These should be in place before you start to render graphics, sounds, and other components, and you should establish a protocol for naming the files so you can organize them for quick retrieval when you need them. These files—called **assets**—should continue to be monitored throughout the project's execution. Chapter 8 provides planning and costing models for a multimedia project, while Chapter 9 discusses the details of managing a multimedia project and its assets.

First Person

The Credit Alligator usually appears late in a multimedia project, and has nothing to do with MasterCard or Visa. This gnarly animal typically lives unseen in the delicate fringes of workgroup politics, but can appear very suddenly, causing great distraction during beta testing, adding moments of personal tension, and occasionally destroying friendships and business relationships.

After hard cash, the most satisfying remuneration for your sweaty effort and creative, late-night contributions to a multimedia project is to see your name listed in the credits for a particular project. Indeed, getting visible credit is a special, high-value currency, in part because it can be added to your portfolio to help you land the next job. The more of this currency you have, the higher your potential wage and the more likely you will remain employed doing what you like to do. Start building defenses against this alligator up front. When you negotiate the original contract with whoever pays the multimedia bill, be sure to include wording such as: "We shall be allowed to include a production credit display on the closing screen or in another mutually agreeable position in the finished work." If you are an individual who is contracting to a producer, be sure it is understood that *if* there is a credit page, your name will be on it.

Not all clients will stand for a credit page. Large companies, for example, use many outside contractors to produce multimedia, but as a policy rarely allow contributors to be credited by name. Some contractors and frustrated employees develop ingenious workarounds for burying these important intellectual credits within their work.

The Credit Alligator raises its bumpy head over the little things, too, and there are often no appropriate defenses for it. For example, if your name begins with a letter that is toward the end of the alphabet, you may never appear first on the list of contributors, even if your contribution was major. Of course, if your name is Walsh or Young, you have endured this ordering system since first-grade lineups. Warning: reversing an alphabetic credit list from last to first will only create or heighten tension; to propose such a list is, in itself, ego-driven and self-serving. Learn to work around it.

The most treacherous place for the Credit Alligator to lurk is in the busy stretch of time during the finalizing of a CD-based project and the "going gold" process of producing a final master. If you are not participating in the final mastering but have contributed a piece or pieces to the project, you must trust the person doing the mastering to do it the right way. But, unfortunately, it doesn't always happen the way you want it to.

One company recently consulted on a job where their work represented the second-greatest contribution from a group of about 15 contributors, all of whom had credit screens. Their contract required credit, but in the final version of the storyboard, they discovered their screen buried at the end of a four-minute linear sequence of all the other credits and advertisements. They asked the producer to move it up. "Sorry," said the producer, "it was an oversight." Then, in the last-minute process of re-sequencing, the producer also switched the contracted company's custom music to his own company's credit screen, leaving the contracted company's screen attached to a pretty ugly leftover sound byte. Because the company was not included in the final feedback and approval loop, they discovered this "little mistake" only after mass replication. It's tough to change 50,000 shrink-wrapped packages, so at that point there was nothing to say.

Crediting creative talent is sensitive stuff. Avoid recurring bouts with the Credit Alligator by publicizing your policy about credit screens. Talk about intellectual credit openly, not as a last-minute thing. Negotiate hard for inclusion of credit in all the projects you undertake for clients. Remember, multimedia doesn't spring from the bankrolls of investors and publishers—it's the result of the hard work of talented, real people.

Communication

Many multimedia applications are developed in workgroups comprising instructional designers, writers, graphic artists, programmers, and musicians located in the same office space or building. The workgroup members' computers are typically connected on a local area network (LAN). The client's computers, however, may be thousands of miles distant, requiring other methods for good communication.

Communication among workgroup members and with the client is essential to the efficient and accurate completion of your project. A combination of Skype video and voice telephone, e-mail, text messaging, and the **File Transfer Protocol (FTP)** may be the most cost-effective and efficient solution for both creative development and project management. In the workplace, use quality equipment and software for your communications setup. The cost—in both time and money—of stable and fast networking will be returned to you.

What You Need: Multimedia Skills

Computer scientists, physicians, and firemen share highest honors as the most respected professions in the United States, according to a recent study of occupations. Are multimedia developers computer scientists? Or are they programmers, graphic artists, musicians, animators, storyboard craftspeople, information specialists, instructional designers, and/or Renaissance authors? However you define them, they come from all corners of the computer, art, literary, film, and audio worlds. Video producers become experts with computer-generated animations and MIDI controls for their edit suites. Architects become bored with two-dimensional drafting and create three-dimensional animated walkthroughs. Oil field engineers get tired of manipulating complex data sets and design mouse-driven human interfaces. Classical painters learn the electronic elements of red, green, and blue and create fantastic, computer-based artwork. A multimedia developer might be any or all of these and typically doesn't fit a traditional management information system (MIS) or computer science mold; many have never seen a line of C++ code or booted up a Linux server. Perhaps, in the broadest definition, multimedia developers might simply be called information technology workers.

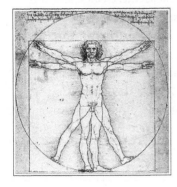

Consider Leonardo da Vinci, the Renaissance man who was scientist, architect, builder, creative designer, craftsman, and poet folded into one. To produce good multimedia, you will need a similar diverse range of skills—detailed knowledge of computers, text, graphic arts, sound, and video. These skills, the **multimedia skill set**, may be available in a single individual or, more likely, in a composite of individuals working as a team. Complex multimedia projects are, indeed, often assembled by teams of artists and computer craftspeople, where tasks can be delegated to those most skilled in a particular discipline or craft. Many job titles and collaborative team roles for multimedia development are being adapted to pull from a mix of motion picture industry, radio and television broadcasting, and computer software industry experiences.

WARNING *A multimedia expert working alone will be hard-pressed to compete with a multidisciplinary team of experts and may be overwhelmed by the sheer amount of effort required to build a complex project single-handedly.*

The Team

A typical team for developing multimedia for television, DVD, mobile, or the Web consists of people who bring various abilities to the table. Often, individual members of multimedia production teams wear several hats: graphic designers may also do interface design, scanning, and image processing. A project manager or producer may also be the video producer or scriptwriter. Depending upon the scope and content of your project and the mix of people required, according to Wes Baker, distinguished professor of communications at Cedarville University in Cedarville, Ohio, a multimedia production team may require as many as 18 discrete roles, including:

> Executive Producer
> Producer/Project Manager
> Creative Director/Multimedia Designer
> Art Director/Visual Designer
> Artist
> Interface Designer
> Game Designer
> Subject Matter Expert
> Instructional Designer/Training Specialist
> Scriptwriter
> Animator (2-D/3-D)
> Sound Producer
> Music Composer
> Video Producer
> Multimedia Programmer
> HTML Coder
> Lawyer/Media Acquisition
> Marketing Director

Project Managers

A project manager's role is at the center of the action. He or she is responsible for the overall development and implementation of a project as well as for day-to-day operations. Budgets, schedules, creative sessions, time

Mere possession of the equipment does not make one into a videographer, film editor, set designer, scriptwriter, audio engineer, animator, and programmer. Some people do possess all of the innate talents required to produce decent multimedia, but few have mastered all the skills required to bring a major project to fruition. More typically, world-class productions are realized through the teamwork of a variety of talented people with specialized experience.

Jeff Burger, Contributing Editor, *NewMedia* magazine

sheets, illness, invoices, and team dynamics—the project manager is the glue that holds it together.

Multimedia Designers

The look and feel of a multimedia project should be pleasing and aesthetic, as well as inviting and engaging. Screens should present an appealing mix of color, shape, and type. The project should maintain visual consistency, using only those elements that support the overall message of the program. Navigation clues should be clear and consistent, icons should be meaningful, and screen elements should be simple and straightforward. If the project is instructional, its design should be sensitive to the needs and styles of its learner population, demonstrate sound instructional principles, and promote mastery of subject matter. But who puts it all together?

Graphic designers, illustrators, animators, and image processing specialists deal with the visuals. Instructional designers are specialists in education or training and make sure that the subject matter is clear and properly presented for the intended audience. Interface designers devise the navigation pathways and content maps. Information designers structure content, determine user pathways and feedback, and select presentation media based on an awareness of the strengths of the many separate media that make up multimedia. All can be multimedia designers.

Interface Designers

Like a good film editor, an interface designer's best work is never seen by the viewer—it's "transparent." In its simplest form, an interface provides control to the people who use it. It also provides access to the "media" part of multimedia—meaning the text, graphics, animation, audio, and video—without calling attention to itself. The elegant simplicity of a multimedia title screen, the ease with which a user can move about within a project, effective use of windows, backgrounds, icons, and control panels—these are the result of an interface designer's work.

Writers

Multimedia writers do everything writers of linear media do, and more. They create character, action, and point of view—a traditional **scriptwriter**'s tools of the trade—and they also create interactivity. They write proposals, they script voice-overs and actors' narrations, they write text screens to deliver messages, and they develop characters designed for an interactive environment.

Writers of text screens are sometimes referred to as content writers. They glean information from content experts, synthesize it, and then communicate it in a clear and concise manner. Scriptwriters write dialog, narration, and voice-overs. Both often get involved in overall design.

The role of an interface designer is to create a software device that organizes the multimedia content, lets the user access or modify that content, and presents the content on screen. These three areas—information design, interactive design, and media design—are central to the creation of any interface, and of course they overlap.

....

Nicole Lazzaro, Designer

Video Specialists

Prior to the 2000s, producing video was extremely expensive, requiring a large crew and expensive equipment. Recently, however, the cost of the equipment and the size of the crew needed have dropped dramatically, and digital video presentation methods have combined increasingly capable hardware and software. The result is that video images delivered in a multimedia production have improved from postage-stamp-sized windows playing at low frame rates to full-screen (or nearly full-screen) windows playing at 30 frames per second. As shooting, editing, and preparing video has migrated to an all-digital format and become increasingly affordable to multimedia developers, video elements have become more and more part of the multimedia mix.

For high-quality productions, it may still be necessary for a video specialist to be responsible for an entire team of videographers, sound technicians, lighting designers, set designers, script supervisors, gaffers, grips, production assistants, and actors. However, for many modest projects, a video specialist may shoot and edit all of the footage without outside help.

Whether working individually or managing a large crew, a video specialist needs to understand how to shoot quality video, how to transfer the video footage to a computer, how to edit the footage down to the final product using a digital nonlinear editing system (NLE), and how to prepare the completed video files for the most efficient delivery on DVD or the Web.

Audio Specialists

The quality of audio elements can make or break a multimedia project. Audio specialists are the wizards who make a multimedia program come alive, by designing and producing music, voice-over narrations, and sound effects. They perform a variety of functions on the multimedia team and may enlist help from one or many others, including composers, audio engineers, or recording technicians. Audio specialists may be responsible for locating and selecting suitable music and talent, scheduling recording sessions, and digitizing and editing recorded material into computer files (see Chapter 4).

Multimedia Programmers

A multimedia programmer or software engineer integrates all the multimedia elements of a project into a seamless whole using an authoring system or programming language. Multimedia programming functions range from coding simple displays of multimedia elements to controlling peripheral devices and managing complex timing, transitions, and record keeping. Creative multimedia programmers can coax extra (and sometimes unexpected) performance from multimedia-authoring and programming

Whether it's recording voice-over talent for a business application, composing a musical score for a shoot-'em up game, or designing sound effects that reflect the particular feel of a product, the end result will rely on knowing the medium going in. By this I mean, for example, at what sampling rate will the audio be delivered? How much space is available for *all* audio combined? Can different sampling rates be applied to voice-over and music to save space and enhance overall quality? In composition will looping be required of individual pieces to provide a seamless score and to save valuable space? And who will do the looping, the composer or the engineer? Will some voice-over talents sound presentable at higher sampling rates but not at lower? Will the producer understand the difference?

Chip Harris,
Composer and Audio Specialist

systems. Without programming talent, there can be no multimedia. Code, whether written in JavaScript, LiveCode, PHP, Java, or C++, is the sheet music played by a well-orchestrated multimedia project.

Producers of Multimedia for the Web

Web site producer is still a relatively new occupation, but putting together a coordinated set of pages for the World Wide Web requires the same creative process, skill sets, and (often) teamwork as any kind of multimedia does. With a little effort, many of us could put up a simple web page with a few links, but this differs greatly from designing, implementing, and maintaining a complex site with many areas of content and many distinct messages. A web site should never be finished, but should remain dynamic, fluid, and alive. Unlike a DVD multimedia product replicated many times in permanent plastic, the work product at a web site is available for tweaking at any time.

The Sum of Parts

Successful multimedia projects begin with selecting "team players." But selection is only the beginning of a team-building process that must continue through a project's duration. **Team building** refers to activities that help a group and its members function at optimal levels of performance by creating a work culture that incorporates the styles of its members. You should encourage communication styles that are fluid and inclusive, and you should develop models for decision making that respect individual talents, expertise, and personalities. This isn't easy, but repeated studies have shown that workgroup managers with well-developed team skills are more successful than managers who dive headlong into projects without attention to team dynamics. Although it's usually a project manager who initiates team building, all team members should recognize their role; gentle collaboration is a key element of successful projects.

The Bureau of Labor Statistics (www.bls.gov) provides descriptions of many occupations related to multimedia in the *Occupational Outlook Handbook* (www.bls.gov/ooh); search on "multimedia." You can also check out career information sites such as www.vault.com, www.monster.com, or www.wetfeet.com for current information on careers in new media.

What You Need: Hardware

This book will help you understand the two most significant platforms for producing and delivering multimedia projects: the **Apple Macintosh** operating system (OS) and the **Microsoft Windows** OS, found running on most Intel-based PCs (including Intel-based Macintoshes). These computers, with their graphical user interfaces (GUIs) and huge installed base of many millions of users throughout the world, are the most commonly used platforms for the development and delivery of today's multimedia.

> For a year and a half I was totally plugged into the Net, checking on our site, looking at stats, and analyzing what was going on in the entertainment/technology industries. This meant keeping Web profession hours rather than banker's hours, which meant it was pretty rare for me to take a day off, even on weekends, and my office became more of my living space than my apartment. To keep from burning out, you have to have a sense of ownership and a passion for what you're doing. In the end, best was that my team members also turned into close friends.
>
> Kevin Edwards, CNET

They offer a compelling combination of affordability, software availability, and worldwide obtainability. Regardless of the delivery vehicle for your multimedia—whether it's destined to play on a computer, a smartphone or tablet, a PlayStation or Xbox, or as bits moving through the cloud—most multimedia will probably be made using a Mac or a Windows PC.

The basic principles for creating and editing multimedia elements are the same for all platforms. A graphic image is still a graphic image, and a digitized sound is still a digitized sound, regardless of the methods or tools used to make and display it or to play it back. Indeed, many software tools readily convert picture, sound, and other multimedia files (and even whole functioning projects) from Macintosh to Windows format, and vice versa, using known file formats or even **binary compatible** files that require no conversion at all. While there is a lot of talk about **platform-independent** delivery of multimedia on the Internet, with every new version of a browser there are still annoying failures on both platforms. These failures in **cross-platform** compatibility can consume great amounts of time as you prepare for delivery by testing and developing workarounds and tweaks so your project performs properly in various target environments.

Selection of the proper platform for developing your multimedia project may be based on your personal preference of computer, your budget constraints, project delivery requirements, and the type of material and content in the project. Many developers believe that multimedia project development is smoother and easier on the Macintosh than in Windows, even though projects destined to run in Windows must then be ported or tested across platforms. Table 7-1 shows the penetration of operating systems.

Windows	Mac	Linux
90.73%	7.68%	1.6%

Table 7-1   Worldwide Operating System Market Share in January 2014 (Source: http://marketshare.hitslink.com)

Windows vs. Macintosh

A Windows computer is not a computer per se, but rather a collection of parts that are tied together by the requirements of the Windows operating system. Power supplies, processors, hard disks, CD-ROM and DVD players and burners, video and audio components, displays, keyboards, mice, Wi-Fi, and Bluetooth transceivers—it doesn't matter where they come from or who makes them. Made in Texas, Taiwan, Indonesia, India, Ireland, Mexico, or Malaysia by widely known or little-known manufacturers, these components are assembled and branded by Dell, HP, Sony, and others into computers that run Windows. If you are handy with a

Phillips screwdriver and can read instructions, you can even order the parts and assemble your own computer "clone" to run Windows—at a considerable cost savings!

In the early days, Microsoft organized the major PC hardware manufacturers into the Multimedia PC Marketing Council, in order to develop a set of specifications that would allow Windows to deliver a dependable multimedia experience. The animated dinosaur in Central Park described in Chapter 5 became part of the theatrical rollout announcement for this effort. Since then, the specifications for a multimedia PC have evolved into "what a computer does."

Unlike Microsoft, primarily a software company, Apple is a hardware manufacturing company that developed its own proprietary software to run the hardware. In 2006, Apple adopted Intel's processor architecture, an engineering decision that allows Macintoshes to run natively with any x86 operating system, same as Windows. All recent models of Macintosh come with the latest Mac operating system, and by using Boot Camp or Parallels software, Macs can also run the Windows operating system.

First Person

In November 1985, during the COMDEX trade show in Las Vegas, members of the computer press were invited to the birthing party for a new Microsoft product called Windows. A crowd of journalists and friends of Microsoft had gathered in a small, low-ceilinged hotel ballroom and were munching on hors d'oeuvres and sipping wine when the swinging doors to the pantry opened suddenly, and Bill Gates drove a golf cart onto the floor, towing a small trailer loaded down with hundreds of blue boxes filled with the new product. A cheer went up, and the boxes disappeared into waiting hands. It was a fun party held in the time before Gates had become the richest man in the world and necessarily employed a personal security force, before his personal income would skew by two dollars the difference between the mean and median income of all Americans. He chatted with a few of us and proudly autographed some User Guides. Mine says "I hope you like the product; thanks for coming, Tay." Back in my office after the show, I loaded the software onto my XT from the five 5.25-inch floppy disks in the box and ran it. Windows was a dog. Indeed, during the ensuing days and months, Windows had a very hard time in the "operating environment" popularity contest and dropped to low-visibility status. But Gates seemed to have a vision, and while we didn't hear too much about Windows during the next years, Gates and Microsoft worked on the product steadily and didn't give up. Windows 3.0, released many years later, changed the world.

Networking Macintosh and Windows Computers

If you are working in a multimedia development environment consisting of a mixture of Macintosh and Windows computers, you will want them to communicate with each other. You will also wish to share other resources among them, such as printers.

Local area networks (LANs) and wide area networks (WANs) can connect the members of a workgroup. In a LAN, workstations are usually located within a short distance of one another, on the same floor of a building, for example. WANs are communication systems spanning greater distances, typically set up and managed by large corporations and institutions for their own use, or to share with other users.

LANs allow direct communication and sharing of peripheral resources such as file servers, printers, scanners, and network routers. They use a variety of proprietary technologies, most commonly Ethernet, to perform the connections either by twisted-pair copper wires or wirelessly using Wi-Fi. If you are operating a cross-platform multimedia development shop, you should install a local Ethernet system so that your PCs and Macintoshes can talk to each other and to your network printers as well. This is many times more efficient than carrying removable media among your machines in a "sneaker network." Ethernet is only a *method* for wiring up computers, so you still will need client/server software to enable the computers to speak with each other and pass files back and forth. The Windows and Mac operating systems provide this networking software, but you may need expert help to set it up—it can be complicated!

Unless you are in a large business or part of government, your WAN is likely the Internet connected to you by an Internet service provider (ISP); the Internet is worldwide and connects tens of millions of computers and other devices! If you are working with people in various time zones (an artist in New York, a programmer in San Francisco, and a client in Singapore), all can communicate and share information with other locations at any time of day or night using the Internet network. Chapter 11 discusses the Internet in greater detail.

Connections

The equipment required for developing your multimedia project will depend on the content of the project as well as its design. You will certainly need as fast a computer as you can lay your hands on, with lots of RAM and disk storage space. Table 7-2 shows various device connection methodologies and their data transfer rates.

If you can find content such as sound effects, music, graphic art, clip animations, and video to use in your project, you may not need extra tools for making your own. Typically, however, multimedia developers have separate equipment for digitizing sound from tapes or microphone, for scanning photographs or other printed matter, and for making digital still or movie images.

Connection	Transfer Rate
Serial port	115 Kbps (0.115 Mbps)
Standard parallel port	115 Kbps (0.115 Mbps)
USB (Original 1.0)	12 Mbps (1.5 Mbps)
SCSI-2 (Fast SCSI)	80 Mbps
SCSI (Wide SCSI)	160 Mbps
Ultra2 SCSI	320 Mbps
FireWire 400 (IEEE 1394)	400 Mbps
USB (Hi-Speed 2.0)	480 Mbps
SCSI (Wide Ultra2)	640 Mbps
FireWire 800 (IEEE 1394)	800 Mbps
SCSI (Wide Ultra3)	1,280 Mbps
SATA 150	1,500 Mbps
SCSI (Ultra4)	2,560 Mbps
SATA 300	3,000 Mbps
FireWire 3200 (IEEE 1394)	3,144 Mbps
USB (Super-Speed 3.0)	3,200 Mbps
SCSI (Ultra5)	5,120 Mbps
SATA 600	6,000 Mbps
Fibre Channel (Optic)	10,520 Mbps

Table 7-2 Maximum Transfer Rates for Various Connections in Megabits Per Second

Vaughan's One-Way Rule

Once you've tried it, you can't go back.

Years ago, a few weeks after HyperCard was released by Apple, I went to work there, designing and building the guided tour for an information management tool used in-house by Apple. I said I didn't know the software, but they said that's okay, nobody else does, either. They gave me a cubicle with my name on it, a Macintosh Plus with a 20MB hard disk, and I was up and running. The Macintosh II had been shipping for a short while, and every department at Apple was attempting to get this latest and hottest color-enabled CPU—but most units were going to the retail channel. There were three Macintosh IIs among about 40 of us.

One afternoon, I sat at a Macintosh II and ran my software. I couldn't believe it! The screen-to-screen dissolves and special effects I had carefully programmed on the old computer went by so fast I couldn't see them. I had to reprogram everything, with a special test to check for CPU speed. If it was a fast machine, I programmed the visual effects to run slower; on a slow machine, faster. But the sad part was that I not only wanted this faster machine, I felt I *needed* it! I had the same experience moving from a dial-up modem to a DSL broadband Internet connection, and knew I'd never go back.

IDE, EIDE, Ultra IDE, ATA, and Ultra ATA

Integrated Drive Electronics (IDE) connections, also known as **Advanced Technology Attachment (ATA)** connections, are typically only internal, and they connect hard disks, CD-ROM drives, and other peripherals mounted inside the PC. With IDE controllers, you can install a combination of hard disks, CD-ROM drives, or other devices in your PC. The circuitry for IDE is typically much less expensive than for SCSI (discussed shortly), but comes with some limitations. For example, IDE requires time from the main processor chip, so only one drive, if there are more than one, can be active at a time.

USB

A consortium of industry players including Compaq, Digital Equipment, IBM, Intel, Microsoft, NEC, and Northern Telecom was formed in 1995 to promote a **Universal Serial Bus (USB)** standard for connecting devices to a computer. These devices are automatically recognized ("**plug-and-play**") and installed without users needing to install special cards or without turning the computer off and on when making the connection (called "hot-swapping"). USB technology has improved in performance since its introduction (see Table 7-2) and has become the connection method of choice for many peripheral devices, from cameras to keyboards to scanners and printers. USB uses a single cable to connect as many as 127 USB peripherals to a single personal computer. Hubs can be used to "daisy-chain" many devices. USB connections are now common on video game consoles, cameras, GPS locators, smartphones, televisions, MP3 players, tablets, and portable memory devices.

FireWire and i.LINK (IEEE 1394)

FireWire was introduced by Apple in the late 1980s, and in 1995 it became an industry standard (IEEE 1394) supporting high-bandwidth serial data transfer, particularly for digital video and mass storage. Like USB, the standard supports hot-swapping and plug-and-play, but it is faster, and while USB devices can be attached to only one computer at a time, FireWire can connect multiple computers and peripheral devices (peer-to-peer). Both OS X and Windows offer IEEE 1394 support. Because the standard has been endorsed by the Electronic Industries Alliance (EIA) and the Advanced Television Systems Committee (ATSC), it has become a common method for connecting and interconnecting professional digital video gear, from cameras to recorders and edit suites. Sony calls this standard i.LINK. FireWire has replaced Parallel SCSI in many applications because it's cheaper and because it has a simpler, adaptive cabling system.

SCSI

The Small Computer System Interface (SCSI—pronounced "scuzzy") adds peripheral equipment such as disk drives, scanners, CD-ROM players, and other peripheral devices that conform to the SCSI standard. SCSI connections may connect *internal* devices, such as hard drives that are inside the chassis of your computer and use the computer's power supply, and *external* devices, which are outside the chassis, use their own power supply, and are plugged into the computer by cable.

The hardware and the drivers for SCSI have improved over the years to provide faster data transfers across wider buses. Unlike the less-expensive IDE scheme described previously, a SCSI controller does not demand CPU time, and because it can support many devices, it is often preferred for real-time video editing, network servers, and situations in which writing simultaneously to two or more disks (mirroring) is required.

> If the label on the cable on the table at your house says you hook up the camera simple as a mouse, but the packets burn a pocket on a socket on the port, then get your receipt and call them to abort.
>
> ....
>
> Tay Vaughan

Memory and Storage Devices

As you add more memory and storage space to your computer, you can expect your computing needs and habits to keep pace, filling the new capacity. So enjoy the months that follow a memory storage upgrade or the addition of a terabyte (TB) hard disk; the honeymoon will eventually end.

To estimate the memory requirements of a multimedia project—the space required on a hard disk, thumb drive, CD-ROM, or DVD, not the **random access memory (RAM)** used while your computer is running—you must have a sense of the project's content and scope. Color images, text, sound bites, video clips, and the programming code that glues it all together require memory; if there are many of these elements, you will need even more. If you are *making* multimedia, you will also need to allocate memory for storing and archiving working files used during production, original audio and video clips, edited pieces and final mixed pieces, production paperwork and correspondence, and at least one backup of your project files, with a second backup stored at another location.

It is said that when John von Neumann, often called "the father of the computer," was designing the ENIAC computer in 1945, there was an argument about how much memory this first computer should have. His colleagues appealed for more than the 2K Dr. von Neumann felt was sufficient. In the end, he capitulated and agreed to install 4K in the ENIAC, commenting "...but this is more memory than you will ever need."

Random Access Memory (RAM)

If you are faced with budget constraints, you can certainly produce a multimedia project on a slower or limited-memory computer. On the other hand, it is profoundly frustrating to face memory (RAM) shortages time after time, when you're attempting to keep multiple applications and files open simultaneously. It is also frustrating to wait the extra seconds required of each editing step when working with multimedia material on a slow processor.

In spite of all the marketing hype about processor speed, this speed is ineffective if not accompanied by sufficient RAM. A fast processor without enough RAM may waste processor cycles while it swaps needed portions of program code into and out of memory. In some cases, increasing available RAM may show more performance improvement on your system than upgrading the processor chip.

Read-Only Memory (ROM)

Unlike RAM, **read-only memory (ROM)** is not *volatile*. When you turn off the power to a ROM chip, it will not forget, or lose its memory. ROM is typically used in computers to hold the small BIOS program that initially boots up the computer, and it is used in printers to hold built-in fonts. **Erasable programmable ROMs** (called **EPROMs**) allow changes to be made that are not forgotten when power is turned off.

Hard Disks

Adequate storage space for your production environment can be provided by large-capacity hard disks, server-mounted on a network. As multimedia has reached consumer desktops, makers of hard disks have built smaller-profile, larger-capacity, faster, and less-expensive hard disks. As network and Internet servers drive the demand for centralized data storage requiring **terabytes** (1TB = 1 trillion bytes), hard disks are often configured into fail-proof redundant arrays offering built-in protection against crashes.

Flash Memory or Thumb Drives

Flash memory data storage devices can be integrated with USB or FireWire interfaces to store from as little as a few megabytes (MB) of data to as much as 128 gigabytes (GB). These devices are available in every color of the rainbow, are extremely portable, and, because they have fewer moving parts, are more reliable than disk drives. Consisting of a small printed circuit board encased in a sturdy metal or plastic casing with a USB connector covered with a cap, the flash drive is convenient to use. Without the USB connector, this same solid-state storage is used in digital cameras, cell phones, and audio recording devices, and for solid-state hard drives (no spinning platters or moving parts) that are found in some tablets, smartphones, and other handheld devices.

CD-ROM Discs

Compact disc read-only memory (CD-ROM) players have become an integral part of the multimedia development workstation and the discs that play in them are an important delivery vehicle for mass-produced projects. A wide variety of developer utilities, graphic backgrounds, stock photography and sounds, applications, games, reference texts, and educational software are available on this medium. CD-ROM players have typically been very slow to access and transmit data (150 KBps, which is the speed required of consumer Audio CDs), but developments have led to double-, triple-, quadruple-speed, 24x, 48x, and 56x drives designed specifically for computer use (not Red Book Audio use, described in Chapter 4). These faster drives spool up like washing machines on the spin cycle and can be somewhat noisy, especially if the inserted compact disc is not evenly balanced.

With a compact disc recorder, you can make your own CDs, using CD-recordable (CD-R) blank discs to create a CD in most formats of CD-ROM and CD-Audio (see Chapter 4). Software, such as Roxio's Toast and Creator, lets you organize files on your hard disk(s) into a "virtual" structure, and then writes them to the CD in that order. CD-R discs are manufactured differently than normal CDs but can play in any CD-Audio or CD-ROM player. These write-once, enhanced CDs make excellent high-capacity file archives and are used extensively by multimedia developers for pre-mastering and testing CD-ROM projects and titles. Because they have become very inexpensive, they are also used for short-run distribution of finished multimedia projects and data backup. A CD-RW (read and write) recorder can rewrite 700MB of data to a CD-RW disc about 1,000 times.

Digital Versatile Discs (DVD)

 In December 1995, nine major electronics companies (Toshiba, Matsushita, Sony, Philips, Time Warner, Pioneer, JVC, Hitachi, and Mitsubishi Electric) agreed to promote a new optical disc technology for distribution of multimedia and feature-length movies called **Digital Versatile Disc (DVD)**. With a DVD capable not only of gigabyte storage capacity but also full-motion video (MPEG2) and high-quality audio in surround sound, this is an excellent medium for delivery of multimedia projects. Commercial multimedia projects will become more expensive to produce, however, as consumers' performance expectations rise. There are three types of DVD, including DVD-Read Write, **DVD-Video**, and **DVD-ROM**. These types reflect marketing channels, not the technology.

Blu-ray Discs

 Driven by the implementation of **High-Definition TV (HDTV)** and by the motion picture industry, a new technology was needed to increase storage capacity and throughput beyond DVD. Two competing and incompatible solutions were promoted and a war was fought in the marketplace between HD-DVD, backed by Toshiba, and **Blu-ray Disc (BD)**, backed by Sony. By 2008, Toshiba had sold about 1 million HD-DVD players, but Sony had sold close to 10 million Blu-ray players, which were also included in popular PlayStation game machines. Toshiba announced it was quitting.

Blu-ray is promoted not only for HDTV recording and high-definition video distribution, but also for high-definition camcorder archiving, mass data storage, and digital asset management and professional storage when used as a recording medium in BD recordable (BD-R) format. Table 7-3 provides a comparison of the DVD and Blu-ray Disc specifications.

DVD Feature	DVD Specification	Blu-ray Disc Specification
Disc diameter	120 mm (5 inches)	120 mm (5 inches)
Disc thickness	1.2 mm (0.6 mm thick disc × 2)	1.2 mm (0.6 mm thick disc × 2)
Memory capacity	4.7 gigabytes/single side	25 gigabytes/single layer
Wave length of laser diode	650 nanometer/635 nanometer (red)	405 nanometer (blue-violet)
Data transfer rate 1x	Variable speed data transfer at an average rate of 4.69 Mbps for image and sound	Variable speed data transfer at an average rate of 36 Mbps for image and sound
Image compression	MPEG2 digital image compression	MPEG-2 Part 2, H.264/MPEG-4 AVC, and SMPTE VC-1
Audio	Dolby AC-3 (5.1 ch), LPCM for NTSC and MPEG Audio, LPCM for PAL/SECAM (a maximum of 8 audio channels and 32 subtitle channels can be stored)	Dolby Digital (AC-3), DTS, and linear PCM
Running time (movies)	Single Layer (4.7GB): 133 minutes a side (at an average data rate of 4.69 Mbps for image and sound, including three audio channels and four subtitle channels)	Single Layer (25GB): Encoded using MPEG-2 video, about two hours of HD content; using VC-1 or MPEG-4 AVC codecs, about 4 hours of HD-quality video and audio

Table 7-3 DVD and Blu-ray Disc Specifications

Input Devices

A great variety of input devices—from the familiar keyboard and handy mouse to touchscreens and voice recognition setups—can be used for the development and delivery of a multimedia project. If you are designing your project for a public kiosk, use a touchscreen. If your project is for a lecturing professor who likes to wander about the classroom, use a remote handheld mouse. If you create a great deal of original computer-rendered art, consider a pressure-sensitive stylus and a drawing tablet. Scanners enable you to use **optical character recognition (OCR)** software so you can convert paper documents into a word processing document on your computer without retyping or rekeying.

Barcode readers are probably the most familiar OCR devices in use today—mostly at markets, shops, and other point-of-purchase locations. Using photo cells and laser beams, barcode readers recognize the numeric characters of the **Universal Product Code** (UPC) that are printed in a pattern of parallel black bars on merchandise labels. With **barcoding**, retailers can efficiently process goods in and out of their stores and maintain better inventory control.

An OCR terminal can be of use to a multimedia developer because it recognizes not only printed characters but also handwriting. This facility may be beneficial at a kiosk or in a general education environment where user friendliness is a goal, because there is growing demand for a more personal and less technical interface to data and information.

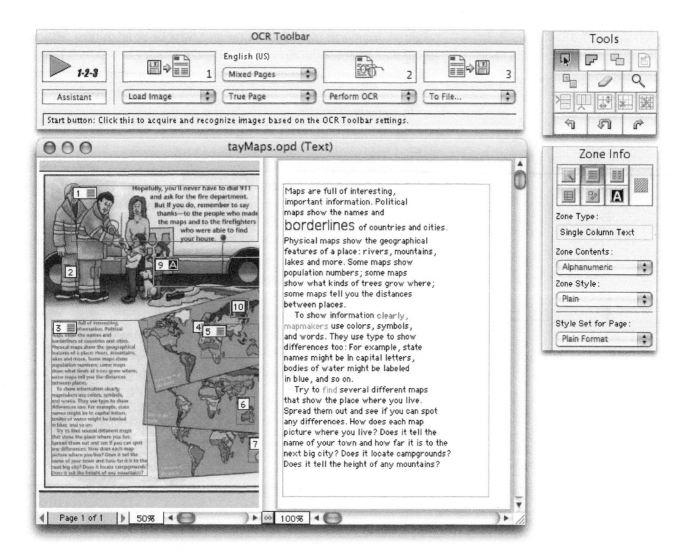

Figure 7-1 Working with a scanner, OCR software can save many hours of rekeying text.

 Quick Response (QR) codes are typically read by the built-in camera on a smartphone or mobile device and may contain link information to quickly access a website. The code might also contain a phone number, a plain text message, or contact information in V-Card format.

For hands-free interaction with your project, try a **voice recognition system**. These behavioral biometric systems usually provide a unidirectional cardioid, noise-canceling microphone that automatically filters out background noise and learns to recognize voiceprints. Most voice recognition systems currently available can trigger common menu events such as Save, Open, Quit, and Print, and you can teach the system to recognize other commands that are more specific to your application. Systems available for the Macintosh and Windows environments typically must be taught to recognize individual voices and then be programmed with the appropriate responses to the recognized word or phrase. Nuance's Dragon NaturallySpeaking takes dictation, translates text to speech, and does command-to-click, a serious aid for people unable to use their hands.

The quality of your audio recordings is greatly affected by the caliber of your microphone and cables. A unidirectional microphone helps filter out external noise, and good cables help reduce noise emitted from surrounding electronic equipment.

Digital cameras use the same technology as video cameras, described in Chapter 6. They capture still images of a given number of pixels (resolution), and the images are stored in the camera's memory to be uploaded later to a computer. The resolution of a digital camera is determined by the number of pixels on the chip, and the higher the megapixel rating, the higher the resolution of the camera. Images are uploaded from the camera's memory using a serial, parallel, or USB cable, or, alternatively, the camera's memory card is inserted into a reader connected to the computer. Digital cameras are small enough to fit in a cell phone and, in a more complicated manner, they can be used in a television studio or spy camera on an orbiting spacecraft.

With the advent of mobile devices, smartphones, and tablets came operating systems that use a trackpad or touch screen for input using multi-touch gestures (see the following illustration).

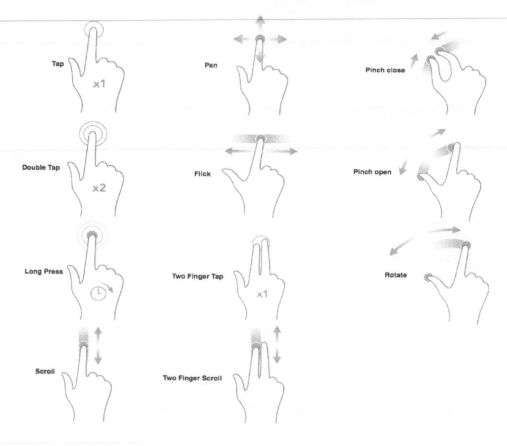

Output Devices

Presentation of the audio and visual components of your multimedia project requires hardware that may or may not be included with the computer itself, such as speakers, amplifiers, projectors, and motion video devices. The better the equipment is, of course, the better the presentation. There is no greater test of the benefits of good output hardware than to feed the audio output of your computer into an external amplifier system: suddenly the bass sounds become deeper and richer, and even music sampled at low quality may sound acceptable.

TIP *Design your project to use many shorter-duration audio files rather than one long file. This simplifies the reaction of your project within your authoring system, and it may also improve performance because you will load shorter segments of sound into RAM at any one time.*

Often the speakers you use during a project's development will not be adequate for its presentation. Speakers with built-in amplifiers or attached to an external amplifier are important when your project will be presented to a large audience or in a noisy setting.

The display you need for development of multimedia projects depends on the type of multimedia application you are creating, as well as what computer you're using. A wide variety of displays is available for both Macintoshes and PCs. High-end, large-screen graphics displays and LCD panels are available for both platforms and have become affordable. Common aspect ratios have evolved from 3:4 (standard TV) to 16:9 (HDTV), resolutions have increased dramatically, and costs have dropped as manufacturing methods improved since the 1980s (see Figure 7-2).

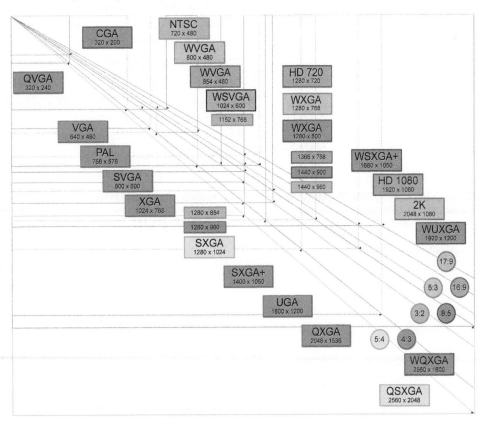

Figure 7-2 Video displays have evolved as hardware performance and manufacturing capabilities have advanced.

Serious multimedia developers will often attach more than one display to their computers and work with several open windows at a time. For example, you can dedicate one display to viewing the work you are creating or designing, and you can perform various editing tasks in windows on other displays that do not block the view of your work.

No other contemporary message medium has the visual impact of video, but keep in mind that good video greatly enhances your project; poor video will ruin it.

When you need to show your material to more viewers than can huddle around a computer display, you will need to project it onto a large screen or even a white-painted wall. **Cathode-ray tube (CRT)** projectors, liquid crystal display (LCD) panels, Digital Light Processing (DLP) projectors, and liquid crystal on silicon (LCOS) projectors are available, as are (for larger projects) Grating-Light-Valve (GLV) technologies. CRT projectors have been around for quite a while—they are the original "big-screen" televisions and use three separate projection tubes and lenses (red, green, and blue). The three color channels of light must "converge" accurately on the screen. Setup, focusing, and alignment are important for getting a clear and crisp picture. CRT projectors are compatible with the output of most computers as well as televisions. Nifty pocket projectors that work with your smartphone (or memory sticks or other sources) are also available.

Graphic print designers often use special color-correction hardware to ensure that what they see on screen matches precisely what will be printed. Multimedia does not usually require the same level of precision—mostly because the multimedia will likely be presented on any number of displays with widely varying color settings.

Hard-copy printed output has also entered the multimedia scene. From storyboards to presentations to production of collateral marketing material, printouts are an important part of the multimedia development environment. Color helps clarify concepts, improve understanding and retention of information, and organize complex data. As multimedia designers already know, intelligent use of color is critical to the success of a project.

Vaughan's Rule for Keeping Up

Upgrade to proven products that lie in the calm water, slightly behind the leading edge of the wave.

What You Need: Software

Multimedia software tells the hardware what to do. Display the color red. Move that tiger three leaps to the left. Slide in the words "Now You've Done It!" from the right and blink them on and off. Play the sound of cymbals crashing. Run the digitized trailer for *Twilight*. Turn down the volume on that MP3 file!

The basic tool set for building multimedia projects contains one or more authoring systems and various editing applications for text, images, sounds, and motion video. A few additional applications are also useful for capturing images from the screen, translating file formats, and moving files among computers when you are part of a team—these are tools for the housekeeping tasks that make your creative and production life easier.

The software in your multimedia toolkit—and your skill at using it—determines what kind of multimedia work you can do and how fine and fancy you can render it. Making good multimedia means picking a successful route through the software swamp. Alligators and learning curves can rise up out of this swamp to nip you in the knees.

You don't have to be a programmer or a computer scientist to make multimedia work for you, but you do need some familiarity with terms and building blocks; as even the simplest multimedia tools require a modicum of knowledge to operate. If someone asks to borrow a metric 13-mm wrench, you should know they are probably working with a nut or a bolt (and if you are an expert, you might know that a 1/2-inch wrench can usually be substituted). If someone sends you a file in Macintosh AIF format, you should know that you're getting *digitized* sound. Don't be afraid of

First Person

After getting my pilot's license for flying small, single-engine airplanes, I traveled from San Francisco to New York on a Boeing 747. Looking out the window at those perfectly circular irrigated farms in Nebraska and Iowa, my lazy thoughts drifted from corn to water to Chevys on levies to girls to football to rope swings splashing into sun-drenched rivers.

There was a small airport below. Would that make a good emergency field for a dead-stick Cessna? Mmmmm, I drifted. What if *this* plane had an emergency?

Mmmmm. What if the crew had been poisoned and we were on autopilot, and a flight attendant had just interrupted the movie to ask if there were a pilot on board? Mmmmm. I knew that if I had to sit in the pilot's seat of that 747

I wouldn't have a clue, and the plane would go down. Thousands of switches, glass screens, levers, pedals, blinking lights, and somewhere a radio, all waiting for me to do something with them. Hollywood's version of this scenario, with

the "tower" talking us down, would never work because I couldn't even turn on the radio.

It's like that when you learn multimedia. The same sinking feeling, frustration, and not knowing. But, because you have this book in hand, you're already in the pilot's seat and are on the way toward a successful landing. Relax. Step-by-step it will get easier. Manuals, online help systems, and instructors are your tower, and you have plenty of fuel. In the same way tens of thousands of pilots have learned to fly, you will learn to make multimedia!

(Photo by Pete McGill, who not only learned to fly heavies, but learned to make multimedia and shoots with a Canon 400D.)

the little things that so easily depress the uninformed. From plumbing to nuclear physics, learning is a matter of time and practice. You will be frustrated as you work your way up the learning curves of multimedia. There will be things you want to do, but you will not know how to work the tools. Take the time to learn the fundamentals of computers and multimedia taught in this book. Then, load up your tools and open the help files; your learning curve will be easier to manage because you have the bigger picture.

TIP *As you explore the workings of multimedia, you should know that web addresses are not guaranteed to be permanent but can abruptly disappear, just like the addresses for physical locations when the house burns down or floats away in a flood.*

Microsoft.com, walmart.com, mcdonalds.com, and visa.com, however, represent such monoliths of business that it seems unlikely that they will float away, at least soon, in the river of time. If, when trying to connect to a URL, you receive a "404 – not found" error message, try stripping away the directories and subdirectories and filenames from the URL and then connect to the domain name itself. If you can connect to the domain name, you may find a menu that will then take you to the relocated document from another direction. If, for example, you are looking for a list of tools useful to web service providers at www.w3.org/hypertext/www/tools/ and the document is not there, connect to www.w3.org/, and then follow the hypertext menus provided to end up at www.w3.org/standards/webdesign/. If none of these efforts brings you joy, you can try entering the web address into one of the search engines listed in Chapter 11.

Keep your tools sharp by upgrading them when new software and features become available, by thoroughly studying and learning each tool, by keeping an eye on the conversations and **Frequently Asked Questions (FAQ)** files online and in Internet blogs, and by observing the practices and products of other multimedia developers. Remember, each new tool has a learning curve.

TIP *Always fill out the registration card for your new software and return it to the vendor, or register online. If the vendor pays attention to product marketing, you will frequently receive upgrade offers, special newsletters, and e-mails with helpful information.*

The tools used for creating and editing multimedia elements on both Windows and Macintosh platforms do image processing and editing, drawing and illustration, 3-D and computer-aided design (CAD), OCR and text editing, sound recording and editing, video and moviemaking, and various utilitarian housekeeping tasks.

First Person

When I left graduate school, I joined the Carpenters Union and built highway bridges, apartment houses, and fine custom homes. The whole-sale tool supply store that catered to the trade had one wall covered with more than a hundred differ-ent hammers—some for nailing big nails, some for tiny upholstery tacks, some for metal work, others with a hatchet on one side for shingles, or with a waffled striking head that would drive slick and wet nails under the roughest conditions. They all came in different weights and

handle lengths and shapes. I tested a few framing hammers and chose a 24-ounce waffle-head framing ham-mer that felt good. With it, I could drive big 16d nails in a single stroke. It had a wicked curved handle. It was a Vaughan hammer.

Next day at noon, the job boss took me aside and quietly told me that he limited hammer weight to 22 ounces, because the older guys on the crew couldn't keep up. My hammer was illegal, and if he saw it the next day, I'd be sent back to

the hiring hall. "Sorry," I said, "jeez, I didn't know." He let me leave early so I could get to the tool store before it closed.

In producing multimedia, no tool is illegal. You should use the best tools that fit your talent, needs, and budget.

Text Editing and Word Processing Tools

A **word processor** is usually the first software tool computer users learn. From letters, invoices, and storyboards to project content, your word processor may also be your most often used tool, as you design and build a multimedia project. The better your **keyboarding** or typing skills, the easier and more efficient your multimedia day-to-day life will be.

Typically, an office or workgroup will choose a single word processor to share documents in a standard format. And most often, that word pro-cessor comes bundled in an **office suite** that might include spreadsheet, database, e-mail, web browser, and presentation applications.

Word processors such as Microsoft Word and Corel's WordPerfect are powerful applications that include spell checkers, table formatters, the-sauruses, and prebuilt templates for letters, résumés, purchase orders, and other common documents.

Many developers have begun to use OpenOffice (www.openoffice.org) for word processing, spreadsheets, presentations, graphics, databases, and more. It can be downloaded and used completely free of charge for any purpose and is available in many languages. It can read and write files from other, more expensive, office packages. In many word processors, you can embed multimedia elements such as sounds, images, and video. Luckily, the population of single-finger typists is decreasing over time as children are taught keyboarding skills in conjunction with computer lab programs in their schools.

OCR Software

Often you will have printed matter and other text to incorporate into your project, but no electronic text file. With OCR software, a flatbed scanner, and your computer, you can save many hours of rekeying printed words, and get the job done faster and more accurately than a roomful of typists.

OCR software turns bitmapped characters into electronically recognizable ASCII text. A scanner is typically used to create the bitmap. Then the software breaks the bitmap into chunks according to whether it contains text or graphics, by examining the texture and density of areas of the bitmap and by detecting edges. The text areas of the image are then converted to ASCII characters using probability and expert system algorithms. Most OCR applications claim about 99 percent accuracy when reading 8- to 36-point printed characters at 300 dpi and can reach processing speeds of about 150 characters per second. These programs do, however, have difficulty recognizing poor copies of originals where the edges of characters have bled; these and poorly received faxes in small print may yield more recognition errors than it is worthwhile to correct after the attempted recognition.

Painting and Drawing Tools

Painting and drawing tools, as well as 3-D modelers, are perhaps the most important items in your toolkit because, of all the multimedia elements, the graphical impact of your project will likely have the greatest influence on the end user. If your artwork is amateurish, or flat and uninteresting, both you and your users will be disappointed. Look in Chapters 9 and 12 for tips on designing effective graphical screens and in Chapter 3 for more about computer graphics.

Painting software, such as Photoshop, Fireworks, and Painter, is dedicated to producing crafted bitmap images. Drawing software, such as CorelDRAW, Illustrator, Designer, and Canvas, is dedicated to producing vector-based line art easily printed to paper at high resolution.

Some software applications combine drawing and painting capabilities, but many authoring systems can import only bitmapped images. The differences between painting and drawing (that is, between bitmapped and drawn images) are described in Chapter 3. Typically, bitmapped images provide the greatest choice and power to the artist for rendering fine detail and effects, and today bitmaps are used in multimedia more often than drawn objects. Some vector-based packages such as Adobe's Flash are aimed at reducing file download times on the Web and may contain both bitmaps and drawn art.

Look for these features in a drawing or painting package:

- An intuitive GUI with pull-down menus, status bars, palette control, and dialog boxes for quick, logical selection
- Scalable dimensions, so that you can resize, stretch, and distort both large and small bitmaps
- Paint tools to create geometric shapes, from squares to circles and from curves to complex polygons
- The ability to pour a color, pattern, or gradient into any area
- The ability to paint with patterns and clip art
- Customizable pen and brush shapes and sizes
- An eyedropper tool that samples colors
- An autotrace tool that turns bitmap shapes into vector-based outlines
- Support for scalable text fonts and drop shadows
- Multiple undo capabilities, to let you try again
- A history function for redoing effects, drawings, and text
- A property inspector
- A screen capture facility
- Painting features such as smoothing coarse-edged objects into the background with anti-aliasing (see illustration); airbrushing in variable sizes, shapes, densities, and patterns; washing colors in gradients; blending; and masking

- Support for third-party special-effect plug-ins
- Object and layering capabilities that allow you to treat separate elements independently
- Zooming, for magnified pixel editing
- All common color depths: 1-, 4-, 8-, and 16-, 24-, or 32-bit color, and gray-scale
- Good color management and dithering capability among color depths using various color models such as RGB, HSB, and CMYK
- Good palette management when in 8-bit mode
- Good file importing and exporting capability for image formats such as PIC, GIF, TGA, TIF, PNG, WMF, JPG, PCX, EPS, PTN, and BMP

If you are new to multimedia and to these tools, you should take time to examine more than one graphics software package. Find someone who is already familiar with graphics applications. You will spend many days learning to use your painting and drawing software, and if it does not fit you and your needs, you will be unhappy. Many artists learn to use a single, powerful tool well.

First Person

Years ago, I founded an accredited maritime school at Pier 66 in San Francisco, where we offered courses in everything from high-tech composite plastics and welding to Rules of the Road and celestial navigation. We also ran several marine trade certification programs. When I talked with Ford, General Motors, Cummins, and Caterpillar about setting up a course for marine diesel mechanics, I was surprised at their competitive interest in supporting the program. It turned out that a widely publicized survey had shown that a mechanic trained to work on a particular brand of engine would stick with it for life, loyally recommending and supporting that brand.

The same holds true for software. By the time you master an application, you have spent many hours on its learning curve. You will likely stay with that product and its upgrade path rather than change to another.

3-D Modeling and Animation Tools

3-D modeling software has increasingly entered the mainstream of graphic design as its ease of use improves. As a result, the graphic production values and expectations for multimedia projects have risen.

3-D is an abbreviation for "three dimensional." Where in a 2-D graphics program, images are painted in the "x" (horizontal or width) and "y" (vertical or height) axes, a 3-D graphics program adds the dimension of depth, labeled as the "z" axis.. Every program that layers objects on the screen must know each object's "z" axis. Web browsers, for example, place objects on the screen using the Cascading Style Sheets (CSS) "z-index" attribute. Some software programs (such as Flash and Toon Boom Studio) can simulate depth by automatically scaling images based on a z-axis value to create a cartoonish or simulated 3-D effect. This differs from true 3-D modeling and rendering, where objects can be rotated and viewed from any direction or angle.

With 3-D modeling software, objects rendered in perspective appear more realistic; you can create stunning scenes and wander through them, choosing just the right lighting and perspective for your final rendered image. Powerful modeling packages such as Vectorworks (see Figure 7-3), Autodesk's Maya and Softimage, and Strata's Design 3D are also bundled with assortments of prerendered 3-D clip art objects such as people, furniture, buildings, cars, airplanes, trees, and plants. Blender is a powerful (and free) cross-platform 3-D modeling program offering an extensive feature set. Google SketchUp is a free 3-D modeling program with limited capabilities but a large online library of components. Important for multimedia development, many 3-D modeling applications include export facilities for creating and saving a moving view or journey through a scene as a Quick-Time or MPEG file.

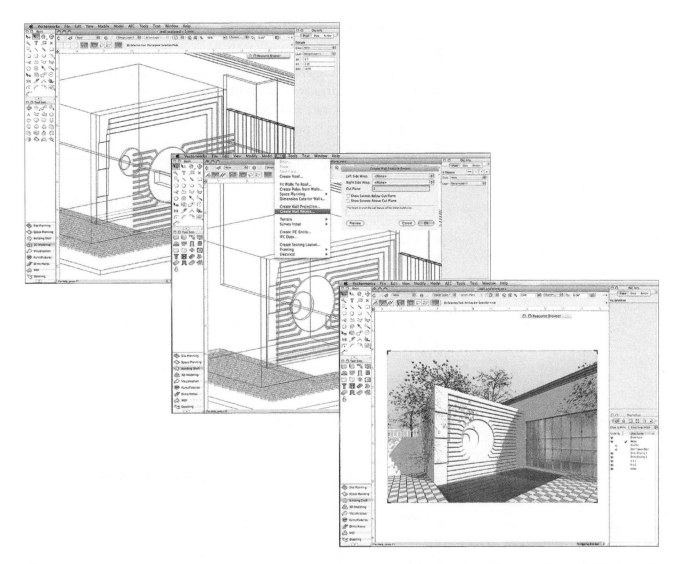

Figure 7-3   Vectorworks and other CAD applications can translate precise 2-D drawings into 3-D perspectives with lighting and shadows, but they can be complicated and very difficult to learn.

Each rendered 3-D image takes from a few seconds to a few hours to complete, depending upon the complexity of the drawing and the number of drawn objects included in it. If you are making a complex walkthrough or flyby, plan to set aside many hours of rendering time on your computer.

TIP   *If there are small errors or things you would like to change in a rendered movie sequence, it may take less time to edit each frame of the affected sequence by hand, using an image-editing program, rather than re-rendering the corrected original.*

A good 3-D modeling tool should include the following features:

- Multiple windows that allow you to view your model in each dimension, from the camera's perspective, and in a rendered preview
- The ability to drag and drop primitive shapes into a scene
- The ability to create and sculpt organic objects from scratch
- Lathe and extrude features
- Color and texture mapping
- The ability to add realistic effects such as transparency, shadowing, and fog
- The ability to add spot, local, and global lights, to place them anywhere, and manipulate them for special lighting effects
- Unlimited cameras with focal length control
- The ability to draw spline-based paths for animation

WARNING *3-D imaging programs require speedy computers with lots of memory, and the learning curve is steep when you enter this world of nurbs, splines, and bump maps.*

Image-Editing Tools

Image-editing applications are specialized and powerful tools for creating, enhancing, and retouching existing bitmapped images. These applications also provide many of the features and tools of painting and drawing programs and can be used to create images from scratch as well as images digitized from scanners, video frame-grabbers, digital cameras, clip art files, or original artwork files created with a painting or drawing package.

TIP *If you want to print an image to a 300-dpi printer for collateral reports and attractive print-matter icons, work with the image in the image-editing application at 300 dpi (every pixel will be a very fine laser printer dot). Then, save your work as a TIFF or BMP file and import it into your word processor. The printed result is a finely detailed image at a high resolution.*

Here are some features typical of image-editing applications and of interest to multimedia developers:

- Multiple windows that provide views of more than one image at a time
- Conversion of major image-data types and industry-standard file formats
- Direct inputs of images from scanner and video sources
- Employment of a virtual memory scheme that uses hard disk space as RAM for images that require large amounts of memory
- Capable selection tools, such as rectangles, lassos, and magic wands, for selecting portions of a bitmap

- Image and balance controls for brightness, contrast, and color balance
- Good masking features
- Multiple undo and restore features
- Anti-aliasing capability, and sharpening and smoothing controls
- Color-mapping controls for precise adjustment of color balance
- Tools for retouching, blurring, sharpening, lightening, darkening, smudging, and tinting
- Geometric transformations such as flip, skew, rotate, and distort, and perspective changes
- The ability to resample and resize an image
- 24-bit color, 8- or 4-bit indexed color, 8-bit gray-scale, black-and-white, and customizable color palettes
- The ability to create images from scratch, using line, rectangle, square, circle, ellipse, polygon, airbrush, paintbrush, pencil, and eraser tools, with customizable brush shapes and user-definable bucket and gradient fills
- Multiple typefaces, styles, and sizes, and type manipulation and masking routines
- **Filters** for special effects, such as crystallize, dry brush, emboss, facet, fresco, graphic pen, mosaic, pixelize, poster, ripple, smooth, splatter, stucco, twirl, watercolor, wave, and wind
- Support for third-party special-effect plug-ins
- The ability to design in layers that can be combined, hidden, and reordered

Sound-Editing Tools

Sound-editing tools for both digitized and MIDI sound let you see music as well as hear it. By drawing a representation of a sound in fine increments, whether a score or a waveform, you can cut, copy, paste, and otherwise edit segments of it with great precision—something impossible to do in real time (that is, with the music playing). The basics of computerized sound are discussed in Chapter 4.

Animation, Video, and Digital Movie Tools

Animations and digital video movies are sequences of bitmapped graphic scenes (**frames**), rapidly played back. But animations can also be made within the authoring system by rapidly changing the location of objects, or **sprites**, to generate an appearance of motion. Most authoring tools adopt either a frame- or object-oriented approach to animation, but rarely both.

To make movies from video, you may need special hardware to convert an analog video signal to digital data. Macs and PCs with FireWire (IEEE 1394) or USB ports can import digital video directly from digital camcorders. Moviemaking tools such as Adobe's Premiere, Apple's Final

Cut Pro, and Corel's VideoStudio Pro let you edit and assemble video clips captured from camera, tape, other digitized movie segments, animations, and scanned images, and audio clips captured from digitized audio or MIDI files. The completed clip, often with added transition and visual effects, can then be played back—either stand-alone or windowed within your project.

WARNING *Digital video editing and playback requires an immense amount of free disk space, even when the video files are compressed.*

TIP *Because digital movie data must stream rapidly and without interruption from your disk drive, be sure that you defragment and optimize your disk with a utility such as Symantec's Norton Speed Disk for Windows (www.norton.com) or iDefrag for OS X (www.coriolis-systems.com/iDefrag.php) before recording and playing back your movie files. If your movie file is fragmented, the read head of the disk drive may need to pause sending data while it physically moves to wildly different locations on the disk; a defragmented file lets the head read sequentially from one adjoining sector to the next. Use disk optimizing utilities with caution, however: accidents have been known to happen, causing permanent data loss.*

Helpful Accessories

No multimedia toolkit is complete without a few indispensable utilities for performing some odd, but oft-repeated, tasks. These are the comfortable and well-worn accessories that make your computer life easier.

On both the Macintosh and in Windows, a screen-grabber is essential. Because bitmapped images are so common in multimedia, it is important to have a tool for grabbing all or part of the screen display so that you can import it into your authoring system or copy it into an image-editing application for custom work. Screen-grabbing to the clipboard, for example, lets you move a bitmapped image from one application to another without the cumbersome steps of first exporting the image to a file and then importing it back into the destination application. In Windows, press the PRINT SCREEN key to place the contents of your screen onto the clipboard (described in Chapter 3). On a Macintosh, press the COMMAND key, the CONTROL key, the SHIFT key, and the number 4 all at the same time, and then drag a rectangle across the screen. Whatever is in the rectangle is then placed on the clipboard, ready for pasting into an image-editing application. In OS X, you can also use the Grab utility (found in Applications/Utilities) to capture the screen.

Format converters are additional indispensable tools for projects in which your source material may originate on Macintoshes, PCs, Unix workstations, or even mainframes. This is an issue particularly with video and audio files, because there are many formats and many compression schemes.

What You Need: Authoring Systems

Multimedia authoring tools provide the important framework you need for organizing and editing the elements of your multimedia project, including graphics, sounds, animations, and video clips. Authoring tools are used for designing interactivity and the user interface, for presenting your project on screen, and for assembling diverse multimedia elements into a single, cohesive product.

Authoring software provides an integrated environment for binding together the content and functions of your project, and typically includes everything you need to create, edit, and import specific types of data; assemble raw data into a playback sequence or cue sheet; and provide a structured method or language for responding to user input. With multimedia authoring software, you can make

- Video productions
- Animations
- Games
- Interactive web sites
- Demo disks and guided tours
- Presentations
- Kiosk applications
- Interactive training
- Simulations, prototypes, and technical visualizations

Helpful Ways to Get Started

Don't be overwhelmed when starting your multimedia project—there may be a lot of things to think about, but there are also a lot of things that have already been done for you. As the cliché goes, "There's no need to reinvent the wheel!" Consider the following tips for making your production work go smoothly:

- Use templates that people have already created to set up your production. These can include appropriate styles for all sorts of data, font sets, color arrangements, and particular page setups that will save you time.
- Use wizards when they are available—they may save you much time and pre-setup work.
- Use named styles, because if you take the time to create your own it will really slow you down. Unless your client specifically requests a particular style, you will save a great deal of time using something already created, usable, and legal.
- Create tables, which you can build with a few keystrokes in many programs, and it makes the production look credible.
- Help readers find information with tables of contents, running headers and footers, and indexes.

- Improve document appearance with bulleted and numbered lists and symbols.
- Allow for a quick-change replacement using the global change feature.
- Reduce grammatical errors by using the grammar and spell checker provided with the software. Do not rely on that feature, though, to set all things right—you still need to proofread everything.
- Include identifying information in the filename so you can find the file later.

Making Instant Multimedia

While this section discusses dedicated multimedia authoring systems, there is no reason to invest in such a package if your current software (or an inexpensive upgrade) can do the job. Indeed, not only can you save money by doing multimedia with tools that are familiar and already at hand, but you also save the time spent on the arduous and sometimes lengthy learning curves involved in mastering many of the dedicated authoring systems. Common desktop tools have become multimedia-powerful.

Some multimedia projects may be so simple that you can cram all the organizing, planning, rendering, and testing stages into a single effort, and make "instant" multimedia.

Here is an example: The topic at your weekly sales meeting is sales force performance. You want to display your usual spreadsheet so that the group can see real names and numbers for each member of the team, but then you want to add an animated, multicolored 3-D bar graph for visual impact. Preparing for your meeting, you annotate the cell containing the name of the most productive salesperson for the week, using sounds of applause found on the Web or a recording of your CEO saying "Good job!" or a colleague's "Wait till next week, Pete!" At the appropriate time during the meeting, you click that cell and play the file. And that's it—you have just made and used instant multimedia.

WARNING *You need special multimedia tools for digitizing your sounds and for creating animations and movies before you can attach these objects to your text, data, or presentation documents.*

You can use a voice annotation, picture, or video clip in many word processing applications (see Figure 7-4). You can also click a cell in a spreadsheet to enhance its content with graphic images, sounds, and animations (see Figure 7-5). If you like, your database can include pictures, audio clips, and movies (see Figure 7-6), and your presentation software can generate interesting titles, visual effects, and animated illustrations for your product demo (see Figure 7-7). With these multimedia-enhanced software packages, you get many more ways to effectively convey your message than just a slide show.

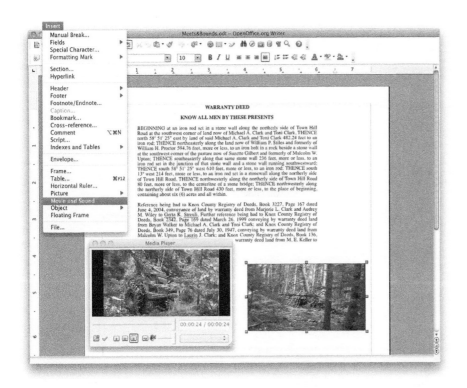

Figure 7-4 Most word processing programs allow you to include various image formats, movies, and digitized sounds (including voice annotations).

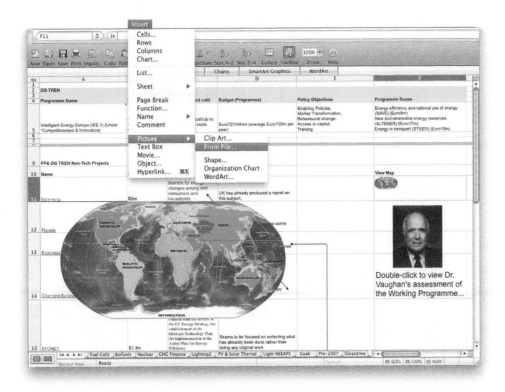

Figure 7-5 Spreadsheets can include embedded objects made with other applications.

Figure 7-6 A FileMaker Pro employee database can include image and sound resources.

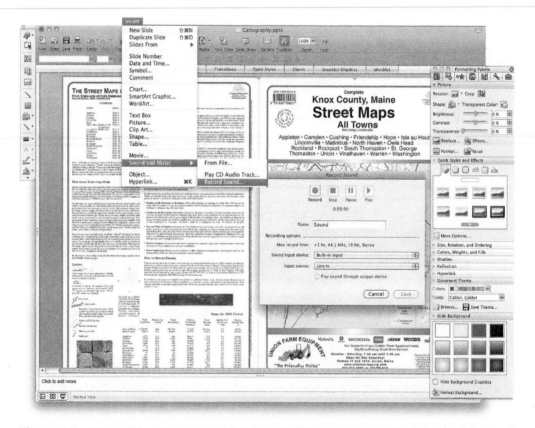

Figure 7-7 Microsoft PowerPoint provides multimedia linking and embedding features.

First Person

Embedding multimedia materials into text documents can be quick, easy, and helpful. For example, a working draft of a manuscript sent to an editor might read:

My father said that Mommy was still in a coma and my little brother was sleeping. We should go home now. So we went out the back way to the physician's parking lot—down the elevator and past the noisy kitchen with its racks of trays, white-uniformed cooks, piles of canned goods, and the steamy smells of institutional stew. The green screen door slammed indelibly into my five-year-old memory, and the attendant waved to my dad; he probably didn't know we were there on family business. It was all pretty serious.

We found Mommy's car behind the police station. I stayed in my seat while my father got out and walked very slowly around the twisted metal. He was calculating the impact forces, visualizing the accident in slow-motion freeze frames, and at one point, he leaned in through the broken glass and ran his hand across the dent in the steel glove compartment where my brother had smashed his face. He went around only the one time, then got back in. "She must have been doing about forty when she hit the pole," he offered as if I were an adult, and we drove out the narrow circular drive alongside the station house. It was a crisp, clear, football-and-pumpkins Saturday afternoon in October.

Note to Sally: Per your comment last week, pick a good illustration from the file of images that I have embedded. One of them should fit the bill... Thanks! See you next week.

Types of Authoring Tools

Each multimedia project you undertake will have its own underlying structure and purpose and will require different features and functions.

E-learning modules such as those seen on PDAs, MP3 players, and intra-college networks may include web-based teaching materials, multimedia CD-ROMs or web sites, discussion boards, collaborative software, wikis, simulations, games, electronic voting systems, blogs, computer-aided assessment, simulations, animation, blogs, learning management software, and e-mail. This is also referred to as distance learning or blended learning, where online learning is mixed with face-to-face learning. The following are several authoring tools for e-learning:

- Adobe Captivate (www.adobe.com/products/captivate)
- Adobe Presenter (www.adobe.com/products/presenter)
- Articulate Storyline and Articulate Studio (www.articulate.com)
- Composica (www.composica.com)
- Claro dominKnow (www.dominknow.com)
- Easygenerator (www.easygenerator.com)
- GoAnimate (http://goanimate.com)
- Harbinger Raptivity (www.raptivity.com)

- iSpring Presenter (www.ispringsolutions.com)
- Lectora Inspire (http://lectora.com)
- Qarbon ViewletBuilder (www.qarbon.com)
- Skilitics Interact and Skilitics Thrive (www.skilitics.com)
- SmartBuilder (www.smartbuilder.com)
- TechSmith Camtasia Studio (www.techsmith.com)
- ZebraZapps (www.zebrazapps.com)

The various multimedia authoring tools can be categorized into three groups, based on the method used for sequencing or organizing multimedia elements and events:

- Card- or page-based tools
- Icon- or object-based, event-driven multimedia- and game-authoring tools
- Time-based tools

Card- or Page-Based Authoring Tools

CARDS & PAGES

Card-based or page-based tools are authoring systems wherein the elements are organized as a stack of cards or pages of a book, respectively. Thousands of pages or cards may be available in the book or stack. These tools are best used when the bulk of your content consists of elements that can be viewed individually, letting the authoring system link these pages or cards into organized sequences. You can jump, on command, to any page you wish in the structured navigation pattern.

Page- or card-based authoring systems such as LiveCode (www.livecode.com) contain media objects: buttons, text fields, graphic objects, backgrounds, pages or cards, and even the project itself. The characteristics of objects are defined by properties (highlighted, bold, red, hidden, active, locked, and so on). Each object may contain a programming script, usually a property of that object, activated when an event (such as a mouse click) related to that object occurs. Events cause messages to pass along the hierarchy of objects in the project; for example, a mouse-clicked message could be sent from a button to the background, to the page, and then to the project itself. As the message travels, it looks for handlers in the script of each object; if it finds a matching handler, the authoring system then executes the task specified by that handler.

Following are some typical messages that might pass along the object hierarchy of the LiveCode authoring system: closeCard, closeStack, idle, mouseDown, mouseStillDown, mouseUp, newBackground, openCard, openStack. Now let's look at specific examples. To go to the next card or page when a button is clicked, place a message handler into the script of that button. An example in the LiveCode language would be

```
on mouseUp
  go next card
end mouseUp
```

The handler, if placed in the script of the card or page, executes its commands when it receives a mouseUp event message that occurs at any location on the card or page—not just while the cursor is within the bounds of a button.

Card- and page-based systems typically provide two separate layers on each card or page: a **background layer** that can be shared among many cards or pages, and a foreground layer that is specific to a single card or page.

Icon- or Object-Based Authoring Tools

Icon-based or **object-based authoring tools** are **event-driven authoring systems** wherein multimedia elements and interaction cues (events) are organized as objects in a structural framework or process. Icon- or object-based, event-driven tools simplify the organization of your project and typically display flow diagrams of activities along branching paths. In complicated navigational structures, this charting is particularly useful during development.

ICONS & OBJECTS

Icon-based, event-driven tools provide a visual programming approach to organizing and presenting multimedia. First you build a structure or flowchart of events, tasks, and decisions, by dragging appropriate icons from a library. These icons can include menu choices, graphic images, sounds, and computations. The flowchart graphically depicts the project's logic. When the structure is built, you can add your content: text, graphics, animation, sounds, and video movies. Then, to refine your project, you edit your logical structure by rearranging and fine-tuning the icons and their properties.

With icon-based authoring tools, non-technical multimedia authors can build sophisticated applications without scripting. By placing icons on a flow line, you can quickly sequence events and activities, including decisions and user interactions. These tools are useful for storyboarding, as you can change sequences, add options, and restructure interactions by simply dragging and dropping icons. You can print out your navigation map or flowchart, an annotated project index with or without associated icons, design and presentation windows, and a cross-reference table of variables.

Time-Based Authoring Tools

Time-based tools are authoring systems wherein elements and events are organized along a timeline, with resolutions as high as or higher than 1/30 second. Time-based tools are best to use when you have a message with a beginning and an end. Sequentially organized graphic frames are played back at a speed that you can set. Other elements (such as audio events) are triggered at a given time or location in the sequence of events. The more powerful time-based tools let you program jumps to any location in a sequence, thereby adding navigation and interactive control.

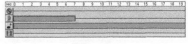

TIME

Each tool uses its own distinctive approach and user interface for managing events over time. Many use a visual timeline for sequencing the events of a multimedia presentation, often displaying layers of various media elements or events alongside the scale in increments as precise as one second. Others arrange long sequences of graphic frames and add the time component by adjusting each frame's duration of play.

Adobe Flash　Flash is a time-based development environment. Flash, however, is also particularly focused on delivery of rich multimedia content to the Web. With the Flash Player plug-in installed in more than 95 percent of the world's browsers, Flash delivers far more than simple static HTML pages. ActionScript, the proprietary, under-the-hood scripting language of Flash, is based upon the international **ECMAScript** standard (www.ecma-international.org) derived from Netscape's original JavaScript.

Adobe Director　Director is a powerful and complex multimedia authoring tool with a broad set of features to create multimedia presentations, animations, and interactive multimedia applications. It requires a significant learning curve, but once mastered, it is among the most powerful of multimedia development tools. In Director, you assemble and sequence the elements of your project, called a "movie," using a Cast and a Score. The **Cast** is a multimedia database containing still images, sound files, text, palettes, QuickDraw shapes, programming scripts, QuickTime movies, Flash movies, and even other Director files. You tie these Cast members together using the **Score** facility, which is a sequencer for displaying, animating, and playing Cast members, and it is made up of frames that contain Cast members, tempo, a palette, timing, and sound information. Each frame is played back on a **stage** at a rate specified in the tempo channel. Director utilizes **Lingo**, a full-featured object-oriented scripting language, to enable interactivity and programmed control.

Objects

In multimedia authoring systems, multimedia elements and events are often treated as **objects** that live in a hierarchical order of **parent and child relationships**. Messages passed among these objects order them to *do* things according to the **properties** or **modifiers** assigned to them. In this way, for example, Teen-child (a teenager object) may be programmed to take out the trash every Friday evening, and does so when they get a message from Dad. Spot, the puppy, may bark and jump up and down when the postman arrives, and is defined by barking and jumping modifiers. Objects typically take care of themselves. Send them a message and they do their thing without external procedures and programming. Objects are particularly useful for games, which contain many components with many "personalities," all for simulating real-life situations, events, and their constituent properties.

Object-based authoring programs typically provide objects pre-programmed with sensible properties, messages, and functions. A video object, for example, will likely have a duration property (how long the video plays) and a source property (the location of the video file) and it will likely accept commands from the system such as "play" and "stop."

Choosing an Authoring Tool

In the best case, you must be prepared to choose the tool that best fits the job; in the worst case, you must know which tools will at least "get the job done." Authoring tools are constantly being improved by their makers, who add new features and increase performance with upgrade development cycles of six months to a year. It is important that you study the software product reviews in the blogs and computer trade journals, as well as talk with current users of these systems, before deciding on the best ones for your needs. The following sections describe what to look for.

Editing Features

The elements of multimedia—images, animations, text, digital audio and MIDI music, and video clips—need to be created, edited, and converted to standard file formats, using the specialized applications described in Chapters 2, 3, 4, 5, and 6, which provide these capabilities. Also, editing tools for these elements, particularly text and still images, are often included in your authoring system. The more editors your authoring system has, the fewer specialized tools you may need. In many cases, however, the editors that may come with an authoring system will offer only a subset of the substantial features found in dedicated tools. According to Vaughan's Law of Multimedia Minimums (see Chapter 4), these features may very well be sufficient for what you need to do; on the other hand, if editors you need are missing from your authoring system, or if you require more power, it's best to use one of the specialized, single-purpose tools.

Organizing Features

The organization, design, and production process for multimedia involves storyboarding and flowcharting. Some authoring tools provide a visual flowcharting system or overview facility for illustrating your project's structure at a macro level. Storyboards or navigation diagrams can also help organize a project and can help focus the overall project scope for all involved. Because designing the interactivity and navigation flow of your project often requires a great deal of planning and programming effort, your storyboard should describe not just the graphics of each screen, but the interactive elements as well. Features that help organize your material are a plus. Many web-authoring programs such as Adobe Dreamweaver include tools that create helpful diagrams and links among the pages of a web site. Planning ahead in an organized fashion may prevent countless moments of indecision, keep the client from changing her mind without periodic sign-offs on the materials included, and, in the long run, save you money.

Programming Features

Multimedia authoring systems offer one or more of the following approaches, as explained in the following paragraphs:

- Visual programming with cues, icons, and objects
- Programming with a scripting language
- Programming with traditional languages, such as Basic or C
- Document development tools

Visual programming with icons or objects is perhaps the simplest and easiest authoring process. If you want to play a sound or put a picture into your project, just drag the element's icon into the playlist—or drag it away to delete it.

Authoring tools that offer a **very high level language (VHLL)** or interpreted scripting environment for navigation control and for enabling user inputs or goal-oriented programming languages—such as Flash, LiveCode, and Director—are more powerful by definition. The more commands and functions provided in the **scripting language**, the more powerful the authoring system. Once you learn a scripting language, you will be able to learn other scripting languages relatively quickly; the principles are the same, regardless of the command syntax and keywords used.

As with traditional programming tools, look for an authoring package with good debugging facilities, robust text editing, and online syntax reference. Other scripting augmentation facilities are advantageous, as well. In complex projects, you may need to program custom extensions of the scripting language for direct access to the computer's operating system.

A powerful document reference and delivery system is a key component of some projects. Some authoring tools offer direct importing of preformatted text, indexing facilities, complex text search mechanisms, and hypertext linkage tools. These authoring systems are useful for development of DVD- and web-based information products, online documentation and help systems, and sophisticated multimedia-enhanced publications.

With scripts, you can perform computational tasks; sense and respond to user input; create character, icon, and motion animations; launch other applications; and control external multimedia devices.

Interactivity Features

Interactivity empowers the end users of your project by letting them control the content and flow of information. Authoring tools should provide one or more levels of interactivity:

- **Simple branching**, which offers the ability to go to another section of the multimedia production (via an activity such as a keypress, mouse click, or expiration of a timer)
- **Conditional branching**, which supports a go-to that is based on the results of IF-THEN decisions or events
- A structured language that supports complex programming logic, such as nested IF-THENs, subroutines, event tracking, and message passing among objects and elements

Performance Tuning Features

Complex multimedia projects require exact synchronization of events—for example, the animation of an exploding balloon with its accompanying sound effect. Accomplishing synchronization is difficult because performance varies widely among the different computers used for multimedia development and delivery. Some authoring tools allow you to lock a production's playback speed to a specified computer platform, but others provide no ability whatsoever to control performance on various systems. In many cases, you will need to use the authoring tool's own scripting language or custom programming facility to specify timing and sequence on systems with different (faster or slower) processors. Be sure your authoring system allows precise timing of events.

Playback Features

As you build your multimedia project, you will be continually assembling elements and testing to see how the assembly looks and performs. Your authoring system should let you build a segment or part of your project and then quickly test it as if the user were actually using it. You should spend a great deal of time going back and forth between building and testing as you refine and smooth the content and timing of the project. You may even want to release the project to others who you trust to run it ragged and show you its weak points.

Delivery Features

Delivering your project may require building a run-time version of the project using the multimedia authoring software. A **run-time version** or **stand-alone** allows your project to play back without requiring the

Why is programming fun? What delights may its practitioner expect as his reward?

First is the sheer joy of making things. As the child delights in his mud pie, so the adult enjoys building things, especially things of his own design. I think this delight must be an image of God's delight in making things, a delight shown in the distinctiveness of each leaf and each snowflake.

Second is the pleasure of making things that are useful to other people. Deep within, we want others to use our work and to find it helpful. In this respect the programming system is not essentially different from the child's first clay pencil holder "for Daddy's office."

Third is the fascination of fashioning complex puzzle-like objects of interlocking moving parts and watching them work in subtle cycles, playing out the consequences of principles built in from the beginning. The programmed computer has all the fascination of the pinball machine or the jukebox mechanism, carried to the ultimate.

Fourth is the joy of always learning, which springs from the non-repeating nature of the task. In one way or another the problem is ever new, and its solver learns something: sometimes practical, sometimes theoretical, and sometimes both.

Finally, there is the delight of working in such a tractable medium. The programmer, like the poet, works only slightly removed from pure thought-stuff. He builds his castles in the air, from air, creating by exertion of the imagination. Few media of creation are so flexible, so easy to polish and rework, so readily capable of realizing grand conceptual structures. (As we shall see later, this tractability has its own problems.)

Yet the program construct, unlike the poet's words, is real in the sense that it moves and works, producing visible outputs separately from the construct itself. It prints results, draws pictures, produces sounds, moves arms. The magic of myth and legend has come true in our time. One types the correct incantation on a keyboard, and a display screen comes to life, showing things that never were nor could be.

Programming then is fun because it gratifies creative longings built deep within us and delights sensibilities we have in common with all men.

From *The Mythical Man-Month: Essays in Software Engineering* by Frederick P. Brooks, Jr., Kenan Professor of Computer Science, University of North Carolina at Chapel Hill

full authoring software and all its tools and editors. Often, the run-time version does not allow users to access or change the content, structure, and programming of the project. If you are going to distribute your project widely, you should distribute it in the run-time version. Make sure your authored project can be easily distributed.

Cross-Platform Features

It is also increasingly important to use tools that make transfer across platforms easy. For many developers, the Macintosh remains the multimedia authoring platform of choice, but 80 percent of that developer's target market may be Windows platforms. If you develop on a Macintosh, look for tools that provide a compatible authoring system for Windows or offer a run-time player for the other platform.

Internet Playability

Because the Web and apps for mobile devices have become significant delivery targets for multimedia, authoring systems typically provide a means to convert their output so that it can be delivered within the context of HTML or DHTML, either with special plug-ins or by embedding Java, JavaScript, or other code structures in the HTML document or for a specific operating system such as iOS or Android. Test your authoring software for Internet or app delivery before you build your project. Be sure it performs as you expect! Test it out for performance stability on as many platforms as you can.

Chapter 7 Review

Chapter Summary

For your review, here's a summary of the important concepts discussed in this chapter.

Describe the four primary stages in a multimedia project

- Planning and costing

- Designing and producing

- Testing

- Delivering

Discuss the intangible elements needed to make good multimedia

- Creativity

- Organization

- Communication skill

Identify the typical members of a multimedia project team and describe the skills that they need for their work.

- The project manager is responsible for the overall development and implementation of a project as well as for the day-to-day operations.

- Instructional designers make sure that the subject matter is clear and properly presented.

- Interface designers devise the navigation pathways and content maps on screen that let the user access or modify that content.

- Information designers structure content, determine user pathways and feedback, and select presentation media. Multimedia writers, sometimes called content writers, create characters, action, and point of view—and they also create interactivity.

- Multimedia video specialists must know the basics about shooting good video, and be thoroughly familiar with the tools and techniques used for digital editing on computers. They also must understand the potentials and limitations of the medium, including interactivity, how it will affect the video, and how these limitations affect the video production itself.

- Audio specialists design and produce music, voice-over narrations, and sound effects. They may also be responsible for locating and selecting suitable music and talent, scheduling recording sessions, and digitizing and editing recorded material into computer files.

- A multimedia programmer or software engineer uses an authoring system or programming language to integrate the multimedia elements of a project into a seamless whole. Sometimes programmers need to build extensions to the authoring and presentation suite in order to extend the system's capabilities.

- Web site producers not only put together a coordinated set of pages for the World Wide Web but also constantly coordinate updates and changes.

Discuss the hardware most often used in making multimedia and choose an appropriate platform for a project

- Windows and Macintosh are the two computer platforms most often used.

- Hardware elements such as hard disks and networked peripherals must be connected together.

- Memory and storage devices include hard drives, random access memory (RAM), read-only memory (ROM), flash memory and thumb drives, and CD-ROM, DVD, and Blu-ray discs.

- Input and output devices such as microphones, recorders, speakers, and displays are required when working with multimedia elements.

Understand common software programs used to handle text, graphics, audio, video, and animation in multimedia projects and discuss their capabilities

- A word processor is usually a regularly used tool in designing and building a multimedia project.

- Image-editing software: bitmapped images provide the greatest choice and power to the artist for rendering fine detail and effects.

- Animations and digital video movies are sequences of bitmapped graphic scenes or frames, rapidly played back.

- With proper editing software, you can digitize video, edit, add special effects and titles, mix sound tracks, and save the clip.

- To master an application, you may have spent many hours learning it, and you will likely stay with that product rather than change to another.

Determine which multimedia authoring system is most appropriate for any given project

- Three metaphors are used by authoring tools that make multimedia: card- and page-based, icon-and object-based, and time-based.

- When choosing an authoring system, consider its editing, organizing, programming, interactivity, performance, playback, cross-platform, and delivery features.

Key Terms

3-D modeling software *(224)*
Advanced Technology Attachment (ATA) *(209)*
Apple Macintosh *(204)*
assets *(198)*
background layer *(235)*
barcoding *(214)*
binary compatible *(205)*
Blu-ray Disc (BD) *(213)*
card-based *(234)*
Cast *(236)*
cathode-ray tube (CRT) *(218)*
client/server software *(207)*
clone *(206)*
compact disc read-only memory (CD-ROM) *(212)*
conditional branching *(239)*
cross-platform *(205)*
Digital Versatile Disc (DVD) *(213)*
drawing software *(222)*
DVD-ROM *(213)*
DVD-Video *(213)*
ECMAScript *(236)*
erasable programmable ROM (EPROM) *(212)*
Ethernet *(207)*
event-driven authoring systems *(235)*
File Transfer Protocol (FTP) *(200)*
filter *(227)*
FireWire *(210)*
format converter *(228)*

frame *(227)*
Frequently Asked Questions (FAQ) *(220)*
handler *(234)*
High-Definition TV (HDTV) *(213)*
hot-swapping *(210)*
icon-based authoring tools *(235)*
image-editing application *(226)*
Integrated Drive Electronics (IDE) *(209)*
Internet service provider (ISP) *(207)*
keyboarding *(221)*
Lingo *(236)*
local area network (LAN) *(207)*
look and feel *(196)*
Microsoft Windows *(204)*
mirroring *(210)*
modifier *(236)*
multimedia skill set *(200)*
object *(236)*
object-based authoring tools *(235)*
office suite *(221)*
optical character recognition (OCR) *(214)*
page-based *(234)*
painting software *(222)*
parent and child relationship *(236)*
platform-independent *(205)*

plug-and-play *(209)*
proof of concept *(196)*
property *(234)*
prototype *(196)*
random access memory (RAM) *(211)*
read-only memory (ROM) *(212)*
run-time version *(239)*
Score *(236)*
scriptwriter *(202)*
scripting language *(238)*
simple branching *(239)*
Small Computer System Interface (SCSI) *(210)*
sprite *(227)*
stage *(236)*
stand-alone *(239)*
team building *(204)*
terabyte *(212)*
time-based tools *(235)*
Universal Product Code (UPC) *(214)*
Universal Serial Bus (USB) *(209)*
very high level language (VHLL) *(238)*
visual programming *(238)*
voice recognition system *(215)*
wide area network (WAN) *(207)*
Wi-Fi *(207)*
word processor *(221)*

■ Key Term Quiz

1. A(n) _____ is a simple, working example that demonstrates whether or not an idea is feasible.

2. A(n) _____ file requires no cross-platform conversion.

3. A file or document containing helpful answers is called a _____.

4. A package of software applications that might include a spreadsheet, database, e-mail, web browser, and presentation applications is called a(n) _____.

5. A program that changes an image from one type of graphics file to another is a(n) _____.

6. A network of workstations located within a short distance of one another that allows direct communication and sharing of peripheral resources such as file servers, printers, scanners, and network modems is called a(n) _____.

7. The type of memory used by a computer to run several programs at the same time is called _____.

8. The type of memory that is not erased when power is shut off to it is called _____.

9. Elements and events are organized along a timeline in a(n) _____ authoring system.

10. Each graphic scene in an animation is referred to as a(n) _____.

■ Multiple-Choice Quiz

1. As you design and build a multimedia project, your most often used tool may be your:
   a. word processor
   b. authoring system
   c. image processor
   d. drawing program
   e. format converter

2. Of all the multimedia elements in a project, the one that will likely have the greatest influence on the end user is the:
   a. video footage
   b. sound effects
   c. graphical impact
   d. packaging
   e. musical background

3. Painting software is dedicated to producing:
   a. vector images
   b. animations
   c. 3-D images
   d. bitmap images
   e. video clips

4. DVD stands for:
   a. Dynamically-Variable Disc
   b. Distributed Video Disc
   c. Data-Vision Disc
   d. Double-Volume Disc
   e. Digital Versatile Disc

5. When you turn off the power to this type of storage, any data stored in it is lost.
   a. CD-ROM
   b. ROM
   c. OROM
   d. EPROM
   e. RAM

6. A barcode reader can:
   a. scan graphics into a computer
   b. read Universal Product Code patterns
   c. provide pressure-sensitive input
   d. recognize spoken words when trained
   e. all of the above

7. Which of these is a common platform for producing and delivering multimedia projects today?
   a. IBM VMS
   b. Windows 3
   c. CPM
   d. Windows 98
   e. Macintosh OS X

8. A scripting language is considered:
   a. a very low level language (VLLL)
   b. an assembler language
   c. a subset of HTML
   d. a form of BASIC
   e. a very high level language (VHLL)

9. For a project whose content consists of elements that can be viewed individually, this type of authoring system is particularly useful during development.
   a. card- or page-based tool
   b. icon-based, event-driven tool
   c. time-based tool
   d. scripting language
   e. All are equally useful.

10. Scripting languages operate by processing small blocks of code when certain events occur. Such a block of code is called:
    a. a function
    b. a handler
    c. a process
    d. a script
    e. a protocol

11. Most card-based programs have a layer that stays constant behind a layer above it that can be different on all other cards. This layer is called the:
    a. master layer
    b. system layer
    c. prime layer
    d. background layer
    e. static layer

12. In multimedia authoring systems, multimedia elements and events are often treated as objects that exist in a hierarchical relationship. This relationship is often called:
    a. servant and master
    b. host and client
    c. property and modifier
    d. creator and creature
    e. parent and child

13. Which of the following is *not* a stage of multimedia production?
    a. testing
    b. planning and costing
    c. designing and producing
    d. marketing
    e. delivering

14. Which of these is *not* a problem you might encounter in porting a program from a Mac to a Windows PC (or from a Windows PC to a Mac)?
    a. Bitmapped images are larger on a PC.
    b. Font sizes and shapes are slightly different.
    c. Special characters are not the same.
    d. Graphics with 256 colors show different colors.
    e. All are potential problems.

15. The most precious asset you can bring to the multimedia workshop is your:
    a. creativity
    b. programming skill
    c. musical ability
    d. film and video production talent
    e. checking account

■ Essay Quiz

1. You are a team leader who has been given six months to produce a multimedia title that will demonstrate your company's capabilities. Write a brief outline describing the timeline and the possible costs associated with the four stages of the project (you do not have to estimate actual amounts, just estimate percentage of budget). Justify your estimates.

2. Consider your own skills, abilities, and goals. Where do you see yourself fitting into a multimedia production team? What abilities would you bring to a team now? What abilities do you need to work to develop? What are your creative abilities? What is your level of mastery of multimedia tools (software and hardware)?

3. You have been assigned to develop for an auto club a complex multimedia kiosk that will allow users with an account to enter a starting point and an ending point, and have a map printed out. What input devices could be used to identify the user? What input devices could be used to enter start and end locations? Could one device do both functions? What about printing out the maps?

4. List the various methods of connecting a computer with the "world," and discuss the benefits and drawbacks of each.

5. Describe the problems you are likely to encounter in creating a cross-platform program, and list several ways to deal with these problems.

Lab Projects

■ Project 7.1

Create the credits for an imaginary multimedia production. Include several outside organizations, such as video production companies and audio mixing/post-production facilities. Don't forget to include copywriters and other content providers. It may be helpful to look at the credits for an actual production.

■ Project 7.2

Visit the web sites of three video-editing programs, and locate a page that summarizes the capabilities of each. List the formats each is able to import from and export or output to. How do they handle clips? Is there an easy, intuitive, "drag-and-drop" interface? How many audio and video tracks are included? How are transitions and filters included? What features do all of them have in common? What unique features does each one have? Document your findings.

■ Project 7.3

You are tasked with formulating a list of software tools needed for a new video multimedia project. Create a list of tools needed, and identify a number of possible commercially available (or free) products for each kind of tool on the list. Compile a final list of software detailing why you chose each specific program over potential alternatives.

■ Project 7.4

Locate a program, such as a paint or sketch program, available both on a full-sized computer and on a mobile device or tablet. Compare which features are available in each version, and identify the advantages and disadvantages of each. Note any differences in cost or feature set.

■ Project 7.5

You have been assigned to manage a major training project. This project is to include a complex simulation of a workplace task and a reference database of images. Create a hypothetical flow diagram that illustrates the relationship between the simulation and the database. Discuss how you might design and produce this project.

## CHAPTER 8

Planning and Costing

In this chapter, you will learn how to:

- Determine the scope of a multimedia project

- Schedule the phases, tasks, and work items required to complete a project

- Estimate the cost, timeline, and tasks required to complete a project

- Write and structure the elements of a multimedia project proposal

BEFORE you begin a multimedia project, you must first develop a sense of its scope and content, letting the project take shape in your head as you think through the various methods available to get your message across to your viewers. Then you must develop an organized outline and a plan that is rational in terms of the skills, time, budget, tools, and resources you have at hand. Proper project planning is as important as planning the layout and content. Your plans should be in place before you start to render graphics, sounds, and other components, and you should refer to them throughout the project's execution.

First Person

When I was nine, my father told me about China. He brought the big spinning globe into the kitchen and used a fork to point out where we were and where China was. He explained that if we dug a hole deep enough in the backyard, eventually we would come out in a place called Peking. After school the next day, I began, unannounced, trenching a pit into the rocky soil of our New England backyard. The first layer was tough sod, then there was some topsoil and loam, and then a thick stratum of moist pea gravel. I was knee-deep into the next layer— hard-packed clay—when my father discovered my work site when he came home at the end of the day. He was pleased I had missed the septic tank by several feet and sternly suggested that more study would be required before I dug any further. This was my first lesson in project planning, not to mention my first experience with project abandonment. Be sure you analyze the requirements of your multimedia project before you go to the toolshed.

The Process of Making Multimedia

Usually something will click in your mind or in the mind of a client that says, "Hey, wouldn't it be neat if we could…" Your visions of sound and music, flashy images, and perhaps a video will solve a business need, provide an attention-grabbing product demo, or yield a slick front end to an otherwise drab computer database. You might want to spark a little interest or a laugh in an otherwise dull meeting, build an interactive photo album for Christmas greetings to your family, or post your company's annual report in a new set of pages on the Web.

Plan for the entire process: beginning with your first ideas and ending with completion and delivery of a finished product. Think in the overview. The stepwise process of making multimedia is illustrated in Figure 8-1. Use this chart to help you get your arms around a new web site, app, or DVD production! Note the feedback loops for revisions based upon testing and experiment. Note also the constant presence of an "evaluation committee" (who could be simply a project manager) to oversee the whole.

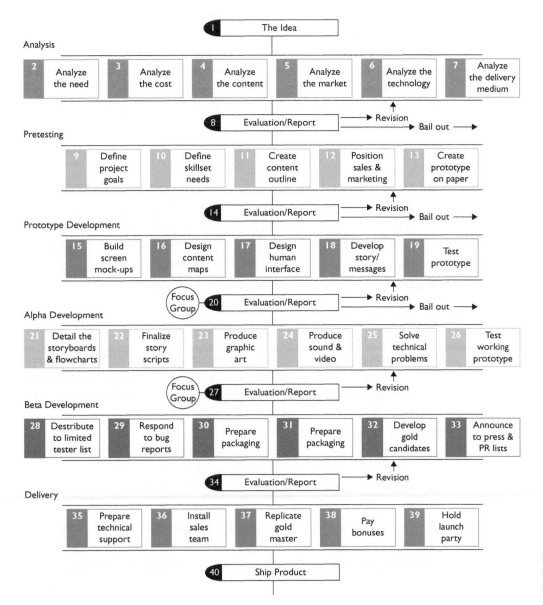

Figure 8-1 The process of making multimedia

> We locked eight people in a room with pizza and out popped a design...
>
> ....
>
> Mike Duffy,
> Chief Technical Officer,
> Software Toolworks, describing
> how the design for the
> "20th Century Almanac"
> was developed

It is, of course, easiest to plan a project using the experience you have accumulated in similar past projects. Over time, you can maintain and improve your multimedia-planning format, just like a batch of sourdough starter. Just keep adding a little rye and water every time you do a project, and the starter for your next job gets a bit more potent as your estimates become tempered by experience.

Idea Analysis

The important thing to keep in mind when you are toying with an idea is balance. As you think through your idea, you must continually weigh your purpose or goal against the feasibility and cost of production and delivery.

Use whiteboard, notepaper, and scratch pads as you flesh out your idea, or use a note-taking or outlining program on your computer. Start with broad brushstrokes, and then think through each constituent multimedia element. Ultimately, you will generate a plan of action that will become your road map for production. Who needs this project? Is it worthwhile? Do you have the materials at hand to build it? Do you have the skills to build it? Your idea will be in balance if you have considered and weighed the proper elements:

- What is the essence of what you want to do? What is your purpose and message?
- Who is your intended audience? Who will be your end users? What do they already know about the subject? Will they understand industry terms (jargon), and what information do they need your project to communicate to them? What will their multimedia playback platforms be, and what are the minimal technical capabilities of those platforms?
- Is there a client, and if so, what does the client want?
- How can you organize your project?
- What multimedia elements (text, sounds, and visuals) will best deliver your message?
- Do you already have content material with which you can leverage your project, such as old videotapes or video files, music, documents, photographs, logos, advertisements, marketing packages, and other artwork?
- Will interactivity be required?
- Is your idea derived from an existing theme that can be enhanced with multimedia, or will you create something totally new?
- What hardware is available for development of your project? Is it enough?
- How much storage space do you have? How much do you need?
- What multimedia software is available to you?
- What are your capabilities and skills with both the software and the hardware?

- Can you do it alone? Who can help you?
- How much time do you have?
- How much money do you have?
- How will you distribute the final project?
- Will you need to update and/or support the final product?

You can maintain balance between purpose and feasibility by dynamically adding and subtracting multimedia elements as you stretch and shape your idea. You can start small and build from minimum capabilities toward a satisfactory result in an additive way. Or you can shoot the moon with a heavy list of features and desired multimedia results, and then discard items one by one because they are just not possible. Both additive and subtractive processes can work in concert and can yield very useful cost estimates and a production road map.

Consider the following scenario: You have a video clip with four head-and-shoulders testimonials that will be perfect for illustrating your message. So add motion video to your list. You will need to purchase special effects software, so add that item and its cost to your list as well. But you want to make your product available at a web site frequented by rural students without high-speed connections who would have to wait minutes for the video to play. Subtract motion video, but add tiny framed still images of the four talking heads using short, one-sentence voice-overs of them speaking (recorded from the video clip). Subtract one of the four testimonials because you discover that particular executive is no longer with the firm and you don't have a signed release. Add animation instead. Subtract. Add. Subtract. In this manner, you will flesh out your idea, adding and subtracting elements within the constraints of the hardware, software, and your budget of cost and expertise.

The time you spend defining your project in this way—reality-testing it against technology and your abilities—might be your most valuable investment, even before you boot up a computer. At any point, you can decide to go forward or bail out.

TIP   *Treat your multimedia idea like a business venture. As you visualize in your mind's eye what you want to accomplish, balance the project's "profit" potential against the investment of effort and resources required to make it happen.*

Idea Management Software

Project management software such as dotProject (www.dotproject. net), OpenProj (https://www.openproject.org), and GanttProject (www. ganttproject.biz, see Figure 8-2), outlining programs such as Microsoft OneNote (http://office.microsoft.com/en-us/onenote/), and spreadsheet software such as Excel (http://office.microsoft.com/en-us/excel/) can be useful for arranging your ideas and the many tasks, work items, employee

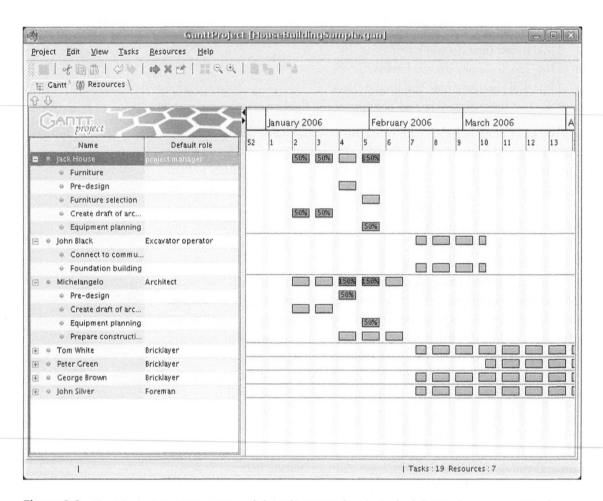

Figure 8-2 GanttProject, an open-source, web-based integrated project scheduling and management tool, generates helpful documents for instructional designers.

resources, and costs required of your multimedia project. Project management tools provide the added benefit of built-in analysis to help you stay within your schedule and budget during the rendering of the project itself.

WARNING *Budget your time if you are new to project management software. It may be difficult to learn and to use effectively.*

Project management software typically provides **Critical Path Method (CPM)** scheduling functions to calculate the total duration of a project based upon each identified task, earmarking tasks that are critical and that, if lengthened, will result in a delay in project completion. **Program Evaluation Review Technique (PERT) charts** provide graphic representations of task relationships, showing **prerequisites**, the tasks that must be completed before others can commence. **Gantt charts** depict all the tasks along a timeline.

The Paper Napkin

While not as high-tech as idea management software, any writing surface can serve as a repository for ideas when you have no other tools at hand. For example, the very early ideas of processing and preliminary planning can be sketched on a paper napkin (a real one is shown in Figure 8-3, which evolved into a complex multimedia project of many months' duration).

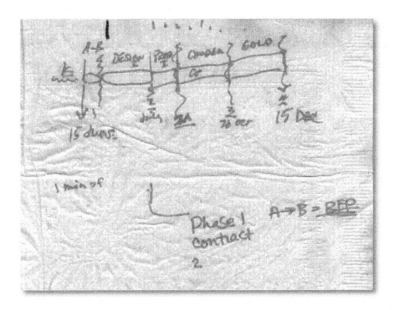

Figure 8-3   The ideas on this luncheon napkin evolved into an animated guided tour for Lotus's multimedia version of 1-2-3 in SmartSuite Millennium.

Around a lunch table, ideas were discussed, refined, and cultivated into a preliminary project plan. A prototype would be built, shown as the A-B portion of the napkin notes, which quite literally answered the question "How do we get from A to B with this idea?" The prototype would then be carefully examined in terms of projected work effort and the technology required for implementing a full-blown version. A more complete plan and cost estimate for full implementation would be developed, and the project would be launched in earnest.

First Person

Last time I took the red-eye home, the guy behind me was pretty ill—sneezing and hawking incessantly over my headrest on the full, hot plane. My glasses blurred with misty droplets, and I wiped the fog away with the damp cocktail napkin under my Coke. That trip cost me four days of being sick in bed, and I promised I would never fly night coach again to make a meeting, no matter how important.

Then I broke my promise and, after a sleepless night on the plane, found myself sitting in the muggy summer air on the bank of the Charles River, having lunch with Rob Lippincott and his multimedia team from Lotus. I pretended to be alert, but residual white noise from the plane ride beat in my ears, and my dry eyes wouldn't focus in the umbrella sunlight. Rob made intelligent notes with a ballpoint pen on a paper napkin while my own input to the creative process

was reduced to grunts and short sentences. The smartest thing I did, though, was slip the paper napkin with its notes into my briefcase as we left the table. After some sleep, I was able to retrieve the napkin and craft those luncheon thoughts into the backbone of a rational project proposal and action plan. We launched the venture, and about ten months later it went gold, shipping with Lotus's new Multimedia product, Lotus SmartSuite Millennium 9.8.

Pretesting

If you decide that your idea has merit, take it to the next step. Define your project goals in greater detail and spell out what it will take in terms of skills, content, and money to meet these goals. If you envision a commercial product, sketch out how you will sell it. Work up a prototype of the project on paper, with an explanation of how it will work. All of these steps help you organize your idea and test it against the real world.

Task Planning

There may be many tasks in your multimedia project. Here is a checklist of action items for which you should plan ahead as you think through your project:

- ❏ Design Instructional Framework
- ❏ Hold Creative Idea Session(s)
- ❏ Determine Delivery Platform
- ❏ Determine Authoring Platform
- ❏ Assay Available Content
- ❏ Draw Navigation Map
- ❏ Create Storyboards
- ❏ Design Interface
- ❏ Design Information Containers
- ❏ Research/Gather Content
- ❏ Assemble Team
- ❏ Build Prototype
- ❏ Conduct User Test
- ❏ Revise Design
- ❏ Create Graphics
- ❏ Create Animations
- ❏ Produce Audio
- ❏ Produce Video
- ❏ Digitize Audio and Video
- ❏ Take Still Photographs
- ❏ Program and Author
- ❏ Test Functionality
- ❏ Fix Bugs
- ❏ Conduct Beta Test
- ❏ Create Golden Master
- ❏ Replicate
- ❏ Prepare Package
- ❏ Deliver or Install at Web Site
- ❏ Award Bonuses
- ❏ Throw Party

In a white paper about producing educational software, elearnity (www.elearnity.com) has allocated percentages of effort, as shown at right:

Task	Percentage of Effort
Analyze need	3%
Draft mission statement	1%
Create audience profile	2%
Write objectives	2%
Analyze and outline content	6%
Lay out course map	2%
Define treatment	2%
Select learner activities	2%
Storyboard the course	19%
Author the course	28%
Evaluate the course	20%
Produce media	13%

Building a Team

Multimedia is an emerging technology requiring a set of skills so broad that multimedia itself remains poorly defined. Players in this technology come from all corners of the computer and art worlds as well as from a variety of other disciplines, so if you need to assemble a team, you need to know the people and skills it takes to make multimedia. (Refer to Chapter 7 for a description of the various skills and talents needed.)

Building a matrix chart of required skills is often helpful to describe the makeup of your team. The skills and software capabilities available to you are not as limiting as your list of required hardware—you can always budget for new and more powerful software and for the learning curve (or consultant fees) required to make use of it. Indeed, authoring software is usually necessary only for development of the project, not its playback or delivery, and should be a cost or learning burden not directly passed to end users.

Figure 8-4 shows a skill matrix developed when four medium-sized multimedia development companies came together to bid on a single, large multimedia project. If you are building a complex web site, substitute Java/Ruby programmer, HTML/CSS programmer, and Server Specialist into the proper row.

Staying at the leading edge is important. If you remain knowledgeable about what's new and expected, you will be more valuable to your own endeavors, to your team, and to your employer or prospective clients. But be prepared for steep learning curves and difficult challenges in keeping your own skills (and those of your employees) current and in demand. And don't neglect team morale as hours grow long, deadlines slip, and tempers flare.

TIP *If you are looking for multimedia talent, try placing a Help Wanted ad in one of the job-hunting/help-wanted sites on the Internet. Or you can try one of these web sites:*

....

www.careerbuilder.com

www.monster.com

www.jobbankusa.com

In a business where success and failure often depends upon our ability to monitor and anticipate emerging technology, job recruiters see multimedia as very challenging. Not only does the fledgling multimedia industry incorporate some of the hottest computer technology tools, it draws on talent that comes from outside the traditional boundaries of data processing and MIS recruitment. The ill-defined but very technical skills needed for multimedia provide us, the industry recruiters, an exceptional opportunity for creativity. Our clients, too, need to be open-minded and flexible about the talent and skills required of multimedia developers.

....

Heinz Bartesch, Director of Sales and Marketing, The Search Firm (San Francisco)

www.dice.com
www.odesk.com
www.elance.com

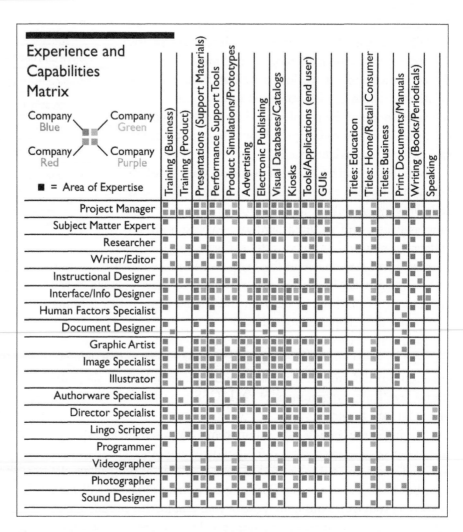

Figure 8-4   A matrix of available skills can assist you in planning for your project.

Prototype Development

Once you have decided that a project is worth doing, you should develop a working prototype. This is the point at which you begin serious work at the computer, building screen mock-ups and a human interface of menus and button clicks. Your messages and story lines will take shape as you explore ways of presenting them. For the prototype, sometimes called a **proof of concept** or **feasibility study**, you might select only a small portion of a large project and get that part working as it would in the final product. Indeed, after trying many different approaches in the course of prototyping, you may end up with several different approaches or candidates.

During this phase you can test ideas, mock up interfaces, exercise the hardware platform, and develop a sense about where the alligators live. These alligators are typically found in the swampy edges of your own expertise; in the dark recesses of software platforms that almost-but-not-quite perform as advertised; and in your misjudgment of the effort required for various tasks. The alligators will appear unexpectedly behind you and nip at your knees, unless you explore the terrain a little before you start out.

Test your prototype along several fronts: technology (will it work on your proposed delivery platform or platforms?), cost (can you do this project within budget constraints?), market (can you sell it, or will it be properly used if it is an in-house project?), and human interface (is it intuitive and easy to use?). At this point you may wish to arrange a focus group, where you can watch potential end users experiment with your prototype and analyze their reactions. The purpose of any prototype is to test the initial implementation of your idea and improve on it based upon test results. So you should never feel committed or bound to any one option, and you should be ready and willing to change things!

Persuade the client to spend a small amount of money and effort up front to let you build a skeletal version of the project, including some artwork, interactive navigation, and performance checks. Indeed, there may be some very specific technology issues that need thorough examination and proof before you can provide a realistic estimate of the work and cost required. The focused experience of this proof will allow both you and the client to assess the project's goals and the means to achieve them.

Include your experimental pilot as the first phase of your project. At the pilot's conclusion, prepare a milestone report and a functional demo. You will be paid for the work so far, and the client will get real demonstration material that can be shown to bosses and managers. If your demo is good, it will be a persuasive argument within the client's management hierarchy for completing the full-scale project.

As part of your delivery at the end of the pilot phase, reassess your estimates of the tasks required as well as the cost. Prepare a written report and analysis of budgets and anticipated additional costs. This is also the proper time to develop a revised and detailed project plan for the client. It allows the client some flexibility and provides a reality check for you. At this point you can also finalize your budget and payment schedule for the continuation of the project, as well as ink a contract and determine overrun procedures.

Difficulties may arise if your client is disappointed in the quantity of material delivered or is otherwise not satisfied with your work. If you have kept good records of the time and effort spent during prototyping, you may be able to smooth the rough waters. Remember that developing multimedia is a "trying" experience—try this, try that, then try this again a bit differently—and the creative process soaks up a lot of hours and cost. Listen carefully to the client's reaction to your prototype, because many problems can be quickly fixed, and all constructive comments can certainly be woven into the next phase of development.

Alpha Development

As you go forward, you should continually define the tasks ahead, because just as if you were navigating a supertanker, you should be aware of the reefs and passages that will appear along your course and prepare for them. With a prototype in hand and a commitment to proceed, the investment of effort will increase and, at the same time, become more focused. More people may become involved as you begin to flesh out the project as a whole. You may wish to prepare an **alpha release**, so a selected few users can exercise your prototype and provide feedback.

Beta Development

By the time your idea reaches the **beta** stage of development, you will have committed serious time, energy, and money, and it is likely too late to bail out. You have gone past the point of no return and should see it through. But by now you have a project that is looking great! Most of the features are working, and you are distributing it to a wider arena of testers. In fact, you are on the downhill slope now, and your concern should be simply successfully steering the project to its well-defined goal.

Delivery

By the time you reach the delivery stage, you are **going gold**—producing the final product. Your worries slide toward the marketplace: how will your project be received by its intended audience? You must also deal with a great many practical details, such as who will answer the support hotline and run the live chat desk, or whether to co-locate a server or trust the current ISP to handle the predicted increased volume of hits. The alpha, beta, and final gold stages of project delivery for apps, CD-ROM, DVD, and the Web are discussed in Chapter 13.

First Person

Not every prototype segues naturally into a full-blown project. Sometimes a project is shut down at this milestone due to reality shock: the client chokes on cost-to-completion estimates. Sometimes it's the Reorg Alligator: new managers with new agendas axe the project. Sometimes the client just plain doesn't like your work. Then sometimes a project simply disappears like a dream forgotten by mid-morning.

My company was invited to prepare the prototype for a large and intricate intranet site behind a corporate firewall—potentially a two-year involvement. We proposed a first phase, an analysis and definition of the company's structure and information-gathering and dissemination needs so that we could lock down major content areas and the navigation design. We wanted to know how many buttons to put on the main menu and what they would say, before we spent long hours creating the bitmaps and animations of a neat interface. "No, no," they said, "our guys have put that together already."

So we negotiated for creation of artwork and HTML page styles that would provide a consistent look and feel throughout the site. We set a fixed price and provided a list of deliverables: (1) graphic style and image elements for main home and subpages; (2) a complete site structure and map with navigationally functional "under construction" pages based on the organizational charts they would provide; and (3) working demo pages for two of the company's departments.

Then we had our first team meeting, and it soon became clear they needed hand-holding while their own MIS people transitioned from other tasks and got up to speed in their new jobs as in-house intranet team and webmasters. None had coded a page of HTML, although some had used editors and builders to get pages working. The database guy was stopped dead by an undefined Java error when accessing his massive SQL database. The server guy was still getting set up. The HTML guy was learning his authoring tools. There was neither a graphic artist nor a handy pool of

company graphic art from which our own contribution might spring. Okay, we thought, so they're on the learning curve. We can start from scratch. We took the group leader aside and quietly suggested that she consider bringing on a full-time graphics person to support her team.

During the next weeks, we developed a classy look and feel and theme. After a couple of feedback/change loops, they loved it. We worked up the more detailed bits and pieces of our deliverable and tightened up the organization of their proposed navigation map. By prototype deadline, we had spent all the hours we had estimated for the job, and they had the site up and working in test mode. We had gotten their motor running.

The last time we saw the SQL database programmer was on the afternoon we picked up our milestone check—he was removing shrink-wrap from a new copy of Photoshop, and the HTML guy was deep into Cold Fusion. We never heard from them again.

Scheduling

Once you have worked up a plan that encompasses the phases, tasks, and work items you feel will be required to complete your project, you need to lay out these elements along a timeline. This will usually include **milestones** at which certain **deliverables** are to be done. If you are working for a client, these are work products that are delivered to the client for approval. To create this schedule, you must estimate the total time required for each task and then allocate this time among the number of persons who will be asynchronously working on the project (see, for example, Figure 8-5). Again, the notion of balance is important: if you can distribute the required hours to perform a task among several workers, completion should take proportionally less time.

WARNING   *Assigning twice as many people to work on a task may not cut the time for its completion precisely in half. According to Brooks' Law, "adding manpower to a late software project makes it later." Consider the administrative and management overhead of communication, networking, and necessary staff meetings required when additional staff is added, and remember Brooks' corollary: "Nine women can't make a baby in one month."*

Scheduling can be difficult for multimedia projects because so much of the making of multimedia is artistic trial and error. A recorded sound will need to be edited and perhaps altered many times. Animations need to be run again and again and adjusted so that they are smooth and properly placed. An MPEG movie may require many hours of editing and tweaking before it works in sync with other screen activities.

Scheduling multimedia projects is also difficult because the technology of computer hardware and software is in constant flux, and upgrades while your project is under way may drive you to new installations and

Project Calc Sheet

c. 5 5		$112,000 Origination Fee	Salary	March 1	2	3	4	April 5	6	7	8	May 9	10
1 Content				5									
	Director		40	**0.1**	**0.1**	**0.1**	**0.1**	**0.1**	**0.1**	**0.1**	**0.1**	**0.1**	**0.1**
		cost		0.22	0.22	0.22	0.22	0.22	0.22	0.22	0.22	0.22	0.22
	Editor		20					**1**	**1**				
		cost		0.00	0.00	0.00	0.00	1.12	1.12	0.00	0.00	0.00	0.00
	Writer A		40	**1**	**1**	**1**	**1**	**1**					
		cost		2.24	2.24	2.24	2.24	2.24	0.00	0.00	0.00	0.00	0.00
	Researcher		16										
		cost		0.00	0.00	0.00	0.00	0.00	0.00	0.00	0.00	0.00	0.00
	subtotal number personnel			1.1	1.1	1.1	1.1	2.1	1.1	1.1	0.1	0.1	0.1
		cost		2.46	2.46	2.46	2.46	3.58	1.34	0.22	0.22	0.22	0.22
2 Art													
	Director		35	**1**	**1**	**1**	**1**	**1**	**1**	**1**	**1**	**1**	**1**
		cost		1.40	1.40	1.40	1.40	1.40	1.40	1.40	1.40	1.40	1.40
	Art 1		18								**1**	**1**	**1**
		cost		0.00	0.00	0.00	0.00	0.00	0.00	0.00	1.01	1.01	1.01
	Art 2		13										
		cost		0.00	0.00	0.00	0.00	0.00	0.00	0.00	0.00	0.00	0.00
	subtotal number personnel			1	1	1	1	1	1	1	2	2	2
		cost		1.40	1.40	1.40	1.40	1.40	1.40	1.40	2.41	2.41	2.41
3 Technical													
	Director		35								**1**	**1**	**1**
		cost		0.00	0.00	0.00	0.00	0.00	0.00	0.00	1.40	1.40	1.40

Figure 8-5   Portion of a spreadsheet used to schedule manpower and project costs

concomitant learning curves. The general rule of thumb when working with computers and new technology under a deadline is that everything will take longer to do than you think it will.

In scheduling for a project that is to be rendered for a client, remember that the client will need to approve or sign off on your work at various stages. This approval process can wreak havoc with your schedule since it takes time and depends upon factors beyond your control. Perhaps more important, the client feedback may also require revision of your work. In order to protect yourself from a capricious client, you need to have points during the project for **client sign-off** on the work, meaning that he or she

First Person

Many times we have heard about the Feedback Alligator. Its mottled skin boasts an Escher-like pattern of lines and marks, showing apparently clear definition along the head and neck, but converging to a brown muddled wash at the tail. When the tail wags this alligator, all hell breaks loose, and multimedia contracts can be severely strained or lost altogether.

Feedback Alligators can appear when you throw a client into the mix of creative people... when necessary-for-client-satisfaction approval cycles can turn your project into an anorexic nightmare of continuing rework, change, and consequently diminished profit. These alligators typically slink out from the damps *after* you have locked down a contract and scope of work, when the creative guys are already being well paid to ply their craft.

For client protection, multimedia creative artists should be hired with a cap on budget and time. They should be highly skilled, efficient, and have a clear understanding of what a project's goals are, and they should be allowed to accomplish these goals with as much freedom as possible. But good multimedia artists should come close to the mark the first time.

They don't always. For example, you agree to compose background theme music to play whenever your client's logo shows on the screen. You master a sample file and pass it to the client. She doesn't quite like the sound but is not sure why. You go back to the MIDI sequencer and try again. The client still isn't sure that's it. Again, you make up a file and e-mail it to her for review. No, maybe it needs a little more Sgt. Pepper... this is our logo, remember?

The process of client feedback can go on and on forever in a resonance of desire-to-please and creative uncertainty unless you have developed rules for limiting these cycles. While your client might always be right, you will still go broke working unlimited changes on a fixed budget.

Projects can also suffer from "scope creep." If you don't clearly delineate the features and specifications of the project expected by your client, you will be tempted to add features, enhancements, and improvements. Before long, the project's scope will exceed the original specifications, the budget, and your timeline.

So do two things to ward off the Feedback Alligator. First, make it clear up front (in your contract) that there will only be a certain number of review cycles before the client must pay for changes. Second, invite the client to the workstation or studio where the creative work is done. For sound, tickle the keyboard until the client says, "That's it!" Make 'em sign off on it. For artwork and animations, let the client spend an afternoon riding shotgun over the artist's shoulder, participating in color and design choices. Get the client involved.

If your client contact isn't empowered to make decisions but simply carries your work up to the bosses for "management approval," you are facing the unpleasant Son of Feedback Alligator. Demand a client contact who has budget and design authority.

has approved the work to that point. If the client changes his or her mind later in the process, then any revisions of the previously approved materials would require a change order, meaning that the client agrees to pay the additional costs for making the changes, rather than your having to eat that unbudgeted cost out of your profit margin.

TIP   *When you negotiate with your client, limit the number of revisions allowed (each revision costs time and money) before you rename the revisions as change orders and bill extra.*

Estimating

In production and manufacturing industries, it is a relatively simple matter to estimate costs and effort. To make chocolate chip cookies, for example, you need ingredients, such as flour and sugar, and equipment, such as mixers, ovens, and packaging machines. Once the process is running smoothly, you can turn out hundreds of cookies, each tasting the same and each made of the same stuff. You then control your costs by fine-tuning known expenses, like negotiating deals on flour and sugar in quantity, installing more efficient ovens, and hiring personnel at a more competitive wage. In contrast, making multimedia is not a repetitive manufacturing process. Rather, it is by nature a continuous research and development effort characterized by creative trial and error—a "trying" experience, as described previously. Each new project is somewhat different from the last, and each may require application of many different tools and solutions. Philosophers will counsel you that experience is something you get only after you need it!

TIP   *To recoup learning-curve costs when you first perform a task, you must factor extra time into your budget; later you can increase your billing rate to reflect your improved skill level.*

In the area of professional services, let's consider some typical costs in the advertising community. According to the national trade association representing the advertising agency business in the United States, the average national 30-second spot for television costs more than $354,000 in 2011. Production of a storyboard for a 30-second commercial spot costs about $50,000. Postproduction editing time in a professional video studio runs upwards of $500 per hour. An hour of professional acting talent costs $350 or more at union scale. The emerging multimedia industry, on the other hand, does not have a track record long enough to have produced "going rates" for its services. A self-guided tour distributed with a software product, for example, may cost $15,000 for one client and $150,000 for another, depending upon the tour's length and polish. A short original musical clip may cost $50 or $500, based on the talent used and the nature of the music. A graphical menu screen might take 2 or 20 hours to develop, depending on its complexity and the graphic art talent applied. Without available going rates for segments of work or entire projects, you must estimate the costs of your multimedia project by analyzing the tasks that it comprises and the people who build it.

Be sure you include the hidden costs of administration and management. It takes time to speak with clients on the telephone, to write progress reports, and to mail invoices. In addition, there may be many people in your workforce who represent specialized skills, for example, a graphic artist, musician, instructional designer, and writer. In this case, you'll need to include a little extra buffer of time and expense in your estimate to pay for these artists' participation in project meetings and creative sessions. Also, remember to include a line item in your budget for **contingencies**, as a little extra padding to cover the inevitable unexpected costs. Adding 10 percent to 15 percent of the total cost is a typical rule-of-thumb contingency amount.

As a general rule, there are three elements that can vary in project estimates: time, money, and people. As illustrated next, if you decrease any one of these elements, you'll generally need to increase one or both of the others. For example, if you have very little time to do a project (an aggressive schedule), it will cost more money in overtime and premium sweat, and it may take more people. If you have a good number of people, the project should take less time. By increasing the money spent, you can actually decrease the number of people required by purchasing efficient (but costly) experts; this may also reduce the time required.

Do your best to estimate the amount of time it will take to perform each task in your plan. Multiply this estimate by your hourly billing rate. Sum the total costs for each task, and you now have an estimate of the project's total time and cost. Though this simple formula is easy, what is not so easy is diligently remaining within the budgeted time and money for each task. For this, you need good tracking and management oversight.

If you are working for an outside client, you will also need to determine a **payment schedule**. Payments are often divided into thirds: one-third up front upon the signing of a contract, one-third as work products are delivered and approved during the alpha and beta development phases, and one-third upon final approval of the completed production.

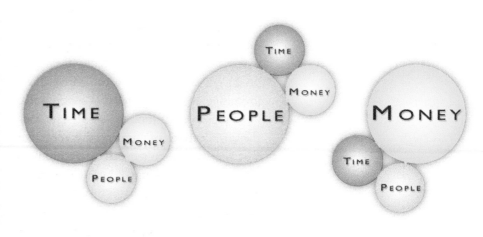

Billing Rates

Your billing rate should be set according to your cost of doing business plus a reasonable profit margin. Typical billing rates for multimedia production companies and web designers range from $65 to $160 an hour, depending upon the work being done and the person doing it. If consultants or specialists are employed on a project, the billing rate can go much higher. You can establish a rate that is the same for all tasks, or you can specify different rates according to the person assigned to a task. The Graphic Artists Guild (www.graphicartistsguild.org) provides its members pricing and ethical guidelines that are based on industry surveys of actual fees charged for graphic arts projects. Pricing guides are also available at www.brennerbooks.com.

Everyone who contributes to a project should have two rates associated with their work: the employee's cost to the employer (including salary and benefits), and the employee's rate billed to the customer. The employee's cost, of course, is not included in your estimate, but you need to know this as part of your estimate—because your profit margin is the difference between the rate you charge the client and the cost to your company, less a proportion of overhead expenses (rental or leasing of space, utilities, phones, shared secretarial and administrative services, and so on). If your profit margin is negative, you should reconsider both your project plan and your long-term business plan.

Multimedia production companies and web site builders with high billing rates claim their skill sets and experience allow them to accomplish more work in a given amount of time, expertly, thus saving money, time, and enhancing the finished quality and reliability of a project. This is particularly the case with larger-scale, complex projects. Smaller and leaner companies that offer lower billing rates may claim to be more streamlined, hungry, and willing to perform extra services. Lower rates do not necessarily mean lower-quality work, but rather imply that the company either supports fewer overheads or is satisfied with a reduced profit margin. The business of making multimedia is a "low entry barrier" enterprise because all you need to get started is some (relatively) inexpensive computer hardware and software, not a 70,000-square-foot factory or expensive tooling. You can make multimedia in a living room, basement, or garage. As more and more multimedia producers and web developers enter this marketplace, the competition is increasing and the free hand of supply and demand is driving prices (down).

Purchasers of multimedia services must, however, thoroughly examine the qualifications of a prospective contracting person or company to ensure that the work required can be accomplished on time and within budget. There is no more difficult business situation than a half-completed job and an exhausted budget.

Contractors and consultants can bring specialized skills such as graphic art, C and Java programming, database expertise, music composition, and video to your project. If you use these experts, be sure your

First Person

Back when floppy disks were common, we were asked by a large institution to complete a project that had fallen on the floor. It was really worse than that—the project had actually slipped through the cracks in that floor. The single known copy of work—representing about $30,000 in paid billings—had been copied to 19 high-density diskettes and stored in a file cabinet. Here, they had been discovered by the secretarial pool and formatted, to be used for WordPerfect documents. The secretaries remembered the whole thing because the stored backups contained protected files, so the disks were unusually difficult to erase! Luckily, bits and pieces of

the project were unearthed on the hard disk of a computer that had been disconnected and stored in the basement. We were able to reconstruct much of the artwork, but not the interactive links.

As we studied the leavings of the embarrassed progenitors, we discovered a trail of missteps and errors. It became clear that the institution made a bad decision in hiring a well-qualified engineering firm at great expense (standard billing rates) to construct a difficult multimedia presentation. CAD/CAM drawings and finite element analysis were the forte of these engineers—not animated icons and colorful bitmaps

with sound tracks. Furthermore, the engineering firm erred in selecting software that performed on the target hardware platform at about the speed of snails chasing a dog. Money had been spent, the product didn't work, and everyone involved was in gray limbo, slinking around, looking for a solution.

We determinedly pulled together the bits and pieces we could find, designed a snappy navigational structure we were proud of, and quickly fixed the big problem for a small fee (based upon our own standard billing rate). The institution, of course, was delighted and became a client of long standing.

billing rate is higher than theirs. Or, if you have a task the client has capped with a not-to-exceed cost, be sure your arrangement with the contractor is also capped. Contractors place no burden on your overhead and administration other than a few cups of coffee, and they should generate a generous profit margin for you during the course of your project. Be sure that contractors perform the majority of their work off-site, using their own equipment; otherwise, federal tax regulators may reclassify these freelancers as employees and require you to pay employee benefits. In 1998, in *Vizcaino v. Microsoft*, the U.S. Supreme Court required Microsoft Corporation to pay employee benefits to hundreds of workers that the court determined were regular employees rather than independent contractors. There are about 20 factors, according to the IRS, in determining whether a worker is an employee or an independent contractor for tax purposes, and companies may be liable for all employment benefits, including (as Microsoft discovered) stock option and stock sharing plans, if the work arrangement is not carefully constructed. However, when these outside workers are not classified as employees, then you run another risk—that they could retain ownership of the work they have created for you, limiting your right to use the material or restrict its use elsewhere. The best way to avoid this is to be sure that your contract with any outside workers clearly specifies the terms of ownership and rights of use of the product for which you are contracting. This "work for hire" issue is discussed in more detail in Chapter 10.

Example Cost Sheets

Figure 8-6 contains groups of expense categories for producing multimedia. If you use these in your own work, be sure to temper your guesses with experience; if you are new to multimedia production, get some qualified advice during this planning stage.

PROJECT DEVELOPMENT COSTS
Salaries
Client meetings
Acquisition of content
Communications
Travel
Research
Proposal & contract prep
Overhead

PRODUCTION COSTS
Management
    Salaries
    Communications
    Travel
    Consumables
Content Acquisition
    Salaries
    Research services
    Fees for licensing content
Content Creation
    All content categories
        Salaries
        Hardware/software
        Consumables
Graphics Production
    Fees for licensing images or animation clips
Audio Production
    Studio fees
    Talent fees
    Fees for licensing music rights
    Data storage

Video Production
    Studio fees
    Talent fees
    Fees for licensing stock footage
    Location fees
    Equipment rental
    Digital capture & editing
Authoring
    Salaries
    Hardware/software
    Consumables

TESTING COSTS
Salaries
Focus groups
    Facility rental
    Printing costs
    Food and incentives
    Coop fees (payment for participation)
Editing
Beta program

DISTRIBUTION COSTS
Salaries
Documentation
Packaging
Manufacturing
Marketing
Advertising
Shipping

Figure 8-6 There are many costs associated with producing multimedia.

First Person

I was downbound from Puget Sound to San Francisco, and the weather was up, with seas running heavy and winds gusting to 80 knots in our face. The Master and the First Mate were on the bridge, the old man sitting curled up in his upholstered high chair on the darkened starboard wing, the First pacing on the rubber mat behind the helmsman. The Third Mate was on watch, leaning over the radar screen and making fluorescent notes with a grease pencil. As I was a guest with no duties, I mostly hung out in the chart room while white water broke over the bows and the shuddering propeller came out of the sea; wind screamed in the vents on the roof of the bridge. There wasn't much conversation that night, but the Master slowed us to five knots, concerned about the containers lashed to the forward deck. When the young Third Mate came into the chart room, I asked, "Where are we?" and he took a sharp pencil, made a fine point on the chart, and drew a tiny circle around the point. Then he smiled, proud to have good radar bearings. The First Mate came in about a half hour later, and when I asked the same question, he circled an area about the size of a walnut.

As the Master left the bridge for his cabin, I asked him, too, where we were. He took his thumb and rubbed it on the chart in a rough oval about the diameter of his fist, saying, "Somewhere in here," and grinned at me as the ship heaved suddenly and we grabbed for the handholds.

The more experience these professionals had, the larger the circle they drew, and the less they relied upon pinpoint navigation. You should be prudent when costing a multimedia production; precision estimating can wreck your project.

RFPs and Bid Proposals

Often, potential clients don't have a clue about how to make multimedia, but they do have a vision or a mandate. You field a telephone call, a voice describes a need or a want, and you explain how you (and your company) can satisfy that need. Much of the talk may be instructional as you teach the client about the benefits and pitfalls of multimedia in all its forms. You seldom will glean enough information during this initial discussion to accurately estimate time or cost, so be prepared to answer these queries in vague terms while you present your available skill sets and capabilities in the most favorable light. If the client is serious and your instruction well received, in short time you may be able to guide this client into good choices and reasonable decisions, working together to conceive and design an excellent product. Discussions will soon turn into design meetings. Somewhere along the way, you will sign a contract.

Occasionally you may encounter a more formal **Request for Proposal (RFP)**. RFPs are typically detailed documents from large corporations that are "outsourcing" their multimedia development work. Figure 8-7 is an example of such a document that provides background information, scope of work, and information about the bidding process. Still, you should note that there is little "hard" information in this document; most bid proposals require contact with the client to fill in details prior to bidding.

Smythe Industries
Request for Proposal

Summary: The objective is to produce a family of materials which will develop a unique personality and visual image for the Smythe Campus in Vancouver, British Columbia, home of multiple Smythe subsidiaries and divisions.

As background, Smythe Industries was launched in 1995 following the acquisition of Wilson Aluminum Foundries, Ltd. (Canada) and Fenwick Rolling Mills, Inc. (U.S.A.) and is based in Vancouver. The site is also the headquarters for Global Aluminum Research, a research and development subsidiary. In addition, there are discussions concerning the establishment of a special alloy research institute at the Vancouver campus.

Each of the entities has unique personality traits, management structures, and business cultures which will need to be recognized and incorporated into the design process.

Audience & Message
Potential Employees – "employer of choice"
Business Development – "partner of choice"
  Metals Companies
  Academic Institutions
Government/Community officials – "good neighbor/citizen"
Smythe Employees – "credible/proud"
Scientific/Engineering Organizations – "credible research/scientifically advanced"

Tone & Manner
Innovative, scientifically advanced, sophisticated, credible
Colorful: jewel colors/crisp/high contrast
Energetic, modern, innovative, cutting edge
Geometric lines & shapes (vs. free form)
A human element: photography, illustration, etc.
Personable, warm, intellectually inviting

Electronic Communications RFP

Multimedia Presentation Capabilities
Summary: The objective is to create a set of tools which will deliver key messages while positioning Smythe Vancouver as an innovative user of technology for communication. There will be two components to this project: a presentation format and a library of images. We would like to develop a library, including still imagery, audio, and video, that can be contained on a DVD and also presented on the corporate web site. Note: all images should be created with the goal of repurposing across different mediums and projects.

The key purpose is to make core messages and the corporate personality come alive by utilizing sound and motion. These multimedia assets will be used for recruiting purposes at career centers, job fairs, and in-house for visiting recruits. They will also serve as presentation support material at scientific and engineering forums.

Smythe will work with the multimedia design firm to create and identify existing television clips, video, and other material which can serve to reinforce key messages.

External Web Site
Summary: As the most visible element of Smythe's Vancouver identity, the web site will set the stage for positioning the company in the research community as an employer of choice and a key player in esoteric alloy and metallurgical research. The web site will provide easy navigation for users to reach the areas of greatest interest to them, e.g. a particular business division, academic papers, employment opportunities, etc.

Figure 8-7 Some RFPs provide great detail.

The multimedia design firm will also be expected to create a library of images which can be utilized to update the site periodically. The design firm should also be prepared to provide input on ways to easily update and cost-effectively maintain the site. In addition, the web site should be created so that audio and live imagery can be incorporated and downloaded easily by users who have the appropriate equipment.

Internal Web Site

Summary: The internal web site is the primary medium for employee communication. It will be a useable, interesting tool for internal users and serve to reinforce corporate messages and the campus culture. Since the web site represents and includes different business entities on campus, this internal site will also introduce employees to activities in which other business units and groups are involved. The site will need to be designed with a template format so that it can be easily updated.

Production Elements for all Electronic Communications

Icons: Develop an illustrative style for a family of icons shared across the CD-ROM, internal web site, and external web site.

Interface Design: Develop an interface design that provides design parameters and a personality for the internal web site and external web site. (Note: Internal and external web sites should carry a similar look and feel; however, it must be easy to distinguish between the two.)

Visual Image: Produce a library of visual images. This will require the additional production of video clips and sound clips.

Photography: A photo shoot schedule and plan will be developed with Smythe to most effectively maximize time and resources in shooting photos which can be used in print, in the web sites, and in multimedia materials.

RFP Process

Quotations: Itemize quotes, e.g. project management, copy writing, editing, design, photography, illustrations, etc. Also provide 3 references.

Note: Smythe will write the HTML directives in-house and will also be posting to a server which is maintained in-house.

All quotes should be submitted to:

Suzanne Petruski
Project Manager
Smythe Industries
65 Silver Foil
Vancouver, BC, CANADA

Figure 8-7   Some RFPs provide great detail. *(Continued)*

A multimedia bid proposal will be passed through several levels of a company so that managers and directors can evaluate the project's quality and its price. The higher a bid proposal goes in the management hierarchy, the less chance it has of being read in detail. For this reason, you always want to provide an executive summary or overview as the first page of your proposal, briefly describing the project's goals, how the goals will be achieved, and the cost.

In the body of the proposal, include a section dealing with creative issues, and describe your method for conveying the client's message or meeting the graphic and interactive goals of the project. Also incorporate a discussion of technical issues, in which you clearly define the target hardware platform. If necessary, identify the members of your staff who will work on the project, and list their roles and qualifications.

The backbone of the proposal is the estimate and project plan that you have created up to this point. It describes the scope of the work. If the project is complicated, prepare a brief synopsis of both the plan and the timetable; include this in the overview. If there are many phases, you can present each phase as a separate section of the proposal.

Cost estimates for each phase or deliverable milestone, as well as payment schedules, should follow the description of the work. If this section is lengthy, it should also include a summary.

TIP *Make the proposal look good—it should be attractive and easy to read. You might also wish to provide an unbound copy so that it can be easily photocopied. Include separate, relevant literature about your company and qualifications. A list of clients and brief descriptions of projects you have successfully completed are also useful for demonstrating your capabilities.*

Finally, include a list of your terms. Contract terms may become a legally binding document, so have your terms reviewed by legal counsel. An example is shown in Figure 8-8. Terms should include the following:

- A description of your billing rates and invoicing policy (for example, what percentage is to be paid up front, how much at certain milestones, and how much upon delivery).
- Your policy on client sign-offs and change order costs.
- Your policy for billing out-of-pocket expenses for travel, telephone, courier services, and so forth.
- Your policy regarding third-party licensing fees for run-time modules and special drivers (the client pays).
- Specific statements of who owns what upon completion of the project. You may wish to retain the rights to show parts of the work for your own promotional purposes and to reuse in other projects segments of code and algorithms that you develop.
- An assurance to the client that you will not disclose proprietary information.
- Your right to display your credits appropriately within the work.
- Your unlimited right to work for other clients.
- A disclaimer for liability and damages arising out of the work.

It is a significant task to write a project proposal that creatively sells a multimedia concept, accurately estimates the scope of work, and provides realistic budget costs. The proposal often becomes a melting pot,

Sample Terms:

We will undertake this assignment on a time-and-expenses basis at our current hourly rate of $___ per hour for __ job title __, $____ per hour for __ job title __, $____ per hour for __ job title __, plus applicable taxes and reimbursement of authorized out-of-pocket expenses. Reasonable travel, express, freight, courier and telecommunication expenses incurred in relation to the project will be considered pre-authorized. [Client] will be responsible for all licensing fees of third-party products incorporated (with [Client]'s knowledge and approval) into the final product. We will invoice [Client] either upon [Client]'s acceptance of the specified deliverables for each work phase specified above, or monthly, whichever is more often. [Client]'s authorization, either written or verbal, to commence a work phase will constitute acceptance of the previous phase's deliverables. Invoices are due and payable upon presentation. To commence work, we require a retainer in the amount of $_____, which will be deducted from the final invoice for the project.

Upon our receipt of final payment, [Client] shall own all rights, except those noted below, to the completed work delivered under this agreement, including graphics, written text, and program code. [Client] may at [Client]'s sole discretion copyright the work in [Client]'s name or assign rights to a third party. Ownership of material provided by third parties and incorporated in our work with [Client]'s knowledge and approval shall be as provided in any license or sale agreement governing said materials. We reserve the right to use in any of our future work for ourselves or any client all techniques, structures, designs and individual modules of program code we develop that are applicable to requirements outside those specified above. Further, our performance of this work for [Client] shall in no way limit us regarding assignments we may accept from any other clients now or at any time in the future.

We shall be allowed to show [Client]'s finished work, or any elements of it, to existing and prospective clients for demonstration purposes. If such demonstration showings would reveal information [Client] has identified to us as proprietary or confidential, we shall be allowed to create a special version for demonstrations which omits or disguises such information and/or [Client]'s identity as the client. We shall also be allowed to include a production credit display, e.g. "Produced by [Our Name]" or equivalent copy, on the closing screen or other mutually agreeable position in the finished work. Following [Client]'s acceptance of this proposal we shall also be allowed to identify [Client] as a client in our marketing communications materials.

In the event it is necessary in the course of this assignment for us to view or work with information of [Client]'s that [Client] identifies to us as proprietary and confidential (possibly including customer lists, supplier data, financial figures and the like), we agree not to disclose it except to our principals, associates and contractors having confidentiality agreements with us.

We make no warranty regarding this work, or its fitness for a particular purpose, once [Client] accepts it following any testing procedures of [Client]'s choice. In any event, our liability for any damages arising out of this work, expressly including consequential damages, shall not exceed the total amount of fees paid for this work.

Figure 8-8   Sample contract terms adapted from language developed by the HyperMedia Group, Inc. (do not use without appropriate legal counsel)

in that you develop the elements of your idea during early conversations with a potential client and add the results of discussions on technique and approach with graphic artists and instructional designers. You blend what the client wants done with what you can actually do, given the client's budgetary constraints, and when the cauldron of compromise cools, your proposal is the result.

The Cover and Package

You have many options for designing the look and feel of your proposal. And though we are often warned to avoid judging a book by its cover, the reality is that it takes about two seconds for executives to assess the quality of the document they are holding. Sometimes, they decide before even touching it. Size up the people who will read your proposal and ferret out their expectancies; tailor your proposal to these expectancies.

If your client judges from the cover of your proposal that the document inside is amateurish rather than professional, you are already fighting an uphill battle. There are two strategies for avoiding this negative first impression:

1. Develop your own special style for a proposal cover and package, including custom fonts, cover art and graphics, illustrations and figures, unique section and paragraph styles, and a clean binding. Do your proposal first class.

2. Make the entire package plain and simple, yet businesslike. The plain part of the approach means not fussing with too many fonts and type styles. This austerity may be particularly successful for proposals to government agencies, where 12-point Times New Roman or 12-point Courier may be not just a de facto standard, but a required document format. If you must submit hardcopy documents in addition to PDF or DOC files, a stapled sheaf of papers is adequate. Don't try to dress up your plain presentation with Trapper Keepers or cheap plastic covers; keep it lean and mean.

Table of Contents

Busy executives want to anticipate a document and grasp its content in short order. A table of contents or index is a straightforward way to present the elements of your proposal in condensed overview. In some situations, you may also wish to include an **executive summary**—a prelude containing no more than a few paragraphs of pithy description and budget totals. The summary should be on the cover page or immediately following. In an electronic submission, you can hotlink to the Table of Contents and to important sections.

Needs Analysis and Description

In many proposals, it is useful to describe in some detail the reason the project is being put forward. This **needs analysis** and description is particularly common in proposals that must move through a company's executive hierarchy in search of approval and funding.

Target Audience

All multimedia proposals should include a section that describes the target audience and target platform. When the end user's multimedia capabilities have a broad and uncertain range, it is crucial to describe the hardware and software delivery platform you intend to provide. For instance, if your project requires a special browser plug-in, you will need to adjust your multimedia strategy by revising the design or by requiring the end user to download the plug-in. Some clients will clearly control the delivery platform, so you may not need to provide detail regarding system components.

Creative Strategy

A **creative strategy** section—a description of the look and feel of the project itself—can be important to your proposal, especially if the executives reviewing your proposal were not present for creative sessions or did not participate in preliminary discussions. If you have a library of completed projects that are similar to your proposed effort, it is helpful to include them with your proposal, pointing the client to techniques and presentation methods that may be relevant. If you have designed a prototype, describe it here, or create a separate heading and include graphics and diagrams.

Project Implementation

A proposal must describe the way a project will be organized and scheduled. Your estimate of costs and expenses will be based upon this description. The project implementation section of your proposal may contain a detailed calendar, PERT and Gantt project planning charts, and lists of specific tasks with associated completion dates, deliverables, and work hours. This information may be general or detailed, depending upon the demands of the client. The project implementation section is not just about how much work there is, but how the work will be managed and performed. You may not need to specify time estimates in work hours, but rather in the amount of calendar time required to complete each phase.

The Waterfall Model

Long the accepted methodology for developing software, in the **Waterfall Model** each stage of a project feeds into the next in a sequential, linear way. The metaphor is appropriate because water does not flow uphill: when a phase is completed or a milestone reached, there is no need to go back to make revisions and changes because that stage of the project is now perfect! It becomes "frozen," and the next stage begins.

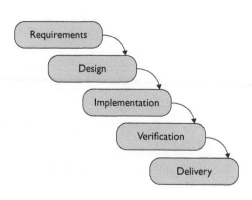

The Agile Approach

In 2001 a group of 17 software developers met at a ski resort in Utah and, after lengthy discussion, published the brief *Manifesto for Agile Software Development* (http://agilemanifesto.org/; see the sidebar). Since then, the Agile "movement" has gained traction as an alternative to developing software in the document-oriented and bureaucratic "code and fix" process implied by the Waterfall Model. Among the advantages of agile software development are closer collaboration among all team members and much greater face-to-face communication and minimization of show-stopping feedback loops. Agile methods (see www.agilealliance.org for more details) with small creative teams are well-suited to developing web sites (often using a content management system [CMS]) and mobile apps. A project simply moves from a description of its requirements to its actual design, to its implementation, and finally to its delivery—and even after delivery, the requirements can be reassessed and the process begun anew:

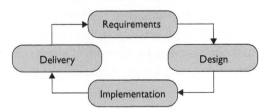

Budget

The budget relates directly to the scope of work you have laid out in the project implementation section. Distill your itemized costs from the project implementation description and consolidate the minute tasks of each project phase into categories of activity meaningful to the client.

Chapter 8 Review

Chapter Summary

For your review, here's a summary of the important concepts discussed in this chapter.

Determine the scope of a multimedia project

- Before beginning a project, develop a sense of its scope and content. Then develop an organized outline and a plan that considers the skills, time, budget, tools, and resources at hand.

- Plan for the entire process, beginning with your first ideas and ending with completion and delivery of a finished product.

- Maintain balance between purpose and feasibility by dynamically adding and subtracting multimedia elements as you stretch and shape your idea.

- Tasks are the building blocks of project management. Allocate an estimated amount of time to each task, and place each one along a calendar-based timeline. The end of each phase is a natural place to set a milestone.

- Project management software can be useful for arranging ideas and tasks; additionally, the software may include built-in analysis to help stay within schedule and budget.

- Build a matrix chart of required skills to help describe the makeup of your team.

- Because there are few concrete standards for multimedia, and developers are constantly "pushing the envelope," consider building a prototype to demonstrate that the idea is feasible and marketable.

Schedule the phases, tasks, and work items required to complete a project

- Lay out the phases, tasks, and work items along a timeline. Scheduling can be difficult to predict due to artistic trial and error and because the technology of computer hardware and software is in constant flux. Include client approval time. Negotiate the number of review cycles to avoid endless reviews.

- Avoid the problem of cost run-ups by requiring clients to sign off at key stages in development and requiring change orders if a client changes specifications on you after signing off on them.

Estimate the cost, timeline, and tasks required to complete a project

- As a general rule, there are three elements that can vary in project estimates: time, money, and people.

- The budget is the total of estimated hours for each task times your hourly billing rate. There is no more difficult business situation than a half-completed job and an exhausted budget.

- Contractors and consultants can bring specialized skills to your project. Be sure they work off-site, using their own equipment, to avoid having them classified as employees.

Write and structure the elements of a multimedia project proposal

- Many projects come about from a phone call or less formal contact.

- Occasionally you may receive a more formal detailed document called a Request for Proposal (RFP), generally from large corporations that are "outsourcing" their multimedia development work.

- A multimedia bid proposal should include an executive summary or overview, a section dealing with creative issues, a description of how the project's goals will be met, and a discussion of technical issues.

- The backbone of the proposal is the estimate and project plan, followed by cost estimates for each phase or deliverable milestone, as well as payment schedules. Finally, include a list of your terms reviewed by legal counsel. Make sure the proposal looks professional.

- All multimedia proposals should include a section that describes the target audience and target platform.

- Your estimate of costs and expenses will be based upon the detailed description of your project.

■ Key Terms

agile software development *(272)*
alpha release *(256)*
beta *(256)*
change order *(260)*
client sign-off *(259)*
contingencies *(261)*
creative strategy *(271)*
Critical Path Method (CPM) *(250)*
deliverable *(257)*
executive summary *(270)*
feasibility study *(254)*
Gantt chart *(250)*

going gold *(256)*
milestone *(257)*
needs analysis *(270)*
payment schedule *(261)*
prerequisites *(250)*
Program Evaluation Review
  Technique (PERT) chart *(250)*
proof of concept *(254)*
Request for Proposal (RFP) *(265)*
scope *(246)*
Waterfall Model *(271)*

■ Key Term Quiz

1. A prototype is sometimes called a proof of concept or _____.

2. When a project reaches the delivery stage, it is said to be _____.

3. In constructing a project timeline, it is important to identify _____, important tasks that must be completed before others begin.

4. A marker that delineates a significant point in a project's timeline—time to deliver work-in-progress, to invoice based upon real work done, to assess or test progress, and/or to solicit and receive constructive feedback—is called a(n) _____.

5. A prototype in which most of the features are working, and you are distributing it to a wide arena of testers, is called a(n) _____.

6. A project management strategy that calculates the total duration of a project based upon each identified task, earmarking tasks that are critical, is called the _____.

7. A(n) _____ provides a graphic representation of task relationships, showing what tasks must be completed before others can commence.

8. A(n) _____ depicts all the tasks along a timeline.

9. A(n) _____ is a detailed document, generally from large corporations who are outsourcing their multimedia development work, asking for companies to suggest projects in response to a defined need.

10. A proposal should begin with the _____, a prelude containing no more than a few paragraphs of pithy description and budget totals.

■ Multiple-Choice Quiz

1. The building blocks of project management are:
   a. budgets
   b. tasks
   c. proposals
   d. milestones
   e. prerequisites

2. The best point to do focus group testing is with the:
   a. concept
   b. prototype
   c. beta
   d. gold master
   e. final version

3. Which of the following is not an area that would need to be tested in a prototype?
   a. technology (Will it work on your proposed delivery platform[s]?)
   b. cost (Can you do this project within budget constraints?)
   c. design (Will the colors and overall interface be attractive to potential users?)
   d. market (Can you sell it, or will it be properly used if it is an in-house project?)
   e. human interface (Is it intuitive and easy to use?)

4. In determining the feasibility of a project, the most common limiting technological factor is:
   a. the hardware on which the project is developed
   b. the network delivering the project
   c. the medium (CD-ROM, DVD, Internet) delivering the project
   d. the end user's hardware
   e. the telecommunications infrastructure

5. A proof of concept or pilot project should probably include all of these except:
   a. some artwork
   b. interface design
   c. packaging mock-ups
   d. interactive navigation
   e. performance checks

6. In the referenced report on producing educational software, the task requiring the greatest percentage of effort was authoring, at 28 percent. The second most demanding task was:
   a. analyze and outline content
   b. lay out course map
   c. select learner activities
   d. evaluate the course
   e. produce media

7. Which of the following is *not* a method typically used by project management software?
   a. Critical Path Method
   b. Feasibility Assessment Review Technique
   c. Program Evaluation Review Technique
   d. Gantt charts
   e. All of these are common methods.

8. Which of the following is *not* a reason why scheduling a multimedia project can be difficult?
   a. Much of the making of multimedia is artistic trial and error.
   b. Market forces may change the demand for the final product.
   c. The technology of computer hardware and software is in constant flux.
   d. Upgrades while your project is under way may add time to learn new hardware and software.
   e. Client feedback loops depend upon factors beyond your control.

9. When calculating the budget for a project, you should use two rates for each employee working on the project: the employee's rate billed to the customer, and:
   a. the employee's cost for tax purposes
   b. the employee's rate for discounted/special clients
   c. the employee's rate for rush/quick-turnaround projects
   d. the employee's cost to the employer
   e. the employee's rate for projects done on spec

10. Typical billing rates for multimedia production companies and web designers range from:
    a. $15 to $30 an hour
    b. $30 to $65 an hour
    c. $65 to $160 an hour
    d. $160 to $200 an hour

11. The business of making multimedia is a "low entry barrier" enterprise because:
    a. those with disabilities can create multimedia
    b. all you need to get started is some (relatively) inexpensive computer hardware and software
    c. there are free or low-cost web hosting solutions available
    d. lots of people can access web sites and DVDs
    e. authoring systems make creating sophisticated projects fast and easy

12. Contractors and consultants should work off-site primarily because if they work on-site:
    a. they may compromise the company's confidential information
    b. they increase the wear on company equipment
    c. providing space for them adds to overhead
    d. they are generally less productive doing so
    e. they may be legally considered employees

13. The first part of a proposal should be the:
    a. executive summary
    b. budget

    c. timeline
    d. project plan
    e. terms and conditions

14. When the end user's multimedia capabilities have a broad and uncertain range, it is very important to describe:
    a. the number of subcontractors working on the project
    b. the authoring system that will be used on the project
    c. the hardware and software platform intended for delivery
    d. the creative strategy that will be used to create the media
    e. the colors and fonts to be used in the interface

15. If the executives reviewing your proposal were not present for creative sessions or did not participate in preliminary discussions, it may be important to include a description of the look and feel of the project itself, called a(n):
    a. creative strategy
    b. executive summary
    c. terms and conditions
    d. needs analysis
    e. table of contents

■ Essay Quiz

1. You have been given the task of finding a new project for a fictional multimedia development company to produce on spec. The project is an instructional game designed to teach learners how to program in Java Script. Justify the project, discussing:
    a. the market for the product,
    b. the objectives of the project,
    c. technical limitations, if any, and
    d. a brief timeline.

2. List and briefly discuss the stages of a multimedia project. Be sure to define the milestones that mark the completion of the phase.

3. List at least ten primary tasks that go into producing a multimedia project. Place these steps in logical order. Comment on these steps with regard to whether they are critical to the timeline (which steps are dependent on the completion of an earlier step).

4. Discuss the factors that affect what a multimedia company might be able to charge for its work. Consider factors that affect overhead, factors related to experience and abilities, and factors related to the project itself.

5. Describe the various technical, management, and creative obstacles to accurately predict the time and resources needed to complete a multimedia project. How might the technical and creative problems be interrelated?

Lab Projects

■ Project 8.1

For a project, choose to build a marketing web site, a corporate intranet, or an online or mobile game. Be creative, and specify the kind of organization for whom you will be creating the project. List the tasks required to develop the project. Specify the stages of development, and provide a timeline for completing each task.

■ Project 8.2

Based on the project specified in 8.1, create a team of at least three people for the project. Specify their titles, internal and external rates, and abilities. Write a one-paragraph bio explaining each team member's relevant experience and capabilities.

■ Project 8.3

Based on projects 8.1 and 8.2, assign specific tasks to your team. Create a chart that identifies the major work items, who is assigned to each, and when each will be completed. Then locate a suitable project management tool, such as dotProject (www.dotproject.net). Download the application, and briefly explore its features. Explain how you might use the features of that tool in your overall plan.

■ Project 8.4

Create a budget based on the task durations and rates for the project you have developed. Calculate both the internal cost (costs × hours) and the billing (rates × hours). Is the project profitable? Don't forget to include a reasonable amount for contingencies and overhead.

■ Project 8.5

Go online and locate an RFP for a project similar to the one you designed for Project 8.1. Suitable RFPs should be fairly large in scope and at least $25,000 estimated cost. Examine the RFP. Write the executive summary for a proposal you might write in response to the RFP.

## CHAPTER 9

Designing and Producing

DESIGNING and building multimedia projects go hand in hand. The best products are often the result of continuing feedback and modifications implemented throughout the production process; projects that freeze a design too early become brittle in the production workplace, losing the chances for incremental improvement. But there is a danger: too much feedback and too many changes can kill a project, draining it of time and money. Always balance proposed changes against their cost to avoid the "creeping features" syndrome.

For a multimedia project bound for a web site, the design may be completed and implemented, yet the web site's content may be regularly updated and changed, so the project may (by its very nature) never be completely frozen. In such cases, it is especially important to set clear deadlines and milestones.

Just as the architect of a high-rise office tower must understand how to utilize the materials with which he or she works (lest the construction collapse on trusting clients), designers of multimedia projects must also understand the strengths and limitations of the elements that will go into their project. It makes no sense, for example, to design the audio elements of a multimedia project in memory-consuming 16-bit, 44.1-kHz stereo sound when the delivery medium will not have sufficient room for it; or to produce lengthy, full-screen, video clips to play at 30 frames per second over the Internet when targeted end users connect by dial-up modems; or to design lovely 1024×768-pixel graphics for elementary school laptops when that environment supports only 800×600-pixel screens. Architects don't design inner-city parking garages with 14-foot ceilings and wide turning radii for 18-wheel big rigs, and they don't build them using wood or mud laid on a swampy foundation.

Designers must work closely with producers to ensure that their ideas can be properly realized, and producers need to confirm the results of their work with the designers. "These colors seem to work better—what do you think?" "It plays smoother now, but I had to change the animation sequence …" "Doing the index with highlighted lines slows it down—can we eliminate this feature?" Feedback loops and good communication between the design and production effort are critical to the success of a project.

In this chapter, you will learn how to:

- Describe various strategies for designing interactive multimedia

- Identify principles for successful production of multimedia projects

The idea processing (described in Chapter 8) of your multimedia project will have resulted in a detailed and balanced plan of action, a production schedule, and a timetable. Now it's time for implementation!

Designing

The design part of your project is where your knowledge and skill with computers; your talent in graphic arts, video, and music; and your ability to conceptualize logical pathways through information are all focused to create the real thing. Design is thinking, choosing, making, and doing. It is shaping, smoothing, reworking, polishing, testing, and editing. When you design your project, your ideas and concepts are moved one step closer to reality. Competence in the design phase is what separates amateurs from professionals in the making of multimedia.

TIP   *Never begin a multimedia project without first outlining its structure and content.*

Depending on the scope of your project and the size and style of your team, you can take two approaches to creating an original interactive multimedia design. You can spend great effort on the **storyboards**, or graphic outlines, describing the project in exact detail—using words and sketches for each and every screen image, sound, and navigational choice, right down to specific colors and shades, text content, attributes and fonts, button shapes, styles, responses, and voice inflections. (Sometimes called **wireframing**, this approach is particularly well suited for teams that can build prototypes quickly and then rapidly convert them into finished goods.) Or you can use less-detailed storyboards as a rough schematic guide, allowing you to exert less design sweat up front and expend more effort actually rendering the product at a workstation.

The method you choose depends on whether the same people will do the whole thing (both the designing and the implementing) or separate teams will be tasked with the design and the implementation, in which case you need a more detailed specification (that is, detailed storyboard and sketches). Both approaches require the same thorough knowledge of the tools and capabilities of multimedia, and both demand a storyboard or a project outline. The first approach is often favored by clients who wish to tightly control the production process and labor costs. The second approach gets you more quickly into the nitty-gritty, hands-on tasks, but you may ultimately have to give back that time because more iterations and editing will be required to smooth the work in progress. In either case, the more planning on paper, the better and easier it will be to construct the project.

On some projects, you may be both the designer and the programmer. This can work well because you will understand how the design features you choose will actually be implemented. Indeed, your design will be tempered, if not defined, by your programming and coding skills, and you will be less likely to specify features that are impossible or overly difficult to realize.

Designing the Structure

A multimedia project is no more than an arrangement of text, graphic, sound, and video elements (or *objects*). The way you compose these elements into interactive experiences is shaped by your purpose and messages.

How you organize your material for a project will have just as great an impact on the user as the content itself. With the explosive growth of the World Wide Web and the proliferation of millions and millions of multimedia-capable HTML documents that can be linked to millions of other similar documents in the cyberspace of the Web, your designs and inventions may actually contribute to the new media revolution: other creators may discover your work and build upon your ideas and methods. You may decide to proactively place your creation into the public domain or use a Creative Commons or copyleft license to make it widely available and reusable (discussed in detail in Chapter 10).

Navigation

Mapping the structure of your project is a task that should be started early in the planning phase, because navigation maps outline the connections or links among various areas of your content and help you organize your content and messages. A **navigation map** (or **site map**) provides you with a table of contents as well as a chart of the logical flow of the interactive interface. While with web sites a site map is typically a simple hierarchical table of contents with each heading linked to a page, as a more detailed design document your map may prove very useful to your project, listing your multimedia objects and describing what happens when the user interacts.

Just as eight story plots might account for 99 percent of all literature ever written (boy meets girl, protagonist versus antagonist, etc.), a few basic structures for multimedia projects will cover most cases: **linear navigation**, **hierarchical navigation**, **nonlinear navigation**, and **composite navigation**. Figure 9-1 illustrates the four fundamental organizing structures used in multimedia projects, often in combination:

- **Linear** Users navigate sequentially, from one frame or bite of information to another.
- **Hierarchical** Also called "linear with branching," users navigate along the branches of a tree structure that is shaped by the natural logic of the content.
- **Nonlinear** Users navigate freely through the content of the project, unbound by predetermined routes.
- **Composite** Users may navigate freely (nonlinearly) but are occasionally constrained to linear presentations of movies or critical information and/or to data that is most logically organized in a hierarchy.

The method you provide to your users for navigating from one place to another in your project is part of the **user interface**. The success of the user interface depends not only upon its general design and graphic art implementations but also upon myriad engineering details—such as the position of interactive buttons or hot spots relative to the user's current activity, whether these buttons "light up," and whether you use the standard pull-down menus of most desktop and laptop operating systems. A good user interface is critical to the overall success of your project.

The nature of your user interface will vary depending on its purpose: browsing, database access, entertainment, information, instruction, reference, marketing, and gaming projects require different approaches and different navigation strategies.

Structural Depth Professor Judith Junger from the Open University of the Netherlands in Amsterdam suggests that when you design your multimedia product, you should work with two types of structure: depth structure and surface structure. **Depth structure** represents the complete navigation map and describes all the links between all the components of your project (see Figure 9-1). **Surface structure**, on the other hand, represents the structures actually realized by a user while navigating the depth structure. Thus the following depth structure

Figure 9-1   The four primary navigational structures used in multimedia

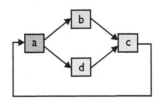

might be realized as the following surface structure:

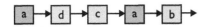

Some surface structures generated by users might look like this:

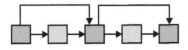

Sequential structure with optional paths

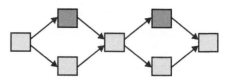

Sequential structure with alternative paths

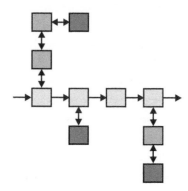

Sequential structure with sidesteps

The following depth structure for a quiz thus consists of three possible surface structures:

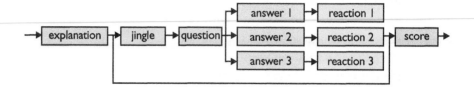

When you design your navigation map, it helps to think about surface structure—to view the product from a user's perspective. Surface structures are of particular interest to marketing firms in tracking users' routes through a web site to determine the effectiveness of the site's design and to profile a user's preferences. When a user's preferences are known, a custom web site experience can be dynamically tailored and delivered to that user. Acquisition and management of such profiling data is a hot topic, with privacy advocates claiming the personal information revealed in these surface structures is akin to a person's medical and health records.

First Person

Dear Tay,

With regard to the creation of interactive fiction, what kinds of software engineering strategies would you recommend for creating stories that maintain a strong sense of cumulative action (otherwise known as plot) while still offering the audience a high frequency of interaction? In other words, how do you constrain the combinatoric explosion of the narrative pathways, while still maintaining the Aristotelian sense of a unity of plot?

—Patrick Dillon, Atlanta, GA

One and one-half T-shirts to Patrick Dillon! Would have been two for your invocation of a famous Greek philosopher, but then I couldn't find "combinatoric" in Webster's. Aristotle himself would have been pleased by the harmonious balance of your reward: you have asked a really good question.

As multimedia and the power of computers begin to change our approach to literature and storytelling, new engineering strategies do need to be implemented.

When fiction becomes nonlinear, and users can choose among alternative plot lines, the permutations can become staggering. To an author, this means each new plot pathway chosen by user interaction requires its own development, and one story may actually become several hundred or more. To constrain this fearsome explosion of narrative pathways, yet retain a high frequency of interaction, try designing your fiction around a single core plot that provides the cumulative action, and use arrays of returning branches for detail and illustration. In this way you can entirely avoid the permutations of alternative universes and still offer the adventure of interactive exploration.

Dear Tay,

I just read your answer to Patrick Dillon's question about interactive fiction in your column. My response is difficult to contain: "Aaarrrrgggh-hhh!!!! You Ignorant Slut!" OK, perhaps I am overreacting, but you are refusing to let go of linearity. Why ever do you want to "constrain the combinatoric explosion of narrative pathways"? Good Lord, that's what makes the gametree bushy. This is exactly the kind of work that's well suited for a computer to perform—grinding out three billion story variations!

—Chris Crawford, San Jose, CA

Chris, I've been called a lot of things over the years (like Fay and Ray), and it's with a smile that I add your gift to my collection. Playing Jane Curtin to your Dan Aykroyd, I'll be happy to counter your counterpoint.

Your challenge represents a serious subject for multimedia designers today. I agree that interactive stories with too few branches are disappointingly flat and shallow. When a plot is broadly nonlinear, however, the permutations of events and possible outcomes become staggering, and the story as a whole becomes difficult to visualize and manage. Producing such work is also an intellectual challenge and costly in time and effort.

A truly open-ended "hypermedia" navigation system for consumer consumption risks death by shock caused by open arterial branches and loss of story pressure, where plot lines become too diffuse and users founder in trivia. Most users may, indeed, *prefer* a structured, organized, and well-defined story environment.

The argument for simplicity is voiced by Steven Levy, the author of *Hackers* and *Artificial Life*, who says, "There's really something to be said for documents with a beginning, middle, and end."

The shape of this new literature made possible by multimedia computers and wide-bandwidth cable and telephone delivery systems is being born in the working designs of developers. The final test for successful multimedia design is the marketplace, where consumers will decide. Your interesting "algorithms for interpersonal behavior, personality models, artificial personality, languages of expression, and facial displays" represent, perhaps, a successful marriage of this computer power with literature containing malleable plots and seemingly endless variations. Indeed, your forthcoming epic game, *Le Morte D'Arthur*, will surely break new ground and quite possibly prove your point. Can't wait to get a copy!

From correspondence in "Ask the Captain," a monthly column by Tay Vaughan in *NewMedia* magazine.

> Because all forms of information—including text, numbers, photos, video, and sound—can exist in a common digital format, they can be used simultaneously as people browse through an information stream, just as people use their various senses simultaneously to perceive the real world.
>
> ....
>
> Bill Gates, Chairman, Microsoft Corporation

Many navigation maps are essentially nonlinear. In these navigational systems, viewers are always free to jump to an index, a glossary, various menus, Help or About… sections, or even to a rendering of the map itself. It is often important to give viewers the sense that free choice is available; this empowers them within the context of the subject matter. Nonetheless, you should still provide consistent clues regarding importance, emphasis, and direction by varying typeface size and look, colorizing, indenting, or using special icons.

The architectural drawings for your multimedia project are the storyboards and navigation or site maps. The storyboards are married to the navigation maps during the design process, and help to visualize the information architecture. A simple navigation map is illustrated in Figure 9-2, where the content of a web site project is organized schematically.

A storyboard or wireframe is organized sequentially, screen by screen, and each screen is sketched out with design notes and specifications before rendering. Figure 9-3 shows the sketch for a single screen in a content

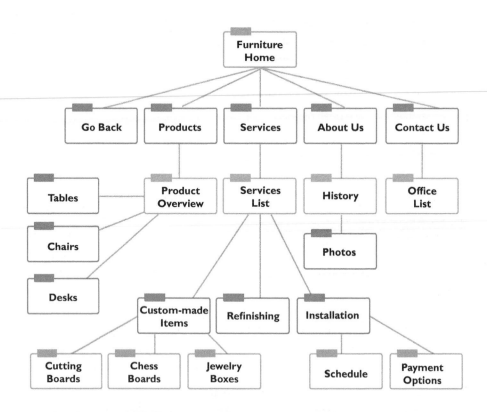

Figure 9-2 A navigation map can help you clarify the structure of your content.

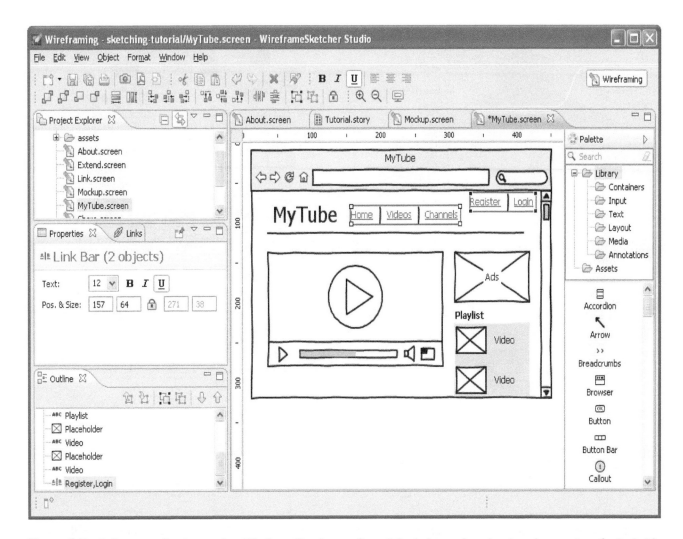

Figure 9-3 Software applications such as WireframeSketcher use "stencils" to help storyboard and mock up projects for Android, iPhone, iPad, Windows Phone, and web sites.

structure storyboard using WireframeSketcher (http://wireframesketcher. com) to organize all the elements.

Schematically or visually organizing the contents of a project during its design phase provides a useful overview for checking logical consistency and size. Many vendors offer both stand-alone and online software for "mindmapping" and for sitemapping the content of existing web sites. Figure 9-4 shows four ways to graphically display a project's content, in this case the documents and links in a single folder at a biographical web site. In a project or at a web site, users can call up this visual representation and then navigate directly to their chosen subject.

Multimedia provides great power for jumping about within your project's content. And though it is important to give users a sense of free choice, too much freedom can be disconcerting, and viewers may get lost.

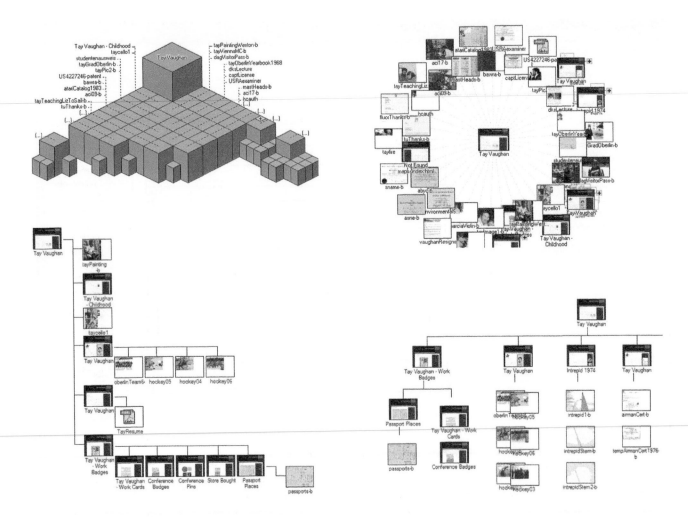

Figure 9-4 PowerMapper (www.powermapper.com) provides many ways to display and organize content through visual navigation maps. Shown clockwise from top left are "Skyscrapers," "PageCloud," "ThumbTree," and "Electrum."

Try to keep your messages and content organized along a steady stream of the major subjects, letting users branch outward to explore details. Always provide a secure anchor, with buttons that lead to expected places, and build a familiar landscape to which users may return at any time.

Hot Spots, Hyperlinks, and Buttons

Most multimedia authoring systems allow you to make any part of the screen, or any object, into a **hot spot**. When users hover over or click a hot spot at that location, something happens, which makes multimedia not just interactive, but also exciting. Hot spots can be given more specific names based upon either their function or their form. For example, if clicking the hot spot connects the user to another part of the document or program or to a different program or web site, it is referred to as a link, **hyperlink**, or **anchor**. If the hot spot is a graphic image designed to look like a push button or toggle switch, it is called a **button**, more formally defined as a meaningful graphic image that you click or "touch" to make something happen.

Hot spots can be text or graphic images. Most authoring systems provide a tool for creating text buttons of various styles (radio buttons, check boxes, or labeled push buttons, for example), as well as graphic buttons.

TIP *Designing a good navigation system and creating original buttons appropriate for your project are not trivial artistic tasks. Be sure you budget sufficient time in your design process for many trials, so you'll be able to get your buttons looking and acting just right.*

Text buttons and their fonts and styles are described in Chapter 2. Graphic buttons can contain graphic images or even parts of images—for example, a map of the world with each country color coded, and a mouse click on a country yields further information. **Icons** are graphic objects designed specifically to be meaningful as buttons and are usually small (although size is, in theory, not a determining factor). Icons are fundamental graphic objects symbolic of an activity or concept:

Once a style has been chosen, you need to determine how your user will know that the button is active or is being selected. Highlighting a button or object, or changing its state, when the cursor rolls over it or the button is tapped, is the most common method of distinguishing it as the object of interest. A mouse click or a second tap is the selection. Highlighting is usually accomplished by altering the object's colors and optionally moving the object a pixel or two or, if text, changing its size. Depending upon how you highlight, you can make a button appear off (not pressed) or on (pressed) as illustrated here.

Or you can use an animated GIF image that animates when the mouse hovers over it. The dove in the illustration at far right begins flying when the mouse passes over the word "Habitat."

Really good software products should be simple, hot, and deep. People need to get into your software in about 20 seconds and get immediate positive feedback and reward; then they are smiling and having a good time and they want to go further. "Hot" means that you've got to be fully cooking the machine, with all its graphics and sound capabilities, conveying something dynamic and exciting that competes with what people are used to seeing in a movie or on TV. In terms of "deep," it's kind of like the ocean where there are people of all ages: some kids will just wade out in a foot of surf, other guys with scuba gear go way out and way deep. Make it possible for me to go as deep as I want, but don't force it on me. Just let the depth of your product unfold to me in a very natural way.

Trip Hawkins, Founder, Electronic Arts

Your navigation design must provide buttons that make sense, so their actions will be intuitively understood by means of their icon or graphic representation, or via text cues. Do not force your viewers to learn many new or special icons; keep the learning curve to a minimum. It's also important to include buttons that perform basic housekeeping tasks, such as quitting the project at any given point, or canceling an activity.

Hot Spots in Web Pages   The simplest hot spots on the Web are the text anchors that link a document to other documents. This is because a browser usually indicates that some specific text is a hot link or anchor by coloring or underlining the text so it stands out from the body. Default colors for anchor text are a user-defined preference, though you can override the default in the <body> tag.

Using Cascading Style Sheets (CSS) in web site design, text can be easily colored and highlighted on hover and hyperlinked or anchored to other document URLs on clicking. Drop-down text menus (see Figure 9-5) allow for a dense hierarchy of menu choices to be displayed.

Other common buttons found on the Web consist of small JPEG or GIF graphic images that are themselves anchor links. Browsers may indicate that an image is hot by drawing a border around it (you can remove this border by placing border="0" into the <img> tag). Larger images may be sectioned into hot areas with associated links; these are called **image maps**.

Figure 9-6 shows a graphic image of a village that has been programmed in HTML to have 32 hot spots, each linking to a document when clicked). The house or barn highlights when the mouse rolls over that area. The code looks like this:

```
<area shape="rect" coords="180,85,230,135" href=" ../vendors/v25/index.html"
onmouseover="set('../vendors/v25/images/logomenu.gif');">
```

Figure 9-5   Drop-down menus at web sites are built using a combination of HTML, CSS, and JavaScript.

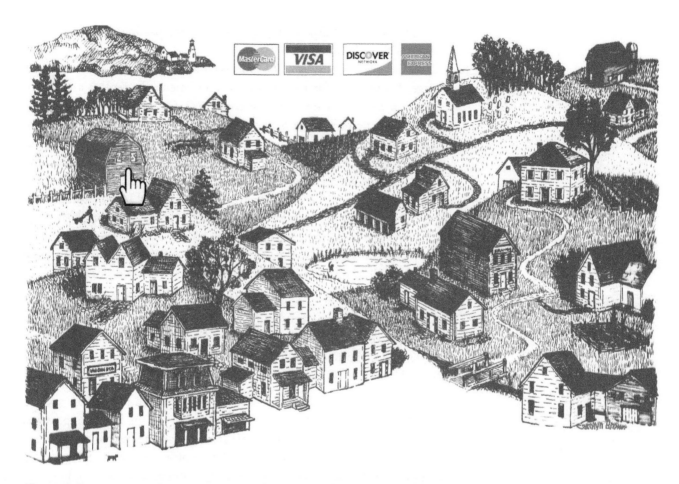

Figure 9-6   Using a large image map and JavaScript embedded in a normal HTML web page, when the mouse rolls over a house or barn, users can actively explore this seaside village to discover what's hidden behind its doors.

Ways to make interesting buttons and interactive graphical interfaces on the World Wide Web are described more fully in Chapter 11.

Icons

In Mac OS X and Windows operating systems, icons have a special meaning, in that they constitute a suite of image resources that is linked to and identifies an application, file, volume, or service.

On the Macintosh, icon image files (.icns) can contain one or more images of 16×16, 32×32, 48×48, 128×128, 256×256, and 512×512 pixels as well as alpha channels for transparency masking. The Mac operating system automatically scales the image(s) to display at other sizes. To use your own icon for a file or folder, open the Get Info panel (COMMAND-I), click once on the icon shown at the top left of the Get Info panel to highlight it, and paste any 512×512-pixel bitmap from the clipboard. The old icon is replaced with the new. You can also highlight an icon in the Get Info panel

Designers will build screens where there are tiny little things going on all over it at different places, and everything has momentous significance. And then the user is supposed to be able to find these momentous things. So people just glaze over. If you want them to hit a button, put a big button right in the middle of the screen.

Trip Hawkins, Chairman & CEO, 3DO Company

and copy it to the clipboard (COMMAND-C) for pasting into your image editor or directly into a project.

Windows 7 icons are 256×256 pixels and are scaled to Extra Large, Large, Medium, or Small sizes in the View menu. To replace a folder or alias icon with your own, simply create a 256×256-pixel PNG file and save it. Then go to a folder or shortcut and right-click it; select Properties. Choose the Customize tab and select Change Icon. Browse to find your saved icon and click OK. In Windows 8, the Start screen consists of "tiles." These are large, square icons (see http://msdn.microsoft.com/en-us/library/windows/desktop/hh127427%28v=vs.85%29.aspx and http://msdn.microsoft.com/en-us/library/windows/desktop/aa511280.aspx for more).

Icons are important when it comes to the small screens on smartphones and tablets, where they must be large enough to recognize yet small enough to allow multiple icons to display at the same time. For more information about Android and iOS icons, see the following, respectively:

- http://developer.android.com/design/style/iconography.html
- https://developer.apple.com/library/ios/documentation/userexperience/conceptual/mobilehig/IconMatrix.html#//apple_ref/doc/uid/TP40006556-CH27-SW1

Building and saving icon files is simpler using an icon editor such as IcoFX (http://icofx.ro/) or the ICOformat plug-in for Photoshop (www.telegraphics.com.au/sw/#icoformat). If you want to use a system icon within your project, it is often quickest to capture or grab it off the screen and place it directly into your project as a bitmap. Use caution, however, because the design of some icons (particularly those using corporate logos) may be protected by copyright or trademark.

Browsers automatically look for a tiny 16×16-pixel icon file named favicon.ico in the root of a web site, which they will display in one or more places in their "chrome" (the toolbars, status bars, sidebars, menus, and navigation elements surrounding the web page itself). In the illustration at left, the Facebook icon is shown by the Firefox browser both in the URL address field and in the tab.

If you wish to identify your own web site with an icon, simply include an ICO file (named favicon.ico) in the root folder of your site. It will be discovered by the browser and used for all pages at the web site. Alternatively,, you can add a link tag in the <head> element of your web page that identifies your icon image to the browser:

```
<link rel="icon" type="image/gif" href="http://www.yourwebsite.com/yourIcon.gif">
```

You may prefer this method because you can use a GIF, JPG, or PNG image. Remember from Chapter 3, you can use transparency in a GIF or PNG image when you don't want your icon to fill the 16×16-pixel box in the corners or edges. Use simple shapes, keep your lines sharp, and experiment in your image editor: it is very hard to make a decent image with only 16×16 pixels to work with.

Apple's handheld touch devices such as iPod touch, iPhone, and iPad use a custom Safari browser to display web clips on a Home screen; they will display a custom icon for your web site if you include in the <head> tag of your page a <link> tag to an appropriate image. Apple recommends a flat (not shiny) and simple 57×57-pixel image in PNG format with sharp 90-degree corners. The display software will then render your icon with rounded corners, a drop shadow, and a reflective shine, as shown in the illustration at far right.

Put the following code into your HTML <head> tag:

```
<link rel="apple-touch-icon" href="/somepath/image.png" />
```

or to force your icon not to be rendered, use

```
<link rel="apple-touch-icon-precomposed.png" href="/
somepath/image.png" />
```

Designing the User Interface

The user interface of your multimedia product is a blend of its graphic elements and its navigation system. If your messages and content are disorganized and difficult to find, or if users become disoriented or bored, your project may fail. Poor graphics can cause boredom. Poor navigational aids can make viewers feel lost and unconnected to the content; or, worse, viewers may sail right off the edge and just give up and quit the program.

Novice/Expert Modes

Be aware that there are two types of end users: those who are computer literate and those who are not. Creating a user interface that will satisfy both types has been a design dilemma since the invention of computers. The simplest solution for handling varied levels of user expertise is to provide a **modal interface**, where the viewer can simply click a Novice/Expert button and change the approach of the whole interface—to be either more or less detailed or complex. Modal interfaces are common on bulletin boards, for example, allowing novices to read menus and select desired activities, while experts can altogether eliminate the time-consuming download and display of menus and simply type an activity code directly into an executable command line. Both novices and experts alike may quickly learn to click the mouse and skip the annoying ragtime piece you chose for background music.

Two readers didn't notice the screen had changed in different circumstances. This happened when the button they clicked on took them to a visually similar screen, and there was no visual effect as the screens changed. One reader was looking at the details of a hostel and clicked the left-hand Next arrow. He arrived at a screen with details about another hostel, but he did not notice he was looking at a different screen. He tried the right-hand Next arrow as well, and the screen changed back to the one he had been viewing initially, but again he did not notice the change and concluded the Next buttons did nothing. A visual effect or animation here would have provided a cue to make the screen changes more noticeable.

....

Lynda Hardman of the Scottish HCI Centre, after focus group testing the "Glasgow Online" hypertext system

Unfortunately, in multimedia projects, modal interfaces are not a good answer. It's best to avoid designing modal interfaces because they tend to confuse the user. Typically, only a minority of users are expert, and so the majority are caught in between and frustrated. The solution is to build your multimedia project to contain plenty of navigational power, providing access to content and tasks for users at all levels, as well as a help system to provide some hand-holding and reassurance. Present all this power in easy-to-understand structures and concepts, and use clear textual cues. Above all, keep the interface simple! Even experts will balk at a complex screen full of tiny buttons and arcane switches, and will appreciate having neat and clean doorways into your project's content.

GUIs

The Macintosh and Windows graphical user interfaces (GUI, pronounced "gooey") are successful partly because their basic point-and-click style is simple, consistent, and quickly mastered. Both these GUIs offer built-in help systems, and both provide standard patterns of activity that produce standard expected results. The following actions, for example, are consistently performed by similar keystrokes when running most programs on the Macintosh or in Windows:

Action	Macintosh Keystroke	Windows Keystroke
New file	⌘-N	CTRL-N
Open file	⌘-O	CTRL-O
Save file	⌘-S	CTRL-S
Quit	⌘-Q	CTRL-Q
Undo	⌘-Z	CTRL-Z
Cut	⌘-X	CTRL-X
Copy	⌘-C	CTRL-C
Paste	⌘-V	CTRL-V

TIP   *Since Cut, Copy, and Paste are used so often, this mnemonic device may help you to remember their keyboard shortcuts: X looks like scissors and is to Cut. C is straightforward; C is for Copy. Think of V as an upside-down insertion caret (used to insert text when copyediting) and you will remember that it is for Paste.*

For your multimedia interface to be successful, you, too, must be consistent in designing both the look and the behavior of your human interface. Multimedia authoring systems provide you with the tools to design and implement your own graphical user interface from scratch. Be prudent with all that flexibility, however. Unless your content and messages are bizarre or require special treatment, it's best to stick with accepted conventions for button design and grouping, visual and audio feedback, and navigation structure.

Stick with real-world metaphors that will be understood by the widest selection of potential users. For example, consider using the well-known trash can icon for deleting files, a hand cursor for dragging objects, and a clock or an hourglass icon for pauses. If your material is time-oriented, develop metaphors for past, present, and future. If it is topic-oriented, choose metaphors related to the topics themselves. If it is polar (the pros and cons of an issue, for example), choose relevant contrasting images.

TIP *Most multimedia authoring systems include tutorials and instructions for creating and using buttons and navigation aids. Typically, they also supply templates or examples of attractive backgrounds and distinctive buttons that serve as an excellent starting place. In a large project, you might want to use a different metaphor as the backbone of each major section, to provide a helpful cue for users to orient themselves within your content. For the Travel section, for example, you could use icons that are sailing ships with various riggings; for the Finance section, buttons that are coins of different denominations; and for the buttons of the International Business section, you could use colorful flags from various countries.*

Users like to be in control, so avoid hidden commands and unusual keystroke/mouse click combinations. Design your interface with the goal that no instruction manual or special training will be required to move through your project. Users do not like to have to remember keywords or special codes, so always make the full range of options easily available as interactive buttons or menu items. And finally, users do make mistakes, so allow them a chance to escape from inadvertent or dangerous predicaments ("Do you really want to delete? Delete/Escape"). Keep your interface simple and friendly.

Graphical Approaches

Designing excellent computer screens requires a special set of fine art skills, and not every programmer or graduate in fine arts may be suited to creating computer graphics. Like programmers who must keep up with current operating systems and languages, computer graphic artists must also stay informed about the rapidly changing canvas of new features, techniques, applications, and creative tools.

Vaughan's General Rule for Interface Design

The best user interface demands the least learning effort.

Throw out your tried and true training or software development methodologies, and pretend that you're Spielberg or Lucas: think of what the viewer sees and hears and how the viewer interacts with the system you deliver. Create an "experience" for the viewer.

....

David A. Ludwig, Interactive Learning Designs

Computer graphics is more left- and right-brained—and not so spontaneous as doing it by hand. The ramp time is tedious; I am used to instant gratification with my fine artwork.

....

Cornelia Atchley, a fine artist creating multimedia art with computers, Washington, D.C.

The artist must make broad design choices: cartoon stick figures for a children's game, rendered illustrations for a medical reference, scanned bitmaps for a travel tour of Europe. The graphic artwork must be appropriate not only for the subject matter, but for the user as well. Once the approach is decided, the artist has to put real pixels onto a computer screen and do the work. A multimedia graphic artist must always play the role of the end user during the design and rendering process, choosing colors that look good, specifying text fonts that "speak," and designing buttons that are clearly marked for what they do.

Things That Work   Here are some graphical approaches that get good results:

- Neatly executed contrasts: big/small, heavy/light, bright/dark, thin/thick, cheap/dear (see Figure 9-7)
- Simple and clean screens with lots of white space (see Figure 9-8)
- Eye-grabbers such as drop caps, or a single brightly colored object alone on a gray-scale screen
- Shadows and drop shadows in various shades
- Gradients
- Reversed graphics to emphasize important text or images
- Shaded objects and text in 2-D and 3-D

Figure 9-7   Contrasts attract the eye—Bud Knight, PGA Junior Champion at the turn of the century, was made thick by stretching him in an image-editing program.

THINK RED
THINK HOT
THINK SMALL

CHARLIE'S CHILIES

Figure 9-8   Use plenty of white space ("noninformation areas") in your screens.

Things to Avoid   Here are some mistakes you will want to avoid in creating computer graphics:

- Clashes of color
- **Busy screens** (too much stuff)
- Using a picture with a lot of contrast in color or brightness as a background
- Trite humor in oft-repeated animations
- Clanging bells or squeaks when a button is clicked
- Frilly pattern borders
- Cute one-liners from famous movies
- Requiring more than two button clicks to quit
- Too many numbers (limit charts to about 25 numbers; if you can, just show totals)
- Too many words (don't crowd them; split your information into bite-sized chunks)
- Too many substantive elements presented too quickly

Most graphic artists will tell you that design is an "intuitive thing," but they will be hard-pressed to describe the rules they follow in their everyday work. They know when colors are not "working" and will change them again and again until they're right, but they usually won't be able to explain why the colors work or don't work. A project with a good navigation design, though it may have been developed with good planning and storyboarding, is indeed more often the result of many hours of crafty finagling with buttons and editors. Visit www.templatemonster.com to see a huge number of web site templates, some of them Flash-based, and many with multimedia features such as animations, dynamic interfaces, and sound.

Audio Interfaces

A multimedia user interface may include important sound elements that reflect the rhythm of a project and may affect the attitude of your audience. Sounds can be background music; special effects for button clicks; voice-overs; effects synced to animation; or they may be buried in the audio track of a video clip. The tempo and style of background music can set the "tone" of a project. Vivaldi or Bach might be appropriate for a banking or investment annual report delivered on DVD. Comic laughs and screeching effects might be appropriate for a clothing web site aimed at preteens. Choose music that fits the content and the atmosphere you wish to create. In all cases, use special effects sparingly. Always provide a toggle switch to disable sound. (Many AOL users prefer to disable the "You've Got Mail!" voice, for example.) And always test a project that contains sound with potential users.

> Developing multimedia can be like taking a joy ride in a washer/dryer. When it's all over you feel like you've been washed, rinsed, spun, and tumble-dried.
>
> Kevin McCarthy,
> Director of Business
> Development,
> Medius IV

Producing

By the time you reach the development phases of your multimedia project and you start building, you should already have taken care to prepare your plan and to get organized. The project plan (see Chapter 8) now becomes your step-by-step instruction manual for building the product. For many multimedia developers, following this plan and actually doing the construction work—being down in the trenches of hands-on creation and production—is the fun part of any project.

Production is the phase when your multimedia project is actually rendered. During this phase you will contend with important and continuous organizing tasks. There will be times in a complex project when graphics files seem to disappear from the server, when you forget to send or cannot produce milestone progress reports, when your voice talent gets lost on the way to the recording studio, or when your hard disk crashes. So it's important to start out on the right foot, with good organization, and to maintain detailed management oversight during the entire construction process. This rule applies to projects large and small, projects for you or for a client, and projects with 1 or 20 people on staff. Above all, provide a good time-accounting system for everyone working on the project. At the end of the week, it's hard to remember how much time you spent on the tasks you did on Monday.

TIP *If your project is to be built by more than one person, establish a management structure in advance that includes specific milestones and the production expectations for each contributor.*

Starting Up

Before you begin your multimedia project, it's important to check your development hardware and software and review your organizational and administrative setup, even if you are working alone. This is a serious last-minute task. It prevents you from finding yourself halfway through the project with nowhere to put your graphics files and digitized movie segments when you're out of disk space, or stuck with an incompatible version of a critical software tool, or with a network that bogs down and quits every two days. Such incidents can take many days or weeks to resolve, so try to head off as many potential problems as you can before you begin. Here are some examples of things to think about:

■ Desk and mind clear of obstructions?
■ Best computers you can afford?
■ Time-accounting and management system in place?
■ Biggest (or most) monitors you can afford?
■ Sufficient disk storage space for all work files?
■ System for regular backup of critical files?

- Conventions or protocols for naming your working files and managing source documents?
- Latest version of your primary authoring software?
- Latest versions of software tools and accessories?
- Communication pathways open with client?
- Breathing room for administrative tasks?
- Financial arrangements secure (retainer in the bank)?
- Expertise lined up for all stages of the project?
- Kick-off meeting completed?

First Person

At 18, I used to hang around with people who drove fast cars, and once volunteered to help an acquaintance prepare his Ferrari Berlinetta for a race at Watkins Glen. My job was to set the valves while my friend went over the suspension, brakes, and later, the carburetor. The car boasted 12 cylinders and 24 valves, and adjusting the clearance between tappet and rocker arm seemed to me akin to a jeweler's fine work. It required special wrenches and feeler gauges and an uncommon touch to rotate the high-compression engine so the cam was precisely at its highest point for each valve. I was blown away by the sheer quantity of moving parts under the Ferrari's long and shiny valve covers—my own fast car had only four cylinders and eight simple valves. It took me about seven exhausting hours (including double-checking) to get it right. As the sun came up, though, the engine sounded great! Tuning up and preparing, I learned, is as important to the race as the race itself. My friend, however, learned a much tougher lesson: he spun out and rolled his Ferrari at the hairpin turn in the seventh lap. He crawled unhurt from the twisted wreckage, but all he was able to salvage from the car was the engine.

Working with Clients

Making multimedia for clients is a special case. Be sure that the organization of your project incorporates a system for good communication between you and the client as well as among the people actually building the project. Many projects have turned out unhappily because of communication breakdowns.

Client Approval Cycles

Provide good management oversight to avoid endless feedback loops—in this situation the client is somehow never quite happy, and you are forced to tweak and edit many times. Manage production so that your client is continually informed and formally approves by signing off on artwork and other elements as you build them. Occasionally, the technology will improve during development and you may be able to offer new features that will improve your project. Develop a scheme that specifies the number and duration of client approval cycles, and then provide a mechanism for change orders when changes are requested after sign-off. For change orders, remember that the client should pay extra and the changes should be costly.

Data Storage Media and Transportation

It's important that the client be able to easily review your work. Remember that either both you and the distant site need to have matching data transfer systems and media, or you need to provide a web or FTP site for your project. Organize your system before you begin work, as it may take some time for both you and the client to agree on an appropriate system and on the method of transportation.

Because multimedia files are large, your means of transporting the project to distant clients is particularly important. Typically, both you and the client will have access to the Internet at high bandwidth. If not, the most cost- and time-effective method for transporting your files is on DVD-ROM by an overnight courier service (FedEx, UPS, or U.S. Postal Service Priority Mail Express). Material completed in time for an afternoon pickup will usually be at the client's site by the next morning.

If you use the Internet to deliver your multimedia to the client, be sure that you set up rules and conventions for naming files placed at an FTP site or in the cloud at, for example, GitHub or Dropbox, and use codes in the subject headers of your e-mail to describe the content of the message. After a project has been under way for a while, there will be many files and many communications, so these keywords and clues will make life easier. This is another place where planning ahead pays off!

Tracking

Organize a method for tracking the receipt of material that you will incorporate into your multimedia project. Even in small projects, you will be dealing with many digital bits and pieces.

Develop a **file-naming convention** specific to your project's structure. Store the files in directories or folders with logical names. **Version control** of your files (tracking editing changes) is critically important, too, especially in large projects. If more than one person is working on a group of files, be sure that you always know what version is the latest and who has the current version. If storage space allows, archive all file iterations, in case you change your mind about something and need to go back to a prior rendering.

Copyrights

Commonly used authoring platforms may allow access to the software programming code or script that drives a particular project. The source code of HTML pages on the Web may also be easily viewed.

In such an open-code environment, are you prepared to let others see your programming work? Is your code neat and commented? Perhaps your mother cautioned you to wear clean underclothing in case you were suddenly on a table among strangers in a hospital emergency room—well, apply this rule to your code. You can insert a copyright statement in your project that clearly (and legally) designates the code as your intellectual property (see Figure 9-9),

Figure 9-9 Typical copyright and ownership statements embedded in <meta> tags at the top of an HTML page

but the code, tricks, and programming techniques remain accessible for study, learning, and tweaking by others.

Hazards and Annoyances

Even experienced producers and developers commonly run into at least some light chop and turbulence during the course of a project's development. The experts, however, never crash when their vehicle shudders or loses some altitude. You can expect the going to get rough at any number of stages—from trying to design the perfect interface, to endless testing, to problems with client sign-off or payment. Expect problems beyond your control, and be prepared to accept them and solve them.

Small annoyances, too, can become serious distractions that are counterproductive. The production stage is a time of great creativity, dynamic intercourse among all contributors, and, above all, hard work. Be prepared to deal with some common irritants, for example:

- Creative coworkers who don't take (or give) criticism well
- Clients who cannot or are not authorized to make decisions
- More than two all-nighters in a row
- Too many custom-coded routines
- Instant coffee and microwaved corn dogs
- Too many meetings; off-site meetings
- Missed deadlines
- Software and hardware upgrades that interrupt your normal operations

If your project is a team effort, then it is critical that everyone works well together—or can at least tolerate one another's differences—especially when the going gets tough. Pay attention to the mental health of all personnel involved in your project, and be aware of the dynamics of the group and whether people are being adversely affected by individual personalities. If problems arise, deal with them before they become hazardous; the mix of special creative talents required for multimedia can be volatile. If you stay organized and flexible throughout, you will complete your project successfully. See Chapter 13 for how to deliver it!

First Person

In 1975, I was hired to deliver a 41-foot cruising sailboat from Fort Lauderdale to the British Virgin Islands for the charter trade. In three days I assembled a crew of strangers, provisioned the boat, and checked all the equipment. Then we took off across the Gulf Stream and into the Bermuda Triangle.

After two days it was clear that the cook was a bad apple. It wasn't just that she couldn't cook—she whined about everything: the stove wouldn't light, the boat heeled too much, her socks were wet, her sleeping bag tore on a cleat, her hair was tangled, she couldn't get her favorite radio station (now a few hundred miles astern). It was unending.

The whining began to envelop her in a smog-colored, onion-like layering, each new complaint accreting to the last one, like growing coral. By the fifth day, her unpleasant aura saturated the entire main cabin, and the rest of us had to

seek sanctuary in the cockpit or the small aft cabin. Efforts were made to solve this bizarre situation, but by then, nobody could get near her (or wanted to). When we pulled into tiny Caicos Island for water and fresh stores, I paid her off and arranged for a room at the quaint waterfront hotel, where she could wait three days for the weekly airplane back to Florida. Everyone felt bad about her disappointment and how it all turned out—for about an hour. The rest of the voyage was jubilant.

Chapter 9 Review

■ Chapter Summary

For your review, here's a summary of the important concepts discussed in this chapter.

Describe various strategies for designing interactive multimedia

■ The best products are often the result of continuing feedback and modifications implemented throughout the production process. However, too much feedback and too many changes can kill a project; always balance proposed changes against their cost.

■ You can either describe the project in great detail before the production, or you can use rough storyboards and refine the design as you produce it.

■ How you organize your material for a project will have just as great an impact on the viewer as the content itself.

■ Start mapping the structure of your project early in the planning phase.

■ Project designs are typically linear, hierarchical, nonlinear, or composite.

■ The method you provide to your viewers for navigating from one place to another in your project is part of the user interface.

■ Depth structure represents the complete navigation map and describes all the links between all the components of your project.

■ Surface structure represents the structures actually realized by a user while navigating the depth structure.

■ Hot spots can be text, graphic, and icon.

■ Stick with accepted conventions for button design and grouping, visual and audio feedback, and navigation structure.

Identify principles for successful production of multimedia projects

■ Production is the phase when your multimedia project is actually rendered.

■ Provide a time-accounting system for everyone working on the project.

■ Check your development hardware and software and review your organizational and administrative setup.

■ Have in place a system for communication between you, the client, and the people actually building the project.

■ Provide management oversight and control the client review process to avoid endless feedback loops.

■ Establish a process in which your client is continually informed and formally approves the project as you develop it.

■ Organize a method for tracking the receipt of material that you will incorporate into your multimedia project.

■ Develop a file-naming convention specific to your project's structure.

■ Version control of your files (tracking editing changes) is critically important, especially in large projects.

■ Key Terms

anchor *(286)*
busy screen *(295)*
button *(287)*
composite navigation *(280)*

depth structure *(281)*
file-naming convention *(299)*
hierarchical navigation *(280)*
hot spot *(286)*

hyperlink *(286)*
icon *(287)*
image map *(288)*
linear navigation *(280)*

modal interface *(291)*
navigation map *(280)*
nonlinear navigation *(280)*
production *(296)*

site map *(280)*
storyboard *(279)*
surface structure *(281)*
user interface *(281)*

version control *(299)*
white space *(294)*
wireframing *(279)*

■ Key Terms Quiz

1. A graphic outline that describes each page of a project in exact detail is called a(n) _____.

2. A multimedia structure in which users navigate sequentially, from one frame or bite of information to another, could be called _____.

3. A multimedia structure in which users navigate along the branches of a tree structure that is shaped by the natural logic of the content could be called _____.

4. A multimedia structure in which users navigate freely through the content of the project, unbound by predetermined routes, could be called _____.

5. A multimedia structure in which users may navigate freely, but are occasionally constrained to linear presentations, could be called _____.

6. The complete navigation map that describes all the links between all the components of your project is known as _____.

7. The structure actually realized by a user while navigating the project's content is known as _____.

8. A fundamental graphic object that represents an activity or concept is called a(n) _____.

9. The standard that ensures that project files are given logical names and stored in folders with logical names is the _____.

10. Making sure that old files are archived and new versions are properly tracked is called _____.

■ Multiple-Choice Quiz

1. Which of these is *not* an advantage of creating detailed storyboards before beginning production?
   a. Constructing the project will be easier.
   b. Less time is required in polishing the final product.
   c. Getting to the production stage is faster.
   d. It is better suited to separate design and production teams.
   e. Clients who like to tightly control the production process prefer it.

2. Which of these is *not* one of the listed types of organizational structures?
   a. linear
   b. hierarchical
   c. nonlinear
   d. composite
   e. recursive

3. The visual representation of a project that includes a table of contents as well as a chart of the logical flow of the interactive interface is often called:
   a. a storyboard
   b. a workflow diagram
   c. a prototype
   d. a navigation map
   e. a master layout

4. The method you provide to your viewers for navigating from one place to another in your project is part of the:
   a. script
   b. user interface
   c. storyboards
   d. depth structure
   e. surface structure

5. The generic term for any area of an image that can be clicked on is:
   a. a hot spot
   b. a storyboard
   c. an image map
   d. a rollover
   e. an icon

6. An interface in which a user can click a button and change the approach of the whole interface is called:
   a. a prototype
   b. a navigation map
   c. a modal interface
   d. a site map
   e. a transitional GUI

7. Having separate novice and expert interfaces for a multimedia program is generally not a good idea because:
   a. it tends to take up too much disk space or bandwidth
   b. novice users tend to get caught in the expert mode
   c. only a minority of users are expert; most users are caught in between and are frustrated
   d. most authoring systems are not capable of handling parallel structures
   e. it makes developing documentation awkward and unwieldy

8. GUI stands for:
   a. general/universal/individual
   b. general utilization instructions
   c. global usage image
   d. guidelines for usability and interaction
   e. graphical user interface

9. The Macintosh and Windows GUIs are successful partly because:
   a. they enable cross-platform file structures
   b. their basic point-and-click style is simple, consistent, and quickly mastered
   c. they are highly customizable, allowing programmers to use program-specific keyboard shortcuts
   d. they tend to make the computer run more efficiently
   e. slick marketing efforts tricked gullible consumers

10. Noninformation areas left intentionally free from visual clutter are often referred to as:
    a. negative space
    b. screen real estate
    c. advanced organizers
    d. white space
    e. depth structure

11. The standards that ensure that project files are given logical names and stored in folders with logical names are the:
    a. usability guidelines
    b. pattern-recognition algorithms
    c. file-naming conventions
    d. review-cycle management
    e. project tracking protocols

12. Perhaps the most significant problem with creating a multimedia program that gives users complete free reign is that:
    a. such freedom is difficult to program
    b. computers cannot yet process so many variables concurrently
    c. too much freedom can be disconcerting to users
    d. it is difficult to organize data into meaningful structures
    e. such interfaces tend to be cluttered and unwieldy

13. Default colors for anchor text are found in which HTML tag?

    a. <head>

    b. <frame>

    c. <link>

    d. <color>

    e. <body>

14. Which of these is probably *not* a good step to take before starting the production process for a multimedia project?

    a. Lock in the design so there are no further changes to delay production.

    b. Establish limits on client review cycles to reduce cost overruns.

    c. Set up an FTP site for sending and receiving production files.

    d. Establish clear file-naming and version control standards.

    e. Check the state of your hardware and software to ensure reliability and capability, and integrate any upgrades.

15. An image on a web page can be sectioned in HTML into areas that are clickable links. This is called:

    a. a sweet spot

    b. a site map

    c. a rollover

    d. a frameset

    e. an image map

■ Essay Quiz

1. You are given the task of managing a design and production team to complete a multimedia web site for your own company. The site is to use the latest plug-ins for interactive 3-D presentation. The design team consists of a writer and a designer, and the production team includes two programmers. Would you make sure the design and storyboards were "nailed down" before beginning production, or would you start and allow the design to be changed during the production process? How would factors such as the client, the technology, and the relationship between the design and production teams affect your approach?

2. List the four different types of multimedia structures. Next, describe four hypothetical projects, one that might be appropriate for each of the four types of structures. For each of these four projects, comment on why the project is best suited to that structure and why each of the other three structures is less appropriate for that project.

3. Discuss the relationship between a program's content, its interface, and its usability. What is the best way to make the content accessible to users without unnecessary complexity? Where are modal interfaces useful? What are their drawbacks? Where are navigation or site maps useful? How might you use "themes" to identify different areas of a program or different approaches to the content's structure?

4. What are the steps you would take in "gearing up" for the production phase of a multimedia project? Organize your thoughts according to the infrastructure (hardware, software, networks, web/FTP site), team management, and client interaction.

5. Describe the tracking process you might use to control the project development process. Be sure to include a discussion of version control, file-naming convention, client review cycles, and team management.

Lab Projects

Project 9.1

Locate three different web sites: a news site, a shopping site, and a social media site. Examine the buttons on each and analyze the navigation options. Comparing the three sites, how does the site design prompt you to do certain actions? What features are present to make your experience as a user more friendly? Consider hot spots, icons, and menus as you explore.

Project 9.2

Locate an online service or project, such as a game or a social media site, that is currently in beta (meaning that it is public and being tested, but not yet commercially released). Use this service, recording your experience as you go. List the elements that work well. List what you feel needs to be redesigned or improved. Once you have completed your critique, locate a place or method on the web site to submit your feedback to the creators.

Project 9.3

Create a site map for a web site that presents the history of the Internet. Imagine it as an interactive timeline, which the user scrolls through to progress. Consider what tools you should provide to the user, such as a glossary or tooltips for specific items on the timeline. Explain three alternative ways to view the timeline: as a compressed version for quick skims; as an elaborate version with more in-depth info; and as a version for mobile viewing.

Project 9.4

Using simple text blocks and icons, create a user interface for the project you developed in Project 9.3. Discuss what buttons are included, how they are logically grouped together, and why. What non-text interface elements might you include to provide navigational cues?

Project 9.5

Devise a method for gathering feedback within the web site you designed in Project 9.3. First draw the design on paper and have a few friends provide feedback on your design. Then describe how you would test your web site online, how you would identify who your audience is, and how you would gain their feedback online.

## CHAPTER 10

Content and Talent

Every multimedia project includes **content**. It is the "stuff" from which you fashion your messages. It is also the information and material that forms the heart of your project, and it is that which defines what your project is about.

Practically, content can be any and all of the elements of multimedia. You might use your collection of wedding photographs and videotapes to create a special multimedia newsletter for family and relatives. Or you might edit portions of the audio track from these videotapes and capture still images to build a multimedia database of aunts, uncles, and cousins. This material is your project's content.

Content can have low and high **production value**. If you hire a team of professionals to shoot your wedding video, and then they digitize images and audio clips at broadcast quality, your content will have high production value. If you persuade Hillary Rodham Clinton to record the voice-over and Garry Trudeau, the "Doonesbury" artist, to retouch the images, it will have yet higher production value.

You must always balance the production value of your project against your budget and the desired result. For aerial photographs of the wedding reception, you would not likely commission the private launch of a spy satellite to achieve highest production value. Instead, you could rent a helicopter with paparazzi and still achieve good production value. Or you could photograph the wedding yourself from a neighboring rooftop and be satisfied with the lower production value. The production value of your project is a question of balance (see Vaughan's Law of Multimedia Minimums in Chapter 4).

Content has to come from somewhere—either you make it or you acquire it. Whether you make it, borrow it, or buy it depends upon your project's needs, your talent and time constraints, and your pocketbook. Content that is destined for sale to the public is also wrapped up in numerous legal issues. Who owns the content? Do you have the proper rights to use it? Copyright laws, for example, establish rights for the creators or owners of literary works; musical works; dramatic works; pictorial, graphic, and sculptural works; motion pictures and other audiovisual works; and sound recordings. Do you have licenses for protected works and signed releases from anyone who appears in your project?

When the Vatican recently made a collection of artwork available on the World Wide Web, they made certain there was a digital "watermark" for each image; they would then know if the artwork was ripped off, without recourse to even higher laws. The Vatican is aware (as you should be) of the nature of the electronic revolution:

> In accordance with international regulations on Intellectual Property and Author's Rights, prior authorization is necessary to reproduce the VIS service, partially or in its entirety, or in the case of electronic re-transmission. In addition, it is always necessary to cite the source (VIS – Vatican Information Service). To obtain permission, as well as to make comments or suggestions, you may write to vis@pressva-vis.va.

This chapter discusses some of the legal issues surrounding content and the use of talent in multimedia projects. It provides examples of contract terms and introduces you to sources and providers of content and talent. Needless to say, always consult an attorney versed in intellectual property law when you negotiate the rights and ownership of content.

Acquiring Content

Content acquisition can be one of the most expensive and time-consuming tasks in organizing a multimedia project. You must plan ahead, allocating sufficient time (and money) for this task.

- If your project describes the use of a new piece of robotics machinery, for example, will you need to send a photographer to the factory for the pictures? Or can you use existing photographs?
- Suppose you are working with 100 graphs and charts about the future of petroleum exploration. Will you begin by collecting the raw data from reports and memos, or start with an existing spreadsheet or database? Perhaps you have charts that have already been generated from the data and stored as TIFF or JPEG files?
- You are developing an interactive guide to the trails in a national park, complete with video clips of the wildlife that hikers might encounter on the trails. Will you need to shoot original video footage, or is there existing content for you to edit?

TIP   *Be sure to specify in your project plan the format and quality of content and data to be supplied to you by third parties. Format conversion and editing takes real time. Worse, if you have specified that images for a client's web site are to be 1024×768 pixels, but the photo files you receive from your client's cousin are 640×480 pixels, there will simply not be enough information in the image to enlarge it to the required resolution.*

This is how you do things on a shoestring. Years ago, we created a basketball product starring Dr. J and Larry Bird. The first thing we knew we had to do was sign a contract with Dr. J. So we found a guy that knew his agent and we made a side deal with him to pay him to convince Julius to do it. And then we went to Julius and we made a deal where we gave him some stock in the company, rather than writing a huge check. And we convinced him of the educational value of what we were doing, instead of just trying to get it to be an arms-length financial deal. So we were able to sign him up with an advance of only $20,000. And he was quite easily the biggest name in basketball and one of the top two or three regarded professional athletes at the time. We got him for a royalty rate of 2 ½ percent (not what you hear today in a lot of cases), so you don't have to do things that have really high royalty rates and advances. By the way, he made a killing on the stock!

Trip Hawkins, Founder, Electronic Arts

Using Content Created by Others

When a work is created, certain rights, such as for the work's public display or performance, its use in a broadcast, or its reproduction, are granted to its creator. Among the rights most relevant to a multimedia producer are electronic rights—the rights to publish a work in a computer-based storage and delivery medium such as on a DVD or on the Web. Investors in the multimedia marketplace have been quietly purchasing electronic rights (the right to reproduce works in electronic form) to the basic building blocks of content—including films, videos, photographic collections, and textual information bases—knowing that in the future these elements can and perhaps will be converted from their traditional form to computer-based storage and delivery. This is smart, but not easy; the many union-supported contract restrictions and performer and producer rights are not only complicated and difficult to trace but also very expensive to acquire.

WARNING *If you negotiate ownership or rights to someone else's content, be sure to get the advice of a skilled copyright and contracts attorney.*

Obtaining the rights to content is not, however, a hopeless undertaking. For example, Amaze, Inc., acquired rights from several sources to produce a series of computer-based daily planners with a cartoon-a-day from Gary Larson's "The Far Side" or Cathy Guisewite's "Cathy," a word-a-day from Random House, or a question-a-day from the Trivial Pursuit game. Random House and Brøderbund's Living Books Division negotiated the rights to the Dr. Seuss books for multimedia use. Multimedia rights to Elvis Presley historical material, to the movie *Jurassic Park*, and to a myriad of other content have been acquired by multimedia developers and publishers.

Depending on the type and source of your content, the negotiations for usage rights can be simple and straightforward, or they may require complicated contracts and a stack of release forms. Each potential content provider you approach will likely have his or her own set of terms that you need to look at carefully, so that the terms are broad enough not to constrain the scope of your multimedia project.

Locating Preexisting Content

Preexisting content can come from a variety of sources, ranging from a trunk of old photographs in your neighbor's attic to a stock house or image bank offering hundreds of thousands of hours of film and video or still images, available for licensing for a fee.

If your needs are simple and fairly flexible, you may be able to use material from collections of **clip art**. Such collections of photographs, graphics, sounds, music, animation, and video are becoming widely available from many sources, for anywhere from fifty to several hundred dollars. Part of the value of many of these packages is that you are granted unlimited use, and you can be comfortable creating derivative versions tailored to your specific application. Carefully read the license agreement that comes with the collection before assuming you can use the material in any manner. In the six-point italicized type on the back of the agreement, you may discover that the licensor offers no guarantee that the contents of the collection are original works. Thus, the licensor bears no responsibility to indemnify you for inadvertently infringing on the copyrights of a third party. Even if the collection is described as allowing "free use," you may discover that the collection comes with severe restrictions on the way material can be used, or that a **royalty** is required for any use beyond wallpaper on your computer.

If your content needs are more specific or complex, a good place to start your search for material might be at a **still photo library**, a **sound library**, or a **stock footage** house. These "stock" resources may be public or private and may contain copyrighted works as well as materials that are in the public domain. **Public domain** means either that the work was never copyrighted in the first place or that its copyright protection has expired over time and has not been renewed; you can use public domain material without a license.

In addition to stock photos and videos clips, there are whole collections of flash animations and components, web site templates, sound effect libraries, and even 3-D models available for downloading and integration into multimedia projects. Many are not free, but stock material may save you many hours of effort.

. . . .

www.flashcomponents.net
www.templatemonster.com
www.sounddogs.com
http://turbosquid.com

. . . .

Mickey Mouse Goes to Washington

Unless you earn your living as an intellectual property lawyer, you probably don't know that the Supreme Court has granted certiorari in *Eldred v. Ashcroft,* a case that will test the limits of Congress's power to extend the term of copyrights. But while copyright may not seem inherently compelling to nonspecialists, the issues at stake in *Eldred* are vitally important to anyone who watches movies, listens to music, or reads books. If that includes you, read on.

Back in 1998, representatives of the Walt Disney Company came to Washington looking for help. Disney's copyright on Mickey Mouse, who made his screen debut in the 1928 cartoon short "Steamboat Willie," was due to expire in 2003, and Disney's rights to Pluto, Goofy, and Donald Duck were to expire a few years later.

Rather than allow Mickey and friends to enter the public domain, Disney and its friends—a group of Hollywood studios, music labels, and PACs representing content owners—told Congress that they wanted an extension bill passed.

Prompted perhaps by the Disney group's lavish donations of campaign cash—more than $6.3 million in 1997–98, according to the nonprofit Center for Responsive Politics—Congress passed, and President Clinton signed, the Sonny Bono Copyright Term Extension Act.

The CTEA extended the term of protection by 20 years for works copyrighted after January 1, 1923. Works copyrighted by individuals since 1978 got "life plus 70" rather than the existing "life plus 50." Works made by or for corporations (referred to as "works made for hire") got 95 years. Works copyrighted before 1978 were shielded for 95 years, regardless of how they were produced.

In all, tens of thousands of works that had been poised to enter the public domain were maintained under private ownership until at least 2019.

So far so good—as far as Disney and its friends were concerned, at least. In 1999, a group of plaintiffs led by Eric Eldred, whose Eldritch Press offers free online access to public domain works, filed a challenge to the statute. Eldred argues that the CTEA is unconstitutional on two grounds: first, because the statute exceeds Congress's power under the Copyright Clause; and, second, because the statute runs afoul of the First Amendment by substantially burdening speech without advancing any important governmental interest.

Eldred lost before the district court and the D.C. Circuit. However, there is good reason to believe that he may yet prevail in the Supreme Court.

Chris Sprigman, Counsel to the Antitrust Group in the Washington, D.C. office of King & Spalding

(Contrary to many predictions, on January 15, 2003, the United States Supreme Court upheld the Act in a 7–2 decision.)

Google claims that the full text of more than twenty million books can now be searched and read online at Google Books (http://books.google.com/) as part of an ongoing effort to scan and digitize entire libraries of books, magazines, journals, and articles from around the world. Certainly a noble idea, to make all known literature searchable and available on the Internet, but many are concerned that Google will, by the very nature of its vast collection, own a monopoly on much of the world's literature, particularly out-of-print "orphan" books, where copyrights are unknown or unclaimed. Lawsuits and haggling are underway involving copyright law, unfair competitive advantages, monetizing, and licensing rights of all kinds.

Google categorizes its holdings into three groups: in-copyright and in-print books, in-copyright but out-of-print books, and out-of-copyright books. For copyrighted and in-print material, users can search for the book, preview portions of it, and then purchase it through a bookseller like Amazon, Barnes & Noble, or Borders. In-copyright but out-of-print books can be previewed and purchased, opening an otherwise dry revenue stream to publishers and authors. Out-of-copyright books can be freely read, downloaded, and printed by the public. The mechanics of this system are being worked out in the courts; it's all about money and control.

The National Archives of the United States (www.archives.gov), the National Archives of the United Kingdom (www.nationalarchives.gov.uk), and the Archives Nationales of France (www.archivesnationales.culture .gouv.fr), among others, are rich sources of content, both copyrighted and in the public domain. Other public sources in the United States include the Library of Congress (www.loc.gov), NASA (www.nasa.gov), and the Smithsonian Institution (www.si.edu), all of which are located in Washington, DC (as is the National Archives). You cannot, however, safely assume that all material acquired from a public source is in the public domain. You remain responsible for ensuring that you do not infringe on a copyright.

In addition to public sources, there are many other repositories of content material. Commercial stock houses offer millions of images, video and film clips, and sound clips, and they often own the works outright—so, when they grant you a license for use of their work, you don't have to worry about possible copyright infringement of the rights of third parties. Some stock sources also specialize in certain subjects. For example, if you want a video clip of a shark, you might contact a stock footage house that specializes in underwater videos.

Copyrights

Laws governing copyright vary from country to country. The following discussion mainly involves laws in the United States. In all cases, you should consult a specialist in the copyright laws of your own country before making decisions about ownership and protection.

Copyright protection applies to "original works of authorship fixed in any tangible medium of expression." The Copyright Act of 1976, as amended (17 U.S.C. §101 et seq.) protects the legal rights of the creator of an original work. Consequently, before you can use someone else's work in your multimedia project, you must first obtain permission from the owner of the copyright. If you do not do this, you may find yourself being sued for **copyright infringement** (unauthorized use of copyrighted material).

Several changes in the law have created confusion over copyright protections. One change is that works now come under copyright protection as soon as they are created and presented in a fixed form. Prior to 1976, protection was only granted upon registration, but now works do not have

> Google's mission is to organize the world's information and make it universally accessible and useful. Today, together with the authors, publishers, and libraries, we have been able to make a great leap in this endeavor. While this agreement is a real win-win for all of us, the real victors are all the readers. The tremendous wealth of knowledge that lies within the books of the world will now be at their fingertips.
>
> Sergey Brin,
> co-founder & president
> of technology at Google,
> October 28, 2008

to be registered with the U.S. Copyright Office to be protected. Because of this there is another crucial change: works no longer need a properly formatted statement of **copyright ownership** (for example, "Copyright © 2014 by Tay Vaughan") to be protected. Many people assume, because of the pre-1976 rules, that if there is not a copyright statement, the work is available to be used. While that may be true for older works, you should start with the assumption that a work *is* protected, unless there is a specific statement that it is in the public domain. There are **fair use** exceptions in which copyrighted material can be used without permission, but they are very limited and specific—primarily for educational and journalistic use and rarely for commercial use—so you should consult an attorney before assuming this exception applies to work you wish to use in a project.

From the U.S. Copyright Office:

The distinction between what is fair use and what is infringement in a particular case will not always be clear or easily defined. There is no specific number of words, lines, or notes that may safely be taken without permission. Acknowledging the source of the copyrighted material does not substitute for obtaining permission.

Owning a copy of a work does not entitle you to reproduce the work, and you still need to obtain permission from the copyright owner to use it. If you buy a painting from an artist, the artist retains the copyright unless it is assigned to you. You do not have the right to reproduce the painting in any form, such as in postcards or a calendar, without permission.

For additional discussion about copyrights as they apply to original works created for a project, visit the U.S. Copyright Office at www.copyright.gov and the UK Copyright Service at www.copyrightservice.co.uk.

Digital Rights Management (DRM)

As rights and ownership are redefined for the information age, various rights management technologies are emerging and competing to become industry standard. Apple's iTunes Store has sold more than 25 billion songs since going online in 2003. Songs downloaded from iTunes prior to April 2009 are protected with a DRM scheme called FairPlay, which works within Apple's QuickTime container structure and limits the number of devices upon which the tune can be played (in 2009, Apple removed the DRM restriction for music tracks, but continues to protect movies and television shows). Microsoft Windows Media Rights Manager (WMDRM, Windows only) and the Windows Media Player 12 format incorporate extensive DRM capabilities. The Association of American Publishers is promoting DRM methodologies for protecting unauthorized copying of e-books. The Internet Streaming Media Alliance (ISMA) offers a content protection specification designed to provide a single, end-to-end encryption scheme for streaming media and file downloading that can be integrated with different key and rights management software and licensed content protection devices. A Digital Object Identifier (DOI), which can be used for identifying and exchanging intellectual property, provides a framework for managing intellectual content, linking customers with content suppliers, facilitating electronic commerce, and enabling automated copyright management for all types of media. The Digital Millennium Copyright Act of 1998 has set the rules of digital copyright into law. For an overview of this emerging battle, check out these URLs:

www.copyright.gov/laws/

www.webopedia.com/TERM/D/DMCA.html

www.doi.org/

First Person

Rights Management at Work

It is well known that professors and teachers who write textbooks do not get rich from the publisher's royalties. For all their hard work, they become famous perhaps, and they gain some bragging rights and add an important credit to their curriculum vitae as they strive toward tenure, but rich? Never.

So it was with some surprise that I received an e-mail from the Authors Registry in New York (www.authorsregistry.org), letting me know that I, as author of *Multimedia: Making It Work*, was owed some royalty monies collected by The Authors' Licensing and Collecting Society (ALCS) in the United Kingdom. For a five-percent fee, the Registry would take care of the paperwork and conversion from Pounds Sterling to U.S. Dollars and

mail me a check. Having in the past received more than one letter from Mr. Obutu in Nigeria offering me millions, I was skeptical.

It turns out that the ALCS (www.alcs.co.uk) is quite legitimate and collects a small fee on behalf of authors when their book (such as the one you are holding in your hands) is photocopied or scanned in schools, universities, businesses, public sector bodies, or libraries or, according to Public Lending Right laws (www.plr.uk.com), each time their book is borrowed from a public library. In fact, the ALCS administers payments due to writers from the Austrian, Dutch, Belgian, French, Spanish, German, and Irish PLR schemes as well.

When the twice-yearly royalty check from the Authors Registry did finally

arrive, less various commissions and fees, it was sufficient to purchase a 25 kg bag of dry dog food for my Sophie. We both wish to thank those of you borrowing and copying readers from Britain and Europe who, most likely without knowing it, participated in a small but generous way in the formal management of writers' rights.

Obtaining Rights

You should license the rights to use copyrighted material before you develop a project around it. You may be able to negotiate outright ownership of copyrighted material. If the owner does not wish to give up or sell ownership rights, however, you may still be able to **license** the rights to use that material. Keep in mind, however, that different rights for the same copyrighted work (for example, rights for public performance, broadcast use, or publication) may be assigned to different parties. When you are negotiating a license, make sure that the party you are dealing with has ownership of the appropriate rights.

There are few guidelines for negotiating content rights for use in multimedia products. If you are dealing with content providers who are professionals familiar with electronic media, you may be given a standard **rate card** listing licensing fees for different uses, formats, and markets. Other content providers or owners may be less familiar with multimedia and electronic uses, and you will need to educate them.

Some **licensing agreements** may be as simple as a signed permission letter or release form describing how you may use the material. Other agreements will specify in minute detail how, where, when, and for what purpose the content may be used. Ideally, you would seek rights for **unlimited use**, which allows you to use the content anytime, anywhere, and in any way you choose; more likely, however, the final license would contain restrictions about how the material may be used. Try to retain the option to renegotiate terms in case you want to broaden the scope of use at a later date.

The following items are but a few of the issues you need to consider when negotiating for rights to use preexisting content:

- How will the content be delivered? If you limit yourself to thumb drives or DVDs, for example, you may not be able to distribute your product over the Internet without renegotiation.
- Is the license for a set period of time?
- Is the license exclusive or nonexclusive? (In an exclusive use arrangement, no one else would be able to use the material in the manner stipulated.)
- Where will your product be distributed? There may be different rates for domestic and international distribution.
- Do you intend to use the material in its entirety, or just a portion of it?
- What rights do you need? You need to be sure you have the right to reproduce and distribute the material. In addition, you may wish to use the material in promotions for your product.
- What kind of credit line or end-credits might the content owner require you to display?
- Does the content owner have the authority to assign rights to you? It is important to ensure you will not be held liable if a third party later sues for copyright infringement.
- Do you need to obtain any additional rights to use the content? For example, if you use a clip from a movie, do you need to get separate

releases from actors appearing in the clip or from the director or producer of the movie?

- Will the copyright owner receive remuneration for the license? If so, what form will it take? A one-time fee? Royalty? Or a simple credit attribution?
- In what format do you wish to receive the content? Specifying formats is particularly important with video dubbed from a master.

Derivative Works   Any text taken verbatim, or any image or music perfectly copied, clearly requires permission from its owner to incorporate it into your work. But there are some other, less clear-cut issues. For example, as a starter for your work, you may wish to incorporate but a tiny portion of an image owned by someone else, altering the image until the original is no longer recognizable. Is this legal? Indeed, how much of the original must you change before the product becomes yours or remains a derivative work? There are no simple answers to these tough questions.

Figure 10-1 shows an original photograph taken by Mark Newman, along with some artwork derived from it. Newman sold certain rights to 21st Century Media, which at the time packaged and sold assortments of stock photographs to computer graphics and multimedia developers on the Web and as CD-ROMs. The CD-ROM product contained these instructions:

> You may make copies of the digitized images contained on the Product for use in advertisements, public or private presentations, business communications, multimedia presentations, and other uses as long as the images are not used to create a product for sale. For example, you may not use the images to create calendars, posters, greeting cards, or books of image collections for sale. You may not use, in whole or in part, or alter a digitized image in any manner for pornographic use.

Figure 10-1   The original photograph by Mark Newman was clipped and manipulated for use in a multimedia project. Who owns the resulting image?

> There is a serious issue facing multimedia developers. Now that they have tools to creatively modify things, how much of someone else's image, music, or video clip needs to be modified before ownership changes? This is up for grabs. There is a law called "fair use," which comes into play in a very limited way here. But I think there needs to be a law called "fair modification."
>
> ....
>
> Trip Hawkins, Founder,
> Electronic Arts

Suppose, however, that the image in Figure 10-1 were scanned from the pages of *National Geographic* or *Time*—what then? If you change 51 percent of the pixels, is the image yours? These questions of ownership will undoubtedly be resolved eventually in the courts.

Use of images, sounds, and other resources from stock houses such as Getty Images, Index Stock Photography, or Corbis is a safe way to go, because ownership and your rights to use the material are clearly stated. Creative Commons licensing (discussed below) also provides a rich source of (freely useable) material.

WARNING   *Beware of clip media claiming to be public domain (where no copyrights apply) that include sounds from popular television shows or motion pictures.*

Permissions   Permission must also be obtained to use copyrighted text. Sample language follows for requesting permission to reprint copyrighted text material, and sample terms that you might expect from the copyright owner. Such a request might look like:

> Dear Sirs:
>
> I am currently producing a computer-based multimedia presentation with a working title of (Title). My publisher is (Publisher, Publisher's Address). The anticipated completion date of the work is (Month/Year).
>
> It will be used for (Use).
>
> This letter is to request your permission to incorporate into this work a brief passage from: (Title, Author, Edition, ISBN, Page).
>
> The text I wish to reproduce is: (Text).
>
> Please process this request at your earliest convenience and use this letter or your own form to return your approval by mail or fax to: (Your Name/Address).
>
> The undersigned, having full authority, hereby grants permission to (Your Name) to copy and reproduce the referenced text for use in the work cited above.
>
> Signed:_____

Here are some typical terms you might expect to receive from a large publishing company:

1. To give full credit in every copy printed, on the copyright page or as a footnote on the page on which the quotation begins, or if in a magazine or a newspaper, on the first page of each quotation covered by the permission,

exactly as "Reprinted with the permission of (Publisher) from (Title) by (Author). Copyright (Year) by (Publisher)."

2. To pay on publication of the work, or within 24 months of the date of granting the permission, whichever is earlier, a fee of: $_____.

3. To forward one copy of the work and payment on publication to the Permissions Department of (Publisher).

4. To make no deletions from, additions to, or changes in the text, without the written approval of (Publisher).

5. That the permission hereby granted applies only to the edition of the work specified in this agreement.

6. That permission granted herein is nonexclusive and not transferable.

7. That this permission applies, unless otherwise stated, solely to publication of the above-cited work in the English language in the United States, its territories and dependencies and throughout the world. For translation rights, apply to the International Rights Department of (Publisher).

8. That unless the work is published within two years from the date of the applicant's signature (unless extended by written permission of (Publisher)) or, if published, it remains out of print for a period of six months, this permission shall automatically terminate.

9. This permission does not extend to any copyrighted material from other sources which may be incorporated in the books in question, nor to any illustrations or charts, nor to poetry, unless otherwise specified.

10. That the work containing our selection may be reproduced in Braille, large type, and sound recordings provided no charge is made to the visually handicapped.

11. That unless the agreement is signed and returned within six months from the date of issue, the permission shall automatically terminate.

Copyleft   Antipodal to copyright is **copyleft**. While perhaps a cute play on words, copyleft represents a serious and growing worldwide effort to (as claimed in the preamble to the Free Art License) "grant the right to freely copy, distribute, and transform creative works without infringing the author's rights." Effectively, copyleft uses the copyright laws themselves to remove traditional copyright protections from a work and offer that work with legal and unlimited permission clearly granted to freely copy, modify, transform, or distribute the work.

In the software world, the GNU General Public License (GNU GPL) is "intended to guarantee your freedom to share and change all versions of a program—to make sure it remains free software for all its users…" From the preamble to the GNU GPL:

> The licenses for most software and other practical works are designed to take away your freedom to share and change the works. By contrast, the GNU General Public License is intended to guarantee your freedom to share and change all versions of a program—to make sure it remains free software for all its users. We, the Free Software Foundation, use the GNU General Public License for most of our software; it applies also to any other work released this way by its authors. You can apply it to your programs, too.
>
> When we speak of free software, we are referring to freedom, not price. Our General Public Licenses are designed to make sure that you have the freedom to distribute copies of free software (and charge for them if you wish), that you receive source code or can get it if you want it, that you can change the software or use pieces of it in new free programs, and that you know you can do these things.
>
> To protect your rights, we need to prevent others from denying you these rights or asking you to surrender the rights. Therefore, you have certain responsibilities if you distribute copies of the software, or if you modify it: responsibilities to respect the freedom of others.

GNU General Public License
Version 3, 29 June 2007
Copyright © 2007 Free Software Foundation, Inc. <http://fsf.org/>

Responsibilities and provisos typically embedded in the copyleft material that you might want to use in a multimedia project include your obligation for "proper attribution of the work to its authors and access to previous versions of the work when possible." The philosophical notion is of a "common work," so if you change, improve, or modify someone else's creative product, you should politely allow others to change, improve, or modify yours. Details of these copyleft licenses are available at:

http://artlibre.org/licence/lal/en
www.gnu.org/copyleft/gpl.html

Creative Commons (CC) Licenses A Creative Commons license (six combinations or modules are most commonly used—see Table 10-1 and visit http://creativecommons.org) grants specific rights to reuse and distribute media. The variations on this license are the result of many years of legal testing, and support the copyleft movement described in the previous section. The licenses can be defined by icon and acronym, as shown in Table 10-2.

Icon	Description	Acronym
(cc)(i)	Attribution alone	BY
(cc)(i)(=)	Attribution + NoDerivatives	BY-ND
(cc)(i)(↻)	Attribution + ShareAlike	BY-SA
(cc)(i)($)	Attribution + Noncommercial	BY-NC
(cc)(i)($)(=)	Attribution + Noncommercial + NoDerivatives	BY-NC-ND
(cc)(i)($)(↻)	Attribution + Noncommercial + ShareAlike	BY-NC-SA

Table 10-1   The Six Most Commonly Used Creative Commons Licenses

Icon	Right	Description
(i)	Attribution (CC BY)	Licensees may copy, distribute, display, and perform the work and make derivative works based on it only if they give the author or licensor the credits in the manner specified by these.
(↻)	ShareAlike (CC BY-SA)	Licensees may distribute derivative works only under a license identical to the license that governs the original work. (See also copyleft.)
($)	NonCommercial (CC BY-NC)	Licensees may copy, distribute, display, and perform the work and make derivative works based on it only for non-commercial purposes.
(=)	NoDerivs (CC BY-NC-ND)	Licensees may copy, distribute, display, and perform only verbatim copies of the work, not derivative works based on it.

Table 10-2   Conditions Under Which a Creative Commons License May Be Granted (see http://en.wikipedia.org/wiki/Creative_Commons_license)

Flickr hosts more than 200 million Creative Commons–licensed photos and claims, "You can browse and search those CC photos by license, or find exactly the one suitable for and available to you by using advanced search, ticking the CC checkbox, and searching for whatever image you are looking for." Figure 10-2 shows Flickr's Creative Commons search page at www.flickr.com/creativecommons. Wikipedia Commons is another collection of more than 20 million media files which link to Wikipedia articles and are typically "freely usable." As with Flickr, the public may also contribute content to the collection. Google also recognizes the Creative Commons licensing levels in its Advanced Search engine (see Figure 10-3), which may make your search for "free" images easier.

Explore / Creative Commons

Many Flickr users have chosen to offer their work under a Creative Commons license, and you can browse or search through content under each type of license.

Here are some recently added bits and pieces:

Attribution License

From HPRMan / From HPRMan / From HPRMan / From HPRMan / From HPRMan

» **51,003,481** photos (See more)

Attribution-NoDerivs License

From _Lehook / From goforchris / From goforchris / From goforchris / From goforchris

» **14,109,150** photos (See more)

Attribution-NonCommercial-NoDerivs License

From Andy E. Nystrom / From Andy E. Nystrom / From Andy E. Nystrom / From Andy E. Nystrom / From Andy E. Nystrom

» **71,459,920** photos (See more)

Attribution-NonCommercial License

From nchenga / From dhgatsby / From nchenga / From nchenga / From nchenga

» **34,217,257** photos (See more)

Attribution-NonCommercial-ShareAlike License

From r_kerber / From Dando una vuelta / From Murtada al Mousawy / From r_kerber / From Murtada al Mousawy

» **74,831,741** photos (See more)

Attribution-ShareAlike License

From TheJRB / From TheJRB / From TheJRB / From TheJRB / From TheJRB

» **23,522,102** photos (See more)

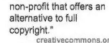

"Creative Commons is a non-profit that offers an alternative to full copyright."
creativecommons.org

Briefly...

Attribution means: You let others copy, distribute, display, and perform your copyrighted work - and derivative works based upon it - but only if they give you credit.

Noncommercial means: You let others copy, distribute, display, and perform your work - and derivative works based upon it - but for noncommercial purposes only.

No Derivative Works means: You let others copy, distribute, display, and perform only verbatim copies of your work, not derivative works based upon it.

Share Alike means: You allow others to distribute derivative works only under a license identical to the license that governs your work.

Add a Creative Commons license to your photostream.

Figure 10-2 Searching for the right image from Flickr's library of millions is made easier with a filter specifying what licensing you need.

Figure 10-3 Google's Advanced Search options allow you to filter results by the associated Creative Commons license.

Ownership of Content Created for a Project

In the process of developing your multimedia project, you or your collaborators will design interfaces, write text, program lines of code, and illustrate original artwork with photographs, animations, musical scores, sound effects, and video footage. Each of these elements is an original work. If you are creating a project single-handedly for yourself, you own the copyright outright. If other persons who are not your employees also contribute to the final product, they may own the copyright of the element created by them or may share joint ownership of the product unless they assign or license their ownership rights to you. Never rely on an oral agreement for assignment of rights. You should make it your practice in every project to get all assignments of rights or licensing terms in writing to protect everyone involved. You and your best friend may collaborate on a project today based on a handshake, but if there is a falling out that results in a dispute over ownership, having the terms in writing will save both of you from an expensive legal battle over who owns what.

The ownership of a project created by employees in the course of their employment belongs solely to the employer if the work fits the requirements of a **work made for hire**. To meet the definition of a work made for hire, several factors must be weighed to determine whether the individual is legally an employee or an independent contractor. Among these factors are where the work is done, the relationship between the parties, and who provides the tools and equipment.

If the individual contributing to a project is not an employee, the commissioned work must fall within one of the following "work made for hire" categories: a contribution to a collective work, a work that is part of a motion picture or other audiovisual work, a translation, a supplementary work, a compilation, an instructional text, a test, answer material for a test, or an atlas (1976 Copyright Act, 17 U.S.C. § 201(b)). Even if the work falls within one of these categories, be sure to get an agreement in writing from every individual contributing to the work that it is being created as a work for hire. Figures 10-4 and 10-5 offer sample contracts with

PROPRIETARY INFORMATION AND INVENTIONS AGREEMENT

NOTICE:

This agreement does not apply to an invention which qualifies fully under the provisions of Section 2870 of the Labor Code of California as an invention for which no equipment, supplies, facility, or trade secret information of (Company) was used and which was developed entirely on the employee's own time, and (a) which does not relate (1) to the business of (Company) or (2) to (Company's) actual or demonstrably anticipated research or development, or (b) which does not result from any work performed by the employee for (Company).

Employee's Name _____

Address _____

Date of Hire _____

In consideration of my employment by (Company) or any of its subsidiary or affiliated companies (all called "the Company") and the compensation paid me by the Company, I agree as follows:

1. I understand that my employment results in a confidential relationship between myself and the Company. It is expected that I will receive, during and for purposes of my employment, information about the Company's products, processes, business, plans, research programs, and like Company information (all called "the Company business"), which information is the property of the Company. I may also conceive of or develop ideas and inventions related to the Company business during or for purposes of my employment. The information received from the Company and information which I conceive or develop pertaining to the Company business are the sole property of the Company and are valuable trade secrets of the Company. I agree to preserve their value as Company property, by complying with the following requirements.

2. Except as required in the course of my employment, I shall not disclose to anyone or use at any time, either during or after my employment, any information about the Company business which is either received from the Company or conceived or developed by me, unless I have the prior written consent of the Company.

3. I agree to disclose promptly to the Company all inventions, ideas or conceptions, developments, and improvements (whether or not patentable or subject to copyright) which are made or conceived by me, either alone or together with others, during or as a result of my employment, provided that they pertain to the Company business. I will keep complete records of such matter and will and hereby do assign such matter to the Company, whether or not it has been tested or reduced to practice. Included are all data processing communications, computer software systems, programs, and procedures, which pertain to the Company business. All such records are and shall be the property of the Company alone.

4. Upon request of the Company, either during or after my employment, I will assist in applying for Letters Patent, or for copyright or Inventors Certificate or other appropriate legal form, on all such Inventions and Ideas, in this and in foreign countries, and will execute all papers necessary thereto, including assignments as may be requested by the Company, without further compensation to me. Such applications shall be filed at the expense of and under the control of the Company.

5. All unpublished data and information relating to the Company business, whether reduced to writing or not, are understood and agreed to be confidential and the sole property of the Company. This extends to all confidential information or data I may receive from or about any of the Company's licensees, customers, or others with whom the Company has a business relationship. I will maintain all such information in confidence and not use it other than as expressly requested by the Company, either during or after my employment with the Company, unless and until such information is published without fault on my part.

6. Upon termination of my employment, I will surrender all records and material relating to the Company business.

7. I am aware of no prior obligations which would prevent my compliance with the terms and spirit of this agreement.

8. This agreement shall be binding upon me and my heirs, executors, administrators, and assigns. The Company shall have the right to assign this agreement to any successor to the business in which I am employed.

Signed at _____ , on _____ , 20_____

Employee (Signature)

Witness (Signature)

(Address of Witness)

Figure 10-4
Sample employer/ employee agreement covering intellectual property and inventions; consult an attorney when preparing your own legal documents.

Confidential

(Date) (Name and Address of Consultant)

Dear (Consultant): This document, when accepted and agreed to by you, will confirm our mutual understanding and agreement concerning your engagement as an independent contractor to render consulting services to (Employer Name).

You will be engaged as an independent contractor to provide such advice, consultation, and other assistance as may, from time to time, be requested by (Employer Name) in furtherance of (Employer Name)'s business in general and particularly for:

(General Statement of Scope of Work)

During the term of this Consulting Agreement, you agree to provide consulting services to (Employer Name), on the terms and conditions contained in Attachment A, "Description of Services and Reimbursement." Twice monthly you will submit a statement, in a form satisfactory to (Employer Name), setting forth the milestone reached and any authorized expenses incurred to be reimbursed by (Employer Name). Payment will be made according to the schedule in Attachment A.

The consulting services that you will provide are to be rendered at such times and at such places as are mutually agreed upon by (Employer Name) and you. You agree that (Employer Name) shall own all intellectual property rights, including but not limited to copyrights, patents, trade secrets, and trademarks in any and all products of your work within the scope of this Agreement. Said products will be copyrighted by (Employer Name) or in such other name as (Employer Name) may designate. You further agree that any work provided hereunder shall be considered "work made for hire" within the meaning of 17 U.S.C. 2201(b). However, (Employer Name) will give proper credit to you in a manner to be mutually agreed upon as appropriate to the creative direction of the work.

In the performance of the consulting services herein contemplated, you are, and shall be deemed to be for all purposes, an independent contractor (and not an employee or agent of (Employer Name)) under any and all laws, whether existing or future, including without limitation, Social Security laws, state unemployment insurance laws, withholding tax laws, and the payments and reports of any taxes and/or contributions under such laws. You will not be entitled to participate in any employee benefits accruing to employees of (Employer Name). You will not be authorized to make any material representation, contract, or commitment on behalf of (Employer Name).

You agree to comply with applicable laws, rules, and regulations in respect to self-employment, including without limitation, the payment of all taxes required, and you agree to furnish (Employer Name) evidence of the payment of such taxes if requested. In addition, you agree to defend, indemnify, and hold (Employer Name) harmless against all losses, liabilities, claims, demands, actions and/or proceedings, and all costs and expenses in connection therewith, including attorney's fees, arising out of your failure to comply with this paragraph. The term of this Consulting Agreement shall be for the period of time described in Attachment A, subject to the following limitations: Upon five (5) days' written notice, either you or (Employer Name) may terminate this Consulting Agreement. Such termination shall be effective at the conclusion of said five-day period.

This Consulting Agreement shall terminate on your death.

Notwithstanding anything herein to the contrary, (Employer Name) may, without liability, terminate this Consulting Agreement for cause at any time, and without notice, and thereafter (Employer Name)'s obligations hereunder shall cease and terminate. The term "cause" shall mean, by way of example, but not by way of limitation:

Misappropriating funds or property of (Employer Name);

Attempting to obtain any personal profit from any transaction related to THIS consulting work which is adverse to the interest of (Employer Name);

Unreasonable neglect or refusal to perform the consulting services agreed to be performed by you under this Consulting Agreement;

Being convicted of a felony;

Being adjudicated a bankrupt; or

A breach of any of the other provisions of this Consulting Agreement.

Upon termination of this Consulting Agreement, for any reason, you will be paid your consulting fee on a pro rata basis, and you will be reimbursed for authorized expenses, to and including the effective date of such termination.

Figure 10-5
Sample employer/consultant agreement in the form of a letter; hire an attorney when preparing your own legal documents.

You agree to hold all Confidential Information in trust and confidence for (Employer Name), and except as may be authorized by (Employer Name) in writing, you shall not disclose to any person, and you shall take such reasonable precautions as may be necessary to prevent the disclosure of, any Confidential Information at all times during and after the term of this Consulting Agreement. For the purposes of this Consulting Agreement, "Confidential Information" shall mean all information obtained by you, or disclosed to you by (Employer Name), at any time before or during the term hereof, which relates to (Employer Name)'s or (Employer Name)'s clients' past, present, and future research, development, and business activities, and any other trade secrets, records, engineering notebooks, data, formulae, computer code, specifications, inventions, customer lists, and other proprietary information and data concerning (Employer Name) or any client, provided that Confidential Information shall not include information that becomes part of the public knowledge or literature (not as a result of any action or inaction on your part) either prior or subsequent to your receipt of such information.

Upon termination or expiration of this Consulting Agreement, you agree to return to (Employer Name) all written or descriptive matter, including but not limited to drawings, blueprints, descriptions, drafts, computer code, computer files, hardware, software, or other papers or documents that contain any Confidential Information.

(Employer Name) does not desire to receive information in confidence from you under this Consulting Agreement.

You represent and warrant that you are under no obligation or restriction nor will you assume any obligation or restriction which would in any way interfere or be inconsistent with the services to be furnished by you under this Consulting Agreement. In that regard, this Consulting Agreement will in no way restrict you from freely entering into other similar consulting agreements with other firms in the field as long as the provisions herein are honored.

(Employer Name) shall have sole discretion to make other consulting arrangements with other persons concerning any or all of the consulting services to be rendered by you under this Consulting Agreement.

(Employer Name) acknowledges and understands that he is the author of the work you are hired to consult on and that he is therefore responsible for its contents. In the event of a third party action against (Employer Name), (Employer Name) agrees to indemnify and hold you harmless if you are made a party to such action; provided however that (Employer Name) shall have no such responsibility to you if such suit arises due to your misconduct or gross negligence. You promise to provide (Employer Name) with all reasonable cooperation and assistance in any such action or proceedings.

If any action at law is necessary to enforce or interpret the terms of this Consulting Agreement, the prevailing party shall be entitled to reasonable attorneys' fees, costs, and necessary disbursements, in addition to any other relief to which such party shall be entitled.

This letter shall constitute the entire agreement between the parties hereto with respect to the subject matter hereof. In the event of any unresolved dispute in respect thereof, the matter shall be submitted to arbitration in accordance with the rules and regulations of the American Arbitration Association, and the decision of the arbitrator(s) shall be final and binding on both parties hereto.

The validity of this Consulting Agreement and any of its terms and conditions, as well as the rights and duties of the parties hereunder, shall be interpreted and construed pursuant to and in accordance with the laws of the State of California.

(Employer Name)

(Employer Signature)

Accepted and agreed to this ____ day of _____, 20__.

Consultant's Signature: _____

Consultant's Social Security Number or EIN: _____

Attachment A to the Consulting Agreement of (Date) between (Employer Name) and (Consultant)

Description of Services and Reimbursement

Figure 10-5
Sample employer/
consultant agree-
ment in the form
of a letter; hire an
attorney when
preparing your own
legal documents.
(Continued)

employees and contractors to precisely specify ownership issues. Although the language of these contracts is consistent with U.S. copyright law, and may be adequate for certain other jurisdictions, you should always seek the advice of an attorney before using sample contracts such as these.

The copyright ownership of works created in whole or in part by persons who fall under the definition of **independent contractor** may belong to that contractor unless the work is specially ordered or commissioned for use and qualifies as a work made for hire, in which case the copyright belongs to the entity commissioning the work.

A copyright can belong to a single individual or entity, or it may be shared jointly by several entities. Make sure that copyright ownership issues have been resolved, in writing, before people contribute to your project.

Acquiring Talent

After you have tested everybody you know and you still have vacant seats in your project, you may need to turn to professional talent. Getting the perfect actor, model, or narrator's voice is critical. You don't want to settle for a narrator or an actor who is not quite polished or is ill suited to the part, or your whole project may have an amateurish feel.

Professional voice-over talents and actors in the United States usually belong to a union or guild, typically **SAG-AFTRA**. (In 2012, the Screen Actors Guild (SAG) and American Federation of Television and Radio Artists (AFTRA) merged to form SAG-AFTRA. See www.sagaftra.org/production-center/new-media/faq.) Other countries may have their own professional associations (see www.actorsguild.co.uk). These actors are usually represented by a talent agent or agency that you can find in the yellow pages.

Partnerships often finish in quarrels; but I was happy in this, that mine were all carried on and ended amicably, owing, I think, a good deal to the precaution of having very explicitly settled, in our articles, everything to be done by or expected from each partner, so that there was nothing to dispute, which precaution I would therefore recommend to all who enter into partnerships; for whatever esteem partners may have for, and confidence in each other at the time of the contract, little jealousies and disgusts may arise, with ideas of inequality in the care and burden of the business, etc., which are attended often with breach of friendship and of the connection, perhaps with lawsuits and other disagreeable consequences.

From the *Autobiography of Benjamin Franklin* (circa 1784)

First Person

We put out a call for a multimedia acting job (male, mid-30s, credible voice, earnest smile), and 18 men showed up for tryouts at a local studio—17 were nonunion and 1 belonged to AFTRA. We videotaped each applicant as he read a prepared script, chatted with all of them, and asked them to walk around and jump up and down. The best choice by far, we thought at the end of a long day, was Dave Kazanjian, the union member.

"Oooh," we said to ourselves, "real union talent! This is going to cost us."

So we got together with the client and ran tapes of half a dozen of the better actors trying out, without saying which one was our favorite. The client's choice was the same as ours, because Dave was very polished and professional and simply perfect for the part. Paying union-scale wages to the actor would double what we had estimated in our original budget, and we had naively assumed we could quickly and easily find the right talent from the nonunion pool. We ran the new numbers past the

client, implying that the second-choice actor was more affordable, even if he wasn't quite perfect. Then we showed Dave's clip next to the other guy, and repeated it a few times, until the difference was really apparent. The comparison was persuasive, and in the end, the client supported the extra cost.

We all learned again that you get what you pay for: Dave did a terrific job. In future proposals, we used union scale in estimating cost, whether we hired a union actor or not.

Locating the Professionals You Need

Before you can safely put a professional in front of a camera or a microphone, you have to find the talent first and then deal with hiring and union contracts.

Begin by calling a **talent agency** and explaining what you need. The agency will probably suggest several clients who might fit your needs, and send you to their web site for video or audio samples of the actors' work. After reviewing the samples, you can arrange **auditions** of the best candidates, at your office or at a studio. You can also get in touch with several agencies and put out a **casting call** for screen or audio auditions. Furthermore, you are not limited to using union talent, and if your call is posted on bulletin boards in public places (in the theater department of a local university, for example), you may find yourself with many applicants, both union and nonunion, who are eager for the work.

TIP   *If you run your own audition, be sure you are organized for it. You will need sign-up sheets for names and phone numbers, a sample script for applicants to read, a video camera or audio recorder, tracking sheets so that you can coordinate actors' names with their video or audio clips, and hospitable coffee and donuts.*

Working with Union Contracts

The two unions, AFTRA and SAG, have similar contracts and terms for minimum pay and benefits. AFTRA has approved an Interactive Media Agreement to cover on- and off-camera performers on all interactive media platforms. Figure 10-6 shows some AFTRA definitions related to interactive media.

DEFINITIONS

"Material": includes all products (audio or visual) derived from the recordation of the live-action performances of performers, whether or not such performances are incorporated into the final version of the fully-edited Interactive Program produced hereunder by Producer.

"Interactive": Interactive describes the attribute of products which enables the viewer to manipulate, affect or alter the presentation of the creative content of such product simultaneous with its use by the viewer.

"Interactive Media" means: any media on which interactive product operates and through which the user may interact with such product including but not limited to personal computers, games, machines, arcade games, all CD-interactive machines and any and all analogous, similar or dissimilar microprocessor-based units and the digitized, electronic or any other formats now known or hereinafter invented which may be utilized in connection therewith;

"Performers": Persons whose performances are used as on or off-camera, including those who speak, act, sing, or in any other manner perform as talent in material for Interactive Media.

Figure 10-6   From the AFTRA Interactive Media Agreement (reprinted courtesy of AFTRA, 260 Madison Avenue, New York, NY 10016)

The AFTRA/SAG contracts are lengthy and detailed and share language and job descriptions (such as principal, voice-over performer, extra, singer, and dancer). Also, both unions have the same wage scales for these jobs. Table 10-3 shows the Screen Actors Guild categories for interactive media work and rates in 2014 (in U.S. Dollars). Note that the **Atmospheric Voices** category is new, driven by the "vocally stressful" and multiple roles often required in video games. Of course, an actor can always negotiate more than minimum wage.

NOTE *With the advent of "new media," some interesting words have entered the lexicon. "Webisodes" are short pieces of multimedia content distributed on the Internet. "Mobisodes" are short pieces (often TV shows) delivered to mobile phones. "Placeshifting" is watching or listening to multimedia at a place not originally intended. "Time-shifting" is watching or listening to content when the user wants, not when the broadcaster distributes it. "Snack-size media" involves a brief few minutes of content, not hours.*

If your talent needs are simple, you can usually get good contract advice directly from the union representative in your area or from the actors themselves. If your needs are elaborate or undefined, you may wish to consult an attorney or agent who specializes in this area and who can oversee the many required clauses and details of the contract.

Talent contracts are filled with quirky details and complicated formulas. Consider, for example, the AFTRA Interactive Media Agreement, which reads:

> If a solo or duo is called upon to Step Out of a group to sing up to fifteen (15) cumulative bars during a session, the solo/duo shall be paid an adjustment of fifty percent (50%) of the solo/duo rate in addition to the appropriate group rate for that day.

Although the concept of "stepping out" may be more in keeping with an MTV video project than with your own multimedia work, you need to keep an eye out for buried clauses that do apply to your project.

WARNING *If you create a multimedia product that incorporates union talent under contract, you will be restricted to using the material only for its initial primary use. Later, if you wish to spin off bits and pieces for other purposes (such as a commercial or as part of a product for sale to the public), you must then renegotiate with the talent and the union and pay for this expanded and supplemental use.*

Sometimes it is very difficult to do certain things because of previous rights that have been given out. For example, not too long ago I asked an executive from a media company if it would be possible to take some of his film footage and put it into a copyright library, to have something available for multimedia software developers to freely use in their interactive products? He said, "Well, we couldn't use a single frame of any film that was ever shot by a director who was a member of the Directors Guild of America." The bottom line is that there are so many rights attached to so many of these things, with so many different people involved, that it is very complicated even to figure out if you have the right to use it in any way, and again that's too bad because again, that is just going to slow us down.

Trip Hawkins, Founder,
Electronic Arts

On-Camera Performers	
Day Performers (including solo/duo singers)	$825.50
3-Day Performers (including solo/duo singers)	2,088.25
Weekly Performers (including solo/duo singers)	2,864.80
6 Day Overnight Location	3,150.90
Group Singers 3–8 (4-hour day)	783.10
Group Singers 9+ (4-hour day)	683.05
Dancers	
Rehearsal Days Only	$485.10
Work Days (no rehearsal): Solo/Duo	825.50
Work Days (no rehearsal): Group 3–8	723.25
Work Days (no rehearsal): Group 9+	631.95
Weekly Option (includes rehearsals): Solo/Duo	2,653.85
Weekly Option (includes rehearsals): Group 3–8	2,432.00
Weekly Option (includes rehearsals): Group 9+	2,212.25
Background Actor Rates	
General Background Actors	$141.35
Special Ability Actors and Stand-ins	177.30
Off-Camera Performers	
Day Performer (Up to 3 voices/4-hour day)	$825.50
Day Performer (1 voice/1 hr)	412.75
Additional Voices (each)	275.15
6–10 Voices/6-hour day	1,651.05
Singers (4 hour day):	
Solo/Duo	$825.50
Hourly Rate	412.75
Group Singers 3–8	437.20
Group Singers 9+	379.60
Group Hourly Rate	244.75
Atmospheric Voices	
Up to twenty (20) Atmospheric Voices [300-word limit] (4-hour session)	$825.50
Unlimited number of Atmospheric Voices (4-hour session)	1,651.00
Up to 3 Voices (1-hour session)	412.75

Table 10-3   From the SAG-AFTRA, Interactive Media Rates 2014

Acquiring Releases

A union talent contract explicitly states what rights you have to the still and motion images and voices you make and use. If, however, your talent is nonunion (a co-worker, perhaps, or a neighbor's child, student actor, waitress, or tugboat captain), be sure to require the person to sign a **release form**. This form grants to you certain permissions and specifies the terms under which you can use the material you make during a recording session.

Figure 10-7 is a sample release form that covers most situations in a multimedia project and provides nearly perfect rights to the producer. Because such forms are legal documents, always consult an attorney to be sure that the specific language of your own release document meets your requirements.

Release Form

This is a release and authorization to use the name, voice, sounds, image and likeness, and writings of the undersigned ("Model"), as obtained in the photography / filming / video / audio session / creative session taking place

_____, at _____ ("the Session"), for commercial purposes by

_____ and his respective successors and assigns (collectively, "Producer").

For valuable consideration, Model hereby authorizes the unlimited use in perpetuity by Producer of all recorded images, likenesses, voice and recorded sounds, and writings of Model obtained during the Session, and of Model's name in connection with such use. Model grants producer the rights to use such sounds, images, and likenesses in any and all media and forms now known or hereafter devised throughout the universe without limitation as to territory or term, including but not limited to advertising, literature, computer demonstrations, and packaging, whether in the form of photography, magnetic or electronic data storage, or any other form, both as obtained and as modified at Producer's sole discretion to suit business purposes of Producer. The compensation stated above shall be the sole compensation for all such use, and no further compensation, including but not limited to royalties, residuals, or use fees, shall be payable at any time.

Model further transfers and assigns all copyrights and all other rights in the recordings, sounds, images and likeness, and writings obtained at the Session to Producer. Producer shall have the right to register the copyright to these in the name of its choice and shall have the exclusive right to dispose of these in any manner whatsoever. This agreement constitutes the sole, complete, and exclusive agreement between Model and Producer.

Name: _____   SIGNATURE: _____

Address: _____   SOCIAL SECURITY NO.: _____

_____   DATE: _____

Phone: _____

Figure 10-7 Sample release form; consult an attorney when preparing your own legal documents.

WARNING   *Do not include any images or voices of people in your multimedia project—even if you yourself recorded and edited the material—unless you have their written consent to use it; it is in the public domain; you are reporting it as news, commentary, or parody (fair use); or it is work unarguably made for hire.*

Chapter 10 Review

■ Chapter Summary

For your review, here's a summary of the important concepts discussed in this chapter.

Acquire content for a project and identify the benefits and drawbacks of various sources of content such as clip art, stock libraries, and public domain sources

■ Content is the information and material that forms the heart of your project—or what your project is about. Content can have both low and high production value. You must always balance the production value of your project against your budget and the desired result.

■ Content acquisition can be one of the most expensive and time-consuming tasks in organizing a multimedia project. Be sure to specify in your project plan the format and quality of content and data to be supplied to you by third parties. If you negotiate ownership or rights to someone else's content, be sure to get the advice of a skilled copyright and contracts attorney.

■ Preexisting content can come from a variety of sources. Clip art collections of photographs, graphics, sounds, music, animation, and video are relatively inexpensive, and you are generally granted unlimited use. If your content needs are more specific or complex, a still photo library, a sound library, or a stock footage house is a good choice. You can also search in many places for "free" material under the Creative Commons license.

Discuss the concepts of copyright, public domain, licensing, and derivative works, and determine who owns the copyright for a work, depending on who contracted the work and for what purpose

■ Some materials are in the public domain, meaning you can use the material without a license. But never *assume* a work is in the public domain, even if it bears no copyright notice.

■ Always make sure you have permission to use copyrighted material, or you may find yourself being sued for copyright infringement. Works come under copyright protection as soon as they are created and presented in a fixed form. Owning a copy of a work does not automatically entitle you to reproduce the work. If the owner does not wish to give up or sell ownership rights, however, you may still be able to license the rights to use that material.

■ Negotiating rights to use preexisting content involves many factors. In some cases you can use materials "derived" from another work, but this is a gray area of copyright law.

■ In general, you own the copyright of works you create for yourself. You also own the copyright of works created by those whom you employ for the purpose of creating the work. If the contributor is not an employee, the work is not work made for hire, and the contributor has not assigned ownership to you, then that contributor holds the copyright for the work. *Work made for hire* is a legal term used in the United States, the United Kingdom, and other jurisdictions covering work made by an employee as part of his or her job for an employer.

Discuss the process of identifying appropriate talent for a production, and recognize issues in using talent, including union rules, contracts, and releases

■ Getting the perfect actor, model, or narrator's voice is critical. Professional talents and actors in the United States often belong to AFTRA or SAG and are represented by a talent agent or agency. The agency will probably suggest several clients who might fit your needs. Arrange auditions of the best candidates.

■ Check out talent contracts carefully, and think about any limitations on future use. If your talent is nonunion, be sure to have the person sign a release form.

■ Key Terms

American Federation of Television
 and Radio Artists (AFTRA) *(19)*
Atmospheric Voices *(327)*
audition *(326)*
casting call *(326)*
clip art *(309)*
content *(306)*
content acquisition *(307)*
copyleft *(317)*
copyright infringement *(311)*
copyright ownership *(312)*
copyright protection *(311)*
Creative Commons license *(318)*
derivative work *(315)*
electronic rights *(308)*
fair use *(312)*

independent contractor *(325)*
license *(314)*
licensing agreement *(314)*
production value *(306)*
public domain *(309)*
rate card *(314)*
release form *(329)*
royalty *(309)*
SAG-AFTRA *(325)*
sound library *(309)*
still photo library *(309)*
stock footage *(309)*
talent agency *(326)*
unlimited use *(314)*
work made for hire *(321)*

■ Key Term Quiz

1. The information and material that forms the heart of your project—what your project is about—is _____.

2. Collections of media generally granted unlimited use are called _____.

3. If a work's copyright protection has expired and not been renewed, it is _____.

4. The term for unauthorized use of copyrighted material is _____.

5. Works come under _____ as soon as they are created and presented in a fixed form.

6. Even if the owner of a work does not wish to give up or sell ownership rights, you may still be able to _____ the rights to use that material.

7. A standard document that lists licensing fees for different uses, formats, and markets is called a(n) _____.

8. If an artist takes another person's work and creates a new work based on the original, such a work is said to be _____.

9. Professional talents and actors in the United States are usually represented by a(n) _____.

10. If your talent is nonunion, be sure to require the person to sign a(n) _____.

■ Multiple-Choice Quiz

1. Which of the following is not content?
   a. photographs
   b. animations
   c. video clips
   d. the graphical user interface
   e. the program's programming code

2. The responsibility for ensuring that content included in a product does not infringe on a copyright belongs to:
   a. the developer
   b. the original creator
   c. the product's purchaser
   d. the U.S. Copyright Office
   e. The Library of Congress

3. A source for free content in the public domain is:
   a. a clip art collection
   b. a stock photo/video library
   c. a government agency
   d. a publishing company
   e. a television network

4. The legal privilege to publish a work in a computer-based storage and delivery medium is often called:
   a. digital watermarks
   b. electronic rights
   c. computer publishing licenses
   d. new media contracts
   e. multimedia/Internet ownership

5. A disadvantage to using a clip art image from a stock library might be:
   a. it is available in high resolution
   b. you are usually granted unlimited use
   c. you can alter the image for derivative works
   d. it is easily downloadable
   e. you do not have exclusive rights

6. If a work is in the public domain:
   a. you can secure a free license through the Public Domain Institute (PDI)
   b. you can license it with a $25 processing fee through the Library of Congress
   c. you can use the material without a license or permission
   d. you can use the material through the public domain contract, where some percentage of the profit is disbursed to nonprofit arts organizations
   e. it is publicly owned and thus cannot be reproduced for any purpose

7. Which of the following issues might you consider when negotiating for rights to use preexisting content?
   a. how the content will be delivered
   b. the license's period of time
   c. how the owner or artist will be credited
   d. whether the copyright owner will receive remuneration for the license
   e. all of the above

8. Works come under copyright protection:
   a. as soon as they have been submitted to the U.S. Copyright Office
   b. as soon as a notice is published in the legal notices of a local newspaper
   c. as soon as they are notarized by a notary public
   d. as soon as they are created and presented in a fixed form
   e. as soon as the original idea, concept, drawing, draft, or intent is communicated to someone else

9. Owning a work entitles you to reproduce that work if:
   a. you have purchased the work and possess a legal bill of sale
   b. you have the permission of the copyright owner
   c. the work is an original, unreproduced work that has not been previously copied
   d. the work's value is less than $100
   e. you have a *really* good lawyer

10. Which of the following are included in the guidelines for creating a work derived in part from another person's work?
    a. There are no clear-cut guidelines.
    b. Less than 10 percent of the original work was used.
    c. Using the work does not impact the sales or value of the original work.
    d. The derivative work is not clearly recognizable as the original work.
    e. The derivative work is in a different medium from the original.

11. In general, you may legally use a work in a project if:
    a. it has a digital approval code
    b. you paid someone to create it for you
    c. the work contains no copyright information
    d. it came from the school library
    e. you got it off the Internet

12. Which of the following unions deals with acting and talent in the United States?
    a. AFTRA
    b. IBEW
    c. AFL-CIO
    d. AFSCME
    e. CIA

13. In general, if you create a multimedia product that incorporates union talent under contract, you:
    a. will have unlimited rights across all media
    b. can use the material only in related media (such as Web/CD, newspaper/magazine, television/radio)
    c. will be required to pay royalties
    d. will have rights to the talent's firstborn children
    e. will be able to use the material only for its initial primary use

14. If you use nonunion talent, you:
    a. probably don't need to worry about getting a release
    b. should require the person to sign a release form
    c. need to notify the local union representative
    d. must state so plainly in the project's credits
    e. must pay a surcharge to the local union

15. You do not need to worry about having someone's written consent to use his or her image or voice in your production if:
    a. it was already used in the *National Enquirer*
    b. the subject is at least a first cousin
    c. it is work product made for hire
    d. the subject is younger than 18 years old
    e. you are recording a public event

■ Essay Quiz

1. List ten different kinds of content. Try to think of as many different variations as you can. List a high production value and low production value example of each.

2. You are assigned to create an interactive DVD about white-water rafting for an exciting startup company. The product is going to be sent to subscribers of a famous outdoors magazine. This magazine's readership has a high level of disposable income. Discuss the creative process you might go through to determine the content you will use in this project. Where will you get it? Will you use clip art? Public domain content? Will you produce new materials? What will the production values be? How will you justify the expense? What talent will you need for the project? Discuss how you will select the talent (on-screen versus voice-over, age, sex, ethnicity, etc.).

3. You are assigned to create a web site for a town's nonprofit historical society. Discuss the creative process you might go through to determine the content you will use in this project. Where will you get it? Will you use clip art? Public domain content? Will you produce new materials? What will the production values be? How will you justify the expense? What are the production values on the project?

4. List five issues related to the rights to license and use someone else's work. Discuss how these issues affect the scope of your project. Will they affect the number of units you may distribute or where, when, and how you may distribute your project? Discuss the advantages and problems associated with hiring union, nonunion, and nonprofessional talent for a production. What factors would affect this decision?

Lab Projects

■ Project 10.1

Go online and locate at least two game development paid asset providers, such as GamePrefabs.com or Arteria3d.com. Find two 3-D models, two 2-D models, two audio assets (music or sound effect), and at least one AI (artificial intelligence) asset. Compare and record the costs of these assets, as well as the general range of the offerings for each provider.

■ Project 10.2

Go online and locate at least two providers of assets licensed under Creative Commons, such as Blender 3D Model Repository and Freesound. Locate as wide a variety of types of assets as you can, with at least one audio, one 2-D model, and one 3-D model. Record the creator's information and the type of CC license for each asset you find. Compare the quality and diversity of these assets with those you found in Project 10.1.

■ Project 10.3

Based on the research you did for Projects 10.1 and 10.2, estimate the total cost for content assets to develop a small game prototype. Assume you will use at least 15 3-D assets, 25 2-D assets, 2 music assets, and 3 SFX assets. You should also specify a game engine to use, such as Unity 3D or Unreal Engine, as well as factoring the cost of using the engine professionally. What are the high and low ranges for these projects?

■ Project 10.4

Contact a creative services agency or talent agency and ask to see the sourcebook. Most large markets have at least one creative sourcebook. These sourcebooks, among other things, often include a number of head shots, or pages with the face and vital statistics for agency talent in the area. Such sourcebooks also include illustrators, photographers, and other creative artists. Select a person to act as a spokesperson, as well as an illustrator, for a learning project. Photocopy the pages you select from the sourcebook. Justify your decision.

■ Project 10.5

Look at the credits of three DVDs. Copy the wording used in crediting various contributors. Look at several different web sites. Do they list credits? Why or why not?

## CHAPTER 11

The Internet and Multimedia

Launched in 1989, the World Wide Web was not originally designed with multimedia in mind, but rather as a simple method for delivering text documents formatted in HTML, with occasional inline graphic illustrations and figures. By 1995, because it was operational, essentially free, and *good enough* to support traffic (see "Vaughan's Law of Multimedia Minimums" in Chapter 4), the Web had become a full-bore information highway of words and pictures with tens of millions of users cruising along it. The Doppler back-draft of passing travelers has exposed the gristle of an overwhelming number of disappointing audio and visual experiences on the Web: "This is my home page; here is a list of my favorite places; this is me with my dog…" To fill this vacuum of content and presentation, inventive multimedia solutions and enhancements now compete for mind share, stretching the capabilities of HTML, web browsers, PCs, smartphones, and the very fabric of the Internet in order to bring multimedia power to this environment. Plain text and pictures are no longer enough for this highway!

WARNING *Powerful multimedia tools can be used to create totally vacuous web pages.*

The material covered in this chapter is designed to give you an overview of the Internet while describing particular features that may be useful to you as a developer of multimedia for the World Wide Web. URLs and other pointers are also included here to lead you to information for obtaining, installing, and using these applications and utilities.

This chapter does *not* provide details about technology for connecting to and using the Internet, about setting up servers and hosts, about installing and using applications, or what to do when you discover that you pressed the wrong key and have broadcast the intimate details of last night's hot date to 532 friends. This chapter investigates and illustrates some methods for developing and presenting the basic elements of multimedia within the constraints of HTML, **Cascading Style Sheets (CSS)**, and the World Wide Web. It is not intended to substitute for a more complete library of HTML, CSS, web design, and Internet how-to texts, but to present basic examples that will get you started.

In this chapter, you will learn how to:

- Discuss the origins of the Internet

- Define what a computer network is and how Internet domains, addresses, and interconnections work

- Discuss the current state of multimedia on the Internet and tools for the World Wide Web

- Employ the basic methods for displaying elements of multimedia on a web page, including using HTML, CCS, and nibbling

- Manipulate the appearance of text on the Web

- Determine which graphics formats are best suited for different types of images and how they can be manipulated

- Play audio on a web page by embedding the sound within the site

- Include animation on a web page

- Include video on a web page with and without the use of plug-ins

Embarrassing yourself on the stage of the civilized world can be avoided by education. Visit your local bookstore, where, along with the work you are now reading, you may discover as many as a hundred helpful volumes about all the simple and arcane aspects of the Internet. Buy one or two of these and dig in. Or, if you are already connected to the Internet, much of the documentation and learning you may require can be found by surfing the Net itself. Use a search engine such as those listed here. Look particularly for documents called **Frequently Asked Questions (FAQs)**, because they contain answers.

AOL Search	*http://search.aol.com*
Ask	*www.ask.com*
Bing	*www.bing.com*
Dogpile	*www.dogpile.com*
Gigablast	*www.gigablast.com*
Google	*www.google.com*
HotBot	*www.hotbot.com*
Lycos	*www.lycos.com*
Yahoo	*www.yahoo.com*

Some search engines on the World Wide Web

Internet History

The **Internet** began as a research network funded by the **Advanced Research Projects Agency (ARPA)** of the U.S. Department of Defense (DoD), when the first node of the **ARPANET** was installed at the University of California, Los Angeles (UCLA) in September 1969. By the mid-1970s, the ARPANET "inter-network" embraced more than 30 universities, military sites, and government contractors, and its user base expanded to include the larger computer science research community. By 1983, the network still consisted of merely several hundred computers on only a few local area networks.

In 1985, the National Science Foundation (NSF) aligned with ARPA to support a collaboration of supercomputing centers and computer science researchers across the ARPANET. The NSF also funded a program for improving the backbone of the ARPANET, by increasing its bandwidth from 56 Kbps to T1 and then T3 (see "Bandwidth" a little later in the chapter for more information) and branching out with links to international sites in Europe and the Far East.

In 1989, responsibility and management for the ARPANET was officially passed from military interests to the academically oriented NSF, and research organizations and universities (professors and students alike) became increasingly heavy users of this ever-growing "Internet." Much of the Internet's polite etiquette and rules for behavior (such as in sending e-mail and posting to newsgroups) was established during this time. These early rules are being revised, of course, by a newer generation's jargon and manners.

More and more private companies and organizations linked up to the Internet, and by the mid-1990s, the Internet included connections to more than 60 countries and more than 2 million host computers with more than 15 million users worldwide. Commercial and business use of the Internet was not permitted until 1992, but businesses have since become its driving force. By 2001 there were 109,574,429 domain hosts and 407.1 million users of the Internet, representing 6.71 percent of the world's population. By the middle of 2012 (see Table 11-1), about one out of every three people around the world (34.3 percent, up from 26.6 percent in 2009) had access to the Internet, and more than 51 million domain names had been registered as "dot coms."

World Regions	Population (2012 Est.)	Population (2009 Est.)	Internet Users Dec. 31, 2000	Internet Users June 30, 2012	Penetration (% Population)	Growth 2000–2012	Users % of Table
Africa	1,073,380,925	991,002,342	4,514,400	167,335,676	15.6 %	3,606.7 %	7.0 %
Asia	3,922,066,987	3,808,070,503	114,304,000	1,076,681,059	27.5 %	841.9 %	44.8 %
Europe	820,918,446	803,850,858	105,096,093	518,512,109	63.2 %	393.4 %	21.5 %
Middle East	223,608,203	202,687,005	3,284,800	90,000,455	40.2 %	2,639.9 %	3.7 %
North America	348,280,154	340,831,831	108,096,800	273,785,413	78.6 %	153.3 %	11.4 %
Latin America/ Caribbean	586,662,468	586,662,468	18,068,919	254,915,745	42.9 %	1,310.8 %	10.6 %
Oceania / Australia	35,903,569	34,700,201	7,620,480	24,287,919	67.6 %	218.7 %	1.0 %
WORLD TOTAL	7,017,846,922	6,767,805,208	360,985,492	2,405,518,376	34.3 %	566.4 %	100.0 %

Table 11-1 World Internet Users and Population Stats (from www.internetworldstats.com)

Internetworking

In its simplest form, a **network** is a cluster of computers, with one computer acting as a **server** to provide network services such as file transfer, e-mail, and document printing to the **client** computers or users of that network. Using gateways and routers, a **local area network (LAN)** can be connected to other LANs to form a **wide area network (WAN)**. These LANs and WANs can also be connected to the Internet through a server that provides both the necessary software for the Internet and the physical data connection (usually a high-bandwidth telephone line, coaxial cable TV line, or wireless). Individual computers not permanently part of a network (such as a home computer or a laptop) can connect to one of these Internet servers and, with proper identification and onboard client software, obtain an IP address on the Internet (see "IP Addresses and Data Packets" later in the chapter).

Internet Addresses

Let's say you get into a taxi at the train station in Trento, Italy, explain in English or Spanish or German or French that you wish to go to the Mozzi Hotel, and half an hour later you are let out of the car in a suburban wood—you have an address problem. You will quickly discover, as you return to the city in the back of a bricklayer's lorry to report your missing luggage and the cab driver, Mauro, who sped away in the rain, that you also have a serious language problem.

If you know how addresses work and understand the syntax or language of the Internet, you will likely not get lost and will save much time and expense during your adventures. You will also be able to employ shortcuts and workarounds.

Top-Level Domains

When the original ARPANET protocols for communicating among computers were remade into the current scheme of **Transmission Control Protocol/ Internet Protocol (TCP/IP)** in 1983, the **Domain Name System (DNS)** was developed to rationally assign names and addresses to computers linked to the Internet. **Top-level domains (TLDs)**, also called **first-level domains,** were established as categories to accommodate all users of the Internet:

TLD	Intended Purpose	Registered # of Sites in 2012
.com	Commercial organizations	103,224,211
.edu	Post-secondary educational institutions	7,341
.gov	Federal, state, and local U.S. government	4,900
.int	Intergovernmental treaty organizations	120
.mil	U.S. military	N/A
.net	Network infrastructure	14,895,641
.org	Nonprofit, noncommercial organizations	9,900,000
Two-letter country codes	Countries and territories	More than 240 countries and territories

In late 1998, the Internet Corporation for Assigned Names and Numbers (ICANN) was set up to oversee the technical coordination of the Domain Name System, which allows Internet addresses to be found by easy-to-remember names instead of one of 4.3 billion individual IP numbers. In the early part of the 21st century, ICANN approved a few additional TLDs:

TLD	Intended Purpose	Registered # of Sites in 2012
.aero	Aviation community	7,819
.asia	Pan-Asia and Asia Pacific community	200,217
.biz	Businesses	2,253,548
.cat	Catalan-speaking community	52,997
.coop	Cooperatives	14,641
.info	Informational resources	7,980,209
.jobs	Employment and careers	45,000
.mobi	Sites optimized for mobile devices	1,043,448
.museum	Museums	442
.name	Personal sites, names, pseudonyms	233,831
.pro	Professional use	137,334
.tel	Contact information	300,000
.travel	Travel industry	26,092
.xxx	Pornography	200,006

In June, 2011, ICANN then approved plans for a major sale of new generic TLDs, and by 2014 it had received 1,930 applications for TLDs such as .poker, .airbus, .google, and .ferrari. Many new names are online and active. Others, where there is competition (such as for .web, .film, and .flowers), have yet to be approved. A full, long list of approved names and applicants is available at www.iana.org/domains/root/db.

As a particular domain name is built up from the top-level domain, it consists of different levels separated by a period (spoken as "dot"). Since we read left to right in English, we tend to think first.second.third, left to right, but domain name levels are numbered right to left. Companies such as Microsoft, Apple, and IBM have second-level domain addresses that read microsoft.com, apple.com, and ibm.com—they are commercial (.com) operations with their second-level domain to the left of the top-level .com domain. Government (.gov) agencies such as the Federal Bureau of Investigation, the Internal Revenue Service, and the White House have addresses that read fbi.gov, irs.gov, and whitehouse.gov.

> Concerns about "rights" and "ownership" of domains are inappropriate. It is appropriate to be concerned about "responsibilities" and "service" to the community.
>
> J. Postel, from the Network Working Group RFC 1591, March 1994

Second-Level Domains

Many second-level domains contain huge numbers of computers and user accounts representing local, regional, and even international branches as well as various internal business and management functions. So the Internet addressing scheme provides for subdomains that can contain even more subdomains. Like a finely carved Russian matryoshka doll, individual workstations live at the epicenter of a cluster of domains.

Within the education (.edu) domain containing thousands of universities and colleges, for example, is a second-level domain for the fictitious Lotus University called lotus.edu. At that university are many schools and departments (medicine, engineering, law, business, computer science, and so on), and each of these entities in turn has departments and possibly subdepartments and many users. These departments operate one or even several servers for managing traffic to and from the many computers in their group and to the outside world. At Lotus, the server for the Computing and Information Systems Department is named cis. It manages about 11,000 departmental accounts—so many accounts that a cluster of three subsidiary servers was installed to deal efficiently with the demand. These subsidiary servers are named minerva, morpheus, and mercury. Thus, minerva lives in the cis domain, which lives in the lotus domain, which lives in the edu domain. Real people's computers are networked to minerva. Other real people are connected to the morpheus and mercury servers. To make things easy (exactly what computers are for), the mail system database at Lotus maintains a master list of all of its people. So, as far as the outside world is concerned, a professor's e-mail address can be simply firstname.lastname@lotus.edu; the database knows he or she is really connected to minerva so the mail is forwarded to that correct final address. In detailed e-mail headers, you may see the complete destination address listed as well as names of the computers through which your mail message may have been routed.

E-mail accounts are said to be "at" a domain (written with the @ sign). There are never any blank spaces in an Internet e-mail address, and while addresses on the Internet are normally case insensitive, conventional use dictates using all lowercase: the Internet will find tay@timestream.com, TAY@TIMESTREAM.COM, and Tay@Timestream.Com to be the same address.

The .us Domain and Country Codes

The two-letter top-level country domains are based on political boundaries and used by federal, state, and local government agencies, high schools, technical/vocational schools, private schools, elementary schools, libraries, fire and police departments, and regular citizens and commercial enterprises. Any computer in the United States can be in the .us domain. Some fictitious examples are as follows:

fs.fed.us	Federal
senate.state.pa.us	State
assembly.state.ny.us	State
mwra.state.ma.us	State
ci.wayland.mi.us	City
co.alameda.ca.us	County
ccsf.cc.ca.us	Public community college
appleton.lib.me.us	Public library
pps.k12.or.us	Public school
perkins.pvt.k12.ma.us	Private school

NOTE *The Internet RFC 1480, http://tools.ietf.org/search/rfc1480, describes the hierarchical rules for addresses in the .us domain.*

Two-letter country codes, based on the International Organization for Standardization (ISO) document ISO-3166, are used in the addresses of all computers located outside the United States. Each country has an administrator who is responsible for organizing the naming hierarchy within that country's domain. Some countries use categories similar to .com, .edu, and .org. Others base their naming hierarchies on political boundaries, as in the .us country code.

schmidt@cage.rug.ac.be	Professor at University of Gent, Belgium
smythe@fiqus.unl.edu.ar	Student at L.C.S.A, Argentina
smith@iskratel.si	Commercial account, Slovenia
smith@laughs.co.uk	Commercial account, United Kingdom
smithe@idsc.gov.eg	Student at Cairo University, Egypt
smithy@udcf.gla.ac.uk	Researcher at University of Glasgow, Scotland
tsmith@library.usyd.edu.au	Scholar at University of Sydney, Australia

TIP   *For a list of all the two-letter country codes and other top-level domains, see: www.iana.org/domains/root/db.*

IP Addresses and Data Packets

When a stream of data is sent over the Internet by your computer, it is first broken down into packets by the Transmission Control Protocol (TCP). Each packet includes the address of the receiving computer, a sequence number ("this is packet #5"), error correction information, and a small piece of your data. After a packet is created by TCP, the Internet Protocol (IP) then takes over and actually sends the packet to its destination along a route that may include many other computers acting as forwarders. TCP/IP is two important Internet protocols working in concert.

The 32-bit address included in a data packet, the **IP address**, is the "real" Internet address. It is made up of four numbers separated by periods; for example, 140.174.162.10. Some of these numbers are assigned by Internet authorities, and some may be dynamically assigned by an **Internet service provider (ISP)** when a computer logs on using a subscriber's account. There are domain name servers throughout the Internet whose sole job is to quickly look up text-based domain name addresses in large distributed databases, convert them into real IP addresses, and then return them to you for insertion into your data packets. Every time you connect to http://www.google.com or send mail to president@whitehouse.gov, the domain name server is consulted and the destination address is converted to numbers.

TIP   *IP addresses and domain names can be used interchangeably. Thus, netflix.com is the same Internet address as 69.53.236.17. There are occasional problems with the Internet's DNS servers, and by using the IP address, you may get connected immediately. With a Ping utility, or using the "whois" function in Unix, you can discover a domain's IP address.*

Connections

If your computer is connected to an existing network at your home, office, or school, it is likely you are already connected to the Internet, either using an Ethernet connection (hardwired) or a wireless Wi-Fi (radio) connection. You will need a broadband cable modem, digital subscriber line (DSL) modem, or other routing equipment to connect to the **backbone** (the ultra-high-bandwidth underlying network operated by AT&T, Sprint, Verizon, and other telecommunications companies) of the Internet through an ISP.

Bandwidth

Bandwidth is how much data, expressed in bits per second (bps), you can send from one computer to another in a given amount of time. The faster your transmissions (or the greater the bandwidth of your connection), the less time you will spend waiting for text, images, sounds, and animated illustrations to upload or download from computer to computer, and the more satisfaction you will have with your Internet experience. To think in bytes per second, divide the rate by eight. Table 11-2 lists the bandwidth of some common data transfer methods.

Type of Connection	Bandwidth (in bits per second) Without Compression	Comment
56K modem	56,000	Maximum analog modem speed for copper wires, (Dial-Up) data compressed using V91 standard. Actual is about 48 Kbps.
ISDN	56,000 to 128,000	Integrated Services Digital Network basic services (128,000 bps if no voice mixed in).
Frame relay	56,000 to 45,000,000	Dedicated service offered by long-distance phone companies.
Ethernet-10	10,000,000	Networking hardware and protocol, commonly uses two twisted pairs of copper wire.
T1 (DS-1 in North America)	1,544,000	Equal to 24 leased lines at 56 Kbps.
E-1 (DS-1 in Europe)	2,000,000	European equivalent of a T1 connection.
DSL	1,500,000 to 100,000,000	Digital subscriber line service available in various technologies (ADSL, HDSL, RADSL, SDSL, and VDSL) with differing data rates, operating distances, and ratios between downstream and upstream speeds.
Cable modem	384,000 upload; 400,000,000 download	Even though copper coaxial TV cable can be used in a bidirectional fashion, it was originally designed to carry limited signals in one direction.
Wireless (Wi-Fi)	802.11a: 22,000,000 802.11g: 22,000,000 802.11n: 54,000,000	Wi-Fi radio connection in the radio frequency (RF) bands of 2.4 GHz or 5.8 GHz.

Table 11-2   Bandwidth of Typical Internet and Computer Connections

Type of Connection	Bandwidth (in bits per second) Without Compression	Comment
T3 (D-3 in North America)	45,000,000	Typical backbone speed of major ISPs in the United States (1996).
VDSL VDSL2	52,000,000 (2001) 100,000,000 (2006)	Very high-rate digital subscriber line.
Fast Ethernet-100	100,000,000	Networking hardware and protocol, commonly uses two twisted pairs of copper wire.
OC-3	155,000,000	Upgrade for ISPs in the United States (1997).
Gigabit Ethernet	1,000,000,000	Used for local network backbones; standard in many computers.
OC-48	2,400,000,000 (2.4 gigabits per second)	Typical speed for intercity fiber-optic lines (called SONET or Synchronous Optical Network).
10-Gigabit Ethernet	10,000,000,000 (10 gigabits per second)	Used for local network backbones
OC-255	13,210,000,000 (13.21 gigabits per second)	Really fast fiber-optic lines using SONET.

Table 11-2 Bandwidth of Typical Internet and Computer Connections

A low-bandwidth connection is the most serious impediment to sending multimedia across the Internet. At low bandwidth, a page of text (3,000 bytes) can take less than a second to send, but an uncompressed 640×480, 8-bit/256-color image (about 300,000 bytes) can take a few minutes; an uncompressed 640×480, 24-bit/16 million-color image (about 900,000 bytes) can take many minutes to send. Occasionally also, even though you may have a high-speed connection, the server delivering your requested file or content may be "throttled down" while it manages many simultaneous requests at once, and yours must wait its turn or share the pipeline.

To work within the constraints of bandwidth bottlenecks, multimedia developers on the Internet can:

■ Compress data as tightly as possible (into ZIP or SIT or TAR files) before transmitting.

■ Require users to download data only once; then store the data in a local hard disk cache (this is automatically managed by most browsers).

■ Design each multimedia element to be efficiently compact—don't use a greater color depth than is absolutely necessary or leave extra space around the edges.

■ Design alternate low-bandwidth and high-bandwidth navigation paths to accommodate all users.

■ Implement streaming methods that allow data to be transferred and displayed incrementally as it comes in (without waiting for the entire data file to arrive).

Bandwidth constraints are becoming less of a problem as more users improve their connections and vendors improve their hardware. According to the Pew Research Center, as of December 2012, only 3 percent of Internet users were using a dial-up modem connection at 56 Kbps. At the time of writing, three of the most popular streaming video providers have the following requirements and recommendations for Internet download bandwidth (speeds):

Netflix

0.5 Mbps: Required broadband connection speed

1.5 Mbps: Recommended broadband connection speed

3.0 Mbps: Recommended for DVD quality

5.0 Mbps: Recommended for HD quality

7.0 Mbps: Recommended for Super HD quality

12 Mbps: Recommended for 3-D HD quality

Hulu Plus

1.5 Mbps for Standard Definition videos

3 Mbps for High Definition videos

Vudu

1 to 2 Mbps for Standard Definition

2.25 to 4.5 Mbps for High Definition

4.5 to 9 Mbps for High Definition X

> 9 Mbps for 3-D HD

Internet Services

To many users, the Internet means the World Wide Web. But the Web is only the most popular of services available today on the Internet. E-mail; file transfer; discussion groups and newsgroups; real-time chatting by text, voice, and video; and the ability to log into remote computers are common as well. Each Internet service is implemented on an Internet server by dedicated software known as a **daemon**. (Actually, daemons only exist on Unix/Linux systems—on other systems, such as Windows, the services may run as regular applications or background processes.) Daemons are agent programs that run in the background, waiting to act on requests from the outside. In the case of the Internet, daemons support protocols such as the **Hypertext Transfer Protocol (HTTP)** for the World Wide Web, the **Post Office Protocol (POP)** for e-mail, or the **File Transfer Protocol (FTP)** for exchanging files. You have probably noticed that the first few letters of a **Uniform Resource Locator (URL)**—for example, http://www .timestream.com/index.html—notify a server as to which daemon to bring into play to satisfy a request. In many cases, the daemons for the Web, mail, and FTP may run on completely different servers, each isolated by a security firewall from other servers on a network.

FTP.ARL.MIL (Army Research Laboratory) Bandwidth Information

ARL has multiple high-speed connections to several significant networks, providing excellent performance for most document transfers:

- **DREN**   This site is a primary node in the Defense Research and Engineering Network (DREN), which sports a variety of OC-12, OC-3, T-3, and T-1 communications links to other US Government facilities.
- **The Internet Backbone**   This site is connected to the Internet "backbone" at strategic locations via a "cloud" of OC-12 ATM paths provisioned over AT&T's nationwide DISC ATM network:
  - MAE-East in Washington DC
  - FIX-West and MAE-West in San Francisco
  - The Sprint NAP in Pensauken, NJ
  - The NAP in Chicago, IL
  - The "Giga-pop" in Washington state
- **NIPRNET (nee MILNET)**   This site is gatewayed to a NIPRNET military Packet Switching Node which has multiple T-1 trunks.

  Moving 1 MByte of data over an OC-3 link takes about 0.1 seconds, if your end is up to it.

  Moving 1 MByte of data over a T-3 link takes about 1 second, if your end is up to it.

  Moving 1 MByte of data over a T-1 link takes about 8 seconds.

  Moving 1 MByte of data over a 56 Kbps link takes about 3 minutes.

  Moving 1 MByte of data over a 28.8 Kbps modem takes about 5 minutes.

Naturally, no single file transfer ever gets the full bandwidth of these communications lines, as they are a shared resource. These figures should help you make a lower-bound estimate on how much time large file transfers might take.

You are free to transfer large files from this site at any time.

Information seekers from all domains are welcome to view this data. It is important that our guests understand that this is an official U.S. Government System for unclassified use only. Use of this system constitutes consent to security testing and monitoring.

webmaster@arl.army.mil

[Source: http://ftp.arl.army.mil/bandwidth.html]

Media Types

To work with multimedia on the Internet, you must work within the requirements of the appropriate protocol, using recognizable documents and formats. A voice attachment to an e-mail message, for example, must be identified by the Post Office daemon for what it is, and then be transmitted with the correct coding to the receiving computer. The receiver must have the proper software (and hardware) for decoding the information and playing it back. To identify the nature of the data transmitted and, by inference, the purpose of that data, the Internet uses a standard list of filename extensions (see www.iana.org/assignments/media-types /media-types.xhtml) called **media types**. These were formerly known as **Multipurpose Internet Mail Extensions (MIME-types)**. Most browsers allow you to define media types and map "helper apps" to the type for decoding and playing. For example, with Firefox you can define Adobe's Acrobat files (PDF files) as a media type and select Acrobat as the player application.

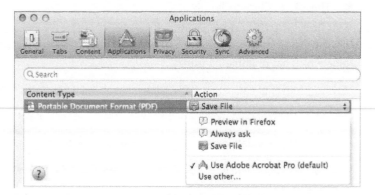

Media types are used not only by the e-mail daemon but, by convention, by other Internet daemons, including the Web's HTTP daemon. Perhaps the most widely installed HTTP software for managing web pages is the open-source application called Apache (www.apache.org). Table 11-3 shows a list of common media types and their uses. (Note that many come from the Unix world, where the Internet was born.) An x before the subtype of a media type means that it is not registered with the Internet Assigned Numbers Authority (IANA). A "vnd" prefix means that the media type is vendor-specific.

Multimedia elements are typically saved and transmitted on the Internet in the appropriate media type format and are named with the proper extension for that type. For example, image files end in .jpg, .jpeg, .gif, or .png; sound files end in .au, .wav, .aif, .mp3, or another conforming format; video clips end in .qt, .mov, .mp4, .mpeg, .avi, or .flv.

Extension	Type	Use
ai	application/postscript	PostScript program
aif	audio/x-aiff	Audio
aifc	audio/x-aiff	Audio
AIFF	audio/x-aiff	Audio
aiff	audio/x-aiff	Audio
au	audio/basic	ULAW audio data
avi	video/x-msvideo	Microsoft video
bin	application/octet-stream	Binary executable
cpio	application/x-cpio	Unix CPIO archive
csh	application/x-csh	C shell program
dcr	application/director	Shockwave animation
dvi	application/x-dvi	TeX DVI data
eps	application/postscript	PostScript program
exe	application/octet-stream	Binary executable
fif	application/fractals	Fractal image format
flv	video/x-flv	Flash video
gif	image/gif	CompuServe image format
gtar	application/x-gtar	GNU tape archive
gz	encoding/x-gzip	GNU zip compressed data
hqx	application/mac-binhex40	Macintosh BinHex archive
htm	text/html	Hypertext Markup Language
html	text/html	Hypertext Markup Language
ief	image/ief	Image
jpe	image/jpeg	JPEG image
jpeg	image/jpeg	JPEG image
jpg	image/jpeg	JPEG image
latex	application/x-latex	LaTeX document
kmz	application/vnd.google-earth.kmz	Google Earth document
man	application/x-troff-man	Unix manual page
me	application/x-troff-me	TROFF document
mov	video/quicktime	QuickTime video
movie	video/x-sgi-movie	SGI video
mpe	video/mpeg	MPEG video

Table 11-3 Some Common Media Types Illustrate the Variety of Data and Formats Used on the Internet *(Continued)*

Extension	Type	Use
mpeg	video/mpeg	MPEG video
mpg	video/mpeg	MPEG video
ms	application/x-troff-ms	TROFF document
pbm	image/x-portable-bitmap	PBM image
pgm	image/x-portable-graymap	PGM image
pnm	image/x-portable-anymap	PBM image
ppm	image/x-portable-pixmap	PPM image
ps	application/postscript	PostScript program
qt	video/quicktime	QuickTime video
ra	audio/x-pn-realaudio	RealAudio sound
ram	audio/x-pn-realaudio	RealAudio sound
ras	image/x-cmu-raster	CMU raster image
rgb	image/x-rgb	RGB image
roff	application/x-troff	TROFF document
rtf	application/rtf	Rich Text Format
sh	application/x-sh	Bourne shell program
shar	application/x-shar	Unix shell archive
sit	application/x-stuffit	Macintosh archive
snd	audio/basic	ULAW audio data
swf	application/ x-shockwave-flash	Flash document
t	application/x-troff	TROFF document
tar	application/x-tar	Unix tape archive
tcl	application/x-tcl	TCL program
tex	application/x-tex	TeX document
texi	application/x-texinfo	GNU TeXinfo document
texinfo	application/x-texinfo	GNU TeXinfo document
text	text/plain	Plain text
tif	image/tiff	TIFF image
tiff	image/tiff	TIFF image
tr	application/x-troff	TROFF document
txt	text/plain	Plain text
vox	audio	VoxWare
wav	audio/x-wav	WAV audio

Table 11-3 Some Common Media Types Illustrate the Variety of Data and Formats Used on the Internet *(Continued)*

Extension	Type	Use
xbm	image/x-xbitmap	X bitmap
xpm	image/x-xpixmap	X pixmap
xwd	image/x-xwindowdump	X Window dump image
z	encoding/x-compress	Compressed data
zip	application/x-zip-compressed	Zip compressed data

Table 11-3 Some Common Media Types Illustrate the Variety of Data and Formats Used on the Internet *(Continued)*

WARNING *Because some media types for multimedia data are new or experimental, not all servers may recognize them. If you have problems with a multimedia file, check with your Internet service provider to be sure your server can serve "experimental" media types. Some ISPs will not install the requisite, and often costly, server software for high-bandwidth streaming media types.*

The World Wide Web and HTML

The World Wide Web (www.w3.org/) started in 1989 at the European Particle Physics Laboratory (CERN) in Switzerland as a "distributed collaborative hypermedia information system." It was designed by Tim Berners-Lee as a protocol for linking a multiplicity of documents located on computers anywhere within the Internet. This new Hypertext Transfer Protocol (HTTP) provided rules for a simple transaction between two computers on the Internet consisting of (1) establishing a connection, (2) requesting that a document be sent, (3) sending the document, and (4) closing the connection. It also required a simple document format called Hypertext Markup Language (HTML) for presenting structured text mixed with inline images.

An HTML document could contain hyperlinks or anchors that referred to other similar documents. With browser software, users could then click on designated areas of hot text in one document and jump to another, which itself might have more hot text pointing to yet other documents. Users could surf from document to document across the Web, with HTML as the underlying buoyant framework. Berners-Lee is currently developing the next evolution, the **Semantic Web**, which "provides a common framework that allows data to be shared and reused across application, enterprise, and community boundaries." Visit www.w3.org/2013/data/ for more information.

The Semantic Web is an extension of the current Web in which information is given well-defined meaning, enabling computers and people to work in better cooperation. The W3C Semantic Web Activity, in collaboration with a large number of researchers and industrial partners, is tasked with defining standards and technologies that allow data on the Web to be defined and linked in a way that it can be used for more effective discovery, automation, integration, and reuse across applications. The Web will reach its full potential when it becomes an environment where data can be shared and processed by automated tools as well as by people.

Tim Berners-Lee and Eric Miller from *The Semantic Web Lifts Off*

Dynamic Web Pages and XML

HTML is fine for building and delivering uncomplicated static web pages. But you will need other tools and programming know-how to deliver dynamic web pages that are built on-the-fly from text, graphics, animations, and information contained in databases or documents. JavaScript and programs written in Java may be inserted into HTML pages to perform special functions and tasks that go beyond the vanilla abilities of HTML—for mouse rollovers, window control, and custom animations.

Cold Fusion and PHP are applications that run side by side with a web server like Apache; they scan an outgoing web page for special commands and directives, usually embedded in special tags. If they find a special tag in the page, the software will do what the tag tells it to do, like "get today's date and put it into that table cell" or "search database xyz for all customers with balances greater than $100 and, after alphabetizing, put that list into a table on the web page being served." Working hand-in-hand with these application servers, relational database management systems (RDBMSs) from Oracle, Sybase, and mySQL offer software to manage Structured Query Language (SQL) databases that may contain not only text but also graphics and multimedia resources like sounds and video clips. In concert with HTML, these tools provide the power to do real work and perform real tasks within the context of the World Wide Web.

Flash animations, Director applications, and RunRev stacks can also be called from within HTML pages. These multimedia mini-applications, often programmed by web developers, use a browser plug-in to display the action and perform tasks such as playing a sound, showing a video, or calculating a date. As with Cold Fusion and PHP, these use underlying programming languages. With the introduction of HTML5, browsers can play multimedia elements such as sound, animations, and video without requiring special plug-ins or software.

Extensible Markup Language (XML) goes beyond HTML—it is the next evolutionary step in the development of the Internet for formatting and delivering web pages using styles. Unlike HTML, you can create your own tags in XML to describe exactly what the data means, and you can get that data from anywhere on the Web. In XML, you can build a set of tags like

```
<fruit>
<type>Tomato</type>
<source>California</source>
<price>$.64</price>
</fruit>
```

and your XML document, according to your instructions, will find the information to put into the proper place on the web page in the formatting style

Flash was created during the PC era—for PCs and mice. Flash is a successful business for Adobe, and we can understand why they want to push it beyond PCs. But the mobile era is about low power devices, touch interfaces and open web standards—all areas where Flash falls short.

The avalanche of media outlets offering their content for Apple's mobile devices demonstrates that Flash is no longer necessary to watch video or consume any kind of web content. And the 200,000 apps on Apple's App Store proves that Flash isn't necessary for tens of thousands of developers to create graphically rich applications, including games. New open standards created in the mobile era, such as HTML5, will win on mobile devices (and PCs too). Perhaps Adobe should focus more on creating great HTML5 tools for the future, and less on criticizing Apple for leaving the past behind.

....

Steve Jobs,
CEO Apple Computer,
Inc., April 2010

you assign. For example, with XML styles, you can declare that all items within the <price> tag will be displayed in boldface Helvetica type.

TIP   *For more information about XML see:*
www.xml.org
www.xml.com

In development as a technique to deliver more pleasing web experiences, AJAX (Asynchronous JavaScript and XML) uses a combination of XML, Cascading Style Sheets (CSS) for marking up and styling information, and JavaScript to generate dynamic displays and allow user interaction within a web browser.

Multimedia on the Web

During the coming years, most multimedia experiences on the Internet will occur on the World Wide Web, programmed within the constraints of HTML, then stretched by the enhanced capabilities provided by XML, Java, JavaScript, AJAX, and special plug-ins like Flash and QuickTime to enable browsers to exceed their limits. These tools are used to build "Web 2.0" sites where there is collaboration and information sharing such as seen in blogs, on wikis, and at social networking sites such as Facebook and Twitter.

To design and make effective multimedia for this environment, developers need to understand not only how to create and edit the elements of multimedia, but also how to deliver it for HTML browsers and plug-in/player vehicles. Well-crafted, professionally rendered sites on the Web include text, images, audio, and animation presented in a user-friendly interface that balances the bandwidth deficit against user patience.

Inside the event horizon of the amazing World Wide Web explosion are many uncertainties and unsolved challenges. The bandwidth deficit will certainly be met with technology solutions that will reach the last mile into homes and businesses. There is a terrific need for high-quality, compelling content; multimedia developers and entrepreneurs will fill this creative void.

Tools for the World Wide Web

In the late 1990s, multimedia plug-ins and commercial tools aimed at the Web entered the marketplace at a furious pace, each competing for visibility and developer/user mind share in an increasingly noisy venue. In the few years since the birth of the first line-driven HTTP daemon in Switzerland, millions of web surfers had become hungry for "cool" enhancements to entertaining sites. Web site and page developers needed creative tools to feed the surfers, while surfers needed browsers and the plug-ins and players to make these cool multimedia enhancements work.

> The Web is becoming much more than a static library. Increasingly, users are accessing the Web for "web pages" that aren't actually on the shelves. Instead, the pages are generated dynamically from information available to the web server. That information can come from databases on the web server, from the site owner's enterprise databases, or even from other web sites.
>
> Charles Goldfarb, who invented SGML (the parent language of HTML and XML) and coined the term "markup language"

A combination of the explosion of these tools and user demand for performance stresses the orderly development of the core HTML standard. Unable to evolve fast enough to satisfy the demand for features (there are committees, international meetings, rational debates, comment periods, and votes in the standards process), the HTML language is constantly being extended de facto by commercial interests. These companies regularly release new versions of web browsers containing **tags** (HTML formatting elements) and features not yet formally approved. By the time (measured in weeks!) millions of users have become dependent upon the features of the new browser versions, the more carefully considered official specification has no choice but to incorporate them. By the time features are "official," of course—after more meetings, votes, and understated demonstrations of power—still newer browser versions have been released with yet newer, unofficial features.

What keeps this cycle from being chaotic are the natural selection forces of the marketplace: developers strive toward a successful product that works better and satisfies more users without mutating so far from the core standard that there are no sales and the company collapses. Developers also complain about the contention among browser vendors because the developers must program workarounds that compensate for the performance differences among the browsers, and they must test the performance of their site on all browsers or as many as possible.

Browsers provide a method for third-party developers to "plug in" special tools that take over certain computational and display activities. They also support the **Java** and **JavaScript** languages by which programmers can create bits of programming script and Java **applets** to extend and customize a browser's basic HTML capabilities, especially into the multimedia realm. Java and JavaScript are only related by name. Java is a programming language much like C++ that must be compiled into machine code to be executed by a computer's operating system. JavaScript is a "scripting language" whose commands are executed at runtime by the browser itself. JavaScript code can be placed directly into HTML using <script> tags or referenced from a file with the ".js" extension.

Thus, while browsers provide the orchestrated foundation of HTML, third-party players and even nonprogrammers can create their own cadenzas to enhance browser performance or perform special tasks. It is often through these plug-ins and applets that multimedia reaches end users. Many of these tools are available as freeware and shareware while others, particularly server software packages, are expensive, though most any tool can be downloaded from the Internet in a trial version. Try it. If you like it or use it, buy it.

The stunning growth of the Internet, including the expansion of wireless mobile device connectivity to the Internet, has caused many multimedia developers to redirect their creative efforts toward providing software solutions for these arenas. Development of apps and games for mobile devices is a new and lucrative frontier, and no developer wishes to be left behind. See Chapter 12 for more about mobile multimedia.

Web Servers

The workings of the Web involve communication between two computers: a server and a client. The server delivers a file when a client asks for it. Because the playback or display performance of your multimedia content—particularly when it is a streaming media type such as RealAudio or Shockwave/Flash or a MPEG video—depends upon the speed and capabilities of the computer and software serving it (as well as the bandwidth and load factors of the Internet), you should know some basics.

A growing number of software vendors provide web servers of varying strength and capacity and for a variety of platforms, all of which meet the requirements of the Hypertext Transfer Protocol. A server is technically not the hardware, but the software—you should invest in server software that will stand up to your intended use and be supported by the vendor. Most vendors will also recommend hardware configurations. This combination of software and hardware is critical to your success and happiness if you wish to optimize response time (less than a second), your connections per second (as many as possible), and your throughput (plenty of room before your Internet connection is overwhelmed by traveling packets).

WARNING *If you do not develop growth predictions based upon sound business practices and install adequate server performance and load balancing, you may discover that those 6,000 hits you received in the hour after you and your brother held up the bedsheet boasting your company's URL during the Super Bowl are being served at 87 bytes per second or refused altogether. At least be sure your choice of server and its connection to the Internet backbone provide a sensible migration path for growth; people don't usually come back to an unsatisfying experience.*

Web Browsers

Your computer's performance is as important as the bandwidth of your connection to the Web. Web **browsers** are applications that run on a user's personal computer (on the client side on the Internet) to provide the interactive graphical interface for searching, finding, and viewing text documents, sounds, animations, and other multimedia resources on the Web. In 1996, as many as 50 browsers competed for market share, each boasting special or unique features, performance, and cost. Rich Santalesa, editor of *NetGuide* magazine, predicted even then that "the browser wars are over—it's a battle between Microsoft and Netscape, and everyone else is going to dry up and blow away." Indeed, by mid-2001, only two serious competitors remained: Netscape and Microsoft, and Netscape, despite more than 40 million registered users, was beginning a chameleon act. Purchased by AOL, then alloyed by a merger with Time Warner (which includes properties such as *Fortune* and *Time* magazines and the 24-hour cable news network CNN), Netscape was repositioned as a "media hub," not a software company, giving the new Netscape a chance to sell advertising across its many media properties and experiment with subscriptions rather than just free services within the AOL-Time Warner media empire. By 2006, Netscape was dead. From Netscape's ashes arose Mozilla Firefox as an open-source competitor to Microsoft Internet Explorer. Apple introduced its own competitor, Safari. Google produced its own Chrome.

Despite the legal and financial seriousness of this competition, manifesting in very real congressional hearings and complicated multimillion-dollar antimonopoly lawsuits, some of those involved kept their sense of humor. Back in October 1997, late in the night after the gala announcement and rollout of Microsoft's new Explorer 4.0 in San Francisco, a group of Microsoft engineers drove 30 miles south to Netscape's headquarters and placed a truck-sized Explorer logo (the world-circling "e") on the front lawn of the competitor's headquarters, accented with a helium balloon saying "We Love You" and a greeting card with the message, "It's just not fair. Good people shouldn't have to feel bad. Best wishes, the IE team." By midmorning, Netscape's own engineers had crowned the Explorer logo with a giant dinosaur (their company mascot, named Mozilla), and nailed up a cardboard sign declaring, "Netscape 72, Microsoft 18" (the companies' market share at that time). Mozilla later spun out of Netscape in a free, open-source effort to standardize the browser's HTML engine.

Today, the majority of visitors to your web site will be using Google Chrome, current winner of the "browser wars" (see Table 11-4). In designing a web site, then, you should be certain that your documents and plug-ins work and look good using Chrome and also Internet Explorer.

Year	Internet Explorer	Firefox	Chrome	Safari	Opera	Unknown
2010	47%	31%	7%	5%	1%	9%
2014	26%	16%	33%	13%	2%	10%

Table 11-4   Browser Market Penetration (from www.w3counter.com)

Search Engines

You should become familiar with the operation of one or more search engines. They will ferret out information for you in seconds, information that would take months to find searching in a traditional library of books. Individualized personal search engines are available that can search the entire public Web, while enterprise search engines can search intranets, and mobile search engines can search mobile devices. **Search engine optimization (SEO)** specialists use arcane schemes to raise their clients' position at a search engine, sometimes gaming the search algorithm with link spamming, manipulation of keyword density, and even spamdexing. Use of unethical methods to improve a site's position is called "black hat SEO." For more about Google's PageRank algorithm for weighting a page's importance, visit www.google.com/competition/howgooglesearchworks.html.

Web Page Makers and Site Builders

To deliver multimedia on the Web today, you should know some HTML, meaning that you must place the proper tags and references into your documents to launch and control your multimedia. Many **HTML editors** and web page–making applications offer to shortcut your HTML learning curve and working effort. If you use one of these editors, enjoy its easing your work effort, but do not shy away from learning the syntax and tags of the language. Often these "helpers" generate extremely complicated HTML code (described by some programmers as "garbage") with the idea that if this code is hidden "under the hood," who cares? As you yourself become more informed and better at HTML coding, you might discover that you are the person who cares!

HTML documents are simple ASCII text files saved to disk without any formatting at all—no bolding, underlining, special fonts, margins, or tabs. Professional web page developers often use only a word processor like BBEdit for the Mac (see Figure 11-1) or WordPad in Windows rather than a souped-up, drag-and-drop, HTML page builder, and they insert text and tags into their documents manually or with personalized short-cut keys and helper scripts. HTML currently includes about 50 tags, and once you understand their properties and uses, coding, or **marking up**, a document and saving it to your web site can be a straightforward process. Plain HTML may not be enough to create dynamic sites on-the-fly, sites based upon user preferences or that display "live" information pulled from databases or spreadsheets. To build these kinds of pages, you should be familiar with programming environments such as Microsoft's Active Server Pages (asp.net); Adobe's ColdFusion (.cfm), which uses ColdFusion Markup Language (CFML); or the open-source and readily available PHP. For other powerful options beyond plain HTML, knowledge of Dynamic HTML (DHTML), Extensible Markup Language (XML), and Cascading Style Sheets (CSS) will enhance your skill set.

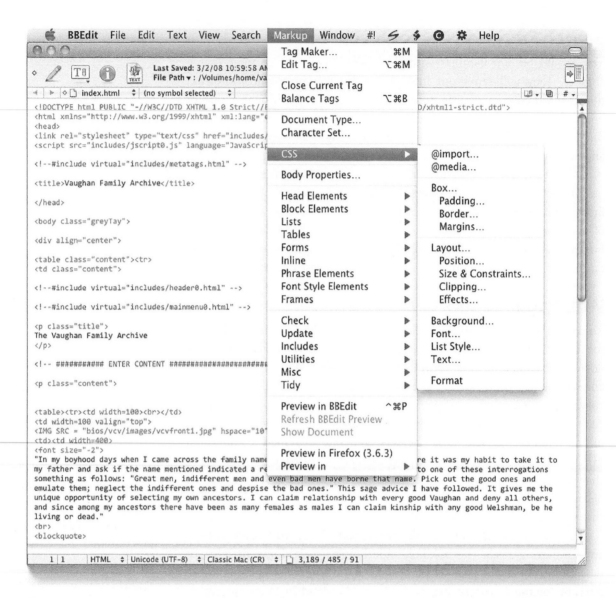

Figure 11-1 BBEdit is a professional programmer's text editor with dedicated features for web page development.

Most web browsers allow you to read the HTML code behind the page you are viewing. In Google Chrome, click the menu icon in the upper-right corner and choose Tools | View Source. In Internet Explorer, choose View | Source. In Firefox, choose Tools | Web Developer | Page Source. In Safari, choose Develop | Show Page Source.

TIP *For tools that add power to HTML pages see:*
www.asp.net
www.adobe.com/products/coldfusion
www.php.net

HTML translators are built into many word processing programs, so you can export a word-processed document with its text styles and layout converted to HTML tags for headers, bolding, underlining, indenting, and so on. Some HTML translators are more powerful than others. These work well for simple text documents but tend to choke on powerful HTML features such as tables, forms, frames, and other extensions. Dedicated editors are usually **WYSIWYG (What You See Is What You Get)** word processors, and they provide more power and more features specifically geared to exploiting HTML. Microsoft Word, for example, automatically opens web pages in a WYSIWYG view. On the downside, these "helpful" features may cause a page with many embedded graphics to load into the word processor very slowly while it interprets and lays out the page as a browser would, instead of just loading the text of the page's HTML code and letting you change a few tags or lines.

First Person

When I was 16, my grandmother loaned me $500 so I could buy my first car. It was a lovely, previously owned, British racing green 1950 MG-TD, happiest doing about 45 miles per hour on tree-lined summer roads in New England. When you hinged up the hood sideways, everything inside was simple and well defined; there was plenty of room to tweak the twin SU carburetors, adjust the distributor, and replace simple parts like the electric fuel pump. I even took the tiny four-cylinder engine entirely out and replaced the shell bearings on the crankshaft. A decade later, with my previously owned 1960 Ford pickup, it was the same—replacing the radiator or changing the starter motor was a piece of cake, and there was plenty of room to work on the engine. But then automobiles got complicated. It started with elaborate emission control systems, then electronic ignitions, then air conditioning, and finally, computers. Opening the hood of a car today, most of us can only stare dumbly at the myriad hoses and wires and color-coded containers for special fluids; and it's so compact a fit, you can't slip a screwdriver between the engine and the fire wall. When the "check engine" light comes on, an expert needs to "pull" the computer codes with a special, expensive reader to see what's wrong.

Writing HTML for the Web today is still simple. But unless you are an expert, you might be staring dumbly at the complex source code created by a new generation of high-powered, special web tools that will deliver mind-boggling multimedia pages built—no muss, no fuss—with simple drag and drop. But like my car today, which is happiest at 70 miles per hour and could cruise at twice that, these HTML engines won't let you do much under the hood without special tools and knowledge.

Among the many tools in this emerging marketplace, InDesign from Adobe saves pages as HTML documents and as **Adobe Acrobat PDF** files. JustSystems' XMetal imports and converts files created in Word, WordPerfect, and other word processors. It has a point-and-click interface for inserting valid HTML tags and elements and provides an enhanced URL editor to manage references and calls to other documents and files. **Adobe Dreamweaver** is a WYSIWYG editor that lets you create and edit text pages, import images, and link to other documents, and offers enhanced integration with Acrobat PDF files. Dreamweaver has become the most popular WYSIWYG HTML editor today.

Managing and maintaining a web site is a serious undertaking when the site contains many thousands of text documents, images, and other resources. Software and expert system tools for automated web page development, document management, and site activity analysis are becoming widely available. Combined with page builders and multimedia editors, these applications will evolve into the ubiquitous "word processors" of the new information age, essential to every home and office with outreach to the Web, and able to integrate and present all the elements of multimedia.

Content Management Systems (CMSs) combine the power and flexibility of a database with the dynamic capabilities of a programming language. Most CMSs are built on a combination of mySQL and PHP. Here's how it works: when a server receives a request for a web page, it looks through that page's code to see if there are any PHP directives to retrieve data from a database. If it finds such a request, it opens the proper database, grabs the data, and inserts it into the web page as programmed.

CMSs offer prepackaged templates of pages with PHP code built in. Open-source Joomla, one of the most popular CMSs, is used in thousands of web sites, large and small. Drupal is another popular, powerful CMS. Concrete5 combines powerful AJAX technology to allow a more interactive experience. CMSs let non-technical computer users add and edit the content of the pages and manage the presentation and ordering of pages at a web site.

Plug-ins and Delivery Vehicles

Plug-ins, **add-ons**, and **extensions** add the power of multimedia to web browsers by allowing users to view and interact with new types of documents and images. **Helper applications**, or **players**, also provide multimedia power by displaying or running files downloaded from the Internet by your browser, but helpers are not seamlessly integrated into the operation of the browser itself. When an unrecognized embedded media type that can't be displayed within your browser is called from an HTML document (sounds, movies, unusual text or image files), most browsers will automatically launch a helper application (if it is specified in the browser's preferences) to view or run it. However, this helper typically starts up and runs separately from the browser.

Many plug-ins are designed to perform special tasks not available without the plug-in installed. If you land on a web page containing embedded, compressed images, for example, and the proper plug-in to decompress those images is not installed, you will not be able to view the images.

Designers work around this problem by including hyperlinks in their pages, which direct the user to the site where the missing plug-in may be found. Users must then download and install the required plug-in, and then restart their browsers. This is all a bit cumbersome. Until the marketplace determines which plug-ins will become de facto standards for the Web, however, developers have no alternative. Because downloading and installing plug-ins is perceived as a hassle for the end user, many tool developers use the Java and JavaScript capabilities already built into today's web browsers. To offer a plug-in's functionality to visitors at your own web site, you may need the addition of MIME-type information to a special setup file on your server that many plug-ins require. If you do not control or operate your own server, you should let your service provider know the MIME-types (media types) that you need to have supported. Setting up servers for some of the multimedia plug-ins is not a trivial task, and many Internet service providers will not support high-bandwidth data streams for fear of overwhelming their Internet connection by serving your streaming voice or video to the world. Indeed, while a plug-in or a player may be free and readily available to anyone who wishes it, the software to actually build, compress, manipulate, and serve the special data (such as for compressed images, compressed audio, streaming video, animations, and VRML worlds) may be difficult and expensive, since the company makes money from the development tool, not the client software.

Text

Text and document plug-ins such as the popular **Adobe Acrobat Reader** get you past the display limitations of HTML and web browsers, where fonts are dependent on end users' preferences and page layout is primitive. In file formats provided by Adobe Acrobat, for example, special fonts and graphic images are embedded as data into the file and travel with it, so what you see when you view that file is precisely what the document's maker intended.

Images

Browsers enabled for HTML5 will read and display bitmapped JPEG, GIF, and PNG image files as well as **Scalable Vector Graphics (SVG)** files. Vector files are a mathematical description of the lines, curves, fills, and patterns needed to draw a picture, and while they typically do not provide the rich detail found in bitmaps, they are smaller and can be scaled without image degradation. Plug-ins to enable viewing of vector formats (such as Flash) are useful, particularly when some provide high-octane compression schemes to dramatically shrink file size and shorten the time spent downloading and displaying them. File size and compression sound a recurring theme on the Internet, where data-rich images, movies, and sounds may take many seconds, minutes, or even longer to reach the end user.

Vector graphics are also **device-independent**, in that the image is always displayed at the correct size and with the maximum number of colors supported by the computer. Unlike bitmapped files, a single vector file can be downloaded, cached, and then displayed multiple times at different scaled sizes on the same or a different web page.

Sound

Sound over the Web is managed in a few different ways. Digitized sound files in various common formats such as MP3, WAV, AIF, or AU may be sent to your computer and then played, either as they are being received (**streaming** playback) or once they are fully downloaded (using a player). MIDI files may also be received and played; as discussed in Chapter 4, these files are more compact, but they depend upon your computer's MIDI setup for quality. Speech files can be specially encoded into a **token language** (a "shorthand" description of the speech components) and sent at great speed to another computer to be un-tokenized and played back in a variety of voices. Sounds may be embedded into QuickTime, Windows Media, and MPEG movie files. Some sounds can be **multicast** (using the multicast IP protocols for the Internet specified in RFC 1112), so multiple users can simultaneously listen to the same data streams without duplication of data across the Internet. Web-based (VoIP, or Voice over Internet Protocol) telephones also transmit data packets containing sound information.

Animation, Video, and Presentation

The most data-intense multimedia elements to travel the Internet are **video streams** containing both images and synchronized sound, and commonly packaged as Apple's QuickTime, Microsoft's Video for Windows (AVI), and MPEG files. Also data rich are the files for proprietary formats such as Keynote, **Microsoft PowerPoint**, and other presentation applications. In all cases, the trade-offs between bandwidth and quality are constantly in your face when designing, developing, and delivering animations or motion video for the Web.

Beyond HTML

When an ingot of pure silicon is "pulled" from a furnace, the process begins with a "seed crystal," around which the ingot forms. HTML is the seed crystal that is shaping and forming the nature of multimedia on the World Wide Web as it extrudes itself onto the Internet's data highway. Within the latticework of HTML servers and browsers, tags such as <object> (browser-specific for Internet Explorer) or <embed> (browser-specific for Firefox) enable text, sound, images, animations, and motion video across the Web. Hooks for powerful platform-independent Java applets and JavaScripts are built into most browsers, so you can design local interaction and activities without a lot of communication between client- and server-based **Common Gateway Interface (CGI)** programming. CGI is a standard for interfacing external applications with information servers, such as HTTP or web servers, and CGI programs can be written in C/C++, Fortran, Perl, TCL, a Unix shell, Visual Basic, or even AppleScript, as long as the language is supported by the server platform.

The following is an example of the combined <object> and <embed> tags used to display a Flash movie in both the Internet Explorer and Firefox browsers. A browser will only act on a tag it understands, ignoring tags it does not recognize (see http://helpx.adobe.com/flash/kb/flash-object-embed-tag-attributes.html).

```
<object classid="clsid:D27CDB6E-AE6D-11cf-96B8-444553540000"
codebase="http://download.macromedia.com/pub/shockwave/cabs/flash/swflash.cab#version=6,0,40,0"
width="550" height ="400" id="myMovieName">
<param name=movie value="myFlashMovie.swf">
<param name=quality value=high>
<param name=bgcolor value=#FFFFFF>
<embed href="/support/flash/ts/documents/myFlashMovie.swf" quality=high bgcolor=#FFFFFF
width ="550" height="400"
name="myMovieName" align="" type="application/x-shockwave-flash"
pluginspage="http://www.macromedia.com/go/getflashplayer">
</embed>
</object>
```

Another work-around is to determine if the browser requesting the object is Internet Explorer and, if so, to provide the appropriate parameters (see http://helpx.adobe.com/flash/kb/object-tag-syntax-flash-professional.html).

```
<object classid="clsid:d27cdb6e-ae6d-11cf-96b8-444553540000"
    width="550" height="400" id="movie_name" align="middle">
<param name="movie" value="movie_name.swf"/>
    <!--[if !IE]>-->
    <object type="application/x-shockwave-flash" data="movie_name.swf" width="550"
height="400">
        <param name="movie" value="movie_name.swf"/>
    <!--<![endif]-->
        <a href="http://www.adobe.com/go/getflash">
            <img src="http://www.adobe.com/images/shared/download_buttons/get_flash_player.
gif" alt="Get Adobe Flash player"/>
        </a>
    <!--[if !IE]>-->
    </object>
    <!--<![endif]-->
</object>
```

3-D Worlds

Three-dimensional environments and experiences on the Web are now possible with Intel's Internet 3-D Graphics hardware using software such as Second Life, papervision3d within Flash, Flash, and **Adobe Director** for development and the Shockwave player for delivery. These have supplanted VRML (Virtual Reality Modeling Language) as an independent environment specifically designed to handle high-performance 3-D worlds containing 3-D text and images, textures, animations, morphs, multiple viewpoints, collision detection, gravity, sounds, and all the arcade elements associated with full-bore game action. With claims that well-executed interactive 3-D content can make nearly any web site more compelling and effective and can better attract, engage, and inform, Intel's algorithms and Adobe's delivery system allow 3-D content to be automatically scaled and tailored to each user's system and available bandwidth. Spinning off from a foundation of vector graphics and animation, 3-D renderings and creative whole worlds present only the latest of multimedia challenges and learning curves for web developers. As this 3-D technology becomes refined and end-user bandwidth increases during the coming years, the very shape of web pages will be altered forever.

TIP   *See the following sites for more information about 3-D tools and technology:*
www.adobe.com/products/director/3d/3dservices
www.autodesk.com/suites/entertainment-creation-suite
www.havok.com
www.maxon.net
www.newtek.com
www.nvidia.com
www.softimage.com

First Person

When I received a press release from Alternate Realities Corporation, a small startup company spun out of a large research effort in North Carolina, I was intrigued. ARC's president, David Bennett, claimed, "We are redefining Virtual Reality!" He went on to describe "a new generation virtual environment that is a 3-D, immersive, full-color, interactive system enclosed in a 16-foot dome or sphere that can be either portable (inflatable or interlocking) or permanent. The system includes a 360-degree projection system with a 180-degree field of view. Imagine a 16-foot helmet that fits over 15 people at the same time and is nonrestrictive! Larger units (in the 24-foot and up range) are in the early development stage."

I knew I had to have one for my experiments with VRML! The 5-meter model, which fits in a 20×20–foot trade-show booth space, was available for $280,000, and the 7-meter model, perfect for my backyard, was only slightly more, at $340,000.

Developing for the Web

In 2001, there were more than 2,000 published books with the word "Internet" in their title. In 2003, there were more than 6,000. In 2006, that number increased to more than 10,000, and in 2010, to more than 42,380. In 2014, there are more than 59,540 books with the word "Internet" in their title!

This section introduces you to basic ways you can put the elements of multimedia onto a web page. You will learn how to use HTML tags with CSS styles rather than rely entirely on web page builders and WYSIWYG editors that never expect you to look under the hood.

As mentioned earlier in the chapter, all modern browsers allow you to examine the HTML code. Look for a menu item such as View Source (refer to "Web Page Makers and Site Builders" for more specific instructions for individual browsers). Use this feature to dig around in the source HTML code of web sites to see how the page is laid out. As you explore, you will discover that some code is neat and clear, some has plenty of embedded descriptive comments, and some is a mess of what programmers call "spaghetti" code.

HTML Is a Markup Language

You should have a basic understanding of HTML and CSS before you begin developing multimedia for the Web. HTML-coded documents, which are the fundamental vehicles for all types of information delivered on the World Wide Web, are explained in Chapter 11, but for this chapter you need to understand the basics of how HTML works.

HTML stands for Hypertext Markup Language. The "Markup Language" part of the name means that tags are used to do such things as format text and embed media. The tags are enclosed by angled brackets: <>. Some tags are bounding tags, requiring both an opening tag and a closing tag. The closing tag is indicated by a leading forward slash inside the angled brackets. This example for bolded text illustrates the use of the two tags:

```
<strong>This text is emphasized</strong>
```

Other tags, such as the tag for inserting an inline image, stand by themselves:

```
<img src="grey_ball.gif">
```

Note that the tags may be written in either upper- or lowercase, although lowercase is preferred by pros; some HTML text editing programs have a switch allowing you to select the case in which you want the tags written in your document. With each version of HTML, some tags have been discontinued or **deprecated**: tags such as <font> or <center> are no longer supported in the HTML standard, yet their use continues to be supported by most browsers.

The Desktop Workspace

Make your web pages look good on a 1024×768 display in true color (millions). Working at this resolution, you will satisfy more than 95 percent of all desktop viewers. Depending upon the browser and preferences set by the user, however, the area of the screen available for your web page, called the **viewport**, will always be less than the full display, and it is not controllable by the designer. Browser "**chrome**" (toolbars and other shiny stuff around the edges of your page's viewport) can be either hidden or shown by the user. If you want to maximize the browser active window size, in Internet Explorer press F11 (function key 11), and go back to regular mode by clicking the mouse; other browsers offer Full Screen toggle switches in the View menu options. So design your web page for a 1,024-pixel-wide display by using tables and images that do not exceed about 1,000 pixels across the page, and you will have room for browser scroll bars. Many designers choose a viewport workspace 960 pixels wide—a number divisible by 3, 4, 5, 6, 8, 10, 12, 15, and 16, making many logical "grid systems" of columns possible.

The Mobile Workspace

Under the hood of many browsers is a layout engine for rendering pages. Versions of those browser engines have been customized to run on small devices such as tablets, e-readers, netbooks, PDAs, and smartphones, and they follow known rules when laying out web pages for smaller viewports. Microsoft Internet Explorer uses the Trident engine; Firefox uses the Gecko engine; Opera uses the Presto engine; and Apple's Safari and Google's Chrome use the WebKit engine. Smartphones use various operating systems: Android, iPhone OS, Linux, Maemo, Palm WebOS, RIM's BlackBerry, Symbian OS, and Windows Phone 8.

To deal with the multiplicity of viewport sizes in the small-device world (320×480, 240×320, 240×400, 854×480, etc.), the Android OS allows programmers to write one application that flexibly covers all display sizes by using virtual **density-independent pixels (dips)**:

> The density-independent pixel is equivalent to one physical pixel on a 160 dpi screen, which is the baseline density assumed by the system for a "medium" density screen. At runtime, the system transparently handles any scaling of the dp units, as necessary, based on the actual density of the screen in use. The conversion of dp units to screen pixels is simple: `px = dp * (dpi / 160)`. For example, on a 240 dpi screen, 1 dp equals 1.5 physical pixels. You should always use dp units when defining your application's UI, to ensure proper display of your UI on screens with different densities.
>
> From the Android "Best Practices" API Guide, http://developer.android.com/guide/practices/screens_support.html

While HTML and CSS do not provide for device independence, if you expect that your project will be widely viewed on small devices, consider designing at 960 pixels to allow the device's browser the most flexibility. Moreover, you should keep in mind that input events on small devices are different from the clicks and drags of a computer with mouse or touchpad: a **double tap** makes the browser zoom in and center on a document; a **touch and hold** will display an information bubble; a **drag** will move the viewport or pan; a **flick** will scroll up or down; and a **pinch open** or **pinch closed** will zoom in or out. There are no mouseOver events without a mouse. Designing for mobile devices is covered in detail in Chapter 12.

Nibbling

A principle you must always keep in mind when designing and making multimedia elements for the Web and particularly for hand-held devices should be called "nibbling." At a serious metal-working supply store, you can buy a power tool called a nibbler—it devours the edges of sheet metal in an ear-damaging staccato of rapid tiny bites. You must apply this concept, for example, to the elegant bitmapped logo you created in Photoshop when you trim it from 24- to 8- to 4-bit color depth and resize it from 96 pixels square to 64 pixels square and create a transparent .png file. Nibble the audio clip of your client's theme song from 44.1 kHz to 11 kHz, and see if it's acceptable at an 8-bit sample size. Text as HTML is cheap: nibble your page design and throw away the pretty shadowed GIF graphic headers and image maps—re-create your text in HTML headers or emphasized text, and try coloring it. Put on your protective headgear—this compromising work is painful for you as the creator—and start nibbling, while constantly seeking a balance between quality and the patience of a user who is downloading your material at 56 Kbps from home. Every choice you make should be tempered by bandwidth worry.

WARNING   *For every image file referenced in an HTML document, a separate Internet HTTP connection must be made between your computer and that image's server before the image itself is downloaded; so using many different tiny images (such as various graphic images for bullets) may not be efficient. After a user has downloaded a file once, however, it should load more quickly from the user's local hard disk, where the browser stores all the images in a cache.*

Text for the Web

In addition to variations in the size of the viewport, browsers used by viewers of your web site may not be displaying the same "preferred" font that you used to design your page, because user preferences in the browsers may alter the way text in your document looks and flows. To make the best of this uncertainty, many developers design their documents in Times Roman for the proportional serif font, Verdana for proportional sans serif, and Courier as the monospaced font. These fonts readily move across platforms and are the default fonts users typically see if they do not set their own preferences. Although you can specify a font, and even alternate fonts, using CSS, a browser can use a specified font only if that font is installed on the end user's computer. Figure 2-3 in Chapter 2 shows a list of the most commonly installed fonts on Windows, Mac, and Linux computers. It is also possible to use a font that is hosted in the cloud. For example, Google Fonts allows you to build a collection of fonts from Google's extensive libraries and link the fonts for use in your HTML page (see www.google.com/fonts for more).

NOTE   *If you wish to absolutely control the look of text on your web page, you must use a graphic bitmap rather than text in your HTML document. Adding images in place of text, however, increases the amount of time necessary to download your page. Embedding graphics into HTML documents is explained later in this chapter.*

You can tag text so that it is displayed as a header, strong, emphasized, or sub- or superscripted. Using CSS, you can specify your "preference" for font face and many text attributes (see Chapter 2), but the viewer's browser ultimately determines if and how these styles are displayed.

The following HTML and CSS code sets up a screen with flowing text (see Figure 11-2). It also includes a background image, a portrait

Figure 11-2   Images, text, and sound can be mixed in an HTML document. Note the use of escape sequences for special characters and an image map for navigation.

image, and an image map that is used for navigation. (Background images and image maps are described later in this chapter.) This document also contains the foreign language special character *ä*, which is called out in the document using HTML's escape sequence for special characters, in this case, "ä". An **escape sequence** begins with an ampersand and ends with a semicolon. Also, note the link to a separate style sheet file holding the CSS code. A MIDI file is embedded in this page to provide background music.

```
<html>
<head>
<title>Annan Lapsuus</title>
<link rel="stylesheet" type="text/css" href="anna.css">
</head>
<body>
<img src="anna.jpg" align="left">
<br>
<h1>Annan Lapsuus</h1>
<p class="annaText">
Min&auml; sain oman huoneen. Sen sein&auml;t on maalattu vihreiksi. Ja yhdelle
sein&auml;lle on maalattu maisema. Mutta joelle ei maalattu joutsenia, koska min&auml; en
halunnut. Niihin voi kyll&auml;sty&auml;niin helposti.
<br><br>
Isi on tehnyt minulle kirjahyllyn. Min&auml; j&auml;rjest&auml;n siihen kaikki tavarat.
Kiiltokuva-albumit ja kirjan. Sen nimi on "Tiina saa suukon". Vaikka on minulla muitakin
kirjoja, mutta en min&auml; en&auml;&auml; sellaisia lastenkirjoja lue.
<br><br>
"T&auml;st&auml; l&auml;htien minun huoneeni on aina hyv&auml;ss&auml;
j&auml;rjestyksess&auml;", sanoin isille.
<br><br>
<img src="navButton.gif" usemap="#thispagemap">
<br>
Isi hymyili.
<br>
<!-- Use image map for click navigation -->
<map name="thispagemap">
<area shape="circle" coords="48,48,12" href="fhelp.htm">
<area shape="polygon" coords="50,50,0,0,100,0" href="fnavmap.htm">
<area shape="polygon" coords="50,50,0,100,100,100" href="f03.htm">
</map>
<!-- play MIDI file on this page -->
<embed src="03/pianobg.mid" width="0" height="2" autostart="true">
</body>
</html>
```

And the following is the accompanying CSS code:

```
body {
    background-image: url(earth.jpg);
    }
h1 {
    font-family: "Lucida Grande", "Trebuchet MS",  Verdana, Helvetica, sans-serif;
    color: #FFFFFF;
    font-size : 24px;
    font-weight: bold;
    }
p.annaText {
    font-family: "Lucida Grande", "Trebuchet MS",  Verdana, Helvetica, sans-serif;
    color: #FFFFFF;
    font-size : 14px;
    font-weight : bold;
    line-height : 18px;
    text-align: left;
    padding-right: 20px;
    }
```

Images for the Web

Theoretically, the Web can support any graphics format the client and server have in common. Practically, even though web standards do not specify a graphics format you must use, browsers recognize four image formats—GIF, PNG, JPEG, and SVG—without resorting to special plug-ins. These formats use built-in **compression algorithms** to reduce file size. (Graphic image formats are described in detail in Chapter 3.) For other graphics formats, such as CGM, CMX, DXF, and fractal- and wavelet-compressed images, special proprietary creation software and browser plug-ins may be required.

GIF and PNG Images

GIF images (Graphic Interchange File, also discussed in Chapter 3) are limited to 8 bits of color depth (256 colors). This is a commercial image format developed by CompuServe Information Services, an online company once owned by Unisys and currently folded into America Online. In late 1994, Unisys announced a patent fee charge to all software developers who use the GIF format. In an angry, industry-wide response, **PNG** (for Portable Network Graphics Specification) was developed as a new "open" format (not requiring fees) to replace GIF. By allowing transparency by single pixel or by alpha channel mask and a 24-bit indexed palette, the PNG format is an improvement on the GIF format it was intended to replace. But it does not support animation. And because it only uses the RGB color model (not CMYK), PNG images may not print well.

First Person

A few years ago somebody told me about an interesting web survey: how does the world pronounce GIF? The results turned out about 50/50 on the hard/soft question, my colleague claimed. Then I spent considerable time using that word (softly) in Europe before realizing everybody was being smirkingly polite about my outlandish pronunciation. In the San Francisco Bay Area, a world center for multimedia development, GIF has the soft "g" of "ginger," "gin," and "gybe." In New York, where little is soft, and in Europe, GIF has a more cutting, hard pronunciation, as in "giggling," "gingham," "girdled," "guilty," or "girls." The real question is whether the written word requires a prefixed dot.

JPEG Images

JPEG (Joint Photographic Experts Group) images may contain 24 bits of color depth (millions of colors). JPEG uses a powerful but **lossy** compression method that produces files as much as ten times more compressed than GIF. Lossy means that information in the original image is lost in the compression process and cannot be retrieved. A **lossless** compression method does not irretrievably discard the original data.

WARNING *Do not edit and reedit files that are in JPEG format. Every time you open a JPEG image and edit it, then recompress and save it as a compressed JPEG, the image degrades. After a few editing/saving cycles, you will be very disappointed. Edit and archive your images in a 24-bit lossless graphic format (such as TIFF, BMP, or PSD), then convert to JPEG (if you need to).*

The JPEG compression scheme compresses about 20:1 before visible image degradation occurs. Test the amount of compression acceptable for your JPEG image; stay inside the "threshold of visible error." To compress an image with JPEG, the image is divided into 8×8–pixel blocks, and the resulting 64 pixels (called a "search range") are mathematically described relative to the characteristic of the pixel in the upper-left corner. The binary description of this relationship requires far less than 64 pixels, so more information can be squeezed into less space. JPEG compresses slowly, about one to three seconds for a 1MB image, depending upon computer speed, but JPEG can compress images as much as 75:1, with loss.

GIF or JPEG?

Use JPEG for photorealistic images containing many colors, and avoid using it for images already forced into a 256-color palette or for line drawings or 1-bit black-and-white images. GIF compresses drawings and

Figure 11-3 Both images at the top were saved in the JPEG format, which compresses image data and trades image quality for small file size. The resulting compressed images at the bottom show the "lossy" and "blocky" nature of compressed JPEGs. The photo at top left is 71K in size when saved as a GIF (not shown) and only 27K saved as a JPEG (bottom left). The drawing at top right is 17K when saved as a GIF (not shown) and 46K as a JPEG (bottom right).

cartoons that have only a few colors in them much better than JPEG, which may introduce visible defects—sharp edges and lines that blur—especially with small-size text. Figures 11-3 and 11-4 show the "blocky" and "lossy" nature of the compressed JPEG images. For the Web, use the JPEG format for photorealistic images that are busy with color; use the GIF format for line art and drawings where there are large areas of the same color.

Using Photoshop

Adobe's Photoshop is the "tool of choice" for most graphic artists, so it is worth taking some time to provide a few suggestions for creating images for use on the World Wide Web. If you use a different image-editing application, follow the same logic and use the commands appropriate for that application. Always work in native Photoshop format using PSD files—these images are typically in RGB mode and use the maximum color depth. They are larger, but they contain more information that can be usefully processed when resizing and

Figure 11-4 Lossy compression schemes save disk space but can also degrade an image. For the Web, line art is often better saved in GIF, PNG, or SVG format than in JPEG.

dithering, and you will get better final results. PSD files also contain layers, a very useful application feature. When creating images for display on a web page, use 72 pixels per inch resolution, which is the resolution of most monitors. When you convert a 24-bit RGB image to an 8-bit indexed image (change its mode), you lose huge amounts of color information that cannot be retrieved, meaning that the fine data is gone forever. So you should follow two practices in order to protect your original image. One is to save the original image in a 24-bit lossless image format (such as PSD, TIFF, or BMP). The other is to do all of your image manipulation (such as resizing, sharpening, and hue adjustments) in RGB mode. Next, save this source image in RGB mode as a PSD file, before reducing the color palette by saving it as a GIF or using a lossy compression like JPEG. By saving the high-quality original and saving the manipulated image in the program's native format, you can return to them if you need to make changes later.

TIP   *When you scan an image, the scanner will often default to print resolution of 300 dpi. When displayed on a 72-dpi resolution monitor, the picture will be displayed more than three times bigger than the original. Never fix this problem by changing the height and width attributes of the <img> tag. Even though this will display the image at the size you want, you still have a huge image file that will slow down the downloading and display of your page. Instead, use Photoshop or another image-editing program to resample the image at a 72-dpi resolution, and use that new image on your page. The same could be said for images sent by e-mail where large size/resolution is not required.*

When you are satisfied with your image and ready to save it as a GIF, PNG, or JPEG file, archive it as described earlier. If you make any mistakes while converting modes or saving, you will still have the original, complete with any layers you might have used. To be very safe, duplicate the original file and open the copy before saving to other formats.

Saving as JPEG Files

To save your image as a JPEG file, you do not need to change Photoshop's mode from RGB, but if you are using layers, you will need to "flatten" the image, merging all layers into a single bitmap. Once an image is flattened and you have edited or saved it, its layers cannot be remade without a great deal of difficult cutting and pasting—so again, archive your original file! You must name your file with the extension .jpg or .jpeg if you will use it on the Web. Then click Save, and choose Maximum, High, Medium, or Low-quality compression in the dialog box that appears. Your file is ready for the Web.

Saving as GIF Files

To save a GIF file using Photoshop, you must first set the mode of your image to Indexed Color, converting it to the best 8-bit palette (256 colors) that will represent the image and be displayed well by web browsers. Note that the option of saving a Photoshop 24-bit RGB file in GIF format will not be available in Windows, and it will be grayed out on the Mac menu until you have converted your image to 8-bit mode: GIF is only for 8-bit images.

TIP   Use GIF files for line art and images that contain large areas of the same color (that can be easily compressed). Use JPEG for photorealistic images.

Palettes   When you change the mode to Indexed Color, you must specify the color depth of the converted image, the color palette to be used, and whether the colors of your image should be dithered (Diffusion or Pattern) or not (None). Figure 11-5 shows the mode-changing dialog box from Photoshop, where the adaptive palette has been selected.

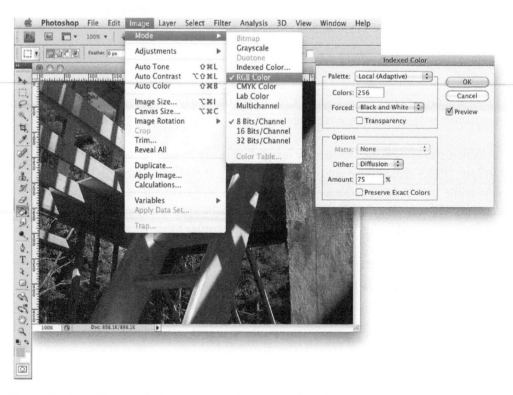

Figure 11-5   In Photoshop, changing the mode of your image from RGB Color to Indexed Color changes the color depth of your image.

Interlaced and Progressive Scans   Both GIF and JPEG images can be saved so that when your browser displays the image as it is being downloaded, you can immediately see a chunky approximation of the final image, with resolution improving as more and more data comes in. While in baseline, or normal configuration, image data is stored as a single top-to-bottom scan; in **interlaced** GIF and **progressive** JPEG files, the data is organized in a different sequence within the file. An interlaced GIF file, for example, is arranged into a series of four passes:

Pass 1: Every 8th row, starting with row 0

Pass 2: Every 8th row, starting with row 4

Pass 3: Every 4th row, starting with row 2

Pass 4: Every 2nd row, starting with row 1

Figure 11-6 shows Photoshop's Save for Web & Devices dialog for saving an image as interlaced, and four increasingly resolved images.

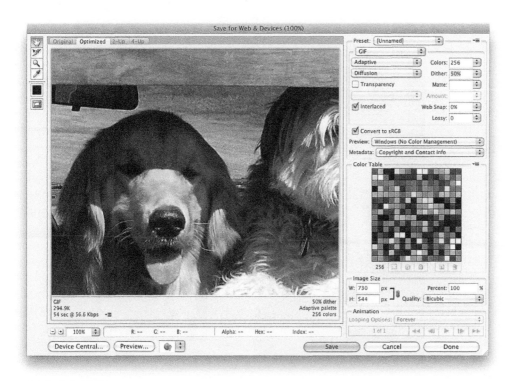

Figure 11-6   Interlacing settings when exporting a GIF89a file from Photoshop. With interlacing, the image incrementally improves its resolution as it downloads.

Transparency The GIF89a and PNG specifications allow for **transparency**: you can save your file with instructions to a browser to use a specific color or palette of colors (with PNG) as your selected transparency color. In many cases, such as for company logos and inline illustrations, it is attractive to let an image float on top of the browser's background.

Images on web pages are displayed as rectangles. The area outside of the circle in Figure 11-7 is filled with a wash of color and would (without transparency) be displayed as a rectangle showing those colors to its edges. To make the part surrounding the circle transparent so that the circle floats on your web page, fill the area outside the circle with a single color, and then save the file, selecting that fill color to be transparent. While white is often used as the transparency color, in this example it would not work because there are white pixels inside of the circle that would also become transparent. Use a fill color not in the area you wish to show; in this case red works. Most image-editing tools provide a palette from which you can select the transparency index color. You cannot make a JPEG file transparent.

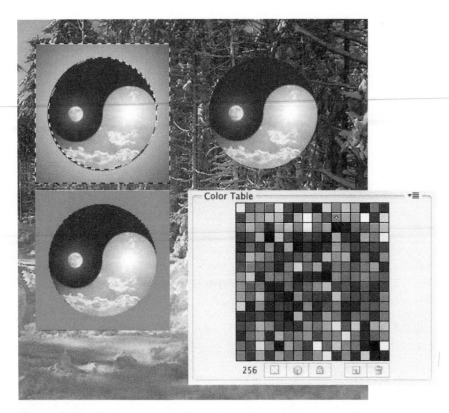

Figure 11-7 Use a transparent GIF or PNG to float a circle or other image on a web page: select the area outside of the circle (upper left), fill it with a single indexed color (red, lower left), choose that color to be transparent (lower right), and save the image as a GIF file. The circle will float on your page (upper right).

Backgrounds

Most browsers allow you to specify an image or color to place in the background of your page or into table cells. Text and images will float on top of this layer.

Background Coloring

You can choose colors for backgrounds, text, and anchors to URL links. Color controls for the entire page are attributes of the **<body> tag** and are set using CSS:

```
body {background-color: #0000FF;}
```

where #0000FF is a hexadecimal red-green-blue (RGB) triplet used to specify the background color, in this case, blue.

Once you have chosen a background color, you will then want to set the color of your text and establish proper contrasts. Red on green shimmers, while black on black is invisible. By setting styles in the <body> tag, you set default styles for the entire document. For white text on a blue background, the CSS code would be:

```
body {color: #FFFFFF;}
```

Background Images

Background images are by default tiled, or repeated, across and down the page until the page or page element is filled, so a randomly distributed "sandy" background image (see Figure 11-8) can easily be made from a very small source image (illustration at right).

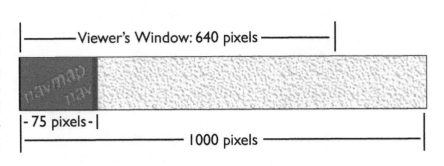

Load a background image into a document by specifying its URL (if it is available somewhere on the Web) or its relative file path (if it is on the same server as the page) in the CSS attributes for the <body> tag; for example:

```
body {background-image: url('paper.gif');}
```

TIP *It is a good idea to specify a background color similar to the prevailing color of the image being used for a background. If the user viewing your page has Image Loading turned off, or if your background image cannot be found for some reason, the page may still look close to the way you designed it. If the image you specify as a background has transparent areas, the background color will show through.*

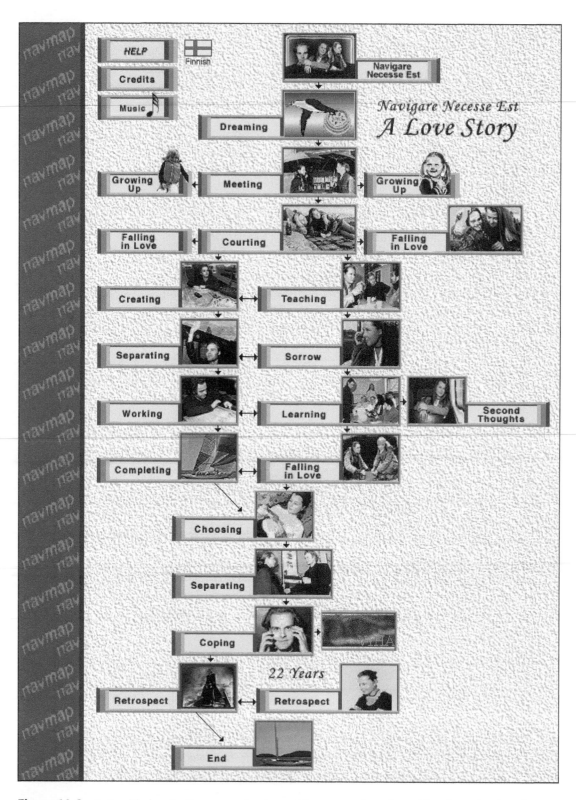

Figure 11-8 A simplified navigation map not only provides an overview of a multimedia project but also contains active links to documents using "hot" areas of the graphic. This is the navmap page from Navigare Necesse Est, a student-built love story.

Sidebars

In the navigation map shown in Figure 11-8, a commonly seen graphic layout was used: a vertical bar containing the word "navmap" is displayed at the left of the screen and in the background. When users scroll up or down, this bar remains stationary. Make the graphic bar at the left as wide as you wish (say 75 pixels); then set the full width of your image to 1,000 pixels. Fill the space to the right of your bar with plain color or a texture. When this background image repeats itself (tiles), it will repeat to the right only if the user widens the viewing window to more than 1,000 pixels; but the image will tile vertically in increments of its height until it reaches the bottom of the window. With CSS you can force the browser to repeat only vertically, only horizontally, or not at all. In this example, adding *background-repeat: repeat-y;* to your CSS code will allow repeats only vertically, even when the window is made wider than 1,000 pixels.

Clickable Buttons

There are three ways to make a graphic image "clickable" so that it links to another document. You can simply include the **<img> tag** inside the bounding tags of an HTML anchor that points to that document's URL:

```
<a href="documentToGoTo.html">
<img src="greenButton.gif">
</a>
```

You can also use the **<a> tag** to provide a link to a larger graphic or even to a video clip from a small, thumbnail-sized image:

```
<a href="bigPicture.jpg"><img src="thumbnail.gif"></a>
```

A second way to make a clickable image is to use the **<button> tag**:

```
<button onClick="window.location='http://www.amazon.com'">
<img src=" thumbnail.gif ">
</button>
```

A third method for creating a clickable button uses the <input> tag found in forms, but is limited to text:

```
<form action="somescript.php">
<input type="image" name="submitimage" src="madre.jpg">
</form>
```

Client-Side Image Maps

Image maps are pictures with defined hot spots that link to other documents when a user clicks on them. Browsers support client-side image maps so that mouse coordinates and their associated document URLs can be included in an HTML document. This is managed by the **<map> tag** and the **usemap attribute** of the <img> tag.

To make a client-side image map with USEMAP, you need three things: an image, a list of coordinates designating hot spots on the image, and the document URL associated with each hot spot. To program the image map into your HTML document, you use the usemap attribute of the <img> tag. Here is the HTML code for the navigation button shown earlier in Figure 11-2 and detailed in Figure 11-9:

```
<img src="compas.gif"usemap="#compass">
<map name="compass">
  <area shape="circle" coords="60,60,10" href="help.htm">
  <area shape="polygon" coords="60,60,0,0,120,0" href="back.htm">
  <area shape="polygon" coords="60,60,0,120,120,120" href="forward.htm">
  <area shape="polygon" coords="60,60,0,0,0,120" href="navmap.htm">
</map>
```

Compas.gif is the transparent image. The usemap="#compass" attribute points to the <map> extension tag that contains the coordinates and URLs. (The pound sign means the <map> tag is located in this same document.) A <map> segment may be placed anywhere in the body of the HTML document and is related to the correct image by the name="xxxxxxx" attribute of the <map> tag. You can have more than one image map in an HTML document, but they must have different names.

Within the <map> tag, the <area> tag defines the shape of the hot spot (as a circle, polygon, or rectangle) and anchors or links it to a URL. Areas are defined by x,y coordinates of the pixels in your bitmap: a circle by the x,y coordinates of its center location and radius (60,60,10), a polygon by a sequence of sets of x,y locations that close automatically (60,60,0,0,120,0 defines a triangle), or a rectangle (two x,y locations defining top left and bottom right).

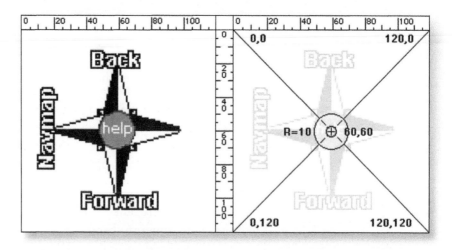

Figure 11-9 This enlarged image illustrates the coordinates used to define hot spots for image maps (the ruler is marked in pixels).

Sound for the Web

In the beginning, when the Internet was primarily a collection of Unix machines, sound files were sent from machine to machine in **AU format** and, when downloaded, were played back using a sound application. As the Web has developed, sound has become more important, and most browsers allow embedding of sounds into documents using the **<audio> tag**. Inside this tag, the **autoplay attribute**, if present, starts the audio playing as soon as it is ready. If **controls** is present, a play/pause control and other controls will be displayed. When **preload** is present, the audio will load when the page does and be ready to run. You can include in the <audio> tag text that will be ignored unless the user's browser cannot understand the <audio> tag:

```
<audio src="LizLaugh.aiff" preload autoplay controls loop>
Sorry, your browser does not support the HTML audio element.
</audio>
```

The <a> anchor tag and <embed> tag can also be used to play sound files:

```
Click <a href="LizLaugh.aiff">here</a> to play sound file.
<embed src="Mozart.mid" autostart="true" loop="false" width="120" height="50" hidden></embed>
```

Chapter 4 describes designing and making MIDI and digitized sound files in detail.

TIP   *Making sound for the Web requires the basic tools and techniques described in Chapter 3. Always nibble at your sound elements and reduce them to the lowest file sizes that will play acceptably. Remember, they will move across the Internet and may be downloaded or played on machines with low-bandwidth connections.*

Animation for the Web

HTML makes no provision for animation, by itself delivering only a static page of text and graphics. Boring, many people said, and programmers went to work devising methods to liven up the view. JavaScript can dynamically change a web page without needing to reload it. JavaScript with XML features combined into **Asynchronous JavaScript and XML (Ajax)** is used for powerful interactive applications such as Google's office suite. The Adobe Flash Player plug-in for browsers offers animation and interaction. HTML5 uses the <canvas> tag to allow two- and three-dimensional drawing to take place within a specified area on a web page under the control of JavaScript. Canvas is particularly useful for creating interactive diagrams.

GIF89a

Browsers implement a little-known animation feature in the final 1989 revision "a" of the GIF file format specification. It is possible to make simple animations by putting multiple images, or frames, into a single GIF89a file and display them with programmable delays (in 100ths of a second) between them.

When you use the <img> tag to embed a GIF89a **multiframe image**, the browser downloads the file and stores it in the cache folder of your local hard disk. Once fully downloaded, the browser plays each frame of the image quickly and smoothly. Limit animated GIFs to small images, and use a more capable plug-in like Flash for animations over larger areas.

Read Chapter 5 to learn the basics of animation. Pick a tool or method and start creating. Lokki, the Shockwaved seagull, was created by a beginner and was flying in just a few hours:

Animation software includes Swish (www.swishzone.com), Flash, Director, After Effects, DHTML, and animated GIF files built using shareware and freeware. Designers must be careful how they use animation though: too much motion and too many flashy colors can cheapen a web site. Subtle animation, however, enhances a site's content and messages.

. . . .

http://webstyleguide.com/wsg2/multimedia/animation.html

http://website.needbeyond.com/templates2.html?flash_intro

www.animationtipsandtricks.com

www.compuphase.com/animtips.htm

For animation styles and tips

. . . .

Video for the Web

To offer a standard method for delivering video to the Web, the HTML5 specification provides a <video> tag, meaning that browsers must contain within themselves the programming code required to recognize a video file, read and decompress both its audio and video components, and play that video on a screen—where and how you, as the designer, specify.

As with the <audio> tag, you can include in the <video> tag text that will be ignored unless the user's browser cannot understand the <video> tag.

```
<video src="myVideo.mpg" preload autoplay controls width="320" height="240">
Sorry, your browser does not support the HTML video element.
</video>
```

There are more than 250 file formats that contain video elements (see www.fileinfo.com/filetypes/video), and there are more than 25 **codecs** from which to choose. And there are many methods and options to capture, compress, edit, store, and distribute video. Introduction of the HTML5 <video> tag is a push in the direction of a standardized few technologies and methodologies that will work for most everyone on the Internet.

The most commonly used codecs are H.264, Theora, and VP8 within MP4, Ogg, and WebM containers. Unfortunately, no one of these will necessarily play in every HTML5-compliant browser. To guarantee playability by all browsers, you may need to encode three separate versions of your video file, including a Flash .flv format as a fallback, and program your HTML <video> tag with all three. The browser will play the first file in the list that it can:

```
<video width="160" height="120" controls autoplay>
<source src="myVideo.mp4" type='video/mp4; codecs="avc1.42E01E, mp4a.40.2"'>
<source src="myVideo.webm" type='video/webm; codecs="vp8, vorbis"'>
<source src="myVideo.ogv" type='video/ogg; codecs="theora, vorbis"'>
<object type="application/x-shockwave-flash" width="160" height="120" wmode="transparent"
data="flvplayer.swf?file=myVideo.flv">
    <param name="movie" value="flvplayer.swf?file=myVideo.flv" />
    <param name="wmode" value="transparent" />
</object>
</video>
```

For more information about making and editing video files, codecs, and distribution methods, see Chapter 6.

Plug-ins and Players

Real animation and programmable power became available to web page developers when Macromedia (prior to its acquisition by Adobe) introduced Shockwave to allow the animation and interactivity of its flagship tool Director to be embedded into pages viewed. Later, Macromedia added Flash to their animation armory, which also uses Shockwave to create an .swf (Shockwave Flash) version of the native .fla file in order to make it displayable on a web page. Players and plug-ins became available for other multimedia tools with animation capabilities (for example, LiveCode), and the view came alive as long as the person viewing your page had installed the necessary plug-in on his or her machine. The QuickTime movie format includes the ability to create Virtual Reality (VR) files, also displayed on a web page via a player. Flash and proprietary viewers can be used to present panoramas. Figure 11-10 shows a real estate sales panorama—when you drag the mouse across this player's window, the scene tracks and rotates in a 360-degree panorama. You can see adjacent rooms, too, by panning the image in a circle.

Figure 11-10 Useful multimedia tools can enhance commercial web sites.

Chapter 11 Review

Chapter Summary

For your review, here is a summary of the important concepts discussed in this chapter.

Discuss the origins of the Internet

- The Internet began as a research network funded by the U.S. Department of Defense in 1969.

- In 1989, the National Science Foundation took over management of the research network, and research organizations and universities (professors and students alike) became increasingly heavy users of this ever-growing "Internet."

- Commercial and business use of the Internet was not permitted until 1992, but businesses have since become its driving force.

Define what a computer network is and how Internet domains, addresses, and interconnections work

- A network is a cluster of computers, with one computer acting as a server to provide services such as file transfer, e-mail, and document printing to the client computers.

- Using gateways and routers, a local area network (LAN) can be connected to other LANs to form a wide area network (WAN). These LANs and WANs can also be connected to the Internet through a server that provides both the necessary software for the Internet and the physical data connection.

- The Domain Name System (DNS) manages the names and addresses of computers linked to the Internet.

- Computers on the Internet manage names in subdomains that are encapsulated so that visitors from outside the local network need not worry about the subdomain names.

- When a stream of data is sent over the Internet by your computer, it is first broken down into packets by the Transmission Control Protocol (TCP).

- The IP (Internet Protocol) address is made up of four numbers between 0 and 255 separated by periods.

- Bandwidth is how much data, expressed in bits per second (bps), you can send from one computer to another in a given amount of time. The bottleneck at a typical user's low-bandwidth modem connection is the most serious impediment to sending multimedia across the Internet.

- When a server receives a request, it is handled by a specific application called a daemon that responds to the request based on the protocol.

- The first part of the URL (Uniform Resource Locator) identifies the protocol to use to handle the request.

- Multimedia elements are typically saved and transmitted on the Internet in the appropriate media type (same as MIME-type—for Multipurpose Internet Mail Extension) format and are named with the proper extension for that type.

- Hypertext Transfer Protocol (HTTP) provides rules for contacting, requesting, and sending documents encoded with the Hypertext Markup Language (HTML).

- HTML documents are simple ASCII text files. HTML currently includes about 100 tags.

- XML (Extensible Markup Language) allows you to create your own tags and import data from anywhere on the Web.

Discuss the current state of multimedia on the Internet and tools for the World Wide Web

- The explosion of tools and user demand for performance is stressing the orderly development of the core HTML standard. The marketplace keeps this cycle from being too chaotic.

- Interactions on the Web involve communication between two computers: a server and a client. The server delivers a file when a client asks for it.

- Browsers are the apps that run on a user's personal computer to provide the interface for downloading and viewing documents and multimedia.

- Professional web page developers often use only a word processor to edit their pages. Many HTML editors and web page–making applications offer to shortcut your HTML learning curve and working effort. Even if you use one of these editors, you should still understand the syntax and tags of the HTML language.

- Plug-ins allow users to view and interact with new types of documents and images. Requiring visitors to download plug-ins can be cumbersome, and servers must be set up to correctly handle requests for special data types.

- Web-enabled 3-D environments promise compelling and interactive multimedia experiences.

Employ the basic methods for displaying elements of multimedia on a web page, including using HTML, CCS, and nibbling

- The World Wide Web was designed as a simple method for delivering text and graphics.

- HTML provides tags for inserting media into HTML documents.

- Use the <img> tag for inline images and use the <audio>, <video>, <object>, and <embed> tags for multimedia objects.

- Specify a font, and even alternates for it, using Cascading Style Sheets (CSS) and/or Google Fonts.

- Use CSS to set text styles across the pages of your web site.

- Use a graphic bitmap if you wish to absolutely control the look of text in your HTML document.

- A viewport 960 pixels wide may be the most flexible choice.

- The overriding principle in designing web pages is to "nibble" away at the content in order to keep the size of the data as small as possible.

Manipulate the appearance of text on the Web

- Choose your fonts carefully: viewers may not have your special fonts installed on their computers.

Determine which graphics formats are best suited for different types of images and how they can be manipulated

- Image formats GIF, PNG, and JPEG use built-in compression algorithms to reduce file size.

- GIF images are limited to 8 bits of color depth, or a palette of 256 colors, while JPEG and PNG images may contain 24 bits of color depth.

- Use GIF files for line art and images that contain large areas of the same color. Use JPEG files for photorealistic images.

- The GIF89a specification allows for a selected transparency color. You cannot make a JPEG file transparent.

- JPEG and PNG use a powerful but lossy compression method that produces files as much as ten times more compressed than GIF.

- Most browsers allow you to specify an image or color to place in the background of your page in the <body> tag. Text and images will float on top of this layer.

- CSS is used to control the color of text in a document.

- Background images are automatically tiled, or repeated, across and down the page unless told not to using CSS.

- Placing an image inside an HTML anchor tag makes the graphic image clickable.

- Image maps are pictures with defined hot spots that link to other documents when a user clicks on them.

Play audio on a web page by embedding the sound within the site

- Audio play is provided by the <audio> tag.

- Always nibble at your sound elements and reduce them to the lowest file sizes that will play acceptably.

Include animation on a web page

- Limit animated GIFs to small images, and use a more capable plug-in for animations over larger areas.

- Flash provides animation on the Web.

Include video on a web page with and without the use of plug-ins

- Play video using the <video> tag.

■ Key Terms

<a> tag *(379)*
<audio> tag *(381)*
<body> tag *(377)*
<button> tag *(379)*
<img> tag *(379)*
<map> tag *(379)*
<video> tag *(382)*
add-on *(360)*
Adobe Acrobat PDF *(360)*
Adobe Acrobat Reader *(361)*
Adobe Director *(364)*
Adobe Dreamweaver *(360)*
Advanced Research Projects Agency (ARPA) *(337)*
applet *(354)*
ARPANET *(337)*
Asynchronous JavaScript and XML (Ajax) *(381)*
AU format *(381)*
autoplay attribute *(381)*
backbone *(344)*
bandwidth *(344)*
browser *(355)*
Cascading Style Sheets (CSS) *(336)*
Chrome *(356)*
chrome *(366)*
client *(339)*
codec *(383)*
Common Gateway Interface (CGI) *(363)*
compression algorithm *(370)*
Content Management System (CMS) *(360)*
controls *(381)*
daemon *(346)*
density-independent pixel (dip) *(366)*
deprecated *(365)*
device-independent *(362)*
Domain Name System (DNS) *(339)*
double tap *(367)*
drag *(367)*
dynamic web page *(352)*
escape sequence *(369)*
Extensible Markup Language (XML) *(352)*
extension *(360)*

Frequently Asked Questions (FAQ) *(337)*
File Transfer Protocol (FTP) *(346)*
first-level domain *(340)*
flick *(367)*
GIF *(370)*
helper application *(360)*
HTML editor *(357)*
HTML translator *(359)*
HTML5 *(352)*
Hypertext Transfer Protocol (HTTP) *(346)*
interlaced *(375)*
Internet *(337)*
Internet service provider (ISP) *(343)*
IP address *(343)*
Java *(354)*
JavaScript *(354)*
JPEG *(371)*
local area network (LAN) *(339)*
lossless *(371)*
lossy *(371)*
marking up *(357)*
media type *(348)*
Microsoft Internet Explorer *(356)*
Microsoft PowerPoint *(362)*
Mozilla Firefox *(356)*
multicast *(362)*
multiframe image *(382)*
Multipurpose Internet Mail Extension (MIME-type) *(348)*
network *(339)*
pinch closed *(367)*
pinch open *(367)*
player *(360)*
plug-in *(360)*
PNG *(370)*
Post Office Protocol (POP) *(346)*
preload *(381)*
progressive *(375)*
Safari *(356)*
Scalable Vector Graphics (SVG) *(361)*
search engine optimization (SEO) *(357)*

■ Key Term Quiz

1. Many web sites include pages that have answers to common inquiries. These pages are known as _____.

2. A cluster of computers tied together to share files and communications is a(n) _____.

3. The set of four numbers separated by periods that points to a domain is a(n) _____.

4. How much data, expressed in bits per second (bps), you can send from one computer to another in a given amount of time is called _____.

5. Each Internet service is implemented on an Internet server by dedicated software known as a(n) _____.

6. HTML formatting elements in HTML-encoded pages are called _____.

7. A(n) _____ is used to compress and decompress video files.

8. A new "open" format that was developed to replace GIF without requiring licensing fees is the _____ format.

9. Web page editors that visually show how a page looks as you are editing are often called _____ editors.

10. Media that is played as it is being received is said to be _____.

■ Multiple-Choice Quiz

1. DNS stands for:
   a. Distributed Numbering System
   b. Device Nomenclature System
   c. Data Networking System
   d. Domain Name System
   e. Digital Neighborhood System

2. The levels of a domain name are separated by:
   a. a period
   b. the @ symbol
   c. forward slashes
   d. hyphens
   e. spaces

3. Which of these is not a top-level domain?
   a. com
   b. edu
   c. gov
   d. mil
   e. cis
   f. home.html

4. Which of the following is a valid IP address?
   a. 192.168.1.1
   b. www.apple.com
   c. activa@midcoast.com
   d. http://www.pages.net/index.html
   e. 12 Dreamcatcher Way, Hope, ME 04847

5. Which of these is the *only* way to ensure that text appears exactly the same across platforms?
   a. Create a bitmap image of the text.
   b. Link to the font at a web site.
   c. Include the font as a download on the server.

> d. Specify the font using Cascading Style Sheets.
>
> e. Embed the font into the HTML code itself.

6. Perhaps the most widely installed HTTP software for managing web pages is the open-source application called:
    a. Apache
    b. Daemon
    c. ISP
    d. Acrobat
    e. Unix

7. Web pages are written in:
    a. MPEG
    b. HTML
    c. QuickTime
    d. TCP/IP
    e. MIME

8. Which of these is *not* an image format supported by most browsers?
    a. GIF
    b. JPEG
    c. PNG
    d. DXF
    e. All are supported by most browsers.

9. An IP address can be exchanged with a(n):
    a. MIME-type
    b. Point-to-Point Protocol
    c. domain name
    d. e-mail address
    e. usenet group

10. HTTP stands for:
    a. High-Technology Transmission Protocol
    b. Help Text Translation Protocol
    c. Hypertext Transfer Protocol
    d. Hardware Testing Tool Protocol
    e. How To Talk Protocol

11. When a browser downloads a file it cannot process itself, it can forward the file to an external application for processing. This external application is sometimes called a:
    a. stand-in
    b. helper application
    c. CGI script
    d. JavaScript
    e. Java applet

12. What is the most colors that can fit into a GIF palette?
    a. 16
    b. 40
    c. 216
    d. 254
    e. 256
    f. 512

13. One criticism of visual page editors is that they:
    a. encrypt the code, making later editing impossible
    b. do not support features such as underlining and bold text
    c. use nonstandard HTML tags
    d. generate extremely complicated HTML code
    e. require the use of plug-ins

14. Which of these tags would most likely be used in HTML to view a multimedia element on the Web?
    a. <blockquote>
    b. <video>
    c. <open>
    d. <mm>
    e. <flash>

15. Which audio file type's sound quality is dependent on the client's computer setup?
    a. AIF
    b. AU
    c. MIDI
    d. Shockwave
    e. WAV

◾ Essay Quiz

1. Bandwidth limitations impose serious limitations on presenting multimedia over the Web. What tools and strategies does a multimedia developer have to deal with the limitations of bandwidth?

2. Describe what the different parts of the URL http://www.secondLevel.topLevel/filename.filetype represent.

3. Briefly describe how a browser requests a URL, how the URL is handled, and how the server responds, in terms of the DNS, encoding schemes, and data protocols.

4. Describe the data rate of a "high-speed" Internet connection. Roughly calculate how long it would take to download a web page consisting of a 5-kilobyte HTML page and 45 kilobytes of image files for that connection.

5. List the most common top-level domains, and describe what categories they are associated with.

6. You have been given the task of creating a new web site for your company. What tools will you use to create the pages? When might you use a word processor? When might you use a WYSIWYG tool? When might you use an HTML text editor? What are the strengths and weaknesses of each?

Lab Projects

◾ Project 11.1

You are given the task of developing a new web site for a cooking magazine. Think about the capabilities of XML to allow you to define your own data tags. What data types would you include? How might you format them? What would be the benefits in this case of being able to define your own tags? Create an outline of how you might structure the data included in a recipe.

◾ Project 11.2

Open a web browser. Locate the "helper applications" preferences panel in the browser. (Note: this option varies among browsers and operating systems, and may not be available for some.)

Find the following media types (MIME-types): audio/x-aiff; application/postscript; application/x-gtar; text /html; image/jpeg; video/mpeg; image/tiff; video/quicktime; audio/x-pn-realaudio. List an application commonly used to read or edit each type.

◾ Project 11.3

Open a word processor that exports to HTML. Create a page of formatted text. Be sure to use different text styles, numerous colors, indenting, tables, and other options. Print the page out from the word processing program.

Export the page to HTML, and then open the HTML page in a Web browser. Print out the page from the browser. How does the browser-rendered page differ from the page in the word processor?

◾ Project 11.4

View the source of the page you created in Project 11.1 in the browser. (Most browsers have a function that allows you to view the source HTML code of a web page.) Print out the source, either from the browser, or by copying the HTML code when you view the source, or by cutting and pasting.

Note how HTML treats various word processing features with its tags.

■ Project 11.5

Go online and compare web hosting packages from three different Web hosts. Most hosting companies offer several options and prices. Select a basic, moderate, and advanced package from each host and describe that package's features and options. Do any of the host providers offer unique or unusual options?

Host _____:

Package	Basic	Moderate	Advanced
Storage space:			
Bandwidth:			
Streaming capabilities:			
Cost			

Comments: _____

Host _____:

Package	Basic	Moderate	Advanced
Storage space:			
Bandwidth:			
Streaming capabilities:			
Cost			

Comments: _____

Host _____:

Package	Basic	Moderate	Advanced
Storage space:			
Bandwidth:			
Streaming capabilities:			
Cost			

Comments: _____

CHAPTER 12

Mobile Multimedia

TABLETS, readers, and smartphones delivering text, images, audio, and video have explosively changed the nature of society in all nations around the world regardless of culture or language. In just a few decades, there has been a phase shift as important as Gutenberg's moveable type (see Chapter 2), and the impact of this profound and disruptive change is felt all across the spectrum of human activity:

- As mobiles entered daily life, lives improved.
- As mobiles entered daily life, more people tripped, fell down stairs, walked into trees, and drove into lakes; dexterous teenagers began looking downward.
- The office is now at your fingertips, at any time and from anywhere.
- Malicious software, thieves, and robbers lurk in the shadows.
- You joined the world of social media.
- Social media has reconnected friends, family, and classmates by making communication easier and more interactive through multimedia.
- E-mail and text messages and video clips are everywhere.
- People took selfies, watched TV, and played a few games.
- They said I love you using two characters: <3.
- Someone blogged OMGOMGOMGOMGOMG i <3 his pants i want to kiss him.
- People called home.
- The call went to voicemail.

According to a 2012 survey published at www.statista.com, in response to the question "If you had to choose between leaving the house in the morning with your wireless mobile device or your wallet, which one would you choose?" 44 percent of the 4,700 survey respondents worldwide indicated they would take their mobile device.

The market for mobile multimedia is enormous and the opportunities for you to contribute are endless.

Digital Revolution Worldwide

As an agent of change, the mobile and multimedia Internet is altering our quality of life, our quality of health, the way we interact socially, the environment, schools and education, the retail marketplace, styles of employment and work, and the organizational patterns that drive business and economies. According to the research organization McKinsey Global Institute, in its May 2013 report "Disruptive Technologies: Advances That Will Transform Life, Business, and the Global Economy" (Manyika et al.), in the United States today about 30 percent of people browsing the Web and 40 percent of people accessing social media use a mobile device. Some pundits say the desktop computer will be gone in a few generations.

Retail

In the retail world, retailers can "push" tailored messages about store specials and sales to shoppers in the vicinity who have signed up to receive such messages via their smartphones equipped with **Global Positioning System (GPS)** or Quick Response (QR) code software (see Chapter 7). People with FOMO, or "fear of missing out," enjoy the pushes. With 3G, 4G, or Wi-Fi access (see "Connections" a bit later), smartphones connect to the Internet from almost everywhere, and if you are lost, they will lead you home. With a Square device (https://squareup.com) or the Venmo app (https://venmo.com), you can easily use credit cards and a mobile device to take retail payments (in 2014, for a fee of 2.75% and 3% per swipe, respectively). Photos and video recorded by mobile devices are high quality; when distributed via the Internet, they can affect the behavior of individuals and governments. They create the **memes** of a culture, the "units" of its ideas, behaviors, and styles.

The true power of civil protest and revolution is no longer in burning tires and furniture barricades; it lies in a raised and recording smartphone linked to the Internet.

Education

Educational and homework assignments are completed by students on tablets provided by schools. Indeed, developed nations are spending considerable resources to teach their children computing skills. In the United Kingdom, for example, learning to program or code apps became a mandatory part of the student curriculum in 2014 (see https://www.gov.uk/government /publications/national-curriculum-in-england-computing-programmes- of-study).

Worrisome to law enforcement and many parents and educators is the increase in sexually explicit images and video sent across the Internet by children, phone to phone and phone to social media sites, where such images can do lasting harm.

Travel

Sending and reading text messages (**texting**) while driving (also called "distracted driving") is an epidemic throughout the world, and most nations have passed laws against it. Both Apple and Google are actively competing with automotive companies to put iOS and Android onto automobile dashboards in a safe and seamless way.

Sending or reading one text is pretty quick, unlike a phone conversation—wouldn't that be okay?

Texting is the most alarming distraction because it involves manual, visual, and cognitive distraction simultaneously. Sending or reading a text takes your eyes off the road for 4.6 seconds. At 55 mph, that's like driving the length of an entire football field, blindfolded. It's extraordinarily dangerous.

Who are the most serious offenders?

Our youngest and most inexperienced drivers are most at risk, with 16% of all distracted driving crashes involving drivers under 20. But they are not alone. At any given moment during daylight hours, over 800,000 vehicles are being driven by someone using a hand-held cell phone.

What can I do to help?

Take the pledge to drive phone-free and turn your cell phone off when you turn your ignition on.

I pledge to:

■ Protect lives by never texting or talking on the phone while driving.
■ Be a good passenger and speak out if the driver in my car is distracted.
■ Encourage my friends and family to drive phone-free.

Excerpts from FAQ and "Take the Pledge" at www.distraction.gov, Official U.S. Government Website for Distracted Driving

If you are traveling long distance by air, you can purchase in-flight Wi-Fi for your tablet or smartphone for varying costs, depending upon the route, airline, and package. Whether the connection is allowed to include a telephone link is currently being argued in the United States: many passengers and airlines wish to avoid the distraction and nuisance of seat neighbors talking loudly. Elsewhere in the world, though, talking on the cell phone is permitted aboard aircraft. If your phone is equipped with **Near Field Communication (NFC)**, in Austria you can pass your phone near the ticket machine and book train travel; the ticket arrives by **short message service (SMS)** message (see Figure 12-1).

With your smartphone and the Uber app, you can hail a taxi in cities in 26 countries, from San Francisco to Berlin. Use the app to position a pin at your location on the map, choose the type of vehicle you want to be picked up in (a taxi, black car, or SUV), and confirm. Other firms recognize this very competitive market: try the mobile apps from Hailo, Get-Taxi, Click A Taxi, Kabbee, Lyft, Sidecar, or Minicabster.

Figure 12-1   NFC standards allow radio communication and secure transactions between smartphones and terminals, in this case a railroad "Handy-Ticket" machine in Austria.

Games, Entertainment, and Home

Replacing the once-ubiquitous Nintendo Game Boy, smartphones use powerful game systems and the new technology of touchscreens and accelerometers. According to Rovio, creator of the game *Angry Birds*, by 2011, players were spending 200 million minutes inside the game every day. When the endless runner game, *Temple Run*, was released by Imangi Studios for Android in 2012, in less than three days it was downloaded 1 million times. Tilt the phone to weave along pathways, swipe to turn, jump, and slide. No more joystick.

With Hulu (www.hulu.com) or xfinity.tv (http://xfinity.comcast.net), your smartphone becomes a television. With the Netflix app (www.netflix.com) or Amazon Instant Video app (www.amazon.com), it becomes a movie theater.

With Spotify, your smartphone becomes a streaming music player with more than 20 million songs. With a Jambox or Boombox Bluetooth speaker system, your smartphone can fill a room with sound.

And it is often smartphones around the world that take photographs of people **planking** or performing variations of that curious fad or meme (an idea or activity that spreads through the Internet like a virus): vadering, teapotting, owling, horsemanning, batmanning, or bradying. See Figure 12-2. If you're a Facebook user, visit https://www.facebook.com/groups/5989617014/ for more images and clues about the propagation of the planking meme. Or search for "planking meme" and the other memes at Google Images.

For the home, your Google Nest or Honeywell Wi-Fi smart thermostat, smoke detector, or carbon monoxide alarm can be read and managed from your smartphone regardless of where you are located.

Figure 12-2   Woman planking in classic position: face down, hands at sides of the body

And when looking for a job with at least one hotel chain in the international hospitality industry, Marriot, you can apply from your mobile device using a custom app that, as claimed in an April 2013 press release, enables Marriot "...to reach a technologically savvy and ever increasing mobile audience, thus enhancing and optimising the recruitment process."

You Are Never More than Six Separations from Anybody—in the Whole World

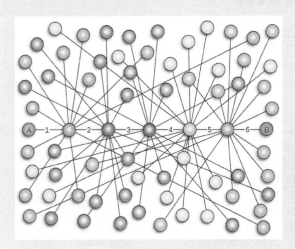

Smartphones and mobile devices and social networks have helped make ours a very small world! In his 1929 short story, *Chains*, Hungarian author and playwright Frigyes Karinthy claimed that a chain of friends-of-friends can connect one person to any other person in the world in a maximum of six steps or six degrees of separation. A parody of this concept is depicted in a commercial for the Visa check card, featuring actor Kevin Bacon (viewable at www.youtube.com/watch?v=afJRKbBEr2Q). When Bacon, playing himself, wants to pay for a book using a check, the bookstore clerk asks for identification, but Bacon has no ID on him. So he leaves the store and returns a while later with a group of five people and tells the clerk, "Okay, I was in a movie with an extra, Eunice, whose hairdresser, Wayne, attended Sunday school with Father O'Neill, who plays racquetball with Dr. Sanjay, who recently removed the appendix of Kim, who dumped you sophomore year. So you see, we're practically brothers."

In June 2006, Jure Leskovec and Eric Horvitz studied a huge anonymized dataset containing more than 30 billion text message conversations among 240 million people from all over the world who were using Microsoft Messenger. Their study, titled *Planetary-Scale Views on an Instant-Messaging Network* (available at http://arxiv.org/abs/0803.0939v1), concluded, in part, with these observations:

…We found strong influences of homophily in activities, where people with similar characteristics tend to communicate more, with the exception of gender, where we found that cross-gender conversations are both more frequent and of longer duration than conversations with users of the same reported gender. We also examined the path lengths and validated on a planetary scale earlier research that found "6 degrees of separation" among people…

We hope that our studies with Messenger data serves as an example of directions in social science research, highlighting how communication systems can provide insights about high-level patterns and relationships in human communications without making incursions into the privacy of individuals.

In a more recent study, from 2011, *Degrees of Separation in Social Networks* (www.aaai.org/ocs/index.php/SOCS/SOCS11/paper/view/4031/4352), Reza Bakhshandeh et al. concluded:

Social networking is a transformative Internet phenomenon. With networks like Facebook and its more than 500 million users, researchers will want to investigate properties of this evolving web of interconnected users and communities. The degree of separation is an important property of such a network and one that is of great interest, especially to social scientists. Twitter's 3.43 degree of separation is surprisingly small (or, rather, we were surprised) and perhaps is indicative of changing social norms. It would be very interesting to do a more definitive study of this number for Twitter and other social networking sites, and then monitor how this changes over time. It reflects the truism that the world gets smaller every day.

Mobile Hardware

At the same time as the hardware used to make and display multimedia has become more capable and more compact, the hardware used for mobile devices has shrunk astonishingly to the size of your palm. And the communications power now in the palm of your hand is immense (see Figure 12-3).

Figure 12-3 On the left, a 26.2-pound Osborne computer; on the right, a business-woman swipes a credit card in a Square Reader, doing business on her 3.95-ounce smartphone in 2014. Separated by 30 years, the tiny smartphone is many times more powerful and orders of magnitude lighter than the now fossilized Osborne. (Photo on right courtesy of Square, Inc.)

Becoming Small

The miniaturization of telephone handsets and the construction of comprehensive radio networks by which to connect these telephones wirelessly have revolutionized human communications. In 2012 there were more than 6.8 billion mobile cellular subscriptions in the world. In the United States, there were 900 cell towers in 1985; in 2014, there are 190,000. The miniaturization of desktop computers into Internet-connected tablets has revolutionized the way people do business and educate themselves and their children. Tablet sales in the year 2013 exceeded 200 million units worldwide (Apple captured 33.8 percent of that market, Samsung 18.8 percent).

Smaller Hardware

The miniaturization and use of touch screens on mobile devices enables **multi-touch gestures** like pinches and swipes and taps (see the diagram in Chapter 7, at the end of the "Input Devices" section). A single mobile device may have four separate radios for not only voice and data communications but also connection to hands-free headsets and microphones and NFC devices (such as the "Handy-Ticket" machine shown earlier in Figure 12-1). With **system-on-a-chip (SoC) technology**, memory, graphics processors, audio components, USB controllers, power management circuits, and a myriad of other essential functions are integrated onto a single chip—meaning shorter wiring and less power consumption. Apple's A7 SoC first appeared in the iPhone 5S and integrates a dual-core CPU, a graphics processing unit (GPU), large memory caches, 1GB of DRAM, and a **Secure Enclave** biometric security device for storing fingerprint IDs. Manufactured by Samsung, the chip includes over 1 billion transistors in an area only 102 mm^2.

The Samsung Galaxy S4 smartphone competes with Apple's iPhone and includes "smart scrolling" and eye-tracking—"smart pause" will halt a video if the user is not looking at the screen. The Samsung Galaxy S4 also includes **3D Touch**—fingertips held above but not touching the glass can still be "felt" by the touch screen.

The Market

During the two months following the Galaxy S4's release in 2013, more than 20 million units were sold in 155 countries. Other manufacturers also compete for market share; according to Gartner, a leading IT research and advisory firm, at the end of 2013 market share for worldwide mobile phone sales was as follows:

Vendor	Percent
Samsung	25.7
Nokia	13.8
Apple	6.7
LG Electronics	4.0
ZTE	3.0
Huawei	3.0
Lenovo	2.9
TCL Communication	2.7
Sony Mobile Communications	2.1
Yulong	1.9
Others	34.2

It is the combination of hardware, operating system, and system programming features that differentiates the many brands of tablets and smartphones available in the marketplace. For a good tool to compare smartphone features, visit www.diffen.com/difference/Special:Compare/Cell_Phones.

Indeed, buying a smartphone (and its service contract) is more difficult than buying an automobile. Does it have a clock, snooze alarm, speaker and mute, font size adjuster, voice texting, a calendar, synced contacts, excellent camera, a flashlight, note taker and recorder, Bluetooth headset, an infrared controller, song identifier, game console, temp and humidity sensors, visual voicemail, blocked phone numbers, an NFC radio, a long-lasting battery, warp-speed processing, crystal-clear display, multiple windows, plenty of storage space, fingerprint sensor, wireless charging? How about a kill switch? How about…

What's the issue?

Incompatibility of chargers for mobile phones is a major environmental problem and an inconvenience for users across the European Union. Currently specific chargers are sold together with specific mobile phones. A user who wants to change his/her mobile phone must usually acquire a new charger and dispose the current one, even if this is in perfect condition. This unnecessarily generates important amounts of electronic waste.

Which is the solution envisaged?

Harmonising mobile phone chargers will bring significant economic and environmental benefits. Following a request from the European Commission and in close co-operation with the Commission services, major producers of mobile phones have agreed in a Memorandum of Understanding ("MoU") to harmonise chargers for data-enabled mobile phones sold in the EU. Industry commits to provide chargers compatibility on the basis of the Micro-USB connector. Once the commitment becomes effective, it will be possible to charge data-enabled mobile phones from any charger compatible with the common specifications.

Who will benefit and how?

Consumers will not need to buy a new charger together with every mobile phone, and they should also benefit from more efficient and cheaper stand-alone chargers. Consumers will be able to charge their mobile phone from the new common charger.

The environmental benefits of harmonising chargers are expected to be very important: reducing the number of chargers unnecessarily sold will reduce the associated generated electronic waste, which currently amounts to thousands of tons. Harmonised chargers are also expected to improve energy-efficiency, thus reducing energy consumption.

Excerpts from "Harmonisation of a charging capability of common charger for mobile phones – frequently asked questions," addressing European Commission MEMO/09/301, June 29, 2009

Looking ahead, smartphones will be adding "augmented reality" (AR) so you can point the smartphone's camera and receive an onscreen overlay of information such as nearby cafes, markets, gas stations, or landmarks (see Figure 12-4). Flexible screens will roll up and fit in a purse. A LED-based **digital light projector (DLP)** will show 2-meter-wide photos on any available wall in your home or office. Voice control using a natural language user interface (LUI or NLUI) such as Siri will supplant texting. 3-D and holographic projections will follow.

Figure 12-4 Augmented reality provides a layer of information superimposed on a real-world camera image, in this case the Wikitude *World Browser* app overlays notes about local geography.

Connections

There is a lot going on "under the hood" to make sure your mobile device is properly connected. Connections are typically by radio, and as many as four radios may be built into a device: one for cell towers, one for Wi-Fi hotspots, one for Bluetooth, and one for NFC (see "Smaller Hardware," earlier in the chapter).

Connection begins with a "**handshake**," a set of complicated but standardized protocols that allows the device and the radio to which it is connecting to identify and authenticate each other. Other protocols guide and modify the connection while it is active and, finally, terminate it. In common use is the Session Initiation Protocol (SIP), which is an international standard (see http://tools.ietf.org/html/rfc3261):

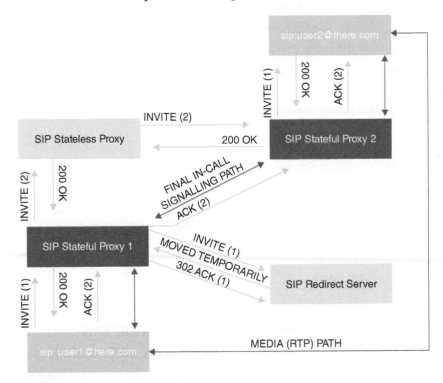

Troubleshooting a Bad Connection on an iPhone—Not as Easy as You Think

Symptoms

Learn how to troubleshoot issues making or receiving calls. If a No Service or Searching message appears in the status bar, follow these steps.

Resolution

Follow the steps below to resolve this issue. Please test after each step.

1. Toggle airplane mode: Tap Settings | Enable Airplane Mode, wait five seconds, then turn off airplane mode.

2. Check your phone settings:

   - Check your Do Not Disturb settings: Tap Settings | Do Not Disturb.
   - Check for any blocked phone numbers: Tap Settings | Phone | Blocked.
   - See if Call Forwarding is turned on: Tap Settings | Phone | Call Forwarding.

3. Ensure that your software is up to date:

   a. Check for a carrier settings update.

   b. Check for an iOS software update.

   Note: Some updates may require a Wi-Fi connection.

4. If the phone has a SIM card, reseat the SIM card.

5. If the iPhone 4 or iPhone 4s is on the Verizon network, dial *228 from the iPhone and select option 2 to update the Preferred Roaming List (PRL). The PRL determines the cellular towers the phone uses for cellular service, selecting those with the best signal strength.

6. Reset the network settings: Tap Settings | General | Reset | Reset Network Settings.

7. Try to make or receive calls in another location.

8. Attempt to isolate to one network band:

   - If you're having the issue on LTE, disable LTE, if possible, and try again.
   - If you're having the issue on 3G/4G, disable 3G/4G, if possible, and try again.

9. Contact the carrier to check the following:

   - Your account is properly configured to use the specific iPhone that has the issue.
   - There are no localized service outages.
   - Your account doesn't have a billing-related block.
   - Your calls don't have errors on the carrier system.

10. Restore the phone as new.

From Apple Support document "iPhone: Troubleshooting issues making or receiving calls," https: //support.apple.com/kb/TS3406

GSM vs. CDMA

Two radio systems are available to connect a smartphone or mobile phone to a cell tower and then onward either to the Internet or to the **public switched telephone network (PSTN)**, which links all telephones in the world using copper wire, optical fiber, satellites, and microwave links. These systems are not interchangeable or compatible.

Code Division Multiple Access (CDMA) is used by Sprint, Verizon, and U.S. Cellular in the United States. **Global System for Mobile Communications (GSM)**, the most widely accepted technology, is used by AT&T and T-Mobile in the United States and reaches more than 5 billion people across 80 percent of the globe. CDMA phones use a single frequency to talk with a cell tower (850 MHz); GSM phones use several frequencies (850/900/1800/1900 MHz) depending on country and provider. On CDMA phones, network and subscriber information is contained within the handset and in a provider database; GSM phones use a **Subscriber Identity Module (SIM) card**, which is a removable card that can be seamlessly swapped among handsets, bringing your phone books, contact lists, and schedulers to a new phone without rekeying or having to make a trip to the provider. For international travel, a GSM phone capable of communicating on all four frequencies is recommended. Figure 12-5 shows the connection methodology for GSM networks.

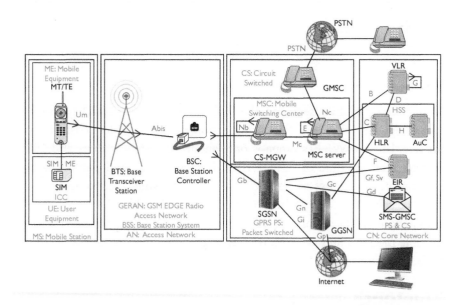

Figure 12-5 The structure of a GSM network showing how a mobile device reaches the telephone network and the Internet

3G vs. 4G

Whether CDMA or GSM, the very important radio link between the mobile device and the cell tower manages voice and data using standard-ized technologies. **3G (Third Generation)** and **4G (Fourth Generation)** are communication protocols that govern this movement of information on the radio connection between handset and tower (see Table 12-1). These terms are particularly useful for marketing because they do not promise a minimum throughput rate or bandwidth and are vague. **LTE (Long-Term Evolution)** and **WiMAX** (Worldwide Interoperability for Microwave Access) are competing 4G technologies.

	3G	4G
Data throughput	Up to 3.1 Mbps, average between 0.5 and 1.5 Mbps	2 to 12 Mbps
Peak upload rate	5 Mbps	500 Mbps
Peak download rate	100 Mbps	1 Gbps
Switching technique	Packet switching	Packet switching, message switching
Network architecture	Wide area cell based	Integration of wireless LAN and WAN
Frequency band	1.8 to 2.5 GHz	2 to 8 GHz

Table 12-1   Comparison of 3G and 4G Protocols

Wi-Fi

Connecting a mobile device to the Internet using **Wi-Fi** 802.11 a/b/g/n technology can provide a faster connection than 4G for less cost, if not for free. But the Wi-Fi's range is only about 30 meters indoors and 100 meters outdoors (line of sight). Many homes, offices, and public places have installed **wireless access points (WAPs)** to which electronic devices connect using radios operating in the unlicensed, public 2.4-GHz spec-trum. These WAPs are often combined with digital subscriber line (DSL) or cable modems and network routers to provide hotspots for connecting to the Internet.

Bluetooth

Sharing the 2.4-GHz spectrum with Wi-Fi, **Bluetooth** is a very short-range, low-power radio technology to interconnect up to seven devices by radio. Typically, Bluetooth is used to connect a mobile phone to a hands-free headset or to an automobile audio system. An innovative use of Blue-tooth is Tile (www.thetileapp.com), which uses Bluetooth to find your stuff by remembering the last place the tile was "seen" and sounding an alert when triggered.

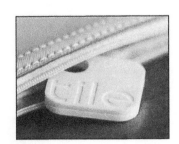

Mobile Operating Systems

An operating system is the software that makes the smartphone or tablet run. The smartphone operating system market is dominated by Google's Android (81%) and Apple's iOS (13%). Windows Phone, Blackberry, and other OSs remain uncompetitive, with market share in the single digits. Depending upon the operating system (and the service provider), users are trapped into a walled garden (explained in Chapter 13) and must download apps for extra features only from the company store: for Android, visit https://play.google.com; for iOS, visit https://itunes.apple.com/us/genre/ios/id36 (substitute *de, fr, gb*, etc. in place of *us* if you are located in a different country).

iOS vs. Android

Android is an open-source operating system for mobile devices based upon the Linux kernel and maintained by Google. **iOS** is a proprietary, closed-source operating system developed and owned by Apple. Together, these OSs are used on more than 90 percent of all mobile devices. Measured not by device but by who uses the Internet more, according to NetMarketShare (www.netmarketshare.com), in February 2014, approximately 53 percent of web users accessing the Internet from mobile devices use iOS; 36 percent use an Android device.

Each of the mobile OSs is relatively new. Android was developed by Android, Inc., a 22-month-old startup purchased by Google in 2005, which became the core of Google's foray into mobile hardware and software. Based on the OS X desktop operating system, Apple's iOS began in 2007 as an OS for the new iPhone, using multi-touch gestures. iOS is never licensed for installation on any hardware except hardware manufactured by Apple, though that may change as Apple partners with automobile manufacturers to bring iOS to the dashboard. Table 12-2 shows the

Codename (Version), API Level	Distribution, February 2014	Release Date
Froyo (2.2), 8	1.3%	May, 2010
Gingerbread (2.3.3–2.3.7), 10	20%	December, 2010
Honeycomb (3.2), 13 (tablet only)	0.1%	February, 2011
Ice Cream Sandwich (4.0.3–4.0.4), 15	16.1%	October, 2011
Jelly Bean (4.1–4.3), 16–18	60.7%	July, 2012
KitKat (4.4), 19	1.8%	September, 2013

Table 12-2   API, Distribution, and Release Date for Android Versions

codename and application programming interface (API) level, distribution (as of February 2014), and release date of the more recent Android versions (not shown are the earlier Cupcake, Donut, and Eclair versions), while Table 12-3 shows the version, distribution (as of February 2014), and release date for iOS versions.

Version	Highest Version For	Distribution, February 2014	Release Date
3.1.3	iPhone (1st generation), iPod touch (1st generation)	4%	February, 2010
4.2.1	iPhone 3G, iPod touch (2nd generation)		November, 2010
5.1.1	iPod touch (3rd generation), iPad (1st generation)		May, 2012
6.1.3	iPhone 3GS	22%	March, 2013
6.1.5	iPod touch (4th generation)		November, 2013
7.0.4	iPhone 4, iPhone 4S, iPhone 5, 5C, iPhone 5S, iPod touch (5th generation), iPad 2, iPad (3rd generation), iPad (4th generation), iPad Air, iPad mini (1st generation), iPad mini (2nd generation)	74%	November, 2013
7.0.5	iPhone 5C and iPhone 5S (China and select European/Asia Pacific models)		January, 2014

Table 12-3 Version, Distribution, and Release Date for iOS

Programming Mobile Apps

Programmers writing apps for iOS use Objective C; they use Java when programming for Android devices. Other programmers use HTML5, CSS, and JavaScript to construct hybrid apps and save themselves the difficulty of learning multiple complex languages. Others use frameworks and integrated development environments (IDEs) such as LiveCode (discussed in the upcoming case study "A Simple Stock Control App"), Adobe Flex and AIR, qui-dev, jQT, jQuery Mobile, Sencha Touch, PhoneGap, Motorola's RhoMobile Suite, WebApp.Net, eMobc, Rare-Wire, Eclipse, and Android Studio.

The responsive web design (RWD) movement is developing methods to deal with the difficulty of programming for the many screen sizes in the mobile and desktop worlds. Typically, the advice is to consider the smallest screen first. For examples of RWD, see "Multi-Device Layout Patterns" by Luke Wroblewski at www.lukew.com/ff/entry.asp?1514 and "Responsive Navigation Patterns" by Brad Frost at http://bradfrostweb.com/blog/web/responsive-nav-patterns/.

From a designer's or programmer's point of view, there is no easy solution to the size issue. Android defines four sizes: small (426×320 dp), normal (470×320 dp), large (at least 640×480 dp), and xlarge (at least 960×720 dp), where dp represents the calculated term density-independent pixel (see Chapter 11), which is used for scaling based upon the actual density of the screen in use. All visual solutions take hard work and often a great deal of trial and error in the simulator/emulator.

There are a great many details and compliance issues to consider when designing, building, and publishing an app for the mobile world. If you are starting from scratch, you will find it initially a steep learning curve; the slope soon gets easier, though, after you master the basic concepts.

Launch Checklist (Android)

Before you publish your app on Google Play and distribute it to users, you need to get the app ready, test it, and prepare your promotional materials.

1. Understand the publishing process
2. Understand Google Play policies
3. Test for core app quality
4. Determine your content rating
5. Determine country distribution
6. Confirm the app's overall size
7. Confirm app compatibility ranges
8. Decide on free or priced
9. Consider In-app Billing
10. Set prices for your apps
11. Start localization early
12. Prepare promotional graphics
13. Build the release-ready APK
14. Plan a beta release
15. Complete the product details
16. Use Google Play badges
17. Final checks and publishing
18. Support users after launch

From Android Developers, http://developer.android.com/distribute/googleplay/publish/preparing.html

and deploy to all platforms.

This stock control app is built using open-source LiveCode (http://livecode.com), a cross-platform development framework that is a card-based multimedia authoring tool (see Chapter 7). Projects authored with LiveCode can be saved as stand-alone apps that run on OS X, Windows, Linux, iOS, and Android platforms. You can code once

Getting Started

For an overview of this case study, visit http://newsletters.livecode.com/february/issue165/newsletter4.html.

accessible in the mobile space so users can add, edit, and delete items. sales and profits, images, and vendor information and makes the data app for the iPad. The app includes variables for item descriptions, costs, This case study shows how to quickly build a simple stock management

Case Study: A Simple Stock Control App

App Store Required Resources (iOS)

There are several things that you are required to provide in your app bundle before submitting it to the App Store:

- Your app must have an Info.plist file. This file contains information that the system needs to interact with your app. Xcode creates a version of this file automatically but most apps need to modify this file in some way. For information on how to configure this file, see "The Information Property List File."

- Your app's Info.plist file must include the UIRequiredDeviceCapabilities key. The App Store uses this key to determine whether or not a user can run your app on a specific device. For information on how to configure this key, see "Declaring the Required Device Capabilities."

- You must include one or more icons in your app bundle. The system uses these icons when presenting your app on the device's home screen. For information about how to specify app icons, see "App Icons."

- Your app must include at least one image to be displayed while your app is launching. The system displays this image to provide the user with immediate feedback that your app is launching. For information about launch images, see "App Launch (Default) Images."

From iOS App Programming Guide, "App-Related Resources," https://developer.apple.com/library/ios/documentation/iphone/conceptual/iphoneosprogrammingguide/App-RelatedResources/App-RelatedResources.html

Download, install, and activate LiveCode. If you want to deploy this app to iOS devices, register at Apple as a developer (https://developer. apple.com/register/index.action) and then download and install the iOS SDK, which is called **Xcode** (https://developer.apple.com/devcenter/ios/). Then configure LiveCode for iOS support. Note that there is a developer program specifically for universities, allowing apps to be tested on devices and distributed within a team but not at the App Store (https://developer. apple.com/programs/ios/university/).

To deploy this app to Android devices, the steps would be similar. On a PC or a Mac, download and install LiveCode. Android is an open environment, so you can download the SDK and the Java SDK for free (http:// developer.android.com/sdk/index.html). You can distribute your Android apps to users in any way you want, using any distribution approach or combination of approaches that meets your needs, from publishing in an app marketplace to serving your apps from a web site or e-mailing them directly to users. You are never locked into any particular distribution platform (http://developer.android.com/distribute/open.html). But the major marketplace is at Google Play, so it might be a good idea to register as a Google Play Developer (https://play.google.com/apps/publish/signup/) and pay a $25 fee.

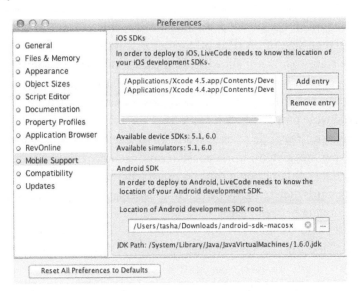

Configure a virtual device. Launch the emulator by starting the virtual device; you can also set up a physical device for testing. As you develop your app, with LiveCode you can test your code directly on the iOS simulator (or Android's emulator) using a one-click button.

Identifying Functions

The purpose of the stock control app is to store information about the stock on the shelves of our fictitious store. We need to be able to add new stock items, delete items, update information, and automatically calculate the profit and value of our stock. We would also like to be able to visit a vendor's web site. Thus, we will create the following fields: name, description, image, vendor, vendor website, stock level, cost price, and sale price. And to manage these, we will need the following functions: add item, edit item, delete item, go to vendor website, sell item, move between items, calculate the profit on an item, calculate the value of our stock. Because we want the data to be persistent between uses of the app, we need to save the data on the device.

Building the Stack

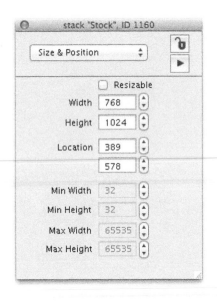

In the LiveCode card-based environment, a project consists of a **stack** of cards. For our app, we need to create a new stack: choose File | New Mainstack, click the Inspector button to open the Property Inspector for the stack, and set the name to **Stock** and the title to **Stock Management**. Next, select Size & Position from the drop-down menu at the top of the Property Inspector and set the width of the stack to 768 and the height of the stack to 1024. For this app, we are allowing only portrait orientation.

The screen size of an iPad in portrait orientation is 768×1024 pixels when the status bar is not showing. If you do want to show the status bar in your app, then set the height of your stack to 1004, allowing 20 pixels for the status bar. If the Resizable check box is checked, uncheck it to turn off the resizable property.

Because a LiveCode stack is made up of a series of cards, we will use one card per stock item; in database terms, each card becomes a record, and each data container on a card becomes a field. We can add new items by adding cards, delete items by deleting cards, and navigate through the stack by moving between cards.

Adding Controls to the Stack

With a new (blank) stack of cards in hand, we add fields, an image, and four buttons that, respectively, go to the vendor web site, add a new stock item, delete a stock item, and sell a piece of stock. In LiveCode you can simply drag field and button controls from the Tools palette to the stack and then use the Property Inspector to name them.

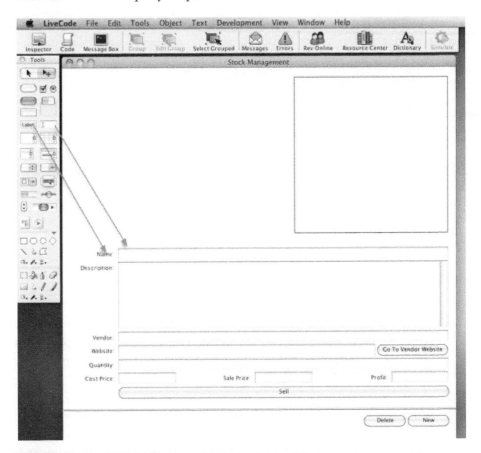

Programming the Link to the Vendor Web Site

To link to the vendor's web site, we can use the LiveCode `launch url` command in the `"vendor website"`, as shown in the following code. Open the Script Editor for the Go To Vendor Website button (click the button while pressing COMMAND-OPTION or CONTROL-ALT) and set the script to

```
on mouseUp
    put field "vendor website" into tVendorWebsite
    launch url tVendorWebsite
end mouseUp
```

The command `launch url` does the work.

Selecting an Image Using iPhonePickPhoto

LiveCode provides special commands to access mobile devices directly. iPhonePickPhoto lets users browse their photo libraries for an image to put into the image containing that command. The command only works for iOS. Open the Script Editor by clicking that image while pressing COMMAND-OPTION or CONTROL-ALT, and set the script of the image to

```
on mouseUp
    ## When iPhonePickPhoto is used the chosen image is placed onto the stack
    ## we want it to appear in the image area and not resize
    set the rect of the templateImage to the rect of me
    set the lockLoc of the templateImage to true
    iPhonePickPhoto "library"
    if the result is empty then
        ## If the result is empty you know the user has chosen an image
        ## and you can start working with it.
    end if
    ## The new image will be the "last" image
    ## We get the text of it, set the text of the stock image
    ## and then delete the "last" image
    set the text of me to the text of the last image of this card
    delete the last image of this card
end mouseUp
```

Adding New Items

To add a new item to our inventory, we simply add a new card to the stack. It should, of course, contain all the controls we have set up for each item—the information fields, buttons, and image. There is a simple way to do this in LiveCode. By grouping the controls together and checking the Behave Like a Background property of the group in the group's basic properties list, the controls will automatically be added to new cards as they are created. Because the image data is not distinct for each card when contained in a background, we will have to copy the product image to each new card separately.

Scripting the New Button

The New button creates a new card and creates an image area. Click the New button while pressing COMMAND-OPTION or CONTROL-ALT to open the Script Editor, and set the script of the button to

```
on mouseUp
newEntry
end mouseUp
```

This script calls a handler named `newEntry`, which is located in the stack script:

```
on newEntry
    ## Add a new card
    ## This will create a new card with the controls group on it
    create card

    ## The long name is a unique identifier
    put the long name of it into tNewCard

    ## We need to create an image separately on the new card
    ## as image data is shared
    copy image "stock image" of card 1 to tNewCard
    set the text of image "stock image" of tNewCard to empty

    ## Put the initial text into the fields
    send "resetControls" to group "controls" of tNewCard

    ## Go to the new card using a visual effect
    visual effect push left
    go to tNewCard

    ## Put the cursor in the name field
    focus on field "name" of group "controls" of tNewCard
    select after field "name" of group "controls" of tNewCard
end newEntry
```

Navigating Between Records

After we have more than one card in the stack, we need to provide the ability to move among them. Because this is an iPad app, we will use a sliding (swipe) movement to navigate to the next or previous card: when moving forward, the old item should slide off the left side of the screen; when moving backward, the old item should slide off the right side. Use the LiveCode command `visual effect push left`.

The following `moveForward` handler is in the stack script, along with an equivalent `moveBack` handler. As with the `newEntry` handler, placing it in the stack script makes it accessible to all the buttons and cards in the stack.

```
on moveForward
    ## If the current card is not the last card go to the next card
    ## If the current card is the last card circle to the first card

    put the number of this card into tCurrentCard
    put the number of cards of this stack into tNumberOfEntries

    if tCurrentCard < tNumberOfEntries then
        visual effect push left
        go to the next card
    else if tCurrentCard = tNumberOfEntries then
```

```
          ## Go to the first card
          visual effect push left
          go to the first card
      end if
end moveForward
```

Using Swipe Gestures

We want to be able to move between records by swiping left or right and moving through the items accordingly. LiveCode provides touchStart, touchEnd, and touchMove messages allowing you to detect swipe gestures. By recording the start and end points of the touch and calculating how far the user has swiped and in what direction, you can detect and manage swipe gestures. Swipe commands are handled in the stack script:

```
on touchStart pID
    ## When the user touches the screen
    put empty into sCoordinateArray["start"]
    put empty into sCoordinateArray["end"]
end touchStart

on touchMove pID, x y
    if sCoordinateArray["start"] is empty then
        put x into sCoordinateArray["start"]
    else
        put x into sCoordinateArray["end"]
    end if
end touchMove

on touchEnd
    put sCoordinateArray["start"] into tStart
    put sCoordinateArray["end"] into tEnd

    ## Compare the x coordinates of the start and end point
    ## This tells us the direction of the movement
    if tStart is not empty and tEnd is not empty then
        if tStart > tEnd and tStart - tEnd > 100 then
            moveForward
        else if tStart < tEnd and tEnd-tStart > 100 then
            moveBack
        end if
    end if
    put empty into sCoordinateArray["start"]
    put empty into sCoordinateArray["end"]
end touchEnd
```

Testing on the Simulator

Now we will use the iPad simulator to test our app. Save the stack, choose File | Standalone Application Setting, and go to the iOS pane:

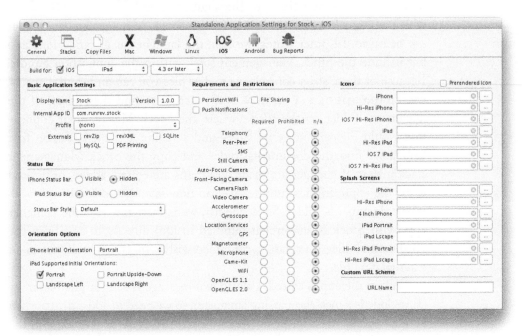

Check Build for iOS, select iPad as the supported device, and choose the minimum iOS version. In the Orientation Options section, check the Portrait check box. Choose the Hidden radio button for the iPad Status Bar setting. In the LiveCode menu bar, click the Simulate button and the app will be launched in the Simulator.

Deleting an Item

You delete an item simply by deleting the card in the stack that holds its information. To enable this, open the script of the Delete button by clicking it while pressing COMMAND-OPTION or CONTROL-ALT, and set its script to

```
on mouseUp
    deleteEntry
end mouseUp
```

The following `deleteEntry` handler goes in the stack script:

```
on deleteEntry
## Delete the current card
visual effect push left
delete this card
end deleteEntry
```

Using a Launcher App

Under iOS safety rules, you cannot save changes to a stand-alone application like Stock Management, so any changes we make to our data could be lost when we quit the app. The solution is to build a launcher app, which in turn launches a version of the Stock Management stack that *can* be saved. In other words, we save the launcher as a stand-alone app but include the Stock Management stack within the application bundle. Because of these strict controls over what files you can and cannot access, we use the `specialFolderPath` function to find the address of the documents folder on the iPad—where the Stock Management application would logically store its data—and save the app there. So, on first launch we find the documents folder and copy the Stock Management stack into it. If changes are made and items are edited, added, or deleted while the application is running, we can now save the updated stack back to the documents folder. Subsequently, we launch and save the launcher app (with Stock Management bundled inside) directly to and from the documents folder. Our data is contained within the stack itself, not in an external data file.

When the app is closed, a shutdown message is sent up the hierarchy (LiveCode is a message-passing language), so we need to add a `shutDown` handler to the stack script in which we tell the stack to save itself to the documents folder before shutting down:

```
on shutdown
    ## When the app is closed save it to preserve data
    save stack "Stock" as (specialFolderPath("documents") & "/Stock.livecode")
end shutDown
```

To create a launcher stack, create another iPad-sized stack, name it **Stock Launcher**, and set its label to **Stock Management**. This stack should never be seen, but we will set the background color to black just in case. You could add a "starting up" message here (such as "Welcome to Amy's Stock Manager"). Add the following handler to its stack script—this is the code that launches the main stack:

```
on openstack
## The first time the app is started copy the Stock stack
## from the application bundle to the documents folder where it can be saved
## The next time the app is started launch the Stock stack in the documents folder

put specialFolderPath("documents") & "/Stock.livecode" into tMainStackPath
if there is not a file tMainStackPath then
## This is the first time the app has been run
put specialFolderPath("engine") & "/Stock.livecode" into tOriginalStackPath
put url ("binfile:" & tOriginalStackPath) into url ("binfile:" & tMainStackPath)
end if

## Launch the main Stock stack
go stack tMainStackPath
end openstack
```

Testing and Skinning on the iPad

You can now deploy your app to an iPad and do some testing; be sure that the gestures work, that you can add, edit, and delete stock items, and that your data is still there the next time you start up!

To make the app more attractive, you can do some very simple skinning. In the example in the lower right we have simply used a background image and some button icons. These are available in a zip file provided by LiveCode in support of this case study (http://newsletters. livecode.com/february/issue165/SimpleStock-ManagementResources.zip). Import the background image using the Import as Control option in the File menu. Then use the Size & Position pane of the Property Inspector to set the layer of the image to 1—this means it will be below all the controls. You can then move the fields, image area, and buttons around to achieve the desired layout.

For a more detailed lesson on customizing the appearance of LiveCode apps, check out http://lessons.runrev.com/spaces/lessons/manuals/2571/lessons/19144-Skinning.

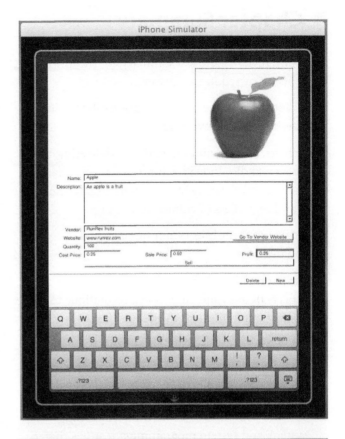

Chapter 12 Review

■ Chapter Summary

For your review, here's a summary of the important concepts discussed in this chapter.

Consider the implications of mobile devices in the worldwide digital revolution

■ Tablets, readers, and smartphones delivering text, images, audio, and video have explosively changed the nature of society in all nations around the world regardless of culture or language.

Describe what mobile/tablet devices can be used for

■ Smartphones and mobile devices are used in all aspects of daily life, from social revolutions to game playing entertainment to calling a taxi.

■ There are more than 6 billion mobile accounts in the world.

Discuss mobile device hardware

■ It is the combination of hardware, operating system, and system programming features that differentiates the many brands of tablets and smartphones available in the marketplace.

■ Mobile devices may have as many as four radios on board.

■ CDMA and GSM are the radio technologies in use today. They are not compatible with each other.

■ A SIM card can be seamlessly swapped among handsets, bringing your phone books, contact lists, and schedulers to a new phone without rekeying or having to make a trip to the provider.

■ 3G and 4G are communication protocols that govern this movement of information on the radio connection between handset and tower.

■ Wi-Fi provides a high-speed connection to wireless access points or hotspots.

■ Bluetooth is a short-range, low-power radio technology.

■ Multi-touch gestures are the new human interface.

Characterize the smallness of the mobile world

■ Smartphones and mobile devices and social networks have helped make ours a very small world! While it has been thought that six degrees of separation among all people is the norm, research on Twitter shows only 3.43 degrees lie between you and anybody else.

Discuss mobile device operating systems

■ iOS and Android are the operating systems used on more than 90 percent of mobile devices.

Program an app

■ Programming mobile apps is not trivial and requires a framework or integrated development environment.

■ To deal with the many screen sizes and pixel densities, the responsive web design (RWD) movement is developing methods to deal with the difficulty of programming for the many screen sizes.

■ Publishing an app at Google Play or Apple's App Store requires registration as a developer and approval of the app.

Key Terms

3D Touch *(399)*
3G (Third Generation) *(404)*
4G (Fourth Generation) *(404)*
agent of change *(392)*
Android *(405)*
Bluetooth *(404)*
Code Division Multiple
  Access (CDMA) *(403)*
digital light projector (DLP) *(401)*
Global Positioning
  System (GPS) *(393)*
Global System for Mobile
  Communications (GSM) *(403)*
handshake *(401)*
hybrid apps *(406)*

integrated development
  environment (IDE) *(406)*
iOS *(405)*
launcher app *(416)*
Long-Term Evolution (LTE) *(404)*
meme *(393)*
multi-touch gesture *(398)*
Near Field Communication
  (NFC) *(395)*
planking *(396)*
public switched telephone
  network (PSTN) *(403)*
responsive web design
  (RWD) *(406)*
Secure Enclave *(399)*

short message service
  (SMS) *(395)*
six degrees of separation *(397)*
stack *(410)*
Subscriber Identity Module
  (SIM) card *(403)*
system-on-a-chip (SoC)
  technology *(399)*
texting *(394)*
Wi-Fi *(404)*
WiMAX *(404)*
wireless access point (WAP)
  (404)
Xcode *(409)*

Key Term Quiz

1. A very short-range, low-power radio technology for mobiles is called _____.

2. The most common radio technology used in Europe to connect smartphones to cell towers is _____.

3. The _____ operating system is owned by Google.

4. A(n) _____ is a unit of cultural behavior and style.

5. _____ is the technology used to connect mobile devices to hotspots.

6. Technology that allows for many key functions to reside on a single chip is called _____.

7. Sending short messages back and forth is called _____.

8. A pinch, swipe, or tap is considered a(n) _____.

9. _____ is the SDK for programming an app for iOS.

10. Apps made for iOS or Android using HTML5, CSS, and JavaScript are called _____.

■ Multiple-Choice Quiz

1. The mobile and multimedia Internet is:
   a. altering our quality of life
   b. an agent of change
   c. at the barricades
   d. available worldwide
   e. all of the above

2. Law enforcement is worried about electronic:
   a. jailbreaking
   b. planking
   c. sexting
   d. bricking
   e. all of the above

3. With the Uber app you can:
   a. virtually fly to Hawaii
   b. call a taxi
   c. replace errors in Microsoft Word
   d. win the lottery
   e. learn German

4. Actor Kevin Bacon once demonstrated:
   a. mobile ventriloquy
   b. multimedia dating
   c. online purchasing
   d. six degrees of separation
   e. distracted driving

5. Which of the following would not be included in system-on-a-chip (SoC) technology:
   a. graphics processor
   b. audio components
   c. USB controller
   d. touch screen
   e. power management circuit

6. What is the screen size (in pixels) of an iPad in portrait mode when the status bar is not showing?
   a. 480×640
   b. 768×1024
   c. 240×320
   d. 900×1200
   e. none of the above

7. In iOS, information that the system needs to interact with your app is contained in the:
   a. README.TXT file
   b. root
   c. Info.plist file
   d. Key.app file
   e. Run.inf file

8. Which is not a size defined by Android?
   a. small (426×320 dp)
   b. normal (470×320 dp)
   c. large (at least 640×480 dp)
   d. xlarge (at least 960×720 dp)
   e. super (at least 768×1024 dp)

9. Which of the following is not a development framework?
   a. Adobe Flex
   b. Sencha Touch
   c. Adobe Illustrator
   d. jQuery Mobile
   e. RhoMobile

10. Which is a named version of Android?
    a. PuddingCup
    b. Cheezit
    c. Hobbit
    d. KitKat
    e. Sugar Baby

11. Which is not an operating system for mobile devices?
    a. Blackberry
    b. Windows Phone
    c. iOS
    d. Android
    e. Linux

12. GSM devices broadcast at:
    a. 850 MHz
    b. 900 MHz
    c. 1800 MHz
    d. 1900 MHz
    e. all of the above

13. Which of the following is not a vendor of mobile phone hardware?
    a. Nokia
    b. Boeing
    c. Huawei
    d. Lenovo
    e. LG Electronics

14. Weird social fads or memes include:
    a. vadering
    b. planking
    c. owling
    d. teapotting
    e. all of the above

15. If a smartphone uses a SIM card, it works with:
    a. CDMA
    b. GSM
    c. CD-ROM
    d. JPEG
    e. HDTV

■ Essay Quiz

1. How does mobile technology facilitate the way we communicate? What are its benefits? What are its drawbacks? How has this technology affected you in your personal life?

2. If you were shopping for a smartphone, what criteria would you use to pick the right device for you? Cost? Available network providers? Fancy features? Would your choice depend on friends' suggestions or on research you conduct on the Internet?

3. You are planning a trip to three foreign countries. Research available mobile options in those countries to see if you can use your current cell phone while traveling. Describe the technologies and service provider restrictions that may prevent you from using your current cell phone. Explore options that will successfully work for you and outline their costs. Explain why features and costs vary.

4. Mobile device chargers and power supplies use many different voltages and many different connectors. Research the current status of the Universal Power Supply movement. Where have billions of electrical transformers (discarded power supplies) been disposed of during the past ten years? What effect will this have on the environment?

5. Consider building a simple custom app to keep track of your family members' birthdays. What operating system would you build it for? Which programming language or languages would you learn? How long would it take you? How would you distribute it to your family members?

Lab Projects

■ Project 12.1

You are tasked with designing a mobile app for teachers. The app must be designed to help teachers with some part of their job, be it grading, distributing homework, helping individual students, or any novel idea you can imagine. Using a wireframe program online or using whatever tools you have at your disposal, create three screens of the app in action. Be sure to also document what the app is meant to achieve and why you made the design choices you did.

■ Project 12.2

Once you have completed exercise 12.1, now you must decide what mobile device and OS to develop the application for. Explore the various options, such as iOS for Apple and Android for Google, and also tablet vs. smartphone. Explain the pros and cons of each option that you considered in your decision-making process.

■ Project 12.3

Using a mobile device, find three mobile apps and download them. Make sure you have at least one game, one image altering or capturing app, and one educational app. Compare the differences and similarities, noting how functional and intuitive each is to use, how the development process of each app might have differed, and if/how the developer makes money from the app. What features seem to make an app better? What features (or lack thereof) detract from an app's usability?

■ Project 12.4

Go online and navigate to http://gamesalad.com/creator and download the latest free version of GameSalad, a simplified game engine for making mobile games and apps. After you have downloaded the GameSalad program, open it, navigate to File | New and create a new GameSalad project; by default the platform should be set to iPhone landscape. Familiarize yourself with the layout, noting the Actor, Behavior, and Media tabs on the top left of the program layout—they will be marked by icons.

Next, locate the sound file you created in Project 4.2 from Chapter 4. Using the import media feature of GameSalad, add the sound file (note: you may need to convert the file type to an .m4a file). Next, add an "actor" by clicking the plus sign on the Actors tab. Select the new actor, label it **Play**, and drag it into the center of the design interface—a white square should appear. Double-click the square to open your actor's Mechanics tab. Now go into the Behaviors tab at the top left, and find the Add New Rule behavior. Drag-and-drop it onto the Mechanics tab. Within the new rule under "when [all] of the following are happening", add the Touch behavior. Under Do, add the Play Music behavior. Now when you test your app, you should be able to play the recording when you click the white square Play actor.

Test your app by clicking the green play arrow at the top of the interface.

■ Project 12.5

Find an app that uses the real world around it to function, such as an astronomy app or an alternate/augmented reality game. Play around with the app you find, taking note of what works well and how the app functions. Now use your imagination and creativity to envision mobile multimedia that somehow interacts with reality (usually called "augmented reality"). What would your program do? Why would people want to use it? Push your creativity and imagine something epic—maybe after finishing this book you'll be on your way to creating it!

Delivering

T EST it—and then test it again; that's the unavoidable rule. You must test and review your project or web site to ensure that it is bug free, accurate, operationally and visually on target, and ready to meet the client's requirements, even if that client is you.

Do this testing before the work is finalized and released for public or client consumption. A bad reputation earned by premature product release can destroy an otherwise excellent piece of work representing thousands of hours of effort. If you need to, delay the release of the work to be sure that it is as good as possible. It's critical that you take the time to thoroughly exercise your project and fix both big and little problems; in the end, you will save yourself a great deal of agony!

One of the major difficulties you face in testing the operation of your multimedia project is that its performance may depend on specific hardware and system configurations and, in the case of the Internet, on end users' connection speeds and choice of browser. If you cannot control the end user's platform, or if the project is designed to be shown in many different environments, you must fully test your project on as many platforms as possible, including heavily loaded, complicated systems. Testing will confirm your **system requirements**, which is a description of the minimum (or recommended) platform.

Game projects that are built to reach as large an audience as possible are designed and tested on mobile, tablet, and desktop platforms. For example, the original *Angry Birds* is designed to function on all these platforms, meaning its creator, Rovio Entertainment, had to determine the game's requirements for each platform. They are listed in the respective **app store** for each platform as indicated in Table 13-1.

ANGRY BIRDS STAR WARS

iPhone iPad Android Kindle
Windows Phone 7 Windows Phone 8
Mac PC Windows 8

DOWNLOAD

Platform	Store	Listed Requirements
Windows desktop	Angry Birds Online Store	Minimum System Requirements OS: Windows 7/Vista/XP SP3 CPU: 1.0 GHz RAM: 512 MB Hard Drive: 60 MB Graphics: Any OpenGL 1.3 compatible device Internet connection required for activation and updates
Mac desktop	Mac App Store	Size: 73.9 MB Compatibility: OS X 10.6 or later
Windows Phone 8	Windows Phone Store	Download size: 24 MB App requires: Xbox Phone identity Data services HD720P (720×1280) WVGA (480×800) WXGA (768×1280)
iPhone, iPad, and iPod touch	iTunes	Size: 42.5 MB Requires iOS 4.3 or later This app is optimized for iPhone 5
Android	Google Play	Size: 44 MB Requires Android 2.3 and up

Table 13-1 Angry Birds' system requirements for different platforms

TIP *Remember to budget for obtaining the hardware test platforms, as well as for the many hours of effort that testing will require. If you are working for a client, clearly specify the intended delivery platform and its hardware and software configuration, and provide a clause in your agreement or contract that you will test only to that platform.*

Few computer configurations are identical. Even identical hardware configurations may be running dissimilar software that can interact with your program in unexpected ways. Because any element of a computer's configuration may be the cause of a problem or a bug, you will spend a good portion of testing time configuring platforms, and additional time reproducing reported problems and curing them. It is not possible for even a well-equipped developer to test every possible configuration of computer, software, and third-party add-ons. Services are available to test your project for a fee. Such companies, for example uTest (www.applause.com), will run your project through its paces and try to identify all the bugs and problems they can wring out of it.

Testing

The terms *alpha* and *beta* are used by software developers to describe levels of product development when testing is done and feedback is sought. **Alpha releases** are typically for internal circulation only and are passed among a select group of mock users—often just the team working on the project. These versions of a product are often the first working drafts of your project, and you can expect them to have problems or to be incomplete. **Beta releases**, on the other hand, are sent to a wider but still select audience with the same caveat: this software may contain errors, bugs, and unknown alligators that slither out of the swamp at day's end to bite startled designers from behind. Because your product is now being shown and used outside the privacy of its birth nest, its reputation will begin to take form during beta phase. Thankfully though, beta-level bugs are typically less virulent than alpha bugs.

TIP   *If your project is a web site, there are a number of online tools that will validate your code, and indicate where you need to make tweaks or repairs. Do a search for "HTML validation" or "CSS validation" tools.*

Alpha Testing

You should remain flexible and amenable to changes in both the design and the behavior of your project as you review the comments of your alpha testers. Beware of alpha testing groups made up of kindly friends who can provide positive criticism. Rather, you need to include aggressive people who will attack all aspects of your work. The meaner and nastier they are, the more likely they will sweat out errors or uncertainties in your product's design or navigation system. In the testing arena, learn to skillfully utilize friend and enemy alike. You will undoubtedly discover aspects of your work that, despite even the most insightful planning, you have overlooked.

Beta Testing

The beta testing group should be representative of real users and should not include persons who have been involved in the project's production. Beta testers must have no preconceived ideas. You want them to provide commentary and reports in exchange for getting to play with the latest software and for recognition as part of this "inside" process.

From a letter with enclosed software, delivered by overnight courier to 240 testers around the world:

We had a bit of a scare on this Beta. Here is the replacement copy for the infected B5 program. For your info, the virus that got past me was a strain of nVir. It was dormant and fooled Virus Detective, Virex, and Interferon. Virex 1.1 listed it as a harmless "Stub" that was left over from a previous cleanup. It wasn't until late yesterday that we discovered that it was real. I must apologize for letting this slip past me and thank the people in our tech support department for their help in calling all the members of the Beta test team and alerting them to this problem. If they didn't get hold of you, it was certainly not for lack of trying.

Ben Calica, letter author and a product manager who claims this product shortened his life span by two years

Managing beta test feedback is critical. If you ignore or overlook testers' comments, the testing effort is a waste. Ask your beta testers to include
a detailed description of the hardware and software configuration at the
time the problem occurred, and a step-by-step recounting of the problem, so that you can re-create it, analyze it, and repair it. You should also
solicit general comments and suggestions. Figure 13-1 presents the search

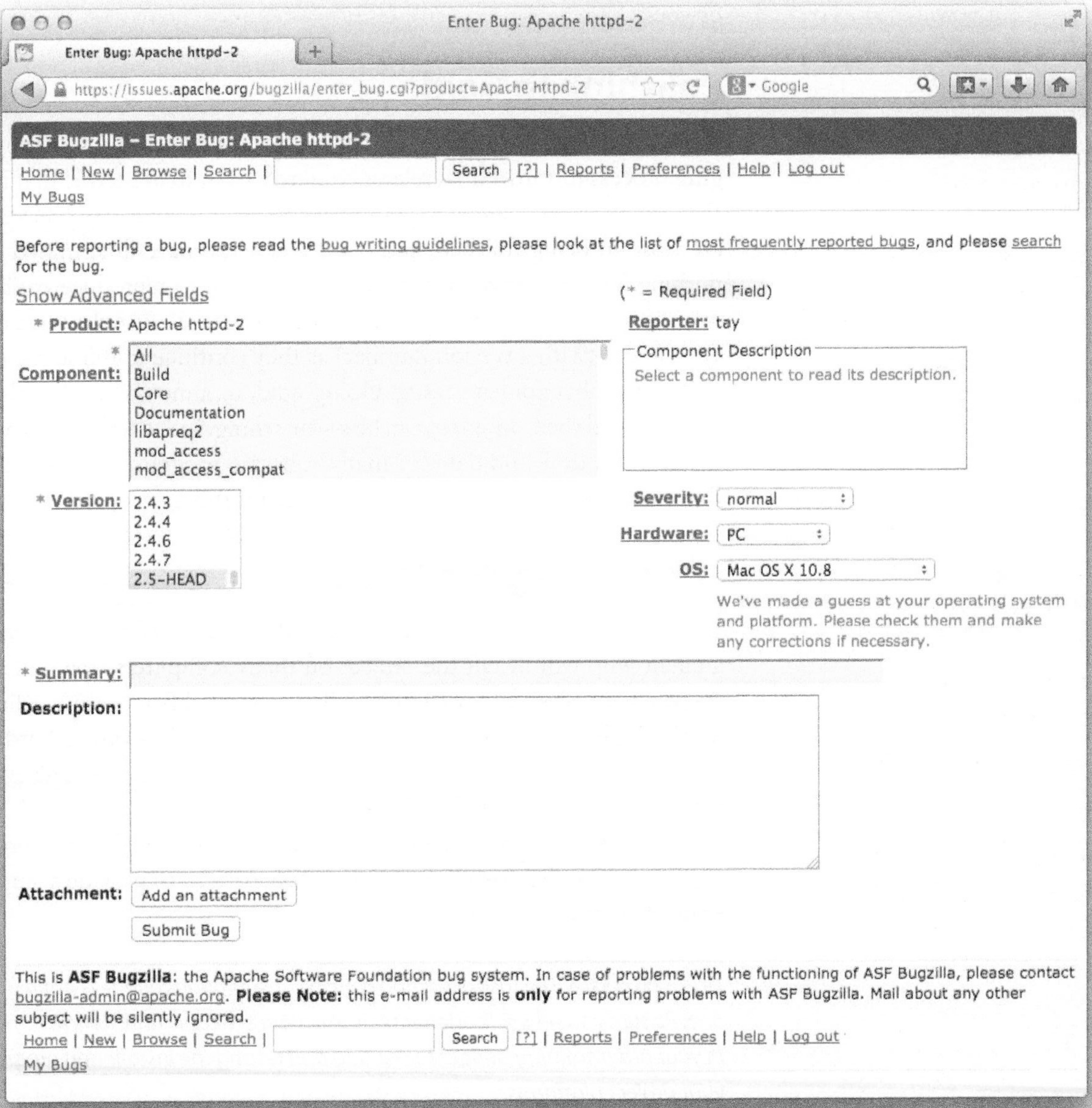

Figure 13-1 This page from a web-based bug reporting system seeks precise and reproducible descriptions of problems. In testing complex applications, thousands of bug reports may be received, and a dedicated quality control team may be tasked to deal with them.

page from a web-based bug reporting system that is database driven and capable of managing thousands of reports about a complicated application in a meaningful way. (Apache is the most widely used HTTP daemon for serving web pages.)

TIP   *Look for testers from a broad range of users, novice to expert. You've been through the program hundreds of times, and you know what's supposed to happen. A new or novice user may get stuck in a place where you thought all is clearly obvious.*

Polishing to Gold

As you move through alpha and beta testing, and then through the debugging process toward a final release, you may want to use terms that indicate the current version status of your project—for example, bronze when you are close to being finished, and gold when you have determined there is nothing left to change or correct and are ready to reproduce copies from your golden master. Some software developers also use the term release candidate (with a version number) as they continue to refine the product and approach a golden master. Going gold, or announcing that the job is finished, and then shipping, can be a scary thing. Indeed, if you examine the file creation time and date for many software programs, you will discover that many went gold at two o'clock in the morning.

Preparing for Delivery

If your completed multimedia project will be delivered to consumers or to a client who will install the project on many computers, you will need to prepare your files so they can be easily transferred from your media to the user's platform. Simply copying a project's files to the user's hard disk is often not enough for proper installation; frequently, you will also need to install special system and run-time files.

So that end users can easily and automatically set up your project or application on their own computers, you may need to provide a single program that acts as an installer.

WARNING   *The task of writing a proper installation routine is not a trivial one. Be sure you set aside adequate time in your schedule and sufficient money in your programming budget for writing and testing the installation program for your project platforms.*

It is important to provide well-written documentation about the installation process so that users have a clear step-by-step procedure to follow. That documentation must include a discussion of potential problems and constraints related to the full range of your target platforms. Because

First Person

We beat on the bronze version of the program right up to the last day, when we had to send a golden master to the duplicator by overnight courier. They were prepared to make 40,000 discs in a matter of hours and then hand-carry them directly to a trade show.

Like kids with sticks at a piñata birthday party, we did everything we could to make all the bugs tumble out of the program. Every time a bug appeared, we killed it. As we pounded and tested, fewer and fewer bugs fell out, until none appeared for about six hours straight, under every condition we could dream up. As the deadline for the courier's airport facility neared, we were ready to apply the finishing touches to the product and stamp it gold. One of the guys waited in his car with engine running, ready for the sprint through commuter traffic to the airport.

We were saving the program every three minutes and nervously backing it up on different media about every ten minutes. We had built in a hidden software routine for debugging this project, and when the product manager clicked Save for the last time, he forgot to reset the program for normal use—we didn't know the master was flawed. Handling the disc like a uranium fuel rod traveling through heavy water, we packed it up and got it to the waiting car. An hour later, our postpartum celebration was interrupted by a painful cry from down the hall—someone had discovered the flaw. By then the courier flight had departed.

We fixed it. Faced with the appalling possibility of 40,000 bad discs being invoiced to us instead of the client, we sent the exhausted product manager out on the midnight flight, without a chance even to go home and clean up. He had a golden master disc in his briefcase, one in his shirt pocket, one in his pants pocket, and one in a manila envelope that would never see an airport X-ray machine.

you likely will not have control over the specification and configuration of the user's platform, it is critical that you include appropriate warnings in your installation document, like these examples:

- 3MB available disk drive space
- Disable all screen savers before running
- Back up older versions before installing this update

Often a file named **README.TXT** or **Read.Me** is a useful thing to include on the distribution disc of your project. This file can be a simple ASCII text file accessible by any text editor or word processing application. It should contain a description of changes or bugs reported since the documentation was printed and may also contain a detailed description of the installation process.

If your project will be deployed from the Web, provide special directions in a FAQ or Help page, where you can describe required plug-ins, browser compatibility, and other issues. You can often do much dynamically using JavaScript "sniffer" routines to alert users when their browser is not compatible. You can serve different versions of your project tailored to a user's particular system or browser.

The clearer and more detailed your installation instructions are, the fewer frustrated queries you will receive from your project's users. If your project is designed for wide distribution, installation problems can cause you many headaches and a great deal of time and expense in providing answers and service over the telephone. Set up a product-related web site with pages for software registration, bug reporting, technical support, and program upgrades.

· ·

From: Christopher Yavelow <Christopher@yav.com>

Subject: The case of the keyboardless kiosk

About ten days ago I posted an announcement to the list about our interactive kiosk installation at the new Netherlands Museum of Science and Technology.

Now I've discovered that science museums at this level are the target of bands of teenage hackers that try to crash all the exhibits. Our exhibit fell prey to such a band last Friday.

Although the software is running inside of a kiosk built into a larger "The Music is the Message" exhibit housing AND the museum visitor has only a trackball and single push button to operate the exhibit AND there is *no* way to quit the software without issuing a command-Q from a keyboard which is double-locked inside the guts of the exhibit housing, some kids were able to get back to the desktop and delete the 60 MB of files associated with the exhibit... and they did so in such a way that Norton Utils (3.5) could not find them for un-erasing (I had to bring over a CD-ROM version and re-install the entire exhibit).

How did they do it? Is there a way to get back to the desktop in such a scenario: a (for all practical purposes) keyboardless kiosk with only a trackball and single button interface and no on-screen option to quit the application? There are no menus, the menubar is hidden, there are no quit buttons, AllowInterrupts is set to false, etc., etc.

Christopher Yavelow
YAV Interactive Media
Brederodestraat 47
2042 BB Zandvoort
The Netherlands
eMail: Christopher@yav.com
wSite: http://www.yav.com

Scary message found at an Internet newsgroup for multimedia programmers

· ·

File Archives

One or more of the files in your project can be compressed or "packed" into a single file, called an **archive**. When that archive is then decompressed, or the files are expanded or extracted, each file in the archive is "reconstituted." Figure 13-2 shows the menu of a zipped archive. Archives are usually identified by filename **extensions** representing the compression software that was used, as shown in Table 13-2.

Figure 13-2   A file archive can contain many compressed files.

Extension	Compression Software	Platform
.arc	ARC	Windows
.cab	Windows Install	Windows
.dmg	Macintosh Install	Macintosh
.exe	Self-extracting	Windows
.gz	Gzip	Internet, Unix
.hqx	BinHex	Internet
.rar	RAR	Windows
.sit	StuffIt	Macintosh
.tar	Tar	Internet, Unix
.zip	7-Zip, WinZip	Windows

Table 13-2   Common Filename Extensions for Compressed File Archives

Self-extracting archives are useful for delivering projects in compressed form. On Windows platforms, these are executable files with an .exe filename extension. Less common on the Mac, these files typically carry the filename extension .sea. With self-extracting archives, the user simply runs the executable archive, and the compressed files are automatically decompressed and placed into a folder on the hard disk.

TIP *Keep a copy of your project archive off-site in case of fire or flood.*

First Person

I recently discovered a group of computer scientists and programmers fully dedicated to exploring and improving the techniques and algorithms used for compression of digital data. These folks are from around the world and hang out on bulletin boards, where they have lengthy and arcane electronic conversations. Programmers and mathematicians such as Huffman, Lempel, and Ziv have been made famous on these services.

The greatest contribution this group has made to computer technology may not be in the area of information condensation, but in the creative spin-off of peculiar new words such as freshen, pack, crunch, squash, shrink, crush, implode, distill, squeeze, stuff, and garble.

When you throw a few atoms and best guesses into this potpourri of words, the language of data compression joins that of modern physics, with its own quarks, gluons, and happy and sad particles. It's a creative and inventive place in the day-to-day forward motion of human endeavor, this place of strange and beautiful compression algorithms.

Delivering on CD-ROM

Many multimedia projects are delivered on CD-ROM or DVD. While the very first users of CD-ROMs were owners of large databases like library catalogs, reference systems, and parts lists, today most computers are shipped with a CD/DVD drive, and software that is not downloaded from the Internet is typically packaged on a disc.

Compact Disc Technology

A compact disc, or CD, is a thin wafer of clear polycarbonate plastic and metal measuring 4.75 inches (120 mm) in diameter, with a small hole, or hub, in its center. The metal layer is usually pure aluminum, sputtered onto the polycarbonate surface in a thickness measurable in molecules. As the disc spins in the CD player, the metal reflects light from a tiny infrared laser into a light-sensitive receiver diode. These reflections are transformed into an electrical signal and then further converted to meaningful bits and bytes for use in digital equipment.

Pits on the CD, where the information is stored, are 1 to 3 microns long, about 1/2 micron wide, and 1/10 micron deep. (By comparison, a human hair is about 18 microns in diameter.) A CD can contain as many as three miles of these tiny pits wound in a spiral pattern from the hub to the edge. A layer of lacquer is applied to protect the surface, and artwork from the disc's author or publisher is usually silk-screened on the back side.

Compact discs are made in what is generally referred to as a **family process**. The glass master is made using the well-developed, photolithographic techniques created by the microchip industry: First an optically ground glass disc is coated with a layer of photo-resistant material 1/10 micron thick. A laser then exposes (writes) a pattern of pits onto the surface of the chemical layer of material. The disc is developed (the exposed areas are washed away) and is silvered, resulting in the actual pit structure of the finished master disc. The master is then electroplated with layers of nickel one molecule thick, one layer at a time, until the desired thickness is reached. The nickel layer is separated from the glass disc and forms a metal negative, or **father**.

In cases where low runs of just a few discs are required, the father is used to make the actual discs. Most projects, though, require several **mothers**, or positives, to be made by plating the surface of the father.

In a third plating stage, **sons**, or **stampers**, are made from the mother, and these are the parts that are used in the injection molding machines. Plastic pellets are heated and injected into the mold or stamper, forming the disc with the pits in it. The plastic disc is coated with a thin aluminum layer for reflectance and lacquer for protection, given a silk-screened label for marketing, and packaged for delivery. Most of these activities occur in a particle-free clean room, because one speck of dust larger than a pit can ruin many hours of work. The mastering process alone takes around 12 hours.

CD-R

Compact Disc: Recordable (CD-R) is an excellent method for distributing multimedia projects. CD-R writers and blank CD-R discs are inexpensive, and for short runs of a product, it is more cost effective to **burn** your work onto CD-Rs and custom-label them with your own printer than to have the discs mastered and **pressed** using the expensive father and son method described previously. Many services with auto-loading equipment and 24-hour turnarounds can make short runs.

CD-R blanks that can hold as much as 84 minutes of Red Book sound (see the next section) or more than 700MB of data are made of a polycarbonate core coated with layers of reflective metals and special photosensitive organic dyes (see Figure 13-3). During the burning process, laser light hits the layer of dye, bakes it, and forms a pit. A 74-minute CD-R disc contains 333,000 sectors × 2048 bytes/sector for a capacity of 650.4MB. An 80-minute disc contains 360,000 sectors × 2048 bytes/sector for a data capacity of 703.1MB.

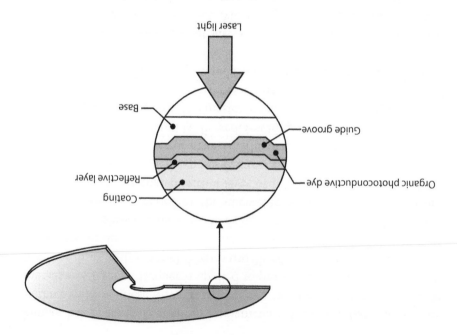

Figure 13-3   As a CD or DVD disc spins, laser light is beamed along a groove or track of lands (high points) and pits (low points). The difference in reflected light as the beam passes over these tiny spots is interpreted as binary data.

Labels in figure:
Base
Guide groove
Reflective layer
Coating
Organic photoconductive dye
Laser light

Compact Disc Standards

In 1979, Philips and Sony together launched CD technology as a digital method of delivering sound and music (audio) to consumers. This collaboration resulted in the **Red Book standard** (named for the color of the document's jacket), officially called the **Compact Disc Digital Audio Standard**. The Red Book standard defines the audio format for the CDs available in music stores today. Later, the Yellow Book covered **Compact Disc Read-Only Memory (CD-ROM)**; the Green Book covered **Compact Disc Interactive (CD-I)**; the Orange Book covered write-once, read-only (WORM) CD-ROMs; and the White Book covered **Video CD** (Karaoke CD).

The Red Book

The Red Book remains the basis for standards that define more elaborate digital data formats for computers and other digital devices. Audio CDs can provide up to 80 minutes of playing time, which is enough for a slow-tempo rendition of Beethoven's Ninth Symphony. This was reported to be Philips and Sony's actual criterion during research and development for determining the size of sectors and ultimately the physical size of the CD itself.

A CD may contain one or more **tracks**. These are areas normally allocated for storing a single song in the Red Book format. CDs also contain lead-in information and a table of contents. Each track on the CD may use a different format; this allows you to create a mixed-mode disc that combines, for example, high-quality CD-Audio with Macintosh **Hierarchical File System (HFS)** CD-ROM or ISO 9660 data formats. Figure 13-4 illustrates the track layouts for Red Book, Yellow Book, Green Book, mixed mode, and for Kodak's **Photo CD** Orange Book layout. Both Macintosh and Windows support commands to access both Red Book Audio and the data tracks on a CD, but you cannot access both at the same time.

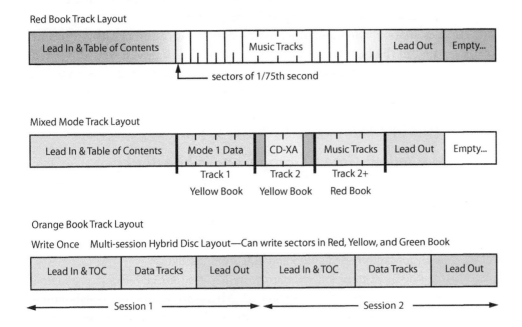

Figure 13-4 CD track layouts

Though a CD contains tracks, the primary logical unit for data storage on a CD is a **sector**, which is 1/75 second in length. Each sector of a CD contains 2,352 bytes of data. After every sector are another 882 bytes consisting of two layers of error-detecting code (EDC) and error-correcting code (ECC) and timing control data. A CD actually requires, then, 3,234 bytes to store 2,352 bytes of data. EDC and ECC allow a scratched or dirty data sector to be reconstructed by software fast enough to avoid dropout of music. Timing codes are used to display song-playing time on an audio CD player.

TIP *Because there is built-in error correction on CDs, small scratches may not affect playback, particularly when the scratch runs in a straight line from center to edge. To really wreck a CD, scratch it in an easy arc from the center to the rim; error correction won't keep up.*

The disc spins at a constant linear velocity (CLV), so data can be read at a constant density and spacing. This means the rotational speed of the disc may vary from about 200 rpm when the read head is at the outer edge, to 530 rpm when it is reading near the hub. This translates to about 1.3 meters (51 inches) of travel along the data track each second. CD players use very sensitive motors so that no matter where the read head is on the disc, approximately the same amount of data is read in each second.

The CD's rotational speed and the density of the pits and lands on the CD allow data to be read at a sustained rate of 150 Kbps in a single-speed reader. This is sufficient for good audio, but it is very slow for large image files, motion video, and other multimedia resources, especially when compared to the high data-transfer rates of hard disk drives. New drives that spin many times faster when reading computer data, and slower for Red Book Audio, have been designed specifically for computers. In any case, CD access speed and transfer rate from CD-ROM is much slower than from a hard disk.

The Yellow, Green, Orange, and White Books

Philips and Sony developed the **Yellow Book** to provide an established standard for data storage and retrieval. The Yellow Book adds yet another layer of error checking to accommodate the greater reliability required of computer data, and it provides two modes: one for computer data and the other for compressed audio and video/picture data.

The most common standard currently used for CD-ROM production evolved from the Yellow Book, with Microsoft joining the collaboration, and it was approved by the International Standards Organization as **ISO 9660.**

WARNING *It is possible to damage your speakers if you play the digital track of a CD-ROM on your audio CD player. The digital data is decoded as full-volume noise by players that do not check for a data flag in the control field of the Q subchannel.*

Later, other standards were developed to deal with specific user requirements, such as synchronized interleaving of compressed audio and visual data in interactive digital movies (**Green Book**), and with formats for **write-once, read-only (WORM)** and magneto-optical CD technologies (**Orange Book**). A CD-R can have several separate images or **sessions** on it, each recorded at different times. **CD-ROM/XA** extends the Yellow Book standard to combine video, audio, and computer data.

The Red, Yellow, Green, and Orange books describe the types of compact discs listed in Table 13-3.

Name	Description	Comment
CD-Audio or CD-DA	Digital audio	Consumer audio discs
CD-ROM High Sierra	Read-only memory	Vestigial standard, seldom used
CD-ROM ISO 9660	Read-only memory	MS-DOS and Macintosh files
CD-ROM HFS	Read-only memory	Macintosh HFS files
CD-ROM/XA	Read-only memory	Extended Architecture
CD-I or CD-RTOS	Interactive	Philips Interactive motion video
CD-I Ready	Interactive/Ready	Audio CD with features for CD-I player
CD-Bridge	Bridge	Allows XA track to play on CD-I player
CD-MO	Magneto-optical	Premastered area readable on any CD player
CD-WO or CD-R	Write-once recordable	May use multiple sessions to fill disc
CD+G	Mixed mode	CD+Graphics—MTV on disc
CDTV	ISO 9660 variant	Commodore proprietary system
Photo CD	Compressed images	Kodak multisession XA system
Video CD or Karaoke CD	Bridge	Karaoke full-motion MPEG video

Table 13-3 Compact Disc Formats

Many multimedia developers place both Macintosh files and PC files on the same CD in a **hybrid format**, letting the user launch the proper applications for the appropriate platform. You can selectively hide the files of either platform when you create a hybrid so that Windows users will not be confused by odd-looking Macintosh files in their directories, and vice versa. Graphics, text, and data files written in common formats such as DOC, TIF, PIC, DBF, and WKS can be read from an ISO 9660 CD and imported into your application, whether the file was generated on a Macintosh or a PC.

Delivering on DVD

Digital Versatile Discs (DVDs) employ a different (multilayer, high-density) manufacturing process than audio and data CDs, and this technology provides as much as 15.9GB of storage on a single disc in the Double-Sided, Dual-Layered format (DVD-18). More common and readily available are Single-Sided, Single-Layered discs offering 4.37GB of storage (DVD-5), often called "4.7GB Media."

In December 1995, nine major electronics companies (Toshiba, Matsushita, Sony, Philips, Time Warner, Pioneer, JVC, Hitachi, and Mitsubishi Electric) agreed to promote a new optical disc technology for distribution of multimedia and feature-length movies. They called this new technology "DVD."

With this medium capable not only of gigabyte storage capacity but also full-motion video (MPEG2) and high-quality audio in surround sound, the bar was raised for multimedia developers: commercial multimedia projects become more expensive to produce as consumers' performance expectations rise.

DVD Standards

Different formats are used to write DVD-video discs and DVD data storage discs. DVD-video discs use a variant of MPEG2 and were designed for set-top boxes connected to televisions. DVD-video is authored by mastering software that allows rudimentary scripting and branching for menu structures, chapter markers, and slide shows, but the format only allows for basic logic (and relies on a simple hand-held remote control input device).

Using a DVD disc as a storage medium, you can create a complex multimedia title using any authoring or programming system, and distribute it on a DVD-ROM disc. Most computers can read or play both DVD-ROM and DVD-video discs. Set-top DVD players are limited to playing DVD-video.

There are three competing sets of standards for data recording on DVD: DVD-R/DVD-RW, DVD+R/DVD+RW, and DVD-RAM. The "R" and "RW" stand for recordable and rewritable respectively. DVD standards are supported by the DVD Forum (www.dvdforum.org). DVD+ standards are supported by the DVD+RW Alliance (www.dvdservices.org). DVD-RAM has better recording features but requires more specialized playback hardware. DVD-R/DVD-RW and DVD+R/DVD+RW are similar and can be played back on most DVD players and drives.

With Dolby AC-3 Digital Surround Sound as part of the DVD specifications, six discrete audio channels can be programmed for digital surround sound, and with a separate subwoofer channel, developers can program the low-frequency doom and gloom music popular with Hollywood. DVD also supports Dolby Pro-Logic Surround Sound, standard stereo, and mono audio. Users can randomly access any section of the disc and use the slow-motion and freeze-frame features during movies. Audio tracks can be programmed for as many as 8 different languages, with graphic subtitles in 32 languages. Some manufacturers such as Toshiba are providing parental control features in their players.

True to marketing principles, DVD manufacturers express DVD capacities in billion-byte quantities, where "billion" or "Giga" means the vernacular $1000 \times 1000 \times 1000$, not the more precise binary definition of $1024 \times 1024 \times 1024$ bytes used by your computer. This makes the advertised capacity of a DVD disc sound about 7 percent bigger than it really is; you will not be able to record more than 4.37GB onto a blank disc!

Blu-ray

Blu-ray Discs were designed to deliver high-definition video material, primarily copies of wide-screen feature films and games. Typically, a single-layer Blu-ray Disc can store about 25GB of data; four-layer discs can store about 128GB.

Wrapping It Up

Packaging is an important area where sales and marketing issues extend the process of making multimedia into the real world of end users. Like the cover of a book, people will judge your work based upon the impression it makes.

If your project is for your own use, you may not need the pretty cover, cardboard box, and shrink-wrap that is required for over-the-counter software sold to consumers. If your project is for a client or for the Web, you may simply need to deliver it on any sufficient storage media or upload it to a server. But if your project is headed for wider distribution within a large company or organization or into retail channels, you will need to think about packaging.

If your project is destined to be sold into the consumer retail channel, then you have made a **title**. Software titles are most often distributed on CD-ROM or DVD. The software itself may, indeed, be only one item (the most important one) in a package that includes a user's manual, a registration card, quick reference guides, hardware adapters, and collateral marketing material from you or other parties with whom you have arrangements.

Retailers claim that consumers typically relate the finish of a package to quality and price of the product inside. The fancier, bigger, and heavier the package is, the higher its perceived value. Software manufacturers juggle the elements of this equation when they determine the cost of goods and shipping/freight add-ons and set the product's price point. Many big software boxes are shipped with plenty of "sailboat fuel" inside, and with cardboard or open-cell foam to hold the thin disc and manuals in place. In fact, the manuals may not be printed, but included on the distribution disc as .PDF files.

The art for your cover should reflect the content and function of the enclosed product; it should also follow normal rules for good design layout. Your company's logo should be prominent, and if this is one of a series of titles, the artwork should conform to the coordinated look or style you are using throughout that series or product line.

When your product reaches the retail channel, it may be displayed on shelves or racks, in kiosks, or it may be hung on brackets. You should be sure to put the name of your title on the front face and on the spine of the package. Use photo-quality images and high-caliber artwork for the front, because this is the most visible face of your package. Many packages are shrink-wrapped with thin plastic to protect them from fingerprints and pilferage at the retail outlet. Even after the shrink-wrap is on your package, there is room for additional artwork: bright stickers can be effective eye-catchers. And some vendors apply specially made holographic stickers to identify their product and to prevent unauthorized bootleg copies from reaching the marketplace.

Some vendors have developed unique or special solutions to make their product stand out. Authorware, for example, was once shipped in a custom-designed briefcase with carry handle. An expensive software package to begin with, this briefcase was easily absorbed in the exorbitant purchase price. Fractal Design Painter, the predecessor of Corel Painter, was at one time shipped in a metal paint can with a colorful paper wrapper, and Eye Candy special effects for After Effects came in a metal movie reel case (see Figure 13-5). But package size and shape options are, more often than not, limited by the common constraints of the floor and shelf space found in retailing outlets and by the expense of fabricating a nonstandard container. Indeed, today most software is delivered via the Internet.

Figure 13-5   Some software comes in interesting packages.

Most industrial cities boast more than one packaging specialist with whom you can consult. These outfits can supply cardboard and plastic boxes, printing, cutting, folding, and wrapping services. Environmentally responsible packaging, especially for compact discs, is popular, and special sleeves and cardboard containers are available. Be sure to consider the weight and bulk of your package—an ounce of extra weight that pushes you over a zone or destination boundary might increase your shipping costs significantly. The outside wrap for shipping should be plain because pilferage, especially for international destinations and customs zones, can be a problem. Look for volume discounts and price breaks.

The current trend in software packaging is toward simplification. Indeed, as the information revolution takes hold, more software and documentation will be available for purchase and downloading directly from the Web, and today's boxes and bright packages will become quaint collector's items.

Delivering on the World Wide Web

Delivering multimedia projects built for the World Wide Web can be as simple as renaming a directory or transferring a group of files to a web server. Servers and networked systems are discussed in Chapters 7 and 11. On the face of it, the mechanics of actually putting a project on the Web are trivial, particularly because you have likely been designing, building, and testing within "web space" throughout the development of your project, anyway. But delivery of your project and activation of your pages by making them available to your intended audience on the Web, whether to the general public or to an intranet of select users behind a firewall, should be approached with caution. Here there are many technical considerations that, while outside the topic of multimedia per se, should be understood if you want your project to be a success.

If you own or host the delivery web server yourself, you will have better security control, better integration of your project into your internal LAN or intranet, and the ability to fine-tune the server's configuration parameters and specify and install any special software you need. On the other hand, you will likely need a full-time webmaster, and you will pay for a high-bandwidth connection directly to the Internet. When you have control of the server, you can provide secure commerce services for credit card transactions, encryption and passwords, special databases, and custom CGI programming. For multimedia projects requiring streaming technologies such as RealAudio or video conferencing, you can purchase and install the necessary software on the server.

If your project will reside at a site hosted by an Internet service provider (ISP) or on a company's own internal intranet, you must discover during the planning phase of your project what the host's limitations might be and design your project within those limitations. It does no good to include SVG images, KML files, or complex Java scripts in your web pages, only to find that your ISP does not or will not support the media type or purchase and install the necessary server software for you.

Internet directories like Yahoo and search engines like Google are important components of the Web's "how-to-find-it" functionality and power: using meta tags, be sure your project will register with the search engines and can be easily found.

> A few years ago I taught a student of mine about HTML, just before she went off to a summer internship working on a traditional book publisher's web site. She returned to school three months later and demonstrated to me how one might use the Web to generate profits—at a time when many doubted it was easy to do. Working for the publisher, she was assigned the job of marketing a book for college students. She did her research and discovered how advertising in the search engines works: by "buying" the word "college" on a few of them, she was able to place an ad on search results that were related to colleges; visitors who clicked on her ad were linked to the publisher's web site, where they could purchase the book online. While explaining the process, she checked the online sales of her book: over 5,000 copies had been sold online within a month of publication—eight of them during the last hour!
>
> Panagiotis Takis Metaxas,
> Associate Professor of
> Computer Science,
> Wellesley College

TIP　*Search engine optimization (SEO) is a service offered by many consultants who will, for a fee, "guarantee" that your web site appears in the top results of a search request. There are strict rules of politeness required by the search engine providers which, if not followed, will cause your site never to appear. Search on "seo rules" for more details.*

Delivering Through an App Store

Much of the financial success of mobile devices, tablets, and smartphones can be attributed to the closed platform environment in which they operate. Amazon's Kindle, Apple's iPod, iPad, and iPhone, Barnes & Noble's Nook, and game platforms, among others, work in a proprietary **walled garden** environment where the operating system is controlled by the manufacturer and apps and media are sold only at the company's approved outlet or store (see Table 13-4). Unless you are developing projects only for devices that have been jailbroken (**jailbreaking** lets Apple's iOS out of "jail") or **rooted** (providing superuser root access to Android devices) and will be selling your software only through a third-party distributor like Cydia (named for *Cydia pomonella*, the worm in the apple), you will need to develop a relationship with the platform/store owner:

Welcome to Cydia
by Jay Freeman (saurik)

Cydia > | saurik >

Cydia is an alternative to Apple's App Store for "jailbroken" devices, at this time including iPhones, iPads, and iPod Touches, specializing in the distribution of all that is not an "app".

Cydia is not available in Apple's App Store, nor is it a website: it is installed on your device using a "jailbreaking" tool, such as evasi0n or redsn0w.

- **Apple**   Enroll in the iOS Developer Program (https://developer.apple.com/programs/ios/)
- **Microsoft**   Register as an app developer at the Windows Phone Dev Center (https://dev.windowsphone.com)
- **Google**   Register as a Google Play Developer and pay a one-time fee (https://developers.google.com/apps-marketplace/listing)
- **Barnes & Noble**   Register as an approved Nook App Developer (https://nookdeveloper.barnesandnoble.com/sell-your-apps)
- **Amazon Kindle Fire**   (https://developer.amazon.com/appsandservices/solutions/devices/kindle-fire)

All these programs offer excellent developer tools, technical help, and discussion forums. But because the owners of the walled gardens control all that occurs within, you must have formal approval before selling any product at their respective app store. Table 13-4 lists details about the major official app stores (some of which details are from http://en.wikipedia.org/wiki/List_of_mobile_software_distribution_platforms [accessed January 2014], which also lists many other sources of apps that are available for "jailbroken" or "rooted" devices).

Owner	Store Name	Device Platform	Available Apps	Installed Base	Developer's Cut per Sale (Typical)
Amazon	Amazon Appstore	Android Kindle	50,000	7 million	70%
Apple	App Store	iOS	1,000,000	500 million	56–71% (varies depending on the developer's country)
Barnes & Noble	Nook Apps	Android (Nook)	Sold at Google Play	Millions	70%
BlackBerry	BlackBerry World	BlackBerry OS, BlackBerry Tablet OS, BlackBerry 10 OS	223,601	75 million	70%
Google	Google Play	Android	1,000,000	500 million	70%
Microsoft	Windows Phone Store	Windows Phone	200,000+	47 million	70%
Nokia	Nokia Store	Qt 4 SDK, Nokia Web Tools, Nokia SDK for Java, Java ME	120,000	885 million	70%
Samsung, Handmark	Samsung Apps	Android, bada, Samsung Smart TV	13,000	100 million bada apps; 20 million Samsung Smart TV apps	70%

Table 13-4   Major Stores for Mobile Apps

Chapter 13 Review

■ Chapter Summary

For your review, here's a summary of the important concepts discussed in this chapter.

List the steps a project should go through as part of the testing process, and describe their significance

- Alpha releases are typically circulated among a select group of mock internal users for testing.

- Beta releases are sent to a wider but still select audience with the understanding that the software may contain errors or bugs.

- Beta testers should include a detailed description of the hardware and software configuration and a step-by-step recounting of the problem so that you can re-create it.

- Fully test your project on as many platforms as possible, including heavily loaded, highly expanded systems. Any element of a computer's configuration may be the cause of a problem or a bug, so plan to spend lots of time configuring and testing various platforms and reproducing and fixing bugs.

- Budget for obtaining the hardware test platforms, as well as for the many hours of effort that testing will require.

- Your contract should clearly specify the intended delivery platform and its hardware and software configuration, and provide a clause that you will test only to that platform.

Determine what steps you need to take to prepare your project for delivery in the marketplace

- You may need to provide a single program that acts as an installation routine, which is not a trivial task.

- Provide well-written documentation about the installation process so that users have a clear step-by-step procedure to follow.

- The clearer and more detailed your installation instructions are, the fewer frustrated users' queries you will receive.

- Use a shareware or commercial compression utility for creating program archives that can then be decompressed and "reconstituted" into the original file structure.

- Self-extracting files allow the user to run the executable archive; compressed files are automatically decompressed and placed on the hard disk.

Discuss CD-ROM technology and standards as they apply to multimedia

- The majority of multimedia products sold into retail and business channels are delivered on CD-ROM or DVD.

- CD-R writers and blank CD-R discs are an inexpensive way to distribute multimedia projects.

- For short runs of a product, it is cheaper to burn your work onto CD-Rs and custom-label them with your own printer.

- The Red Book standard defines the CD audio format; Yellow Book is for CD-ROM; Green Book is for CD-I (Interactive); Orange Book is for write-once, read-only (WORM) CD-ROMs; and White Book is for Video CD (Karaoke CD).

- A single-speed reader allows data to be read at a sustained rate of 150 Kbps, much slower than from a hard disk.

- Although you can access all files on the CD from either platform, a PC executable program will not run on a Macintosh, and vice versa.

- A hybrid format places both Macintosh files and PC files on the same CD, with both PC and Macintosh executable programs.

- The ISO 9660 standard is the most widely used digital data file format for CDs.

Discuss DVD standards and capacities as they apply to multimedia

- Digital Versatile Discs (DVDs) are made with a multilayer, high-density manufacturing process that provides 4.7GB of storage.

- Set-top DVD players for movie viewing at home do not play data-formatted DVDs.

Determine the type of packaging needed for different multimedia projects

- Packaging is an important consideration in marketing your project.

- Although users often equate quality with large boxes, high-caliber artwork, and fancy packaging, the current trend in software packaging is toward simplification.

Assess the technical considerations of project delivery on the World Wide Web

- Delivering multimedia projects built for the World Wide Web can be as simple as renaming a directory or transferring a group of files to a web server. On the other hand, hosting your own server for delivering your project means tackling a variety of issues, including security, server-side configuration, and access.

Discuss delivering software through an app store

- Apps are usually available only at stores within a device manufacturer's walled garden.

- Jailbreaking and rooting allow owners to install a wide variety of apps.

■ Key Terms

■ Key Term Quiz

1. The test release of a product that is typically for internal circulation only and is passed among a select group of mock users is the _____.

2. The test release of a product that is sent to a select group of external users with the understanding that the software may contain errors and bugs is the _____.

3. The final release of a product when there is nothing left to change or correct and it is ready to be reproduced is the _____.

4. The test release of a product with a version number as the developers continue to refine the product and approach a final version is called a(n) _____.

5. A program that saves all necessary run-time files to the user's hard drive is called a(n) _____.

6. Many projects include a plain-text file containing a description of changes or bugs reported since the documentation was printed and a detailed description of the installation process. This file is often named _____.

7. When several files are compressed into a single file, it is usually called a(n) _____.

8. Compressed files can be saved with the ability to automatically decompress themselves and save the individual files. Such a compressed file is called a(an)_____.

9. A CD-ROM that contains both Macintosh files and PC files on the same CD is a(n) _____.

10. A CD-R can have several separate images on it, each recorded at different times. Each of these is called a(n) _____.

■ Multiple-Choice Quiz

1. When delivering a project, you should:
   a. not bother testing; it'll probably work
   b. test once on your development computer
   c. test on a couple of other computers
   d. test on several other computers at least once
   e. test on as many different computers as many times as you can

2. Hacking into the operating system of an iOS device such as an iPhone in order to install your own operating system or app is called:
   a. rooting
   b. booting
   c. jailbreaking
   d. tweaking
   e. fencing

3. A service offered by many consultants who will, for a fee, "guarantee" that your web site appears in the top results of a search request is called:
   a. SearchUppping
   b. EngineRevving
   c. sitelining
   d. search engine optimization
   e. milestone tweaking

4. The beta testing group is best composed of:
   a. the internal development team
   b. users typical of the target group for the software
   c. a cross-section of the computer-using public
   d. computer neophytes
   e. other programmers who are familiar with the authoring system used

5. Which of the following is an extension for a compressed file or archive of compressed files?
   a. .pdf
   b. .psd
   c. .jpg
   d. .zip
   e. .svg

6. Which of the following is *not* an option for delivering a project?
   a. Burn CD-Rs of the project.
   b. Use a father disc to press CDs.
   c. Use a mother disc to press CDs.
   d. Use a son disc to press CDs.
   e. Deliver the project via the Web.

7. Compact discs are manufactured by etching a negative master, then pressing a positive imprint of that master, and then using a third-generation negative imprint from the positive to stamp out production discs. This process is called the:
   a. etching process
   b. stamper process
   c. milling process
   d. positive-negative process
   e. family process

8. Each sector of a CD contains 2,352 bytes of data. After every sector are another 882 bytes used for:
   a. copyright information
   b. encryption key storage
   c. file directory indexing and linking
   d. writing additional information
   e. error detection and correction

9. What is the maximum amount of data that a CD-R (compact disc-recordable) can hold?
   a. 44MB
   b. 128MB
   c. 256MB
   d. 700MB
   e. 4.7GB

10. The Compact Disc Digital Audio Standard used for consumer audio CDs available in music stores today is also known as:
    a. ISO 9660 standard
    b. Red Book standard
    c. Orange Book standard
    d. High Sierra standard
    e. CD-ROM/XA standard

11. The most widely used format for storing digital data in files on CDs is the:
    a. ISO 9660 standard
    b. Yellow Book standard
    c. White Book standard
    d. CD-ROM/XA standard
    e. DVD-ROM standard

12. The compact disc standard that allows both computer data and compressed audio data and video/image information to be read and played back, apparently simultaneously, is called the:
    a. Red Book standard
    b. Yellow Book standard
    c. Green Book standard
    d. DVD-ROM standard
    e. CD-ROM/XA standard

13. The CD-I (Interactive) standard is proprietary to:
    a. Apple
    b. High Sierra
    c. JVC
    d. Kodak
    e. Philips

14. CD-ROM packages are shrink-wrapped with thin plastic:
    a. to prevent outgassing of harmful chemicals used in the manufacturing process
    b. to inhibit oxidation of the CD-ROM surface
    c. to protect them from fingerprints and pilferage at the retail outlet
    d. to reduce unauthorized bootleg copies
    e. for a more professional look

15. Which of the following is *not* a benefit of hosting your own web server for a product delivery site on the Web?
    a. ability to specify and install any special software you need
    b. better security control
    c. ability to fine-tune the server's configuration parameters
    d. easy access to technical support
    e. ability to provide secure commerce services

■ Essay Quiz

1. List the testing stages involved in preparing a project for delivery. What type of testers should be part of each stage's testing team?

2. List the benefits and capabilities of file compression and archiving software.

3. Describe the two methods of copying CD-ROMs, and discuss the benefits and drawbacks of each method.

4. Cite the two primary methods for delivering a project, and discuss the benefits and drawbacks of each method.

5. List the various DVD formats and summarize their purposes and capabilities.

Lab Projects

■ Project 13.1

Find three multimedia projects that are delivered over the Internet for free, and can be used in a browser without downloading an application to your local platform. Examples might include interactive stories, online games, or even online multimedia authoring programs. What are the advantages and disadvantages of delivering multimedia projects this way? How do these products earn money?

■ Project 13.2

Create a form that beta testers can return after testing, and be sure to include information regarding the conditions surrounding bugs.

■ Project 13.3

Use a shareware or freeware compression utility to compress three files—for example, a text file, a JPEG image, an executable file (an application). What percentage compression can you achieve? Repeat the compression, saving the files as self-extracting archives. Document your findings by creating a table that compares original size, compressed size, and size compressed as self-extracting file.

Project 13.4

Locate five computer systems and compare their configurations. Document your findings by creating a table with the following information:

- What operating system and version is installed?
- What is the processor and what is its speed?
- How much RAM is installed?
- How much hard-drive space is available?
- Is QuickTime installed?
- What is the video card/monitor's resolution and color depth?
- What are the system's sound capabilities?

Project 13.5

Go to http://store.steampowered.com and click Install Steam Now to download the latest Steam application. Once installed, mouse over the Community section and select the Greenlight option. Scroll down to the Submit Concept option. Here, independent game developers can create concepts for the Steam community, which in turn votes and provides feedback. Using the framework that Steam provides for idea submission, write up a game concept and include your design for a 512×512-pixel branding image.

Glossary

This glossary is intended as a quick reference to the key terms, not a comprehensive reference with full definitions. The number or numbers in parentheses following each definition identify the chapter or chapters in which the term is explained.

\<a\> tag   Enables you to provide a link to a larger graphic or even to a video clip from a smaller, thumbnail-sized image. (11)

\<audio\> tag   Allows most browsers to play sound files in web pages. (11)

\<body\> tag   Enables you to choose colors for backgrounds, format text, and insert anchors to URL links. Color controls for the entire page are attributes of this tag and are set using CSS. (11)

\<button\> tag   Enables you to make an image clickable and link it to another document or page. (11)

\<img\> tag   Enables you to insert inline images. (11)

\<map\> tag   Enables you to insert image maps (pictures with defined hot spots that link to other documents when a user clicks on them). (11)

\<video\> tag   Offers a standard method for delivering video to the Web. (11)

1080p   Ultra-high resolution format included in the international HDTV standards. It is progressive scan, not interleaved (as is 1080i), and is considered top of the line for HDTV. (6)

16:9   The aspect ratio for HDTV, provides high resolution, and allows viewing of Cinemascope and Panavision movies. (6)

2-D animation   Animation occurring on the flat Cartesian x and y axes. (5)

2½-D animation   Adds an illusion of depth (the z axis) to an image through shadowing and highlighting, but the image itself still rests on the flat x and y axes in two dimensions. (5)

3-D animation   Animation occurring in three axes, x, y, and z. (5)

3-D modeling software   Tools for creating 3-D images and animations. (7)

3D Touch   Samsung Galaxy S4 smartphone feature that enables users to make gestures with their fingertips held above, but not touching, the glass. (12)

3G (Third Generation)   Communication protocol for cell phone to tower radio. (12)

4G (Fourth Generation)   Communication protocol for cell phone to tower radio. (12)

acoustic fingerprint   A music recognition system that uses a combination of tempo, spectrum, and other components that identify the sound to match it against tens of thousands of known samples either systematically gathered or submitted by users. (4)

acoustics   A branch of physics that studies sound. (4)

activation   Going gold in web space; making pages available to their intended audience on the Web. (13)

add-on   A piece of software that adds the power of multimedia to web browsers by allowing viewers to view and interact with new types of documents and images. (11)

additive color   Color created by combining colored light sources in three primary colors: red, green, and blue. (3)

Adobe Acrobat PDF   A widely used technique for integrating formatted text and graphics in a single file. (11)

Adobe Acrobat Reader   An application for viewing Acrobat PDF files. (11)

Adobe Director   Software for developing three-dimensional environments and experiences on the Web. (11)

Adobe Dreamweaver   A WYSIWYG, HTML editor that is part of the Adobe suite of programs. (11)

Adobe PostScript   A page description and outline font language. (2)

Advanced Research Projects Agency (ARPA)   A branch of the Department of Defense that created a research network that was the beginning of the Internet. (11)

Advanced Technology Attachment (ATA)   Also called Integrated Drive Electronics (IDE), connects up to four peripherals mounted inside a PC. (7)

agent of change   Something that alters the quality of life. (12)

agile software development   An alternative to developing software in the document-oriented and bureaucratic "code and fix" process implied by the Waterfall

Model. It advocates closer collaboration among all team members and much greater face-to-face communication and minimization of show-stopping feedback loops. (8)

AIFF   File format for storing sound data; preferred format for the Macintosh. AIF is the three-letter file extension for the AIFF file format. (4)

alpha release   Test release of a product that is typically for internal circulation only and is passed among a select group of mock users. (8, 13)

anamorphic widescreen   A coding system to squeeze 16:9 widescreen image data into a DVD's standard 4:3 aspect ratio format. (6)

anchor   A reference from one document to another document, image, sound, or file on the Web. (2, 9)

Android   Open-source operating system for mobile devices; owned by Google. (12)

animated GIF   A collection of still images in a single file played back in a timed sequence to provide animation. (5)

animation   Collection of images rapidly displayed to provide visual change over time. (5)

anti-aliasing   Blends the colors along the edges of graphic objects and characters to create a soft transition between the letters/objects and the background. (2)

app store   Official web site through which a company sells apps and media for its own operating system. (13)

Apple Macintosh operating system (OS)   Apple's platform for producing and delivering multimedia projects. (7)

applet   A program written in Java that can be included in an HTML page. (11)

archive   A set of files compressed into a single file. The individual files are decompressed and reconstituted into the original, separate file. (13)

ARPANET   Origin of the Internet, established at the University of California at Los Angeles in September 1969 for researchers working for the Advanced Research Projects Agency (ARPA) of the Department of Defense. (11)

ASCII   American Standard Code for Information Interchange, a 7-bit character coding system most commonly used by computers. (2)

aspect ratio   Ratio of the width to height of a display device. (2)

assets   Rendered graphics, sounds, and other components that are part of a multimedia project. (7)

Asynchronous JavaScript and XML (Ajax)   A technique to deliver more pleasing web experiences that uses a combination of XML, CSS (Cascading Style Sheets CSS) for marking up and styling information, and JavaScript to generate dynamic displays and allow user interaction within a web browser. (11)

Atmospheric Voices   A Screen Actors Guild (SAG) category for interactive media work and rates issued in 2014, driven by the "vocally stressful" and multiple roles for actors often required in video games. (10)

attack   How quickly a sound's volume increases. (4)

attributes   Text style characteristics, such as underlining and outlining; properties of an HTML tag. (2)

AU format   The format for audio files based on the international telephone format of uLaw. The two-letter file extension is .au. (11)

audio resolution   Determines the accuracy with which a sound can be digitized, and is measured in bits, such as 8-bit or 16-bit. (4)

audition   Tryout for talent role or part. (10)

authoring tools   Tools designed to manage and manipulate individual multimedia elements and provide user interaction. (1)

autoplay attribute   If present in the <audio> tag, the audio for a web page starts playing as soon as it is ready. (11)

autotracing   A process that computes the boundaries of the shapes of colors within a bitmap image and then derives the polygon object that describes that image. (3)

B-roll   The collection of general footage that supports the main theme or narration. (6)

backbone   The ultra-high bandwidth of the Internet's underlying network operated by AT&T, Sprint, Verizon, and other telecommunications companies. (11)

background layer   A graphic layer behind other layers—often shared by multiple foreground layers. (7)

bandwidth   A description of the size or measurement of a pipeline through which data is sent, as well as how much data, expressed in bits per second (bps), you can send from one computer to another in a given amount of time. (1, 11)

barcodin   Printing or recognizing characters arranged in a pattern of parallel black bars. (7)

beta   Pre-release testing stage of a project or application. (8)

beta release   A test release of a product that is sent to a select group of external users with the understanding that the software may contain errors and bugs. (13)

Bézier   Type of curve that not only creates graphic shapes but represents motion paths when creating animations. Vector drawing tools use Bézier curves or paths to mathematically represent a curve. (3)

binary   Characterizes the two-state nature of a bit, which is either on or off, black or white, or true (1) or false (0). *See also* bit. (3)

binary compatible   Describes a file that requires no conversion when used on various computer platforms. (7)

bit   The simplest element in the digital world, an electronic digit that is either on or off, black or white, or true (1) or false (0). (3)

bit depth   Amount of data used to represent a digital sample. (4)

bitmap   A matrix of the individual pixels that form an image. (3)

bitmapped font   A table containing an exact representation of the pixels of every character in every size. (2)

Blu-ray Disc (BD)   A Sony product with increased storage capacity and throughput beyond DVD for high-definition video, high-definition camcorder archiving, mass data storage, and digital asset management. (7)

blue screen   Shooting against a blue background, making that color transparent, and replacing it with other footage. (6)

Bluetooth   Low-power radio communication technology for very short distances. (12)

BMP   A Windows bitmap image file format; designated with the .bmp file extension. (3)

breadcrumbs   An array of menu items that represents a map of the virtual forest and often the "trail" users have taken, like the edible markers placed by Hänsel und Gretel along the way in the Brothers Grimm's famous fairytale. (2)

bronze   Test release of a product when it's close to being finished. (13)

browser   An application such as Internet Explorer or Google Chrome for reading web pages. (1, 11)

buffer   A place where data is stored temporarily. (4)

burn   To copy data onto a recordable CD-ROM or DVD disc. (13)

burner   Hardware device used for reading and making CDs and DVDs. (1)

busy screen   A cluttered display. (9)

buttons   Graphic objects, with or without text, that generate an action when clicked or tapped. (2, 9)

CamelCase   A word that includes an uppercase letter in the middle. Also called an intercap. (2)

card-based authoring system   System in which elements are organized as a stack of cards or pages of a book. (7)

Cartesian coordinates   A pair of numbers that describe a point in two-dimensional space as the intersection of horizontal and vertical lines (the x and y axes). (3)

Cascading Style Sheets (CSS)   A method of page layout in HTML offering detailed control of text and other styles; an individual CSS file defines the attributes of text displayed on a web page. (2, 11)

case insensitive   Both the uppercase and lowercase forms of a character are considered by a computer program to be the same. (2)

case sensitive   Uppercase and lowercase letters are treated as distinct characters by a computer program. (2)

Cast   In Adobe Director, a visual database of the multimedia elements of a project. (7)

casting call   Announcement for tryouts for talent roles or parts. (10)

cathode-ray tube (CRT)   Type of screen on which colored phosphors glow red, green, or blue when they are energized by an electron beam. (6, 7)

CD-I (Interactive)   Early CD format designed to play sound and pictures on a consumer-grade player connected to a television set. (13)

CD quality   Digitized sound at 44.1 kHz and 16-bit depth. (11)

CD-ROM (compact disc read-only memory)   *See* compact disc read-only memory (CD-ROM).

CD-ROM/XA (Extended Architecture)   A format for reading and writing CDs enabling several recording sessions to be written and read on a single CD-R (recordable) disc. (4, 13)

CDR   A proprietary file format to store images for Corel. (3)

cel   Clear celluloid sheet used for drawing each frame in an animation. (5)

cel animation   A method of overlaying layers of images and sequencing them into an animation. (5)

change order   Revision requested by a client. (8)

character entities   The characters that make up an alphabet recognizable to web browsers according to ISO standards. They are indicated by a word or numbers prefixed by an ampersand and followed by a semicolon. (2)

character mapping   Similar to font mapping, allows bullets, accented characters, and other curious characters that are part of the extended character set on one platform to appear correctly when text is moved to the other platform. (2)

character metrics   General measurements applied to individual text characters. (2)

charge-coupled device (CCD)   A sensor in a video camera that converts light to an electronic signal. (6)

chat-speak   Word shortcuts to pack the most meaning into the fewest characters, such as U (you) or XOXO (hugs & kisses). Used in such communications as Twitter tweets, which allow only about 160 characters per message (140 bytes). (2)

chroma key   A color or range of colors that can become transparent, allowing another image to be inserted in place of the color(s). (6)

chroma key editing   A useful tool easily implemented in most digital video editing applications is blue screen, green screen, Ultimatte, or chroma key editing. (6)

chrome   Toolbars and other shiny stuff around the edges of your page's viewport when making your web pages. (11)

Chrome   Google's web browser. (11)

CIE   A color model that describes color values in terms of frequency, saturation, and illuminance (blue/yellow or red/green). (3)

client   A computer that is part of a network and makes requests to one or more network servers. *See also* network. (11)

client sign-off   Approval from a client to proceed with the client's project; should be obtained at the end of each major stage of a project to ensure that the client approves of the work performed to that point. (8)

client/server software   Enables computers to speak with each other and pass files back and forth. (7)

clip art   Art or other media elements obtained from collections. (10)

clipboard   An area of memory where data such as text and images is temporarily stored when you cut or copy. (3)

clipping   Distortion to the top and bottom of a waveform that occurs if the value of each sample is rounded off to the nearest integer (quantization), and if the amplitude is greater than the intervals available. (4)

clone   When competitors reverse-engineer a product and then produce knockoffs using similar approaches and techniques. If you are handy with a Phillips screwdriver and can read instructions, you can even order the parts and assemble your own computer "clone" to run Windows. (7)

cloud   Dedicated computer farms and storage facilities offering apps and other services from the Internet. (1)

CMYK   Subtractive color scheme consisting of cyan, magenta, yellow, and black, used in printing. (3)

codecs   Digital video and audio compression schemes that code and compress data for delivery and then decode it for playback. (4 ,6, 11)

Code Division Multiple Access (CDMA)   A standard for connecting cell phones. (12)

COLLADA   An ISO standard XML file format for passing 3-D files among applications (from Collaborative Design Activity, http://collada.org). (3)

color cycling   Rapidly altering the colors of an image according to a formula. (5)

Common Gateway Interface (CGI)   Standard for interfacing external applications with information servers. CGI programs are server-based program scripts. (11)

Compact Disc Digital Audio Standard   The Red Book standard for audio CDs. (13)

Compact Disc: Interactive (CD-I)   Early CD format designed to play sound and pictures on a consumer-grade player connected to a television set. (13)

compact disc read-only memory (CD-ROM)   A storage medium for computer data that a computer can read but not write to; typically stores about 700MB of data or 80 minutes of full-screen video or sound. (1, 7, 13)

Compact Disc: Recordable (CD-R) An excellent and cost-effective method for recording and distributing multimedia projects because the discs are inexpensive. (4, 13)

complementary metal-oxide semiconductor (CMOS) image sensor A special sensor that converts light that passes through a video camera lens into an electronic signal. Also called a charge-coupled device (CCD). (6)

component Signal output in which each channel of color information (red, green, and blue) is transmitted as a separate signal on its own conductor. This is the preferred method for higher-quality and professional analog video work. (6)

composite Video recording standard in which all video signals are mixed together and carried on a single cable as a composite of the three color channels and the sync signal. (6)

composite navigation A multimedia structure in which users may navigate freely but are occasionally constrained to linear presentations. (6, 9)

compression algorithm Algorithm built into web image formats such as GIF, PNG, JPEG, and SVG to reduce file size. (11)

condensed Text in which characters are squeezed closer together than with regular spacing. (2)

conditional branching Navigation control based on the results of an IF-THEN decision. (7)

content The text, images, sounds, and video contained in a multimedia project. (1,10)

content acquisition Obtaining the text, images, sounds, and video contained in a multimedia project. (10)

Content Management System (CMS) Software package that combines the power and flexibility of a database with the dynamic capabilities of a programming language. Most CMSs are built on a combination of MySQL and PHP. (11)

contingencies Elements worked into planning and budgeting to allow for unexpected problems, expenses, and delays while developing a project. (8)

controls If this attribute is present in the <audio> tag, play/pause and other controls are displayed on the web page. (11)

convergence Melding of computer-based multimedia with entertainment and games-based media. (1)

copyleft Antipodal to *copyright* and represents a serious and growing worldwide effort to "grant the right to freely copy, distribute, and transform creative works without infringing the author's rights." *See also* Creative Commons license. (10)

copyright infringement Using copyrighted material without permission. (10)

copyright ownership Ownership of the legal rights to use and license a copyrighted asset. (10)

copyright protection Legal rights belonging to the creator of an original work wherein protection is automatically assigned to "original works of authorship fixed in any tangible medium of expression." (10)

Creative Commons license Grants specific rights to reuse and distribute media. The variations on this license are the results of many years of legal testing, and support the copyleft movement. *See also* copyleft. (10)

creative strategy Techniques and presentation methods relevant to a project when planning; description of the look and feel of a project. (8)

Critical Path Method (CPM) A scheduling function to calculate the total duration of a project based upon each identified task, earmarking tasks that are critical and that, if lengthened, will result in a delay in project completion. (8)

cross-platform Describes multimedia that is functional on more than one computer platform. (7)

DAE Digital asset exchange file format used in the COLLADA standard; has the extension .dae. (3)

daemon An agent program that runs in the background, waiting to act on requests from the outside. (11)

decay How long a note takes to fade away, as determined by the software on a MIDI keyboard (or another MIDI device). (4)

decibels (dB) A logarithmic measurement of the sound pressure level (loudness or volume) of a sound. (4)

degaussing Electronic process of readjusting the magnets that guide the electrons in a CRT. (6)

deliverables Work products that must be provided to the client. (8)

density-independent pixel (DPI) Virtual unit of measurement equivalent to one physical pixel on a 160 dpi screen. Using DPIs enables Android OS programmers to deal with the multiplicity of viewport sizes in the small-device world by writing one application that flexibly covers all display sizes. (11)

deprecated In the context of HTML, describes a tag that is no longer supported by the standard but whose use may remain supported by most browsers. (11)

depth structure The complete navigation map, which describes all the links between all the components of a project. (9)

derivative work Material that is derived from another work. (10)

device dependent Performance depends upon the device used, for example, for playback of a sound. (4)

device independent Performance sounds the same, regardless of the device used, for example, to play a sound. (4, 11)

device-independent bitmap (DIB) Also known as a BMP, a common Windows palette–based image file format similar to PNG. (3)

DHTML *See* Dynamic HTML (DHTML).

digital audio Audio represented as a series of binary numbers. (4)

digital audio tape (DAT) Magnetic tape used for recording audio in a digital format. (4)

digital equalization (EQ) Modifying a recording's frequency content. (4)

digital light projector (DLP) LED-based wall projector. (12)

Digital Rights Management *See* DRM.

digital signal processing (DSP) Processing a sound with reverberation, multitap delay, chorus, flange, and other special effects. (4)

Digital Television (DTV) Transmission of digitally processed audio and video signals. (6)

Digital Versatile Disc (DVD) Disc medium stores 4.7GB of data, more in dual layers, typically used for video, data, and delivery of multimedia projects. (1, 6, 7, 13)

Digital Visual Interface (DVI) connector Connector through which a computer display provides purely digital component input, along with the analog component (red, green, blue) input provided through a 15-pin VGA connector. The display may use an HDMI connector instead of, or in addition to, the DVI connector to provide purely digital component input. (6)

digitally manipulated Photos, sounds, text, video, and other multimedia elements that have been edited using a computer. (1)

distributed resources Information and multimedia assets located at various places on the data highway. (1)

dithering Mathematical process used in reducing the number of colors in a palette, whereby the color value of a pixel is changed to the closest matching color value in a target palette; pixels of different colors are then intermixed to create the appearance of a color not in the new, limited palette. (2, 3)

Domain Name System (DNS) System developed to rationally assign names and addresses of computers linked to the Internet. (11)

dot pitch Spacing (size) of the phosphorescing, colored-chemical dots found on the back of the glass face of a monitor. (3)

dots per inch (dpi) Description of screen or printer resolution. (2)

double tap On small touchscreen devices, makes the browser zoom in and center on a document. (11)

downsample Examine an existing digital recording and reduce the number of samples of a sound. Also called resample. (4)

drag On small touchscreen devices, gesture that moves the viewport or pan. (11)

drawing software Software for producing vector-based line art that is easily printed to paper at high resolution. (7)

DRM Digital Rights Management, technology to control copying, printing, and viewing copyrighted works. (4)

DTV (Digital Television) *See* Digital Television (DTV).

DVD *See* Digital Versatile Disc (DVD).

DVD-ROM DVD-Read Only Memory, a DVD used for storing data that is to be read by a computer. (7)

DVD-Video A DVD used for recording video for playback. (7)

DXF Proprietary format for exchanging architectural and engineering drawings across platforms. Largely replaced by IGS. (3)

Dynamic HTML (DHTML)   A collection of software technologies including HTML, JavaScript, and CSS that provides a powerful extension of HTML to improve control of page layouts and presentation. (1, 2)

dynamic web page   A web page constructed using server-side scripts that provide dynamic user interaction. (11)

e-readers   Display text, graphics, and multimedia, most using E Ink screens between five and ten inches diagonal, some with touch screens, some with Wi-Fi and 3G connectivity, and all with varying and sometimes nonstandard input formats. See Table 2-2 for a list of formats. (2)

easing   An animation software tool that allows the user to choose the elasticity of an object, the amount of gravity, and the length of the fall of an object. (5)

eBooks   Books digitized and formatted to be read using an e-reader. (2)

ECMAScript   International language standard derived from Netscape's original JavaScript. (7)

EDL (edit decision list)   List of time and location data for video clips organized into a sequence. (6)

electronic rights   Rights to reproduce or use material in electronic form. (10)

emoji   Japanese-invented ideograms or pictographs (*e* = "picture" and *moji* = "letter") incorporated into Unicode and used in phones and e-mail services; also available in both the Macintosh and Windows operating systems. (2)

emoticons   Symbols used in Internet conversation to express mood, such as "smiley" symbols. Emoticons originally were made up entirely of text and punctuation characters. They have been replaced by both custom-made graphic symbols and official type characters as part of the international Unicode library (Block 1F600..1F64F). (2)

envelope   MIDI data that comprises the attack (how quickly a sound's volume increases), the sustain (how long the sound continues), and the decay (how quickly the sound fades away); provided in addition to MIDI data regarding the instrument and the note. (4)

environment   The combination of hardware and software that governs the limits of what can happen in the GUI of a multimedia project. (1)

erasable programmable ROM (EPROM)   A microchip that allows changes to be made and to be retained when power is lost. (7)

escape sequence   Used in HTML to define special characters; begins with an ampersand and ends with a semicolon. (11)

Ethernet   Method of wiring computers to be part of a network. (7)

event-driven   A programming paradigm in which the flow of the program is determined by events such as user actions and sensor inputs. (7)

executive summary   The first part of a proposal, used to briefly describe the project's goals, how the goals will be achieved, and the project's cost. (8)

expanded   Text in which the characters are spaced further apart from each other than with regular spacing. (2)

Extensible Markup Language (XML)   Allows creation of custom HTML tags and importing of data from anywhere on the Web. (1, 11)

extensions   Drivers and other parts of system software that enable certain functions. (11, 13)

extrude   Extend an object's shape some distance, either perpendicular to the shape's outline or along a defined path. (3)

fair use   Limited exceptions to copyright protection in which copyrighted material can be used without permission. (10)

family process   Process of pressing CDs from a glass master using fathers, mothers, and sons. (13)

FAQ   *See* Frequently Asked Questions (FAQ).

father   A step in the process of pressing CDs from a glass master using fathers, mothers, and sons. (13)

feasibility study   A test to see if a task is doable; often involves selecting only a small portion of a large project and getting that part working as it would in the final product. Also called a prototype or proof of concept. (8)

File Transfer Protocol (FTP)   Method for exchanging files among computers connected to a network. (7, 11)

filename extension   The set of letters (and occasionally numbers) after the last dot of a filename that identifies what method of data organization is used within the file. (4)

file-naming convention   Agreed-upon rules for naming files. (9)

filters   Used by image-editing software to produce special effects. (7)

FireWire   Introduced by Apple in the late 1980s and standardized in 1995 (IEEE 1394), supports high-bandwidth serial data transfer, particularly for digital video and mass storage. (7)

first-level domain   Last dot-separated identity in a domain name; for example, .com or .edu. Also called a top-level domain (TLD). (11)

flare   Place(s) on an image where light is most intense. (3)

flick   On small touchscreen devices, gesture that scrolls the picture up or down. (11)

font   A collection of characters of a single size and style belonging to a particular typeface family. (1, 2)

font mapping   Specifying an appropriate matching font when crossing platforms. (2)

font stack   A comma-separated list of fonts that can be built in the font-family property and can include the exact names of both Windows and Macintosh fonts. A browser will look on the local computer for the first font specified in the list; if it is not available, the browser will check for the next, then the next, and so on until it finds a match. (2)

font substitution   Substituting a font when the original font is unavailable on the target machine. (2)

footage   A legacy term from the film and analog world meaning "feet on a roll of movie film." Now includes digital video clips. (6)

format converters   Indispensable tools for projects in which your source material may originate on Macintoshes, PCs, Unix workstations, or even mainframes. (7)

foundry   A place where typefaces are created. (2)

frame   In animation and digital video, one in a sequence of graphic images. (7)

Frequently Asked Questions (FAQ)   List of common questions and answers that provides useful information. (7, 11)

Gantt chart   Planning chart that depicts tasks along a timeline. (8)

General MIDI   Method for creation and playback of digital music files that uses a numbering system ranging from 0 to 127 to identify musical instruments. (4)

generation loss   Loss of quality that occurs when you copy analog video from one tape to another. (6)

generic font   A font catch-all ("serif" or "sans serif") added to the end of a font stack to cover an instance when your all specified fonts are unavailable. (2)

GIF   Graphics Interchange Format, a proprietary bitmap image format limited to a palette of 256 colors and widely used on the Web. (3, 11)

GIF89a   A version of the GIF image file format specification that allows collection of still images into a single file to be played back in a timed sequence to provide animation. (5)

Global Positioning System (GPS)   A navigation system that enables a properly equipped device to locate its position on the earth. (12)

Global System for Mobile Communications (GSM)   A radio system for connecting a cell phone to a cell tower and then onward either to the Internet or to the public switched telephone network (PSTN). (12)

going gold   Finalizing and shipping a project. (8, 13)

gold   Term to describe current version status of a project when there is nothing left to change or correct and it is ready to reproduce copies. (13)

golden master   Final release of a product when there is nothing left to change or correct and it is ready to be reproduced. (13)

GPS (Global Positioning System)   *See* Global Positioning System (GPS).

graphical user interface (GUI)   The collection of multimedia elements displayed on a computer screen for user interaction. GUI is pronounced "gooey." (1, 2)

Green Book   Standard for CD-I format. (13)

green screen   Green background that is made invisible when merged with another electronically generated image. When the two videos are mixed together, wherever there is green it is replaced by the background image, frame by frame. (6)

GSM (Global System for Mobile Communications)   *See* Global System for Mobile Communications (GSM).

GUI   *See* graphical user interface (GUI).

handler   In a message-passing programming language, code that tells the application what to do when an event occurs. (7)

handshake   A set of complicated but standardized protocols that allows a device and the radio to which it is connecting to identify and authenticate each other. (12)

HDTV (High-Definition Television)   Digital TV with theater-quality pictures and CD-quality sound, providing high resolution in a 16:9 aspect ratio. (6, 7)

helical scan   Method of recording in which analog video and audio signals are written to tape by a spinning recording head that changes the local magnetic properties of the tape's surface in a series of long diagonal stripes. Because the head is canted or tilted at a slight angle compared with the path of the tape, it follows a helical (spiral) path. (6)

helper applications   Applications that run files downloaded by a browser, but are not integrated into the browser itself. (11)

hexadecimal   Two-byte numbering system expressing 16 values from 0 to F; numbering system used for designating colors displayed by web browsers; rather than using values between 0 and 255, it uses a combination of two numbers or letters (1–9 and A–F). (3)

Hierarchical File System (HFS)   An older Macintosh file management system. (13)

hierarchical navigation   A multimedia structure in which users navigate along the branches of a tree structure that is shaped by the natural logic of the content. (9)

High-Definition Multimedia Interface (HDMI)   Type of connector used by HDTV sets to provide purely digital input. (6)

High-Definition Television (HDTV)   *See* HDTV (High-Definition Television).

hints   Special instructions to help improve the resolution of text created with Type 1 PostScript fonts. (2)

hot spot   Clickable area on an image or screen. (9)

hot-swapping   Replacing computer components without shutting down the system. (7)

HSB   A model or methodology based upon hue, saturation, and brightness used to specify colors in computer terms. (3)

HSL   A model or methodology based upon hue, saturation, and lightness used to specify colors in computer terms. (3)

HTML   *See* Hypertext Markup Language (HTML)

HTML editor   Application designed to make it easier to create HTML documents. (11)

HTML translator   Program built into a word processing program to allow you to export a document as an HTML document by automatically adding the necessary tags. (11)

HTML5   HTML standard that enables browsers to play multimedia elements such as sound, animations, and video without requiring special plug-ins or software. (11)

hues   Shades of color. (3)

hybrid apps   Apps made for iOS or Android using HTML5, CSS, and JavaScript. (12)

hybrid format   CD-ROM that is playable on both Windows and Macintosh computers. (13)

hyperlink   Connects the user to another part of the document or program or to a different program or web site. (9)

hypermedia   A structure of linked elements through which users can navigate interactive media. (1, 2)

hypertext   Words keyed or indexed to associate them with other words and/or content. (2)

Hypertext Markup Language (HTML)   Code used to create web pages. (1, 2)

hypertext system   System in which keyed or indexed words allow rapid electronic retrieval of associated information. (2)

Hypertext Transfer Protocol (HTTP)   Protocol providing rules for requesting, sending, and closing documents between two computers on the Internet. (11)

icon-based, event-driven authoring system   A tool that provides a visual programming approach to organizing and presenting multimedia. (7)

icons   Symbolic representations of objects and processes common to the graphical user interfaces of many computer operating systems. (2, 9)

ignition frisson   A mild shiver experienced by many multimedia designers when they pull down the New menu and draw their first colors onto a fresh screen. (3)

IGS or IGES (Initial Graphics Exchange Standard)   Has largely replaced DXF as the format for exchanging architectural and engineering drawings among applications. (3)

image map   A large image that is sectioned into hot spots with associated links. (9)

image-editing applications   Specialized and powerful tools for enhancing and retouching bitmapped images. (7)

independent contractor Worker who works for himself or herself and is hired for a particular task; unless provided otherwise in the contract for his or her services, ownership of any work created is retained by the independent contractor. (10)

inks In computer animation terminology, special methods for computing color values, providing edge detection, and layering so that images can blend or otherwise mix their colors to produce special transparencies, inversions, and effects. (5)

installer Program that saves all necessary run-time files to the user's hard drive. (13)

integrated development environment (IDE) A framework to simplify developing applications. (12)

Integrated Drive Electronics (IDE) Hardware standard for connecting up to four input/output devices mounted inside a PC. Also called Advanced Technology Attachment (ATA). (7)

integrated multimedia The final presentation in which the source documents such as montages, graphics, video cuts, and sounds are weaved together. (1)

interactive multimedia The end user or viewer controls what and in what sequence the elements of multimedia are delivered. (1)

Interactive TV (ITV) Interactive TV technology provides interactivity with TV-related content. (1)

intercap An uppercase letter in the middle of a word. (2)

interlaced The data making up an image is delivered to a display screen in alternating lines. (11)

interlacing Process of building a single video frame from two fields to help prevent flicker; process of displaying a GIF image, line by line. (6)

Internet Worldwide network of linked computers. (11)

Internet service provider (ISP) Company or organization that provides connections to the Internet and other Internet-related services. (7, 11)

inverse kinematics Linking objects, such as hands to arms, and defining their relationships and limits (for example, elbows cannot bend backward). (5)

iOS A proprietary closed-source operating system developed and owned by Apple for its mobile devices. (12)

IP address Set of four numbers separated by periods defining the location of a device on the Internet. (11)

ISO 9660 Format for storing digital data in files on CDs. (13)

jaggies Ragged edges around the boundary of an object or text character. (2)

jailbreaking To let Apple's iOS out of "jail," allowing you to make changes to the distributed "official" iOS. (13)

Java Object-oriented cross-platform programming language. (11)

JavaScript A "scripting language" whose commands are executed at runtime by the browser itself. JavaScript code can be placed directly into HTML using <script> tags or referenced from a file with the ".js" extension. (11)

JPEG Joint Photographic Experts Group, a designation for a bitmap image file format widely used on the Web for photorealistic images; designated by the .jpg or .jpeg file extension. (3, 11)

Karaoke CD *See* Video CD (Karaoke CD).

kerning Controlling the space between individual character pairs in a line of text. (2)

key color The blue or green screens for backgrounds. (6)

keyboarding Typing on a computer keyboard. (7)

keyframes The first and last frame of an action. (5)

kinematics Study of the movement and motion of structures that have joints. (5)

KML Keyhole Markup Language (KML), an XML text-based format used by Google in its mapping software and on mobile devices to place lines, overlays, images, polygons, 3-D models, text, placemark locations, and interactive buttons onto maps. Each item placed onto a map using KML always contains latitude, longitude, and altitude data. (3)

KMZ A zipped package of KML files and images. (3)

landscape Wider-than-tall orientation for printing. (2)

lathe Creating a 3-D object by rotating a profile of the shape around a defined axis. (3)

launcher app An application used to launch other applications. (12)

leading Distance from one line of text to another. (2)

license Legal document allowing use of copyrighted material. (10)

licensing agreement Signed document describing how copyrighted material may be used. (10)

light-emitting diode (LED)   Low-energy semiconductor light source used in flat screen displays. (6)

linear multimedia   A multimedia structure in which users navigate sequentially, from one frame or bite of information to another. (1)

linear navigation   A multimedia structure in which users navigate sequentially, from one frame or bite of information to another, starting at the beginning and running through to the end. (9)

Linear Pulse Code Modulation (LPCM)   Sampling method used for consumer audio CDs; often shortened to PCM. (4)

Lingo   Programming language of Adobe Director. (7)

link   Navigational connection between conceptual elements. (2)

link anchor   In HTML, the clickable link to associated content. (2)

link end   Destination node linked to a link anchor. (2)

liquid crystal display (LCD)   Panel for displaying computer output; supersedes CRT monitors. (6)

local area network (LAN)   Collection of computers connected together in a local area. (7, 11)

localization   Translating or designing into a language or culture other than the one originally intended. (2)

Long-Term Evolution (LTE)   See LTE (Long-Term Evolution).

look and feel   Combination of graphic screen elements and how they respond to user interaction. (7)

lossless   Compression method that does not lose data or quality. (3, 11)

lossy   Compression method that loses image, audio, or video quality in favor of reducing file size. (3, 4, 11)

lowercase   Small letters. (2)

LTE (Long-Term Evolution)   Communication protocol for cell phone to tower radio. (12)

marking up   Specifying the look and presentation of a web page by adding tags to a document. (11)

media type   A standard list of filename extensions used by the Internet to identify the nature of the data transmitted and, by inference, the purpose of that data. Formerly known as MIME-type. (11)

meme   A unit of cultural ideas, behaviors, and styles. (12)

Microsoft Internet Explorer   A web browser application. (11)

Microsoft PowerPoint   Presentation software. (11)

Microsoft Windows   Brand of operating system that runs on a PC. (7)

MIDI   Musical Instrument Digital Interface, an instruction-based system for creating music. (4)

MIDI keyboard   Keyboard used to generate MIDI instructions. (4)

milestone   Point in the development of a project that marks the end of a phase. (8)

MIME-type   See Multipurpose Internet Mail Extensions (MIME-type).

mirroring   Writing simultaneously to two or more disks. (7)

modal interface   Typically, enables a viewer to click a Novice/Expert button and change the approach of the whole interface to be either more or less detailed or complex. (9)

modeling   Creating objects using a 3-D application. (3)

modifiers   Properties of objects that establish how the objects should respond to messages. (7)

morphing   Smoothly blending two images so that one image seems to melt into the next. (3, 5)

mother   In the process of stamping a CD, a metal positive image of a glass master made of nickel. (13)

Moving Picture Experts Group (MPEG)   Organization tasked with developing standards for digital representation of moving pictures and associated audio and other data. (6)

Mozilla Firefox   A web browser and an open-source competitor to Microsoft Internet Explorer. (11)

MP3   File format for storing sound data that uses a compression scheme developed by MPEG. (4)

MPEG   Motion Picture Experts Group, the file format standards and compression specifications for video and audio data. (4)

MPEG-1   1992 specifications for the delivery of 1.2 Mbps of video and 250 Kbps of two-channel stereo audio using CD-ROM technology. (6)

MPEG-2   1994 specifications for 3 to 15 Mbps data rates for higher picture quality; the video compression standard required for digital television (DTV) and for making DVDs. (6)

MPEG-4   1998/89 specifications providing a content-based method for assimilating multimedia elements. (6)

multi-touch gestures   Pinches, swipes, and taps used in touch-screen interfaces. (7, 12)

multicast   Transmission type that enables multiple users to simultaneously receive the same data streams without duplication of data across the Internet. (11)

multiframe image   Type of image used to make simple animations by putting multiple images or frames into a single file. (11)

multimedia   Any combination of text, art, sound, animation, and video delivered by computer or other electronic or digitally manipulated means. (1)

multimedia developers   People who weave multimedia into meaningful tapestries. (1)

multimedia elements   Text, graphics, animation, sound, and video. (1)

multimedia project   The software vehicle, messages, and the content presented on a computer or television screen; the process of making multimedia; its end result. (1)

multimedia skill set   Detailed knowledge of computers, text, graphic arts, sound, and video. (7)

multimedia title   A multimedia project shipped or sold to end users. (1)

Multipurpose Internet Mail Extension (MIME-type)   Standard list of filename extensions used to identify the nature of data transmitted on the Internet; replaced by "media type." *See also* media types. (11)

National Television Standards Committee (NTSC)   A television signal format with a resolution of 525 lines in a 3:4 aspect ratio used in the United States, Japan, and many other countries prior to high-definition TV. (6)

navigation map   Structural representation of the entire content of a project. Also called a site map. (9)

Near Field Communication (NFC)   Secure short-distance communications by radio. (12)

needs analysis   Early part of the planning process; determines the reason a project is being put forward. (8)

network   A collection of computers connected together. (11)

NFC (Near Field Communication)   *See* Near Field Communication (NFC).

node   Conceptual elements linked together in a hypertext system. (2)

nonlinear editing (NLE)   Type of software that allows assembly of a final video from video, image, and audio elements stored in various files on a computer. (6)

nonlinear navigation   A multimedia structure in which users navigate freely through the content of the project, unbound by predetermined routes. (9)

normalize   Adjust the level of a number of tracks to bring them all to about the same sound level. (4)

notation software   Provides a way for composers and musicians to create and arrange scores using MIDI instruments. (4)

NTSC   *See* National Television Standards Committee (NTSC).

object   A basic construction element of many multimedia authoring systems. (3, 7)

object-based, event-driven authoring system   A tool that provides a visual programming approach to organizing and presenting multimedia. (7)

office suite   Software that typically includes spreadsheet, database, e-mail, web browser, and presentation applications. (7)

OpenType   Standard-driven method for displaying typefaces on the Web. (2)

optical character recognition (OCR)   Scanning printed text and converting that image to a word processing computer file. (7)

Orange Book   Standard for WORM (write-once, read-only) CD-ROMs. (13)

outline font   Font whose strokes are generated from mathematical equations and Bézier curves. (2)

overscan   Broadcast of an image larger than will fit on a standard TV screen so that the "edge" of the image seen by a viewer is always bounded by the TV's physical frame, or bezel. (6)

page-based authoring system   System in which elements are organized as a stack of cards or pages of a book. (7)

painting software   Software for producing crafted bitmap images. (7)

PAL (Phase Alternate Line)   An analog broadcast television or video standard of 25 frames per second made up of 625 individual scan lines, used in Europe, China, and other countries. (6)

palettes   Mathematical tables that define the color of a pixel displayed on a screen. (3)

parent and child relationship   Programming objects that are arranged in a hierarchical order. (7)

path animation   Motion created by moving an object along a determined path. (5)

payment schedule   Contract element that defines when a client must make payments. (8)

PCX   One of the original bitmap image file formats; used in MS-DOS applications. (3)

pels   Picture elements or, more commonly, pixels; tiny dots that make up an image on a computer monitor. (3)

pencil test   Penciled frames are assembled and filmed to check smoothness, continuity, and timing for the path an animated action takes. (5)

persistence of vision   The chemical mapping that remains on the eye's retina for a brief time after viewing. (5)

Phase Alternate Line (PAL)   See PAL (Phase Alternate Line).

phi   The human mind's need to conceptually complete a perceived action. (5)

Photo CD   Kodak's format for storing high-resolution images on CD-ROMs. (13)

PICT   Image file format for Macintosh. (3)

pillars   Empty space on either side of the TV screen where the 4:3 image doesn't quite fit the 16:9 frame. (6)

pinch closed   On small touchscreen devices, gesture that zooms out. (11)

pinch open   On small touchscreen devices, gesture that zooms in. (11)

pixelation   Creating a blocky, jagged look when resizing a bitmapped image by duplicating pixels. (3)

pixels   Picture elements (or pels); tiny dots that make up an image on a computer monitor. (2, 3)

planking   Strange social media fad showing photos of people lying face down with their hands to their sides. (12)

plasma   A technology for flat screen, all-digital displays. (6)

platform   Combination of hardware and operating system used to prepare or deliver multimedia. (1)

platform independent   Software that is not limited to a single computer or operating system. (7)

player   Add-in to extend the capabilities of a web browser, allowing users to play programs or files downloaded from the Web that are not directly supported by the browser. (11)

plug-and-play   Devices that are automatically recognized and installed without users needing to install special cards or turn the computer off and on when making the connection. (7)

plug-in   Add-in to extend the capabilities of a web browser, allowing users to view and interact with documents and images not directly supported by the browser. (11)

PNG   Portable Network Graphics, a bitmap image file format created as a free alternative to the GIF format. (3, 11)

point   Description of the vertical size of a text font, about 1/72nd of an inch. (2)

portrait   Taller-than-wide orientation for printing. (2)

Post Office Protocol (POP)   Protocol for retrieving e-mail from a mail server. (11)

post-production, post-session   In the world of professional film and video production, the time during which sound is incorporated, after all the film and video footage has been assembled. (4)

preload   If this attribute is present in the <audio> tag, the audio will load when the web page does and be ready to run. (11)

prerequisites   Tasks that must be completed before other tasks can commence. (8)

pressed   Making CDs using the family process. (13)

primitives   Geometric shapes such as blocks, cylinders, spheres, and cones used to create objects in 3-D applications. (3)

production   The stage in the development of a multi-media project when the plans are implemented and the project is created. (9)

production value   Value of the assets used in producing a project; the degree to which a media asset adds value and interest to a project. (10)

Program Evaluation Review Technique (PERT) chart   Graphic representation of task relationships, showing prerequisites—the tasks that must be completed before others can commence. (8)

progressive scan   Drawing or scanning the lines of an entire video frame in a single pass on a CRT, without interlacing; method of storing and downloading a JPEG image so it displays more of the image as data becomes available. *See also* interlacing. (6, 11)

proof of concept   A prototype or working test of creative and engineering ideas for a project. Also called a feasibility study. (7, 8)

properties   Characteristics of objects and elements such as shape, color, texture, shading, and location; characteristics that define the behavior of objects. (3, 7)

prototype   A working test of creative and engineering ideas. Also called a proof of concept or feasibility study. (7)

public domain   Material without copyright restrictions. (10)

public switched telephone network (PSTN)   Links all the telephones in the world. (12)

quantization   Rounding off the value of each sound sample to the nearest integer. (4)

quantum theory   An explanation of how light is produced by atoms, developed by physicist Max Planck. (3)

QuickTime movie (.mov)   A standard file format for displaying digitized motion video and other multimedia elements without special hardware. (4)

RAID (Redundant Array of Independent Disks)   A hard disk system that supports high-speed data transfer rates. (6)

random access memory (RAM)   Main memory chips in a computer; they lose their memory when power is lost. (7)

raster image   Another name for a bitmap. *See* bitmap. (3)

rasterizing   The process of converting letters such as the letter *A* from a mathematical representation to a recognizable symbol displayed on the screen or in printed output. The computer must know how to represent the letter using tiny square pixels (picture elements), or dots. (2)

rate card   A list of licensing fees covering the different uses of media assets, different formats, and their use in different markets. (10)

read-only memory (ROM)   Chips that are made for a specific purpose; memory is never lost. (7)

README.TXT, Read.Me   A plain-text file containing a description of changes or bugs reported since the documentation was printed. (13)

real estate   Viewing area on a display screen. (3)

Red Book audio standard   International standard, ISO 10149, for digitally encoding audio data on consumer music CDs. (4, 13)

Redundant Array of Independent Disks (RAID)   *See* RAID (Redundant Array of Independent Disks).

release candidate   Test release of a product with a version number as the developers continue to refine the product and approach a final version. (13)

release form   Legal document transferring the rights to use images, sounds, or other copyrighted multimedia content to the producer of the project. (10)

render farm   A farm of many computers hooked together; may also be called a "cluster of workstations," or COW. The engineer who maintains such a render farm is called a "render wrangler." (3)

rendering   Applying intricate algorithms and special effects to 3-D objects to create a final view. (3)

Request for Proposal (RFP)   Document that defines a client's need, requesting a proposed solution. (8)

resample   Examine an existing digital recording and reduce the number of samples in it. Also called downsample. (4)

responsive web design (RWD)   An approach to web development with the aim of developing sites that display optimally across a wide range of device sizes by adapting or responding to the screen size of the device. (12)

RGB   Red, green, and blue; combined in the additive color method to create specific colors. (3)

rollover   Occurs when the mouse cursor passes over a screen object, eliciting a reaction. (2)

rooted   Another word for jailbroken (see *jailbreaking*). Used with the Android OS. (13)

rotated   When you lathe a shape, a profile of the shape is *rotated* around a defined axis (you can set the direction) to create the 3-D object. (3)

ROY G. BIV The colors of the rainbow, the ascending frequencies of the visible light spectrum: red, orange, yellow, green, blue, indigo, and violet. (3)

royalty Continuing payment for use of licensed content or other materials. (10)

run-time version A version of a project that allows it to play back without requiring the full authoring software and all its tools and editors. Also called a stand-alone. (7)

Safari Apple's web browser. (11)

safe title area An area of a TV screen where title content will not be cut off due to overscan. (6)

SAG-AFTRA Screen Actors Guild–American Federation of Television and Radio Artists. Association of professional actors and voice-over talent. (10)

sample Digital information about a sound taken every nth fraction of a second. (4)

sample size Number of binary digits used to represent the value of a sample. (4)

sampling rate Frequency at which samples of a sound are taken. (4)

sans serif A type style characterized by letters without a decoration at the end of the letter stroke. (2)

Scalable Vector Graphics (SVG) A file format supported by browsers on most mobile phones and tablets because the files can be saved in a small amount of memory and are scalable without distortion. (3, 11)

scene Collection of objects arranged in a 3-D layout. (3)

scope of work All the tasks and efforts required of a project. (8)

Score Sequencer for displaying, animating, and playing cast members in Adobe Director. (7)

scripting Outlining of the content of a project using words. (1)

scripting language Programming language that uses natural-sounding phrases. (7)

scripts Used by Unicode to describe the shared symbols of a language unified into a collection of symbols. (2)

scriptwriter Person who creates character, action, and point of view through dialog and narration. (7)

search engine optimization (SEO) A service offered by many consultants who will, for a fee, "guarantee" that your web site appears in the top results of a search request. SEO specialists use arcane schemes to raise their clients' position at a search engine. (11, 13)

SECAM (Sequential Color and Memory) See Sequential Color and Memory (SECAM).

sector Storage block on a CD, 1/75 second in length, that contains 2,352 bytes of data. (13)

Secure Enclave Area of secure memory to store fingerprint data on Apple devices. (12)

self-extracting archive A program file that stores other compressed files that can be run to decompress and reconstitute the original files. (13)

Semantic Web Provides a common framework that allows data to be shared and reused across application, enterprise, and community boundaries. (11)

Separate Video (S-Video) Lower quality analog video signal using two channels that carry luminance and chrominance information. (6)

sequencer software Programs used to record and edit MIDI scores. (4)

Sequential Color and Memory (SECAM) An analog television signal format used in France, Russia, and a few other countries. (6)

serif A type style characterized by letters with a decoration at the end of the letter stroke. (2)

server Software that serves files and documents to a network; popular use also applies the term to the computer upon which the server software is running. (11)

session One of several separate images on a CD-R disc, each recorded at different times. (13)

shading Calculation by a 3-D program of the effect of light on an object within the scene, resulting in lit and shaded areas on the surface of objects. (3)

shape Base from which you model an object to place in your scene. You can create a shape from scratch or import a previously made shape from a library of geometric shapes called primitives, typically blocks, cylinders, spheres, and cones. (3)

short message service (SMS) Short message sent when texting. (12)

SIM (Subscriber Identity Module) card See Subscriber Identity Module (SIM) card.

simple branching Simple navigation to another section of a multimedia project (via an activity such as a keypress, mouse click, or expiration of a timer). (7)

site map   Representation of the entire content of a web site, usually clickable. Also called a navigation map. (9)

six degrees of separation   A theory that a chain of friends-of-friends can connect one person to any other person in the world in a maximum of six steps (12)

Small Computer System Interface (SCSI)   System for adding peripheral devices to a computer. (7)

SMS (short message service)   *See* short message service (SMS).

software robots   Programs that visit millions of web pages and index the content of entire web sites. (2)

son, stamper   Metal mold for mass-producing CDs. (13)

sound library   Collection of recorded sounds available for a project. (10)

sound synthesizer   Hardware that creates a sound from a mathematical representation. (4)

sprites   Graphic objects in a multimedia authoring system, often animated. (7)

stack   Metaphorical stack of cards used by LiveCode's authoring system. (12)

stage   The visible screen in an Adobe Director project. (7)

stand-alone   Version of a project that allows it to play back without requiring the full authoring software and all its tools and editors. Also called a run-time version. (7)

static web page   Uncomplicated web page using only HTML. (11)

still photo library   Collection of photos available for a project. (10)

stitch   Connect a sequence of photos together via a software program such that you can adjust them precisely into a single seamless bitmap, where the right edge attaches to the left edge and the color and lighting differences among the images are smoothed. (3)

stock footage   Video footage purchased or licensed for use from a library of video resources. (10)

storyboarding   Creating drawings or sketches to visualize the content of a project. (1)

storyboards   Graphic and text outlines that describe each part of a project in exact detail. (9)

streaming   A method of delivering sound and video files over the Web; the computer begins playing the file as it continues to receive the rest of it, keeping ahead so playback does not pause or break up. (4, 11)

streaming latency   The wait period before a streaming sound or video file begins to play. (4)

Structured Query Language (SQL)   Method for structuring and accessing data from a database. (11)

STV (Standard Television)   Signal providing the NTSC's resolution of 525 lines with a 3:4 aspect ratio, but in a digital signal. (6)

style   An attribute of a text character, such as boldface and italic. (2)

Subscriber Identity Module (SIM) card   Card for a mobile device, typically a cell phone, containing ID and other information; it is a removable and can be seamlessly swapped among handsets. (12)

subtractive color   Color created by combining colored media such as paints or ink that absorb (or subtract) some parts of the color spectrum of light and reflect the others back to the eye. (3)

surface structure   Represents the structures actually realized by a user while navigating the project's content (depth structure). (9)

sustain   An indication of how long a sound continues, and is part of the envelope of a sound. (4)

SVG (Scalable Vector Graphics)   *See* Scalable Vector Graphics (SVG).

system requirements   A description of the minimum (or recommended) platform. (13)

system-on-a-chip (SoC) technology   Enables many key functions to reside on a single chip. (12)

tags   Codes that specify the visual display of web page content; used to mark up a document in HTML. (2, 11)

talent agency   Company that represents and solicits work for actors, voice-over artists, and other talent. (10)

TCP/IP (Transmission Control Protocol/Internet Protocol)   Rules for sending data to and receiving data from the Internet. (11)

team building   Creating a group of talents for collaboration; activities that help a group and its members function at optimum levels of performance. (7)

terabyte   One trillion bytes. (7)

text-speak English acronyms and instant messaging words such as XOXO (hugs & kisses), U (you), and NME (enemy). Also known as "chat-speak." (2)

texting Sending short text-only messages. (12)

texture Color, patterns, and bitmap images applied to the surface of an object to make the object more realistic. (3)

Theora A common container for video. (6)

TIFF Tagged Interchange File Format, a universal bitmapped image format. (3)

time stretching Altering the length (in time) of a sound file without changing its pitch. (4)

time-based authoring system A tool in which multimedia elements and events are organized along a timeline. (7)

title A project destined to be sold into the consumer retail channel. (13)

token language A shorthand description of speech. (11)

tooltip Displays information about an icon when the mouse pointer or cursor hovers for a short time above the icon. Sometimes called a "hover box" or "screen tip." (2)

top-level domain (TLD) Last dot-separated identity in a domain name; for example, .com or .edu. Also called a first-level domain. (11)

touch and hold For small touchscreen devices, gesture that displays an information bubble. (11)

touchscreen Touch-sensitive display. (12)

track An area normally allocated for storing a single song in the Red Book CD format. (13)

tracking Adjusting the spacing among characters in a line of text; fine adjustment of the tape during playback so that the tracks are properly aligned as the tape moves across the playback head. (2, 6)

translate Move from one location to another location. (5)

Transmission Control Protocol/Internet Protocol (TCP/IP) See TCP/IP (Transmission Control Protocol/Internet Protocol).

transparency In the GIF89a specification, allows you to instruct a browser to use a specific color or palette of colors (with PNG) as your selected transparency color. (11)

trimming Removing blank space or "dead air" at the beginning or end of a recording. This is your first sound-editing task and is typically accomplished by dragging the mouse cursor over a graphic representation of your recording and choosing a menu command such as Cut, Clear, or Erase. (4)

TrueType An outline font methodology developed jointly by Apple and Microsoft. (2)

tweening Drawing the series of frames in between the first and last frames in an action. (5)

typeface A family of graphic characters that usually includes many type sizes and styles. (2)

Ultimatte Process of shooting video against a blue or green background, making that color transparent, and replacing it with other footage. (6)

underscan Computer displays showing a smaller image on the display's picture tube, leaving a black border inside the bezel. (6)

Unicode Worldwide effort to include the characters from all known languages and alphabets in a standards-based methodology for display and printing. (2)

Uniform Resource Locator (URL) Address of a document or file on the Internet. (11)

Universal Product Code (UPC) International barcoding system used in tracking and selling consumer goods. (7)

Universal Serial Bus (USB) A standard promoted by a consortium of industry players in 1995 for connecting devices to a computer. USB devices are automatically recognized and installed without users needing to install special cards or turn the computer off and on when making the connection. (7)

unlimited use Grant to use material, such as content for a project, everywhere, anytime, and in any medium. (10)

uppercase Capital letters. (2)

usemap attribute In an <img> tag, indicates which <map> tag to use to specify hot spots in an image. (11)

user interface Blend of a project's graphical elements and its navigation system. (9)

vector A drawn line that is described by the location of its two endpoints. (3)

vector-drawn graphic An image created from vector objects. (3)

version control Making sure that old files are archived and new versions are properly tracked. (9)

very high level language (VHLL) Programming facility offered by multimedia authoring systems to provide precise control of activities. (7)

VGA connector A 15-pin analog input component (red, green, blue) in displays for computers. (6)

video cassette recorder (VCR) A machine that records analog audio and video on a removable magnetic tape cassette. (6)

Video CD (Karaoke CD) CD format allowing mix of video and audio. (13)

video stream A video file that streams into a computer in the background, keeping ahead of what has already been played so the playback doesn't pause or break up. (11)

viewport The area of the screen available for your web page. (11)

visual programming Authoring environment that uses drag-and-drop icons or objects. (7)

voice recognition system Used with a microphone to recognize spoken words as input to a computer. (7)

walled garden An environment where the operating system is controlled by the manufacturer and apps and media are only sold at the company's approved outlet or store. (13)

Waterfall Model Software development model in which each stage of a project feeds into the next in a sequential, linear way. (8)

wave format (WAV) File format for storing sound data, native to the Windows operating system. (4)

Web 2.0 Web sites where there is collaboration and information sharing such as seen in blogs, on wikis, and at social networking sites such as Facebook and Twitter. (11)

web site A collection of pages and other multimedia assets on the Internet that are viewable/playable with a browser. (1)

What You See Is What You Get (WYSIWYG) When the display screen shows exactly what the printed output will look like. (2, 11)

white balance Corrects for bluish, orange, or greenish color casts resulting from an uneven distribution of colors in the spectrum your eye tells you is white, but your less forgiving digital camera says is not quite white. (6)

White Book Standard for Video CD (Karaoke CD). (13)

white space Roomy blank areas in a screen or page layout. (2, 9)

Wi-Fi Wireless radio standards and protocols. A wireless radio connection. (7, 12)

wide area network (WAN) A network that connects groups of local networks. (7, 11)

WiMAX Communication protocol for cell phone to tower radio. (12)

wireframing Another word for storyboarding. (9)

wireless access points (WAPs) Hot spots for connecting to the Internet. (12)

word processor Tool for creating and editing formatted text documents. (7)

work made for hire Ownership of a project created by employees in the course of their employment belongs solely to the employer, although several factors must be weighed, such as where the work is done, the relationship between the parties, and who provides the tools and equipment. (10)

write-once, read-only (WORM) A CD-ROM that cannot be overwritten or written to later, once writing has stopped. (13)

WYSIWYG *See* What You See Is What You Get (WYSIWYG).

x-height Height of the lowercase letter x. (2)

Xcode Apple's SDK for developing iOS apps. (12)

XML *See* Extensible Markup Language.

YCC A photo model developed to provide a definition that enables consistent representation of digital color images from negatives, slides, and other high-quality input. YCC is used for PhotoCD images. (3)

Yellow Book Standard for CD-ROM format. (13)

YIQ A quadrature amplitude modulation color model developed for broadcast TV (composite NTSC). It is based on luminance and chrominance expressed as the amplitude of a wave and the phase of the wave relative to some reference. (3)

YUV A color model developed for broadcast TV (composite NTSC). It takes human perception into account when masking broadcast transmission errors. (3)

z dimension Depth; the third axis of a 3-D coordinate system. (3)

Index

Symbols

@ (ampersand), use in e-mail addresses, 342

Numbers

1080p (progressive scan), 171, 173
1081i (interleaved), 171
1394 standard. *See* FireWire (IEEE 1394)
16:9 aspect ratio, in HDTV, 170
2 1/2-D animation, 146, 149–150
2-D animation, 146, 149–150
3-D animation
    overview of, 149–151
    software, 147
3-D drawings
    drawings and renderings, 84–89
    vector drawing and, 81
3-D modeling
    creating 3-D objects, 85–88
    Papervision3D for, 154
    Poser (Smith Micro) for, 151
    shading/rendering 3-D shapes, 87–88
    software for, 224–226
3-D touch, on Samsung Galaxy, 399
3-D worlds, Internet, 364
3D Invigorator (Zaxwerk's), 146
3D Studio Max (.max) format, 153
3D Studio Max (.max) format, 153
3G vs. 4G, 404
4.7GB Media, 437

A

<a> tag. *See* anchors
AAC (Advanced Audio Coding), audio file
    formats, 126
acoustic fingerprint, keeping track of your
    sounds, 132
acoustics, 108–110
Acrobat. *See* Adobe Acrobat
action items, in task planning, 252–253
ActionScript
    built on ECMAScript standard, 236
    controlling audio playback, 129
activation, of Web pages, 441
add-ons, Web browser, 360
additive color, 92–93
Adobe Acrobat
    displaying PDFs, 38, 360
    text and document plug-ins for Acrobat
        Reader, 361
Adobe After Effects
    animation software, 382
    titles and text in video and, 188
    working with 2-D animation, 147
Adobe Digital Editions, 40

Adobe Director
    3-D worlds and, 364
    animation file formats
        (.dir and .dcr), 153
    animation software, 382
    bitmap software, 77
    configuring workspace real estate, 71
    controlling audio playback, 129
    time-based authoring tools, 236
    video for Web and, 383–384
Adobe Dreamweaver, as WYSIWYG
    editor, 360
Adobe Fireworks
    examples of painting software, 222
    working with 2-D animation, 147
Adobe Flash
    3-D worlds and, 364
    animation file formats (.fla and .swf),
        153
    animation for Web and, 381
    animation software, 382
    audio quality and, 135
    codec wars and, 176–177
    configuring workspace real estate, 71
    controlling audio playback, 129
    creating animation, 154
    digital video containers, 174
    for Internet video, 167
    Papervision3D, 154, 364
    shortcomings for mobile devices, 352
    time-based authoring tools, 236
    vector-based drawing program, 222
    video for Web and, 383–384
Adobe Illustrator
    bitmap software, 77
    examples of drawing software, 222
    SVG format and, 83
    working with 2-D animation, 147
Adobe InDesign, 77
Adobe Photoshop
    bitmap software, 77
    creating images for Web, 372–373
    examples of painting software, 222
    ICOformat plug-in in, 290
    rolling ball animation example, 155–156
    saving images as GIFs, 374–376
    saving images as JPEGs, 373
Adobe Photoshop Elements, 77
Adobe PostScript. *See* PostScript fonts
Adobe Premiere
    NLE (nonlinear editing) software, 189
    working with video, 227–228
Adobe Shockwave
    3-D worlds and, 364
    animation file formats, 153
    video for Web and, 383–384

Advanced Audio Coding (AAC), audio file
    formats, 126
Advanced Research Projects Agency
    (ARPA), 337
Advanced Technology Attachment (ATA)
    connections, 209
Advanced Television Systems Committee
    (ATSC), 210
After Effects. *See* Adobe After Effects
AFTRA (American Federation of Television
    and Radio Artists)
        locating professionals, 325
        working with union contracts, 326–328
agent of change, mobile multimedia as, 392
Agile software development, 272
AIFF (Audio Interchange File Format)
        audio file formats, 125
        sound over Web, 362
        system sound files in Windows
            OSs, 124
AJAX (Asynchronous JavaScript and XML)
        animation for Web and, 381
        Concrete5 and, 360
        multimedia on Web and, 353
Alchemy Mindworks GIF Construction
    Set Pro, 149
algorithms
        compression algorithms, 370
        Heckbert's algorithm, 96
        search algorithms, 63
alpha releases
        overview of, 256
        testing, 426
alphabets, in world languages, 50
Amaze, Inc., 308
Amazon Instant Video, using smartphone as
    movie theatre, 396
Amazon Kindle Fire, 442
American Federation of Television and Radio
    Artists (AFTRA)
        locating professionals, 325
        working with union contracts, 326–328
American Standard Code for Information
    Interchange. *See* ASCII (American
    Standard Code for Information
    Interchange)
ampersand (@), use in e-mail addresses, 342
analog video
        comparing with digital, 168
        converting to digital, 227
        overview of, 168–169
anamorphic widescreen, DVDs, 182
anchors
        clickable buttons and, 379
        color options, 377
        hypermedia structures, 61–62
        use in text, 28